Evidence

BLACK LETTER OUTLINES

Evidence

by Christopher B. Mueller

Henry S. Lindsley Professor of Law
University of Colorado School of Law

Laird C. Kirkpatrick

Louis Harkey Mayo Research Professor of Law
George Washington University Law School

THIRD EDITION

WEST®

A Thomson Reuters business

Mat #41058356

© West, a Thomson business, 2005, 2008
© 2012 Thomson/Reuters
   610 Opperman Drive
   St. Paul, MN 55123
   1–800–313–9378

ISBN: 978–0–314–26723–8

Preface to the Third Edition

Evidence is a foundational course in all law schools across the United States. It is a "building block" course that is often required for trial practice and advanced clinical offerings. The subject of evidence is tested on the bar examination of almost every state. Knowing evidence law well is critical for trial lawyers, and important even for lawyers who never set foot in a courtroom because anticipating the possibility of litigation and taking appropriate steps to put clients in the best position is part of the task of "transactional" lawyers, even if they never try cases.

Evidence is also one of the most interesting courses in the curriculum, for both students and teacher. Perhaps more than any other course in law school, evidence combines issues of great theoretical complexity with the most practical concerns. It draws on assumptions and understandings about human nature and principles of communication because its very purpose is to regulate the impact of various forms of evidence on juries.

The good news about studying evidence law is that the subject can be mastered by every law student willing to put some time and energy into the task. It consists of a manageable number of discrete rules that in most jurisdictions have been codified in a straightforward way.

The bad news is that some of the rules are technical, and particularly the all-important hearsay doctrine requires students to look at the uses and role of language in new ways. And there are some subtle distinctions between rules and some surprising relationships among rules that are not always readily apparent.

The purpose of this Outline is to provide you with what we might call a roadmap to the subject. You can use this Outline with any of the major evidence coursebooks. It covers evidentiary principles applicable in all states, but places special emphasis on the Federal Rules of Evidence because they are the source of evidence law for federal courts and 43 out of the 50 states.

This Outline should supplement the primary reading in your coursebook, not supplant them. Reading the primary material, which likely includes classic cases in the field that every lawyer is expected to know, and working through problems and questions provided by your professor or found in your regular reading, are important in developing your understanding, as is classroom discussion.

By serving as a roadmap, this Outline provides you an overview of the terrain (a glimpse of the forest as well as the trees), showing where the pathways intersect, and making it clear how one gets to various destinations. But a roadmap is not a substitute for an atlas, and this Outline is not a substitute for a treatise when more detailed explanation or exploration of a subject is needed.

At various places in this Outline, we refer the reader seeking further elaboration or supporting citations to our treatise: Christopher B. Mueller & Laird C. Kirkpatrick, Evidence (Aspen Law and Business, 5th ed. 2012). Other student books provide excellent coverage of the subject, including Graham Lilly, Daniel Capra, and Stephen Saltzburg, Principles of Evidence (5th ed. 2009), Roger C. Park, David P. Leonard, Aviva A. Orenstein, and Steven H. Goldberg, Evidence Law (3d ed. 2010); and McCormick on Evidence (Kenneth Broun 6th ed. 2006).

For use in a practice setting (either after law school or while clerking), the following treatises are recommended: Christopher B. Mueller, Laird C. Kirkpatrick, and Charles H. Rose III, Evidence Practice Under the Rules (3d ed. 2009); McCormick on Evidence (Practitioner Series, Kenneth S. Broun, General Editor, 6th ed. 2006); Stephen A. Saltzburg, Michael M. Martin, & Daniel J. Capra, Federal Rules of Evidence Manual (9th ed. 2006).

For the most comprehensive and detailed treatment of the subject, the following four multi-volume treatises are available: Christopher B. Mueller & Laird C. Kirkpatrick, Federal Evidence (3d ed. 2007) (six volumes); Michael H. Graham, Handbook of Federal Evidence (6th ed. 2006–2010); Charles Wright & Kenneth Graham, Federal Practice and Procedure (volumes 21–26) and 27–28 (Charles Wright & Victor Gold). See also The New Wigmore (Richard Friedman, ed., 2002) (volumes on privileges, expert testimony, and relevancy and its limits presently available).

We wish you well and hope that you enjoy your study of the subject.

LAIRD C. KIRKPATRICK
Washington, DC

CHRISTOPHER B. MUELLER
Boulder, Colorado

January 2012

Summary of Contents

APPENDICES

App.

Table of Contents

APPENDICES

App.

Capsule Summary

This Capsule Summary is intended for review at the end of the semester. Reading it is not a substitute for mastering the material in the main outline. Numbers in brackets refer to the sections in the main outline where the topic is discussed.

■ CHAPTER 1. PRELIMINARY MATTERS: OVERVIEW OF THE TRIAL PROCESS

A. Preliminary Matters

1. Codification

Although evidence law originally developed, in the manner of common law, out of the reason and experience applied in trial court rulings and appellate review of those rulings, now rules of evidence are codified in most jurisdictions. Evidence law serves multiple purposes. These include regulating juries, furthering accurate factfinding, controlling the scope and duration of trials, and favoring or disfavoring certain kinds of litigants or certain claims or defenses (substantive policies *related to litigation*). Evidence law also protects certain private relationships (such as the relationships between client and lawyer and between spouses), and thus furthers what might be called substantive policies *unrelated to litigation,* and insures a perception of fairness about the trial process. **[See Ch. 1, Sec. A]**

The Federal Rules of Evidence (cited throughout as "FRE," or referred to as "the Rules" or "the Federal Rules") were promulgated by the Supreme Court in 1972 and enacted by Congress in 1975 for the federal court system. These Rules constitute the most influential statement of American Evidence law in the early years of the twenty-first century. Forty-three of the fifty states had adopted evidence codes modeled after the Federal Rules of Evidence as of 2011. **[See Ch. 1, Sec. B]**

2. **Proceedings Governed by the Federal Rules of Evidence**
   The Rules apply to both civil and criminal proceedings, subject to a limited number of exceptions. The Rules do not apply to grand jury proceedings, preliminary hearings, bail release hearings, sentencing or revocation hearings, the issuance of search or arrest warrants, and extradition proceedings. **[See Ch. 1, Sec. C]**

3. **Preliminary Questions**
   Sometimes minitrials are necessary to resolve preliminary questions affecting the admissibility of evidence. For example, before certain kinds of hearsay are admissible the person making the out-of-court statement must be shown to be unavailable. The judge must decide, in a hearing under FRE 104(a), whether the person is unavailable before admitting the hearsay statement. For some preliminary questions, the judge plays only a screening role and decides whether there is evidence **sufficient to support a jury finding** of the preliminary fact that is necessary to make the evidence relevant. **[See Ch. 1, Sec. E]**

4. **Making a Record**
   In order to preserve, for purposes of appellate review, a claim of error in a ruling on an evidence point, the party making this claim must make a proper record. In the case of error in admitting evidence, a proper objection must have been made that is timely and states a specific and correct ground. In the case of error in excluding evidence, a proper offer of proof must have been made. Such an offer involves putting into the record (usually outside the jury's presence) a statement describing the nature of the evidence being offered, or sometimes actually adducing the testimony by putting the witness on the stand and asking questions and getting answers, so an appellate court

can determine whether its exclusion was prejudicial. If a proper objection or offer of proof is not made, any error in the ruling of the trial judge is normally considered to be waived. **[See Ch. 1, Sec. F]**

5. **Limited Admissibility**

   Often evidence is admissible for some purposes and not others, or against some parties but not others. In such cases the proponent can be required to specify the purpose for which it is being offered, or name the parties against whom it is being offered. Where evidence is inadmissible for some purposes or against some parties, the other side is entitled on request to a limiting instruction under FRE 105, meaning that the court tells the jury about the proper scope and use of the evidence, and sometimes tells the jury what purposes or uses are not allowed. **[See Ch. 1, Sec. G]**

6. **Rule of Completeness**

   When a party offers part of a writing or recorded statement, FRE 106 allows an adverse party to require the introduction at that time of any other part or any other writing or recorded statement that ought in fairness to be considered at the same time. This rule prevents a party from unfairly presenting part of a writing taken out of context. **[See Ch. 1, Sec. H]**

7. **Appellate Review**

   Evidentiary error is a basis for reversal on appeal only if it is shown to affect the substantial rights of the appellant. Error that does affect such rights is known as prejudicial or reversible error. Error not affecting the substantial rights of a party is known as harmless error. Courts may affirm where evidence was excluded on the wrong ground if it was excludable on some other ground, or where evidence was admitted on the wrong theory if it was admissible on some other theory. Courts may also refuse to reverse where the error was invited by the appellant, or where the appellant opened the door to such evidence by offering inadmissible evidence to which the challenged evidence is a fair response. Interlocutory appeals of evidentiary rulings are generally not allowed. **[See Ch. 1, Sec. I]**

■ CHAPTER 2. RELEVANCY

B. Relevancy

The most fundamental principle of evidence law is that evidence must be relevant to be admissible.

1. **Logical Relevance**

   Under FRE 401, relevance means any tendency to make the existence of a fact that is of consequence to the action more probable or less probable than it would be without the evidence. Thus evidence having only small probative value qualifies. Relevance can only be determined in context. It depends on the issues raised by the pleadings, the applicable substantive law, and other evidence already in the case. FRE 401 merges the concepts of relevance and materiality by providing that the fact to be proved must be of consequence to the determination of the action, which essentially means relevant and material. **[See Ch. 2, Sec. B]**

2. **Judge Decides Most Relevancy Questions**

   Most of the time the judge alone decides the **relevancy** of evidence. Only if the judge decides that is relevant does the jury get to hear it. During deliberations, the jury decides what weight, if any, to give to the evidence. **[See Ch. 2, Sec. D1]**

3. **Jury Decides Preliminary Questions Affecting Relevancy**

   Sometimes relevancy turns on resolving some preliminary question of fact, as happens when a document is offered and it is relevant only if it is genuine or if it was signed or written by a party to the suit. If the document is a forgery or was written or signed by someone else, it may have no relevance. Such cases are said to involve issues of **conditional relevancy.** Here the judge does not resolve the preliminary question (whether the document is genuine or was signed or written by a party), and instead decides only whether there is **sufficient** evidence to support a **jury finding** on such points. If there is sufficient evidence, the judge admits the document and lets the jury make the final decision whether it is genuine (or was written or signed by a party). If the jury finds the document to be a forgery (or concludes that it was not written or signed by a party), the jury is told to disregard the evidence as irrelevant. If the jury resolves the preliminary question in favor of the party offering the document, the condition is satisfied and the document is relevant and the jury can consider it and give it whatever weight it deserves. **[See Ch. 2, Sec. D2]**

4. **Connecting Up**

   The judge has discretion to admit evidence before the proponent has offered proof bearing on the relevant preliminary questions. Thus, for example, if the prosecutor offers a gun that was found near the scene of a homicide, the judge may admit the gun before the prosecutor proves, by means of ballistics or other tests, that it was used in the homicide. In such cases, it is said that the evidence is admitted **subject to connection,** and if the additional "connecting up" proof is never offered, the judge may **strike the evidence** and instruct the jury to disregard it. Alternatively, the judge may require the "connecting up" evidence to be offered first—asking the prosecutor to prove the results of tests indicating that the gun was used in the homicide, for example, before admitting the gun itself. Thus FRE 104(b) says that conditionally relevant evidence may be admitted "upon" or "subject to" some additional proof that is necessary to make the evidence relevant. Normally a court strikes evidence only if asked by the party against whom the evidence was offered, and if the prejudice caused by admitting evidence that was never "connected up" is too extreme, a mistrial may be necessary. [See Ch. 2, Sec. D2c]

5. **Pragmatic Relevance**
   Offsetting FRE 401's broad definition of relevance, FRE 403 grants trial judges discretion to exclude relevant evidence where its probative value is substantially outweighed by the dangers of unfair prejudice, confusion of the issues, or misleading the jury, or by considerations of undue delay, waste of time, or needless presentation of cumulative evidence. Appellate courts give substantial deference to rulings of trial judges under FRE 403 and generally reverse only for clear abuse of discretion. Since credibility determinations are for the jury, evidence may not be excluded under FRE 403 merely because the judge does not find the evidence to be credible. [See Ch. 2, Secs. F & G]

■ CHAPTER 3. THE DEFINITION OF HEARSAY

C. **The Definition of Hearsay**

1. **The Hearsay Doctrine**
   One of the most important exclusionary doctrines is the rule against hearsay. Under FRE 802, hearsay is generally inadmissible. FRE 803 contains 23 exceptions to the hearsay rule that apply regardless whether the declarant is

unavailable, and FRE 804 lists five more that apply where the declarant is shown to be unavailable. FRE 807 establishes a catchall exception for trustworthy hearsay that does not satisfy any of the other exceptions. In addition to these exceptions, FRE 801(d) lists eight types of out-of-court statements that are simply **defined** as not hearsay (even though they otherwise fit the definition of hearsay), hence are not subject to exclusion by the hearsay doctrine. In substance if not form, these "not hearsay" categories are also exceptions to the hearsay doctrine.

a. Hearsay defined

FRE 801(a) and (c) define hearsay as an out-of-court assertion, which can be verbal or nonverbal, when it is offered to prove the truth of the matter asserted. **[See Ch. 3, Sec. A]**

b. A narrower definition

Some authorities define hearsay as an assertion by an **out-of-court declarant** offered to prove the truth of the matter asserted. This definition is narrower than the federal definition because it does not classify statements as hearsay, even if made out-of-court, if the declarant is in court subject to cross-examination.

c. A broader definition

Some authorities define hearsay as evidence of words or conduct outside of court, whether assertive or nonassertive in character, if it is offered to prove the truth of the facts stated or implied by such words or conduct, or to prove that the speaker or actor believed those facts to be true. This definition is broader than the federal definition because it classifies as hearsay nonassertive conduct that demonstrates the actor's belief that some condition exists, or that some act or event occurred, when offered to prove such points.

2. Rationale for Rule Against Hearsay

There are several traditional policy justifications for the rule against hearsay. Perhaps most importantly, the rule protects the right of cross-examination. To the extent that the hearsay rule forces or encourages live testimony, it adds the safeguard of an oath to statements by a witness and allows the jury to see and assess the demeanor of the witness. In criminal cases, the hearsay doctrine has constitutional underpinnings. The Confrontation Clause of the

Sixth Amendment guarantees criminal defendants the right to confront the witnesses against them, which includes the right of cross-examination. **[See Ch. 3, Sec. B]**

3. **Hearsay Dangers**

There are four dangers connected with all human statements and all human testimony. Those dangers relate to **perception, memory, narration, and veracity.** A person may misperceive an act, event, or condition, or may misremember what she saw, or she may speak about the act, event, or condition in an ambiguous or inaccurate way, or may simply be untruthful (whether lying outright or stretching a point). When testimony is presented by a live witness, these dangers can be tested and explored by cross-examination. When an out-of-court statement is introduced to prove such points (hearsay), these dangers are more serious because the declarant is normally not present and cannot be cross-examined. Hence these dangers are known as the hearsay dangers. **[See Ch. 3, Sec. C]**

4. **Hearsay v. Personal Knowledge**

An objection based on hearsay may overlap with an objection based on lack of personal knowledge. A witness who did not perceive an event and only heard about it from others lacks personal knowledge, which FRE 602 requires for all lay witnesses (experts are allowed more latitude, and may more freely rely on outside sources). If the witness does not testify to statements by others, the appropriate objection is lack of personal knowledge. If the witness does testify to statements by others, the appropriate objection is hearsay. Often both objections are proper. **[See Ch. 3, C5]**

5. **Verbal Expressions as Hearsay**

A verbal expression is hearsay if it contains an assertion and is offered to prove the truth of that assertion. Most verbal expressions contain one or more assertions, regardless what their grammatical form may be. Assertions are not limited to declarative sentences. Even requests, questions, and commands can contain assertions. Whether something is an assertion depends on the intent of the maker. Under the Rules, a verbal assertion is any *intentional* expression or communication of ideas or information using words. Some verbal expressions, like saying hello or singing a song, are normally not intended by the declarant as assertions, hence are not hearsay. **[See Ch. 3, Sec. D1]**

6.   Conduct as Hearsay

a.   Assertive conduct

Out-of-court conduct **that is intended to be assertive** is hearsay if offered for its truth (although like verbal hearsay it can sometimes be admitted under an exception). Assertive conduct, like pointing or nodding to signal agreement, is simply a communicative substitute for words and is hearsay if offered to prove the act, event, or condition that the actor was trying to express or communicate. **[See Ch. 3, Sec. D2]**

b.   Nonassertive conduct

Nonassertive conduct is conduct that was not intended by the actor to make an assertion. Sometimes evidence of such conduct is offered to support a two-step inference from act to belief, and from belief to the fact believed. The first step in the inference draws on the observed conduct of the actor, which might involve, for instance, putting up an umbrella, and the inference is that the actor thinks it is raining. The second step in the inference draws on the apparent belief of the actor (he thinks it is raining), and the inference is that it must in fact be raining. When nonassertive conduct is offered for this purpose (to prove what the actor believed, hence that what he believes is actually happening), hearsay dangers arise. The actor may have misperceived the event, or misremembered it. Or his behavior may be an ambiguous or misleading, so that inferences about his belief are likely to be mistaken. Because of these parallels to the hearsay risks, the leading common law case of *Wright v. Doe d. Tatham* held that nonassertive conduct is hearsay when offered to support this two-step inference. The Federal Rules and modern evidence codes take the opposite view: Nonassertive conduct is not hearsay because there is less danger of inaccuracy (and no danger of lying) if the actor did not intend to make an assertion, so putting up an umbrella is not hearsay when offered to prove that it is raining, at least in the ordinary case in which there is no reason to think that the person putting up the umbrella is trying to express or communicate the fact that it is raining (he is just trying to keep dry). **[See Ch. 3, Sec. D3]**

c.   Distinguishing assertive conduct from nonassertive conduct

FRE 801 requires attorneys and courts to distinguish between assertive and nonassertive conduct because only assertive conduct can be hearsay in federal courts. The distinction is less important at common law because conduct can be hearsay, whether it is assertive or nonassertive. Whether conduct is assertive or nonassertive depends on whether the actor **intended** to make an assertion. The burden is on the objecting party (the party claiming that the conduct is hearsay) to persuade the court that the conduct was assertive. If the objecting party fails to carry this burden, then the court must find the conduct to be nonassertive and admit it. [**See Ch. 3, Sec. D4**]

7. **Offered to Prove Truth of Matter Asserted**
An out-of-court statement is hearsay only if it is offered to prove the truth of the matter asserted. The proponent may be required to state the purpose for which the statement is being offered, and the court can instruct the jury to limit its consideration of the statement to that purpose. There are many nonhearsay uses for out-of-court statements (that is, uses other than proving their truth). When a statement is offered for a nonhearsay purpose, the rule excluding hearsay does not apply. [**See Ch. 3, Sec. E2**]

a. **Impeachment**
A statement is nonhearsay if it is used only to impeach trial testimony by the declarant who is now a witness on the stand. The fact that he testified to one version of the facts at trial but gave a different version in his earlier statement may undermine credibility in the eyes of the jury. The jury does not need to decide whether the out-of-court statement was true. It has impeaching value simply because it represents vacillation: The witness tells the story in different (and apparently conflicting) ways at different times. This vacillation makes his trial testimony less believable. [**See Ch. 3, Sec. E3**]

b. **Verbal acts**
Verbal acts are words that have independent legal significance regardless of their truth. They are described as verbal acts because the law assigns consequences to the act of uttering the words. Words are a part of a broader course of conduct, such as making verbal threats in the course of a bank robbery. Merely uttering certain words may have legal consequence, such as making an offer or acceptance under contract law. Assuming the words are being offered for a purpose other than to prove their truth, they are not hearsay. Sometimes the proponent intends to prove the **falsity** of verbal acts, as in the case of perjury or fraud, which also involves a nonhearsay use. [**See Ch. 3, Sec. E4**]

c. **Effect on listener**

A statement is not hearsay if it is offered only to prove the effect of the statement on a listener or reader. Sometimes out-of-court statements operate to notify, warn, or even threaten the recipient. When the statements are offered only to prove that they had (or should have had or might have had) a particular effect on the person hearing or reading them, they are nonhearsay. **[See Ch. 3, Sec. E5]**

d. **Verbal markers**

A statement is nonhearsay if it is offered only as a verbal marker, and the words serve as identifying characteristics **without any need to rely on their assertive aspect.** Thus evidence of a verbal identifier on a product ("Coca Cola" or "Jello," for example) is usually admitted as nonhearsay to the same extent as a nonverbal identifier (the characteristic Coke can or bottle, the small oblong colorful box). Normally a foundation must be laid establishing the marker as **distinctive** to a particular product or something that is regularly affixed during the course of manufacture. **[See Ch. 3, Sec. E6]**

e. **Circumstantial evidence of state of mind**

Out-of-court statements are sometimes admitted as nonhearsay on the theory that they constitute **indirect** or circumstantial evidence of the state of mind of the declarant. For example, evidence of angry comments directed toward a particular person might be admitted to show hostility or anger on the speaker's part toward the person. **Direct** assertions by the declarant about his state of mind, e.g., "I love her more than anyone I have ever met," are hearsay but are admissible under the state of mind exception. In this area the cases often conflict: Some might say that a statement is sufficiently indirect to fit this nonhearsay category, but others might say that the same statement is really direct and that it must be considered hearsay. The debate is largely academic. Even if the statement is so direct that it must be classified as hearsay, it is usually admissible under the state-of-mind exception that allows even direct statements to prove state of mind. See FRE 803(3). **[See Ch. 3, Sec. E7]**

f. **Circumstantial evidence of knowledge, memory, or belief**

A statement is nonhearsay if it is offered as circumstantial evidence of the declarant's knowledge, memory, or belief. This is a narrow nonhearsay category, because a **direct** statement of knowledge, memory, or belief is normally hearsay if offered to prove the fact asserted, and the state-of-mind exception cannot be used to admit such a statement because the exception does not reach statements offered to prove "the fact remembered or believed." A statement fits this nonhearsay category only where it displays knowledge that can only be explained by some experience, familiarity, or contact on the part of the witness, which the statement is offered to prove, and in this setting it is possible to say that the statement proves the point **without having to rely on the statement in its assertive aspect. [See Ch. 3, Sec. E8]**

8. **Admissible as Not Hearsay–Prior Statements of Testifying Witnesses**
   Under FRE 801(d)(1), three categories of statements by testifying witnesses are defined as not hearsay. In fact, such statements often fit the definition of hearsay, because they are made out of court and offered to prove what they assert. But they are defined out of the hearsay rule and classified as not hearsay primarily because the declarant can be cross-examined about them at trial. (If for any reason the declarant is not subject to cross-examination about them at trial, they cannot be admitted under this Rule.) The *Owens* case held that a witness who has forgotten the underlying event can still be considered subject to cross-examination about his statement within the meaning of FRE 801(d)(1). **[See Ch. 3, Sec. G3a]**

   a. **Prior inconsistent statements**
      Not *all* prior inconsistent statements are admissible under this Rule, even where the witness is subject to cross-examination about them. See FRE 801(d)(1)(A). The only statements that qualify are prior inconsistent statements given under oath subject to the penalty of perjury at a trial, hearing or other proceeding, or in a deposition. Under the majority view, the mere giving of an affidavit at a police station does not qualify as an other proceeding. **[See Ch. 3, Sec. G3b]**

      i. **Cross-examination not required**
         Under FRE 801(d)(1)(A), it does not matter whether the witness was subject to cross-examination in the earlier proceeding. Under FRE 801(d)(1)(A), all that is required is that she was under oath subject to penalty of perjury in the earlier proceeding. Therefore grand jury testimony is admissible against the accused under FRE 801(d)(1)(A) even though the accused had no opportunity, in grand jury proceedings, to cross-examine the declarant.

ii. **Degree of inconsistency required**

The prior statement does not have to be completely inconsistent with (in the sense of being diametrically opposite from) the trial testimony. The majority view is that there must be only sufficient inconsistency between the trial testimony and the earlier statement to raise doubt about the credibility of the trial testimony.

iii. **Loss of memory**

Under the majority view, a prior statement about an event can be inconsistent with trial testimony claiming lack of memory about that event, thereby making the earlier statement admissible under FRE 801(d)(1)(A). But some courts hold that the prior statement is admissible only if the trial judge finds that the witness's claim of loss of memory at trial is feigned.

b. **Prior consistent statements**

Prior consistent statements are admissible under both common law and the Federal Rules to rehabilitate a witness. But at common law prior consistent statements are hearsay and can come in only to rehabilitate a witness. They are not to be considered for the truth of what they assert, and a limiting instruction is required. FRE 801(d)(1)(B) goes beyond the common law by allowing certain prior consistent statements to be admitted not only for rehabilitation but also for their truth. **[See Ch. 3, Sec. 3c]**

i. **No oath required**

Prior consistent statements offered under FRE 801(d)(1)(B) need not have been made under oath and need not have been made at a proceeding.

ii. **Rebut certain attacks**

Prior consistent statements qualify as not hearsay under FRE 801(d)(1)(B) only when they are offered to rebut an express or implied charge against the declarant of recent fabrication or improper influence or motive.

iii. **Time sequence**

In the *Tome* case, the Supreme Court held that prior consistent statements offered as substantive evidence under FRE 801(d)(1)(B) must have been made **prior** to the motive to fabricate. The rationale for this rule is that a statement made after the motive to fabricate does not tend to rehabilitate the witness: Because it was made after the motive to fabricate arose, such a statement may be just as tainted as the trial testimony.

c. **Prior statements of identification**

A statement of identification of a person is admissible as substantive evidence under FRE 801(d)(1)(C) provided that the declarant testifies and is subject to cross-examination about the statement. The paradigm for this exception is the police line-up, and the thought is that statements identifying suspects, made at this time, are more trustworthy than trial testimony, at least when the witness is also present at trial and can be cross-examined. There is no requirement that the statement be made under oath or at a proceeding. In its most powerful use, FRE 801(d)(1)(C) allows use of earlier identifications when the witness cannot repeat the identification at trial. The Rule also paves the way to admit such statements where the witness *is* able to make the same identification at trial, which means that this provision overlaps the one allowing prior consistent statements. If a witness makes an identification of a person at trial and that identification is challenged as a recent fabrication, an earlier statement making the same identification is admissible **both** as a prior consistent statement and as a prior statement of identification. [**See Ch. 3, Sec. G3d**]

■ CHAPTER 4. HEARSAY EXCEPTIONS

D. **Hearsay Exceptions**

1. **Admissions**

Under FRE 801(d)(2), out-of-court statements **by** a party are defined as not hearsay if offered **against** that party at trial. Common-law doctrine classified these statements as an exception to the hearsay rule. FRE 801 classifies them as not hearsay because the factors of necessity and trustworthiness do not play roles in the rationale for admitting them. In this respect, admissions are fundamentally different from the other hearsay exceptions, which turn in large measure on notions of necessity and trustworthiness. Admissions are statements by a party and if they are wrong, the party who made them can take the stand and try to correct any errors. The admissions doctrine is broader than other hearsay exceptions. Admissions need not rest on personal knowledge, and they can be in the form of opinions. **[See Ch. 4, Sec. B]**

a. Individual admissions

Out-of-court statements by a party are admissible against that party at trial. See FRE 801(d)(2)(A). Thus a confession made voluntarily by a criminal defendant is admissible (provided that *Miranda* warnings were given if the defendant was in custody and being questioned by police when the statement was made). The statement is admissible only against the party who made it, not against other parties. The *Bruton* doctrine bars use of a statement made by one criminal defendant that implicates another codefendant by name or obvious reference, and holds that limiting instructions are not enough to protect the latter's rights under the Confrontation Clause. **[See Ch. 4, Sec. B2]**

b. Adoptive admissions

If a party has expressly adopted an out-of-court statement made by a third person, that statement becomes an admission of that party. See FRE 801(d)(2)(B). Sometimes adoption occurs by silence, as happens when a party does not deny or refute a statement by a third person under circumstances in which a reasonable person would do so. Cases split on the question whether the issue of adoption should be resolved by the judge under FRE 104(a) or the jury under FRE 104(b). **[See Ch. 4, Sec. B3]**

c. Authorized admissions

If a party authorizes a third person to speak for her, statements by that person within the scope of his speaking authority are treated as admissions of the party. See FRE 801(d)(2)(C). Sometimes speaking authority is implied from the nature of the relationship, as in the case of the relationship between attorney and client. The statement itself can be considered in determining whether the third person had speaking authority, but is not necessarily sufficient to establish authority. **[See Ch. 4, Sec. B4]**

i. **Current pleadings**

Unless amended, pleadings are binding on those who file them, and procedural law produces this outcome without reference to the admissions doctrine. Statements in pleadings are binding as judicial admissions.

ii. **Other pleadings**

Amended or superseded pleadings, or pleadings filed by a party in other lawsuits, are generally admissible against the party who signed them or authorized them to be filed. Statements in such pleadings are not binding and can be contradicted by the party at trial. They are considered evidentiary admissions only.

iii. **Interrogatories**

Answers to interrogatories are viewed as authorized admissions, both in the suit in which they are filed and in later suits. But they are evidentiary admissions only and may be contradicted by a party's testimony.

iv. **Requests to admit**

Responses to requests for admission filed under FRCP 36 and its state counterparts are judicially binding in the lawsuit in which they are filed, but are inadmissible in any other litigation, even when offered against the party who filed them originally.

d. **Admissions by agents and employees**

At common law, statements by an agent or employee were admissible against the employer only when the agent or employee had speaking authority. Thus statements by a truck driver after an accident were often excluded because the driver lacked authority to speak for the employer. Under FRE 801(d)(2)(D), statements by an employee are admissible against the employer if the employee was speaking about a matter within the scope of his duties, regardless whether the employee *had authority* to speak. **[See Ch. 4, Sec. B5]**

e. **Coconspirator statements**

Under FRE 801(d)(2)(E), statements by one conspirator can be admitted against another if (1) declarant and defendant conspired, (2) the statement furthered the conspiracy, and (3) the statement was made during the pendency of the venture. Under *Bourjaily,* the judge acting under FRE 104(a) must find these facts by a preponderance of the evidence before admitting a statement under this exception. Even if the judge finds a conspiracy to exist for purposes of admitting the statement, the jury can ultimately decide that there was no conspiracy, because the jury has an independent fact-finding function and is governed by a beyond-reasonable-doubt standard. In deciding whether there was a conspiracy, the judge may consider the statement itself (despite the bootstrapping problem), but the statement is not itself **sufficient** to establish the existence of a conspiracy, and additional evidence beyond the statement is required. **[See Ch. 4, Sec. B6]**

2.   Exceptions Not Requiring Declarant Unavailability
Many important exceptions apply to out-of-court statements regardless whether or not the declarant is available to testify. **[See Ch. 4, Sec. C]**

a.   Present sense impressions
FRE 803(1) recognizes an exception for statements describing or explaining a condition made while the declarant was perceiving it, or immediately thereafter. The statement must have been made contemporaneously with the event, or at most only a few seconds afterwards, and must describe that event. **[See Ch. 4, Sec. C1]**

b.   Excited utterances
FRE 803(2) reaches statements relating to a startling event made while the declarant was under the stress of excitement caused by the event. The court must find that the statement was an excited utterance before it may be admitted. Under the modern view, the statement itself can be considered as evidence that the startling event occurred (despite the bootstrapping problem). Because the stress of excitement can last for minutes and sometimes even hours, the allowable time period after the event for a statement to be considered an excited utterance is much longer than the time lapse permitted for present sense impressions. **[See Ch. 4, Sec. C2]**

c.   State-of-mind
FRE 803(3) creates a critically-important exception for statements by a declarant describing her current physical condition or mental state. Such

statements may be used to prove (a) the mental state itself, or (b) future conduct by the speaker. But state-of-mind statements admitted under FRE 803(3) cannot be used to prove the truth of memories or beliefs about events in the past (unless they relate to execution, revocation, or terms of the declarant's will). See FRE 803(3). **[See Ch. 4, Sec. C3]**

i. **Physical condition**

Statements describing current ailments, pains, and injuries fit the exception even if not made to a doctor. The statements must relate to current physical condition, and they can support some inferences about the recent past and immediate future. For example, it may be inferred that a declarant who complains of a broken arm in the morning is probably not practicing violin that afternoon.

ii. **Proving mental state**

Often the mental state of the declarant is an issue in a case, particularly if the declarant is a victim or a party. Statements by the declarant revealing that mental state may be highly relevant. For example, out-of-court statements by an alleged extortion victim may be highly probative in proving that he was put in a state of fear by defendant's conduct.

iii. **Proving future conduct**

The mental state of the declarant, as shown by his state-of-mind statement admitted under FRE 803(3), can be used to prove his future conduct. If he says he intends to do something, he is more likely to do it (although this conclusion is less than certain because we do not always do what we intend to do). In the *Hillmon* case, the Supreme Court approved use of a statement of intent (I intend to go with Hillmon) to prove future conduct (declarant did go with Hillmon). In an ambiguous phrase, the Court seemed to suggest that the declarant's statement could be used to prove not only the declarant's future conduct but Hillmon's as well. The House Report to FRE 803(3) says that the *Hillmon* doctrine should be limited, and that state-of-mind statements are admissible to prove **declarant's** future conduct, but not future conduct by another person. Modern decisions, both state and federal, are not in complete agreement on this matter. Some modern state cases allow statements of intent to prove what another person did with the declarant, and other modern cases (both state and federal) take this approach if there is additional evidence tending to prove what the other person did.

d. Medical diagnosis or treatment

FRE 803(4) creates an exception for statements made for purposes of medical diagnosis or treatment. Such statements may describe the declarant's medical history or her past or present symptoms. They may also describe the inception or external source of the injury or condition. Such information must be reasonably pertinent to diagnosis or treatment rather than simply ascribing fault in causing the injury or condition. The statements need not be made **by** the person receiving treatment, and need not be made to a doctor. Many child abuse cases allow statements identifying the abuser, on the theory that removing the child from an abusive environment is part of treatment. **[See Ch. 4, Sec. C4]**

e. Past recollection recorded

When a witness is unable to testify fully and accurately about an event, an earlier memorandum or record describing the event may be admissible under FRE 803(5). The exception applies only when the witness cannot remember, which means that the examining lawyer usually can resort to the exception only if she first tries but fails to refresh the recollection of the witness. The record must have been made by the witness, or, if made by another, then adopted by the witness. The making or adoption must have occurred when the matter was fresh in the memory of the witness. The record must also be shown to reflect her knowledge accurately. The past record is a substitute for live testimony and is not entitled to greater emphasis than live testimony. Hence the writing may be read to the jury under FRE 803(5), but does not itself come in as an exhibit (meaning that it does not go to the jury room during deliberations) unless offered by an adverse party. **[See Ch. 4, Sec. C5]**

f. Business records

Records of regularly conducted activity are admissible under FRE 803(6), provided they satisfy certain requirements. Such records are usually described as business records, but the exception includes records of nonprofit organizations as well. To invoke the exception, the proponent must lay a foundation. There are four requirements. First, the record must be regularly kept in the course of a regular business (which includes professions and nonprofit enterprises). Second, the source of the information must be someone with personal knowledge acting in the course of employment. Third, the record must have been made at or near the time of the events recorded or the conditions observed. Fourth, the custodian of records or other qualified witness (someone who can describe the making of the proffered record, or at least similar records) must offer testimony on the foregoing points, although this fourth point can be satisfied by offering a certificate that complies with FRE 902(11) or 902(12). These provisions envision an affidavit by a knowledgeable witness showing that the basic requirements of the exception are satisfied, which allows the proponent to bypass the necessity of actually calling the custodian of records or other qualified witness to lay the foundation. **[See Ch. 4, Sec. C6]**

i. **Multiple hearsay**
Business records often raise problems of multiple hearsay. If a record contains (sets forth or draws upon) statements by an outsider (someone who does not work for the business, thus lacks a business duty to be accurate), the exception does not apply unless the outsider's statement itself fits an exception. See FRE 805 (hearsay within hearsay admissible if each statement fits an exception). But if a record contains (sets forth or draws upon) multiple statements, each made by someone within the business acting in the course of her duties, then the record fits the exception even though it contains multiple layers of hearsay.

ii. **Untrustworthiness**
Even though the foundation is otherwise established, a business record may be excluded under FRE 803(6) if the source of information or the method or circumstances of preparation indicate lack of trustworthiness. In evaluating trustworthiness, courts consider many factors, including whether the record was made in anticipation of litigation, its utility apart from litigation, the presence or absence of motives to fabricate among those preparing the record, the simplicity or complexity of matters recorded, the training or experience of the preparers, and whether the record is offered by or against the entity that prepared it.

g. **Absence of records or entry**
For reasons similar to those underlying the business records exception, there is also an exception for proving the absence of such records or entries. See FRE 803(7). Under this provision, if an act, event, or condition would normally generate an entry or record, then evidence

that no such entry or record exists is admissible to show that the act or event did not occur or that the condition did not exist. **[See Ch. 4, Sec. C6d]**

h. Public records
Under FRE 803(8), public records are admissible to prove the activities of a public office or agency, or matters observed and reported under official duty, or certain investigative findings. **[See Ch. 4, Sec. C7]**

i. Activities of office or agency
Public records may be used to prove almost anything public agencies do, such as serving papers, issuing tickets, maintaining equipment, or responding to fires or other emergencies. See FRE 803(8)(A)(i).

ii. Matters observed
Under FRE 803(8)(A)(ii), public records may be used to prove things observed and recorded by a public agency as part of its legal duties, such as a Weather Bureau recording meteorological conditions or a social services agency the ways that a child is being cared for in a foster home. The source of the information must be someone with a duty to report, most commonly a public employee (usually within the agency), rather than a private citizen. The rule expressly bars use in criminal cases of public reports or records prepared by police officers or other law enforcement personnel. This "use restriction" protects the accused from being deprived of an opportunity to confront witnesses against him. The *Oates* case interprets the term "law enforcement personnel" to include government chemists who conduct laboratory analyses of drugs, and the principle reaches essentially all personnel in public forensic laboratories performing such work as fingerprint or ballistics analysis, and many related undertakings. *Oates* also holds that since the lab report is inadmissible under FRE 803(8), it should not be admitted under the business records exception in FRE 803(6) or the catchall exception now found in FRE 807. Despite the bar against use of law enforcement reports or records against the accused, leading decisions allow use of the exception for routine and nonadversarial records (like checkpoint records of the license tags on cars crossing a national border).

iii. Investigative findings
Public agencies investigate a wide range of matters, from civil rights complaints to airline crashes. FRE 803(8)(A)(iii) authorizes use of

reports reflecting the results of such investigations in civil cases and against the government in criminal cases. They cannot be admitted against criminal defendants. Unlike reports covered by Clause A(ii), investigative findings fit Clause A(iii), even when they rest on information gleaned from sources outside government, such as information obtained from private citizens. Investigative findings can be excluded when the sources of information or other circumstances indicate lack of trustworthiness. According to the ACN, factors to be considered in evaluating trustworthiness include the timeliness of the investigation, the skill or expertise of the investigator, whether a hearing was held, and possible motivational problems.

i. **Learned treatises**

In contrast to common law tradition, FRE 803(18) allows use of a learned treatise as substantive evidence (proof of whatever it asserts), provided that an expert is on the stand who can be examined about it. Before the treatise can be used, it must be established as a reliable authority by the testimony of the witness, by other expert testimony, or by judicial notice. **[See Ch. 4, Sec. C8]**

j. **Vital statistics**

Complementing the public records exception is a narrower one for vital statistics, reaching records of births, deaths, and marriages reported to a public office by legal requirement. See FRE 803(9). **[See Ch. 4, Sec. C9]**

k. **Absence of public record or entry**

FRE 803(10) creates an exception for a properly authenticated certification by a public agency that a diligent search failed to disclose a particular record or entry. **[See Ch. 4, Sec. C9]**

l. **Ancient documents**

FRE 803(16) recognizes an exception for statements in documents in existence for 20 years or more the authenticity of which is established. **[See Ch. 4, Sec. C9]**

m. **Commercial lists**

This exception reaches market reports and commercial catalogues when offered to prove points like selling price. It also reaches city directories and mortality tables. See FRE 803(17). **[See Ch. 4, Sec. C9]**

n. Reputation

Reputation of a person among associates in the community is admissible under an exception created by FRE 803(21). Reputation is hearsay when offered to prove the truth of that reputation, because reputation is a distillation of out-of-court statements by members of the community about the person. This exception is necessary to allow reputation evidence to be admitted to prove character under FRE 404, 405, and 608. **[See Ch. 4, Sec. C9]**

o. Court judgments

Under FRE 803(22), felony convictions are admissible to prove any fact essential to sustain the judgment. For example, in a wrongful death action, evidence that the defendant was previously convicted of murdering the victim could be admitted as evidence that defendant did in fact commit the killing. Modern liberalization of the doctrine of collateral estoppel often makes it unnecessary to rely on this exception. **[See Ch. 4, Sec. C9]**

3. Exceptions Requiring Declarant Unavailability

Some hearsay exceptions can be used only if the declarant is shown to be unavailable. See FRE 804. **[See Ch. 4, Sec. D]**

a. Unavailability defined

Five types of unavailability are listed in FRE 804(a). **[See Ch. 4, Sec. D1]**

i. Privilege

The declarant is exempted from testifying by ruling of the court on the ground of privilege.

ii. Refusal

The declarant refuses to testify despite an order of the court to do so.

iii. Lack of memory

The declarant can no longer remember the subject matter of the statement he made before, meaning essentially that he cannot remember the acts, events, or conditions described in his earlier statement.

iv. Death or illness

The declarant is unavailable to testify because of death or illness. If it appears that the declarant will be able to testify at some later time in the trial, the court may defer taking the testimony of the declarant, in preference to admitting his hearsay statement, particularly in criminal cases where the testimony relates to some critical point.

v. Absence

The proponent is unable to procure the attendance of the declarant by process or other reasonable means.

b. Wrongful procurement

None of the above grounds is sufficient to pave the way for statements under FRE 804(b) if the unavailability of the witness is due to the procurement or wrongdoing of the proponent of a statement for the purpose of preventing the witness from attending or testifying. Failure by the government to grant immunity to the declarant does not normally constitute wrongful procurement of declarant's unavailability. [**See Ch. 4, Sec. D1f**]

c. Constitutional unavailability

In addition to the grounds of unavailability listed in FRE 804(a), the Sixth Amendment right of confrontation has been interpreted as imposing a constitutional unavailability requirement in criminal cases. In *Barber v. Page*, the Supreme Court held that the prosecutor must show a good faith effort to produce the declarant before his out-of-court statements can be admitted under the former testimony exception. Normally compliance with FRE 804(a) satisfies the constitutional unavailability requirement, but the latter operates independently and can be more stringent. [**See Ch. 4, Sec. D1eii**]

d. Forfeiture of hearsay objection

A party who causes a declarant to be unavailable cannot, by that stratagem, invoke an exception created in FRE 804(b) for the purpose of offering statements by the declarant. In fact a party who causes the unavailability of a declarant, if it is done purposefully by wrongful conduct in order to keep the declarant from testifying, may wind up **forfeiting** the right to exclude hearsay statements by the declarant. See FRE 804(b)(6) (creating hearsay exception for statements "offered against a party that has wrongfully caused—or acquiesced in wrongfully causing—the declarant's unavailability as a witness, and did so intending that result"). If, for example, a court finds by a preponderance that a criminal defendant murdered a declarant to prevent him from testifying at trial, the defendant cannot **offer** statements by the declarant that might fit the against-interest exception in FRE 804(B)(3) because the defendant **procured** the unavailability of the declarant. At the same time, the prosecutor can offer against the defendant **any** statement made by the same declarant, such as his grand jury testimony, because the defendant has **forfeited** his right to exclude such statement as hearsay or as violating defendant's rights under the Confrontation Clause. **[See Ch. 4, Sec. D1f]**

e. **Former testimony**

A particularly reliable form of hearsay is former testimony, since statements in this form (unlike most forms of hearsay) were given under oath subject to cross-examination at a trial, hearing or deposition. In cases where the declarant is shown to be unavailable, FRE 804(b)(1) recognizes an exception for former testimony when it is offered **against** a party who had an **opportunity** at the earlier proceeding to examine the declarant and develop the testimony by direct, cross, or redirect examination. The party also must have had a **similar motive** to develop (or challenge) the testimony at the earlier proceeding as in the current proceeding. (In civil cases, it is sufficient if a **predecessor in interest** of the party against whom the former testimony is now offered had an opportunity and similar motive to develop the testimony.) **[See Ch. 4, Sec. D2]**

i. **Depositions**

The FRCP and FRCrimP also make depositions admissible under certain circumstances. Depositions allowed pursuant to a procedural rule are admissible even if they do not also satisfy the requirements of FRE 804(b)(1).

ii. **Grand jury testimony**

Grand jury testimony does not fit the former testimony exception when offered against criminal defendants, because they are not allowed to cross-examine witnesses at grand jury hearings, or even attend such hearings. If the defendant offers the grand jury testimony of an unavailable witness **against the government,** then the issue is whether the government had a similar motive to develop the testimony at the grand jury proceeding as it does at trial. In the *Salerno* case, the Court held that the defendant must show that the government had a similar motive, and courts split on the question whether prosecutors in this setting have a motive similar to the motive they have at trial. In *Salerno*, the Court rejected the argument that since the government refused to immunize the witness (which would have made him available to testify at trial), notions of adversarial fairness should block the government from arguing lack of motive to cross-examine during the grand jury proceedings. The Court held that the requirements of opportunity and similar motive are to be strictly applied even when defendants offer grand jury testimony against the government.

f. Dying declarations

A venerable hearsay exception admits statements by a declarant who believes he is dying which describe the cause or circumstances of what the declarant believes to be his impending death. At common law, such statements were only admissible in homicide cases, but FRE 804(b)(2) admits them in civil cases as well. The latter provision does not actually require that the declarant be dead, so long as he **thought** he was dying when he spoke, but the declarant must be unavailable or the exception cannot be used. **[See Ch. 4, Sec. D3]**

g. Statements against interest

This exception admits statements by an unavailable declarant that are so much against her interest that a reasonable person in his position would not have made the statement unless he believed it to be true. Under FRE 804(b)(3), statements can qualify if they are against the pecuniary or proprietary interest of the declarant, tend to subject him to civil or criminal liability, or render invalid his claim against another. **[See Ch. 4, Sec. D4]**

i. Subjective standard

The declarant must understand the statements are against her interest. If the declarant believes the statements advance her interests, they do not fit the exception.

ii. Conflicting interests

Often a person has several conflicting interests. When such multiple interests appear, the court should compare and weigh them and admit the statement if it seems to give up more than it gains.

iii. Fact versus statement

Sometimes it is the **fact asserted** that is against interest, sometimes it is the **making** of the statement, and often it is both. If either the fact asserted or the making of the statement is against interest, courts tend to apply the exception.

iv. Against penal interest

The common law exception did not extend to statements against **penal** interest because of concern about either false confessions by a third party or false testimony that a third party confessed to the charged crime. FRE 804(b)(3) allows statements against penal interest, but when offered by or against a criminal defendant the proponent must show corroborating circumstances clearly indicating the trustworthiness of the statement. Statements made by a declarant who is no longer in danger of criminal prosecution, for example, because of the running of the statute of limitations, are not considered against interest. Statements made by a declarant to curry favor with the authorities also are not considered against interest.

v. Collateral statements

Often when a declarant makes statements against interest, he also makes statements providing additional information that is not itself against the declarant's interest. Such neutral statements are known as collateral statements. In the *Williamson* case, the Supreme Court held that only statements shown to be against the declarant's interest are admissible under FRE 804(b)(3) and not collateral statements. Thus *Williamson* prevents a prosecutor from offering an out-of-court statement by an accomplice identifying the defendant as one of the participants in the crime **unless** the prosecutor could show on the facts of the case that naming others involved in the crime was against the **declarant's** penal interest. *Williamson* was not a constitutional decision so it is not binding on state courts. Many states follow *Williamson*, but some do not.

h. Catchall exceptions

The catchall exception provides flexibility by allowing courts to admit trustworthy hearsay that does not satisfy any of the exceptions described above. See FRE 807. Five requirements must be satisfied before hearsay may be admitted under the catchall exception. **[See Ch. 4, Sec. E]**

i. Trustworthiness

The hearsay must have equivalent circumstantial guarantees of trustworthiness. In civil cases, courts often consider the presence or absence of corroborating evidence in determining whether the statement is trustworthy. In criminal cases, however, *Idaho v. Wright* held that the existence of corroborating evidence does not count in evaluating the trustworthiness of hearsay when a confrontation objection is made to it. Hence courts are unlikely to consider it in evaluating trustworthiness for purposes of the catchall exception, at least when the hearsay is offered against the accused rather than against the government.

ii. Material

To fit the catchall, the hearsay must bear on a material fact. In practice, this requirement means only that the hearsay must be relevant under FRE 401–402.

iii. More probative

The hearsay offered under the catchall must be more probative than anything else available.

iv. Interests of justice

Hearsay may be admitted under the catchall only if it serves the interests of justice. In practice, courts usually say that the interests of justice are served when the hearsay seems reliable and not served when the hearsay seems unreliable.

v. Notice

In order to admit hearsay under the catchall exception, the proponent must provide notice to the adverse party sufficiently in advance of the trial or hearing to provide the adverse party an opportunity to meet it. The notice must specify the particulars of the statement and provide the name and address of the declarant.

■ CHAPTER 5. CONFRONTATION

E. Confrontation

The Sixth Amendment of the United States Constitution guarantees a criminal defendant the right to be confronted with the witnesses against him. The

Confrontation Clause applies not only in federal courts but also in state courts as part of due process of law under the Fourteenth Amendment.

1. **Right to be Present, to Face Prosecution Witnesses, and to Cross–Examine**

   The most fundamental right secured by the Confrontation Clause for criminal defendants is the right to cross-examine prosecution witnesses. Performing this critical function presupposes the presence of the defendant at his own trial and the presence of prosecution witnesses. **[See Ch. 5, Sec. A3]**

2. **Right to Impeach**

   If a statute or court ruling unduly interferes with a defendant's ability to impeach a prosecution witness, it may be unconstitutional under the Confrontation Clause. **[See Ch. 5, Sec. A3e]**

3. **Right to Exclude Testimonial and Some Other Hearsay**

   The term "witness against" in the Confrontation Clause has been interpreted to include hearsay declarants.

   a. **Testimonial hearsay**

      The Clause entitles defendants to exclude "testimonial" hearsay, which includes *at least* statements given by eyewitnesses to police investigating crimes, and the right to exclude such material is critical to criminal defendants. This doctrine originated in the Court's decision in *Crawford v. Washington*, 541 U.S. 36 (2004). If the declarant *testifies at trial* and can be cross-examined on what he told police, however, the Confrontation Clause no longer stands in the way. Even so, the hearsay doctrine blocks the use of at least some such statements. If the declarant *has testified* in a previous proceeding or trial, and was then *actually* cross-examined by the defendant, once again the Confrontation Clause no longer stands in the way, and some such statements may be admissible as a matter of hearsay law because they fit exceptions like the one for former testimony in FRE 804(b)(1), at least if the witness is unavailable to testify at trial. **[See Ch. 5, Secs. A & B]**

   b. **Nontestimonial hearsay**

      The Supreme Court has held that the Confrontation Clause does not apply to nontestimonial hearsay. The Clause entitles the accused to confront anyone who is a "witness against" him, and this expression covers only those who make "testimonial" statements. In extreme cases, admitting even nontestimonial statements might deprive the accused of a fair trial, and in such cases the Due Process Clause may well require exclusion. Many states also regulate the use of hearsay against the accused under provisions of their constitutions that are similar to the Confrontation Clause, and at least some of these states continue to apply their own state versions of the old standard of *Ohio v. Roberts*, 448 U.S. 56 (1980) that used to be the basis of federal confrontation law. At least sometimes, states taking this approach continue to require the prosecutor to show that the hearsay declarant is unavailable. In addition, generally these states (following their versions of the *Roberts* standard) require a showing that a statement is reliable. Reliability is assumed if a statement fits one of the "firmly rooted" exceptions, such as the ones for business records or excited utterances, but reliability is not assumed if a statement does not fit such an exception and is offered under a newer or less established exceptions, such as the ones covering child victim hearsay or the against-interest exception as applied to statements against penal interest, or the catchall. In any such case, admissibility depends on a particularized showing that the statement is reliable. **[See Ch. 5, Sec. B8]**

4. **Limits of Confrontation, and Forfeiture of Objection**

   a. **Certain exceptions approved**
      Consistently the Supreme Court has approved the use of certain hearsay exceptions to admit out-of-court statements against the accused. Thus *Crawford* indicates approval of the exceptions for coconspirator statements and business records, and *Crawford* hints at the possibility that dying declarations might be admissible (without resolving the question). The exceptions for present sense impressions, excited utterances, state-of-mind statements, and medical statements, probably continue to have clear sledding when they are not testimonial in nature. This means that many statements made in purely private conversations are admissible when they fit those exceptions, but that such statements are excludable if made to police in the course of investigating crimes (again assuming that the declarant does not testify). **[See Ch. 5, Secs. B2 & B4]**

   b. **Nonhearsay uses**
      Probably nonhearsay uses of out-of-court statements do not violate the Confrontation Clause, as *Crawford* suggested. **[See Ch. 5, Sec. B5]**

c. Forfeiture of right to exclude

If the defendant is shown to have caused the unavailability of the declarant for the purpose of silencing him (as by murder or frightening him into refusing to testify, for example), he forfeits his right to exclude his prior statements on grounds of either hearsay or confrontation. The Court in *Crawford* approved this principle, and it is embodied in FRE 804(b)(6). **[See Ch. 5, Sec. B6]**

■ CHAPTER 6. CHARACTER AND HABIT EVIDENCE

F. Character and Habit Evidence

1. Character to Prove Past Conduct

Evidence of a person's character is generally excluded, but with important exceptions, if offered to prove that he acted in accordance with that character on a particular occasion. For purposes of evidence law, character generally means a propensity to engage or not engage in certain behavior, such as drinking excessively, driving carefully, or being truthful, law-abiding, or peaceable. Thus each person has multiple traits of character. **[See Ch. 6, Sec. E]**

a. First exception: Criminal defendants

A criminal defendant is allowed to offer evidence of a pertinent trait of his own character to prove that he did not commit the crime. Thus a defendant charged with assault can offer evidence of his peacefulness and a defendant charged with embezzlement can offer proof of his honesty. The prosecutor cannot be the first to introduce evidence of defendant's character, but if defendant offers such evidence the prosecutor can introduce character evidence in rebuttal. Also, if the defendant offers evidence of a trait of character of the alleged victim under FRE 404(a)(2), the prosecutor may introduce evidence of the *same* trait of character of the defendant: If, for example, defendant in a trial for assault offers proof that the alleged victim was a violently aggressive person (in support of the claim that the victim started the affray), then the prosecutor may offer proof that *defendant* is a violently aggressive person (to refute the defense and prove that defendant started the affray). In these and most instances, character must be proved by reputation or opinion evidence, not specific instances. But on cross-examination of a witness who testifies to the character of another person, inquiry is allowed into specific instances of conduct by the other person. **[See Ch. 6, Sec. E1]**

b.   Second exception: Crime victims

Evidence of a pertinent trait of character of a crime victim is admissible when offered by (a) the accused or (b) the prosecution to rebut this evidence. Thus a defendant charged with assault may introduce evidence that the victim had a violent character to support a self-defense claim, and the prosecutor can rebut by offering evidence that the victim had a peaceful character. Again character must be proved by reputation or opinion evidence, not specific instances. Again on cross-examination of the witness who testifies to the victim's character, inquiry may pursue specific instances of conduct by the victim. **[See Ch. 6, Sec. E2]**

i.   Rape shield statutes

Under FRE 412, and similar state rape shield statutes, the defendant is generally prohibited from introducing character evidence about the complainant's past sexual behavior or sexual predisposition as evidence that she likely consented to the acts for which defendant is being tried.

ii.   Exceptions to FRE 412

There are four exceptions to FRE 412: The first allows the defendant to prove other sexual behavior by the complainant in order to show that some third person was the source of the semen, injury, or other physical evidence of sexual contact. The second allows defendant to prove prior instances of sexual behavior by the complainant **with the defendant** in order to show that the complainant consented on the occasion in question. The third exception allows defendant to prove the sexual history or predisposition of the alleged victim if *excluding* the evidence would violate the constitutional right to present a defense. A fourth, which applies only in civil cases, allows evidence of the sexual behavior or sexual predisposition of the complainant if it is otherwise admissible and if probative value substantially outweighs the danger of harm to the victim or unfair prejudice to a party.

iii. Procedural requirements

A party offering evidence under any of these exceptions must serve notice at least 14 days before trial. The notice goes to the parties and also to the complainant. The court must conduct an *in camera* hearing to rule on admissibility, and the parties and complainant have a right to attend and be heard.

c. Third exception: Witnesses

In criminal and civil cases, evidence of the character of a witness is admissible to the extent allowed under the rules governing impeachment of witnesses, such as FRE 607, 608, and 609. This exception is necessary to prevent a conflict between the general prohibition of FRE 404(a) against using evidence of character to prove conduct and the rules governing impeachment, which allow evidence of a witness's untrustworthy character to prove that the witness may be untruthful while testifying. The defendant's character may be proved only by reputation or opinion evidence. On cross-examination, inquiry is allowed into specific instances of conduct. [See Ch. 6, Sec. E3]

d. Fourth exception: Sexual assault cases

FRE 413–415 apply in sexual assault and child molestation cases, and these provisions in effect override the restrictions that FRE 404(a) would otherwise impose. In some instances, FRE 413–415 pave the way to prove the character of the defendant as a way of proving his conduct. Specifically, FRE 413 and 414 allow evidence that he has committed other sexual assaults or child molestations, in order to show that he committed the assault or molestation for which he is being tried. The prosecutor must give advance notice before offering evidence under these rules. FRE 415 adopts the same principle in civil suits advancing claims based on conduct amounting to an offense of sexual assault or child molestation. [See Ch. 6, Sec. E4]

2. Character as an Element

Character evidence is admissible when a person's character is an element of a charge, claim, or defense. In criminal cases, character is almost never an element in a charge or defense. In civil cases, character is an element in a claim or defense in a small handful of situations, including negligent entrustment cases (where plaintiff must prove the character of defendant's agent in order to show that defendant was negligent in entrusting responsibility to the agent). Pursuing such a claim after an auto accident, for example, might require plaintiff to prove that the person driving defendant's car was a bad driver generally (plaintiff must also prove that the driver was negligent at the time of the accident). In cases where character is an element of a claim or defense, the proof may take the form of opinion or reputation testimony, and it may also show specific instances of conduct. **[See Ch. 6, Sec. F]**

3. **Prior Bad Acts**

Evidence of other crimes, wrongs, or acts by a person are admissible under FRE 404(b) for narrower purposes, like proving motive, opportunity, intent, preparation, plan, knowledge, identity, or absence of mistake or accident. The purposes listed in FRE 404(b) are **examples,** not an exclusive listing. Prior crimes, wrongs, or acts are potentially admissible when offered for **any** relevant purpose that does not require a general inference from character to conduct. But evidence offered under FRE 404(b) is subject to exclusion under FRE 403 when its probative value on the specific point for which it is offered is substantially outweighed by the danger of unfair prejudice or misleading the jury. **[See Ch. 6, Sec. G]**

a. **Extrinsic acts versus intrinsic**

FRE 404(b) regulates and potentially excludes only prior acts that are **extrinsic** to the charged offense, such as drug possession on a prior occasion. Offenses that are **intrinsic** to the charged offense are admissible without having to satisfy FRE 404(b). For example, in a trial for selling drugs, the prosecutor can prove that defendant possessed the drugs prior to the sale. Because possession is intrinsic to the act of selling, the prosecutor may prove defendant's possession without having to justify the proof under FRE 404(b).

b. **Degree of similarity required**

FRE 404(b) does not necessarily require that the prior act be similar to the charged crime. Some uses of prior acts, such as showing motive, does not require similarity to the charged crime. Other uses, such as proving knowledge, may require similarity or the evidence would be irrelevant. When offered to prove *modus operandi*, the prior act must have a high degree of distinctive similarity in order to show that the charged offense bears the signature of the accused.

c. **Showing that the act was committed**

In federal courts under the Supreme Court's decision in *Huddleston,* a prior act can be shown under FRE 404(b) by proof sufficient to support a finding that defendant committed the act. Whether he did is a question for the jury under FRE 104(b) rather than a question for the judge under FRE 104(a). Some states do not follow *Huddleston,* and instead require that a prior act be shown by a preponderance of the evidence (or even clear and convincing proof), and assign this issue to the judge to resolve under FRE 104(a). It is thought that the latter course provides more protection for the defendant.

4. Habit Evidence

While character evidence is generally excluded when offered to prove past conduct (subject to important exceptions discussed above), habit evidence is generally admissible for this purpose. Habit is viewed as more probative because the invited inference is stronger and more specific. Also habit evidence does not carry the moral overtones associated with character evidence. **[See Ch. 6, Sec. H]**

a. Meaning of habit

Habit means particular behavior in a specific setting. The three criteria that courts find most useful in distinguishing among them are the specificity and regularity of the behavior and the degree to which it is automatic or unreflective.

b. Proof of habit

Habit is usually proved by witnesses testifying to prior specific instances of conduct. There must be a large enough sample to establish a pattern of behavior and sufficient consistency of response. Most modern courts also allow habit to be proved by opinion testimony.

c. Common law limitations rejected

FRE 406 rejects two limitations on habit evidence that were imposed by the common law. Those requirements were corroboration and absence of eyewitnesses. Under FRE 406, habit evidence is admissible regardless whether corroborated and regardless whether there were eyewitnesses.

■ CHAPTER 7. RELEVANCY: SPECIFIC APPLICATIONS

G. Relevancy: Specific Applications

Even though relevant, some Rules in Article IV require exclusion of some kinds of evidence. These exclusionary rules are partly designed to implement important policy objectives, such as encouraging settlement negotiations, plea bargaining, and subsequent remedial measures. They also serve to provide uniform and predictable treatment for important categories of evidence. Such evidence may satisfy the minimal standard of relevancy (see FRE 401), but much of it would likely be excluded on an ad hoc basis as unfairly prejudicial, confusing, or misleading (see FRE 403).

1. Subsequent Remedial Measures

Post-accident measures, taken in order to prevent future accidents of the same nature, are excludable under FRE 407 when offered to prove negligence, culpable conduct, a defect in the product or its design, or a need for warning or instruction. **[See Ch. 7, Sec. B]**

a. Rationale

Subsequent remedial measures are generally excluded because they have low probative value in showing fault (conditions may have been safe before, even though there was an accident), and parties should be encouraged (not penalized) for making conditions safer still.

b. Application

The exclusionary principle covers not only physical changes to premises or machines involved in accidents, but to changes in design, labels, warnings, instructions, and personnel or procedures.

c. Product liability suits

As amended in 1997, FRE 407 covers product liability suits, but many states do *not* apply the exclusionary principle in this setting, and did not follow the federal lead in amending their state counterpart to extend it to such cases.

d. *Erie* problem

Arguably state law on subsequent measures is substantive (hence should apply in diversity cases under *Erie*) because it is designed to affect conduct outside the courtroom (either encouraging or not encouraging subsequent repairs). Particularly after FRE 407 was amended so that it *expressly* applies in product cases, however, most federal courts apply the federal rule in this setting, and not state law.

e. Exceptions

There are several exceptions to FRE 407 under which evidence of subsequent remedial measures may be admitted.

i. Impeachment

Sometimes a defending party offers testimony that the machine or premises in question has a particular safety feature or that certain procedures are always followed. Proof of post-accident modifications or changes in procedures may be admissible if it would tend to refute such testimony, thereby impeaching the witness.

ii. Feasibility

Sometimes a defending party offers evidence that it would be impossible or impracticable to make a particular change that would prevent similar accidents. Here too, proof of subsequent measures is admissible if it tends to refute the testimony. But such evidence can be admitted to prove feasibility only if defendant has denied feasibility. If defendant says only that the conditions were reasonably safe at the time of the accident, and not that they were as safe as possible, then the door is *not* opened for the plaintiff to prove that remedial measures were later implemented.

2. Civil Settlement Offers and Negotiations

In order to encourage the settlement of civil claims, settlement agreements and offers to settle or compromise are generally inadmissible under FRE 408. The same is true of statements made in the course of settlement negotiations, including statements that concede or suggest that certain facts are true or that certain things happened, which might otherwise be relevant and compelling evidence of those facts or acts or events. Settlement agreements are excludable if offered in later civil suits or, by virtue of an amendment adopted in 2006, if offered in later criminal prosecutions. "Conduct or statements" made in civil settlement negotiations with agencies exercising "regulatory, investigative, or enforcement authority" are excludable from later civil suits, but (again under the 2006 amendment) they are **not excludable** from later criminal cases. Thus, for example, a nurse who faces license revocation for misconduct cannot exclude any statement that he or she makes in the course of civil negotiations with a regulating agency if later criminal charges are brought that arise out of the conduct leading to the revocation. [**See Ch. 7, Sec. C**]

a. Claim

The exclusionary principle applies only to agreements, offers, and statements that are made or entered into after a claim is advanced that the other side has not conceded. A claim is advanced by filing a lawsuit, but also by taking other steps indicating that a party seeks or expects redress for a grievance.

b. Dispute

FRE 408 applies only to disputed claims, and does not apply if the other side promptly acknowledges liability or promises to pay. In this situation, there is no dispute, and statements acknowledging responsibility or promising to pay are admissions under FRE 801(d)(2), and are generally admissible. Even if suit has been filed, the exclusionary principle does not apply to responses by a defendant who concedes (or does not dispute) the validity or the amount of the claim.

c. Settlement agreements

Ordinarily a settlement agreement is performed and results in dismissal of the underlying suit. If it is not performed, and if the suit is resumed or refiled, the exclusionary principle normally operates and the agreement is excludable. But if the plaintiff sues to enforce the agreement itself rather than the underlying claim, the exclusionary principle does not apply.

d. Settlements with a third party

FRE 408 also applies to a settlement with a third party, at least when such a settlement is offered as evidence bearing on the validity of the claim in litigation or its amount.

e. Exceptions

There are two recognized exceptions to the general principle. Until 2006, there was a third *possible* exception.

i. Proving bias

If a party settles with a nonparty who testifies as a witness, the settlement may be explored on cross if it bears on bias.

ii. Refuting claim of undue delay

If a party is charged with undue delay in settling, proof of attempts to settle are admissible by way of defense.

iii. Impeachment

Before 2006, it was not settled whether statements made in course of settlement negotiations could be used to impeach a party's testimony at trial, but an amendment to FRE 408 that was adopted in that year extended the exclusionary principle to the use of any statement made in settlement negotiations to impeach by "contradiction" or as "a prior inconsistent statement." It is to be expected that most states with Rules based on the federal model will follow the federal lead on this point.

3. Payment of Medical Expenses

Proof that one party paid the medical or similar expenses of another is inadmissible under FRE 409 when offered to show that the party is liable for the injury. The rationale is to avoid penalizing persons who act as Good Samaritans. **[See Ch. 7, Sec. D]**

4. Pleas and Plea Bargaining

Just as FRE 408 generally excludes evidence of settlement negotiations in civil cases, FRE 410 generally excludes evidence of plea bargaining that goes forward in criminal cases, at least if such evidence is offered, in a later case (either civil or criminal), against the person who was the defendant in the earlier criminal case. **[See Ch. 7, Sec. E]**

a. Withdrawn pleas

Sometimes courts, on a showing of good cause, allow a guilty plea to be withdrawn and the defendant proceeds to trial. FRE 410 prohibits the withdrawn guilty plea from being introduced as evidence against the defendant. If it were otherwise, the purpose in allowing defendant to withdraw the plea would be undermined.

b. Nolo pleas

Courts have discretion to accept pleas of nolo contendere (no contest) to allow a person charged with a crime to avoid a criminal trial without admitting to civil liability. To implement this purpose, nolo pleas are excludable from later civil litigation.

c. Plea bargaining statements

Statements made in the course of plea bargaining by the defendants or their lawyers are excludable if plea bargaining is unsuccessful and the case goes to trial.

i. Statements to police

Statements given by suspects to the police are generally not excludable as plea bargaining. One reason is that FRE 410 is limited to negotiations involving attorneys rather than police and suspects. Another reason is that police do not conduct plea bargaining, or have authority to do so. But if the prosecutor gives police officers authority to negotiate a plea, or if police act as if they can bargain and defendant reasonably believes the talks amount to plea bargaining, the exclusionary principle may apply after all.

ii. Impeachment or substantive evidence

Obviously FRE 410 requires exclusion of plea bargaining statements by the defendant when offered against him as substantive evidence. Legislative history makes it clear that FRE 410 also blocks the use against the defendant of plea bargaining statements offered to impeach any testimony he might give at a trial after the attempt to dispose of the case by a plea bargain has failed.

iii. Exceptions

In the rare case in which a defendant introduces his own plea bargaining statement, the prosecutor may sometimes introduce defendant's related statements (also made during plea bargaining), since language in FRE 410 echoes the principle embodied in FRE 106 under which a related statement may be admitted if it ought in fairness to be considered with other statements that have come in. Plea bargaining statements by the defendant are also admissible in trials for perjury or false statement.

5. Liability Insurance

Proof that a party was or was not covered by liability insurance cannot be admitted on the issue of negligence or other wrongful conduct. **[See Ch. 7, Sec. F]**

a. Rationale

Liability coverage is excluded for two reasons. First, it is thought to be irrelevant on the question whether a party was acting with due care at the time of the accident. Second, evidence of insurance coverage might tempt juries to find liability where none exists or boost recovery unjustifiably, and the absence of coverage might persuade juries to find against liability or reduce recovery unjustifiably.

b. Exceptions

There are several important exceptions to the rule excluding evidence of liability coverage.

i. Proving agency, ownership, control

The purchase of liability coverage for a car or premises indicates that the purchaser has an interest in it, and evidence of this fact is admissible for this purpose.

ii. Impeachment

When insurance investigators testify to the substance of eyewitness statements, or when written proof is offered in which investigators or adjusters played a role, their connection with liability carriers may be shown when it bears on possible bias in their testimony.

■ CHAPTER 8. COMPETENCY OF WITNESSES

H. Competency of Witnesses

The term competency is sometimes used in a general sense to refer to evidence that is admissible, as distinguished from evidence that is incompetent (meaning inadmissible). But competency is also a term of art referring to the qualifications expected of witnesses who take the stand and give testimony. A witness must be competent to testify. **[See Ch. 8]**

1. Almost Everyone is Competent as a Witness

Under FRE 601, everyone is competent to testify, except persons specifically made incompetent by the rules. Among the most important categories of persons who are incompetent to testify are judges (who are incompetent to serve as witnesses in cases in which they preside) and jurors (who are incompetent to testify in the cases in which they sit). These are important but very narrow exceptions to the general principle that very nearly every person is competent to be a witness.

2. Mentally Disabled Witnesses

Even witnesses suffering from serious mental incapacities may testify under FRE 601, provided they have relevant evidence to offer. Paradoxically, courts can authorize a voir dire examination if serious questions of mental capacity arise, presumably in order to bar testimony by a witness who suffers from some serious mental disability on grounds that such testimony could not reasonably affect the matters to be decided (and in that somewhat peculiar sense it is irrelevant or perhaps excludable under FRE 403 as a waste of time or as introducing confusion and unnecessary complication). It is at least doubtful that courts have authority to **order** a prospective witness to submit to a mental examination, but courts probably have authority **to refuse to allow testimony** by a witness who has very serious mental problems and is unwilling to be examined.

3. **Drug or Alcohol Use or Addiction**

The fact that a witness was under the influence of drugs or alcohol at the time of the event (or was an alcoholic or drug addict) generally does not make her incompetent. To the extent drug or alcohol use at the time of the events may have impaired her perception or memory, it may be raised by way of impeachment. If she is under the influence of drugs or alcohol at the time of testifying, the usual solution is to delay her testimony until she recovers.

4. **Hypnotized Witnesses**

Because of the danger that hypnotized witnesses will remember facts that never happened, most states regulate the testimony of hypnotized witnesses. Some bar hypnotically-refreshed testimony entirely (or at least new memories produced as a result of hypnosis). Some bar it unless certain procedural safeguards are followed. Some admit it subject to impeachment by the adverse party. In the *Rock* case, the Supreme Court held that an absolute bar against hypnotically-refreshed testimony by a criminal defendant is unconstitutional.

5. **Children**

At common law, children below a certain age were presumptively incompetent to testify, and a few states continue in this tradition. The Federal Rules do not impose special restrictions or qualifications on child witnesses, although many courts continue the tradition of voir dire examinations of children to test their understanding of the duty to tell the truth and their ability to deal with direct and cross-examination. In cases where a child is unable to testify in court, or would be psychologically damaged by doing so, many states now have provisions allowing children to testify by deposition or by closed-circuit television from outside the courtroom.

6. Lawyers

Although no evidence rule bars lawyers from testifying in cases that they are trying, such dual roles of advocate and witness are prohibited by ethics codes.

7. Judges

As noted above, judges cannot testify in cases in which they preside.

8. Jurors: Trial Testimony

As noted above, jurors may not testify in the trials in which they sit.

9. Jurors: Impeaching Verdicts

In addition from being barred from testifying in cases where they sit, jurors are not allowed, after returning a verdict, to give evidence impeaching that verdict. Under FRE 606(b) testimony or affidavits by jurors describing any matter or statement during deliberations, the effect of anything on the mind of any juror, and the mental processes of any juror are generally excluded. This exclusionary principle covers virtually everything that a juror might say after a verdict that would be relevant in showing that it is somehow improper, but the Rule also makes three large exceptions that result in admitting proof in some cases:

a. Extraneous information

One exception allows the use of juror testimony or affidavits to prove that they were provided extraneous prejudicial information, often in the form of media reports about the trial or events in litigation. Sometimes jurors act on their own by going to the scene of a crime or accident, or by conducting outside investigations or by performing experiments with physical evidence in the jury room, and information gleaned in these ways also qualifies as extraneous prejudicial information that can be proved by affidavit.

b. Outside influence

A second exception allows the use of juror testimony or affidavits to prove outside influence, such as bribes or threats to themselves or their families.

c. Error on verdict form

The third exception, added by language amending FRE 606(b) in 2006, allows the use of juror testimony or affidavits to prove that a mistake was made in entering the verdict onto the verdict form, such as omitting a critical zero (if the form said "$10,000" and the intent was to say "$100,000," juror testimony or affidavits would be admissible to prove this point).

10. Dead Man's Statutes

Many states have such statutes in varying forms. They block or restrict parties who sue the estates of decedents from testifying as witnesses. A primary purpose of such statutes is to prevent claimants from giving false testimony that the estate cannot rebut because the decedent cannot reply. There is no federal Dead Man's Statute, but federal courts must defer to such state statutes in diversity cases litigated in federal court.

■ CHAPTER 9. DIRECT AND CROSS–EXAMINATION

I.   Direct and Cross–Examination

When witnesses are called to the stand, they are first questioned on direct examination by the calling party. Cross-examination by the adverse party follows, unless the adverse party has no questions to ask. Usually direct and cross-examination bring matters to an end for each witness, but sometimes questioning continues. There may be redirect by the calling party, and then recross by the adverse party, and such further redirect and recross as may be necessary. Under FRE 611(a), the trial judge can invite or limit further questioning: The Rule provides that the judge has discretion to control the mode and order of interrogating witnesses. The judge may allow the witness to testify by presenting a narrative rather than requiring him to respond to a series of specific questions propounded by counsel, even though this question-and-answer process is by far the most common means of adducing testimony by witnesses. **[See Ch. 9, Secs. A & B]**

1.   Leading Questions

The fundamental rule of direct examination is that a party generally cannot put leading questions to its own witnesses. A leading question is one that suggests the answer sought by the questioner, by phrasing, tone, or larger context. There are, however, several exceptions to the rule barring leading questions on direct.

a. **Preliminary matters**

Courts may allow leading questions seeking background information about a witness, such as his name, address, place of employment, or similar details. Such matters are usually uncontested, and leading questions can cover the territory faster.

b. **Adverse or hostile witness**

Leading questions are generally proper when one party calls and questions an adverse party, or a witness identified with an adverse party, or a witness who is for some other reason hostile to the cause of the calling party.

c. **Forgetful or frightened witness**

Courts often allow leading questions to develop the testimony of witnesses who are forgetful or frightened.

d. **Child witness**

Courts often allow attorneys greater leeway to lead child witnesses, especially a very young child, because otherwise it may take longer or actually prove impossible to develop what such a child has to say.

2. **Refreshing Recollection**

When a witness lacks full or partial recollection about a matter, an attorney may attempt to refresh his memory by letting him review a document that may revive his memory. If memory is refreshed, he may then testify on that basis. If not, the document or other matter is not necessarily admissible to prove the point. It must qualify under other rules, such as the hearsay exception for past recollection recorded (FRE 803(5)) or the rule covering prior inconsistent statements of testifying witnesses (FRE 801(d)(1)(A)). The adverse party is entitled to examine writings used to refresh recollection, to use them on cross-examination, and to introduce portions that relate to the testimony of the witness. [**See Ch. 9, Sec. B5**]

3. **Cross–Examination**

Cross-examination is a fundamental trial right. If a witness cannot be cross-examined by the adverse party, her direct testimony may be stricken and sometimes a mistrial must be declared. [**See Ch. 9, Sec. C**]

a. Scope of cross

The majority rule is that cross-examination is limited to the scope of direct. A minority of jurisdictions follow a wide open approach allowing cross-examination on new matters. FRE 611(b) generally limits cross-examination to the scope of direct, but gives trial courts discretion to permit examination into new matter by nonleading questions.

b. Leading questions

Leading questions are allowed on cross-examination, except in special circumstances. One of these is the situation in which one party calls an adverse party as a witness. Here it is sensible to allow the calling party to ask leading questions (because the witness is adverse) and to limit the attorney for the witness to nonleading questions because the lawyer is actually examining his own client.

c. Harassment of witnesses

Cross-examination should not be used simply to badger or demean a witness. FRE 611(a) authorizes trial judges to exercise reasonable control over questioning in order to protect witnesses from harassment or undue embarrassment. Ethics codes impose similar constraints.

d. Questioning by judge

In addition to calling witnesses on their own initiative under FRE 614(a), judges may question witnesses called by a party under FRE 614(b). Parties may of course object if such questions become improper or if the judge misuses the power by questioning that is excessive or that communicates to the jury, in a fashion that is too heavy-handed, the judge's opinion on the merits of the case. See FRE 614(c) (allowing objection "at the time" or at "the next available opportunity" when jury is not present).

e. Exclusion of witnesses

At the request of a party, the court must exclude from the courtroom witnesses who have not yet testified so they do not hear testimony by other witnesses. See FRE 615. The court may also make such an order on its own motion. But certain people cannot be excluded, including parties, representatives of corporations or governmental entities, and other persons essential to the presentation of a party's cause. Also statutes or special rules in the federal system and in most states block courts from excluding certain categories of people who are victims of the crimes that lead to the charges being tried in the case (often these provisions reach relatives of victims too).

■ CHAPTER 10. IMPEACHMENT AND REHABILITATION

J. Impeachment and Rehabilitation

All witnesses are subject to impeachment, which involves questioning or extrinsic evidence attacking credibility. There are five recognized methods: Witnesses may be impeached by showing that (1) they are **biased** for or against a party, (2) they have a **defect in sensory or mental capacity,** (3) that they have **bad character for truthfulness** (as shown by prior bad acts, convictions, or by reputation or opinion evidence), (4) they have made **prior inconsistent statements,** or (5) their testimony is false or mistaken on some important point, as indicated by evidence that **contradicts** something to which they have testified. Although these methods of impeachment are permitted in federal courts, not all are covered by the Rules. The common law voucher rule, which prevented a party from impeaching its own witness, has been abolished. Instead, FRE 607 provides that the credibility of a witness may be attacked by any party, including the party calling him. **[See Ch. 10, Secs. A & B]**

1. **First Method of Impeachment: Showing Bias**
   A witness may be impeached by showing that she is biased for or against a party, and bias is a broad term that includes such things as sympathy, financial connection, friendship, animus, and bribery. There is no federal rule governing bias, but the Supreme Court recognized bias in the *Abel* case as a proper method of impeachment. The bias of a witness is always relevant. **[See Ch. 10, Sec. C]**

   a. **Types of bias**
      Many facts may indicate bias, including a personal, social, romantic, sexual, or business relationships with a party or financial interest in the

outcome of the suit. Other points that show bias are fear of retaliation, settlement of a claim between witness and party, the prospect of criminal proceedings against a witness who testifies for the government in another case, or the existence of a plea agreement committing the witness to testify for the government.

b. Proving bias

Bias is usually brought out on cross-examination, although it can also be proved by extrinsic evidence (meaning, for the most part, testimony by other witnesses) because, as courts often say, bias is never "collateral." To save trial time, however, some courts require that the witness be asked about bias on cross, allowing extrinsic evidence only if the point could not be adequately covered on cross, or if the witness has had a chance to explain the charge of bias. The calling party may develop matters relating to bias on direct, so jurors do not think the calling party is hiding important information from them.

c. Restricting proof of bias

Parties are entitled to prove bias on the part of an adverse witness, and imposing undue restrictions on such proof may be reversible error. In a criminal case, unreasonable limits on a attempt to impeach a witness for bias may also violate the Sixth Amendment right of confrontation. But the trial judge has discretion to limit attacks attempting to establish bias in order to prevent harassment of witnesses, confusion of issues, waste of time, and unfair prejudice to parties.

2. Second Method of Impeachment: Showing Defect in Sensory or Mental Capacity

A witness may be impeached by showing a defect in her sensory or mental capacity affecting either her ability to observe at the time of the events or to recollect and recount the events at trial. Common examples include bad eyesight, poor hearing, or failing memory. The attacking party may also bring out deficiencies in the opportunity to observe, such as poor lighting or being far away from the acts, events or conditions that the witness describes in her testimony. Although this method of impeachment is universally accepted, it is not specifically addressed by any Federal Rule. [**See Ch. 10, Sec. D**]

a. Form of proof

A defect in sensory or mental capacity (or opportunity to observe) may be brought out on cross-examination or proved by extrinsic evidence.

b. Alcohol or drug use

Both perception and memory may be affected by the use of drugs and alcohol, so it is proper to impeach a witness by showing her alcohol or drug use at the time of the event to which she testifies. If she is under the influence of alcohol or drugs at the time of trial, that can be explored too.

c. Mental illness or disability

The attacking party may show by cross-examination or extrinsic evidence that the witness suffers (or once did) from a mental illness that could affect her ability to perceive or recall the events at issue.

3. Third Method of Impeachment: Showing Bad Character By Means of Prior Bad Acts

A witness may be asked about specific instances of conduct that suggest untruthfulness. In most jurisdictions, this method of attack is one that can only be mounted on cross-examination. **[See Ch. 10, Sec. E]**

a. Truthfulness

Some jurisdictions allow inquiry into past acts bearing on general morality, but FRE 608(b) limits the inquiry to acts bearing on truthfulness—those involving such things as fraud, falsehood, or deception. More general moral shortcomings, such as drug use or prostitution, do not qualify.

b. Focus on act

The question is whether the witness did the act, not whether she was arrested for it. Thus the questioner should **not** ask "Isn't it true that you were arrested for embezzlement?" Instead the questioner should ask "Isn't it true that you embezzled funds from your employer?"

c. Good faith basis

The judge can require the questioner to show a good faith basis before going forward. It is improper to ask about past conduct when the questioner lacks any basis for believing such conduct occurred. A groundless accusation, even though emphatically denied, may unfairly taint the witness.

d. Discretion to exclude

Trial judges have discretion under FRE 608(b), as well as FRE 403 and 611, to bar questions that have low probative value and are overbalanced by the need to protect parties from prejudice, witnesses from harassment and embarrassment, juries from confusion, and trials from being prolonged. Although FRE 608(b) does not contain a time limit, courts have discretion to exclude acts that are remote in time.

e. No extrinsic evidence

Under FRE 608(b), extrinsic evidence of untruthful acts is not admissible. (If the conduct resulted in conviction, the conviction may be admissible under FRE 609, as discussed in the next subsection.) If the witness denies the act on cross-examination, FRE 608(b) blocks the attacking party from proving the act by extrinsic evidence. It is said that the impeaching party must take the answer of the witness, and that extrinsic evidence on the point is "collateral."

4. Third Method of Impeachment (continued): Showing Bad Character By Means of Prior Criminal Convictions

Prior convictions may sometimes be used to impeach a witness. The theory is that a witness who committed certain types of crimes may be dishonest. This method of impeachment is controversial, however, because many convictions bear no direct or immediate relationship to veracity. Also such evidence can be prejudicial, particularly when the witness is the accused and must defend himself against other criminal charges. [**See Ch. 10, Sec. F**]

a. Automatic admissibility

FRE 609(a)(2) provides that convictions for crimes involving dishonesty or false statement are admissible to impeach a witness, regardless whether they are felonies or misdemeanors. Courts narrowly construe the rule in accordance with its legislative history and generally limit it to crimes such as perjury, forgery, fraud, and embezzlement (crimes that actually involve deceit, untruthfulness, or falsification).

b. Discretionary admissibility

FRE 609(a)(2) provides for discretionary admissibility of prior **felony** convictions to impeach, subject to a balancing test. The **possible** punishment rather than the actual punishment determines whether the crime was a felony, and the law of the jurisdiction where the conviction was obtained controls on classification as a felony.

c. Balancing tests

For witnesses other than the accused, prior felony convictions are admissible to impeach subject to Rule 403, which means they should be excluded if probative value is substantially out-weighed by the danger of unfair prejudice, confusion of issues, and related concerns. If the accused testifies, there is a more protective balancing test: Prior felony convictions are admissible to impeach only if their probative value outweighs their prejudicial effect to the accused.

d. Factors considered in balancing
In balancing probative value against prejudice, courts consider the nature of the prior crime and the extent to which it bears on veracity, its recency or remoteness, its similarity to the charged crime (which greatly increases prejudice), the entire criminal record of the witness, the importance of his testimony, and the importance of credibility issues in the trial.

e. Ten-year limit
FRE 609(b) in effect creates a presumption that convictions more than ten years old are not admissible for impeachment. The ten years are measured from the date of conviction or the release of the witness from confinement for that conviction, whichever is the later date. But a court may admit convictions more than ten years old if it determines on specific facts and circumstances that their probative value outweighs their prejudicial effect, and notice must be given to the opponent of the intent to use such convictions so that the opponent can contest their use.

f. Proof of conviction
The prior conviction may be proved either by getting the witness to admit it or by extrinsic evidence, such as a certified copy of the judgment of conviction. The calling party may bring out the prior convictions of its own witness on direct examination in order to take the sting out of anticipated cross-examination and to avoid appearing to conceal the witness's criminal past from the jury.

g. Details of conviction
Generally the impeaching party is allowed to bring out only the date and nature of the conviction and the punishment imposed, and sometimes the location where the conviction was obtained.

h. Effect of pardon or annulment
A conviction may not be introduced if it has been the subject of a pardon, annulment, or other equivalent procedure that is based on a finding of innocence or rehabilitation accompanied by a showing that the witness has no later felony convictions.

i.   Juvenile adjudications

A juvenile adjudication is generally not admissible to impeach a witness. But in criminal cases a juvenile conviction may be admissible to impeach a witness other than the accused if it would be admissible to attack the credibility of an adult and allowing the impeachment is necessary for a fair determination of guilt or innocence.

j.   Pendency of appeal

A conviction may be admitted even if it is being appealed, but evidence that an appeal has been taken is also admissible.

5.   Third Method of Impeachment (continued): Showing Bad Character By Means of Reputation or Opinion Evidence

A witness may be impeached by reputation or opinion evidence showing that he has an untruthful character. The character witness presenting this type of attack cannot be asked to describe specific instances of untruthful conduct, but must limit the testimony to a general conclusion. **[See Ch. 10, Sec. G]**

a.   Foundation

Before adducing testimony by one witness (the "character" witness) indicating that the reputation of another witness (the "target" or "principal" witness) is not good, the attacking party must show that the character witness is familiar with reputation of the target witness. Before presenting the opinion of the character witness that the target witness is not a truthful person, the attacking party must show that the character witness has an adequate basis for such an opinion.

b.   Cross-examination

A character witness may be impeached like any other witness. In this particular situation, the impeachment may involve asking the character witness about specific instances of conduct on the part of the target witness that undercut the substance of the opinion or reputation to which the character witness has testified, or that suggests that the community (in the case of reputation testimony) or the character witness herself (in the case of opinion testimony) lacks sufficient information or has misjudged the character of the target witness. The only permissible use for such questions is to help the jury appraise whether reputation or opinion has been given, and these questions may not be used as proof that the target witness did or did not do whatever acts are being asked about.

6. **Fourth Method of Impeachment: Showing Prior Inconsistent Statements**
A witness may be impeached by evidence that he made earlier statements inconsistent with his trial testimony. **[See Ch. 10, Sec. H]**

a. **Inconsistent**
A statement is inconsistent if it differs in any significant way from trial testimony or if comparing the prior statement with the trial testimony suggests that the witness has changed his view or made a mistake that matters in the case. If a prior statement omits a material detail, which under the circumstances would likely have been included if true, the statement is inconsistent with trial testimony that includes this detail. Most courts view a claim of lack of memory at trial as inconsistent with an earlier affirmative statement about a point, although some courts find the earlier statement to be inconsistent only where the claim of memory loss at trial appears to be feigned.

b. **Foundation required**
FRE 613(a) provides that a lawyer cross-examining a witness about her prior statement need not first show or make known the contents or substance of the statement before asking questions about it, and thus rejects common law tradition requiring the cross-examiner to observe this nicety. The same provision, however, requires the cross-examiner on request to show or disclose the substance of the statement to opposing counsel.

c. **Opportunity to explain**
FRE 613(b) provides that extrinsic evidence of a prior inconsistent statement can be admitted only if the witness is afforded an opportunity to deny or explain the statement, unless the interests of justice otherwise require. The opportunity to explain or deny can occur after the witness was impeached by questions asking her about the statement.

d. **Collateral matters**
Courts normally block attempts to impeach a witness by means of prior inconsistent statements that go only to collateral matters. If such a statement tends **neither** to undermine an assertion by the witness on some substantive point **nor** to demonstrate or refute the existence of some bias, capacity, or truthful disposition on the part of the witness, then the statement relates to a collateral matter and may be excluded.

e. **Abuse of FRE 607**

While FRE 607 lets the calling party impeach its own witness, most courts have concluded that calling a witness for the primary purpose of impeaching him by inconsistent statements that are likely to be taken as substantive evidence is an abuse that should be disallowed. Here prior statements should be excluded under FRE 403. At common law, this danger was avoided by a rule excluding prior inconsistent statements unless the impeaching party was both **surprised and damaged** by the trial testimony. Some commentators urge judicial adoption of the common law approach under FRE 607.

f. **Impeaching by silence**

Sometimes the fact that a testifying witness remained silent on some prior occasion seems inconsistent with the substance of positive statements that the witness makes on the stand, at least in cases where it seems likely that the witness would have spoken out before, in a manner similar to his trial testimony, rather than remaining silent.

g. **Impeaching and Miranda rights**

It is settled that statements given by the accused during the course of custodial questioning that proceeds in violation of *Miranda* rights can be used to impeach the accused if he takes the stand and testifies in a way that is inconsistent with those statements. Thus statements made by the accused during custodial interrogation when *Miranda* warnings should have been given but were not may be used in this way, as well as statements made during questioning that went forward after warnings were given despite the fact that the accused requested counsel (when questioning should have ceased). It is different with silence after *Miranda* warnings. If the accused receives such warnings and declines to say anything, then his post-warning silence may not be used to impeach, even if that silence seems inconsistent with positive trial testimony by the accused.

7. **Fifth (and Last) Method of Impeachment: Contradicting the Witness**

A witness may be impeached by contradictory evidence in the form of counterproof that something the witness said is not true (whether a purposeful falsehood or simply a mistake). The counterproof may raise doubts not only about the specific point contradicted but about the credibility of the witness more generally: If he is wrong on one point, how many others is he wrong about? Often impeachment by contradiction is accomplished by extrinsic evidence (testimony by other witnesses or physical evidence), but sometimes it can be accomplished simply by close questioning that gets the witness to admit that something he said in his direct testimony was wrong. **[See Ch. 10, Sec. I]**

a. **Dual relevancy requirement**

Under the traditional view, evidence to contradict a witness is *not* admissible if its *only* relevance is to prove the witness wrong on some specific point of her testimony. Instead the evidence must have dual relevancy, meaning that it must also be relevant for some *additional* reason, such as to prove a substantive point going to the merits of the case or to prove bias, defect of capacity, or untruthful disposition on the part of the witness. Some authorities recognize an exception to the dual relevancy requirement if the counterproof tends to refute a linchpin point that the witness simply could not be mistaken about if he is being truthful: If, for example, a witness says he was returning from a visit to his son, and the cross-examiner can show that the witness never had children, the point may be shown to contradict what the witness has said, even though the counterproof serves *only* to contradict, and doesn't prove a fact that counts in any other way in the case.

b. **Setting up witness**

Ordinarily impeachment by contradiction can be used only to attack testimony given on direct. Courts are reluctant to allow lawyers to set up a witness by questioning that allows them to open their own door to contradictory evidence that would not otherwise be admissible.

c. **Illegally-seized evidence**

Direct testimony may be contradicted by illegally-seized evidence as a check on perjury. Under the *Havens* case, even testimony on cross-examination can be contradicted by the use of illegally-seized evidence, provided the question on cross was reasonably suggested by the defendant's direct testimony.

8. **Rehabilitation or Repair**

Once a witness has been impeached, a calling party may try to rehabilitate or repair her credibility. But a party cannot repair until the witness has been attacked, because offering supporting testimony would violate the rule against bolstering one's own witness. It is permissible, however, for the calling party to bring out impeaching evidence on direct, in order to take the sting out of cross-examination and avoid the appearance of hiding important information from the jury. There are three common forms of rehabilitation. **[See Ch. 10, Sec. J]**

a. **Allowing witness an opportunity to explain**
The most common and simplest means of repair is to give the witness an chance to explain the impeaching matter, as by going into why or whether she made a prior inconsistent statement, or whether it really is inconsistent with what she is trying to say now.

b. **Showing character for truthfulness**
Once character for truthfulness is attacked, a supporting character witness can testify in the form of reputation or opinion that the principal witness has a truthful disposition. In attesting to this truthfulness disposition, the character witness cannot also say he thinks the testimony given by the principal witness is true or that the character witness believes what the principal witness is saying. Rather, the supporting character witness can only describe the general truthfulness of the principal witness.

i. **Attack on character**
This method of rehabilitation is proper only after the principal witness has been impeached in a way that amounts attacks her truthfulness. Impeachment that opens the door to this method of repair includes testimony giving negative character evidence under FRE 608(a), questioning that asks the principal witness about prior acts bearing on veracity under FRE 608(b), or bringing out her prior convictions under FRE 609. Normally impeaching attacks that show bias or inconsistent statements do not amount to attacks on character. But sometimes such impeachment, because of particular facts or context, leaves little room for any other explanation, and where the only likely explanation is that the witness is lying, then character has been attacked and showing good character becomes a proper method of repairing credibility after all.

ii. **Foundation for character testimony**
Before character evidence may be offered to rehabilitate, the party supporting the witness in this way must show that the character

witness is acquainted with the principal witness (if opinion evidence is offered) or with community sentiment about her (if reputation evidence is offered).

iii. Cross-examining the character witness

The supporting character witness may be asked about specific instances of conduct by the principal witness that bear on her veracity. The proper purpose of such inquiry is not to prove prior conduct by the principal witness, but only to call into question the extent of the knowledge of the character witness (in the case of opinion testimony) or the extent of knowledge in the community (in the case of reputation testimony), or to call into question the judgment of the character witness (in the case of opinion testimony) or the judgment of the community (in the case of reputation testimony).

9. Prior Consistent Statements

Evidence that a witness made prior statements consistent with trial testimony may be admissible to rehabilitate. If such statements are offered to rebut an express or implied charge against the declarant of recent fabrication or improper influence or motive, they are admissible under FRE 801(d)(1)(B) not only for rehabilitation but also as substantive evidence. When offered under this rule, the *Tome* case requires that the earlier statements were made before the motive to fabricate arose.

■ CHAPTER 11. OPINION AND EXPERT TESTIMONY

K. Opinion and Expert Testimony

Special rules govern the admissibility of opinion evidence and testimony by expert witnesses.

1. Lay Opinions

At common law, lay witnesses (anyone who was not an expert) generally could not give opinion testimony, with some exceptions. In contrast, FRE 701 permits lay opinion testimony if it rests on personal perception and is helpful to the trier of fact. **[See Ch. 11, Sec. A]**

a. **Collective facts doctrine**
The collective facts doctrine allows lay opinions that are based on an aggregation of specific details observed by the witness.

b. **Personal perception**
FRE 701(a) requires that lay opinions be rationally based on the perception of the witness. Thus opinions that are mere speculation or conjecture are excluded. But categorical certainty is not required, and a witness may qualify his testimony by saying he thinks or believes a fact to be true, provided that his opinion rests on firsthand knowledge.

c. **Helpfulness requirement**
Under FRE 701(b), a lay witness may give opinion testimony only if it helps understand the balance of his testimony or help determine the facts at issue. Opinion testimony is excludable if it merely tells jurors what they already know or how they should decide the case.

2. **Expert Opinions**
Unlike lay witnesses, expert witnesses may give opinions about matters that they did not personally perceive. Their knowledge, skill, and experience can qualify them to express an opinion despite their lack of firsthand knowledge about the matter or event. But expert opinions (like lay opinions) must assist the trier of fact or they are not admissible. See FRE 702. **[See Ch. 11, Sec. B]**

3. **Qualifications of Expert**
There are no uniform or rigid credentials required to qualify a witness as an expert. Under FRE 702 qualification as an expert witness may rest on knowledge, skill, experience, training, or education. Before a witness is allowed to testify as an expert, the calling party must lay a foundation showing such qualifications. Deciding whether the witness qualifies as an expert is up to the judge under FRE 104(a), but what weight to give the testimony is up to the jury. **[See Ch. 11, Sec. B1]**

4. **Bases for Expert Testimony**
There must be an adequate basis for an expert opinion, and FRE 703 sets out the three permissible bases. **[See Ch. 11, Sec. D]**

a. Facts perceived by expert

Expert opinion testimony may rest on personal perception. If the expert has examined the relevant facts or data firsthand, she may rely on what she learns in this way. Unlike lay opinion testimony, however, which *must* rest on such firsthand observation, expert testimony *need* not rest on firsthand knowledge. When the expert does rely on such firsthand knowledge, the calling party may bring out this basis during direct examination of the expert.

b. Facts made known to expert at trial

Expert opinion may also rest on facts or data made known to the witness at the trial or hearing, which may be accomplished by having the expert listen to testimony by other witnesses or by asking him hypothetical questions that recite the facts necessary for the opinion being sought (which facts must be supported by evidence already admitted).

c. Facts reasonably relied on

Expert opinion may also rest on outside information obtained from a variety of sources, provided that the information is of a type reasonably relied on by experts in the field in forming the kinds of opinions to which the expert is to testify. The information may come from treatises or other authorities, reports by third parties, test results, interviewing bystanders, and independent investigation. It is not necessary that such information already be provided in the case by evidence, and in fact the such information is usually in the form of hearsay that might not even be admissible. When the expert does rely on inadmissible hearsay as the basis for an opinion, FRE 703 bars the proponent from disclosing such hearsay to the jury unless the court determines that probative value *in helping the jury evaluate the expert's opinion* substantially outweighs their prejudicial effect. Under FRE 705, however, the adversary may question the expert about such material on cross-examination.

5. Ultimate Issue Rule Rejected

At common law, a witness could not testify about an ultimate issue because such testimony was thought to invade the province of the jury. FRE 704(a) repudiates this objection and allows testimony on ultimate issues, but the opinion must still meet the helpfulness requirement of FRE 701 or FRE 702. **[See Ch. 11, Sec. C]**

6. **Testimony About Mental Condition**

   FRE 704(b) prohibits experts from testifying that a criminal defendant had the mental state constituting an element of the crime charged or a defense thereto (this change was enacted after John Hinckley was acquitted, on grounds of insanity, of charges that he tried to kill President Reagan). **[See Ch. 11, Sec. C3]**

7. **Expressing Opinion Without Disclosing Underlying Facts**

   FRE 705 allows an expert to express an opinion and give the underlying reasons without first testifying to the supporting facts or data, unless the court otherwise requires. The purpose of this Rule is to reduce the use of hypothetical questions, which are criticized as confusing and time-consuming and susceptible to misuse as slanted minisummations in the middle of trial. **[See Ch. 11, Sec. E]**

8. **Appointing Expert Witnesses**

   Under FRE 706, the trial court may appoint expert witnesses at the request of the parties or on its own motion. In civil cases (other than condemnation actions), the expense of such experts must be borne by the parties in a proportion determined by the court and is assessed like other costs of the proceeding. The court has discretion whether to disclose to the jury (or allow the parties to disclose) that the court appointed the expert witness. **[See Ch. 11, Sec. F]**

9. **Scientific Evidence**

   Scientific evidence is almost always offered through testimony by experts and is regulated by the rules on expert testimony, by rules governing relevancy as opposed to confusion and prejudice (FRE 401–403), and by a special standard that once applied specifically to scientific evidence. At common law, the *Frye* rule required that scientific evidence reflect ideas or principles that had won general acceptance in the relevant scientific community. The *Daubert* decision discarded the *Frye* standard and required the judge to take a more active role, and specifically to pass on the reliability on evidence offered as science. The decision in *Kumho Tire* expanded the reach of *Daubert* to all expert testimony of a technical nature (not just "scientific" expertise). FRE 702 now incorporates criteria designed to implement the *Daubert* standard, and they require that (1) expert testimony rest on sufficient facts or data, (2) expert testimony reflect the application of reliable principles and methods, and (3) the principles and methods were reliably applied.

Whether a technique is reliable is a preliminary question for the court under FRE 104(a). In making this determination, the Supreme Court in *Daubert* suggested five factors to be considered (although none is conclusive): Courts should consider (1) whether the theory or technique can be tested, (2) whether it has been subject to peer review or publication, (3) known or potential rates of error, (4) the existence of established standards relating to the technique, and (5) whether the technique is generally accepted in the pertinent scientific community. **[See Ch. 11, Sec. G]**

■ CHAPTER 12. AUTHENTICATION

L.   Authentication

Before an exhibit of any sort (such as a document, photograph, or gun) is introduced, the proponent must "lay the foundation" by offering enough evidence to support a jury finding that the thing is what the proponent claims it is. Usually laying the foundation involves offering testimony or other evidence, and the "authentication requirement" (as the process is also called) actually applies to essentially all forms of nontestimonial evidence (from tape recordings to phone calls). **[See Ch. 12, Sec. A]**

1.   **Role of Judge and Jury**
     The judge decides whether enough evidence has been offered to support a finding that the exhibit is what its proponent claims. If the sufficiency standard is met, the exhibit is admitted and goes to the jury, which makes the ultimate determination whether the exhibit is authentic. This matter is viewed as raising issues of conditional relevancy under FRE 104(b): The exhibit is relevant if the condition is satisfied that it is what the proponent claims that it is. If the jury finds it to be authentic, the jury decides what weight to give it. If the jury finds the exhibit not to be authentic, the jury is instructed to give it no weight at all. **[See Ch. 12, Sec. A3]**

2.   **Steps in Process**
     Authenticating an exhibit involves (1) having it marked for identification, (2) proving that it is what the proponent claims, usually by offering the

testimony of someone with knowledge, (3) offering the exhibit in evidence, (4) letting counsel for the other side examine it, (5) allowing opportunity for objection, (6) obtaining the ruling of the court, and (7) in some cases, requesting permission to have the exhibit, if admitted, presented to the jury by reading it to them or having it passed among them. (The order of these steps varies according to local custom.) [See Ch. 12, Sec. A2]

3. **Pretrial Authentication**

Particularly in civil cases, discovery and pretrial proceedings often resolve authentication issues. In criminal cases, some of these issues are resolved prior to trial by stipulation, but usually some remain for trial. [See Ch. 12, Sec. A5]

4. **Sample Foundations**

Although many different foundations suffice to meet the authentication requirement (i.e., producing evidence sufficient to support a finding of authenticity), FRE 901(b) lists ten examples of foundations that satisfy the authentication requirement as a matter of law. [See Ch. 12, Secs. B & C]

a. **Testimony of person with knowledge**

This is the most widely used authentication method. A witness shown to have knowledge of the exhibit identifies it as what its proponent claims it to be. For example, a photograph can be authenticated by a person familiar with the scene depicted who testifies that it is a fair and accurate representation. For some exhibits, such as a gun or knife, the witness may be required to explain how she is able to identify it. [See Ch. 12, Sec. B1]

b. **Chain of custody**

If the evidence lacks distinctive markings and is essentially fungible (such as drugs seized from a suspect or found in a dwelling or car), chain-of-custody evidence is usually necessary. Here each person who had custody of the material any time from seizure to trial is called to identify it, to testify that it was not altered or tampered with, and to describe how it came into his possession and who he gave it to. A missing link in the chain is usually not fatal, however, and goes to weight rather than admissibility. [See Ch. 12, Sec. B2]

5. **Writings**

There are several methods available to authenticate writings:

a. Lay opinion on handwriting

A signature or document written by human hand can be authenticated by the testimony of a person familiar with the handwriting of the person in question. The witness need not have observed the signing or preparation of the document. [See Ch. 12, Sec. C1]

b. Comparison by trier or expert witness

Handwriting and other forms of script (like documents made by an office printer hooked to a computer) can be authenticated by introducing exemplars (specimens from the same source that have been authenticated) or by expert testimony that the exemplars match the document being offered. Alternatively the trier of fact may sometimes make such comparisons and reach such conclusions on its own. In this latter situation, the court submits the exemplars and exhibits to the jury only if it concludes, after making its own comparison, that there is enough similarity to support a jury finding of match. [See Ch. 12, Secs. C2 & C3]

c. Distinctive characteristics

Evidence may be authenticated by its distinctive characteristics (appearance, contents, internal patterns, etc.), considered in conjunction with other circumstances. A writing may be authenticated by showing that only the person said to be the author would likely know the facts reflected in the writing. Under the reply letter doctrine, a letter may be authenticated on the basis of its content as being from A by showing that it is a **reply** to a letter previously sent to A. A signature on a document, however, is not enough to authenticate the document as having been written by that person, unless it is shown that the signature is that of the person in question. [See Ch. 12, Sec. C4]

d. Public records or reports

There are many ways to authenticate public records, including identification by a person with knowledge, handwriting testimony, and use of certified copies. A public record may also be authenticated by showing that it was authorized by law to be recorded and filed, that it was recorded or filed in a public office, and that it is kept in the office where such records are normally kept. [See Ch. 12, Sec. C5]

e. Ancient documents

Writings may be authenticated as ancient documents if they are shown (1) to be in such condition as to create no suspicion about their authenticity, (2) to be in the place where they would be expected to be found if they were authentic, and (3) to have been in existence 20 years or more. A written date on a document is not enough by itself to establish age. There is a matching hearsay exception for ancient documents (FRE 803(16)) that can overcome a hearsay objection. **[See Ch. 12, Sec. C6]**

6. **Recordings**

A recording of a conversation may be authenticated by showing how it was made and identifying the participants. Usually the required foundation has two elements. One involves showing what process was followed and why it is reliable. The other involves showing who participated in the conversation. A witness can identify a voice heard on a tape recording as being that of a certain person on the basis of familiarity with the person's voice. **[See Ch. 12, Sec. D]**

7. **Photographs**

Photographs can be authenticated by the testimony of a witness with knowledge of the thing or scene depicted, if he states that the photograph accurately depicts the thing or scene at the time. The witness need not be the one who took the photograph. **[See Ch. 12, Sec. E1]**

8. **Medical images**

Authentication of medical image (fluoroscopy, ultrasound, magnetic resonance, x-rays) proceeds means of testimony describing the process and its use in the case. The description should cover the capability of the equipment and should indicate that it generally used and accepted by people knowledgeable in the field. The description should cover the qualifications of the operator, the procedures followed, and any process used to create the images being offered, as well as the date of preparation and what the images show. **[See Ch. 12, Sec. E2]**

9. **Computer Output**

Authentication of computer output requires a description of the process and a showing that it produces an accurate result. See FRE 901(b)(9). If computer output embodies out-of-court statements of persons, the hearsay doctrine must be satisfied, and often it can be if the records contain business entries that satisfy FRE 803(6) or constitute public records that satisfy FRE 803(8). **[See Ch. 12, Sec. E3]**

10. Telephone Conversations

A party to a phone conversation can identify the person on the distant end either on the basis of voice or, if the identifier is the person who placed the call, by testifying to the number he dialed and showing it is the number assigned to the person in question. If a calling party cannot identify the party receiving the call on the basis of voice identification, then another method is authorized by the rules. If the call was to a particular phone (whether a landline in a residence or business or a cellphone of a particular person), the conversation can be authenticated on the basis of evidence that the number dialed was the number assigned to that residence or business or person and that circumstances, including self-identification, show the person answering to be the one called. In the case of calls to a **business,** the conversation can be authenticated by showing that the number dialed was the one assigned to the business and the call related to business reasonably transacted over the telephone. [**See Ch. 12, Sec. F**]

11. Self–Authentication

Some written materials are self-authenticating, which means they may be taken at face value and no authenticating witness is required. A self-authenticating document is not necessarily admissible, because it remains subject to other objections (such as hearsay). Being self-authenticating does not mean the matter of authenticity is conclusively settled, and even if the document is admitted the opponent may offer counterproof contesting its authenticity. The following are examples of self-authenticating documents. [**See Ch. 12, Sec. G**]

a. Public documents

Original public documents are self-authenticating, provided that they are certified. Domestic public documents bearing a seal and signature of execution or attestation are admissible under FRE 902(1). Domestic public documents not bearing a seal are admissible if certified by an officer with a seal pursuant to FRE 902(2). Foreign public documents are admissible if the more elaborate certification process of FRE 902(3) is satisfied.

b. Copies of public records

A properly certified copy of a public record, or an officially recorded document, is self-authenticating under FRE 902(4).

c. **Official publications**
Official publications, such as government books and pamphlets, are self-authenticating. See FRE 902(5).

d. **Newspapers and periodicals**
Printed materials that appear on their face to be newspapers and periodicals are self-authenticating under FRE 902(6) (but taking newspapers or periodicals to be authentic does not resolve any hearsay issues in the use of such materials to prove matters asserted in articles or other writings contained in them).

e. **Trade inscriptions**
Labels on commercial products and similar inscriptions or signs affixed in the course of business are self-authenticating to the extent of establishing ownership, control, or origin of the product or instrumentality to which they are affixed. See FRE 902(7).

f. **Acknowledged documents**
Notarized documents are self-authenticating. See FRE 902(8).

g. **Commercial paper**
Some commercial documents and signatures thereon are self-authenticating. See FRE 902(9).

12. **Subscribing Witnesses**
FRE 903 rejects the general common law rule requiring that subscribing or attesting witnesses be called (or shown to be unavailable) before a subscribed document may be admitted. Some states continue to follow this requirement for at least certain important documents, such as wills. In federal courts, subscribing witnesses must be called only if the law of the state governing the validity of the writing so requires. **[See Ch. 12, Sec. H]**

■ CHAPTER 13. BEST EVIDENCE DOCTRINE

M. Best Evidence Doctrine

Proving the content of a writing, recording, or photograph normally requires producing the original of the thing itself, unless it is unavailable or an exception applies. Under the Rules, a duplicate (meaning essentially a machine-made copy) is nearly as acceptable as the original. When content is at issue, the writing itself (or a duplicate) is far more reliable than testimony describing content (the most likely alternative). **[See Ch. 13, Sec. B]**

1. **Definitions**
    The common law version of the doctrine applied only to writings, but the Rules expand coverage to include recordings and photographs as well.

    a. **Writings**
        The doctrine applies to all types of writings, including letters, memoranda, notes, books, and computer output (hardcopy printouts and contents of disks). Courts sometimes exercise discretion to treat inscribed chattels, like a stopsign or policeman's badge number or laundry initials on a shirt, as falling beyond reach of the doctrine.

    b. **Recordings**
        The doctrine reaches letters, words, numbers, or their equivalent captured by magnetic impulse or mechanical or electronic recording.

    c. **Photographs**
        Photographs include still photographs, medical imaging of all sorts from fluoroscopic images to x-rays, videotapes, and motion pictures.

    d. **Original**
        An original is the writing, recording, or photograph at issue in the case. What constitutes an original depends on the nature of the claim or defense, surrounding circumstances, party intention, and substantive legal principles. There can be multiple originals, because the definition includes any counterpart intended to have the same effect (such as multiple executed copies of a contract).

    e. **Duplicate**
        A duplicate is a photocopy or other machine-made copy, meaning virtually anything made by a modern office copier or generated commercially by similar machines operated by copycenters.

2. **General Rule**
    Under FRE 1002, a party seeking to prove the content of a writing, recording, or photograph must offer the original unless it is unavailable or an exception

applies. The key concept is proving content, and the Best Evidence Doctrine applies in two common situations. Sometimes substantive law requires proof of content, as in a libel case where plaintiff must prove the content of the allegedly defamatory writing. Sometimes a party proves content as a matter of strategy or choice, even though doing so is not required legally—as happens, for example, when a party introduces medical records to prove medical costs or diagnosis. In both situations—both when substantive law requires proof of content and when parties choose to prove content—the Best Evidence Doctrine applies because it is *content* that is being proved. The Doctrine does not apply, however, to proving *absence* of content—as happens, for example, when a party shows that a particular transaction did not occur by testifying that the records that would likely reflect the transaction in fact contain no entry for it. **[See Ch. 13, Sec. C]**

3. **Matters Incidentally Recorded**

The fact that a party tries to prove some fact that also happens to be reflected or described or depicted in a writing, recording, or photograph does not *by itself* bring the Best Evidence Doctrine into play. If the party chooses to prove the facts without using the writing, recording, or photograph, that is all right. Thus a participant in a conversation may testify to the content of the conversation even it was recorded, and even if the recording is "better evidence" in the sense that it captures the conversation verbatim, and the memory of a witness cannot recreate it in similar detail or with similar accuracy. **[See Ch. 13, Sec. C3]**

4. **Admissibility of Duplicates**

Under FRE 1003, duplicates are admissible to the same extent as originals, except where a genuine question is raised as to the authenticity of the original or in circumstances in which it would be unfair to admit the duplicate in lieu of the original. **[See Ch. 13, Sec. E]**

5. **Production of Original Excused**

When the original is unavailable, production is excused and secondary evidence is admissible to prove content of a writing, recording, or photograph. Production is excused when the original has been lost or destroyed (unless the party seeking to prove content destroyed the original in bad faith), or is beyond reach of judicial process, or in possession of the opponent, or collateral (not closely related to critical issues in the case). **[See Ch. 13, Sec. F]**

6. **Degrees of Secondary Evidence**

   If production is excused because the original is unavailable, *any* form of secondary evidence is admissible to prove content. FRE 1004 rejects the common law rule recognizing degrees of secondary evidence, which required that the most reliable form of secondary evidence be introduced in preference to less reliable forms. In practice, this approach meant that a party seeking to prove content might have to prove that various preferred forms of proof were unavailable, not just that the *original* was unavailable. **[See Ch. 13, Sec. F6]**

7. **Public Records**

   It is hard to get and offer original public records because government offices are often unwilling to release originals, even for use in court. Ordinarily duplicates are obtained instead. Although duplicates are generally admissible under FRE 1003, FRE 1005 imposes the special requirement that public records be certified or that they be compared copies. **[See Ch. 13, Sec. G1]**

8. **Summaries**

   Where writings are too voluminous to be conveniently examined in court, written or testimonial summaries may be used instead, subject to certain restrictions. Summaries are admissible only if the originals have been made available for inspection and copying. Summaries are admissible only if, and to the same extent as, the writings themselves would be admissible. Finally, the proponent who offers a summary must authenticate both originals and summary. Summaries admitted under FRE 1006 as a substitute for originals are themselves evidence. But summaries used only for pedagogical purposes to **illustrate or explain** original writings, rather than to substitute for them, are not governed by FRE 1006 and are usually not considered evidence. **[See Ch. 13, Sec. G2]**

9. **Written or Testimonial Admission**

   The content of writings, recordings, or photographs may be established by an adverse party's written or testimonial admission, relieving the proponent of the duty of offering originals or proving that they are unavailable. **[See Ch. 13, Sec. G2c]**

10. **Judge and Jury**

    Most Best Evidence issues are for the judge to decide under FRE 104(a). Thus the judge decides whether a writing has been destroyed, or is beyond reach of process, or is collateral. But FRE 1008 reserves three issues for the jury to determine under FRE 104(b): One is whether the writing ever existed; another is whether another writing, recording, or photograph produced at the trial is the original; the third is whether other evidence correctly reflects contents. **[See Ch. 13, Sec. H]**

■ CHAPTER 14. PRIVILEGES

N. Privileges

Evidence, whether it takes the form of testimony or written material, may be excluded on grounds of privilege. Most privileges protect important relationships, like attorney-client, psychotherapist-patient, and husband-and-wife. The privilege against self-incrimination serves a different purpose. It acts as a restraint on government and protects one from being forced to be his own accuser. Most privileges protect only confidential communications, but a few (like the spousal testimonial privilege and the privilege against self-incrimination), are broader and protect the holder from being compelled even to testify.

1. Sources of Privileges

In many states, privilege rules are codified. Congress threw out the privilege provisions proposed by the framers of the Federal Rules. FRE 501 leaves federal privileges to common law development. FRE 501 also provides that where state law supplies the rule of decision (primarily diversity suits) state law also governs issues of privilege. **[See Ch. 14, Sec. A]**

2. Attorney–Client

The attorney-client privilege protects confidential communications between attorney and client made for the purpose of obtaining professional legal services. **[See Ch. 14, Sec. B]**

a. Client

The holder of the privilege is the client, who may be a person, organization, or entity. One becomes a client by consulting a lawyer for purposes of securing professional legal services. The privilege applies even though no fee is paid and even if the lawyer ultimately declines to represent the client. **[See Ch. 14, Sec. B2a]**

b. Lawyer
A lawyer is a person authorized to practice law in any jurisdiction, or any person whom the client reasonably believes to be such. The privilege covers not only lawyers, but also representatives of lawyers (including secretaries, receptionists, and outside experts hired to assist). **[See Ch. 14, Sec. B2b]**

c. Legal services
The privilege applies only when the lawyer provides legal services (although the litigation need not be involved), and it does not extend to situations in which lawyers give other kinds of advice, in areas such as finances or business or accounting. **[See Ch. 14, Sec. B2c]**

d. Communications
The privilege covers communications (oral or written) between lawyer and client, and nonverbal conduct that is communicative in nature. It applies only to the communications themselves, not to the facts embodied in communications. The privilege does not cover pre-existing writings of the client, even if they are turned over to the lawyer to assist in the representation. Most jurisdictions recognize a two-way privilege that covers the lawyer's communications to the client as well as the client's to the lawyer. **[See Ch. 14, Sec. B2d]**

e. Confidentiality
The privilege applies only to communications that are intended to be confidential. The necessary intent may be inferred from circumstances. A communication remains confidential even if made in the presence of a representative of the lawyer or client, or in the presence of a communicative intermediary, or in the presence of someone covered by the privilege. But the presence of an outsider destroys confidentiality. The privilege is not lost, however, if overheard by an eavesdropper, assuming that the client took *reasonable precautions* to protect confidentiality. **[See Ch. 14, Sec. B2e]**

f. Joint clients
If two or more clients consult one lawyer on a matter of common interest, communications between clients and lawyer are privileged as against

outsiders. But there is no privilege as between the joint clients if they later become adversaries in litigation. **[See Ch. 14, Sec. B3]**

g. **Pooled information**

When two or more separately represented clients consult on matters of mutual interest, the privilege applies as against outsiders and perhaps (although the point is not settled) between the clients themselves. Thus if two defendants and their lawyers meet and discuss a case involving three or more defendants, what the two say in confidence in mapping out strategies is privileged against outsiders (like prosecutors and additional defendants not participating in the consultation). Whether it is also privileged among participating defendants (so neither could offer what was said against the other) remains unclear, although often participating defendants sign a confidentiality agreement that amounts to an attempt to preserve the privilege in this setting. **[See Ch. 14, Sec. B4]**

h. **Corporate client**

The privilege applies to corporations, but the scope of the privilege varies among jurisdictions. Corporations communicate only through representatives, so the question is how broadly the privilege covers the various people who might speak for the corporation to the lawyer. Under one view, the privilege extends only to representatives in the **control group** of the corporation (officers and directors) who have authority to act on any advice given. By another view, the privilege applies to communications by any employee, so long as she speaks on a **subject matter** within the scope of her job or responsibilities to the corporation. Federal courts follow the *Upjohn* decision, which rejected the control group test as too narrow and in effect adopted something very close to the **subject matter** standard. But *Upjohn* is written in modest tones, and it did not purport to adopt a definitive standard. The opinion suggested that the following factors should be considered:

i. **Obtain legal advice**

The purpose of communication was to obtain legal advice for the corporation (which is a general requirement of the privilege in all settings), and the employee knew of this purpose.

ii. **Request by superior**

The person speaking to the lawyer acted at the request of his bosses or superiors of the employee.

iii. Scope of duties

The communication relates a matter within the scope of duties of the employee, which is the **subject matter** standard, or something very close to it.

iv. Treated as confidential

The communication was treated as confidential and was not generally circulated or shown to others, even within the corporation itself. **[See Ch. 14, Sec. B5]**

i. Shareholder litigation

When shareholders bring a derivative or other suit alleging corporate mismanagement, the corporate attorney-client privilege is qualified rather than absolute. The reason is that managers have a conflict of interest and might assert the corporation's privilege to shield their own misconduct rather than to represent the best interests of the corporation. Under the *Garner* decision, shareholders can overcome a claim of privilege by making a showing of good cause that justifies granting them access to the privileged information. **[See Ch. 14, Sec. B5g]**

j. Client identity, fee arrangements

Ordinarily the identity of the client is not covered by the privilege because it is not a confidential matter, and opposing litigants are entitled to know who they are up against. The same is true of fee arrangements, the identity of the fee payer, dates of consultation, and other points which are normally not privileged because they do not involve communications going to the substance of the legal advice. But if disclosing the identity of the client or fee arrangements **would reveal the substance of the confidential communications,** then courts refuse to require disclosure of client identity or fee arrangements. For example, if disclosing a billing statement would reveal the nature of the legal advice given, it is privileged. **[See Ch. 14, Sec. B6a & b]**

k. Lawyer's observations of client

The privilege does not apply to observations that lawyers make about the appearance or demeanor of clients. These matters are neither communications nor confidential. A more difficult situation arises when a lawyer is asked to testify about his client's mental state because his opinion may rest not only on observations of behavior but also on client confidences. To the extent lawyers can testify about the client's mental state without relying on or disclosing confidential communications, courts allow them to do so. **[See Ch. 14, Sec. B6c]**

l. **Evidence delivered to lawyer**

Ethical rules bar attorneys from receiving physical evidence from a client or third person for the purpose of concealing or destroying it, and from counseling a client to conceal or destroy evidence. The prevailing view is that a lawyer must turn over to the prosecutor any physical evidence received from a client or third party that is either an instrumentality or a fruit of the crime. But if the client brings the item in question to the lawyer, most courts say the privilege applies and the attorney cannot be required to disclose that the source was his client. If the lawyer goes to the place where the item is located and **removes** it after being guided to it by his client, the *Meredith* case holds that the attorney may be compelled to disclose the location from which she took it, on the theory that her action may have prevented police from discovering the item. **[See Ch. 14, Sec. B6d]**

m. **Future crime or fraud exception**

The privilege shields statements relating to past misconduct, but not ongoing or future crimes or frauds. The party seeking disclosure must make a prima facie showing that the client was engaging in criminal or fraudulent conduct and that the attorney's assistance was obtained in furtherance of such activity. In the *Zolin* case, the Supreme Court held that material claimed to be privileged may be examined *in camera* by the judge to determine whether the crime-fraud exception applies. **[See Ch. 14, Sec. B7a]**

n. **Breach of duty exception**

In suits by a lawyer against her client (typically to collect fees) and suits by a client against her lawyer (typically for malpractice), an exception to the privilege is recognized to the extent disclosure is necessary to prove the claims and defenses raised. **[See Ch. 14, Sec. B7b]**

o. **Claimants through same deceased client**

The privilege survives the death of the client, but there is an exception for communications by a deceased client in suits between parties claiming through that client. The theory is that the deceased client would *want* the communications revealed to determine which of the competing claimants is entitled to his estate, and the privilege does not apply. [**See Ch. 14, Sec. B7c**]

p. Duration of privilege

The privilege continues to protect confidential communications of a client who is a person, even if she has died. It is unclear whether the privilege survives the death of a client that is an institution (corporation or partnership or government agency). [**See Ch. 14, Sec. B8**]

q. Claiming the privilege

The privilege is not self-enforcing. It must be claimed when matter covered by the privilege is sought, or the privilege is lost. The lawyer has an ethical obligation to claim the privilege for the client when necessary, and the lawyer's authority to do so is presumed (absence of evidence to the contrary). Current corporate management can assert or waive the privilege on behalf of a corporate client, even with respect to communications by former officers. [**See Ch. 14, Sec. B9**]

r. Appellate review

Ordinarily interlocutory review of a privilege ruling is not available, and the trial court's resolution of a privilege issue can only be challenged on appeal from a final judgment. If a privilege claim is rejected and the claimant is held in *criminal* contempt, he can obtain immediate review of the contempt citation and test the privilege ruling in that way. If the claimant is held in *civil* contempt, the availability of interlocutory review depends on whether he is a party. If he is, most appellate courts refuse to review the merits of the privilege ruling because the claimant holds the key to his own discharge and can obtain review by taking an appeal from final judgment in the case in which the privilege was claimed and rejected. If the claimant is not a party, he may appeal any contempt citation and obtain review of the privilege ruling, since final judgment in the suit does not provide an opportunity for a nonparty to appeal. If the witness who must disclose despite a privilege claim is an attorney who claims the privilege on his client's behalf, the *Perlman* doctrine lets the client intervene and appeal immediately. The reason is that otherwise the privilege may be lost without chance for review because the lawyer may be unwilling to go to jail to protect his client's rights. [**See Ch. 14, Sec. B9g**]

s.   **Waiver by voluntary disclosure**
Voluntary disclosure of any significant part of matters covered by a privilege waives the privilege, as does failure to claim the privilege when disclosure is sought. Waiver may occur at trial, during discovery, or in informal settings outside the litigation context. Disclosing facts underlying a privileged communication (such as telling a neighbor how the accident happened) does not waive the privilege, which protects the **communication with lawyers,** not the client's knowledge of the facts. If a privileged writing is used to refresh the memory of a witness who is not covered by the privilege, then the privilege is waived. If a privileged writing is used to refresh the memory of a **client,** the privilege is not waived, but the trial judge probably has discretion to order disclosure under FRE 612 so the adverse party can review the documents and use them on cross-examination. **[See Ch. 14, Sec. B10]**

t.   **Waiver by inadvertent disclosure**
Privileged material may be disclosed inadvertently, as happens if it is mistakenly sent to a third party or disclosed during discovery. Under new FRE 502, the disclosure does not operate as a waiver if the holder took reasonable steps to prevent disclosure and promptly took reasonable steps to rectify the error, such as asserting the privilege and reclaiming the material after disclosure. **[See Ch. 14, Sec. B11]**

u.   **Waiver by claim assertion**
Where a client asserts a claim or defense based on privileged communications, substantial authority holds that this tactic amounts to waiver, at least where discovery of the communications is necessary for a fair response by the other side. Thus when a party defends by claiming reliance on advice of counsel, plaintiff is entitled to know the advice given. **[See Ch. 14, Sec. B12]**

3.   **Spousal Testimony**
Federal courts and most states recognize a privilege covering testimony by the spouse of the defendant, when offered against him in a criminal case. **[See Ch. 14, Sec. C]**

a.   **Holder**
In federal courts and many states, the witness-spouse holds the privilege and can refuse to testify or waive the privilege and testify. The defendant

does not hold the privilege and cannot prevent her testimony. In other states, defendant holds the privilege and can block his spouse from testifying against him. In a few jurisdictions, both spouses hold the privilege, so the witness-spouse can refuse to testify and (even if she is willing) the party-spouse can block the testimony.

b. Scope

Where it applies, the privilege covers all testimony by the spouse, including testimony relating observations and matters occurring before the marriage. It is not limited to confidential marital communications.

c. Marital relationship

The privilege requires that the witness and the defendant be legally married when the testimony is sought. In several states, same sex couples are allwed to marry and can obtain the benefit of this privilege. Some states also allow civil unions or domestic partnerships that provide for the same privileges that are available to married couples. Courts sometimes refuse to recognize marriages that are sham or in poor repair (spouses permanently separated or in process of separating and headed toward divorce).

d. Exceptions

Most courts recognize an exception for cases in which one spouse is charged with a crime or tort against the person or property of the other, or against a minor child of either. Many courts also recognize an exception covering cases in which the spouses are **joint participants** in a crime.

4. Marital Confidences

Federal courts and almost all states recognize a privilege for marital confidences that covers private communications between spouses during marriage. This privilege applies in both civil and criminal cases. **[See Ch. 14, Sec. D]**

a. Holder

In most jurisdictions, both spouses hold the privilege, meaning that each can refuse to disclose and can block the other spouse from disclosing any confidential communication that occurred between them.

b. **Scope**

The privilege covers communications, not observed conduct (except conduct intended to be communicative). It covers only communications that are confidential and made *during* marriage, not before or after. But for communications during the marriage, the privilege continues for all time, even if the marriage ends in divorce or death.

c. **Marriage relationship**

The privilege applies only to partners in a legal marriage. This can include same sex couples in some states. Also some states provide for civil unions or domestic partnership agreements for same sex couples that recognize this privilege. Courts may refuse to apply the privilege to marriages that are sham or moribund.

d. **Exceptions**

The privilege does not apply where one spouse is charged with a crime or tort against the person or property of the other or a minor child of either.

5. **Psychotherapist–Patient Privilege**

This privilege is recognized by statute in almost all states, and the Supreme Court decision in *Jaffee* adopted it for federal proceedings. The privilege covers statements made in confidence to a psychotherapist for purposes of treatment. The privilege normally does not apply where the patient, or someone acting on her behalf, relies on her mental condition as an element of a claim or defense. **[See Ch. 14, Sec. F]**

6. **Other Professional Privileges**

Most states have a statutory physician-patient privilege, which was not recognized at common law. This privilege is riddled with exceptions—for court-ordered examinations, medical conditions that doctors are required to report to authorities, and cases where the patient puts his own medical condition in issue. Almost all jurisdictions recognize a privilege for confidential disclosures to a member of the clergy for purposes of spiritual counseling. Journalists have a qualified privilege that allows them to protect the confidentiality of their sources. A few states recognize a privilege for accountants. **[See Ch. 14, Secs. E & G]**

7. **State Secrets**

The government holds a privilege to prevent disclosure of military or diplomatic information that amount to state secrets. The government must demonstrate that the information should not be divulged in the interests of national security, and the required showing may be made *in camera* and *ex parte*. If the government is a party to the litigation and refusal to disclose deprives the other side of information important to a claim or defense, the court may adopt appropriate remedies, such as striking testimony, finding against the government on an issue, or dismissing the action. **[See Ch. 14, Sec. G9a]**

8. **Official Information**

   A qualified privilege protects information collected by government agencies for use in policy deliberations or during investigations. The privilege is designed to encourage an uninhibited exchange of views among policy makers and to protect investigative material (sources, suspects, investigative techniques, etc.). The privilege is qualified, and the court balances the need for accurate fact-finding against the public interest in effective governmental functioning. To make the necessary decision, courts sometimes order disclosure of the underlying material for *in camera inspection.* **[See Ch. 14, Sec. G9b]**

9. **Informer's Identity**

   The government holds a qualified privilege to refuse to disclose the identity of an informer who provides information assisting law enforcement. The privilege is qualified and requires balancing the public interest in protecting the flow of such information against the accused's right to prepare his defense. In undertaking this balancing, courts consider the nature of the charge, possible defenses, and the significance of the informer's testimony. In proceedings testing whether there was probable cause for an arrest or search, defendants often seek to have the identity of the informer revealed. If the government produces independent evidence of the reliability of the informer, disclosure of his identity is not required. But if the court doubts the credibility of the witness attesting to the existence or reliability of the informer, the court may order that the informer be produced or identified. **[See Ch. 14, Sec. G9c]**

10. **Privilege Against Self–Incrimination**

    The privilege against self-incrimination created by the Fifth Amendment applies in both federal and state proceedings. It protects a witness from being compelled to give testimony that may be incriminating. **[See Ch. 14, Sec. H]**

    a. **Persons protected**

       The privilege applies only to individuals and cannot be asserted by corporations, labor unions, or other entities. The privilege is personal, and one defendant in a criminal case cannot raise the Fifth Amendment privilege of another. Criminal defendants cannot even be called to the stand by the prosecutor. Witnesses other than criminal defendants can be called in order to have the judge rule on any claim of privilege.

b. **Testimonial**

The privilege protects only against compelled statements (whether in oral or written form) or compelled communicative acts (such as re-enacting a crime). Nontestimonial evidence, such as fingerprints and blood and hair samples, may be obtained over the protest of the defendant.

c. **Incrimination**

The privilege applies only to statements that might subject the speaker to the risk of criminal prosecution, not to statements that might be damaging in other ways. The court determines whether an answer might tend to incriminate a witness. There must be an actual danger of prosecution, and a privilege claim should be denied where reprosecution is barred by the Double Jeopardy Clause or the statute of limitations has run.

d. **Immunity**

A person may be required to make self-incriminating statements if he is given use immunity barring later use of the statements against him, and he is not entitled to transactional immunity blocking the government from prosecuting him for any underlying crime on the basis of other evidence. Thus a grant of use immunity allows the government to prosecute the defendant with evidence obtained *independently* of any statement that he is compelled to make. It is often hard for the government to prove that its independent evidence was not in some way related to or tainted by his compelled statements.

e. **Adverse inferences**

Under the *Griffin* case, it is a violation of due process for the court to instruct the jury, or for the prosecutor to argue, that the jury should draw an inference of guilt against a criminal defendant because he does not take the stand. An accused is entitled, on request, to an instruction advising the jury that it should not consider the fact that he did not testify or that he claimed the privilege. The *Griffin* rule does not apply in civil cases.

f. Act of production

Pre-existing documents, such as financial records, are not subject to the privilege against self-incrimination (even if incriminating), because their making was not compelled by the government. But the compelled **act of producing** those documents in response to a subpoena may violate the privilege to the extent production is communicative and amounts to an assertion by the party that these are the documents requested. The prosecutor may be able to avoid the problem by granting immunity for the act of production and authenticating the documents by some means other than the fact that the defendant produced them in response to the subpoena.

g. Required reports

Sometimes in the course of its regulatory authority the government requires the keeping or filing of certain reports. Such reports may contain incriminating information that is later used to prosecute their maker. Because such reports are prepared under government compulsion (there are usually penalties for noncompliance), defendants sometimes argue that use of them for purposes of prosecution violates the privilege against self-incrimination. Courts find no violation of the privilege where the government can show that the reports were required for a genuine regulatory purpose and not simply as a pretext to assist law enforcement. Courts also usually require that any claim based on the privilege against self-incrimination be made at the time the report is required to be made or filed rather than at a later date when it is offered into evidence.

■ CHAPTER 15. BURDENS AND PRESUMPTIONS

O. Burdens and Presumptions

1. Two Meanings of Burden of Proof

The term burden of proof can mean either the burden of production or the burden of persuasion. **[See Ch. 15, Sec. A]**

a. **Burden of production**

This term refers to the obligation of a party to produce sufficient evidence to support a jury finding in its favor on an issue. If sufficient evidence is not produced, the issue does not go to the jury, and the party with the burden loses on the point as a matter of law (by judgment as a matter of law or summary judgment).

b. **Burden of persuasion**

This term refers to the obligation to persuade the jury (or judge serving as factfinder) on an issue. If the factfinder is not persuaded because the evidence favors the other side or because the evidence seems equally strong for both sides, then the party who bears the burden of persuasion loses on the issue.

2. **Three Common Standards of Proof**

There are three commonly used standards of proof that govern the degree to which the factfinder must be persuaded: The preponderance standard, the clear and convincing standard, and the standard of proof beyond a reasonable doubt. The first applies in most civil cases, the second in special cases (often fraud claims and mental commitment proceedings), and the third applies in criminal prosecutions. **[See Ch. 15, Sec. B]**

3. **Burdens of Pleading, Production, and Persuasion Generally Coincide**

In most situations, the party who pleads an issue also has the burden of production and the burden of persuasion on that issue. Plaintiffs generally must plead and prove claims and defendants must plead and approve affirmative defenses. Sometimes the burdens of pleading, production, and persuasion diverge: In suits to collect on a promissory note, for example, plaintiff must allege nonpayment, but defendant must not only plead payment, but also carry the burdens of production and persuasion on this issue at trial. **[See Ch. 15, Sec. C]**

4. **Criminal Cases**

In criminal cases, as a matter of federal constitutional law, the prosecutor has both the burden of production and the burden of persuasion on every element of the charge, and every element must be proved beyond a reasonable doubt (highest standard known to law). The defendant can be required to carry the burdens of production and persuasion on affirmative defenses that raise new matters, but not on defenses (such as consent in a rape trial) that negate an element of the charge. [**See Ch. 15, Sec. D**]

5. **Inferences**

   An inference is a rule of law that says that *if* a particular basic fact is established, *then* the jury (or judge as factfinder in a bench trial) *may* find some other fact. An inference may satisfy the burden of production and even satisfy or help satisfy the burden of persuasion. But since the jury (or judge in a bench trial) is not required to draw the permitted inference, the actual effect of the formal inference rule depends on what the jury (or judge in a bench trial) decides to do. [**See Ch. 15, Sec. E**]

6. **Presumptions**

   A presumption is a rule of law that says that *if* a particular basic fact is established, *then* a certain presumed fact **must** be found in absence of evidence rebutting the presumed fact. If a presumption comes into play and is not rebutted, it satisfies both the burden of production and the burden of persuasion with respect to the presumed fact. [**See Ch. 15, Sec. E**]

7. **Contesting Basic Fact**

   The opponent may contest the basic fact giving rise to the presumption, in which case the jury is told to find the presumed fact only if it first finds the basic fact. [**See Ch. 15, Sec. I**]

8. **Contesting Presumed Fact**

   If the opponent contests the presumed fact, there are differing views on what effect the presumption should have. Under the common law bursting bubble view (also known as the Thayer view), the presumption disappears when counterproof is offered that is sufficient to support a jury finding of the nonexistence of the presumed fact. FRE 301 appears to adopt this view, although the matter is not fully settled. Under URE 301 and the Morgan view, a presumption does not disappear in the face of evidence contesting the presumed fact, and instead the presumption shifts the burden of persuasion to the opponent to establish the nonexistence of the presumed fact. There are also intermediate positions between these views that do not shift the burden of persuasion but require a higher level of counterproof to rebut the presumption. [**See Ch. 15, Secs. J & K**]

9. **State Presumptions in Federal Civil Cases**

   Under FRE 302, federal courts are required to follow state rules governing presumptions in diversity cases and other cases where state law supplies the rule of decision. [**See Ch. 15, Sec. L**]

10. **Presumptions in Criminal Cases**

Presumptions in favor of the prosecution on an element of the offense are unconstitutional, because they undercut the government's obligation to prove every element of the charge beyond a reasonable doubt. The burden of persuasion cannot be shifted to the defendant. It would also be unconstitutional to shift the burden of production to the defendant in the sense of requiring a finding against the defendant if he failed to produce evidence on an element of the charge. **[See Ch. 15, Sec. M]**

11. **Inferences in Criminal Cases**

Inferences in favor of the prosecution are generally permitted in criminal cases, provided the inferred fact follows more likely than not from the basic facts. **[See Ch. 15, Sec. N]**

■ CHAPTER 16. JUDICIAL NOTICE

P. Judicial Notice

FRE 201 authorizes courts to take judicial notice of adjudicative facts.

1. **Substitute for Evidence**
   Judicial notice allows facts to be established without formal proof, providing a substitute for evidence. **[See Ch. 16, Sec. A]**

2. **Four Concepts**
   The term judicial notice sometimes refers to four distinct processes, including notice of (a) adjudicative facts, (b) basic facts (communicative and evaluative), (c) legislative facts, and (d) law. FRE 201 regulates only judicial notice of adjudicative facts. **[See Ch. 16, Sec. A]**

3. **Adjudicative Facts**
   These are facts to which the law is applied, that are normally for the factfinder (jury, or judge in bench-tried cases) to determine. A fact is adjudicative if a party would be required formally to prove it if notice were not taken. **[See Ch. 16, Sec. B]**

4. **Beyond Reasonable Dispute**

    Under FRE 201(b), an adjudicative fact may be judicially noticed only if it is not subject to reasonable dispute. The party requesting judicial notice has the burden of establishing indisputability. The opponent may offer counterproof to show that the matter is subject to reasonable dispute, hence that notice should not be taken. **[See Ch. 16, Sec. A]**

5. **Generally Known**

    A fact is beyond reasonable dispute if it is generally known in the community. It need not be universally known, provided that it is known by informed persons in the jurisdiction. That a judge *personally* knows something, however, is not enough if the point is not generally known. **[See Ch. 16, Sec. B]**

6. **Verifiable**

    A fact may also qualify as beyond reasonable dispute if it is subject to verification by sources whose accuracy cannot reasonably be questioned. Thus notice is often taken of dates, times of sunrises and sunsets, high tides, and geographical locations, because reliable sources readily available establish such facts. **[See Ch. 16, Sec. B2]**

7. **Initiating Notice**

    Courts may take judicial notice on their own or at the request of a party. If notice is requested, the court must take notice if it has been supplied with the necessary information. **[See Ch. 16, Sec. C1]**

8. **Opportunity to Be Heard**

    Parties are entitled on timely request to an opportunity to be heard on the propriety of taking judicial notice. This request may be made after notice was taken if there was no prior notification. **[See Ch. 16, Sec. C2]**

9. **When Notice Can Be Taken**

    Although judicial notice is usually taken during trial, adjudicative facts may be noticed at any stage of the proceeding, from pretrial through the appeal process. However, in criminal cases, notice generally cannot be taken after a jury has rendered its verdict. **[See Ch. 16, Sec. C3]**

10. **Instructing the Jury**

    In civil cases, the jury is instructed to accept the noticed fact as conclusively established. In criminal cases, the jury is instructed that it may, but is not required to, accept the noticed fact. FRE 201(g) does not allow a mandatory judicial notice instruction against a criminal defendant because he is entitled to have the jury decide every factual issue. **[See Ch. 16, Secs. C4 & C5]**

11. **Basic Facts**

Basic facts are those facts that are known by jurors when they come to court. Basic facts include communicative facts, such as the ordinary meaning of words and phrases in the English language. We assume that jurors know the language, or else they would not understand the testimony in the case, or even the preliminary procedures by which they are empaneled. Another subset of basic facts is evaluative facts, which includes human knowledge of the ways of the world and society that enable jurors to appraise and evaluate the evidence. If a flowerpot falls from a third-floor window ledge and strikes a pedestrian, it is assumed that jurors understand what a flower pot is, and the operation of gravity on the pot, and the likely consequences to a person if she is struck by the falling pot. This presumed basic knowledge of jurors is sometimes referred to as jury notice. No specific instruction is given on matters in the realm of jury notice, and notice of basic facts is not regulated by FRE 201. **[See Ch. 16, Sec. E1]**

12. **Legislative Facts**

Legislative facts are the ones that courts consider when ruling on matters of law. Such facts are considered (judicially noticed) when courts construe statutes or constitutions, create new common law claims or recognize new meanings of common law principles, or rule on motions (such as for summary judgment or dismissal). Notice of legislative facts may be taken by both trial and appellate courts. Notice of legislative facts is not regulated by FRE 201. **[See Ch. 16, E2]**

13. **Notice of Law**

Courts take judicial notice of federal and state law, including constitutional provisions, statutes, case law, and administrative regulations. Knowledge of such law by the court is necessary in order to instruct the jury and make appropriate legal rulings. In this context, taking judicial notice means that a party does not have to prove the content of law by calling witnesses or offering admissible evidence, although courts may still burden parties with researching and demonstrating the content of the law by means of briefs and citations. **[See Ch. 16, Sec. F]**

CHAPTER 1

Preliminary Matters: Overview of the Trial Process

CHAPTER OVERVIEW

Here are the key points in this chapter:

- There are many reasons for the development of evidence law, and mistrust of juries is perhaps the most important of them all.

- Evidence law originated at common law but now has been codified in most jurisdictions.

- Evidence law applies in most but not all types of court proceedings.

- The same rules of evidence generally apply on both the civil and the criminal side of the docket, and in both jury trials and court trials.

- Sometimes the admissibility of evidence depends on resolving preliminary questions, such as whether a hearsay declarant is unavailable to testify (if so, her statement may fit a hearsay exception; if not, the statement could not fit the exception).

- Preliminary questions affecting admissibility of evidence are decided by the court, but questions of conditional relevancy are decided by the jury.

- When the court decides preliminary questions, most rules of evidence do not apply, but privilege rules still do apply.

- When evidence is admissible for one purpose and not others, or against one or more parties but not against others, a limiting instruction must be given upon request.

- To prevent part of a writing from being taken out of context, a party offering that part can be required to offer other parts that ought to be considered at the same time.

- Appellate courts generally do not review evidentiary rulings unless a proper objection or offer of proof was made.

- Appellate courts reverse judgments on account of error on evidentiary rulings only if they are shown to affect the substantial rights of the complaining party.

A. PURPOSES OF EVIDENCE LAW

1. Regulate Jury Trials

Evidence law began to develop in England in the 1500s, as juries began to assume their modern form. The purpose was to control and limit the types of evidence that juries can consider. There has long been a concern that juries might overvalue certain evidence (such as information about the background and character of a criminal defendant) or might otherwise be too easily misled, confused, or emotionally influenced for or against litigants by certain types of evidence. Mistrust of juries is an important reason for the law of evidence.

2. Further Accurate Factfinding

Many evidence rules are designed to ensure more accurate factfinding, thus aiding the search for truth. The hearsay doctrine, for example, helps ensure that juries get live descriptions of events, rather than secondhand accounts in the form of testimony describing what others have said. And the authentication requirement provides at least a minimal safeguard against forgery or fabrication of documents or other exhibits.

3. Control the Scope and Duration of Trials

Without limits on the evidence that attorneys can present (such as the fundamental requirement of **relevance**), trials could be interminable, and could venture far afield from the dispute that brought the parties into litigation.

4. Favor or Disfavor Certain Litigants or Claims

Some evidence rules are designed to favor certain outcomes. For example, the presumption that persons holding themselves out as husband and wife are lawfully married helps protect a child born in the relationship, and helps vindicate the expectations of the putative spouses too. To take another example, the requirement of clear and convincing evidence helps assure that claims of fraud carry the day only if they have clear merit. Likewise the requirement of proof of guilt beyond reasonable doubt in criminal cases is designed to protect against the terrible risk of sending an innocent person to jail (or putting him to death) by mistake.

5. Protect Private Relationships

Privilege rules are designed to protect certain private relationships outside the courtroom. Included are relationships between patients and psychotherapists, members of the clergy and the believers who come to them for spiritual advice or counseling, or in observance of religious rituals, and husbands and wives.

6. Further Other Substantive Policies Unrelated to the Litigation

In addition to protecting certain relationships, some evidence rules further other social policies unrelated to litigation. For example, the "repair rule" encourages parties to make property, practices, machinery, or products safer after an accident by blocking proof of remedial measures from being introduced against them.

7. Ensure Due Process and a Perception of Fairness

Apart from the purposes listed above, evidence rules also help ensure that litigants have a fair hearing that goes forward in accordance with common understandings of "due process of law." For example, the right to confront and cross-examine adverse witnesses is independently important (apart from its contribution toward more accurate fact-finding) because a litigant would likely feel that he was unfairly treated if he were denied this right. In order to make judgments entered by courts generally acceptable in society at large, judicial proceedings must be **perceived** as following fair procedures.

B. CODIFICATION OF EVIDENCE LAW

For several centuries, evidence law was almost entirely a creature of common law development. Lawyers would appeal from judgments seeking reversal on account of evidentiary rulings by trial judges, and appellate decisions established a body of rules regulating admissibility and resolving other recurrent evidentiary issues. These rules restrained the discretion of trial judges and provided guidance for judges and litigating lawyers alike. Eventually states enacted miscellaneous statutes that governed narrow points of evidence: Some of these set up a business records exception to the hearsay rule, for example, and many statutes created various evidentiary privileges. But comprehensive evidence codes did not appear until the twentieth century.

1. Early Codes

Some scholars, including Dean Wigmore, made initial attempts to codify the law of evidence during the first part of the last century. See John Wigmore, Code of Evidence (1909).

2. Model Code of Evidence (1942) (MCE)

The American Law Institute (source of Restatements of various areas of law) completed the Model Code of Evidence in 1942. Professor Edmund Morgan of Harvard Law School was the primary drafter. It was called a Model Code rather than a Restatement because it made significant departures from the common law. For example, it repealed much of existing hearsay doctrine. American lawyers and legislators considered the MCE to be too radical, and it was not adopted anywhere.

3. Original Uniform Rules of Evidence (1953) (URE)

In 1953 the National Conference of Commissioners on Uniform State Laws approved the Uniform Rules of Evidence. This codification was shorter and did not depart from common law nearly as far as the MCE. The Uniform Rules were also less technical and complex than the Model Code. Still the Uniform Rules did not achieve widespread acceptance, although they did become the basis for evidence codes adopted in Kansas, New Jersey, and Utah.

4. California Evidence Code (1965)

The California legislature approved a comprehensive evidence code in 1965. It was drafted by a Law Revision Commission and drew heavily on the URE as well as the MCE.

5. Federal Rules of Evidence (Court Approval 1972; Enacted 1975) (FRE)

The Federal Rules of Evidence were drafted by a distinguished Advisory Committee comprised of lawyers, judges, and law professors. Professor

Edward Cleary of the University of Illinois served as Reporter. The Committee's draft was approved by the U.S. Supreme Court in 1972 and, pursuant to the Rules Enabling Act, would have become effective on July 1, 1973. But Congress exercised its prerogative to suspend the effective date of the Rules, and it subjected them to rigorous consideration and considerable revision. Congress enacted its amended version of the Rules into law, effective July 1, 1975. The Advisory Committee Note (ACN) to each Rule explains the Rule as proposed by the Advisory Committee, and the House and Senate Reports explain amendments made by Congress.

6. Revised Uniform Rules of Evidence (1974 and 1999) (URE2)

After the Supreme Court approved the proposed Federal Rules of Evidence in 1972, the National Commissioners on Uniform State Laws withdrew the 1953 Rules and adopted new Uniform Rules based on the proposed Federal Rules. Because the URE2 did not adopt the congressional amendments to the proposed Federal Rules, there are discrepancies between the URE2 and the Federal Rules as ultimately enacted. In 1999, the Uniform Rules underwent substantial revision.

7. State Codes Based on the FRE (or URE2)

Since the Federal Rules were adopted, 43 states have adopted Codes or Rules of Evidence modeled on the Federal and Uniform Rules. Those states are Alabama, Alaska, Arizona, Arkansas, Colorado, Connecticut, Delaware, Florida, Hawaii, Idaho, Illinois, Indiana, Iowa, Kentucky, Louisiana, Maine, Maryland, Michigan, Minnesota, Mississippi, Montana, Nebraska, Nevada, New Hampshire, New Jersey, New Mexico, North Carolina, North Dakota, Ohio, Oklahoma, Oregon, Pennsylvania, Rhode Island, South Carolina, South Dakota, Tennessee, Texas, Utah, Vermont, Washington, West Virginia, Wisconsin, and Wyoming.

C. PROCEEDINGS GOVERNED BY EVIDENCE RULES

1. FRE Applicable

a. Civil proceedings

The Federal Rules apply to civil trials and proceedings generally, including admiralty and maritime cases and bankruptcy proceedings.

b. Criminal proceedings

The Federal Rules apply to criminal trials and proceedings, subject to the exceptions listed below.

c. Contempt proceedings

Contempt proceedings are governed by the Federal Rules, except those in which the court may act summarily.

d. Habeas corpus proceedings

The Federal Rules are applicable to habeas corpus proceedings to the extent not inconsistent with statute.

2. FRE Inapplicable

FRE 1001(d) provides that the Rules of Evidence, other than rules of privilege, do not apply in the following proceedings:

a. Preliminary questions of fact

Often the question whether an item of evidence is admissible turns on resolving a question of fact. In criminal cases, for example, common suppression motions require courts to determine the legality of a police search or seizure. Such hearings are not governed by the Federal Rules (apart from privilege rules).

b. Grand jury proceedings

Because there is no judge or defense attorney at grand jury proceedings, the Federal Rules are inapplicable (apart from privilege rules). State statutes often require, however, that a grand jury indictment be supported by sufficient admissible evidence.

c. Preliminary hearings

In criminal cases, preliminary hearings (or examinations) are informal in nature, and their purpose is to determine whether there is "probable cause" to hold a defendant for trial. Because the evidentiary standard is so low, application of the Federal Rules is not considered necessary (apart from privilege rules).

d. Bail release hearings

Bail release hearings are informal proceedings, and their purpose is to determine the risk of flight (and perhaps danger to the community) presented by the accused, and the Rules of Evidence do not apply (apart from privilege rules).

e. Sentencing or revocation proceedings

Sentencing hearings occur only after a determination of guilt. Sentencing is often affected by factors that would not be proper to admit at trial, such as information about the defendant's prior criminal history. Again the Rules do not apply (apart from privilege rules), but sentencing procedures in federal and state courts have drawn increased attention and are now subject to elaborate rules, and the Supreme Court has intervened to limit what can be covered in this setting. See *Blakely v. Washington*, 542 U.S. 296 (2004) (in state court, sentencing defendant to a term more than three years longer than 53–month statutory maximum for charged offense, on basis of finding by sentencing judge that defendant acted with deliberate cruelty, violated Sixth Amendment right to jury trial); *Apprendi v. New Jersey*, 530 U.S. 466 (2000) (any fact that increases the penalty for crime beyond statutory maximum, apart from prior convictions, cannot be established during sentencing proceedings and must be proved to jury beyond reasonable doubt).

f. Arrest warrants and search warrants

Arrest and search warrants are often issued on the basis of affidavits showing "probable cause" to believe that defendant committed a crime or possesses contraband. Such affidavits constitute hearsay and would not be admissible in trials conducted under the Rules of Evidence. But some protection is provided by the constitutional requirement that informants must be shown to be reliable.

g. Extradition proceedings

Extradition proceedings are informal hearings to determine whether an accused should be returned to another jurisdiction to stand trial. They are not governed by the Federal Rules (apart from privilege rules).

3. Court Trials

The Federal Rules apply equally in judge-tried and jury-tried cases. But judgments based on decisions by judges without juries are less likely to be reversed on evidentiary grounds than judgments based on jury verdicts. Even if a judge in a case tried without a jury admits inadmissible evidence, reviewing courts usually presume that the judge did not give any weight to evidence that should not have been admitted.

4. Rules Apply to Civil and Criminal Trials

The Federal Rules apply equally in civil and criminal trials, with minor exceptions. For example, in criminal trials the rules pertaining to judicial notice and presumptions are different. In some states, there are different evidence codes for civil and criminal cases.

5. Proceedings Governed by the Federal Rules of Civil Procedure (FRCP)

In some cases the extent to which evidence rules govern certain proceedings is specified by the Rules of Civil Procedure.

a. Summary judgment motions

Under FRCP 56(e), affidavits supporting or opposing motions for summary judgment must "set forth such facts as would be admissible in evidence." Thus the affidavit itself need not be admissible (and at trial most affidavits would be excludable as hearsay), but the affidavit offered in summary judgment proceedings must show facts that would be provable at trial, and must indicate that the affiant (maker of the affidavit) or someone described in the affidavit could competently testify to such facts if the case went to trial.

b. Discovery

Under FRCP 26(b)(1), parties may obtain discovery regarding any matter not privileged, that is "relevant to any party's claim or defense." Thus information may be discoverable even if not admissible at trial, so long as it is "reasonably calculated to lead to the discovery of admissible evidence."

6. Nonjudicial Proceedings

Many important types of hearings occur outside the judicial system and are not governed by either the Federal Rules of Evidence or Procedure.

a. Administrative hearings

Administrative proceedings are not governed by the Rules of Evidence. See Administrative Procedures Act (APA) § 556(d) (1996). Nonetheless privileged evidence and illegally-seized evidence are generally excluded in agency hearings, and less reliable forms of evidence may be given less weight.

b. Arbitration hearings

Arbitration hearings are conducted by private arbitrators rather than judges and are not subject to the rules of evidence unless the parties agree otherwise. See American Arbitration Association Commercial Arbitration Rules, Rule 31 ("conformity to legal rules of evidence shall not be necessary"). However, evidence principles play a greater role in arbitration proceedings than is often recognized. For example, often arbitrators give less weight to evidence such as hearsay that would be inadmissible in a judicial proceeding.

D. THE TRIAL PROCESS

1. Stages of a Trial

Generally a trial proceeds along the following steps: Jury selection ("voir dire" of jurors); Opening statement of plaintiff (or prosecutor); Opening statement of defendant; Case-in-chief of plaintiff (or prosecutor); Case-in-chief of defendant; Case-in-rebuttal of plaintiff (or prosecutor); Case-in-rebuttal of defendant (sometimes called case-in-rejoinder); Closing argument of plaintiff (or prosecutor); Closing argument of defendant; Rebuttal argument of plaintiff (or prosecutor); Jury instructions; Jury deliberation; Verdict and entry of judgment; Post-trial motions; Appellate review.

2. Discretion to Control or Alter Order of Proceedings

Under FRE 611(a), the trial judge can control or alter the order of presenting evidence. For example, he can require a party to prove one point before going on to second point that depends on the first point, or can allow a party to prove the second point first. And the judge can allow a party to reopen its case-in-chief if something was omitted, or can refuse to allow a party to do so if it appears that there was no good reason for the omission or that the party is purposefully abusing the system. Often the discovery of new evidence that could not have been obtained earlier justifies reopening a case, as does the need to respond to some particular point proved by the opponent after the case-in-chief was completed.

3. Motions in Limine

A motion *in limine* (literally "at the threshold") is a motion seeking a court ruling to exclude (or sometimes to admit) anticipated evidence. Usually the motion is filed and heard before trial, but sometimes it is filed during trial in anticipation that objectionable evidence will be offered later. The purpose of a motion *in limine* is to obtain an advance ruling so jurors are not exposed to potentially inadmissible evidence and litigants can plan trial strategy. Raising the issue in advance also allows parties to brief it more thoroughly. Courts are sometimes reluctant to make evidentiary rulings in advance, however, because the admissibility of the challenged evidence may depend on what issues are raised and what other evidence is admitted at trial–in short, the judge may need to see the fuller context that trial will provide, and may for that reason feel unready to rule on the matter in a preliminary motion.

4. Sidebars

A sidebar conference is one in which attorneys approach the bench and confer with the judge outside the hearing of the jury. FRE 103(c) requires that steps be taken to prevent the jury from being exposed to inadmissible evidence, and a sidebar is one way to achieve this objective.

5. Conference in Chambers

Sometimes evidence issues are raised with the judge at a conference in chambers. Such a conference ensures that the discussion cannot be overheard by jurors. This setting is also better adapted to the task of making a verbatim record (with the court reporter present) than is a sidebar conference. If there is to be an extended presentation or argument about an evidentiary issue, however, the judge may prefer that it be done in the courtroom during a recess with the jury excused. Often judges prefer, for example, for offers of proof to be made in court rather than in chambers, again with a court reporter present and a full record being made, in a public setting and with all the usual formalities in place.

E. PRELIMINARY QUESTIONS AFFECTING ADMISSIBILITY

Sometimes admissibility cannot be determined until a preliminary question is resolved. For example, a witness cannot give an opinion as an expert until the court makes a preliminary determination that she is a qualified expert on the matter. And an out-of-court statement is not admissible under the "excited utterance" exception in FRE 803(2) until the court makes the preliminary determination that the utterance was made in a state of excitement.

1. Judicial "Minihearings"

Often courts conduct "minihearings" during trial to decide preliminary questions that determine whether evidence is admissible.

2. Most Preliminary Questions are for the Court Under FRE 104(a)

a. Types of preliminary questions for the judge

Under FRE 104(a), the judge decides qualifications of a witness (whether one is competent to testify and whether one qualifies as an expert), the existence of a privilege, and questions of admissibility generally.

b. Rules of Evidence do not apply

When the preliminary question is for the judge under FRE 104(a), the Rules of Evidence do not apply, except for privilege rules. Inadmissible evidence, such as hearsay affidavits, may be presented.

☛ EXAMPLES AND ANALYSIS

Baxter's conviction for armed robbery of a liquor store is reversed on appeal and sent back for a new trial. At the second trial, the prosecutor offers a transcript of testimony given by Rudy (liquor store clerk) at the first trial. The prosecutor claims that since the first trial Rudy has disappeared and cannot be found. The prosecutor submits affidavits from two different investigators describing their extensive but futile efforts to locate Rudy.

Under the former testimony exception to the hearsay doctrine that is found in FRE 804(b)(1), testimony given in Baxter's first trial is admissible in Baxter's second trial only if the declarant is shown to be unavailable. (Otherwise he would be expected to appear in person at the second trial and testify again, presumably repeating much of what he said the first time.) Under FRE 804(a)(5), a declarant is "unavailable" if the party offering what he said in another trial can show that despite all reasonable efforts he is unable to locate the declarant or procure his attendance. It is for the court to decide the preliminary question whether Rudy is unavailable. If the judge decides that he is unavailable, the hearsay statement (Rudy's former testimony) may be admitted (there are other requirements that must be satisfied). If the judge decides that Rudy is not unavailable, his former testimony will likely not be admitted because it doesn't fit the former testimony exception. It is proper for the court to consider inadmissible evidence, such as affidavits by investigators or statements by the prosecutor, in deciding this preliminary question, even though the former would be excluded as hearsay and the latter would not constitute "evidence" if the setting was the trial itself, as opposed to a hearing under FRE 104(a).

---

c. Burden of persuasion on proponent

The burden of producing evidence and persuading the court on a preliminary question rests on the proponent of the evidence. Thus the burden is on the prosecutor in the above example to establish Rudy's unavailability because it is the prosecutor who seeks to introduce Rudy's former testimony.

There is one important exception to this general rule: A party seeking to exclude evidence under a claim of privilege bears the burden of producing evidence and persuading the court that the privilege applies. In other words, here is an instance in which the objecting party bears the burdens of production and persuasion, rather than the proponent who offers the evidence. **[See Ch. 14, Sec. B9c]**

d. Preponderance standard

Preliminary questions for the court under FRE 104(a) are generally decided by a preponderance of the evidence standard. See *Bourjaily v. United States*, 483 U.S. 171 (1987).

e. Jury may be excluded

"Minihearings" on preliminary questions are sometimes conducted in the presence of the jury and sometimes outside their presence. FRE 103(c) requires that the minihearing be conducted outside the presence of the jury when necessary to prevent inadmissible evidence from being suggested to the jury. FRE 104(c) requires that hearings on the admissibility of challenged confessions shall in all cases be conducted out of the hearing of the jury because of the prejudice that would result from a jury hearing about a confession that is ultimately ruled inadmissible.

f. Even when court decides in favor of admissibility, opposing party may challenge evidence

If the court decides preliminary questions relating to admissibility in favor of the proponent (the offering party), the evidence is then admitted. Under FRE 103(e), however, the opponent is still entitled to introduce evidence relevant to weight or credibility. By way of illustration, even if the court allows Rudy's former testimony in the preceding example (after finding him to be "unavailable"), Baxter can still introduce evidence attacking Rudy's credibility (see FRE 806) and can urge the jury to disregard his testimony totally. Baxter can even argue that the prosecutor could have produced Rudy if greater efforts had been made to do so.

3. Preliminary Questions for the Jury Under FRE 104(b)

Some preliminary questions are for the jury under FRE 104(b), although it is more accurate to recognize that both the judge and the jury have a role under FRE 104(b).

a. FRE 104(b) questions

When the relevance of evidence depends on a preliminary question of fact, the jury ultimately determines the preliminary question. Thus the jury decides whether a witness has personal knowledge under FRE 602. The jury also decides whether an exhibit or other evidence is authentic under FRE 901. Both these matters are preliminary questions covered by FRE 104(b).

☛ EXAMPLE AND ANALYSIS

While driving home from a tavern, Raymond collides with a car driven by Ethel. She suffers severe injuries and sues Raymond for damages. At trial, as proof that

Raymond was driving while intoxicated, Ethel offers what she describes as a letter written by Raymond to his girlfriend that contains the following statement: "I was really smashed driving home last night and ran into some old lady. Hurt her pretty bad."

Before Ethel can introduce this letter as an admission by Raymond, the preliminary question that must be answered is whether it was actually written by Raymond. If it is a forgery (or was written by some other Raymond about some other accident), it is irrelevant. In the words of FRE 104(b), the relevancy of this letter "depends on whether a fact exists," meaning a finding that the letter was in fact written by Raymond. The *jury* ultimately determines whether this letter is authentic. If the jury finds it to be authentic, the letter may be admitted and given whatever weight the jury deems appropriate. If the jury finds the letter not to be authentic, the letter should be disregarded as irrelevant in the case, and an instruction to this effect would normally be given.

---

b. Role of judge under FRE 104(b)

Although the jury makes the *ultimate* decision whether the letter is authentic, the judge has an important screening function to perform: Under FRE 104(b), the judge decides whether there is **sufficient** evidence to support a **jury finding** that the letter is authentic. This function differs from what the judge does under FRE 104(a), where he simply decides whether a fact is established by a **preponderance** of the evidence. Thus in the example above, Ethel must lay a foundation for the letter (meaning that she "authenticates" it): If she offers enough evidence to enable a jury reasonably to decide that the letter was written by Raymond, then the court admits the letter (absent some other reason for excluding it) and asks the jury to resolve this question finally. Laying a foundation means producing sufficient evidence (such as handwriting identification) to allow a reasonable jury to find the letter to be authentic. See Chapter 12.

c. Opponent may introduce rebutting evidence

Even if the court finds that the offering party has offered enough evidence of authenticity under FRE 104(b), the opponent can offer rebutting evidence. If Ethel's evidence that Raymond wrote the letter is sufficient, for example, Raymond can still introduce evidence that he did not write the letter (it is a forgery, or some other Raymond wrote it) and urge the jury to disregard it. See FRE 104(e). After hearing the evidence for and against authenticity, the jury ultimately decides whether the letter is genuine.

F. MAKING A RECORD

To preserve for review any error in ruling on evidence matters, the party claiming error must make a proper record. In the case of error in admitting evidence, a proper objection must be made. In the case of error in excluding evidence, an offer of proof must be made. Absent proper objection or offer of proof, error is considered waived.

1. Objecting to Evidence

To protect the right to urge error on appeal, a party who wishes to exclude evidence offered by the other side ordinarily must object.

a. Mechanics

To be adequate, an objection must satisfy two important criteria.

i. Timely

The objection must be timely, which means it must normally be stated after the question but before the answer. If the witness "jumps the gun" and answers before the opposing party has a reasonable opportunity to object, an objection after the answer will still be considered timely.

ii. Ground

The objection must state a specific ground, unless the ground is apparent from the context. The trite and threadworn objection that evidence is "irrelevant, immaterial, and incompetent" should be avoided because it is a "general objection" that is inadequate to preserve a more specific point (like "hearsay") for review.

b. Limits

An objection advanced on one ground preserves a claim of error only on that ground. Thus a "hearsay" objection preserves a claim of error in admitting evidence if it amounts to hearsay, but does not preserve a claim that admitting the evidence violated the rule against using character to prove conduct. Of course a party can object on more than one ground.

c. Identify objectionable evidence

Usually context makes clear what evidence a party objects to. In the event of doubt, the objecting party must specify and explain to the court which evidence is the target of the objection. If a party objects to a question that is detailed or elaborate, or objects to a large body of material, and if the objection relates only to part of the question or the body of material, the objecting party must tell the judge what part is objectionable.

2. Reasons for Requiring Objections

There are three reasons to require objections.

a. Inform court

First, objections help the trial judge play her role in applying the Rules of Evidence by calling her attention to the evidence in question and alerting her to the rule or principle involved in deciding whether to admit or exclude.

b. Alert offering party

Second, objections help the offering party make whatever adjustments may be necessary to present competent proof.

c. Finality and fair chances

Third, requiring timely objections helps ensure that parties have reasonable but not endless chances to protect their interests. If objections were not required at trial and could still be advanced on appeal, many more undetected errors would be made at trial and many more appeals could be taken. The thought is that taking this course would give parties *more* protections than warranted, and at far higher cost to the system because litigation would drag on far longer and produce less finality than it does now.

3. Motion to Strike

Where a witness replies to an improper question before objection can be made (or gives an improper response to a proper question), a party can preserve the error by moving to strike the answer. Even if the motion is granted, the answer is not actually "stricken" from the court reporter's transcript. "Striking" the evidence merely means that the judge and jury are not to consider it in deciding the case. In jury cases, normally a motion to strike is accompanied by a request for an instruction advising the jury not to consider the evidence.

4. Offer of Proof

If the judge errs in *sustaining* an objection, the proponent of the evidence must make an offer of proof to preserve the claim of error. An offer of proof is unnecessary only when the substance of the evidence is apparent from the context.

a. Making of offer

An offer of proof involves showing on the record the substance of the evidence. In this way the excluded evidence becomes part of the trial transcript even though the jury does not hear it.

b. Reasons for requiring an offer of proof

Offers of proof are required for the same three reasons as objections. First, offers of proof help the trial judge understand the nature of the evidence issue, so she can rule properly on the issue at hand. Second, an offer of proof helps the objecting party more accurately formulate her position on the evidence issue at hand. Third, requiring an offer of proof helps accord to the offering party an adequate opportunity to make her case, without introducing into the system the added costs that would come if cases could be retried even if the offering party did *not* take the step of explaining with some care the matter being offered. There is yet another reason to require offers of proof, which is that in the absence of an offer the reviewing court would have a hard time knowing what was being kept out, and would as a practical matter be unable to appraise claims of error (unable to figure out whether excluding the evidence likely affected the result).

c. Form of offer

There are two traditional ways to make an offer of proof. One is for the attorney offering the evidence simply to state for the record the substance of the excluded evidence (what he believes the witness would have said if allowed to answer the question, for example). The second method is to make the offer of proof in question-and-answer form by posing the excluded questions to the witness and allowing the witness to answer. The trial judge has discretion to require the offer to be made in this form.

d. Normally made outside presence of jury

Almost always an offer of proof is made outside the presence of the jury. The court reporter must be present to take down the offer for the record. If the offer goes only to a preliminary question that does not cause prejudice (such as whether a hearsay declarant is unavailable, which can be determined without revealing what she has said), the offer can be made in the presence of the jury.

5. "Exceptions" to Judge's Ruling No Longer Required

In an earlier era, it was necessary to file "exceptions" to a trial judge's rulings on evidentiary matters to take an appeal from them—"Your Honor, I request an exception to that ruling." The requirement of filing exceptions has been abolished by modern procedural codes. See FRCP 46.

G. LIMITED ADMISSIBILITY

1. Purpose for Which Evidence Offered

There are often many purposes for which evidence might be offered, and evidence admitted without objection or limitation can normally be considered for any relevant purpose. But often evidence is admissible for some purposes and inadmissible for others, or admissible against one party but inadmissible against others.

2. Proponent Can Be Required to Specify Purpose

When evidence is admissible for some uses but not others, the proponent can be required to specify the purpose for which it is being offered. Then the court can decide whether an objection should be sustained or whether a limiting instruction is necessary.

3. Limiting Instruction

Where evidence is admissible for only limited purposes, or against fewer than all parties, an opponent on request is entitled to a limiting instruction under FRE 105. Such an instruction restricts the evidence "to its proper scope." Because such an instruction may be ineffective, and might even be counterproductive in suggesting a purpose that the jury might never consider if it were not mentioned, usually such instructions are given only if the opposing party requests.

4. Alternatives to Limiting Instruction

a. Exclusion

Sometimes the permissible use of the evidence is *de minimus* in comparison to the danger of its misuse by the jury for an impermissible purpose. In such cases, the court has discretion to exclude the evidence entirely under FRE 403.

b. Redaction

In some cases, particularly involving writings, the objectionable portion of the evidence can be redacted (by excising it or covering it up) so the jury will not see it or use it for the forbidden purpose.

c. Separate trials

In some cases where evidence is admissible against one defendant but not others, the danger of misuse is so great that a jury instruction is inadequate and separate trials are required. See *Bruton v. United States*, 391 U.S. 123 (1968) (admitting a statement by one defendant in a criminal case that incriminates another defendant by name is constitutional error under Confrontation Clause of Sixth Amendment where the statement is admissible against the declarant but not against the other defendant incriminated by name in the statement; limiting instruction is not adequate to protect constitutional rights of codefendant, as jury is not likely to follow the instruction).

H. RULE OF COMPLETENESS

1. Common Law Rule

At common law, if a party offers part of a writing during its case, the opponent is allowed to introduce other relevant parts during its case (or to inquire about them on cross-examination).

2. FRE 106

FRE 106 takes the common law rule one step further. When a party offers part of a writing or recorded statement, "an adverse party may require the introduction *at that time* of any other part or any other writing or recorded statement which ought in fairness to be considered contemporaneously with it." FRE 106 thus prevents a litigant from unfairly presenting part of a writing taken out of context even during its own case-in-chief.

I. APPELLATE REVIEW

1. Standard of Review

Under FRE 103(a), a party "may claim error in a ruling to admit or exclude evidence only if the error affects a substantial right." Thus a successful appeal of an evidence ruling requires three elements: First, the record must show that appellant made a proper objection or offer of proof at trial. Second, appellant must establish that the trial court's evidentiary ruling was error. Third, the reviewing court must be persuaded that the error was harmful.

2. Harmless Error

If the appellate court is not persuaded that the evidentiary error affected a substantial right, the error is **harmless.** If a substantial right of the party is affected, the trial court ruling is deemed **reversible error** or **prejudicial error.**

3. Grounds for Refusing to Reverse

a. Evidence admitted, wrong ground of objection

Even if there was error in admitting evidence, an appellate court generally affirms if the attorney did not object on the right ground at trial. A trial judge is responsible only for ruling on the objection made, not for considering all other possible grounds of objection.

b. Inadmissible evidence excluded on wrong ground

Even if it was error to exclude evidence on the basis of the objection made, most appellate courts do not reverse if the evidence was properly excludable on *some other ground.* Appellate courts are reluctant to find prejudicial error in a ruling excluding evidence, if it actually was inadmissible, merely because the evidence was excluded for the wrong reason.

c. Evidence admitted on wrong theory

Sometimes evidence is admitted on an improper theory. For example, a trial judge might admit hearsay under the wrong exception. If the evidence was admissible under some other exception, the error is generally considered harmless.

d. Curative instruction

Sometimes evidentiary error is found to have been "cured" when the record shows that the trial judge gave the jury an instruction to disregard the challenged evidence.

e. Invited error

Sometimes a reviewing court refuses to reverse because the evidentiary error was "invited" by the appellant. If, for example, a defendant in a criminal case asks the investigating officer, "Isn't it true that you only focused on my client because you didn't like his looks," the officer might answer by saying, "No that's not the reason. I focused on your client because I saw him lighting up a joint on the street." In this example, the question invited the response given, and any "error" in admitting evidence that defendant lit a joint on the street was likely invited by defense counsel.

☞ EXAMPLE AND ANALYSIS

The defense in an automobile accident case cross-examines Arnold, who is the plaintiff, as follows:

Q. On direct you said you weren't speeding at the time of the collision.

A. Yes, that's what I said and that's the way it was.

Q. And I suppose you're going to tell the jury that you never speed and always drive carefully.

A. Well, in fact you're right. I don't ever exceed the speed limit, and I've never gotten a speeding ticket in my life.

On redirect, Arnold expands on his driving habits, testifying that he abides by the rules of the road and that he has never been in an accident before this one. The defense objects to this line of questioning.

The objection should be overruled. It is true that Arnold could not ordinarily prove that he was a careful driver (or that he had a spotless driving record) during his case-in-chief because such proof is viewed as "character evidence." FRE 404 generally bars such proof in civil cases if the purpose is to prove due care on the occasion in question. See Chapter 6. But when the defendant in effect challenges Arnold's perfectly proper and focused testimony about his speed at the time of the accident, and broadens the inquiry by asking him whether he claims he never speeds, Arnold can answer that question directly, and can even defend the answer by further testimony and directly responds to the question that was put to him. Any "error" in letting Arnold testify go into this matter was invited by the defense. Hence the defense is not likely to win a reversal on appeal, particularly with respect to Arnold's initial answer to the defense question, and probably with respect to his additional response on redirect.

---

f. "Opening the door" doctrine

Otherwise inadmissible evidence can sometimes properly come in if it is offered in response to evidence introduced by an opponent. It is said that parties are allowed to "fight fire with fire," or the opponent's tactic "opens the door" to proof that might otherwise be inadmissible. Usually the appropriate response to inadmissible evidence offered by an opponent is to object, in order to keep the evidence out, rather than stand silent and then offer rebuttal evidence that is also inadmissible. But often courts allow the rebuttal.

Example. Henry, a local businessman, is charged in state court with sexual abuse of a minor. At trial Henry takes the stand, denies committing the offense, and states: "As an upstanding citizen of this community, I am shocked by these charges. In my entire life, I've never been in trouble with the law before." In rebuttal the prosecutor offers evidence that during the last five years Henry has been convicted twice for robbery and once for illegally selling narcotics. Assume that evidence of these prior convictions is otherwise inadmissible, as is likely on these facts. Nevertheless, Henry "opened the door" to evidence about his past criminal record by testifying to his unblemished past, and a reviewing court is unlikely to reverse his conviction for that reason.

g. Overwhelming evidence

Sometimes evidentiary error is found to be harmless because there is overwhelming evidence in support of the verdict. Thus, the verdict would not likely have changed even if the trial judge had ruled correctly on the disputed evidence issue.

4. Constitutional Error

In criminal cases, when the claim of error is constitutional rather than evidentiary, different standards of review apply. Thus rulings admitting physical objects seized in violation of the Fourth Amendment (as might happen if officers lacked a warrant when they searched a residence), or a confession illegally taken in violation of the Fifth Amendment (as might happen if officers failed to give *Miranda* warnings when interrogating a suspect in custody), are reviewed under a special constitutional standard. In rare cases, constitutional error results in automatic reversal. Usually, however, the constitutional standard requires reversal unless it is shown that the error was harmless beyond a reasonable doubt. *Chapman v. California,* 386 U.S. 18 (1967). In the case of constitutional error in jury instructions, the applicable standard turns on whether there is a reasonable likelihood that the jury has applied the challenged instruction in a way that would violate the Constitution. *Estelle v. McGuire,* 502 U.S. 62 (1991).

5. Plain Error

When an error is both obvious (a clear violation of a well-understood principle) and serious (probably having a major effect on outcome), appellate courts sometimes invoke the plain error doctrine to reverse a judgment even though the appellant made no objection at trial. Reversal for plain error is unlikely when the appellant complains about a ruling excluding evidence but failed to make an offer of proof at trial because the record usually fails to disclose anything about the proof. Reversal is somewhat more likely in cases of error in admitting evidence, particularly if the ground for exclusion is obvious even though it was not raised by objection. Reversals on ground of plain error are more common in criminal than in civil cases because of the heightened level of concern about securing fairness for criminal defendants. Also, if egregious evidentiary error in a criminal case is not addressed in the original appeal, defendant is likely to raise the claim later in a post-conviction proceeding attacking the competency of his trial counsel. In any event, reversals for plain error are rare.

6. Interlocutory Appeals

The general rule is that appellate courts do not grant interlocutory review (review prior to final judgment) of evidence rulings. Trials would be interminable if every evidence ruling could immediately be taken to an appellate court. Review of evidence rulings usually occurs only during appeal from a final judgment.

a. Privilege rulings

There is a narrow exception to the general policy against interlocutory appeal of evidence rulings that sometimes comes into play in connection with rulings denying claims of privilege. If a witness is ordered to testify over a claim of privilege, he sometimes refuses to do so and is held in criminal contempt, which is an appealable order that can lead to a review of the underlying ruling on the privilege claim. In effect, the criminal contempt is viewed as a separate proceeding in which the merits of the privilege claim can be reviewed. See Chapter 14.

b. Appeal by prosecutor from rulings suppressing evidence

Often criminal defendants file pretrial motions to suppress evidence. Usually such motions assert constitutional claims: Often the claim is that the evidence was obtained from the defendant in violation of his rights under the Fourth, Fifth, or Sixth Amendment. If the trial judge grants the motion to suppress, the prosecution may face the prospect of a trial without evidence critical to its case. In the event of an acquittal, the Double Jeopardy Clause would bar the prosecutor from retrying the defendant even if the trial court erred in excluding the evidence. For these reasons, prosecutors have a limited right to take an immediate appeal from pretrial rulings suppressing evidence. See 18 U.S.C. § 3731.

REVIEW QUESTIONS AND ANSWERS

Question: Why do we have rules of evidence?

Answer: Evidence rules serve many purposes. They protect against juries becoming unfairly prejudiced against a party or unduly sympathetic toward a party on the basis of factors not bearing on the immediate dispute. They are designed to further accurate factfinding and to keep juries from being confused or misled. The fundamental requirement of relevance helps control the scope and duration of trials. Burdens and presumptions have the effect of favoring or disfavoring certain claims or outcomes. Privileges protect various personal and professional relationships from being impaired by the compelled disclosure of confidential information. Other evidence rules, such as the rule prohibiting evidence of subsequent remedial measures, are intended to encourage socially constructive behavior outside the courtroom or at least to avoid penalizing a party for it. Some rules of evidence help ensure a perception of fairness that results in greater public acceptance of verdicts and judgments reached in court proceedings.

Question: Can evidence objections be waived?

Answer: Yes. The Rules of Evidence are not self-enforcing. It is expected that the parties, not the trial judge, will decide when to make an evidentiary objection. For reasons of trial strategy, a party may consciously choose not to make an evidentiary objection even when it is likely to be sustained. Failure to assert an objection results in waiver and generally forecloses any opportunity to raise the issue on appeal. An objection is also waived when it is not timely, fails to state a correct ground, or does not clearly identify the objectionable evidence.

Question: What is required to have an erroneous evidentiary ruling reversed on appeal?

Answer: As a general matter, a ruling on a point of evidence can lead to reversal only if three requirements are satisfied. First, the trial record must show that a proper objection or offer of proof was made (unless the nature of the objection or offer is made clear by the context). Second, the appellate court must find the trial court's ruling to be error. On some issues, trial courts are granted broad discretion, and their rulings are reversed only for abuse of discretion. Finally, the appellate court must be persuaded that the error affected a substantial right of a party. Only in such cases is the trial court's ruling considered to be prejudicial or reversible error. Otherwise, it is labeled harmless. Even if these three requirements are satisfied, courts sometimes affirm judgments for other reasons, as happens when the complaining party invited the error.

EXAM TIPS

Important Note: Some **General Pointers** are set out below, and then some **Specific Pointers** arranged by subject heading follow after each chapter. Bear in mind that the Specific Pointers **do not summarize everything** you need to know. Instead, they select points that are salient and sometimes overlooked by exam takers. In other words, don't take these Specific Pointers as complete descriptions of the doctrines to which they relate.

Here are some **General Pointers** about exam-taking in the Evidence course.

Broad questions. Questions on an evidence exam may provide an account of a trial, including a transcript reflecting questions and answers, offers and objections. Here your task may be to analyze issues raised by the lawyers, determine the right outcome on an objection or offer of proof, or determine whether the court did the right thing.

Specific questions. Questions on an evidence exam may ask specific questions, in the setting of short factual accounts. Here your task may be to decide whether a proffered item is admissible, whether a stated ground of objection or reason to admit is correct, or to say what rule ought to control and what the outcome should be.

Objective questions. An evidence exam may contain true/false or multiple choice questions. Here your task may be to recall specific points, to apply a specific doctrine, or to recognize mistakes in suggested choices.

Substantive law and process issues. Some evidence law relates to process issues rather than substantive points. Hence you should take care, in reading the questions, to determine whether the professor wants you to discuss process issues or only substantive points. If the question doesn't say, the safest course is to address both in your answers.

Process issues include the requirement to object and offer proof, various provisions requiring the parties to give pretrial notice of intent to invoke certain rules (catchall exception) or offer evidence (prior acts by the complainant in a sexual offense case), the doctrines allocating responsibility between judge and jury, and doctrines relating to burdens and presumptions.

Substantive points include the hearsay doctrine, the rules on character evidence, privileges, the Best Evidence doctrine, and, in fact, most of the rules, statutes, and doctrines you studied.

Constitutional points. Evidence rules may have constitutional dimensions, or may be limited or affected in their operation by constitutional concerns. For instance, the operation of the catchall exception in criminal cases is limited by the Supreme Court's decision in *Wright* requiring courts to examine statements for trustworthiness without considering corroborating evidence (and satisfying the exception doesn't necessarily satisfy the Constitution).

Be prepared to discuss constitutional decisions and doctrines when appropriate.

The professor may not want you to discuss such issues, so don't do it if the question or instructions tell you not to.

Remember that some Supreme Court decisions, such as *Williamson* (on against-interest statements) and *Tome* (on prior consistent statements) and *Trammel* (on the spousal testimony privilege) do not apply the Constitution, and they may be relevant in discussing evidence issues even if you are not expected to discuss constitutional matters.

Catchall exception. The catchall exception could be invoked for almost every out-of-court statement, but a good rule of thumb is to discuss specific (categorical) exceptions first, and go on to the catchall if there is time. Your professor may not want you to discuss the catchall, so be sure to look for general instructions (or indications in the question) that direct you not to apply it.

Answer what the question asks.   In Evidence, as in other courses, pay attention to the question, and answer what it asks. If the question or general instructions on the exam **direct you to specifics** (does a particular hearsay exception apply?), you should concentrate on them and need not discuss other points that typically arise in almost every setting, like the mechanics of objecting.

CHAPTER 2

Relevancy

Chapter Overview

The key points in this chapter are

- Only relevant evidence is admissible.

- Relevance means having any tendency to prove a legally significant fact.

- The definition of materiality is merged with the definition of relevancy under FRE 401.

- Relevant evidence is admissible unless otherwise provided by constitution, statute, or rule.

- Considerations of relevancy underlie many other Rules of Evidence.

- Judges decide the relevance and admissibility of evidence, and juries decide its weight.

- When relevancy depends on a preliminary fact, the jury makes the ultimate determination of that preliminary fact.

- Courts have discretion under FRE 403 to exclude relevant evidence on several grounds, including unfair prejudice and confusion of issues.

- Appellate courts give considerable leeway to trial court rulings under FRE 403 and reverse only for abuse of discretion.

A. EVIDENCE MUST BE RELEVANT TO BE ADMISSIBLE

1. Relevancy Is Threshold Requirement

The most fundamental requirement of admissibility is that evidence be relevant. Irrelevant evidence is inadmissible. Assessing relevancy should ordinarily be the starting point of any evidentiary analysis.

2. Reason for the Relevancy Requirement

The relevancy requirement is necessary to constrain the length of trials, control the cost of litigation, and confine litigated issues to manageable proportions. If litigants could offer evidence without limitation, trials could drag on interminably, jurors would become confused, and the judicial system would no longer provide a rational factfinding process.

B. DEFINITIONS

1. Relevant

Under FRE 401, evidence is relevant if it has any tendency to make the existence of any fact that is of consequence to the determination of the action more probable or less probable than it would be without the evidence. FRE 401 is broad. Even evidence having only slight probative value qualifies. It does not have to establish that a fact is more probable than not or provide sufficient basis for sending the issue to the jury. It can be a small piece of a mosaic tending to make the existence of a fact more or less likely. As commentators have observed, "a brick is not a wall," and even a brick is admissible. Also, not every witness "can make a home run," and even single-base hitters can testify. See ACN to FRE 401 (containing these quotations).

a. Only logical relevance required

FRE 401 adopts the view of Professor Thayer requiring only **logical** relevance and rejects Dean Wigmore's standard of **legal** relevance, which would require each item of proof to carry a "plus value" (something more than slight probative value). But even though FRE 401 establishes a low threshold, evidence having only marginal probative force is more likely to be excluded under FRE 403 for reasons of unfair prejudice, confusing or misleading the jury, undue delay, waste of time, or needless presentation of cumulative evidence.

b. Does not address specific categories of evidence

FRE 401 sets forth a general standard for all types of evidence. Other rules in Article IV address relevance and admissibility of specific categories of evidence. See Chapter 6 on Character and Habit Evidence (FRE 404–406 and FRE 412–415) and Chapter 7 on other specific relevancy rules (FRE 407–411).

c. A relational concept

The relevancy of an item of proof cannot be judged in isolation, but only in the context of the specific issues raised by the parties (in pleadings, indictments, or arguments), the other evidence in the case, and the applicable substantive law.

d. Need not be in dispute

Evidence can be relevant even when offered to prove a point that is not contested, although exclusion under FRE 403 is more likely. A party is not automatically deprived of the right to offer evidence on an issue in its case merely because the opponent does not contest it.

e. Impeachment evidence

Relevant evidence includes not only evidence tending to advance a party's own case but also evidence that refutes an opponent's case or impeaches the credibility of opposing witnesses.

2. Materiality

a. Legally significant

Evidence is material if it has legal significance in the case and is immaterial if it does not. For example, if under the substantive law assumption of risk is not a defense to a claim, evidence offered to prove assumption of risk is immaterial.

b. Merged in FRE 401

Relevancy and materiality are treated as separate concepts at common law, but they are merged in FRE 401. Materiality is part of the definition of relevance because of the requirement that the fact to be proved must be "of consequence to the determination of the action."

3. Direct Evidence

Evidence is "direct" in nature when it *asserts* the existence of the fact to be proven, or, in the case of tangible evidence, *embodies* or ***represents*** the fact. An example is testimony by an eyewitness that she saw the defendant shoot the murder victim, which is direct evidence of the shooting. By definition, direct evidence is always relevant if the fact it proves is of consequence to the action.

4. Circumstantial Evidence

Circumstantial evidence is proof that does not actually assert or represent the fact to be proved, but from which the factfinder can infer an increased probability that the fact exists. Defendant's fingerprint on the murder weapon is circumstantial evidence in a trial for murder. Most questions of relevance pertain to circumstantial evidence because often the reasonableness of an inference can be debated. Courts generally do not consider circumstantial evidence to be an "inferior" form of proof. A legal finding, including a criminal conviction, can rest entirely on circumstantial evidence.

C. RELEVANCY REQUIREMENT UNDERLIES OTHER RULES OF EVIDENCE

The concept of relevancy embodied in FRE 401–402 is also a component of other Rules found elsewhere in the code. The following are examples:

1. Particularized Rules of Relevancy

FRE 404–415 are particularized rules of relevancy in which the probative value of certain forms of evidence (like subsequent remedial measures) is balanced against competing considerations (like the social policy of encouraging repairs after an accident) as a matter of law. By obviating the need for case-by-case balancing, these Rules advance goals of consistency and predictability. See Chapters 6 and 7.

2. Personal Knowledge Requirement

The personal knowledge requirement of FRE 602 helps insure that witnesses testify only about matters personally known to them rather than engaging in conjecture and speculation (which would be irrelevant). See Chapters 2 and 11.

3. Lay Opinion

Opinions by lay witnesses (nonexperts) are admissible under FRE 701 only if they are based on the personal perception of the witness and are helpful to the trier of fact. These requirements help insure that only relevant opinions are admitted. See Chapter 11.

4. Expert Opinions

Expert opinions are admissible under FRE 702 only if the expert is qualified and the opinion assists the trier of fact. Again these requirements help insure the relevance of expert opinions. See Chapter 11.

5. Authentication

FRE 901 requires that a party offering exhibits (and certain other evidence) make a preliminary showing that the items are what their proponent claims them to be. Authentication is simply a more specific application of the relevancy requirement. See Chapter 12.

D. ROLE OF JUDGE AND JURY

1. FRE 104(a)

Most of the time, it is the judge who decides the relevancy of evidence at the time it is offered. Only if the judge determines that it is relevant does the jury get to hear it. During deliberations the jury decides what weight, if any, to give it.

2. FRE 104(b)

Sometimes relevancy depends on a **preliminary question of fact** (whether a document is genuine or a forgery, for instance). Such cases involve issues of **conditional relevancy.** Here both judge and jury play roles, and the situation differs from the one governed by FRE 104(a).

a. Role of judge

The judge does not resolve the preliminary question (genuineness of the document), but decides only whether there is **sufficient** evidence to support a jury finding of genuineness. If there is, the judge submits the document to the jury to make the ultimate decision whether it is genuine. See discussion in Chapter 1.

b. Role of jury

If the jury finds the document was forged, it should disregard it as irrelevant. If the jury finds the document genuine (hence relevant), the jury can give it whatever weight the jury deems appropriate.

c. Connecting up

Under FRE 104(b), the judge has discretion to submit the document to the jury before the proponent makes a preliminary showing of genuineness, provided the proponent agrees to "connect up" the evidence later by putting on evidence of genuineness.

i. Admit subject to later proof

The proponent might promise to call a handwriting expert later in trial to testify that the document is genuine. Under FRE 104(b), the court has discretion to admit the document subject to later introduction of the authenticating evidence.

ii. **Failure to connect up**
If the proponent fails to connect up by producing the promised evidence of genuineness, the opposing party can move to strike the document (withdrawing it from evidence, not submitting it to the jury) and request an instruction telling the jury to disregard it. A mistrial may be required if the jury's exposure to the improper evidence has caused prejudice.

E. RELEVANT EVIDENCE ADMISSIBLE UNLESS OTHERWISE PROVIDED

FRE 402 provides that all relevant evidence is admissible except as otherwise provided by the Constitution, federal statutes, other Federal Rules of Evidence, or other rules prescribed by the Supreme Court, such as the Federal Rules of Civil Procedure (FRCP or Civil Rules) or Federal Rules of Criminal Procedure (FRCrimP or Criminal Rules).

1. U.S. Constitution
Under the constitutional exclusionary rule, evidence seized in violation of constitutional guarantees may be excluded even though relevant. For example, statements by defendants taken during custodial interrogation by police without *Miranda* warnings and physical evidence seized during illegal searches may be excluded.

2. Federal Statutes
There are a number of federal statutes that exclude evidence at trial, even though it may be relevant. See, e.g., 18 U.S.C. § 2510–2520 (excluding unlawfully obtained wiretap evidence).

3. Other Evidence Rules
Numerous Federal Rules exclude evidence even though relevant. See FRE 403–405, 407–412, 501, 602, 605, 606, 610, 701, 702, 802, 901, 1002.

4. Federal Rules of Civil Procedure
Several provisions of the Civil Rules restrict the admissibility of evidence. See FRCP 26(b)(3) (creating qualified immunity for work product); FRCP 36(b) (response to request for admissions not usable in other proceedings); FRCP 37(b)(2) (exclusion for failure to comply with discovery rules); FRCP 68 (evidence of unaccepted offer of judgment inadmissible).

5. Federal Rules of Criminal Procedure

Some provisions of the Criminal Rules block the use of evidence. See FRCrimP 6(e) (grand jury proceedings secret); FRCrimP 11(e)(6) (statements made in plea agreements inadmissible); FRCrimP 12.1(d) and 12.2(d) (requiring exclusion of defense evidence of alibi or insanity for failure to give pretrial notice); FRCrimP 16(d)(2) (requiring exclusion of evidence for failure to comply with discovery order).

F. JUDICIAL DISCRETION TO EXCLUDE RELEVANT EVIDENCE

To offset the broad definition of relevancy contained in FRE 401, FRE 403 grants trial judges discretion to exclude evidence of unquestioned relevance when its probative value is substantially outweighed by the dangers of unfair prejudice, confusion of the issues, or misleading the jury, or by considerations of undue delay, waste of time, or needless presentation of cumulative evidence.

1. Balance in Favor of Admissibility

FRE 403 authorizes exclusion only when probative value is "substantially" outweighed by competing considerations. Thus the Rule is slanted in favor of admissibility. When probative value is equally balanced against, for example, the risk of unfair prejudice, the evidence is to be admitted.

2. Stipulations

An offer to stipulate counts in rulings under FRE 403. The trial judge has discretion to exclude evidence when the opposing party is willing to stipulate to the point being proved. If, for example, a prosecutor offers a photograph of the body of a murder victim to establish its location at the crime scene, defendant might offer to stipulate to location. But the other side is not necessarily required to accept an offer to stipulate. Courts can reject stipulations when they are incomplete or would unfairly deny a party the full force of the evidence it wants to offer. In the narrow setting in which prosecutors offer proof of prior convictions to establish that the defendant is a repeat offender (typically "felon in possession cases," in which the charge is that defendant is a convicted felon who was illegally in possession of a handgun), the Supreme Court concluded that a defense offer to stipulate to prior convictions does block the prosecutor from proving them in other ways, but the Court was careful to distinguish this situation from the situation in which prior crimes are relevant in tending to prove such things as intent under FRE 404(b). See *Old Chief v. United States*, 519 U.S. 172 (1997). *Old Chief* is not a constitutional holding, but rather a construction of FRE 403 in the exercise of the Court's supervisory responsibilities, so state courts are free to accept or reject this holding.

3. Surprise

FRE 403 does not recognize surprise as an independent ground for exclusion. The ACN states that "granting of a continuance is a more appropriate remedy [for surprise] than exclusion of the evidence." But surprise may sometimes be a factor in finding that evidence will result in unfair prejudice, confusion of the issues, and undue delay.

4. Credibility Determinations

Evidence may not be excluded under FRE 403 merely because the trial judge does not find the evidence to be credible. Although the court may consider probative value of the evidence in undertaking the required balancing, nothing in FRE 403 alters the principle that questions of credibility are for the jury.

5. Relation to Other Rules

FRE 403 generally allows the trial judge discretion to exclude evidence even when it is admissible under another rule:

a. Prior crime impeachment

FRE 609(a)(1), which authorizes impeachment by evidence of prior convictions, expressly incorporates FRE 403 as a limit for impeaching witnesses other than the accused. (For the accused, FRE 609(a)(1) contains its own balancing principle, under which prior felony convictions should be excluded unless probative worth exceeds risk of prejudice–a standard providing *more* protection against prejudice by *reversing* the standard stated in FRE 403, under which exclusion is authorized only if unfair prejudice *exceeds* probative worth.) But most courts hold that FRE 403 cannot be used to prevent impeachment by convictions involving dishonesty or false statement under FRE 609(a)(2). See discussion in Chapter 10.

b. Prior acts

FRE 403 is frequently used to limit proof of bad acts under FRE 404(b) (see Chapter 6) and inquiry into acts bearing on truthfulness or untruthfulness of a witness under FRE 608(b) (see Chapter 10).

c. Cross-examination of character witnesses

FRE 403 is used as a restraint on the scope of cross-examination of character witnesses about specific instances of conduct under FRE 405(a). See Chapter 6.

6. Appellate Review

Appellate courts give substantial deference to rulings of trial judges under FRE 403 and generally reverse only for clear abuse of discretion.

G. GROUNDS FOR EXCLUSION UNDER FRE 403

1. Unfair Prejudice

The most common ground for exclusion under FRE 403 is "unfair prejudice." The qualification "unfair" was included in order to recognize that relevant evidence could be said to be "prejudicial" to the opposing party by its very nature—all evidence that is relevant may aid the proponent and to that extent harm the case of the opposing party, and this tendency is not "unfair" prejudice. In other words, FRE 403 asks courts to distinguish between prejudice resulting from the persuasive force of the evidence and prejudice resulting from either of two other qualities or tendencies in the evidence. One is the tendency to evoke anger or emotion that would lessen the ability of the jury to behave rationally or reasonably. The other is the tendency to tempt the jury to misuse the evidence—to use evidence that has one legitimate or permissible use for some other illegitimate or forbidden use. It is only these latter kinds of prejudice that count as "unfair."

a. Excessive emotionalism

One type of unfair prejudice arises from the injection of **excessive emotionalism, arousing hostility, passion, anger, or sympathy** on the part of the jury. Courts may exclude evidence that is "inflammatory," "shocking," or "sensational." Evidence may also be excluded when it evokes the anger or punitive impulses, or unfairly puts a party or witness in a negative light, or appeals to prejudice, or gives rise to overly strong sympathetic reactions.

Example.   Bland is charged with being a felon in possession of a firearm. The prosecutor offers evidence that his felony conviction, handed down years ago, was for child abuse resulting in injury—the torture and murder of a seven-year-old girl. This evidence of the **nature** of the prior conviction should have been excluded because it might inflame the jury against the accused and make the jury believe that if they acquitted they would be "releasing an exceedingly dangerous child molester and killer." *United States v. Bland,* 908 F.2d 471, 473 (9th Cir. 1990).

Example.   In a suit for invasion of privacy by a woman pictured in *Hustler* magazine, the trial court erred under FRE 403 in admitting a slide show of 128 of the magazine's "worst pictures." *Douglass v. Hustler Magazine, Inc.,* 769 F.2d 1128, 1142 (7th Cir. 1985).

b. Jury unable to limit use

A second type of unfair prejudice results when the jury is likely to misuse the evidence in some way or to be unable to follow a limiting instruction.

Example. In a classic case in which a doctor was charged with murdering his wife, the Supreme Court rejected use of the wife's statement shortly before she died, saying "Dr. Shepard has poisoned me" for the limited purpose of showing her will to live and the unlikelihood that she committed suicide, but not for the purpose of proving what she actually said–that defendant had poisoned her. The Court concluded: "Discrimination so subtle is a feat beyond the compass of ordinary minds. The reverberating clang of those accusatory words would drown out all weaker sounds. It is for ordinary minds, and not for psychoanalysts, that the rules of evidence are framed." *Shepard v. United States,* 290 U.S. 96, 103–104 (1933) (Cardozo, J.).

c. Undue weight

Evidence may be excluded as unfairly prejudicial when the jury is likely to give it undue weight.

Example. In the trial of a postmaster for improperly opening a package, it was reversible error to admit "highly prejudicial" testimony by a postal inspector that defendant was investigated because of "information" that he was "taking out packages which had been missent." *United States v. Lamberty,* 778 F.2d 59, 60–61 (1st Cir. 1985).

d. Demonstrative evidence

Demonstrative evidence, such as photographs, "day-in-the-life" films, computer-generated visual imagery, courtroom displays of wounds, and experiments, can sometimes have an unfairly powerful emotional impact on the jury justifying exclusion under FRE 403.

Example. In the trial for manslaughter of a father who allegedly caused the death of his seven-month-old daughter by shaking her, the prosecutor called an expert on "shaken baby syndrome." The expert did a courtroom demonstration by repeatedly and violently shaking a rubber mannequin. The appellate court reversed, concluding that probative value was "overwhelmed" by unfairly prejudicial effects that came from seeing an "adult male repeatedly shaking a representation of an infant." The government "failed to establish that either the degree of force or the number of oscillations bore any relationship to the defendant's actions." *United States v. Gaskell*, 985 F.2d 1056, 1061 (11th Cir. 1993).

2. Confusion of the Issues

Evidence may be excluded when it is likely to confuse the issues, as by distracting the jury with collateral matters.

Example. In a criminal trial, the defendant offered evidence that other persons allegedly involved in the conspiracy were not prosecuted. This evidence was properly excluded under FRE 403 as confusing the issues. *United States v. Steffen*, 641 F.2d 591, 596 (8th Cir. 1981).

3. Misleading the Jury

FRE 403 gives the judge discretion to exclude evidence that is likely to mislead the jury.

Example. Brewer files an action against the Jeep Corporation for personal injuries suffered in a rollover accident. He alleged that the rollover resulted from certain negligence and breaches of warranty. At trial, Brewer offered a film of a simulation of the accident with dummies riding in the jeep as passengers. The trial court properly excluded the film as misleading because the dummies "admittedly did not have the ability to even attempt to hold on to anything" and the film showed them "flailing about in the vehicle and losing legs, heads and arms in the process." *Brewer v. Jeep Corp.*, 546 F.Supp. 1147, 1149 (W.D. Ark. 1982).

4. Waste of Time or Undue Delay

Evidence can be excluded that would simply waste time or result in undue delay. In the immortal words of Justice Holmes, providing trial judges with discretion to exclude on such grounds is a "concession to the shortness of life" (Justice Holmes lived to age 94!).

Example. In the trial of Patty Hearst for bank robbery and other crimes, the trial court properly refused to admit a tape of a psychiatric interview of the defendant lasting almost two hours. The information on the tape was already sufficiently established by other evidence, and the tape would have resulted in unnecessary consumption of time. *United States v. Hearst*, 563 F.2d 1331 (9th Cir. 1977).

5. Needless Presentation of Cumulative Evidence

It is sometimes hard to decide when evidence is "needlessly cumulative" because it is hard to know how much evidence on a particular issue is necessary to convince the jury. But under FRE 403 courts have discretion to limit the number of witnesses called and to prevent unnecessary repetition.

Example. In a personal injury suit against the manufacturer of a farm combine, the judge admitted evidence of three similar accidents. The judge could then exclude evidence of six others because the court has discretion to exclude "unnecessarily cumulative" evidence. *Melton v. Deere & Co.*, 887 F.2d 1241 (5th Cir. 1989).

H. RECURRING ISSUES OF RELEVANCE

There are a number of recurring issues of relevance involving the admissibility of circumstantial proof. See generally, Christopher Mueller and Laird Kirkpatrick, *Evidence* §§ 4.5–4.8 (5th ed. 2012) (hereinafter "M & K").

1. Evidence of Guilty Mind

Evidence indicating consciousness of guilt is generally relevant to prove that the actor was involved in wrongful conduct.

a. Flight

The most common example of evidence indicating consciousness of guilt is flight. When a defendant flees the scene of a crime, or flees after learning that police are looking for him, his conduct suggests the possibility of a guilty mind, which in turn suggests possible guilt of the charged crime. Sometimes it is unclear whether conduct really is flight (as opposed to an innocent journey or something else), or whether flight really indicates a guilty mind (as opposed to fear of police, or something else), and whether a guilty mind relates to the charged crime (as opposed to some other). Judges must assess such possibilities in deciding whether the proffered evidence is relevant and whether it should be excluded for unfair prejudice even if it is relevant.

b. Other examples

Other examples of evidence indicating consciousness of guilt include resisting arrest, escape, use of aliases, wearing a disguise, fabricating or destroying evidence, bribing a witness, threatening or killing a witness, making false exculpatory statements, refusing to comply with a lawful order to furnish fingerprints or similar identifying data, and attempting suicide.

c. Entitled to little weight

Courts generally hold that evidence of consciousness of guilt is insufficient, standing alone, to support a conviction, and jury instructions usually add cautions indicating that there may be innocent explanations for what the party did.

2. Other Accidents

The general rule is that evidence of prior accidents is not admissible to prove negligence or contributory negligence in the accident giving rise to the lawsuit.

a. Admissible for narrower purposes

Evidence of prior accidents may be admissible to prove an element of a negligence claim, such as the existence of a condition or the dangerousness of the condition. Other accidents may also show that the condition *can* cause an accident or injury of the type in suit, or that it *did* cause the accident at issue, or that the defendant knew (or should have known) about the condition and its dangerousness.

b. Substantial similarity requirement

To be admissible, even for these narrower purposes, other accidents must be "substantially similar" to the one at issue.

c. Remoteness

Accidents or mishaps occurring at remote times in the past or under different conditions are usually excluded as irrelevant.

d. Absence of accidents

A party defending against a claim may show the *absence* of other accidents involving the same or like place or instrumentality as counterproof on the issues of dangerousness, causation, or knowledge. The substantial similarity of conditions requirement must be satisfied.

3. Other Contracts or Business Transactions

Evidence of other contracts or business transactions is sometimes admitted to prove the existence of a contract in litigation, its terms, or their intended meaning. Thus if the terms of an oral contract are disputed, a prior written contract between the parties involving the same matters may be circumstantial evidence of the nature of the oral agreement.

a. Same parties

Other contracts are most likely to be admitted when they are between the same parties and involve the same or similar subject matter. Occasionally evidence of contracts between a litigant and third persons is admissible to show the usual practice of a party on such points as including or excluding a particular provision in such contracts.

b. Parol evidence rule

Evidence of prior agreements between the parties may be barred by the parol evidence rule (a rule of substantive law rather than evidence) if offered to *vary or change* the terms of an integrated or complete written agreement. But the Uniform Commercial Code recognizes the relevance of evidence pertaining to "course of dealing" and "usage of trade" in *interpreting and supplementing* the terms of a contract.

4. Industry Standards

Evidence of conformity or nonconformity to industry standards is often admitted as bearing circumstantially on negligence. But the standard must be so general or well known that the actor may be charged with knowing it or with being negligent if he does not know of it. The weight given to industry standards is for the jury to determine. Evidence of conformity is not enough to establish due care, and evidence of nonconformity does not by itself prove negligence.

5. Governmental Safety Standards

Safety standards promulgated by governmental agencies are often admitted to assist the trier of fact in determining negligence or, in a product liability action, whether the product was unreasonably dangerous. Such standards provide evidence of the care expected of employers or manufacturers. But nonconforming with agency safety standards normally does not constitute negligence per se.

REVIEW QUESTIONS AND ANSWERS

Question: What is the difference between relevancy and materiality?

Answer: Common law cases distinguished between an objection that evidence was irrelevant and an objection that it was immaterial. Irrelevance meant the evidence lacked probative value—it did not raise or lower the probability of the fact for which the evidence was offered. Materiality meant that the fact being proved had legal significance in the case. The definition of relevancy in FRE 401 merges these concepts of relevancy and materiality by defining relevant as having any tendency to make the existence of a fact of consequence to the action more probable or less probable than it would be without the evidence. The reference to a fact "of consequence" means a material fact. Thus an objection under FRE 401 that evidence is "irrelevant" incorporates and preserves an objection that the evidence is immaterial. In federal courts and in states adopting a counterpart of FRE 401, a separate objection on grounds of immateriality no longer needs to be made.

Question: What is the difference between the role of the judge and the role of the jury in determining questions of relevance?

Answer: Most questions of relevance are for the court to decide under FRE 104(a). Since relevance is a relational concept, the court must consider issues raised by the parties (in their pleadings or arguments), other evidence in the case, and applicable substantive law. The court may conduct a "minihearing" under FRE 104(a) to obtain additional information useful in assessing probative value before deciding whether to admit evidence over an objection going to relevance. If the court finds that the evidence meets the generous standard of FRE 401 and admits it, the jury decides what weight it deserves, if any. Sometimes relevancy depends on a preliminary finding of fact (that a document is genuine, for example, rather than forged). In some such cases, the matter goes to the jury as an issue of **conditional relevancy,** and the jury ultimately determines the **preliminary question** (whether the document is genuine or forged). Here the court plays only a screening role, deciding whether there is sufficient evidence to support the necessary jury finding (that the document is genuine). If there is enough evidence to answer the preliminary question in the appropriate way, then the proof is admitted and the jury makes the ultimate decision (that the document is genuine). Once the jury makes the necessary preliminary finding, it goes on to decide how much weight the evidence deserves. If the jury decides the preliminary question the other way (that the document is forged), then the jury should give it no weight.

Question: On what grounds can relevant evidence be excluded?

Answer: Finding evidence to be relevant is only the first step in assessing its admissibility. It can still be excluded under FRE 403 if its probative value is substantially outweighed by the dangers of unfair prejudice, confusing the issues, or misleading the jury. It can be excluded if it violates any other rule of evidence, such as hearsay, privilege, or the Best Evidence Doctrine. Finally, even if it does not violate any evidentiary rule, it can still be excluded by statute or constitutional provision, or in federal courts by the FRCP and FRCrimP.

Exam Tips

Here are some pointers about relevance issues:

Relevance includes both the concepts of probative worth (does the proof support the point for which it is offered?) and materiality (does the point matter in the case?).

The standard of probative worth is generous, and proof can be relevant without being sufficient ("a brick is not a wall").

Seldom is proof irrelevant in the sense of having *no* logical tendency to support the point for which it is offered, but sometimes proof is irrelevant because the point doesn't matter.

Even *relevant* evidence may be excluded if its probative worth is substantially outweighed by risks of unfair prejudice or for other reasons (most important being confusion and waste of time), and exclusion on these grounds is far more common because lawyers seldom offer evidence that truly has no logical tendency to support any provable point in a case.

Unfair prejudice refers to **emotional impact arousing anger or passion** (bloody pictures of murder victims, for example), and unfair prejudice also refers to **jury misuse** (out-of-court statements being admissible only to prove state of mind, for example, but also tending to prove acts, events or conditions, which involves an improper use).

CHAPTER 3

The Definition of Hearsay

CHAPTER OVERVIEW

The key points in this chapter are

- FRE 801 defines hearsay as an out-of-court assertion offered to prove the matter asserted.

- Some jurisdictions have broader or narrower definitions of hearsay.

- FRE 802 makes hearsay inadmissible unless it fits an exception found in rule or statute.

- The hearsay doctrine implements our preference for having live in-court accounts rather than descriptions of what others have said. In-court accounts bring great advantages, usually described as the three "trial safeguards." First, the witness is subject to cross-examination. Second, he is under oath as he testifies. Third, the factfinder, which is often a jury, can watch him as he testifies (appraise his "demeanor").

- Lacking the trial safeguards, hearsay statements bring increased risks in four areas, usually described as the "hearsay risks." These are (1) problems of perception (or the risk of misperception), (2) problems of memory (or the risk of failed memory), (3) problems of narration (or the risk of "narrative ambiguity"), and (4) problems of candor (or the risk of untruthfulness). These hearsay risks are at least lessened by the trial safeguards that accompany live testimony.

- Hearsay can include both verbal expressions and nonverbal conduct.

- Under the Rules, conduct is hearsay if it is assertive in nature (including nonverbal conduct), but nonassertive conduct is not hearsay even if it is used to prove some act, event, or condition in the world (nodding the head "yes" in answer to the question whether the truck ran a red light is assertive conduct and it is hearsay if offered to prove that the truck ran the red light; putting up an umbrella is nonassertive conduct and is not hearsay, even if it is offered to prove it was raining).

- Out-of-court assertions can be offered for purposes other than proving the truth of what they assert. If so, they are not hearsay.

- There are cases in the borderland of hearsay where it is hard to decide whether there is an out-of-court assertion of any sort and, if so, whether its use in the case involves using the assertion as proof of what it asserts (in which case it is hearsay) or not (in which case it is not hearsay).

- Prior statements, even by testifying witnesses who are subject to cross-examination at trial, are hearsay when offered for their truth, except for certain prior inconsistent statements, prior consistent statements, and prior statements of identification that are *defined* in FRE 801(d)(1) as "not hearsay" (even though they would be hearsay if they weren't defined that way).

- Prior inconsistent or consistent statements or prior statements of identification are not admissible for their truth unless the declarant testifies at trial and is subject to cross-examination about them.

A. THE DEFINITION OF HEARSAY

There are differing views about how hearsay should be defined, although today the vast majority of states follow the federal definition.

1. Federal Definition

Under FRE 801(a) and (c), hearsay is an out-of-court assertion, whether verbal or nonverbal, when offered to prove the truth of the matter asserted.

2. A Narrower Definition

Some authorities define hearsay as an assertion by an **out-of-court declarant** offered to prove the truth of matter asserted. This definition is **narrower** than the federal definition because it does not classify statements as hearsay, even if made out-of-court, if the declarant (the person making the statement) is in court subject to cross-examination. See Model Code of Evidence Rule 503(b) (hearsay is admissible if the declarant "is present and subject to cross-examination"). And see Cal. Ev. Code § 1235 (prior inconsistent statements by testifying witnesses are admissible for their truth).

3. A Broader Definition

Some authorities define hearsay as words or conduct outside of court, assertive or nonassertive, offered to prove the truth of facts stated or **implied** in them, or to prove that the declarant **believed** them to be true. This definition is **broader** than the federal definition because it classifies as hearsay nonassertive conduct that demonstrates the actor's belief, hence the fact believed. By this broad definition, putting up an umbrella would be hearsay if offered to prove that it was raining, even if the person with the umbrella was not trying to assert anything at all. See Section D. This expansive view of hearsay was adopted by the early common law and was the law of England until 2010. Compare *Regina v. Kearley*, 2 App. Cas. 228 (H.L. Eng. 1992) with Regina v. Chrysostomou (Mark), 2010 Crim. L.R. 942 (Ct. App. Cim. Div. 2010). And see Tex. R. Crim. Ev. 801(c) (hearsay includes "any matter implied by a statement, if the probative value of the statement as offered flows from declarant's **belief** as to the matter").

Example. In an action to recover for personal injuries suffered in an automobile accident, Elaine seeks to prove that her injuries are permanent. She testifies that her treating physician, Dr. Bowen, told her that her injuries were permanent. Dr. Bowen is not in the courtroom. The statement by Dr. Bowen to Elaine is hearsay under any of the definitions suggested above. It is offered to prove the truth of what it asserts (that Elaine's injuries actually are permanent) and Dr. Bowen was not testifying at the trial when he said it.

Example. Same as above. This time Elaine offers a properly authenticated medical report by Dr. Bowen saying that Elaine's injuries resulting from the accident are permanent. Once again Dr. Bowen's written statement is hearsay, and for the same reasons. The hearsay rule applies equally to oral and written statements.

Example. Same as above. This time Dr. Bowen is on the stand testifying when his report is offered, and he can be cross-examined about it. Now under a narrow view of hearsay, the report is not hearsay because the declarant (Dr. Bowen) is subject to cross-examination at trial. But under the broader and more common view that is also found in FRE 801, the report is still hearsay because it is an out-of-court statement offered for its truth.

Example. Same as above. To prove her injuries are permanent, this time Elaine testifies that Dr. Bowen mailed her a booklet telling how to apply for permanent disability benefits from the Social Security Administration. Such evidence of Dr. Bowen's conduct would be hearsay under a broad definition because the evidence indicates conduct by Dr. Bowen that tends to prove *his belief that Elaine suffered permanent injuries*, hence to prove that *indeed Elaine's injuries are permanent*. Dr. Bowen's conduct would not amount to hearsay under the federal definition if he did not intend to assert his belief that Elaine's injuries were permanent by mailing the booklet, but the conduct would be hearsay if he did intend to assert this point. Absent special facts, Dr. Bowen's conduct seems nonassertive and could be proved in order to show that he thought Elaine's injuries are permanent, hence that they probably are indeed permanent.

B. THE RATIONALE FOR THE RULE AGAINST HEARSAY

1. Policy Justifications

There are three traditional policy justifications for the rule against hearsay:

a. Cross-examination

In preferring live testimony over out-of-court statements, the hearsay doctrine helps protect the rights of parties to cross-examine witnesses. Cross-examination is a critical component of the search for truth in trials. So important is this testing process that direct testimony may be stricken if the witness cannot be cross-examined, as may happen if he becomes suddenly ill after his direct testimony. The trial safeguard of cross-examination would mean little if out-of-court statements were freely admissible even if the declarant never testified.

b. Oath

To the extent that the hearsay rule encourages live testimony, it brings with it the additional safeguard of the oath, which at least quells casual impulses to lie and may bring home to the witness the obligation to take care and to be serious in her testimony. Note well, however, that sworn out-of-court statements are not freely admissible: In other words, the oath alone does not pave the way to admit things like affidavits, which are formal out-of-court statements made under oath. Affidavits are hearsay and are generally inadmissible as such, although they are of course used freely in resolving motions for summary judgment in civil cases.

c. Demeanor

To the extent that the hearsay leads to the use of live testimony in preference to out-of-court statements, it also brings with it demeanor evidence, meaning that the factfinder (judge or jury) can watch the witness as she testifies and assess credibility in part on the basis of mannerisms, voice pressure, facial expressions, and other visible and audible clues.

2. Constitutional Underpinnings

In addition to these policy considerations, the hearsay rule also has constitutional underpinnings. The Sixth Amendment guarantees criminal defendants the right to confront the witnesses against them, including the right to cross-examine. The hearsay doctrine and the rights secured by the Confrontation Clause are not coterminous, but they do overlap, and pretty clearly we could not scrap the hearsay doctrine completely in criminal cases without violating defense confrontation rights. Under the modern *Crawford* doctrine (named for a 2004 decision by the Supreme Court), the Confrontation Clause blocks the use against the accused of "testimonial" hearsay, meaning *at least* statements given in testimony in earlier court proceedings *and* statements given by eyewitnesses to police investigating crimes. The *Crawford* doctrine, however, gives way if the declarant can be cross-examined at trial or was cross-examinable by the defendant in earlier proceedings. Modern confrontation jurisprudence is discussed in Chapter 5.

C. THE TESTIMONIAL DANGERS

1. Types of Potential Error

All testimony by witnesses at trial and all out-of-court statements by hearsay declarants are subject to at least four types of potential error, often referred to as the hearsay risks:

a. Perception

The witness or declarant may have misperceived the event she is describing because of sensory error (such as that caused by poor eyesight or hearing), physical circumstances (such as that caused by poor lighting or being too far away), or other factors (such as distraction or stress). This is **the risk of misperception.**

b. Memory

Even if the witness or declarant accurately perceived the event, she may not remember it very well. She may have forgotten important details or confused them with the circumstances of some other similar event. This is the risk of **faulty or failed memory.**

c. Narration

There is also the danger of misstatement or ambiguity in narration. When a witness or declarant describes a vehicle as "red" she may have really seen a color that could more aptly be described as burgundy or maroon, and when she says the vehicle swerved to the left she may have meant to say to the right. This is the risk of **ambiguity or faulty narration.**

d. Veracity

A speaker may lie or distort (consciously or unconsciously) in reporting about the perceived event. This is the risk of **insincerity or lack of candor.**

2. Cross–Examination as a Check on These Testimonial Dangers

With trial witnesses, these risks can be minimized or reduced because of the trial safeguards, the most important of which is **cross-examination**. (The other trial safeguards include putting the witness under **oath** and letting the jury watch her **demeanor** as she testifies.) When hearsay is admitted, there may be no opportunity to cross-examine if the declarant is not also a witness. Even if the declarant *does* also testify, cross-examination is not contemporaneous with her prior statement: Trial lawyers think that cross-examination can only be truly effective if it is brought to bear right away while the witness is giving her story and that "deferred" cross-examination, that must take up what the witness said before, is inferior. Hence the use of hearsay brings large risks that cannot be minimized or reduced by the trial safeguards, and hearsay is far less desirable than live testimony.

3. Diagram Illustrating the Testimonial Dangers

The risks of introducing hearsay can be illustrated by a diagram (Figure 3–1). Assume the **declarant** is a person who saw an event and made an out-of-court statement about it. The **witness** is a person who heard the out-of-court statement and relates it in court.

The four risks of misperception, failed memory, narration or ambiguity, and insincerity or lack of candor apply to both the hearsay declarant and the trial witness. The trial witness may have misheard the hearsay statement or remembered it inaccurately. The trial witness may also misspeak or even fabricate when testifying about the statement in the courtroom. But these are *not* considered hearsay dangers. The reason is that the trial witness is in court, testifying under oath in front of the jury, and therefore can be cross-examined on these matters. The risks about which the hearsay rule is concerned (the **hearsay risks)** are risks that come with statements made by a declarant out of court. The declarant may have misperceived or misremembered the event, and the dangers of faulty narration or lack of veracity apply to the declarant's statement about the event. These four hearsay dangers cannot be addressed by cross-examining the witness who reports what the declarant said because it is the declarant's statement (rather than the testimony given by the witness describing the statement) that is the source of information about the act, event, or condition described in the statement.

Example.   In the example discussed above, Elaine might be lying when she testifies that her doctor said that her injuries were permanent. But *this* is not a hearsay danger because she can be cross-examined, and the questioner may delve into the question whether she actually heard Dr. Bowen make such a statement. There is no greater danger that she is fabricating this aspect of her testimony than any other aspect, such as how the accident occurred. The dangers of concern to the hearsay rule arise because the declarant is Dr. Bowen, and he is not in court under oath when he speaks, and his demeanor is not on display to the trier of fact as he speaks, and most importantly he is not subject to cross-examination when he speaks, so he cannot be tested in that way about what he thinks and says about Elaine's injuries.

FIGURE 3-1

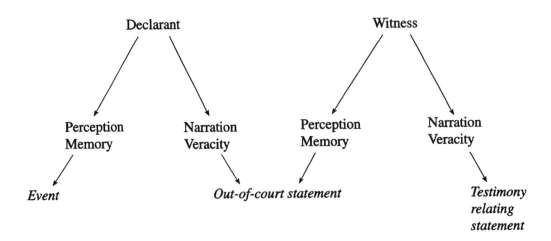

4. Impeachment of Hearsay Declarant as Partial Substitute for Cross-Examination

Although a hearsay declarant is normally not subject to cross-examination, FRE 806 provides a partial substitute for cross-examination. It allows the hearsay declarant to be impeached by the same methods that could be used if the declarant had testified as a witness. These include showing that the declarant had a bad character for truth and veracity, or that he made prior inconsistent statements, or that he had a defect in sensory ability, or that he was biased. See the discussion of impeaching witnesses in Chapter 10.

☞ EXAMPLE AND ANALYSIS

In a trial for murder, the facts indicate that Vince was shot, and shortly afterwards he died from his wounds. The prosecution introduces a statement Vince made a few seconds before his death identifying David as the murderer. Assume this statement is admissible under the dying declaration exception to the hearsay rule.

FRE 806 would allow David to impeach this hearsay statement by showing that the shot was fired from a point such a great distance from Vince that he could not have seen who was shooting at him, particularly given that Vince was nearsighted. This showing tends to impeach Vince by showing a problem in sensory perception. David would also be allowed to show that Vince had a long-standing grudge against him that might prompt a false accusation (impeachment by showing bias).

5. Distinction Between Hearsay and Lack of Personal Knowledge

There is a difference between a hearsay objection (FRE 802) and an objection that the witness lacks personal knowledge (FRE 602), and yet the two objections overlap. A witness who did not see an event, but did hear about it from others, lacks personal knowledge. Assuming that she testifies but makes no reference to what she was told, the other side might well raise a lack-of-knowledge objection on learning during cross that the witness did not herself see what she described. (Ordinarily such a situation would not arise because the calling party would lay a foundation showing that the witness did see the accident before asking questions about it, but sometimes this foundation is overlooked or, more likely, it comes out on cross that the witness was indeed at the scene but was not looking when the accident happened.) Here the right objection is lack of personal knowledge under FRE 602. To be sure, a court might entertain a hearsay objection here, but FRE 602 is the stronger ground because no out-of-court statement was offered or even mentioned. But if the witness, in answering the question, quotes or describes a statement made to her by another, then the hearsay objection becomes appropriate, and an objection might well stress both lack of knowledge under FRE 602 and hearsay under FRE 802. A witness who offers to testify to an out-of-court statement that is admissible under some exception need not have personal knowledge of the underlying facts asserted in the statement. Such a witness only needs personal knowledge of the statement itself, meaning essentially that she heard the declarant make the statement. See ACN to FRE 602.

☞ EXAMPLE AND ANALYSIS

At trial, the police officer who investigated an automobile accident is called to testify that defendant's car ran the red light. Before the officer can go forward in this vein, defense counsel gets the court's permission to question the officer outside the presence of the jury in aid of an objection (this process is called "voir dire," which means finding out whether the witness has a basis for the testimony that he appears ready to give). The officer admits that he did not see the accident or have any other basis for his conclusion, and is relying on statements made to him by bystanders.

Here the most appropriate objection is lack of personal knowledge. But if the officer recites any of the statements (or indicates to the jury anything about their substance), the most appropriate objection would be hearsay. In such cases it may be wiser to object under both FRE 602 and FRE 802, stressing both lack of knowledge and hearsay. See Chapter 1 on making a proper record.

D. DEFINITION OF A HEARSAY STATEMENT

FRE 801(a) defines a statement for purposes of the hearsay rule as "(1) an oral or written assertion or (2) nonverbal conduct of a person, if it is intended by the person as an assertion."

1. Verbal Expressions as Hearsay Statements

a. Assertive intent

The definition of hearsay usually includes the term "statement," which in turn is usually defined as an "assertion." Almost every verbal utterance, oral or written, is both a statement and an assertion. While neither the Rules nor the cases define "assertion," the ACN to FRE 801(a) provides an important clue, which is that "nothing is an assertion unless intended to be one." This comment means that the intent of the declarant is crucial. When a person speaks or writes words, she is making an assertion if that is what she intends to do, and she is asserting whatever she intends to assert. Practically speaking, an assertion is always an attempt to communicate with someone or to express ideas or information in words, with *very* few exceptions. And practically speaking, every use of words involves an attempt to communicate with someone or to express ideas, again with *very* few exceptions. In the case of diaries or notes to oneself, the words are expressive even if they are not intended for anyone else's eyes (hence they are not communicative). We should nonetheless view them as assertions just because they express ideas in words. A good working definition is that a verbal assertion is any intentional expression or communication of ideas or information using words.

b. Form of expression

Since almost all uses of words involve intentional expressions or communication of ideas or information, almost all words are assertions. That means the hearsay doctrine reaches statements that have many different grammatical forms:

i. Declarative sentences

Perhaps the most obvious assertion is a simple declarative sentence: "John is pointing his gun at me." Here we have subject, verb, and object, and a strong factual claim that expresses ideas or information: John is pointing his gun at the declarant.

ii. Requests or commands

Often requests and commands do not make strong factual claims with the simplicity of a declarative sentence, but usually requests and commands do express ideas and information, even though indirectly. Suppose the declarant says "John, don't shoot me." Here the main purpose is to communicate the speaker's request asking John not to shoot, and the statement implies (in the strong sense of intentionally suggesting) that the speaker does not want to be shot. The words make these points directly. But indirectly the declarant is also asserting that John is apparently poised to shoot the declarant. This indirect meaning is also part of what the declarant intends to express, and the statement should be viewed as hearsay if offered to prove this point.

iii. Questions

Some cases hold that questions cannot be assertions, apparently on the ground that the declarant is "just asking a question" and is therefore not making any strong claim that something is so. But suppose a declarant says "You're not going to shoot me, are you, John?" Even if we suppose the main purpose is to gather information (declarant wants to know whether John plans to shoot him), still he is intentionally expressing the same point that we found in the other statements set out above: John is poised to shoot at the declarant. On the realistic assumption that the declarant isn't simply trying to learn whether John intends to shoot, but is in fact trying to persuade John not to shoot, it is even clearer that the words express and therefore assert that John is poised to shoot.

Example. Dan is charged with bank robbery. The bank teller identifies the gun that was pointed at her as a .38 special. As evidence that Dan once owned such a gun, the prosecutor offers testimony by Rose that she heard Daryl ask Dan "Do you still own that .38 special? I'd like to buy it." Because this question asserts that Dan once owned a .38 special, it is hearsay if offered to prove that point, even though the words referring to the gun are contained in a statement that is grammatically cast as a question.

c. Multiple assertions

A single verbal expression may contain many factual assertions. The expression is hearsay if offered to prove the truth of any of them.

Example. Assume an airline pilot says to the passengers: "Because we've used a lot of fuel facing these high winds, we're going to have to make an emergency landing in Peoria." This verbal statement makes at least three assertions: First, the plane is low on fuel. Second, the flight has been experiencing high winds. Third, the pilot intends to land in Peoria. The statement is hearsay if offered to prove any of these points.

d. Indirect assertions

An assertion may directly assert a simple fact: "That car is speeding." Assuming we know some context (like what car the statement refers to and what "speeding" means), interpretation is easy. But the interpretive task can be more challenging because people make statements that express facts indirectly, sometimes because it is easier or more tactful and sometimes because people have other purposes. A declarant who says "Watch out for that speeding car" is mainly trying to convey a warning. Her statement does not directly say there is a car that is speeding. Still her words express or communicate this point indirectly, and it seems clear that she *means* to express or communicate it. Hence her statement is hearsay if offered to prove that a speeding car was approaching the person to whom she was speaking. The same is true if she said "They ought to give that guy a ticket, as fast as he was going." (When we consider these indirect meanings, we eventually come to points that may or may not have been included in the assertive intent of the speaker, and we consider this subject in Section F below under the heading "Borderland of Hearsay.")

Example. Richard, who serves as treasurer of his church, is charged with embezzlement of church funds. At trial the prosecutor offers the testimony of Gertrude that she heard a heated argument between Richard and his sister Ruth, where she said "At least I've never stolen money from my church." The prosecutor offers this testimony as evidence of Richard's guilt. It should be excluded as hearsay. In her statement, Ruth implies that Richard stole money from his church, which is to say that it was Ruth's intention to assert this point, and her statement is offered to prove the point that she asserted indirectly in this way.

e. Nonassertive verbal expressions

Some verbal expressions are not intended by the declarant to make factual assertions, hence are not hearsay. For example, singing a song, acting a play, or reciting poetry are normally not intended by the declarant to assert the truth of whatever words he sings, speaks as lines, or recites. Similarly common social pleasantries ("hello," "good morning," "goodbye") have little or no assertive intent, although arguably they do assert that the speaker means to be polite and to acknowledge that she is looking at the person she addresses, and perhaps even to suggest that she harbors friendly or cordial or collegial feelings about that person.

2. Nonverbal Assertions

Normally when we think of hearsay we think of out-of-court *verbal* statements (oral or written). But the hearsay doctrine is broader. It also encompasses (and therefore can exclude) out-of-court *nonverbal* conduct. Under all the definitions of hearsay, out-of-court conduct that is intended as an assertion is hearsay if offered to prove its truth (although like verbal hearsay it sometimes fits an exception). It may seem surprising that out-of-court conduct can be hearsay, but on further reflection it becomes obvious why this is true. Sometimes an actor intends conduct to be a communication or expression of ideas or information, and the conduct is in fact just a substitute for words. We may nod our heads instead of saying "yes," shake our heads instead of saying "no," and point to identify a person or indicate a direction.

Example. Eunice, who is mute, observes an auto accident. By use of sign language she gives her version of what happened to Mary, who is a qualified sign language interpreter. Mary testifies at trial about Eunice's observations. (Eunice does not appear.) Mary's testimony describing what Eunice has communicated to her is subject to a hearsay objection. The hearsay doctrine applies to the messages communicated by Eunice in sign language because Eunice is expressing and communicating ideas and information in conduct that is the equivalent of words.

Example. The DEA investigates a marijuana smuggling ring operating just across the Mexican border. Sometimes the drugs are hidden in motor homes and driven across the border. On other occasions they are hidden in fishing boats and smuggled into the country by sea. Rodriguez, a DEA informant, infiltrated the ring in Mexico. He agreed to send up a signal flare to alert DEA agents that a shipment was being sent and how it was being transported— one flare if by land, and two flares if by sea. On October 20, Rodriguez sent up two signal flares. If evidence of his conduct is offered to prove that a drug shipment was sent by sea on that day, it would be hearsay.

Example.   Hank is about to be released from prison after serving a lengthy prison term. Uncertain whether his wife Marge wants him to return home, he writes and asks her to tie a yellow ribbon to the tree in front of their house if she wants him back. He tells her he will be on a bus going through town and will stop only if he sees the yellow ribbon. Marge drapes not only the tree but the entire front yard with yellow ribbons. If evidence of her conduct is offered to prove that Marge wants Hank back, it is hearsay. It is assertive even though she speaks no words. Although her conduct is hearsay, what she did (what she "said" with ribbons) would likely be admissible under the state-of-mind exception in FRE 803(3) to prove that she wanted him back.

3. Nonassertive Nonverbal Conduct

Conduct is nonassertive if the actor does not intend to make an assertion. Evidence of nonassertive conduct is commonplace in trials, and rarely raises hearsay concerns.

a. Two-step inference

A hearsay issue is likely to arise with nonassertive conduct if it is offered to support a two-step inference about some act, event, or condition in the world. Here is the first step: The act suggests what the person is thinking (he put up an umbrella, so he thinks it is raining). Here is the second step: Since the actor thinks something is so (and he is in a position to know), it probably is so (he thinks it is raining and he is outside, so he's probably right; it is in fact raining).

Example.   Surviving relatives of persons lost at sea bring suit against Farway Shipping Company for sending out an unseaworthy ship that sank. As evidence that the ship was seaworthy, Farway offers proof that it was piloted by an experienced captain who inspected the ship before departing and took his family along on the voyage. This classic example is drawn from a 19th century English decision in *Wright v. Doe d. Tatham*, 112 Eng. Rep. 488 (1837), and Baron Parke took the position that this conduct is hearsay if offered for this purpose. Analytically this conduct involves the two-step inference described above. It is offered to establish that (1) the captain believed the ship to be seaworthy after his inspection (or he wouldn't have sailed away and taken his family along), and therefore (2) the ship was seaworthy in fact.

b. Hearsay dangers in nonassertive conduct

At least three of the four hearsay dangers apply to nonassertive conduct offered in support of the two-step inference. This use of such conduct brings risks of misperception, failed or faulty memory, and ambiguity. In the example described above, the captain may have overlooked something in making his inspection and thus **misperceived** the seaworthiness of the ship. He might have forgotten a dangerous condition after making the inspection, so his conduct brings the risk of **faulty memory**. His conduct is subject to misinterpretation because he may have thought that the ship needed maintenance or repairs but elected to go on the voyage anyway because no other transportation was available or some opportunity would be lost by delay, so his conduct brings the risk of **ambiguity** when offered to prove that the ship is seaworthy. Isn't cross-examination of the sea captain necessary to check against these dangers? Shouldn't this evidence be classified as hearsay? For reasons discussed further below, the answer of the early common law to both these questions is Yes, but the answer of the Federal Rules and modern codes is No.

c. Common law view

i. Wright v. Doe d. Tatham

This classic case was a will contest. Sandford Tatham was cousin and sole heir at law to John Marsden, who died leaving a valuable estate. In his will Marsden left real property to his steward George Wright. Tatham sued to set aside the will and claimed that Marsden was mentally incompetent. Wright defended the will and Marsden's competence to make it, offering three letters written to Marsden before his death, all by persons who had themselves died before trial. The writers each wrote to Marsden as though he were competent, thus suggesting that they believed that he was competent. One of the writers discussed a business matter and urged Marsden to tell his attorneys to propose terms of agreement that would settle a dispute with the Township.

ii. Baron Parke's opinion

In *Wright*, Baron Parke wrote one of the most famous opinions in the history of evidence law. He concluded that the letters were hearsay and should not have been admitted. In effect, his opinion advanced the broad proposition that whenever human conduct is offered in support of the two-step inference, it is hearsay. He said that in such cases conduct by a person (writing letters) is offered to prove the belief of the actor in a fact (he thinks the recipient is competent), for the ultimate purpose of proving the fact itself (the recipient really is competent), and this proof involves proving an *implied statement* of the fact in question. Hence it is hearsay. *Wright* went far to establish the common law rule that conduct is hearsay when offered to prove the truth of the belief underlying the actor's conduct. Parke gave several examples of nonassertive conduct that would be inadmissible hearsay under this broad view, including payment of a wager to prove that an event happened contrary to the bet of the losing party and payment by an insurance company as evidence that a particular insured event or loss occurred. Parke also cited the example of the ship's captain inspecting the vessel, described in the example above. This expansive view of hearsay took root in a number of American cases, and in 1992 it was reaffirmed as the law of England. See *Regina v. Kearley*, 2 App. Cas. 228 (H.L. Eng. 1992). But in 2003, the UK changed the statutory definition of hearsay, and in Regina v. Chrysostomou (Mark), 2010 Crim. L. 942 (Ct. App. Crim. Div. 2010), the Court of Appeals concluded that drug inquiries found on defendant's cellphone were not hearsay, apparently rejecting the earlier view.

d. **Federal Rules view**

Although there remains some uncertainty about the scope of FRE 801, this much is clear. The Rules reject the broad view of Baron Parke in *Wright* that nonassertive conduct can be hearsay. FRE 801(a) defines nonverbal conduct of a person to be hearsay only "if it is intended by the person as an assertion." Under FRE 801, nonassertive conduct is *never* hearsay.

i. **Hearsay dangers still exist**

The drafters of the Federal Rules did not deny that hearsay dangers lurk in nonassertive conduct. As noted above, when nonassertive conduct is offered to prove that the actor had a certain belief about a factual matter and that this belief was true (the two-step inference described above), at least three of the four hearsay dangers exist: The actor may have misperceived the matter, failed to remember it accurately, or miscommunicated his true belief about the matter. But the fourth hearsay risk of **insincerity or lack of candor** does *not* appear if the actor did not intend to assert or communicate his belief. For example, if the sea captain who set sail with his family did not intend to assert to anyone that the ship was seaworthy, how can he be said to be insincere or to lack candor on this matter?

ii. **Hearsay dangers are less when no assertion was intended**

The absence of this fourth hearsay risk persuaded the drafters to exclude nonassertive conduct from the definition of hearsay in the Federal Rules. The ACN to FRE 801 states that hearsay risks in nonassertive conduct "are minimal in the absence of an intent to assert and do not justify the loss of the evidence on hearsay grounds." Thus evidence of the ship captain's conduct is admissible under FRE 801, but it is hearsay under common law. The drafters of the Federal Rules may also have been influenced by a practical consideration: Nonassertive conduct as possible hearsay is an issue that is rarely spotted by trial lawyers or judges. Does it make sense to have a hearsay ground for exclusion that is so seldom recognized?

4. Distinguishing Assertive Conduct from Nonassertive Conduct

a. Difference between Federal Rules and common law

FRE 801 requires courts and lawyers to distinguish sharply between assertive and nonassertive conduct because only the former can be hearsay under the Rules. This distinction has less importance at common law because conduct can be hearsay whether assertive or not. Thus in *Wright*, for example, it was not necessary for the court to decide whether the writers of the letters intended to assert anything about Marsden's competence because the letters were hearsay even if viewed as nonassertive conduct tending to show the belief of the writers. A determination of their intent would be necessary to resolve the admissibility of the letters under FRE 801.

☞ EXAMPLE AND ANALYSIS

In a wrongful death suit filed on behalf of Adrien (who was killed in an automobile accident), it is important to know when Adrien died because it bears on the issue of damages for pain and suffering prior to his death. As evidence that Adrien died at the scene of the accident, defendant calls Officer Johnson to testify that he saw the emergency paramedic check for a pulse and then pull a sheet over Adrien's face before loading him into the ambulance.

At common law this testimony would be hearsay. The evidence is offered for the two-step inference. Here is the first inference: From the conduct of the paramedic, the factfinder is invited to infer that he believed that Adrien was dead. Here is the second inference: From the paramedic's belief, the factfinder is invited to infer that indeed Adrien was dead. Under FRE 801, the admissibility of this evidence depends on whether the paramedic's conduct was assertive or not. The likely conclusion here is that the conduct was nonassertive, although the point can be argued either way. If nonassertive, the conduct would not be hearsay under FRE 801 and the evidence would likely be admitted. But if pulling the sheet over Adrien's face is seen as an expression by the paramedic of the idea that Adrien is dead, the conduct would be assertive, and therefore hearsay. It might be admitted anyway under the exception for present sense impressions found in FRE 803(1), but it would be viewed as hearsay.

---

b. **Intent of actor**

Whether conduct is assertive or nonassertive depends on the intent of the actor. Deciding whether apparently nonassertive (usually wordless) conduct is or is not assertive requires a preliminary decision whether the actor intended to assert something. How does a court answer this question? The actor is usually not in court and cannot be examined. Thus it is, for example, hard to decide whether the paramedic in the problem intended to communicate that Adrien was dead or was engaging in an act of courtesy or respect for the dead (probably as a result of his paramedic training) that was not intended to be communicative.

c. **Burden of proof**

The drafters of the Rules recognized the difficulty of making this determination of the actor's intent, so they included an important statement in the ACN to FRE 801(a):

> When evidence of conduct is offered on the theory that it was not a statement, and hence not hearsay, a preliminary determination will

be required to determine whether an assertion is intended. The rule is so worded as to place the burden upon the party claiming that the intention existed; ambiguous and doubtful cases will be resolved against him and in favor of admissibility.

Thus the burden is on the objecting party (the party claiming the conduct is hearsay) to persuade the court that the conduct was assertive. If the objecting party fails to carry this burden, the court should find that the conduct was nonassertive and treat it as nonhearsay.

5. Silence, Noncomplaint as Hearsay

a. Proving absence of occurrence or condition

Sometimes a party offers evidence of silence or noncomplaint to prove absence of a certain occurrence or condition. For example, a restaurant sued by a customer for serving spoiled food might offer evidence that no other customers complained when served the same food. The silence of the other customers is offered to support the two-step inference: First, the conduct of the other customers indicates that they did not think anything was wrong with the food. Second, the fact that they didn't think anything was wrong (and were in a position to know) indicates that in fact there was nothing wrong with the food. Because their conduct (being silent and not complaining) is nonassertive, it is not hearsay under the Federal Rules.

b. Hearsay if intended as an assertion

Silence or noncomplaint can be hearsay if it is intended as an assertion. For example, if a doctor tells a patient to speak up if a certain procedure hurts and the patient agrees to cooperate in this way, his silence when the doctor performs the procedure is his assertion that the procedure did not hurt. It is hearsay if offered to prove the truth of that "statement."

6. Negative Results of Inquiry

Evidence of fruitless inquiry is sometimes admitted to establish that a person cannot be found.

Example. An investigator for plaintiff testifies that he tried to locate Xavier in Laredo, Texas, making inquiry of the people who would most likely know where he is, and that nobody that he talked to in Laredo had seen or heard of him. The defendant objects that the testimony conveys hearsay because it relies on (and reveals) statements of townsfolk whom Xavier questioned. Courts often fail to see (or choose to ignore) the hearsay issue and allow such testimony, at least when the inquiry is only one aspect of the search and the investigator also relies on his own observations and investigatory techniques.

The issues here are subtle. If the investigator directly quotes the townspeople ("They told me Xavier moved to Houston") and those quoted statements are offered to prove what they assert (that Xavier moved to Houston, hence was no longer in Laredo), the court is likely to sustain a hearsay objection, which is the right outcome. But if the investigator limits his testimony to saying that he made inquiries in Laredo among people who knew Xavier, and that nobody knew where he was, then what the investigator describes is simply the absence of knowledge among people who would surely have such knowledge. Even in this case, one might imagine that the responses embedded in this report (many people told the investigator essentially, "I haven't seen hide nor hair of Xavier") embody hearsay, but arguably the state-of-mind exception would apply and those statements would be admissible to prove absence of knowledge. From the absence of knowledge that one would expect at least some of these people to have, one can then infer that Xavier was no longer in Laredo.

7. Hidden Hearsay

Sometimes attorneys try to evade the hearsay rule by having a witness suggest what the declarant must have said while not actually quoting him. Alert opposing counsel should object, and perceptive courts will not allow such an end run around the hearsay rule.

Example.   Defendant is charged with starting a fight in a bar. The prosecutor poses the following questions to the arresting officer and gets the following answers: Q. "Did you ask the bartender who started the fight?" A. "Yes, I did." Q. "Without telling us what the bartender said, would you just tell us what you did next?" A. "Yes, I arrested the defendant." Even though the arresting officer never says what the bartender told him, the questions and answers make it clear that the bartender must have told the officer that defendant started the fight. A hearsay objection should be sustained.

8. Machine or Animal Hearsay

a. FRE 801 covers only statements of a "person"

FRE 801(b) defines a "declarant" for purposes of the hearsay rule as a "person" who makes a statement. Hence statements by machines or animals are not hearsay under the Federal Rules. There was confusion on this point at common law. See *State v. Storm,* 238 P.2d 1161, 1176 (Mont. 1951) (rejecting bloodhound tracking evidence as hearsay because dog could not be cross-examined).

b. Machine hearsay

An alarm clock or an automated factory whistle "telling" listeners the time is not a hearsay statement, nor is a blood-alcohol reading taken by a Breathalyzer. But subtle issues lurk here. The output of a machine such as a computer is hearsay if it is merely a recapitulation of human statements. Business records stored on a computer represent statements by persons and are subject to the hearsay rule. On the other hand, purely mathematical calculations made by a computer are not hearsay.

E. OFFERED TO PROVE THE TRUTH OF THE MATTER ASSERTED

An out-of-court statement is hearsay only if it is offered to prove the truth of the matter asserted. Thus hearsay analysis is always a two-step process: (1) Is there an out-of-court statement? and (2) Is the statement offered to prove the truth of the matter asserted?

1. Identifying Purpose for Which Evidence Is Offered

A most difficult aspect of the hearsay doctrine is the task of determining whether an out-of-court statement is offered to prove the truth of the matter asserted. This determination can be made only if one knows the purpose for which the statement is offered. In a trial, an attorney may ask an opponent to specify the purpose for which she is offering an out-of-court statement, so the attorney can determine whether a hearsay objection should be made.

Practice Tip

If the proponent specifies a narrow, permissible, nonhearsay purpose for introducing a statement, a limiting instruction may be requested that directs the jury to limit its consideration of the statement to the proper purpose. See FRE 105 (authorizing limiting instructions).

---

2.   Nonhearsay Uses

a.   Purposes other than truth

Why would an out-of-court statement be offered if not to prove the truth of what it asserts? Perhaps surprisingly, there are actually many nonhearsay uses for out-of-court statements. For example, the fact that the declarant made a statement could be used to prove that he was alive at the time, that he was conscious enough to speak, that he could speak English, that he was involved with another in a conversation, and there are many other purposes that do not depend on the truth of a statement.

b.   Six common nonhearsay uses

Most of the time when an out-of-court statement is offered for a nonhearsay purpose–a purpose other than proving its truth–it falls into one of the following six categories.

1.   Impeachment

2.   Verbal acts (or parts of acts)

3.   Proof of effect on listener or reader

4.   Verbal objects

5.   Circumstantial evidence of state of mind

6.   Circumstantial evidence of memory, knowledge, or belief

c.   Nonhearsay uses not listed in Federal Rules

These nonhearsay categories are not listed in the Federal Rules. FRE 801 provides a definition of hearsay, and FRE 802 says that hearsay is not admissible unless otherwise "provided by these rules" or other by rules or statutes. Neither of these provisions goes on to list or define other nonhearsay uses, but the framers of these Rules knew very well that there were such uses, and decisions following common law tradition recognize all of the nonhearsay uses described above. They are also well known to trial lawyers and judges.

3.   Impeachment

A statement is nonhearsay if it is used only to impeach the trial testimony by the declarant testifying as a witness. The fact that he testifies to one version of facts at trial, while having given a differing (inconsistent) version earlier, may undermine his credibility in the eyes of the factfinder (judge or jury). The prior statement can have this effect regardless whether the factfinder believes or credits that statement. It is the fact that a witness vacillates–the fact that he tells the same story in different, perhaps conflicting, ways–that makes his trial testimony less believable. In McCormick's apt phrase, the witness "blows hot and cold," and it is this inconstancy that undercuts credibility.

☞ EXAMPLE AND ANALYSIS

Cody is charged with holding up a 7–11 store at approximately 9:30 P.M. and murdering the clerk. He asserts an alibi defense, claiming he was at a movie with his girlfriend Dixie at the time. Dixie testifies that she and Cody were at a movie together from 8 P.M. to approximately 11 P.M. that day. On cross-examination, Dixie is asked whether she told police the morning after the murder that she and Cody were together at their apartment for the entire evening and did not go out.

Dixie's earlier statement is admissible for the nonhearsay purpose of impeaching her trial testimony. The prosecutor certainly isn't trying to prove the truth of Dixie's earlier statement that Cody was at the apartment at the time of the murder. But the fact that Dixie has made inconsistent statements about Cody's whereabouts makes it less likely that the jury will believe her alibi testimony at trial.

4. Verbal Acts (or Parts of Acts)

a. Words as acts

A statement is nonhearsay if it is a verbal act or part of an act. Usually verbal acts refer to utterances that have operative effect under substantive legal principles. Thus words of offer and acceptance can form a binding contract, and words demanding that a victim relinquish his wallet can be part of the crime of robbery. In such areas, the usual dichotomy between words and conduct disappears: Uttering words is a form of conduct, and words are acts or parts of acts.

b. Examples

Some crimes can be committed by words alone, such as fraud, forgery, perjury, intimidation, extortion, and solicitation. Some torts can be committed by words alone, such as libel, slander, misrepresentation, and harassment.

c. Words as part of an act

Perhaps more often, words accompany and become parts of an act. Thus a rapist who physically attacks a woman and threatens harm if she does not cooperate is using words and physical actions in committing a crime. And one who lends his car to another, perhaps turning over the keys while asking the other "to return the car by Monday and not to drive it into the mountains," has accomplished a conditional transfer (or loan or bailment) in which possession of the car changes hands, but only for a time, and with restrictions on use of the vehicle. In these examples, the words are being offered for their operative effect and not as assertions. The words have effect not because the speaker simply *asserts* something but because the speaker *does something* with words.

d. Independent legal significance

As noted above, it is often said that words constituting verbal acts have independent legal significance. The mere fact that they were uttered brings legal consequences, and the proponent is not using words as assertions to prove a truth that depends on the perception, memory, candor, or verbal accuracy of the speaker. In some of the examples described above, like perjury, fraud, and libel, the proponent intends to prove that the words were false.

☛ EXAMPLE AND ANALYSIS

Zeke is charged with bank robbery. Judy, the bank teller, testifies that Zeke pointed a gun at her and said "Give me all your money. If you do anything dumb, someone is going to get hurt."

Zeke's statement is admissible as the verbal part of the act of robbing a bank. His pointing a gun at Judy and uttering those words (which represent both a demand and a threat) is an act of force that is an element of robbery. The prosecutor is not offering Zeke's words to prove that he intended to hurt someone. Even if he didn't intend to hurt anybody (assume he had only a fake gun), his threatening words and conduct still constitute the act of bank robbery and can be proven without violating the hearsay rule.

5. Proof of Effect on Listener or Reader

A statement is not hearsay if it is offered to prove its effect on a listener or reader. Sometimes out-of-court statements notify, warn, or threaten the person who hears them. When the statements are offered only to prove that they had (or may or should have had) a particular effect on the person hearing or reading them, they are nonhearsay.

☞ EXAMPLE AND ANALYSIS

While taking out her garbage, Evelyn slips on the icy steps in back of her apartment building and suffers serious injuries. She files a civil suit for damages against Trump, the owner of the building. In his answer, Trump alleges that Evelyn was partially at fault in going down the stairs when she knew they were covered with ice. To prove his defense, Trump calls Jack (his maintenance man), who testifies that just before the fall he yelled to Evelyn: "Lady, please don't go down those stairs until I get them cleaned off. They're really icy." Evelyn ignored his warning.

Jack's out-of-court statement is admissible as nonhearsay because it is offered to prove that Evelyn was on notice of the icy condition, hence that in continuing to descend the stairs after being warned, she was negligent. Trump is not offering the statement to prove its truth—he is not using the statement to prove that the steps were "really icy," which would be against his interest. Presumably the fact that ice was on the steps has already been established by the plaintiff's evidence.

---

6. Verbal Markers

a. Words as Identifying Characteristics

Where a statement, or more precisely the *physical embodiment of a statement in written characters*, is attached to or associated with an object, it can help identify that object. Such a statement (its physical embodiment) can distinguish the object from other objects in much the same way that descriptions of shape or color or texture perform this role. In this sense words can be identifying characteristics of objects, or what we may call verbal markers. This use of words as verbal markers is a nonhearsay use. Suppose a witness testifies that he saw the robber arrive at the bank in a red Ford pickup truck, license number ZBD7769, and another witness testifies that an hour later he saw a red Ford pickup truck, tagged ZBD7769, driving north on Riverside. These descriptions use the word indicating the make of the truck ("Ford"), and the numbers and letters on the tag, as verbal markers. Treating such evidence as hearsay would be foolish because the word "Ford" and the letters and numbers on the tag are used as identifying characteristics of the truck, just as color is.

b. Verbal Markers With Assertive Aspects

Most words assert something, and this point applies to verbal markers too. In the previous example, the word "Ford" on the truck amounts to the manufacturer's assertion "This truck is a Ford" or "This truck was made by the Ford Motor Company." But the assertive content does not undercut the points made above: Testimony describing the truck by its make does not involve using the word "Ford" in its assertive aspect. The purpose of the testimony is not so much to prove that the truck is a Ford, but to prove that a particular truck (one that has the word "Ford" on it, and is red and has certain tag letters and numbers) was seen at a robbery and was later seen headed north on Riverside.

c. Verbal Markers as Hearsay

For the reasons noted above, brand names on manufactured articles can raise hearsay issues. The word "Ford" on a truck, and the word "Coke" on a can or bottle, both assert the nature of the product and its origin, and similar examples could be multiplied endlessly. If the purpose is to prove that indeed a truck is a Ford or indeed a can contains Coke, then using the label to prove the point is arguably hearsay. There are two possible answers to such a hearsay objection: First, it can be argued that trucks bearing the label Ford are *the sorts of trucks* one would expect Ford Motor Company to make, so the word Ford is circumstantial evidence that the truck is in fact a Ford. Second, as a practical matter, FRE 902(7) states that trade inscriptions "purporting to have been affixed in the course of business" can be accepted as proof of the nature of an object (authenticating it to that degree) when such inscriptions indicate "ownership, control, or origin." In effect, FRE 902(7) simply *sidesteps* the hearsay problem.

☞ EXAMPLES AND ANALYSIS

1. Duane is prosecuted for stealing Sally's portable Apple computer from the library at 10:15 P.M. while Sally went to the restroom. Although the computer was never recovered, Sally testifies that Duane was the only other person studying in that area of the library at the time she left her computer unattended and that he did not have a computer with him. George testifies that he saw Duane running down the steps of the library at approximately 10:17 P.M. carrying a computer with the insignia "Apple" on it. Duane objects that George's testimony is hearsay if offered to prove that the computer Duane was carrying was an Apple.

Most courts would overrule this objection. The insignia "Apple" is a verbal marker that helps identify the type of computer Duane was carrying. If Sally has testified that her computer is an "Apple" and described it as having this insignia, then George's testimony that he saw Duane with a computer bearing the same insignia involves use of the insignia "Apple" as a verbal marker, and it is nonhearsay. This approach is reinforced by FRE 902(7), which in effect simply avoids hearsay issues by providing that a brand name affixed to an object by the manufacturer is proof that the object was made by that manufacturer.

2. Bill Winter is prosecuted for illegal possession and interstate transportation of narcotics after a briefcase with his name tag on it is found unclaimed in the baggage area of the local bus station. (The baggage in that area had just been unloaded from a bus arriving from another state.) Acting on a tip from an informant, police open the briefcase and find it stuffed with packages of cocaine. On the handle of the briefcase is a luggage tag with an American flag on one side and the name "Bill Winter" on the other. Winter objects to introduction of the briefcase at trial. He claims that the name tag is hearsay if offered to prove that the briefcase belongs to him.

Argument to exclude: The prosecutor is relying on the assertive aspect of the tag, which in essence says "This briefcase belongs to Bill Winter." Hence the tag does *not* qualify as a nonhearsay verbal marker. It is offered to prove the truth of this statement of ownership, and is hearsay. The words cannot be offered as an admission by Winter because the prosecutor has not proved that Winter wrote the tag.

Argument to admit: The prosecutor is offering the words "Bill Winter" as an identifying characteristic, like the American flag on the other side of the name tag. This argument is stronger if the prosecutor has a witness who testifies that she has often seen Bill Winter carry a briefcase with such a name tag. Other corroborating circumstantial evidence will also help, like proof that Bill Winter was riding the bus that delivered this luggage or usually carries a briefcase identical to this one. The name tag would also be admitted if an expert could identify the written "Bill Winter" as being the handwriting of the defendant. See *United States v. Snow*, 517 F.2d 441 (9th Cir. 1975) (admitting briefcase with defendant's name tag on it as nonhearsay circumstantial evidence; there was additional evidence linking defendant to the briefcase).

---

d. Criticism of classifying verbal markers as nonhearsay

Some commentators argue that verbal markers offered to identify the nature, origin, or ownership of a tangible object are used to prove the truth of what they assert and should be classified as hearsay. See M. Graham, *Handbook of Federal Evidence* § 801.6 (5th ed. 2001) (but they should be admitted under the residual exception to the hearsay rule).

7. Circumstantial Evidence of State of Mind

a. Indirect evidence

An out-of-court statement is sometimes admissible as nonhearsay on the theory that it constitutes circumstantial evidence of the state of mind of the declarant.

☛ EXAMPLE AND ANALYSIS

Martha sues under Title VII alleging sex discrimination when she is denied a promotion to store supervisor, a position for which she was qualified. As evidence that she was denied the promotion for discriminatory reasons, she offers the testimony of a witness who heard Walter, the company president, say at a staff meeting: "Women don't make good managers."

Walter's out-of-court statement is not being offered to prove the truth of what it asserts. (Obviously that is not a view Martha would endorse.) Instead it is offered as circumstantial evidence of Walter's state of mind, indicating his beliefs about women, which in turn constitutes some evidence that he discriminates and may well have discriminated against Martha because of her sex. This statement could equally be described as hearsay, however, since Walter openly discloses his state of mind, in effect saying that he "thinks" or "believes" that women don't make good managers, even though the words "think" or "believe" are not uttered. Viewed this way, the statement *is* offered to prove his state of mind, after all. Then the statement is hearsay, but almost certainly it would be admitted under the state-of-mind exception in FRE 803(3) (discussed in Chapter 4).

b. Direct assertions of state of mind are hearsay

A statement cannot be described as "circumstantial" evidence if it *expressly* describes the declarant's state of mind. If, for example, Walter had actually included in his statement the words "I think" or "I believe," then his comment about women managers is direct and not circumstantial evidence of his views. The same is true of words like "I love you," "I hate you," "I am worried," or "I am in pain," when they are offered to prove those states of mind. These words are hearsay. Once again, however, such direct statements by declarants about their state of mind are admissible under FRE 803(3), as we will see in Chapter 4.

c. Nonhearsay or hearsay within the state-of-mind exception

Not surprisingly, courts and commentators don't always come to the same conclusion when the question is whether a statement is direct or circumstantial evidence of state of mind. For some, the key is the literal language of the declarant. For others, the key is the declarant's expressive intent, rather than the actual words. Since statements like this are likely to be admitted regardless how they are analyzed (either as nonhearsay circumstantial evidence or as hearsay within the state-of-mind exception), the debate is academic.

Exam Tip

When a statement revealing a declarant's state of mind is indirect, first argue that it qualifies under this category of nonhearsay. But be sure to point out that even if the statement so directly asserts the declarant's current state of mind that it must be treated as hearsay, it is still likely admissible under the state-of-mind exception in FRE 803(3).

☞ Examples and Analysis

1. Parry is charged with conspiracy to distribute illegal drugs. He denies the charge, claiming that he thought he was working as a government informant leading undercover agents to drug sources. As evidence that he believed he was working as a government agent, he offers testimony by his mother that several times after completing a phone call from their home Parry would tell her "That was the federal agent with whom I am working."

This statement is admissible as nonhearsay circumstantial evidence of his state of mind. See *United States v. Parry*, 649 F.2d 292 (5th Cir. 1981). Even if the court had found the statement to be hearsay, it would be admissible under FRE 803(3).

2. The question has arisen whether Duane is mentally competent. There is evidence that Duane walked around town telling everyone he met that "I am Louis XIV."

Most courts treat such out-of-court statements as nonhearsay, and admit them. The statements are not offered to prove their literal truth (that Duane is Louis

XIV). Instead they are offered to prove that he is incompetent. Some commentators argue that Duane's statements are the equivalent of saying "I think I am Louis XIV," in which case arguably they are hearsay because they *expressly* say what Duane thinks and are offered to prove what he thinks. Of course they would still be admissible under the state-of-mind exception in FRE 803(3).

There is another argument for nonhearsay treatment. *Saying such things,* whether or not Duane begins his comments with "I think," amounts to *bizarre behavior* indicating that something is wrong with Duane's mental condition. His statements are evidence on this point *regardless whether* we take them as proof that he *thinks* he is Louis XIV. If he does think so, something is wrong. If he doesn't, but says it anyway, something is still wrong. In short, these statements have both an *assertive aspect* indicating that something is wrong, and a *performative aspect* indicating the same thing. See M & K, *Evidence* §§ 8.20 and 8.22 (5th ed. 2012).

---

8. Circumstantial Evidence of Knowledge, Memory, or Belief

Some rather rare statements can reasonably be viewed as nonhearsay circumstantial evidence of declarant's knowledge, memory, or belief. This tricky and narrow nonhearsay category brings real dangers because an express statement of knowledge, memory, or belief is normally hearsay, and normally such a statement *cannot* be admitted under the state-of-mind exception contained in FRE 803(3) if the purpose is to prove the act, event, or condition that is remembered, as opposed to merely the memory itself. A statement fits this nonhearsay category only if it displays knowledge that is sufficiently distinctive so that relevant inferences can be drawn without relying on the truth of the statement.

☞ EXAMPLE AND ANALYSIS

Dirk is charged with kidnapping Amy, a nine-year-old girl, keeping her confined in his apartment for nine days and sexually abusing her. Amy is so psychologically traumatized by the incident that she is unable to testify at Dirk's trial. The prosecutor is able to prove most of its case by physical evidence, medical testimony, and the testimony of other witnesses. But as additional proof that Amy was in Dirk's apartment, the prosecutor offers testimony by her parents that Amy recited detailed facts from a diary she says she read while being confined in her abductor's apartment. (During the hours she was left alone while imprisoned, the only book she had to read was her abductor's diary.) In addition to Amy's statements to her parents about what she read, the prosecutor offers Dirk's diary, which was seized from his apartment. The details Amy recited to her parents correspond exactly with what Dirk wrote in his diary. The prosecutor further offers evidence that Amy never knew Dirk, never had been in his apartment, never had access to his diary before the kidnapping, and that there was no way she could learn the information she recited except by reading Dirk's diary during her captivity.

Amy's out-of-court statements to her parents are admissible nonhearsay. They are circumstantial evidence of her memory that could only have been acquired by being in Dirk's apartment. Amy's statements are not offered for their truth. The linkage between the details recalled by Amy and the contents of Dirk's diary tends to prove she was in his apartment. We do not have to rely on the truth of her statement that she learned these details from reading a diary, because other evidence has shown that this is the only way she could have such knowledge.

This example rests on the famous case of *Bridges v. State*, 19 N.W.2d 529 (Wis. 1945), in which out-of-court statements by a child describing the apartment where she was taken and sexually abused were admitted on the same nonhearsay theory. *Bridges* is a harder and more controversial case because the child's description of the abductor's apartment did not demonstrate unique knowledge as convincingly as the description of the contents of the diary in this example.

F. HARD CASES—THE BORDERLAND OF HEARSAY

1. Mixed Conduct and Verbal Expression

a. The difficulty of classification

For purposes of applying the hearsay doctrine, it is sometimes hard to know whether to classify some types of evidence as speech or nonassertive conduct. For example, should what happened in *Wright v. Tatham* (discussed above) be classified as nonassertive conduct (because it involved the *act* of proposing to do business with Marsden) or as assertive conduct (because the letters made statements)?

b. Why classification makes a difference

If an act containing a verbal expression is classified as nonassertive conduct, then it is hearsay only if the assertive aspect of the act is important in proving the point for which the evidence is offered.

c. Performativity analysis

Sometimes lawyers and judges mistakenly assume that certain evidence has to be classified as *either* assertive *or* nonassertive conduct when in fact it is *both*. Instead of insisting on a dichotomy that cannot be maintained, it is more useful to assess the extent to which the words serve as a performative acts. The greater the performative aspect of the evidence, the more appropriate it is to classify it as nonassertive conduct rather than as a verbal assertion. See generally M & K, § 8.22 (3d. ed. 2003).

☞ EXAMPLE AND ANALYSIS

Derrick is prosecuted for vehicular homicide for driving away from a party while drunk, colliding with another vehicle, and killing three people. As evidence that Derrick was drunk when he left the party, the prosecutor calls Wanda. She was a guest at the party, and could testify to the following: (1) Abe, another guest, said to Derrick just before he drove away, "You can't drive, you're stinking drunk"; (2) Burt, host of the party, tried to take away Derrick's car keys, but Derrick held on and eventually drove away; (3) Before Derrick left, Carl, another guest, dialed for a cab and said to Derrick: "Please wait. I've got a cab coming for you in three minutes."

Abe's statement is clearly hearsay: He says that Derrick is so drunk that he can't drive, and the statement is offered to prove that Derrick is too drunk to drive. In contrast, however, Burt's behavior is probably nonassertive conduct demonstrating his belief that Derrick was unfit to drive. One might plausibly argue that Burt, in trying to take away Derrick's keys, is also *saying* or *asserting* that Derrick is drunk. If interpreted in this latter way, one can *still* point out that Burt is doing *more than* asserting that Derrick is drunk because Burt is also trying to take away the keys to prevent Derrick from driving. If this behavior is assertive, it is assertive behavior with an important performative aspect. Carl's conduct is harder to appraise in terms of the hearsay doctrine: Like what Burt did (and said), Carl's conduct is a mix of nonassertive conduct (getting a cab for Derrick shows, under the circumstances, that Carl thought Derrick was drunk and shouldn't drive home) and speech (Carl tells Derrick to wait because Carl has summoned the cab). Arguably the performative aspect of Carl's behavior counts for more than the assertive aspect, and what Carl did is closer to what Burt said and did than it is to what Abe said. That means that what Carl said and did (his words and his acts) should be admitted as nonhearsay. But these mixed cases present challenging issues for the hearsay doctrine, and there is continuing controversy among courts and commentators about how they should be handled.

d. Lying as hearsay

Sometimes out-of-court statements that are lies are offered as evidence.

☞ EXAMPLE AND ANALYSIS

Ed is prosecuted for bank robbery. While the crime was under investigation, his wife Ellen falsely told police that Ed was out of state on a business trip at the time of the robbery.

If the prosecutor offers her statement into evidence, clearly it is not being offered to prove its truth. Hence it is not hearsay if analyzed as a verbal assertion. Probably it is better to classify what she did as nonassertive conduct in any event. Ellen's conduct (telling a lie) is offered to support a two-step inference: First, her lying statement suggests that she thinks that her husband committed the crime and she's covering up for him. Second, the fact that she thinks he committed the crime suggests that in fact he did commit the crime. There are hearsay dangers, and such evidence might be excluded in a jurisdiction that recognizes nonassertive conduct as hearsay. But nonassertive conduct is not hearsay under FRE 801 and a hearsay objection would be overruled.

One might object to this evidence on other grounds: Helen might have had other reasons for misleading police: For example, she might not know where Ed was or whether he committed the crime, or might lack an adequate basis for whatever opinion she holds. In other words, the proof might be viewed as only marginally relevant and excluded under FRE 403 as confusing, or it might be excluded because Helen lacks personal knowledge or has an inadequate basis for whatever she might think. Finally, statements to police during an investigation are often excludable as violating the Confrontation Clause under the *Crawford* doctrine, although nonhearsay uses of such statements might be allowed. The *Crawford* doctrine is discussed in Chapter 5.

2. Proving Facts Assumed or Apparently Believed by the Declarant

Sometimes a statement reveals facts that are assumed or apparently believed by the declarant without directly stating them. This type of statement is sometimes referred to as an **implied assertion.**

a. Two meanings of "implied assertion"

This term has two very different meanings and can be misleading. Caution is required.

i.   Indirect but intended assertions

The term implied assertion sometimes refers to an assertion advanced indirectly, in which the intended meaning is a message that differs from the literal meaning of the words, but in which the declarant still does purposefully express or communicate that meaning. Such assertions are hearsay if offered to prove their truth. See Section D.

> **Example**.   A man named Kay and a woman companion are charged with interstate transportation of another woman for purposes of prostitution. As evidence against Kay, the government proves that the companion talked with the alleged victim prior to trial and told her: "It would be better for us two girls to take the blame than Kay because he couldn't stand to take it." This statement is hearsay because it "plainly implies" that Kay is guilty. The assertion is indirect, but it appears that Kay intended to assert this point. See *Krulewitch v. United States*, 336 U.S. 440 (1949) (reversing conviction for error in admitting this hearsay).

ii. Statements containing unintended messages

Sometimes a statement supports an inference about acts, events, or conditions in the world even if the declarant did not intend to express or communicate anything about such points. Such inferences are nevertheless plausible when the statement reveals facts assumed or believed by the declarant even though he was not trying to say anything about them. It is confusing and potentially misleading to speak of statements of this type as "implied assertions" for two reasons. First, the term "imply" normally refers to something that the speaker intended to communicate, so referring to an unintended message as an implied assertion amounts to a misuse of the term "imply." Second, the term "assertion" also carries with it an idea of intent to express or communicate, and FRE 801 uses this concept in exactly that way: Under FRE 801 there is no such thing as an "assertion" that is "unintended." See ACN to FRE 801(a) ("nothing is an assertion unless intended to be one").

iii. The problem of figuring out declarant's intent

Often it is hard to know what the declarant intended to convey, and what he did not intend to convey, in an out-of-court statement.

Often the declarant is not available to be asked about his intent, and even he may not know (looking back on it) exactly how much he meant to communicate. Moreover, even if the declarant had one primary purpose in saying what he said, he may also have had secondary purposes covering other points in his statement.

☞ EXAMPLE AND ANALYSIS

Kearley is charged with operating an illegal drug-distributing scheme out of a house that he rents, where he spends a lot of time. During a raid of the house, the phone rings six times, and police answer each time: All six callers ask to purchase illegal drugs, and try to make arrangements and agree on a price. At trial, the prosecutor calls the officers to testify to the substance of these calls, as proof that the callers (whose identities remain unknown) thought they could purchase drugs from Kearley, hence as some evidence that indeed Kearley deals drugs out of that house. Kearley objects to this testimony as hearsay.

Argument for Hearsay Treatment: Arguably the callers are asserting, by implication even if not expressly, that drugs are dealt at the number (and place) being called, hence that Kearley is involved in drug dealing. Assume the callers say, in effect, "How much do I have to pay for thus-and-such and when could you get me X quantity?" Arguably what they intend to communicate, beyond their interest in purchasing drugs, is that "I know you're in the business and I want to do business with you." Viewed in this way, the words are hearsay if offered to prove that Kearley deals drugs.

Argument Against Hearsay Treatment: The callers do not intend to assert anything about what happens at the house or what Kearley does. The callers are simply *acting on unstated knowledge or assumptions* about what goes on at the house. They don't need or intend to assert anything about what Kearley does or what happens at the house. At most they reveal that the callers thought or assumed Kearley was a drug dealer, but the callers had no need or intent to assert that fact to Kearley or anyone else. Concluding that the callers don't assert anything about what happens at the house doesn't mean their statements don't tend to prove it: After all, a person who gathers his lapels close around his neck, hunches his shoulders, and fumbles in his pocket for his gloves is doing something that would lead any observer to think he must be cold even if the actor has no intention of expressing or communicating this point. Most American courts admit incoming drug calls, of the sort described in this example, as nonhearsay. In the UK, however, incoming drug calls were until recently viewed as hearsay regardless whether the callers intended to express or communicate anything about what goes on in the house. See *Regina v. Kearley,* 2 App. Cas. 228 (H.L. Eng. 1992). But see *Regina v. Chrysostomou (Mark)* 210 Crim. L. 942 (Court of Appeals, Criminal Div. 2010) (concluding, under revised statutory hearsay definition, that such statements are not hearsay). For an informative discussion of *Kearley* and the issues it raises under American evidence law, see *Symposium on Hearsay and Implied Assertions: How Would (or Should) the Supreme Court Decide the Kearley Case?*, 16 Miss. C. L. Rev. 1 (1995).

---

iv. Conduct rather than speech

Most American courts that admit evidence of incoming phone calls attempting to purchase drugs (or place bets) do so on the theory that such calls represent conduct rather than speech. The callers are primarily engaged in the *act* of buying drugs (or placing bets) rather than making statements about the occupation of the person they have called. In other words, the *performative aspects* of such statements justify treating them as nonhearsay even though they also have *assertive aspects.*

G. PRIOR STATEMENTS BY TESTIFYING WITNESSES

We think of hearsay as being an out-of-court statement by a third person (the declarant) that is described in court by a witness. But what if the witness and the declarant are the same person? What if the witness quotes her own earlier statement?

1. General Rule

At common law, the definition of hearsay reaches any statement made out-of-court (if offered for its truth), even if the person making the statement comes to court at the time of trial and is available to be cross-examined. In other words, what counts is that the *statement was made out-of-court*, not that the *declarant came into court*. FRE 801(c) generally adopts this position by defining hearsay as "a statement that . . . the declarant does not make while testifying," offered "to prove the truth of the matter asserted." But as we will see in the next section, FRE 801(d)(1) qualifies this definition by defining *certain* prior statements by testifying witnesses to be admitted as "not hearsay."

Example.   Shirley saw an automobile accident, and she testifies as a witness. Asked to describe what she saw, she answers "Well, I told the investigating police officer what happened; I told him that it was the pickup truck that ran the red light." Under both the common law and the Federal Rules, Shirley's testimony about her earlier statement is hearsay. She is relating an out-of-court statement, even though she is the one who made it and even though she is subject to cross-examination about it.

Practice Tip

In the situation described in this example, the attorney has several options. First, she can ask "And was that statement you made to the police officer an accurate version of what happened?" If Shirley adopts her earlier statement as her current trial testimony, the hearsay problem is solved. See ACN to FRE 801(d)(1) ("If the witness admits on the stand that he made the statement and that it was true, he adopts the statement and there is no hearsay problem."). Second, the attorney can try to get Shirley to testify now to the same points she made in her statement, by asking something like this: "Without referring to any earlier statements you may have made, could you please tell the jury what you saw at the time of the accident?"

---

2. Criticism of General Rule

Scholars have criticized the general rule on the ground that the reasons for excluding hearsay (the hearsay risks) disappear when the declarant testifies and is subject to cross-examination about what he said before.

a. Reformist view

Some reformers argue that hearsay should be defined as an out-of-court statement by a nontestifying declarant (if offered for its truth). Under this view, prior statements by testifying witnesses would not be hearsay because the declarants can be cross-examined at trial. Under this view, Shirley's statement to the police officer in the example would not be hearsay because Shirley is in court and can be cross-examined.

b. Criticism of reformist view

The reformist view is not beyond criticism. Admitting all prior statements by testifying witnesses would have significant ramifications for the trial process. Delayed cross-examination (cross-examining at trial about a statement made earlier) is arguably not as effective as cross-examination that follows immediately after the statement was made, which is what happens when a witness is cross-examined about his *testimony*, as opposed to his prior statement. And the spontaneity of direct examination would be undercut if a witness could write out her direct testimony in advance, then come to court and read her statement, and then face cross-examination about what she'd prepared before trial.

c. California view

Some jurisdictions (notably California) adopted the reformist view in part by providing that prior *inconsistent* statements by testifying witnesses are not hearsay. See Cal. Ev. Code § 1235 (prior inconsistent statements of testifying witnesses are admissible for their truth, provided that the witness can be cross-examined about them).

Example.   In a California murder prosecution of Mark and Neville arising out of a drive-by shooting, the state calls Wanda as a witness, and she identifies Mark as the shooter. On cross-examination by Mark's attorney, she admits telling police officers afterwards that it was Neville who fired the gun. Her prior statement identifying Neville as the shooter is admissible not only to impeach her trial testimony, but also as nonhearsay evidence that can be considered as proof of what it asserts–that indeed Neville was the shooter. Because Wanda is subject to cross-examination about her earlier statement, and because it is inconsistent with her trial testimony, California treats her earlier statement as nonhearsay, and would admit it for all purposes. By common law tradition (and under the Federal Rules), Wanda's earlier statement is considered hearsay, but it might still be used for the more limited purpose of impeaching her trial testimony. See Chapter 10.

d. FRE 801 partially adopts reformist view

i.   **FRE 801(c)**

Standing alone, FRE 801(c) adopts the common law rule that earlier out-of-court statements by testifying witnesses are hearsay. But FRE 801(c) does not stand alone, and is in effect modified by FRE 801(d)(1). The latter simply *defines* certain prior statements by a testifying witness as "not hearsay," provided that the witness is cross-examinable "concerning" those statements. In this "not hearsay" category are *some* (but not all) prior inconsistent statements, prior consistent statements when offered for certain purposes, and prior statements of identification.

ii.   Compromise

FRE 801(d)(1) represents a compromise between the common law and reformist views because it places some prior statements by a testifying witness outside the definition of hearsay. Unfortunately the terminology is confusing, because FRE 801(d)(1) simply *defines* as "not hearsay" what *would certainly be* hearsay under the definition set forth in FRE 801(c). It would be clearer if FRE 801(d)(1) had listed these three types of statements as exceptions–as statements that are admissible even though they are hearsay.

3.   Prior Statements of Testifying Witnesses That Are "Not Hearsay"

As a qualification to the definition of hearsay in FRE 801(c), FRE 801(d)(1) provides that a statement is not hearsay if "[t]he declarant testifies at the trial or hearing and is subject to cross-examination about the prior statement, and the statement (A) is inconsistent with the declarant's testimony and was given under penalty of perjury at a trial, hearing or other proceeding, or in a deposition; (B) consistent with the declarant's testimony and is offered to rebut an express or implied charge that the declarant recently fabricated it or acted from a recent improper infuence or motive in so testifying; or (C) identifies a person as someone the declarant perceived earlier."

a.   Subject to cross-examination

No prior statement in any of these categories is admissible unless the declarant testifies at trial and is subject to cross-examination about what he said before. Prior statements are not admissible, for instance, if the declarant dies prior to trial or if he testifies but refuses to answer questions about what he said before.

Example.   While crossing the street, Peter is severely injured when struck by a car driven by Dan. Peter sues Dan, and Peter's lawyer deposes Betty, who saw the accident. In her deposition, she supports Peter's version of the facts by testifying that Peter was in a crosswalk when struck. Three years later at trial, Betty testifies that Peter was outside the crosswalk. Her deposition testimony that Peter was in the crosswalk can come in as a prior inconsistent statement, and can be used both to impeach her trial testimony and to prove what it asserts. She is subject to cross-examination at trial about what she said in her deposition, which qualifies as "not hearsay" under FRE 801(d)(1)(A).

i. **Loss of memory about underlying event**

What if the witness claims to have forgotten the underlying event described in her statement? FRE 801(d)(1) requires only that she be subject to cross-examination "about the statement," so arguably not remembering the event described in the statement does not matter.

Example. In *United States v. Owens*, 484 U.S. 554 (1988), a prison guard was severely injured after being hit on the head by an inmate. At trial, the guard could not remember the assault but did remember making a statement to an FBI agent identifying defendant as his assailant. The Supreme Court held that FRE 801(d)(1)(C) was satisfied because the declarant was adequately cross-examinable, in a decision that addressed only the meaning of the Rule, and not constitutional issues.

ii. **Loss of memory about making statement**

What if the declarant cannot remember making the earlier statement? What if he denies making it? Is the Rule's requirement that the declarant be subject to cross-examination still satisfied? In *Owens*, the Court suggested in dictum that the requirement would still be satisfied, provided that the declarant responds to questions about the statement at trial and that he be subject to the usual forms of impeachment. It is questionable whether such cross-examination could be meaningful, and states are not required to follow *Owens* on this point.

b. Prior inconsistent statements

A prior inconsistent statement by a testifying witness is generally admissible to impeach her trial testimony. But when such a statement is admitted for impeachment, it is not to be used as substantive evidence (not to be used as proof of what it asserts). The jury is supposed to use the prior statement only as a basis for appraising the credibility of the witness, who has apparently "blown hot and cold" on the same point. FRE 801(d)(1)(A) is important in allowing the attacking party to use the prior statement not only to impeach, but also to prove what the statement asserts.

i. **Limitations**

FRE 801(d)(1)(A) does not cover all prior inconsistent statements by testifying witnesses. Unlike the California rule, which covers all prior inconsistent statements, the Federal Rule covers only inconsistent statements that were given (a) "under penalty of perjury" and (b) "at a trial, hearing or other proceeding, or in a deposition."

ii. Nature of prior proceeding

The Rule covers statements made in a prior trial, hearing, deposition, or "other proceeding." Under the majority view, the term "other proceeding" does not reach the situation in which a witness gives to police an affidavit at a stationhouse. While an affidavit is a statement made "under oath," and therefore satisfies *that* requirement of the Rule, the setting of the police station does not satisfy the "prior proceeding" requirement. Some courts, however, read the language broadly as reaching this situation. See *State v. Smith*, 651 P.2d 207 (Wash. 1982) (affidavit given by crime victim at police station admissible under state counterpart).

iii. Prior cross-examination not required

Although FRE 801(d)(1)(A) covers testimony given in a prior proceeding, there is no requirement that the declarant was *then* cross-examinable. In many prior proceedings, the declarant *would be* cross-examinable, as would be true if the declarant testified at an earlier trial of the same case, or in a deposition given in the same case, or in a preliminary hearing (where both the prosecutor and the defense can question the declarant). But the Rule does not require that there be *prior* cross-examination. Hence grand jury testimony is covered by FRE 801(d)(1)(A), even though the defense has no opportunity in a grand jury proceeding to cross-examine (because the defendant is not even a party to such a proceeding).

☛ EXAMPLE AND ANALYSIS

Vivian is taken to the hospital after being badly beaten. In an unsworn statement, Vivian tells police that her assailant was armed with a baseball bat. At a grand jury hearing, Vivian testifies that her boyfriend Bart accosted her on the street in front of her apartment and beat her. At the trial of Bart for the assault, Vivian has a change of heart and testifies that she was assaulted by someone unknown to her and that her assailant was unarmed and struck her with his fists.

Because Vivian is subject to cross-examination at trial, the prosecutor may offer her prior inconsistent grand jury testimony under FRE 801(d)(1)(A), not only to impeach her trial testimony but to prove the truth of what it asserts. The jury can properly use what she told the grand jury as proof that Bart assaulted her on the street. Vivian's statement to police that her assailant had a baseball bat, however, can be used only to impeach her trial testimony that her assailant was unarmed. That statement was not made under penalty of perjury, and most courts would say that the setting of a stationhouse interview with police is not a "prior proceeding."

When you read the material dealing with defense confrontation rights under the *Crawford* doctrine (Chapter 5), you will see that both of Vivian's statements are "testimonial" in nature, and might well have to be excluded under the Confrontation Clause if there were no opportunity for the defendant to cross-examine Vivian. The fact that Vivian is subject to cross-examination at trial, however, likely satisfies the Confrontation Clause, and it would not block use of her grand jury testimony. Nor would it block use of her prior statement to police, although the hearsay doctrine continues to block at least the substantive use of that statement.

---

iv. **Degree of inconsistency**

The prior statement does not have to be completely inconsistent with trial testimony, but there must be enough inconsistency so that the earlier statement could reasonably raise doubt about the credibility of the trial testimony.

v. **Loss of memory at trial can be inconsistent with earlier statement**

Under the majority view, a prior positive statement that describes an act, event, or condition in the world event can be inconsistent with trial testimony that claims a lack of memory about that same act, event, or condition. Thus the earlier statement can be admissible as a prior inconsistent statement under FRE 801(d)(1). Some courts hold that in this situation the prior statement is admissible only if the trial judge finds that the claimed loss of memory at trial is feigned. In the typical context in which it is the prosecutor who called the testifying witness, it is not uncommon to encounter a "waffling" witness who simply has changed his mind about testifying, sometimes in fear of the defendant and sometimes because the witness "promised too much" in earlier conversations with the prosecutor. Hence courts conclude with some frequency that claimed lack of memory at trial is simply an escape from testifying, and that the witness really does remember the acts, events, or conditions he described before (which makes the prior statement admissible because the claimed lack of memory is feigned).

> **Example.** Daryl is tried for robbing a liquor store. At a grand jury proceeding, William testifies that Daryl used a gun to carry out the robbery. But at trial William says he can't remember whether the robber was armed. Is William's earlier grand jury testimony (in which William said that Daryl used a gun during the robbery) inconsistent enough with William's trial testimony (where he says he can't remember whether the robber was armed) to be admitted? Under the majority view, the answer is yes. (Some courts, however, would admit William's grand jury testimony only if the trial judge concludes on the facts that William is only pretending to have forgotten whether the robber was armed.).

c. Prior consistent statements

i. For rehabilitation or repair

Prior consistent statements are admissible under both the common law and the Federal Rules to rehabilitate a witness (to "repair" credibility). But at common law, prior consistent statements are admissible only to rehabilitate, and not as proof of what they assert (a hearsay use), and a limiting instruction would be in order.

ii. To prove truth of matter asserted

FRE 801(d)(1)(B) goes beyond the common law by allowing the use of certain prior consistent statements only for rehabilitation but also to prove what they assert. This change makes sense because a jury is not likely to understand why it can consider what the witness says at trial for its truth but not an earlier statement by the same person saying the same thing. When a prior consistent statement is admitted under FRE 801(d)(1)(B), a limiting instruction is not in order.

iii. Types of prior consistent statements

Unlike prior *inconsistent* statements offered as substantive evidence under FRE 801(d)(1)(A), prior *consistent* statements offered under FRE 801(d)(1)(B) need not be made under oath or in a proceeding.

iv. "Not hearsay" only when offered to rebut certain attacks

Not all prior consistent statements qualify as "not hearsay" under FRE 801(d)(1)(B). They qualify only when offered "to rebut an express or implied charge that the declarant recently fabricated it or acted from a recent improper influence or motive in so testifying." Sometimes prior consistent statements are used to rehabilitate or repair a witness who has been impeached in other ways, but FRE 801(d)(1)(B) does not apply in these settings.

☞ EXAMPLES AND ANALYSIS

1. On March 12th, eighty-five-year-old Clarence is sitting on his porch swing when he sees a train strike and kill Rodney as he crosses the tracks in his pickup truck. Rodney's family brings a wrongful death suit against the railroad. Clarence testifies for the plaintiffs that the train did not blow its whistle, but on cross the lawyer for the railroad brings out that Clarence has a bad memory and cannot remember other details about what happened on March 12th (or other days near that time). To rehabilitate, plaintiffs offer a statement Clarence made to a police officer immediately after the accident, to the effect that the train "didn't blow its whistle."

   What he told the police officer is a statement that is consistent with what Clarence said in his testimony (the train didn't blow its whistle). It is likely admissible to repair his credibility, but it does not qualify as "not hearsay" under FRE 801(d)(1)(B) because the railroad has not suggested that Clarence has fabricated his testimony or that he has some improper motive or influence. Here a limiting instruction might be in order (if the railroad requested it), telling the jury not to consider what Clarence told the police officer as additional proof that the train did not blow its whistle, and to consider that statement only as it might bear on the question whether Clarence suffers from lack of memory.

2. Same problem as above. This time the railroad's lawyer suggests on cross that Clarence only testified that there was no whistle because plaintiffs promised Clarence a share of any recovery from the suit.

   Now FRE 801(d)(1)(B) applies because the attack on credibility suggests that Clarence fabricated his testimony and has been improperly influenced, and is motivated by a desire to share in plaintiff's recovery. (The charges of "recent fabrication" and "improper influence or motive" tend to be brought together and are usually part of a single picture.) Hence the prior statement by Clarence to the investigating officer qualifies as "not hearsay" and may be used both for rehabilitation and to prove what it asserts.

v. **Earlier statement must precede motive to fabricate**
The Supreme Court interprets FRE 801(d)(1)(B) as requiring that prior consistent statements offered as substantive evidence must have been made before the motive to fabricate arose. Thus a statement made after the motive to fabricate came into being does not fit FRE 801(d)(1)(B). See *Tome v. United States*, 513 U.S. 150 (1995). The rationale is that a statement made *after* the motive to fabricate does not rehabilitate because the motive to fabricate taints such a statement just as much as it taints the trial testimony. To put it another way, a post-motive statement that is consistent with trial testimony simply does not refute the claim that the witness is being untruthful–the motive affects what he said after the motive came into being just as much as it affects what he says still later in his trial testimony.

> **Example.**   Same problem as above. Assume plaintiff's alleged offer to give Clarence a share of any recovery was made 60 days prior to trial. Assume that 30 days later Clarence says the train didn't blow its whistle. This prior consistent statement is not admissible under FRE 801(d)(1)(B). It is prior to the trial testimony but not prior to the event giving rise to the motive to fabricate.

d. **Prior statements of identification**
An out-of-court statement identifying a person is admissible if the declarant testifies and is subject to cross-examination about the statement.

> **Example.**   Sharon, a bank teller, picks Dunston out of a police lineup as the person who robbed the bank. At the trial of Dunston for robbery, Sharon cannot say whether the defendant is the one who did the deed. A police officer who was present at the lineup may testify that Sharon picked Dunston as the robber at the lineup. What she said then fits FRE 801(d)(1)(C).

i. **Need not be under oath or in a proceeding**
Unlike prior inconsistent statements offered under FRE 801(d)(1)(A), there is no requirement that earlier statements of identification be made under oath or in a proceeding.

ii. **Can supplement trial identification**
Although the primary purpose is to admit earlier identifications when the witness cannot repeat the identification at trial, the Rule

covers statements of identification even if the witness does repeat the identification at trial. The earlier statement may still be more convincing, simply because the circumstance of a trial is invariably highly suggestive: A witness can easily figure out who the defendant is, and when she answers the question whether "she sees the person who robbed her in the courtroom today," she is likely to be very much affected by her knowledge that the defendant has been charged with the crime (and by her guess that there must be lots of other evidence against him or he wouldn't be sitting there).

iii. **Overlap between prior consistent statements and prior statements of identification**

Obviously FRE 801(d)(1)(C) can overlap with the other two provisions in FRE 801(d). Some prior inconsistent statements made under oath in proceedings that satisfy FRE 801(d)(1)(A) also satisfy FRE 801(d)(1)(C), and some prior consistent statements that satisfy FRE 801(d)(1)(B) similarly satisfy FRE 801(d)(1)(C). Hence prior statements of identification might be admissible under two provisions.

REVIEW QUESTIONS AND ANSWERS

Question: What does it mean to say an out-of-court statement is nonhearsay or "not hearsay"?

Answer: When an out-of-court statement is classified as nonhearsay, it means the statement is not offered to prove its truth, but for some other purpose. Thus it falls outside the definition of hearsay, which includes only out-of-court statements for their truth. Such a statement can also properly be described as "not hearsay." The Federal Rules create some confusion in terminology because FRE 801(d) simply *defines* various out-of-court statements as "not hearsay" *even when they are offered for their truth* and therefore fit the definition of hearsay in FRE 801(c). FRE 801(d) paves the way to admit three types of prior statements by testifying witnesses as well as admissions by a party-opponent. This special "not hearsay" category created by FRE 801(d) is really a qualification on the definition of hearsay in FRE 801(c). In other words, statements covered by FRE 801(d) can be admitted to prove what they assert. They are "not hearsay" only because the drafters of the Rules decided to call them "not hearsay" rather than classifying them as exceptions (as statements that are admissible even though they are hearsay). But they should be distinguished from other nonhearsay statements that are not offered to prove their truth: These are not hearsay because they do not fit the definition of hearsay. Sometimes the distinction is made by using quotation marks when referring to statements admissible under FRE 801(d) that are "not hearsay" only because the rule classifies them as such.

Question: Where can one find a list of the possible nonhearsay uses for an out-of-court statement?

Answer: The Federal Rules don't provide a list. The basic hearsay doctrine, which is codified in FRE 801 and 802, simply excludes out-of-court statements when offered for their truth (unless they fit an exception or are defined as "not hearsay"). The doctrine does not apply when statements are offered for some other purpose. A nonhearsay use can be any relevant use of an out-of-court statement other than proving the truth of the matter asserted. The most common nonhearsay uses, all of which are discussed above, are impeachment, verbal acts, proof of effect on listener or reader, verbal objects, circumstantial evidence of state of mind, and circumstantial evidence of knowledge, memory, or belief.

Question: Is an out-of-court statement admissible over a hearsay objection if the person who made it takes the stand and is subject to cross-examination about the statement?

Answer: Generally not, with three important exceptions. The question whether this result is right divides the commentators. Some scholars argue that the hearsay dangers disappear when the declarant can be cross-examined at trial about earlier out-of-court statements, so such statements *should not be excluded* by the hearsay rule. Others argue that delayed cross-examination, conducted long after the statement was made, is simply not as effective as cross-examination about what the witness says at trial, so the earlier out-of-court statements *should be excluded* as hearsay. They also argue that if the declarant appears at trial, she should be required to give her current account of the act, event, or condition in issue, rather than introducing her past statements about it. The Rules take a compromise position. FRE 801 generally treats prior statements by testifying witnesses as hearsay, but FRE 801(d)(1) admits three categories of out-of-court statements, provided the declarant is subject to cross-examination about them:

The first is prior inconsistent statements given under oath subject to the penalty of perjury at a trial, hearing, or other proceeding, or in a deposition. The second is prior consistent statements offered to rebut an express or implied charge against the declarant of recent fabrication or improper influence or motive. The third is prior statements of identification of a person made after perceiving the person.

Question: Jan is prosecuted for murdering Jed, her former boyfriend. She claims self-defense. Jed had been stalking her for several months and made repeated threats to injure or kill her if she did not take him back. Late one night after Jan returned from a date with Bill, Jed called her on the phone and said, "I told you I'd kill you if I ever saw you out with another man" and hung up. Jan was terrified. She called police, who told her there was nothing they could do unless Jed appeared at her house. Jan then got a pistol that her father had given her and sat wide-awake on her bed. She heard a loud pounding at her front door and, just as she got to the hallway, Jed broke down the door and burst in. Jan shot him. To prove that she had a reasonable apprehension that Jed would kill her, Jan seeks to testify about the threat Jed made on the phone. Should her testimony be allowed?

Answer: Yes, Jed's statement is admissible as nonhearsay. It is being offered to prove its effect on Jan, not to prove its truth. Under the substantive criminal law, the use of force against another person is justifiable when the defendant believes that such force is immediately necessary for the purpose of protecting herself against the use of unlawful force by the other person. What is important is that Jan "believed" she was in danger. It is not necessary for her to prove that she actually was in danger or that Jed intended to carry out his threat. All Jan needs to show is that Jed made the threat, that she heard the threat, and that such threat caused reasonable apprehension on her part, justifying her use of deadly force.

EXAM TIPS

Here are some pointers about issues relating to the hearsay doctrine:

Definitions of hearsay vary slightly among jurisdictions, but all reach both oral and written assertions made out of court, as well as assertive behavior (pointing, nodding, or shaking the head) if offered to prove the truth of the matter asserted.

Whether something is hearsay turns *both* on whether it is an assertion ("the light was red") *and* on whether it is offered to prove what it asserts (light was in fact red).

Even if an assertion is *not* offered to prove what it asserts, it is sometimes excluded as prejudicial because of the *risk* that a jury will misuse it as proof of what it asserts.

Commonly the term "statement" is used interchangeably with the term "assertion."

A statement is hearsay if offered to prove what it literally asserts *and* if offered to prove what the declarant intends to express or communicate, even though the statement doesn't literally say it.

The statement "John is pointing his gun at me" is hearsay if offered to prove that John is pointing his gun at the speaker because the statement *directly asserts* that point.

The statement "John, don't shoot me" is hearsay if offered to prove that John is poised to shoot the declarant because the statement *indirectly asserts* the same point.

Most jurisdictions follow the rule that nonassertive conduct is not hearsay, even if offered in support of a two-step inference that leads to a conclusion about acts, events, or conditions in the world. Thus putting up an umbrella is nonhearsay evidence that it is raining. Here is the two-step inference: The act suggests that the person *thinks* it is raining. The fact that he thinks so suggests that it *is* raining.

Remember the six common nonhearsay uses for out-of-court statements:

Impeachment (usually a prior inconsistent statement)

Verbal acts or parts of acts (such as contract or threatening words during a holdup)

Effect on listener or reader (such as threats or warnings)

Circumstantial evidence of state of mind (such as "I am Louis XIV," offered to prove the speaker is out of his mind)

Circumstantial evidence of memory or belief (such as knowledge of the content of a secret diary, offered to prove the speaker had seen the diary)

Verbal markers (usually written words on an object that somebody saw, to which she refers at trial to describe the object)

Remember that some prior statements by testifying witnesses are defined as "not hearsay" in FRE 801, so they may be used as proof of what they assert. The declarant must testify and be cross-examinable about these statements:

Inconsistent statements in proceedings under oath

Consistent statements offered to rebut claims of improper influence or motive or recent fabrication.

Statements identifying a person after perceiving the person.

CHAPTER 4

Hearsay Exceptions

CHAPTER OVERVIEW

The key points in this chapter are

- Hearsay exceptions pave the way to admit statements even though they *are* hearsay.

  - The list is long, but only about a dozen exceptions are heavily used.

  - Necessity and trustworthiness underlie the exceptions, and these concepts vary in meaning from one setting to another.

- Reform efforts often target the hearsay exceptions, and many reforms would expand the admissibility of hearsay.

- Two kinds of hearsay (prior statements by testifying witnesses and admissions by party opponents) are defined as "not hearsay" by FRE 801, but this definition is best understood as creating hearsay exceptions (for statements that really are hearsay, despite what the definition suggests, but are admissible anyway).

- Hearsay fitting an exception may be excluded for other reasons, since fitting an exception answers a hearsay objection, but not other objections.

- Admissions are statements by a party offered against the party. There are five kinds:

    - Individual admissions, which are statements by a person offered against that person.

    - Adoptive admissions, which are statements made by another that a person adopts. Sometimes silence adopts, and we speak of tacit admissions.

    - Authorized admissions, which are statements by someone like a broker or lawyer, who is authorized to speak for the person or entity (admissible against such person or entity).

    - Admissions by agents or employees, which are statements by such persons relating to matters within the scope of their authority or duties, and these statements are admissible against the principal or employer regardless whether the person making the statement had authority to speak.

    - Coconspirator statements, which are statements by persons who conspire with the person against whom such statements are offered (usually the defendant in a criminal conspiracy case), which must meet three criteria: First, the declarant must have **conspired** with the person against whom the statement is offered; second, the statement must have been made **during the pendency or course of** the conspiracy; third, it must have it **furthered** the conspiracy.

- Present sense impressions. Key elements are **immediacy, description,** and **perception.** The statement must describe acts, events, or conditions existing or occurring **as the speaker speaks** and perceives these things.

- Excited utterances. Key elements are **external stimulus, excitement,** and **relation to an act or event.** There must be an act or event that catches the attention of the speaker; she must be excited by it; her statement must relate to it.

- State-of-mind statements. Key elements are that the statement must describe **existing physical condition or mental state** of the speaker. This exception is one of the most important and most difficult in application.

    - Existing physical condition. A statement fits the exception in describing the speaker's existing physical condition. Some inferences backward and forward in time are permissible, but the exception does not reach statements describing either a past condition or the past cause of present condition.

- Mental state as end in itself. Statements describing existing mental state fit the exception when offered to prove mental state *as an end in itself*. Such statements may prove, for instance, that an extortion victim was afraid. But the exception does not allow use of a statement to prove some act, event, or condition that caused the fear.

- Mental state to show later behavior. Statements shedding light on intent fit the exception when offered to prove intent where the ultimate purpose is to show *that the speaker acted accordingly*. The *Hillmon* doctrine endorses this result. But a statement offered to show intent, hence later behavior, does not fit the exception if used to prove an act, event, or condition that produced the intent. *Hillmon* invites use of statements of intent to prove the later conduct of the speaker *with another person*, but this use is problematic.

- Wills cases. In wills cases, the exception is broader. It reaches any statement by a decedent relating to the execution or revocation of his will or similar document, or behavior by family members, or the mental state of the decedent.

- Medical statements. Key elements are that the statement must describe **condition** or **symptoms** (including history and cause) and must be **reasonably pertinent to** treatment or diagnosis. The exception reaches statements by people other than the patient, but not those that cast blame or ascribe fault.

- Past recollection recorded. Key elements are (1) **insufficient memory** on the part of the witness, (2) statement **correctly reflecting** past memory, (3) **made or adopted** when (4) the matter was **fresh** in his recollection.

- Business records. The exception reaches (1) records **regularly kept** by a business, (2) based on information from a **source within the business with personal knowledge**, (3) **prepared contemporaneously** with the event reported, as shown by (4) **foundation testimony** by the custodian of records or other knowledgeable witness, or by a certificate or affidavit that lays out these other foundational element. Such records may be still excluded as untrustworthy.

- Public records. This exception reaches three categories, and is subject to use restrictions that not merely prevent some things from fitting the exception but actually block resort to some other exceptions.

  - **Activities of office or agency.** The exception covers records reflecting activities of the office or agency.

  - **Matters observed.** The exception covers records reflecting matters observed by public agencies, like temperature and weather conditions. Special language in FRE 803(8)(A)(ii) creates a **use restriction** for criminal cases preventing prosecutors from proving **police or law enforcement reports.** This restriction blocks not only the use of FRE 803(8) to prove such points, but also blocks resort to the catchall and business records exceptions. Resort to the exception for past recollection recorded, however, may be appropriate. Police records that are **routine and nonadversarial** may be admitted as public records, however.

  - **Investigative findings.** Under FRE 803(8)(A)(ii), the exception reaches "factual findings" based on official investigations, such as reports on the cause and spread of diseases. Such findings may rest on information from outsiders. Another use restriction blocks the government from offering such material against criminal defendants.

  - **Trustworthiness factor.** Even records and reports that fit the exception may be excluded as untrustworthy.

- Learned treatises. This exception reaches books like medical texts, if shown to be authoritative and either relied upon or called to the attention of expert witnesses.

- Unavailable declarants. A handful of exceptions apply only if the testimony by the declarant is **unavailable:** This requirement is satisfied if he cannot be found or subpoenaed, or if he makes a claim of privilege that a court sustains, or simply refuses to testify, or lacks memory of underlying events.

- Former testimony. This exception requires the declarant to be unavailable. The exception reaches **testimony in depositions or other proceedings** if (1) the party against whom the testimony is offered **could cross-examine** in the deposition or other proceedings, and (2) had **similar motive and opportunity** to do so.

- Dying declarations. This exception requires the declarant to be unavailable. The declarant must have a settled expectation of imminent death, and the statement must relate to the "cause or circumstances."

- Against-interest statements. This critical exception requires the declarant to be unavailable and reaches statements **against both pecuniary or proprietary interest and penal interest**.

  - Context is critical. Facial meaning may show a statement is against interest ("I killed the President"). But context must be carefully scrutinized. Context may show a statement is against interest even if facial meaning does not, or that a statement is not against interest even though facial meaning suggests that it is.

  - Interests may conflict. Where the speaker has conflicting interests, a statement is against interest if it gives up more than it gains.

  - Collateral statements. The Supreme Court's 1995 decision in *Williamson* held that the federal exception reaches only statements that are **themselves** against interest, and not **collateral statements** that are spoken along with against-interest statements. *Williamson* involved statements by H to police describing H's and W's role in the crime later charged to W, and the Court thought that the description of W's role was collateral and did not fit the exception. H was probably trying to **curry favor,** so what he said about W was collateral and not against his interest.

  - *Williamson* did not put an end to the problem of using against the defendant a statement by an alleged co-offender to police because the Court in *Williamson* acknowledged that some statements mentioning others could be against interest. In 2004, the Court decided in the *Crawford* case that the Confrontation Clause of the Sixth Amendment bars the use of "testimonial" statements against the accused. This category of "testimonial" statements clearly includes statements of the sort involved in *Williamson,* in which a co-offender incriminates the defendant in a statement to police investigating crime. *Crawford* did largely solve the problems raised by cases like *Williamson.*

  - *Williamson* remains important because it establishes the general principle that the against-interest exception does not reach "collateral" statements that are not themselves against the declarant's interest. *Williamson* also remains important because statements by alleged co-offenders to *persons other than law enforcement* officers may not be "testimonial" and thus may not be covered by *Crawford*. Finally, *Williamson* also remains important because *Crawford* holds that a chance to cross-examine the declarant (at trial or before) satisfies confrontation concerns, which leaves room for a statement by one co-offender, if he testifies and can be cross-examined, to be used against another, even if the statement is made to police investigating crime.

- **Pecuniary, proprietary interest**. Subject to the above caveats, a statement may be against pecuniary or proprietary interest if the speaker is saying that he owes money to someone, or has been paid (which thus cancels a claim that he might have against another), or has committed acts that could give rise to tort liability.

- Statements against **penal interest** that *implicate the defendant*. As indicated above, *Williamson* limits use of the against-interest exception to admit statements by a co-offender that implicate the defendant. Some statements by co-offenders may constitute evidence against the defendant even if they do not mention the defendant, and these statements do not raise the same kinds of concern over "collateral" statements that appeared in *Williamson*. If, for example, L is tried for robbing a store and M (who is unavailable) says to his friend N, "I was waiting in front in the truck," then what M told N might tend to incriminate both M and L (if the two were seen later in the truck) and could fit the exception. If M says in substance, "L and I robbed the store," some courts say the reference to L does not fit the exception, but others say it does.

- Statements against **penal interest** that *exonerate the defendant*. If K is charged with murder and J (who is unavailable) says he did the deed, K can probably introduce J's statement. If J said, "I did it, and K wasn't involved," some courts say the latter comment is "collateral" under the *Williamson* doctrine, hence not against interest and not within the exception, but other courts apply the exception to both parts of the statement.

- Forfeiture-by-wrongdoing exception. If a party (typically defendant in a criminal case) kills a witness *with the idea of keeping her from testifying,* thus intentionally procuring the unavailability of the witness, FRE 804(b)(6) permits the use against that party of anything the witness has said. The idea is that wrongful behavior of this sort, aimed at keeping another from testifying, **forfeits the right** to claim the protection of the hearsay doctrine. The Court in *Crawford* pointedly stated that it accepted the same principle as a matter of confrontation law, indicating that the same conduct that forfeits the right to exclude evidence under the hearsay doctrine also forfeits the right to exclude evidence under the Confrontation Clause.

- Catchall. Hearsay that does not fit a "categorical exception" described above may be admitted if it fits what we call the "catchall" exception contained in FRE 807 (also called the "residual" exception). The central requirement is "circumstantial guarantees of trustworthiness." Also the proponent must give pretrial notice, and must show that a statement proffered under the exception is more probative than anything else reasonably available.

A. INTRODUCTION

The hearsay doctrine requires exclusion of many out-of-court statements offered as proof of what they assert. A long list of exceptions, however, paves the way to admit many such statements. If an exception applies, an out-of-court statement is not excluded because it is hearsay. It may still be excluded for other reasons, but in the absence of such reasons it may be admitted to prove what it asserts after all.

1. Few Important Exceptions

There are many exceptions: Counting admissions and certain statements by testifying witnesses (covered by FRE 801(d)(1), as discussed in Chapter 3), the number of standard exceptions is more than 35. But only about a dozen are in common use. Most of the rest arise infrequently, and some are truly obscure (like the one in FRE 803(13) covering engravings on urns, crypts, and similar things).

2. Rationale of Exceptions

Most hearsay exceptions are justified by appeals to **trustworthiness** and **necessity.** That is to say, statements covered by the various exceptions are considered either trustworthy (reliable) or necessary in the quest for truth, or some combination of both.

a. Trustworthiness

Many factors count in favor of trustworthiness, including spontaneity (one reason for the excited utterance and state-of-mind exceptions), organizational routine (one reason to admit business records), and need for accuracy (one reason to admit medical statements). These "trustworthiness factors" eliminate or lessen the hearsay risks (perception, memory, narration or ambiguity, veracity or candor), and justify admitting statements despite lack of oath and demeanor evidence, and inability to cross-examine. Critics sometimes argue that these factors do not insure trustworthiness, or that they are outweighed by other concerns: Spontaneity, for instance, may indicate that the declarant was truthful, but may also show that she spoke so quickly that she could not exercise care in observation or speech.

b. Necessity

This factor too takes many different forms. Sometimes necessity means that the speaker is unavailable to testify, so the choice is to admit what he said or do without his observations. (Some exceptions *require* and partly rest on this kind of necessity, including the ones for dying declarations, former testimony, and against-interest statements. See FRE 804(b).) Sometimes necessity takes very different forms: Excited utterances are considered necessary because they describe fleeting events for which proof is scarce, such as a violent crime or an automobile accident, and public records are considered necessary because officials shouldn't be constantly summoned away from their duties to testify.

3. Reform Proposals

The hearsay doctrine is well established in American law. Despite ongoing calls for reforms that would admit more hearsay, the doctrine remains stable, resilient, and remarkably resistant to change. Some argue that hearsay should be generally admissible if the speaker either testifies or is unavailable. In the former situation, whatever he said can be tested at trial; in the latter, his unavailability justifies admitting the next best thing. Under this approach, the hearsay doctrine would actually exclude statements only if the witness could be summoned but is not. Others argue that hearsay should be generally admitted in civil cases. England takes this approach, but England also did away with civil juries. Still others argue that our approach should be changed: Alternatives include admitting hearsay on the basis of pretrial notice, or admitting hearsay if the proponent offers enough evidence to enable juries properly to evaluate it, or using a cost-benefit analysis under which a party might be excused from the obligation to produce the declarant as a witness, and allowed to use his hearsay statements instead, if the adverse party is in a better position to produce the declarant to testify as a witness.

4. Terminology

Two kinds of out-of-court statements are sometimes called "not hearsay" and sometimes "hearsay within an exception." Those are prior statements by testifying witnesses and admissions.

a. Prior statements by testifying witnesses

Under FRE 801(d)(1), some statements by testifying witnesses are defined as "not hearsay." In fact, such statements are made out of court and often are offered to prove what they assert, which means they fit the basic definition of hearsay. Calling them "not hearsay" can be justified by the fact that FRE 801 requires the declarant to be cross-examinable about them during trial, which makes them different from almost all the "true" exceptions set forth in FRE 803 and 804(b).

b. Admissions

Under FRE 801(d)(2), statements made by a party and offered against that party (admissions) are defined as "not hearsay." Here again, such statements are made out of court and are often offered to prove what they assert, so they fit the basic definition of hearsay. Calling them "not hearsay" can be justified by the fact that admissibility does not depend on ideas of necessity and trustworthiness that underlie standard exceptions. Admissions don't need to be trustworthy and the declarant is usually able to respond because he is right there. The "admissions doctrine" expresses the philosophy of the adversary system in a free society—everyone is responsible for making (or breaking) her own case. And if statements that come into the case admissions are false or mistaken for some reason, the party may take the stand and say why.

5. Exceptions Only Overcome Hearsay Objection

Applying an exception means that a proffered statement need not be excluded as hearsay. It does not follow that the statement must be admitted. If a statement that fits an exception would be irrelevant or violate some other exclusionary rule, it must still be excluded. Thus a statement by a criminal defendant that might qualify as an admission is still subject to constitutional restrictions such as the *Miranda* doctrine, and to exclusionary doctrines such as the rule against admitting proof of prior crimes (FRE 404), subsequent remedial measures (FRE 407), offers to plead guilty (FRE 410), and similar restrictions. If a defendant in a civil case says, for example, "I repaired the loose tread on the steps," these words constitute the admission of the defendant for purposes of the hearsay doctrine and so a hearsay objection would not require exclusion. The words also describe what might be a subsequent remedial measure for purposes of FRE 407, and an objection under the latter provision might well require exclusion.

6. Double and Multiple Hearsay

If one out-of-court statement contains (reports the substance of) a second out-of-court statement, and the purpose is to prove the truth of the matter asserted in the second statement, the situation presents an issue of double hearsay. Although it rarely happens, the second statement might report the substance of a third, and so on (multiple hearsay).

a. Each statement must fit exception

With double or multiple hearsay, a hearsay objection can be overcome if each statement satisfies an exception. See FRE 805. Suppose Witness testifies to a statement by Abe reporting what Bob said, and the purpose is to prove the matter asserted by Bob. Abe's statement is hearsay when offered to prove that Bob said something, and Bob's statement is hearsay when offered to prove the truth of what Bob said. A hearsay objection to this testimony can be overcome if what Abe said and what Bob said both fit exceptions.

b. Written statements

It is easy to overlook the fact that the same double or multiple hearsay problem can arise when a written statement reports the substance of a second oral statement. If a party offers a writing by Ann reporting a statement by Betty, the writing is Ann's out-of-court statement and it is hearsay if offered to prove Betty said something. And again, what Betty said is hearsay if offered for its truth. Again a hearsay objection can be overcome only if Ann's written statement and Betty's oral statement both fit exceptions. See FRE 805.

B. ADMISSIONS BY PARTY OPPONENT

All jurisdictions agree that the hearsay doctrine should not block one party from using against another statements that the latter has made.

1. Broad Admissibility

In many important ways, the admissions doctrine is very broad. First, there are no limitations other than identity (must be, or be affiliated with, the adverse party), which means that admissions need not be against interest to be admitted at trial. Second, admissions (other than coconspirator statements) generally come in regardless whether the speaker had personal knowledge, which makes the doctrine different from standard exceptions that require or assure such knowledge. Third, admissions usually come in even if they are conclusory (simply conceding fault or liability), while many standard exceptions reach only statements with high factual content.

☞ EXAMPLE AND ANALYSIS

Five-year-old Allen is bitten by Fido, who is owned by an adult named Bernard. Fido had escaped from a fenced dog run while Bernard was at work, and he only learned of the event afterwards. His neighbor Carla told him about the incident. After talking with her, Bernard comments to a clerk at the Animal Control Department, which had taken Fido to the pound, that "It's probably my fault that the child got attacked, since Fido has just gotten to be too big for that fence." At trial, Bernard raises a hearsay objection to testimony by the clerk describing what Bernard had said, pointing out that "the statement is conclusory and he didn't even know what had happened and was relying entirely on what Carla told him."

The objection should be overruled. Conclusory statements fit the exception, and lack of personal knowledge doesn't matter, although it may affect weight. This result usually makes sense, since most such statements reflect at least "circumstantial knowledge" on the part of the speaker. Bernard presumably knows something about what Fido might or might not do, and the fact that he apparently accepts what he was told is at least some indication that Bernard considers Fido to be capable of such behavior, which is some indication that indeed Fido is capable of it.

---

2. Individual Admissions

In suits by or against an individual, whatever he says personally that is relevant is generally admissible. See FRE 801(d)(2)(A).

a. *Bruton* doctrine

In addition to constitutional limits like the *Miranda* doctrine, application of the admissions doctrine is limited by constitutional holding of *Bruton v. United States*, 391 U.S. 123 (1968). The crux of *Bruton* is that, in a trial of more than one defendant (call them A and B), a statement by A that implicates B by name may not be admitted, even if the judge gives limiting instructions telling the jury that the statement is evidence only against A. It is worth noting that the hearsay doctrine does not permit A's statement to be used against B, and the usual way of dealing with this problem is to do what the trial court did in *Bruton,* which is to admit the statement and tell the jury not to consider it as evidence against B. What *Bruton* adds is this: In a criminal case, admitting such a statement (a statement by one codefendant incriminating another by name or reference) violates the Confrontation Clause and a limiting instruction is not good enough to satisfy this constitutional provision. There are ways to accommodate the *Bruton* limit:

i.   Sever trials

If A and B are tried separately, admitting A's statement in A's trial cannot violate B's rights. Using two juries in one trial, excusing the jury that is to consider B's guilt when A's statement is admitted, can achieve the same result.

ii.   Edit A's statement

Sometimes A's statement can be effectively edited (the technique is called "redaction") to delete references to B. This approach can work with written statements, but is not promising with oral statements because it is hard to tell a witness to testify truthfully while omitting reference to parts of A's statements naming B. Moreover, redaction is hard to do effectively. In *Gray v. Maryland,* 523 U.S. 185 (1998), the Supreme Court held that redaction did not offer adequate protection where the edited statement by defendant Bell said "me, blank, and a few other guys" in answer to the question "Who hit and kicked" the victim. Substituting "blank" for "Gray" did not adequately protect Gray because the jury would know that "blank" referred to Bell's codefendant Gray. The decision in *Gray* suggests that redaction satisfies *Bruton* only if it is truly effective, but the Court also implied that redaction might be adequate if the statement had been edited to say "me and a few other guys," which suggests that the use of neutral pronouns might be sufficient, even though a jury might interpret those as referring to particular codefendants. The redaction approach does not work if deleting references to B distorts the statement to the detriment of the person who made it, or leaves an obvious gap that would be understood as a reference to B, or (in a trial of three or more defendants) might reasonably be interpreted as incriminating yet another defendant who was not actually mentioned in the original (unedited) statement.

iii. Cross-examine the declarant

If A testifies and B can cross-examine, B's right of confrontation is satisfied. But note that A's statement **still** is not admissible against

B (if it is admitted only as A's own admission), and note that during its case in chief the prosecution cannot be sure that A will testify, and neither the prosecutor nor codefendant B can call A as a witness.

iv. Limits of doctrine

Bruton applies only in criminal cases (because Sixth Amendment confrontation applies only in criminal cases). Also, *Bruton* does not apply to statements by A that do not refer expressly or by implication to B, even if A says things that might be relevant against B. If the two are prosecuted for bank robbery, for example, and A admits that "the getaway car was a blue sedan," *Bruton* does not require exclusion of A's statement, although a limiting instruction might be appropriate because A's statement is *relevant* in the case against B but is *still inadmissible* against B.

b. Restrictions

Occasional statutes restrict the use of statements that would normally fit the admissions doctrine. Some states, for example, have statutes blocking use of statements by accident victims who might—in a weak moment while suffering shock or serious injury—make ill-considered statements, and some statutes block the use of admissions gathered by claims investigators. Admissions can also be excluded under FRE 403 if they are unduly confusing or prejudicial.

c. Admission by "privies"

By common law tradition, a statement by a person in "privity" with another could be attributed to the latter for purposes of the admissions doctrine. If J and K were joint tenants, for example, and J sued to enforce rights linked to this tenancy, the other side could offer K's statements against J. Similarly if L sued as personal administrator of the estate of M, the other side could offer against L what M said.

i. Wrongful death suits

The same rule could apply in wrongful death suits, although here some courts hold that the privity rule does not apply because the claim belongs to the survivor and was not something inherited or acquired from the decedent.

ii. No privity doctrine in FRE

The Federal Rules do not contain a "privity" doctrine for admissions. Statements formerly offered under that rubric may now be admitted, assuming the declarant is unavailable to testify, if they fit the against-interest exception, as they often do.

3. Adoptive admissions

If X signs a written statement prepared by another or expressly agrees (orally or in writing) with an oral statement by another, X is said to have adopted what the other has written or said. X has in effect "made the statement his own," and it becomes an admission by X. See FRE 801(d)(2)(B).

a. Tacit admissions

If Y makes a statement in the presence of X or writes something to X, and X is silent or makes a responsive comment of some sort (written or oral), this silence or responsive comment may or may not show that X agrees to what Y said. Here, when there is no express adoption, the question of adoption turns on many factors. Most important are the nature of the statement and the setting. Adoption is indicated if X would likely deny or disagree if he considered the statement false or mistaken.

☞ EXAMPLE AND ANALYSIS

In a July conversation among Abe, Bob, Carl, Don, and other casual acquaintances in a restaurant, Abe asks Bob, "Where can I get a good pilot to bring in a load of coke?" Bob replies, "Carl brought some stuff in from Colombia last week, and he's a good pilot and reliable too." Don comments, "Yeah, he showed real courage since that line of work is dangerous nowadays." In a trial of Carl and Don for importing cocaine from Colombia in July, the state offers the statement by Bob as an adoptive admission by Carl and Don.

The statement should be admitted: Bob said Carl committed a crime, and the nature of that statement is such that Carl would have denied or disagreed if Bob were lying or mistaken, a point that is reinforced by the presence of acquaintances who might spread rumors or tell police. In silence, Carl made a tacit adoption of Bob's statement. Don responded verbally to what Bob said, and the response builds on and implicitly agrees with Bob. Hence Don too adopted Bob's statement.

b. Judge/jury role

Cases conflict on whether adoption is to be determined by the judge as an issue relating to admissibility of evidence under FRE 104(a), or by the jury as an issue relating to conditional relevancy under FRE 104(b). Most courts say the latter, which means the judge simply screens the proof to decide whether a reasonable person could find that the objecting party meant to agree with what was said. This approach may fail to provide adequate protection against the dangers of hearsay, at least where a statement has plausible factual content, since such a statement is clearly *relevant* even if the party against whom it is offered did not mean to agree to it. In the example above, a jury would likely consider Bob's statement to be evidence against Carl even if it thought that Carl did not mean to agree with it.

4. Authorized Admissions

When one person K authorizes another person L to speak, statements by L that are within the scope of his speaking authority are admissible against K. Under familiar substantive principles, K is a principal and L is an agent, and agency law would make what L says relevant in claims against K, and sometimes binding. If L were to negotiate deals on behalf of K, L's statements would be admissible as "verbal acts" in suits against K. Under FRE 801(d)(2)(C), much of what L says is admissible against K even if those statements were not verbal acts.

a. Authority

If the relationship between K and L requires L to speak in order to be effective, authority to speak is implied, and it does not matter that there is no additional indication that L is authorized to speak. Examples include brokers and lawyers. In other situations, the relationship does not necessarily bring speaking authority, and additional proof is necessary: Thus the spousal relationship does not imply authority by one to speak for the other.

b. Pleadings, briefs, argument

Unless amended, pleadings are binding on those who file them in that case, and procedural law produces this outcome without reference to the admissions doctrine.

i. Prior pleadings

Superseded pleadings and pleadings from other cases are generally viewed as authorized admissions by the person on whose behalf they were prepared. But when any such pleading represents an attempt by the pleader to take advantage of the procedural doctrine permitting alternative and inconsistent pleadings, exclusion may be warranted, lest the opportunity to plead in this manner be compromised. Answers to interrogatories are authorized admissions too, both in the suit in which they are filed and in later suits.

    ii.   Briefs, argument

A few cases apply the same principle to appellate briefs and even oral argument by lawyers, although considerations peculiar to context means caution is warranted.

    iii.   Requests to admit

Responses to requests for admission filed under FRCP 36 and its state counterparts are *inadmissible* in later actions. Such materials are *judicially binding* in the suit in which they are prepared, and excluding them from later suits represents an attempt to make this mechanism attractive and workable by limiting the risk to parties who file such admissions.

c.   **"Internal statements"**

Authorized admissions include so-called "internal statements," meaning conversations between the party and the spokesperson. Thus in suits involving K, what L says to K on the subjects within his authority are authorized admissions by K.

d.   **Personal knowledge**

As is true generally of admissions, authorized admissions do not require personal knowledge on the part of the speaker.

☞ EXAMPLE AND ANALYSIS

Broker Fran is authorized to sell a barn for owner Everett. Fran tells buyer Greg "the barn was built ten years ago." After the sale, the barn burns down. Greg sues Everett for breach of contract, alleging that the barn "was not built to code" because it lacked a sufficient sprinkler system. Everett claims the barn "was built 30 years ago and complied with the building requirements of that day." At trial, Greg proposes to testify to what Fran said, as proof that the barn was built ten years ago.

Fran's statement fits the exception when offered against Everett, even if Fran did not have personal knowledge of the construction date.

---

e. Independent evidence

Prior to *Bourjaily v. United States*, 483 U.S. 171 (1987), the rule was that speaking authority had to be proved by evidence apart from the statement itself. The problem with using the statement to prove the speaker's authority is that this use involves a circularity or bootstrapping problem (statement itself used to prove its own admissibility). In *Bourjaily*, however, the Supreme Court considered a similar situation, and said that a coconspirator statement could itself be used to prove the conspiracy that needs to be established to make the statement admissible, as long as there is independent evidence as well. Courts now apply the same logic to the present situation, and FRE 801(d)(2) was amended in 1997 to adopt this approach for authorized admissions, statements by agents or servants of a party, and coconspirator statements. As amended, this provision authorizes courts to consider the very statement being offered, although its content "does not by itself establish" authority, agency, or the existence of a conspiracy for purposes of these various parts of the admissions doctrine. Hence *some* additional or "independent" evidence is still required.

f. Judge and jury

In the common situation where the authority of the speaker affects the merits (as is true if Buyer sues Owner to enforce a deal negotiated by Broker, where Owner denies Broker's authority), both judge and jury address the question of authority. This "coincidence" of function raises sticky theoretical questions, but the prevailing approach is that the judge decides the authority question **solely to apply the admissions doctrine** and the jury then decides the same question **solely to decide the merits.**

5. Admissions by Agents and Employees

Traditionally, what an agent or employee said was admissible against his employer only if the employee had "speaking authority." Agents who act for their principal, and truck drivers and others whose work sometimes leads to accidents and suits against the employer (under the respondeat superior doctrine) might lack such authority, so what they said would not be admissible against the employer. Modern courts hold that speaking authority is unnecessary, so long as the employee or agent speaks on a matter that is within the scope of his duties. A truckdriver employed by Acme Company who comments to a bystander after an accident, "I ran a red light," is speaking an a matter within the scope of his duties, so what he said is admissible against Acme Company under this branch of the admissions doctrine. See FRE 801(d)(2)(D). Of course the truckdriver's statement is also admissible against him personally under FRE 801(d)(2)(A), so the statement could be offered against both the truckdriver and the company in the event that someone injured in the accident brings suit against both.

a. Reach of rule

In suits against employers, this principle is broad and crucial. It reaches statements that an alleged tortfeasor makes about his own conduct (truck driver says he was speeding), statements by a supervisor describing things done by people under her supervision, descriptions of a place or piece of equipment for which the speaker is responsible, and accounts of company practice or policy in areas of the speaker's responsibility.

b. Multiple hearsay

In discrimination suits, courts split on the question whether statements by Supervisor to Claimant describing what "someone else in the company said" about policies or employment decisions fit the exception when offered against the Company. Courts are concerned about multiple hearsay, even though it is plausible to suppose that Supervisor would not convey statements by people who lacked the requisite authority, and the exception could be invoked twice–once for what Supervisor said and again for the statement by "someone else" that the Supervisor conveys. See FRE 805. At least where it appears that Supervisor is communicating something that was given to him by a higher-up in the company, as is usually the case, most courts now admit the statement, which seems the right result.

c. Personal knowledge

While some have argued that personal knowledge should be required in the setting of statements by employees offered against their employers, a landmark modern case refused to adopt this requirement. See *Mahlandt v. Wild Canid Survival & Research Research Center, Inc.*, 588 F.2d 626 (8th Cir. 1978) (in suit against company that owned wolf, admitting statement by animal's keeper indicating that wolf bit child, despite fact that keeper lacked knowledge).

d. Independent evidence

As in the case of authorized admissions, courts traditionally required independent evidence to avoid bootstrapping, so the proponent had to offer other proof showing the employment and duties of the speaker. But the decision in *Bourjaily* (coconspirator statement can be used to prove the conspiracy that needs to be shown to make the statement admissible, as long as there is some independent evidence too) led to a change in FRE 801(d)(2), which now says that the very statement being offered must be considered, although it "does not by itself establish" employment or duties.

e. Judge and jury

As in the case of authorized admissions, where the authority of the speaker affects the merits (as would be true if an injured pedestrian sued Company for negligence of truck driver), both judge and jury address the question of authority. Again this "coincidence" or overlap of function raises sticky theoretical questions. Once again, under the prevailing modern approach, the judge decides the authority question **solely to apply the admissions doctrine** and the jury decides the same question **solely to decide the merits.**

6. Coconspirator Statements

In federal courts, this exception is invoked more than any other because there are so many drug conspiracy trials. See FRE 801(d)(2)(E).

a. Predicate facts

To invoke the exception against a criminal defendant, the prosecutor must show that (1) declarant and defendant conspired, (2) the statement was made during the pendency of the venture, and (3) the statement furthered the conspiracy.

i. Conspiracy

Usually the exception is invoked in cases that include charges of conspiracy, but the exception *can be invoked* even if no conspiracy charges are brought, if such charges are brought and dismissed, and even if such charges are pursued but they lead to acquittal.

ii. Pendency

Statements made before or after a conspiracy do not fit the exception. But statements made by conspirators before the defendant joined are usually admissible against him, on the theory that he adopted whatever was said or done before. Statements made by a conspirator after his arrest usually do not fit the exception when offered against other conspirators, but statements by conspirators still at large are usually admitted against an already-arrested member of the venture.

iii. Furtherance

Statements further a conspiracy if they seek to drum up business ("you can count on X to get what you need"), encourage continued adherence to the venture ("don't worry, we can count on X"), or keep conspirators abreast of developments ("X found a substitute pilot"). Statements made to undercover agents can satisfy the requirement too. The **purpose** of the speaker may be to further the venture even if they do not achieve that purpose (in other words the purpose of the speaker is enough), but statements knowingly made to police do not fit the exception.

b. Mere narrative

The exception does not reach "mere narrative" or "idle chatter" that do not somehow advance (at least seek to advance) the aims of the conspiracy. These are statements that fail the furtherance requirement.

c. Procedural issues

Under *Bourjaily*, judges determine the predicate facts of the exception despite the fact that one of the predicate facts (defendant and declarant conspired) usually coincides or overlaps with a question for the jury to decide. *Bourjaily* also holds that the preponderance standard applies, despite the fact that usually coconspirator statements are offered by prosecutors against criminal defendants. Finally, *Bourjaily* holds that in deciding the admissibility question the judge may consider the statement itself (despite the circularity or bootstrapping problem), although the Court did *not* say the statement itself would suffice to prove these points, and FRE 801(d)(2) was amended in 1997 to adopt in the Rule this part of *Bourjaily*, making it clear that contents of the statement itself "are not alone sufficient" to establish these points.

C. UNRESTRICTED EXCEPTIONS

These exceptions may be invoked regardless whether the declarant testifies or is available as a witness. These exceptions are set out in FRE 803. See generally M & K §§ 8.35–8.62 (5th ed. 2012).

1. Present Sense Impressions

These statements are considered reliable because the immediacy requirement reduces risks of memory loss and deception. See FRE 803(1). This exception, and also the next two (excited utterances and state-of-mind), rely on notions of spontaneity and grew out of the common law "res gestae" notion (statements should be admitted when they are closely connected with "what happened"). For present sense impressions, there are three requirements:

a. Immediacy

This requirement is strict: The statement must describe an act, event, or condition that happens or exists **at the moment of speaking**. A statement may fit the exception if it follows a fleeting event by a few seconds (the federal provision reaches statements "immediately thereafter"), but not minutes or hours.

b. Perceiving

The speaker must **perceive** what she describes. Usually that means "seeing," but many cases admit statements describing what the speaker has heard, and often what is described is a phone call.

c. Descriptive

The statement must **describe** an act, event, or condition. In the landmark case and modern origin of this exception, a woman commented to a man (as they were riding in a car together) that the people in a passing car must be drunk, and "we would find them somewhere on the road wrecked if they keep that rate of speed up." See *Houston Oxygen Co. v. Davis*, 161 S.W.2d 474 (Tex.Com.App. 1942) (admitting woman's statement to prove the manner of driving).

☞ EXAMPLE AND ANALYSIS

In the trial of Booth for murdering Ross, the state offers testimony by Regina that she telephoned Ross between 5:30 and 6:00 P.M. on the day of his murder, and that Ross told Regina that his friend Brenda was talking to "some guy" at the door. Other evidence indicated that Booth had gone to the house of a friend of Brenda's.

What Ross told Regina on the phone fits the exception: It was spontaneous, as the events were happening at the moment of speaking. It described those events at the very time when the speaker was perceiving them. See *Booth v. State*, 508 A.2d 976 (Md. 1986).

---

2. Excited Utterances

This traditional exception also rests on spontaneity and is crucial in paving the way for statements by accident and crime victims describing what has happened to them, and often the exception is applied to admit statements by victims of violent identifying or describing the perpetrator. Of course the exception also reaches statements by eyewitnesses (bystanders) who see such events and then describe them. See FRE 803(2).

a. External stimulus

The first requirement is a **startling or exciting event**. The idea is that such an event rivets the attention of the speaker, assuring personal knowledge and full perception.

b. Excitement

The requirement is that the speaker **must be excited** as he speaks. The idea is that the stress of excitement reduces or eliminates concerns over candor and draws the attention of the speaker to whatever is happening, and in fact rivets her attention on the events. The standard is subjective, but in practice a court cannot psychoanalyze the declarant. Instead, it decides whether a person like the declarant and in her position at the time would be excited under the circumstances. Indicators include demeanor, content of the statement, and nature of the event described. Unlike present sense impressions, which must be truly contemporaneous with what they describe, the excited utterance exception can reach statements that are made some minutes or even hours after the events described, provided that the speaker is indeed excited as she speaks.

c. Related to event

An excited utterance must **relate to an exciting act, event, or condition**, but the required connection is looser than what is required for present sense impressions (which must *describe* a contemporaneous act, event, or condition). A landmark decision in *Murphy Auto Parts v. Ball*, 249 F.2d 508 (D.C. Cir. 1957) approved a postaccident statement by a driver saying he "had to call on a customer and was in a bit of a hurry to get home." The reviewing court decided that the statement explaining the circumstances of the accident satisfied the relational requirement even though it did not describe the physical realities of the accident itself.

d. Proving agency

A statement fitting this exception can be used to prove the speaker was an agent for another (crucial in respondeat superior suits) and was acting within the scope of his agency. Statements by an alleged agent, offered on the theory that they are **admissions** by the principal, cannot prove agency by themselves because of the circularity or bootstrapping problem. The requirements for excited utterances do not include showing that the speaker was an agent for someone, so using an excited utterance to prove agency does not the same problem. In *Murphy Auto Parts,* supra, the excited utterance was offered for this purpose.

e. Procedural issues

The court decides whether the exception applies, which includes deciding whether an exciting event occurred. Some courts say that the court, in deciding this point, cannot rely on the statement itself because doing so would reintroduce the circularity or bootstrapping problem. The better rule, however, and the modern trend in decisions, is to allow the statement to be considered. Usually there is at least some additional evidence that something exciting happened, and the demeanor of the speaker or other aspects of her conduct at the time may indicate that she was excited, and so it is seldom necessary to rely on what the statement itself asserts to conclude that the speaker was excited.

3. State-of-Mind Statements (Includes Bodily Condition)

This exception also rests on spontaneity. It paves the way for statements describing existing physical condition, existing mental state as an end in itself, existing mental state as basis for drawing inferences about later behavior by the speaker, and facts about the speaker's will. See FRE 803(3).

a. Rationale

The theory is that each person is the best source of information on mental and physical states, that there is little or no risk of misperception, and that spontaneity tends to insure candor.

b. Present, not past

Apart from wills cases, there is an important limit: Statements must show **existing mental or physical states**, not past states. Thus the exception reaches the statement "My head aches," but not "Three days ago I had a headache." And it reaches the statement "I intend to go to Chicago," but not "Last week I hoped to get to Chicago." In the nature of things, however, Wednesday's state of mind (or aches and pains) may carry forward to Friday or backward to Monday. As indicated below, statements admitted under the exception as reflecting Wednesday's state of mind (or aches and pains) are only *sometimes* allowed to support *past* (backward-looking) inferences about Monday, but usually *are* allowed to support *future* (forward-looking) inferences about Friday.

c. Existing physical condition

Statements describing ailments, pains, and injuries fit the exception. They don't need to be made to a doctor.

i. Reasonable past inference

Statements that prove present physical condition can support some inferences about the past: If X says at noon "My arm broke in the crash, and I can't move it," the exception permits use of the statement to prove X was not practicing the violin at 11 A.M. Absent proof that X was fine at 11 A.M. and broke his arm later, this conclusion is a deduction from knowing his condition at noon. But as noted below, statements cannot be admitted under the exception to prove *prior* acts, events, or conditions. Hence the exception does not allow use of the statement to prove X was in a crash, which depends on the fact that the statement mentions a crash, and cannot be a deduced from knowing his condition at noon.

ii.   Future inferences

If a statement tends to prove present mental or physical condition, using it to draw inferences into the future is generally allowed. What X said could be used to show he didn't practice the violin that afternoon, or for some time thereafter.

d.   Mental state: Issues of form

All agree that the exception reaches statements describing mental states expressly or by necessary implication: "I intend to go to Chicago" or "I'm not going to deal with Acme any more" or "I'm afraid of Bob" clearly fit, when offered to prove the mental states they describe. Courts disagree on whether the exception reaches fact-laden statements when offered to prove mental condition. The following examples tend to prove the same states of mind, but *in form* they simply assert facts: "My boss told me to go to Chicago," "Acme sells inferior merchandise," "Bob says he's going to kill me." Courts that refuse to apply the exception to such statements might still admit them as *nonhearsay circumstantial evidence* of state of mind, subject to objections under FRE 403 for potential prejudice.

e.   Mental state: Facts remembered

As shown by these fact-laden examples, mental states tend to form around and reflect acts, events, or conditions. If the exception reached statements offered to prove such points, it would swallow the hearsay doctrine: Every statement could prove mental state, which could in turn prove any acts, events, or conditions it reflected. To avoid this result, this use of the exception is not allowed. See *Shepard v. United States*, 290 U.S. 96 (1933) (statement by victim saying her husband "has poisoned me" should not have been admitted to prove her will to live; jury could not confine its consideration to this issue, and using statement to prove *cause* of mental state would put "an end, or nearly that, to the rule against hearsay"). See also FRE 803(3) (exception does not reach statements offered to prove a "fact remembered or believed").

f. Mental state as end in itself

Whether it is the intent of a criminal defendant, the mental state of customers who are discouraged from patronizing a business, or fear in an extortion victim, statements describing mental state fit the exception.

g. Mental state: Later conduct

One way to prove a person did something is to prove he intended to do it. Under what is usually called the *Hillmon* doctrine, the state-of-mind exception can be used in this way. If the question is whether Y went to Chicago on Monday afternoon, proof that on Monday Y said "I'm going to Chicago this afternoon" could be used to prove the point.

i. *Hillmon* case

In *Mutual Life Ins. Co. v. Hillmon*, 145 U.S. 285 (1892), a beneficiary of policies on the life of John Hillmon sued the insurance carriers to collect. The question was whether a body found at Crooked Creek was that of Hillmon or Adolph Walters. The companies claimed Hillmon and Walters went west from Wichita, and that Hillmon and another killed Walters to collect on Hillmon's policies. The companies offered letters from Walters to his fiancée and sister saying he was "going [west] with a man by the name of Hillmon," who "promised me more wages than I could make at anything else." The Court approved. The letters were "competent not as narratives of facts" nor as proof that Hillmon "actually went away from Wichita," but the letters could be used to show Walters "had the intention of going, and of going with Hillmon, which made it more probable both that he did go and that he went with Hillmon."

ii. Construing *Hillmon*

Narrowly read, *Hillmon* means only that statements of intent can prove *later conduct by the speaker*, which is noncontroversial. Broadly read, *Hillmon* could mean that what *one person* (Walters) said can be used to prove what *another person* (Hillmon) did *with* the speaker. This use violates the principle that statements offered under the exception cannot prove prior acts, events, or conditions. The reason is that what Walters wrote in his letters only proves what Hillmon and Walters did together if the letters are taken as proof that the two had previously discussed their plans and agreed to travel together. The ACN to FRE 803(3) comments cryptically that the *Hillmon* doctrine "allowing evidence of intention as tending to prove the doing of the act intended is . . . left undisturbed," but a House

Report says that FRE 803(3) limits the *Hillmon* doctrine by allowing use of statements admitted under the exception only to prove the *declarant's* future conduct, and "not the future conduct of another."

iii. *Alcalde* case

In many cases, including *People v. Alcalde*, 148 P.2d 627 (Cal. 1944) and *United States v. Pheaster*, 544 F.2d 353 (9th Cir. 1976), *cert. denied*, 429 U.S. 1099 (1977), a murder victim tells another, shortly before being killed, that he or she is going to meet the defendant. In *Alcalde*, the murder victim told a friend she was going out with Frank (defendant), and in *Pheaster* the victim of a kidnapping (who was later murdered) commented, shortly before disappearing forever, that he "was going to meet Angelo" (defendant). Both cases approved use of these statements. In *Alcalde*, however, Justice Traynor argued in dissent that this use of the exception was improper. And the opinion in *Pheaster* (which was tried before the Federal Rules took effect) is ambiguous, since it might be interpreted to mean that under the Rules this use of the exception would be *improper* (and the judge was right to admit the letters *only* because the Rules were not yet in effect).

iv. Modern compromise

Perhaps because statements describing the intent of the speaker to meet another seem highly probative, and in cases like *Hillmon*, *Alcalde*, and *Pheaster* the speaker is dead and better proof of what happened is in short supply, courts are reluctant to exclude such statements. And of course state courts are not bound by the limiting language of the House Report mentioned above. On facts similar to *Alcalde* and *Pheaster*, some courts continue to admit such statements, see *State v. Terrovona*, 716 P.2d 295 (Wash. 1986). And there are signs of a modern compromise, under which such statements are admitted if there is other proof of the behavior of the second person or some other reason to think the contemplated events happened. See *People v. James*, 717 N.E.2d 1052 (N.Y. 1999) (admit such statements only if, among other things, there is "independent evidence of reliability" and proof that the future acts "were at least likely to have taken place"). See also *United States v. Annunziato*, 293 F.2d 373 (2d Cir.) (famous opinion admitting statement by company president that union leader called and asked for bribe; forward-looking statement of intent is more reliable as proof of past fact that motivates speaker than as proof that speaker later acted as he intended), *cert. denied,* 368 U.S. 919 (1961).

h. Statements of fear by murder and extortion victims

Another difficult situation arises when victims of murder or extortion have told others that they are afraid of the defendant. Such statements may simply report fear ("I'm afraid X is going to kill me") or may be fact-laden statements in which the speaker indirectly says he is afraid ("X keeps threatening to kill me").

i. Prejudice, misuse

Fact-laden statements are challenging because the asserted facts are relevant (threatening behavior makes it more likely that defendant committed murder or extortion). But even statements that just report fear suggest that defendant did something threatening to cause the fear. These points raise concerns over unfair prejudice because the jury cannot properly use such statements to draw inferences about what defendant did. Courts can exclude such statements under FRE 403 for this reason.

ii. Exclude in murder cases

In murder cases, courts usually exclude such statements because the victim's state of mind is not an element of a charge or defense. That state of mind is still relevant because it suggests that defendant behaved in a hostile or threatening manner, and nonhearsay evidence of fear (proof that victim always fled when defendant appeared) would be admissible to prove that defendant behaved in this way. But statements indicating fear are usually excluded because the state-of-mind exception cannot properly support inferences from the victim's statement to the defendant's conduct. However, such statements are sometimes admitted if defendant claims self-defense or that the victim committed suicide or died from accidental causes (these defenses make the state of mind of the victim relevant in itself).

iii. Extortion cases

Here courts usually admit statements of fear by the victim because part of what the state must prove in order to get a conviction is that the victim was afraid of the defendant. Hence proving the victim's state of mind becomes more important.

iv. Wills cases

In wills cases, statements by the decedent are admissible to prove not merely state of mind, but acts, events, and conditions relating to a will. Special language in FRE 803(3) *exempts* wills cases from the general prohibition against using state-of-mind statements to prove facts "remembered or believed." Thus statements by the decedent can explain references in a will ("my wife" means Shirley), and they can show that the decedent executed (or revoked) a particular document and where and when he did, and such statements can prove behavior by members of his family that might bear on the question of undue influence. In this setting, the state-of-mind exception is an open-ended provision, allowing use of the decedent's words to prove state of mind, later conduct, previous conduct, and conduct by others.

4. Medical Statements

At common law, there has long been an exception for statements by patients to treating physicians describing the history and present nature of symptoms and feelings. The exception rested on the idea that patients seeking medical help are motivated to speak carefully and accurately. In its modern formulation in FRE 803(4), the exception is broader: It reaches not only statements made for **treatment,** but statements made for **diagnosis,** which paves the way for statements to a doctor hired only to testify (no treatment given). The reason for this expansion is that doctors who testify are allowed to rely on such statements, and often the statements come out as part of the basis for opinion testimony, so it was thought that juries should not be asked to try to limit their consideration of such statements as evidence merely of the basis for the opinion. Some states continue to adhere to the common law principle, under which statements to a physician who only diagnoses the patient do not fit the exception.

a. First requirement: Condition or symptoms

Unlike the state-of-mind exception (where statements must describe *present* conditions), the medical statements exception reaches statements describing present condition or symptoms, *and* their history and cause, *and* past symptoms relating to the present symptoms or conditions. As set forth in FRE 803(4), the exception expressly embraces statements relating to "past or present" symptoms and "their inception or their general cause."

b. Second requirement: Medical purpose

The statement must be made for the purpose of obtaining treatment or diagnosis.

c. Third requirement: Pertinent

The statement must be pertinent to the treatment or diagnosis sought. This limit excludes statements ascribing fault or blaming others. See ACN to FRE 803(4) (statements ascribing fault "would not ordinarily qualify").

d. By, to whom

While the exception envisions statements by the patient to her doctor, it applies more broadly. For instance, it can reach statements by parents describing the history and symptoms of a child, statements by Good Samaritans who bring an injured person to a hospital from an accident scene, statements to admitting clerks and emergency room personnel, and statements by one doctor to another.

☞ EXAMPLES AND ANALYSIS

1. In a suit arising out of a car-bus accident, plaintiff offers testimony by his own treating physician that plaintiff said the accident happened "when the bus ran a red light and sideswiped me in the intersection."

The reference to the red light would be excluded as a statement ascribing fault. (The statement that plaintiff was hurt when his car was sideswiped might fit the exception, as a description of the cause of his injuries).

2. In a suit against an employer for a leg injury, plaintiff offers records of his doctor to show that he hurt his ankle while negotiating rusted-out steps at work.

While it is arguable that he has described the history and cause of his injury, it is also arguable that the reference to work, and even to the rusted-out steps, go beyond what a doctor would need to know in treating a leg injury. Most courts exclude such statements when offered to support claims that an injury was sustained at the workplace. See *Rock v. Huffco Gas & Oil Co., Inc.*, 922 F.2d 272 (5th Cir. 1991).

e. Child abuse cases

In child abuse cases, courts are split on the question whether the exception may be used to identify the abuser. Decisions permitting this use of the exception often comment that effective treatment depends on separating the victim from her abuser (often a member of her household), so in that sense the identity of the abuser relates to treatment. See *Blake v. State*, 933 P.2d 474 (Wyo. 1997) (stressing "special character of diagnosis and treatment" in such cases). Decisions barring this use of the exception argue that identity of the abuser is simply irrelevant to medical treatment, and essentially reject the idea that adequate psychotherapy depends on this point, arguing that this standard would pave the way to admit any and every statement under the exception. See *Commonwealth v. Smith*, 681 A.2d 1288 (Pa. 1996) (disapproving this use of the exception). Those jurisdictions in the former category got a boost when the Supreme Court refused to condemn this use of the exception. See *White v. Illinois*, 502 U.S. 346 (1992) (rejecting constitutional challenge in case applying state version of exception to admit statements identifying babysitter as abuser).

5. Past Recollection Recorded

This exception complements the trial technique of refreshing memory described in Chapter 9. The difference is that the exception for past recollection recorded paves the way for prior statements by a testifying witness as proof of what they assert, while refreshing memory allows use of prior statements (by the witness or others) only for the purpose of enabling the witness *now* to describe what she had forgotten. For the federal version of the exception for past recollection recorded, see FRE 803(5).

a. First requirement: Insufficient memory

The exception applies only when the witness cannot remember, which means that the examining lawyer can resort to the exception only if she first tries but fails to refresh the recollection of the witness. It is not necessary to show total loss of memory, and forgetting a single point should be enough to justify use of the exception to prove that point.

Example.   Eyewitness describes an automobile accident but says she does not remember who had the green light. Shortly afterwards, she made and signed a statement that she gave to a police officer saying "the light was green for the Jeep Cherokee." At trial her lack of memory about the light justifies admitting this part of her statement, assuming other requirements of the exception are met.

b. Second requirement: Correctly reflect memory

The statement must correctly reflect memory that the witness once had. Typically police officers and insurance adjusters persuade witnesses to sign statements that contain accuracy clauses ("This statement truthfully and accurately reflects what I saw and know"), but the exception contemplates *trial testimony* that the statement accurately reflects what the witness once knew. Since she has forgotten at least something about subject matter of her statement, she may not be sure whether it accurately reflects memory that is now gone. Courts usually accept testimony that "I remember making sure that the statement was accurate," and some courts accept a general claim that "I wouldn't sign anything that was false."

c. Third requirement: Made or adopted

The witness must have **made** the statement herself, or **adopted** a statement prepared by another. There is no signature requirement, and a writing made by the witness can fit the exception even if it is unsigned. When a writing is prepared by someone other than the witness, an indication of adoption (typically a signature by the witness) is necessary. The exception also reaches recorded statements.

d. Fourth requirement: Made while memory fresh

The statement must have been made while the matter was **fresh in the mind** of the witness, but there is no hard-and-fast time limit. It is not necessary that the statement be made contemporaneously with events, or within moments of their occurrence. Factors that count are the relative importance of the event in the life of the witness and indications of care in preparing or crafting the statement (like corrections in something drafted by another).

e. Jointly produced statements

Sometimes one person sees or hears something and conveys a description to another person, who writes it down. In a bank robbery case, for example, a Good Samaritan may see the culprits drive off and might describe the car or provide the license number to the bank guard, who writes down what he's told. Or two people might take an inventory of supplies or equipment, where one person actually examines the scene and gives a count and description of what's there, which the other person then records. Here the exception can apply, but both participants are needed to lay the foundation: One person must testify that he lacks memory that he once had, and that he accurately conveyed what he knew while it was fresh. The other person must testify that he accurately recorded what he was told.

f. Not taken to jury room

Past recollection recorded substitutes for live testimony, and probative force is directly connected with the credibility of the witness. Hence most courts do not allow the writing itself to be taken to the jury room. See FRE 803(5) (writing may be read to jury, but "may be received as an exhibit only if offered by an adverse party").

6. Business Records

This critical exception is very broad: It reaches not only inventories and personnel records, but memoranda describing business meetings, driver logs, accident reports, and records of medical procedures and patient care. It reaches not only ledgers and other writings, but also computer databases.

a. Requirements

Most jurisdictions impose four requirements. These are designed to insure trustworthiness, but it is recognized that most business records are in some sense self-serving, and this fact does not alone disqualify them.

i. Regular business; regularly kept record

The exception applies only to **business** records that are **regularly kept,** not to personal records (checkbooks, mileage logs, diaries kept for personal reasons). Business is defined broadly: It reaches one-person operations (also records an employee keeps in connection with his job, like a waiter's tip tally), professions (like medicine and law), and companies and corporations. It reaches charitable institutions, even illegal activities like gambling. Key factors are an **ongoing enterprise** that follows a **routine.** The exception reaches only records that are routinely made, which means that records must be made on a repetitive basis, like daily or weekly or every time an event occurs, by people acting in regular course of their work.

ii. Source with knowledge

The source of what is recorded must have personal knowledge and must be acting in the course of employment. The exception embraces layered hearsay (information passed along a chain of people or among an array and ultimately recorded in the document offered), but the source must be a person who saw or observed what has been recorded.

iii. Contemporaneity

When a record reflects an event, like the temperature of a patient or medication administered, the record must be made close to the time of that event. Reports made long afterwards that summarize transactions do not fit the exception because they fail this requirement. But this requirement does not block use of computer output generated long after information has been entered into memory (so long as the entering process satisfies the requirement) nor does it block investigative findings analyzing, for instance, the cause of an accident (although accident reports are sometimes excluded as untrustworthy).

iv. Foundation testimony or certificate

Invoking the exception requires testimony by someone who knows how the record was prepared (FRE 803(6) speaks of testimony by the "custodian or another qualified witness"), or a certificate (meaning affidavit) by such a person. See FRE 902(11) and (12) allowing the foundation for business records to be established by certificate. Ideally the foundation witness (or the person who makes the certificate) is someone who actually helped prepare the record and can describe how it was made, but courts accept less-than-the-ideal, and it usually suffices that the witness (or person who signs the certificate) has "circumstantial knowledge" and can describe the routines and steps involved in preparing similar records, even if he knows nothing about the record being offered and even if he was not employed when the record was made.

☞ EXAMPLE AND ANALYSIS

A police officer investigates an accident, examining the scene and gathering information from eyewitnesses. He writes up an accident report, which is later offered in evidence to prove what happened.

Insofar as the report rests on information from eyewitnesses, it does not satisfy the requirement that the source must be a person employed by the business having personal knowledge and acting in regular course. Eyewitnesses may get it right, but there is no routine that helps insure that they will, and they are not subject to the performance pressures of the workplace. See *Johnson v. Lutz*, 170 N.E. 517 (N.Y. 1930) (classic case refusing to apply exception in this situation). Under the Federal Rules, police accident reports should be analyzed as public records under FRE

803(8). In civil cases an accident report can satisfy the latter exception insofar as it reflects the opinion of the officer, which brings it within FRE 803(8)(A)(ii). Insofar as it rests partly on what eyewitnesses say, the report can fit FRE 803(8)(A)(iii). But many jurisdictions refuse to admit such reports under either their business records exception or their public records exception, sometimes because of express language blocking such material.

b. Multiple hearsay

When a business record sets forth information provided by an outsider, it may be admissible if a second exception is available that covers what the outsider said. (For police accident reports, usually no exception covers what eyewitnesses relate, although the excited utterance exception might apply if the officer appears quickly.) In three common situations, such piggybacking is often possible, although other problems may appear.

i. Hospital and doctor records

Records prepared by hospital personnel or doctors in their office practice may contain information provided by outsiders. Sometimes the outsider is the patient: What he tells doctors or hospital personnel may fit the medical statements exception if it is germane to diagnosis or treatment, see FRE 803(4). If the record is offered against the patient himself, anything he says fits the admissions doctrine, see FRE 801(d)(2)(A). Sometimes the outsider is a doctor in another office or hospital: Her statements may also fit the medical statements exception (she is helping diagnose or treat the patient), and her own record for the patient is a business record too. If a hospital or doctor routinely records such information from the patient or another doctor, then both levels of hearsay are covered. The record can prove what the outsider said (patient or other doctor), and what the outsider said can prove whatever it asserts.

☞ EXAMPLE AND ANALYSIS

Bob sues Dixon Clothiers, a retail store, for personal injuries he claims to have sustained in a slip-and-fall accident on the premises. He alleges that a greasy substance on the floor caused his fall, but Dixon denies negligence and contends that Bob never fell in the store. Bob dies from unrelated causes before trial, and his surviving spouse Amy is substituted as plaintiff. A medical record prepared by Bob's treating physician Clark contains an entry indicating that "Bob presented with back pain, apparently caused by a fall on a greasy floor at Dixon Clothiers as he ran through the store." If Amy offers the Clark record to prove place and cause, can Dixon exclude it as hearsay? If Dixon offers the Clark record to prove Bob was running, can Amy exclude it as hearsay?

There are two levels of hearsay: The first level is the Clark record itself, which is hearsay if offered to prove what Bob said (the record is Clark's statement that Bob told him something). For this purpose, however, it fits the business records exception if Clark routinely records patient accounts of their injuries because they aid in diagnosis or treatment, regardless which side offers the record. The second level of hearsay is Bob's statement, and here it matters who offers it. When offered by Amy, Dixon's hearsay objection will be sustained. At least when the records are offered to prove where Bob was hurt and negligence on the part of Dixon, most courts hold that the medical statements exception does *not* apply to what Bob said because (1) it ascribes fault and (2) the place of injury is not relevant to diagnosis or treatment. When offered by Dixon, Amy's hearsay objection will be overruled. Some courts would say Bob's statement fits the admissions doctrine because he is in privity with Amy or should be viewed as a party even after his death because he is the one who originally brought the suit. Others would say his statement fits the against-interest exception because it undercuts his claim against Clark (and of course he is unavailable as a witness). See FRE 804(b)(3).

---

ii. **Entries based on records of another business**

Often one business incorporates into its own records the content of records from another business. As indicated above, hospitals and doctors may record information from doctors in other hospitals. Invoices or packing lists that accompany shipments may become the basis for entries in the records of the recipient. Both levels of hearsay are covered, in effect, by applying the business records exception twice. Both theory and sound practice require foundational testimony for both records, but courts sometimes make do with foundation testimony only from the second business.

iii. **Hotel registration**

When a guest registers at a hotel by writing his name and address, the hotel's record rests on outside information. If the record is offered to prove some person X stayed at the hotel, no obvious exception covers the guest's statement that he is X. Notions of authentication and hearsay overlap: Handwriting analysis might confirm that guest was X, and the hearsay issue would all but vanish. But without such proof, using what the guest says to prove that he is X and that it is X who registered would be hearsay. Still, some modern courts accept such evidence if the clerk verifies identity by asking the guest for identification. Most clerks simply take a credit card imprint, and arguably this too should suffice. But it is hard to square this result with the demands of the hearsay doctrine. See generally *United States v. Lieberman*, 637 F.2d 95, 101–102 (2d Cir. 1980).

c. Trustworthiness factor

Records that satisfy the objective requirements may still be excluded if they are untrustworthy. This doctrine recasts the logic of *Palmer v. Hoffman*, 318 U.S. 109 (1943), which held that an accident report, prepared by a railroad after its train killed a motorist at a grade crossing, was inadmissible in the surviving husband's wrongful death suit, on the ground that the business of a railroad is railroading, not investigating accidents. *Palmer* could be read to mean the exception reaches only records that are central to the commercial purpose or as creating a per se rule excluding accident reports. Instead, *Palmer* has been read as a general caution against untrustworthy material.

i. Factors that count

Courts usually refuse to apply the exception to records prepared in anticipation of litigation, and when they contain important mistakes or contradictions, or reveal shortcomings in method. Other factors that bear on the inquiry are (a) importance of the record apart from litigation, (b) other uses to which record is put, (c) presence or absence of motives to fabricate among those involved in preparing the record, (d) involvement in or independence from the dispute generating the suit, (e) simplicity versus complexity of the matters recorded, (f) training and experience of preparers, and (g) whether record is offered by or against the entity that prepared it (when offered *against* the preparer, it may fit the admissions doctrine and is in any event more likely to be received).

ii. Self-serving

A famous comment in the opinion of the Court of Appeals in *Palmer* remarked that a rule excluding self-serving records would effectively destroy the exception (even a grocer's account book would not fit), so the trustworthiness standard does not require exclusion merely because a record or entry is in some way self-serving.

iii. Burdens

Under standard principles, the *proponent* must show the specific requirements of the exception are met. The objecting party bears the burden of raising the trustworthiness issue and of showing that a record that satisfies the specific criteria should be excluded anyway. See FRE 803(6) (records qualify when they meet objective criteria and neither "the source of information" nor "the methods or circumstances of preparation" indicate untrustworthiness).

iv. Accident reports

Many cases exclude accident reports, especially in settings like *Palmer* where the preparer offers the report in defense against negligence claims. But sometimes courts admit accident reports, even in this setting. See *Lewis v. Baker,* 526 F.2d 470 (2d Cir. 1975) (in railroader's personal injury suit, admitting personal injury report prepared and offered by railroad; court stresses that federal agency requires such reports, and that they are filed every month).

v. Internal investigations

When a business undertakes an internal investigation into problems in the workplace, the resulting report is likely to contain multiple hearsay, as the person (or team) assigned to investigate and write the report talks to people in the know. If a company routinely prepares such reports, or hires an outsider to prepare the report and the outsider routinely prepares such reports, the report itself might fit the business records exception insofar as it reports what others in the company have said. But statements by these others (themselves witnesses to the events being investigated) usually do *not* satisfy the requirement of being made in routine of business, although they are likely to fit the exception for authorized admissions because the company is likely to authorize its employees to cooperate in the investigation. See FRE 801(d)(2)(C). Consequently, such reports may well be admissible when offered *against* the company but not when offered *by* the company. Compare *Norcon v. Kotowski,* 971 P.2d 158 (Alaska 1999) (admitting against defendant company an internal report on incidents of sexual harassment, combining exceptions for business records and admissions) with *Bean v. Montana Board of*

Labor Appeals, 965 P.2d 256 (Mont. 1998) (excluding report prepared and offered by employer, which determined that employee engaged in misconduct; exception did not apply because report was prepared in anticipation of litigation).

d. Absence of records

When an act, event, or condition would normally generate an entry or record, evidence that no such entry or record exists is some proof that the act or event did not occur or the condition did not exist. For reasons similar to those underlying the business records exception itself, there is also an exception for proving the absence of such records. See FRE 803(7).

7. Public Records

Under modern formulations of this exception, public records are admissible to prove the activities of a public office or agency, matters observed and reported under official duty, and certain investigative findings. Unlike the business records exception, which is bounded by specific criteria, the modern formulation of the public records exception contains general descriptive phrases and "use restrictions" limiting the admissibility of public records as evidence against defendants in criminal cases. See FRE 803(8).

a. Activities of office or agency

Public records may be used to prove almost anything public agencies do—serving papers, issuing tickets or citations, disbursing checks, erecting signs or monuments, hiring and firing people, buying, selling, or maintaining equipment, and so forth. See FRE 803(8)(A)(i) (public records may prove "the office's activities").

b. Matters observed

Public records may be used to prove things like temperature and weather conditions, building code violations, geographical features, and prices of commodities studied or regulated by the government. See FRE 803(8)(A)(ii) (public records may prove "matters observed while under a duty to report").

i. Inside sources

Like the business records exception, this provision requires the source of information to be someone within the organization (here a public agency or office). Clause A(ii) does not reach information supplied by citizens.

ii. **Use restriction**

Clause B has a use restriction blocking use of public records in criminal cases to prove "matters observed by law-enforcement personnel." While this language bars all use of such records, clearly the main concern was to block the government from offering such records against the accused. See further discussion of criminal cases below.

c. **Investigative findings**

Public agencies and hearing officers conduct studies over a wide range of subjects, and the exception may be used to prove the results of such studies. Included are reports on the nature, causes, and spread of diseases, on product safety, on discrimination in housing or workplace, on incidence of crime, on educational attainments, and so forth. See FRE 803(8)(A)(iii) (public records may prove "factual findings from a legally authorized investigation").

i. **Factual findings**

The phrase "factual findings" invites an interpretation that excludes "evaluations" or "conclusions." But in *Beech Aircraft Corp. v. Rainey*, 488 U.S. 153 (1988), the Court interpreted the language broadly, citing the "analytical difficulty" in distinguishing facts from conclusions and telling courts to focus on trustworthiness. *Rainey* approved a report that power rollback caused a military training plane to crash.

ii. **Outside sources**

Unlike material covered by clause B, investigative findings can rest on information gleaned from sources outside government, whether gathered in field investigations or in hearings. The point, however, is to admit *official findings*, not simply the findings or conclusions of outsiders who testify or give information to the government.

iii. **Use restriction**

Clause A(iii) has a use restriction blocking use against criminal defendants of public reports containing investigative findings (clause A(iii) applies "a civil case and against the Government in a criminal case"). See further discussion of criminal cases below.

d. **Civil cases**

The use restrictions do not apply in civil cases. Here public records can prove the full range of points described above.

☞ EXAMPLE AND ANALYSIS

After working for a manufacturer of airplanes, Sara is diagnosed with a serious neurological ailment. She sues American Plastics, which makes the resin her employer uses in the planes, alleging that fumes from the resin caused her ailment. She offers an OSHA report describing conditions in her factory that contains data on resin fumes, and a CDC study indicating that such fumes can cause the ailment from which she suffers.

Both these reports fit the public records exception. Defendant might hope to exclude them under the trustworthiness clause (discussed below), but the expertise of the agencies in the subject areas makes such a challenge difficult. If the methods underlying the CDC study failed the *Daubert* standard, the defense might exclude it on that ground. If the defense could show the data underlying either report were inadequate, such a showing might also lead to exclusion. The *Daubert* standard is discussed in Chapter 11.

e. Criminal cases

The use restrictions implement special concerns to protect defense confrontation rights under the Sixth Amendment.

i. Police reports

A landmark decision interprets the restriction in clause A(ii) broadly. The restriction bars reports of matters observed by "law-enforcement personnel" and the decision concludes that this language applies to a Customs Service chemist who conducted a laboratory analysis of white powder seized from defendant and determined that it was heroin. See *United States v. Oates*, 560 F.2d 45 (2d Cir. 1977) (restriction covers officers/employees of any governmental agency "which has law enforcement responsibilities"). *Oates* has been followed, and the holding is realistic in recognizing that investigative personnel who work with prosecutors and police have a motive to secure convictions. Admitting their hearsay would undercut confrontation rights.

ii. Investigative findings

The use restriction in clause A(iii), covering factual findings resulting from an investigation, states that this provision may only be invoked in civil cases and "against the Government" in criminal cases.

iii. *Crawford Doctrine*

The concerns over the limits imposed by the Confrontation Clause, which led to the restrictions in the public records exception described above, proved providential. In *Crawford v. Washington*, 541 U.S. 36 (2004), the Court largely threw out the existing approach to the Confrontation Clause, and adopted a new standard under which "testimonial" hearsay cannot be offered against the defendant. *Crawford* indicates that "testimonial" hearsay includes statements by eyewitnesses to investigating officers describing crimes, and almost certainly the category also reaches police reports. But *Crawford* also stated emphatically that the Confrontation Clause would not stand in the way if the declarant was subject to cross-examination about his statement in prior proceedings, or if the declarant testifies at trial and can be cross-examined about his statement at that time. Hence objections based on the Confrontation Clause would largely disappear if, for example, a police officer who prepared a report also testifies at trial. The impact of the Confrontation Clause is discussed in Chapter 5 of this Outline. Under the Rules, however, testifying at trial would *not* change application of the public records exception: Even when the officer testifies at trial, FRE 803(8) does not pave the way to use of the officer's report against the accused.

☞ EXAMPLE AND ANALYSIS

Frank is charged with burglarizing a grocery. Police write a report describing the scene. The report says the safe was opened rather than blown. It describes clues about the perpetrator, including a work glove found by the safe and footprints where he entered. The report says, on the basis of employment records and statements by the owner, that Frank was employed at the store. Finally, the report says that, according to the owner, only Frank and two others had the combination.

The report is inadmissible against Frank. Insofar as it describes the crime scene and clues found there, clause A(ii) applies. Since police prepared the report, the use restriction bars its use against Frank. Insofar as the report asserts that Frank worked at the store, it states an official conclusion resting on outside information (statements by the owner and records). Clause A(ii) cannot apply (Frank's working there is not "a matter observed"), and this part of the report must be analyzed under clause A(iii) (Frank's working there is a "factual finding"). The use restriction in clause A(iii) blocks use of the report against Frank (investigative findings are only admissible in civil cases or against the government). Insofar as the report conveys the claim by the owner that only Frank and two others knew the combination, the report restates third-party hearsay rather than official findings. This part would not qualify under clause A(ii) because it does not state matters observed by police, and it does not qualify under clause A(iii) because it does not state an official conclusion. This part could not be admitted even if there were no use restrictions.

As interpreted in the *Crawford* case, the Confrontation Clause also requires exclusion of the police report, although objections based on the Confrontation Clause would fail if the officer who prepared the report testifies at trial and is subject to cross-examination about the report. This fact, however, would not open the door to admit the report under the public records exception.

---

iv. Routine and nonadversarial reports

When police reports reflect routine and nonadversarial observations, the concerns underlying the use restriction in clause A(ii) recede. Such reports are not prepared with a motive to build a case against a defendant, and we can be more confident about the objectivity of police. The alternative may be testimony that would not be better or more reliable than the reports themselves. In what amounts to a judge-made exception to the use restriction in clause A(ii), courts admit even police reports that contain routine and nonadversarial observations. See *United States v. Orozco*, 590 F.2d 789 (9th Cir.) (admitting computer data generated by customs official at border crossing between California and Mexico indicating that car owned by defendant crossed back and forth on night when he told agents he was on double date in Los Angeles), *cert. denied*, 439 U.S. 1049 (1978).

f. Nature of use restrictions in FRE 803(8)

There is good reason to interpret the use restrictions in clauses A(ii) and A(iii) not merely as limits on the exception, but as exclusionary principles. If they were only limits on the exception, prosecutors could offer official records and reports against a criminal defendant if they fit another exception, such as the one for business records.

i. The *Oates* holding

In *Oates*, the court considered the question whether a laboratory report, which would be excluded under the use restrictions in clause

A(ii) or A(iii), could be admitted under the business record or catchall exceptions. *Oates* concluded that the use restrictions were exclusionary principles, and when they apply the government cannot resort to other exceptions. See *United States v. Oates*, 560 F.2d 45 (2d Cir. 1977).

ii. *Oates* **may be too broad**

Oates seems right in restricting easy access to other exceptions, but may be too broad in interpreting the use restrictions as barring resort to all other exceptions, for two reasons.

In the first place, some authorities approve use of the exception for past recollection recorded: This approach is realistic because even a live witness may forget important points in such reports, and using this exception assures the defense a witness who can be cross-examined.

In the second place, some specific exceptions authorize courts to admit public records that might also be embraced by the broader terminology of clauses A(ii) and A(iii) and by the use restrictions. Hearsay covered by such narrow and specific exceptions is admissible against defendants. See FRE 803(9), covering records of vital statistics (births, deaths, marriage).

iii. **Specific state statutes admitting lab reports**

Because of the limitations of FRE 803(8) with respect to admitting lab reports, as illustrated by *Oates*, most states enacted special statutes that override their state counterparts of FRE 803(8) and specifically allow the admission of lab reports. These statutes typically provide either that **prosecutors must, if defendants raise the point, call the technician who prepared the report** or that **defendants are entitled to call the technician who prepared the report.**

iv. *Crawford Doctrine; Melendez–Diaz*

The limitations implemented by the *Oates* decision are also mandated by the Confrontation Clause as interpreted in *Crawford v. Washington*, 541 U.S. 36 (2004). *Crawford* requires exclusion of "testimonial" statements unless the declarant was cross-examinable at trial or in prior proceedings.

In *Melendez–Diaz v. Massachusetts*, 129 S.Ct. 2527 (2009) the Supreme Court held that lab reports are testimonial and may not be admitted unless the prosecution makes a lab technician available for cross examination. Thus a state statute that puts the burden on the defendant to call the lab technician is unconstitutional.

In *Bullcoming v. New Mexico*, 131 S.Ct. 2705 (2011), the Court again considered the impact of *Crawford* on the use of forensic lab reports. *Bullcoming* involved use of gas chromatography to measure blood alcohol content, and the state offered a report prepared by the state chemist who conducted the test, along with testimony by a lab supervisor who had nothing to do with the test itself. This procedure violated defense confrontation rights, the majority held. In *Bullcoming*, however, four Justices dissented and one (Justice Sotomayor) offered a concurring opinion that may limit the reach of the decision. The case did *not* entail, Justice Sotomayor wrote, a test conducted for "an alternate purpose" (such as providing medical treatment), nor did it involve testimony by someone who had "a personal, albeit limited, connection with the tests," not did it involve testimony by an expert offering his own "independent opinion" about the results of the test under FRE 703, nor did it involve use of "only machine-generated results, such as a printout from a gas chromatograph." When any such factors appear, Justice Sotomayor's opinion suggests, the confrontation issue might be resolved the other way, and the fact that four other dissenters would not have excluded the testimony offered in *Bullcoming* increases the likelihood that one or more of these factors could lead to admitting lab reports along with testimony by someone not involved in their preparation.

g. Trustworthiness factor

As in the case of business records, even public records that satisfy the specific criteria may still be excluded if they are untrustworthy. The trustworthiness proviso in FRE 803(8) could be read to apply only to investigative findings in clause A(iii), but it probably applies to clauses A(i) and A(ii) too.

i. Factors that count

Investigative findings may be excluded as untrustworthy if underlying testimony or evidence does not suffice to support the conclusions or if delay or shortcomings in methodology appear, and courts have excluded public records prepared in anticipation of litigation. According to the ACN, factors that count in the trustworthiness calculus include skill or expertise of an office or agency, whether a hearing was held and how careful or thorough it was, possible motivation problems, and timeliness of the investigation.

ii. Burdens

Under standard principles, the *proponent* must show that the specific requirements of the exception are met. The objecting party bears the burden of raising the trustworthiness issue and showing that a record that fits the specific criteria should be excluded anyway. See FRE 803(8) (records qualify when they meet specific criteria unless "sources of information or other circumstances indicate" untrustworthiness).

8. Learned Treatises

Modern practice allows limited use of learned treatises (like medical texts) as proof of what they assert. Under FRE 803(18), a treatise may be used to the extent it is "called to the attention" of an expert on cross or to the extent the expert relies on the treatise "in direct examination," *if* the treatise is shown to be "reliable authority" by the testimony of the witness or by "other expert testimony" or judicial notice. This development is a departure from common law tradition, where treatises were background that could be used only on cross to impeach experts.

a. First factor: Authoritative

To fit the exception, a treatise must be "reliable authority." The purpose here is not to limit the exception to works like maps and almanacs that report universally accepted and elemental data, but rather to prevent the mere fact of publication from being determinative. This element may be established even by an expert who disagrees with the treatise on important points. The exception reaches standard works like the Merck Index of Chemicals and obscure works like a treatise on Industrial Oil and Fat Products.

b. Second factor: Attention, reliance

Under the exception, treatises must be offered in conjunction with expert testimony. Whether the proponent seeks to satisfy this requirement by showing the expert relied on the treatise or by calling it to her attention on cross, the important thing is to prevent a hide-the-ball approach and insure that the expert's view on the pertinent passage is made known, or at least can be made known if the adverse party considers it appropriate.

9. Minor Exceptions

In addition to these important exceptions, many minor exceptions have long been recognized. Here are some of the more useful exceptions in this lesser list:

a. Absence of entries or records

For both business and public records, related exceptions cover the absence of records or entries. See FRE 803(7) (absence of business record or entry) and 803(10) (absence of public record or entry). Reliability is insured by the requirement that regular records or entries be made, so the absence of such record or entry becomes itself a reliable indicator.

i. Use

These exceptions are used to show an act or event did not occur, or a condition did not exist, that would generate a record or entry if the contrary were so. They may also be used to show that no record or entry was made, which may be important in itself.

ii. Manner of proof

Absence of public records may be proved by a certificate indicating that a search was made and nothing was found. Absence of a business record or entry may be proved by testimony or by offering related material, from which the relevant omission can be detected.

b. Vital statistics

Complementing the public records exception is a narrower one for "vital statistics," reaching records of births, deaths, and marriages reported to a public office by legal requirement. See FRE 803(9).

c. Family records, statements, certificates

Three exceptions cover statements about family history and events. There is a family records exception covering statements about family history recorded in Bibles, genealogies, charts, and so forth. See FRE 803(13) ("an engraving on a ring, inscription on a portrait, or engraving on an urn or burial marker"). There is another exception for birth, marriage, and baptismal certificates. See FRE 803(12). And if the speaker is unavailable, yet another exception reaches statements about his own family history or relationships. See FRE 804(b)(4).

d. Property records and documents

Narrow exceptions cover dispositive property documents (deeds, easements) and recorded property documents. These rest on the notion that the serious matters reflected in such documents, and the care expected in their preparation and execution, suffice to make them trustworthy on the points they recite. See FRE 803(14) (recorded documents) and 803(15) (dispositive documents).

e. Ancient documents

Age does not establish the reliability of a document, but does provide assurance that it was written before the forces generating the litigation came into play. Age also brings a relative scarcity of living memories that could generate reliable testimony. At common law, ancient meant 30 years or more, but the modern rule cuts the time to 20 years. See FRE 803(16).

f. Commercial lists

This exception covers commercial catalogues and published market reports when offered to prove points like selling price. The exception also reaches city directories (that list names, addresses, phone numbers) and mortality and morbidity tables (expected lifespans, survival rates with disease). See FRE 803(17).

g. Reputation

Reputation evidence is admissible in three areas. One exception covers reputation among family members on birth, adoption, marriage, relationship, ancestry, and similar matters. See FRE 803(19). Another exception covers reputation in the community relating to boundaries or customs affecting lands, provided that the reputation arose before the controversy. See FRE 803(19). A third very broad exception reaches reputation "among a person's associates in the community" relating to one's "character." See FRE 803(21). It is the latter provision that paves the way to prove conduct by means of character under FRE 405, in the situations allowed in FRE 404, and to prove points relating to "truth and veracity" under FRE 608. In these settings, the fact that "reputation" evidence is actually hearsay, for which an exception is needed, is usually overlooked entirely.

h. Court judgments

Judicial decrees are operative documents that may be used in the proceedings that generate them without any need for a hearsay exception. Final judgments also have res judicata and collateral estoppel effects, and these aspects of judgments also require no aid from a hearsay exception. In other situations, however, judgments may be merely evidence of some point, and hearsay exceptions are needed if they are to operate in this manner.

i. Felony convictions

One exception covers felony convictions, when offered to prove what FRE 803(22) calls "any fact essential" to the judgment. An old decision in *Kirby v. United States*, 174 U.S. 47 (1899), held, in a trial for receiving stolen property, that a conviction of another for theft could not be used to prove the property was stolen. To accommodate *Kirby*, FRE 803(22) has language barring use of the exception against defendants to prove convictions of others, except when such convictions are used to impeach.

ii.   Judgments relating to history or boundaries

Another narrow exception covers judgments when offered to prove matters of "personal family" history or "general history" or "boundaries," whenever "reputation" evidence would also be admissible on such points. See FRE 803(23). This provision complements FRE 803(19)–(21), and rests on the idea that judgments are at least as reliable on such points as reputation.

D. EXCEPTIONS: DECLARANT UNAVAILABLE

A small group of exceptions paves the way to admit hearsay if the declarant is unavailable as a witness. In effect these exceptions depend less on trustworthiness and more on necessity, conceived to mean that without the exception the court would have to do without whatever the declarant knew. See FRE 804(b).

1.   Unavailability Defined

What is crucial is the unavailability of *testimony* by the declarant on the "subject matter" to which her prior statement relates. See FRE 804(a). It doesn't matter whether she herself can be brought into court, or whether she testifies on other subjects. She is unavailable, even if present and even if she testifies on other points, if her testimony on points covered by her prior statement cannot be had. Note that being unavailable does not by itself make her prior statement admissible as proof of what it asserts. The statement must *still* fit one of the exceptions that require unavailability.

a.   Exempt by privilege

If a declarant takes the stand and successfully claims a privilege blocking questions on the subject matter of her prior statement, she is unavailable under FRE 804(a)(1). This provision contemplates actually calling her, and hearing and ruling on her privilege claim. Advice from counsel that she would claim a privilege is usually insufficient. But where a prosecutor offers against several defendants a statement by one of them, calling the declarant is unnecessary and would indeed be improper (prosecutors may not even call a defendant).

b. Refuses to testify

Simple refusal to testify makes a declarant unavailable under FRE 804(a)(2). Again the proponent is usually expected to go through the motions: Declarant is called; her testimony is sought; she refuses; the court instructs her to answer and warns her that refusal puts her in contempt. (Actually holding her in contempt is not necessary.)

c. Lack of memory

When a declarant testifies that he lacks memory on the subject matter of a prior statement, the modern trend is to consider him unavailable with respect to that subject matter. See FRE 804(a)(3). If a witness said "the light was red for the truck" and at trial he testifies that he "doesn't remember what color the light was," he is unavailable for purposes of that subject, and what he said before may be admitted *if* it fits one of the exceptions contained in FRE 804(b). The fact that the witness remembers *making a statement* does not change the result. He is still unavailable if he does not remember the facts (what color the light was).

d. Death, physical or mental illness

Obviously death makes a declarant unavailable. So does physical or mental illness, if shown by the proponent of the statement, except that courts sometimes prefer to defer decision on the matter if it appears that the declarant may be able to testify later in the trial. See FRE 804(a)(4).

e. Unavoidable absence

If the proponent tries unsuccessfully to find and serve the declarant, or if she is beyond reach of subpoena, she is generally considered unavailable. Ordinarily in state court the subpoena power runs statewide in both civil and criminal cases. In federal courts, the subpoena power normally runs statewide in civil cases (FRCP 45(b)(2)(C) extends federal subpoena power as far as state court subpoena power extends), plus 100 miles from the courthouse ("bulge service" extends federal subpoena power that far even if the end point is outside the district or state), and nationwide in criminal cases. See FRE 804(a)(5), under which this form of unavailability is complicated by three additional points:

   i. Inviting, bringing in witness

   Even if the declarant cannot be subpoenaed, some jurisdictions require the proponent to show that *additional efforts* were made to produce him, such as inviting him and offering travel expenses. See FRE 804(a)(5) (declarant unavailable if he cannot be brought in by subpoena or "other reasonable means"). In practice, this requirement is invoked most often against prosecutors, both because they may have the means to take such steps and because of sensitivity over the confrontation rights of the accused.

ii. Constitutional dimension

The Supreme Court has held that prosecutors have a constitutional duty to bring the declarant to court, rather than offering her prior testimony. This duty is of uncertain dimension, but it may require more than FRE 804(a). Compare *Barber v. Page,* 390 U.S. 719 (1968) (in state criminal trial, error to admit preliminary hearing testimony by witness incarcerated in federal prison in nearby state; defendant was not represented by counsel in preliminary hearing; state could have sought federal cooperation to obtain the witness at trial) with *Ohio v. Roberts,* 448 U.S. 56 (1980) (defense called witness in preliminary hearing and engaged in "functional equivalent" of cross; witness had left state and disappeared; Court approves use of her preliminary hearing testimony even though state might have taken further steps to locate her by calling social worker who had contact with witness in distant state).

iii. Deposition preferred

A little-cited proviso in FRE 804(a)(5) requires the proponent, as a condition of invoking most of the exceptions in FRE 804(b), to show that he could not bring the declarant, *and* could not obtain his "testimony" in another form (meaning mostly deposition). If noticed and taken seriously, this proviso would force proponents to try to take the deposition of a declarant in preference to offering his statement under one of the exceptions contained in FRE 804(b)(2), but if the declarant has disappeared or refused to cooperate in other ways, it is doubtful that anything would be gained by forcing the proponent to go through the motions of trying to subpoena the declarant for a deposition or trying to get the declarant to testify if he has refused to do so in another setting. In any event, the proviso is seldom invoked.

f. Procurement or wrongdoing

When a declarant is unavailable because of conduct by one of the parties, remedial measures may be appropriate. Clearly a party who engages in misconduct to make a declarant unavailable should not be able to take advantage of this stratagem. See FRE 804(a) (blocking resort to exceptions contained in FRE 804(b) when "procurement or wrongdoing" by the proponent made the declarant unavailable).

i. **Proponent's misconduct**

If the **proponent** kills a declarant, or threatens or bribes such a person and thus persuades him to evade process or refuse to testify, it is common doctrine that the proponent cannot invoke one of the exceptions normally triggered by unavailability. Sometimes lesser forms of misconduct prevent prosecutors from invoking hearsay exceptions, see *Motes v. United States*, 178 U.S. 458 (1900) (unconstitutional for government to use former testimony exception when declarant escaped custody because of official negligence), but refusing to grant use immunity (which would overcome a claim of privilege against self-incrimination because committing not to use what a witness says means he no longer has that privilege) does not have this effect.

ii. **Adverse party's misconduct**

A hearsay exception adopted in 1997 paves the way to admit, *against* a party who has "wrongfully caused" or "wrongfully acquiesced in causing" a declarant to be unavailable, any statement made by the declarant, if the intent of the wrongdoer was to make the declarant unavailable to testify. See FRE 804(b)(6), discussed further below.

2. Former Testimony

This exception paves the way for statements that are most like trial testimony: It reaches former testimony given in a trial, hearing, or deposition in which the declarant was sworn and examined. See FRE 804(b)(1). There are three requirements:

a. First requirement: Unavailability

The exception applies only if the declarant is unavailable at trial. A proviso in FRE 804(a) says a party who offers statements under other exceptions in FRE 804(b) must show *both* that declarant's trial testimony is unavailable *and* that his deposition could not be taken. But a party who offers statements that fit the former testimony exception need not show the declarant's deposition could not be taken. The idea is that one kind of former testimony is as good as another.

b. Second requirement: Hearing or proceeding

Prior trials of the same or another case satisfy the "hearing or proceeding" requirement. So do preliminary hearings and grand jury proceedings, and almost any trial or pretrial hearing in which live testimony is taken. Administrative hearings also satisfy the requirement. See FRE 804(b)(1) (language does not require "judicial" hearing or proceeding).

c. Third requirement: Opportunity and motive for prior cross

Oversimplifying slightly, the key requirement is that the party *against whom* former testimony is offered had "opportunity and similar motive" in the prior proceeding to cross-examine the declarant. Actual cross is not required. "Similar motive" means the motive to cross-examine the declarant now is similar to the motive to cross-examine in the prior proceedings. The idea behind this element (the key to the exception) is that if there was opportunity and similar motive to cross-examine, we can be sure that mistakes and falsehood in the testimony would have been exposed in the prior proceedings.

d. Issues and parties

At common law, the third requirement was framed in *structural* terms: An identity of issues and parties was necessary, the notion being that prior testimony could be admitted *only if* the issues and parties were the same in the proceeding in which the testimony was given and the later proceeding in which it was offered. Only then could one be confident that the party hurt by the testimony either tested the witness in the prior proceeding or forswore the chance because the witness got it right. The prevailing modern view favors a *functional* approach allowing more flexibility, see FRE 804(b)(1), under which some changes in parties and issues do not affect application of the exception, but others do.

i. Changes in issues

Adding or subtracting issues between a first and second trial should not require exclusion of testimony from the first trial, when offered in the second, in cases where this change in issues would not lead to different motivations or strategies in challenging the testimony. But if motivation or strategy in the second trial would differ because of such changes, the first-trial testimony should be excluded.

ii. Adding and subtracting parties

A similar observation applies to changes in parties. Adding a party to the second trial, or subtracting one who had been in the first trial, makes no difference if the testimony in the first trial (now being offered in the second) does not relate to or bear in any way on the claims or defenses made by the party in the second suit against whom the testimony is offered. But if the contrary is true, then the motivation or strategy of a party who would challenge the testimony may itself change between one trial and the other, and the testimony should be excluded.

☞ EXAMPLES AND ANALYSIS

1. In his criminal trial for sexually assaulting Helen in June, Greg claims consent. The state calls Ike, who testifies that he and Greg, along with Helen and others including Laura, had pizza at a restaurant before Greg and Helen left together. Later Ike dies in a plane crash. Still later Greg is tried for selling cocaine to Laura in July. In his drug trial, Greg testifies that he never met Laura. Invoking the former testimony exception, the state offers Ike's testimony from the sexual assault trial to prove the contrary.

   Greg objects, and should prevail. In his sexual assault trial, Greg had no incentive to refute Ike's testimony that Laura was in the group at the restaurant, even if that testimony were false. The issues in the drug trial are completely different, and here he does have an incentive to refute what Ike said about Laura's presence at the restaurant.

2. While driving his car with Oscar, Ned collides with a Ford truck driven by Roger, in which Sally was a passenger. Ned sues Roger and Ford Motors. He alleges that Roger was negligent and the truck had a design defect, in the form of a blind spot caused by the rearview mirror design that kept the driver from having an adequate view of the passing lane. Called by Ned, Sally testifies that (a) Roger was talking with and looking toward her as he pulled into the passing lane at the time of the collision, and (b) when she drove the truck she had trouble seeing enough of the passing lane through the mirror to know when it was safe to enter that lane. On cross, Roger tries to get Sally to admit that he glanced into the rearview mirror and over his left shoulder before pulling into the passing lane. After trial, Sally moves permanently to France. Oscar brings a second suit, only against Roger, seeking recovery for injuries in the accident. In this suit, Oscar invokes the former testimony exception and offers Sally's testimony. Roger objects.

   Roger probably cannot exclude Sally's testimony that he was looking toward her when he pulled left into the passing lane, since Roger had as much motive and incentive in the first suit as he would have in the second to attack and refute this point on cross. The fact that Ford was named in the first suit but not the second would not make any difference. But Roger has a good argument to exclude Sally's testimony on the adequacy of the mirror: This point had only a small bearing on the question whether Roger was negligent, and Roger might have counted on Ford to attack this part of Sally's testimony in the first suit, thus not pursuing it himself.

e. Use against new parties

For the most part, the exception can only be invoked against someone who *was a party* in the prior proceeding in which the testimony was given. Only on rare occasions can the exception be invoked against new parties, who did not participate in the prior proceedings.

i. Philosophical dispute

Some argue that the exception should be available for use against someone who was not party to the prior proceedings, if some other party to those proceedings had similar motive and opportunity to test the witness. Others argue that it is unfair to saddle someone with strategic decisions made by another, even if the other had similar motive and opportunity to attack the testimony.

☞ EXAMPLE AND ANALYSIS

Business partners JB Wright and JC Wright lose their building to fire. JB Wright is charged with arson, and Eppler and Brown testify that he hired them to burn the building. Insurance carriers then sue JB and JC Wright for a declaratory judgment of nonliability on their fire policies because of the arson. Eppler and Brown invoke their privilege against self-incrimination and refuse to testify. The carriers offer their testimony from the arson trial. JB Wright does not have a good objection (as defendant in the arson trial, he had motive and opportunity to attack Eppler and Brown). But is the testimony admissible against JC Wright?

A famous pre-Rules case held that it was: In the arson suit, JB Wright had "the same interest and motives" that JC Wright had in the second suit, so the standard requiring "substantial identity of parties and issues" was satisfied. See *Travelers Fire Ins. Co. v. Wright*, 322 P.2d 417 (Okla. 1958). If the case arose under FRE 804(b)(1), the question would be, not whether JB had the same opportunity and motive to cross-examine in the first trial as JC would have in the second trial, but whether he was a predecessor in interest of JC. A strong argument can be made that he was.

ii. **Congress decides**

The Federal Advisory Committee favored a broad exception. Early drafts did not require the party against whom the exception was invoked to have been a party in the prior proceedings. Congress would not go along, and added new language: As enacted, FRE 804(b)(1) is available only against someone who was a party in the prior proceedings, or whose "predecessor in interest" was a party, with similar motive and opportunity to cross-examine.

iii. **"Predecessor in interest"**

Congress didn't spell out what it meant by that phrase, but apparently the purpose was to require a close or formal connection of some sort. By one reading, the phrase embodies a property concept similar to the idea of "privity," which means a grantor of property is the predecessor in interest to her grantee. By a broad reading, the phrase means "community of interest" in which a party to the prior proceedings is a "predecessor" to a party in the present proceedings if the former represents the interests of the latter. See *Lloyd v. American Export Lines, Inc.*, 580 F.2d 1179 (3d Cir. 1978) (in license revocation proceedings against seaman L, Coast Guard was predecessor in interest to seaman A; proceedings against L arose from a shipboard altercation between L and A, and there was sufficient "community of interest" between Coast Guard and A to satisfy "predecessor in interest" requirement), cert. denied, 439 U.S. 969. But unless representation requires an "official" or "formal" nexus, this broad interpretation would read "predecessor in interest" out of the Rule, since any prior party could be said to "represent" a later party merely by having the same motive to attack the prior testimony.

iv. *Wright* **reconsidered**

Under the *broad* reading of the "predecessor in interest" proviso described above, arguably JB Wright (in the EXAMPLE AND ANALYSIS described above) had the same interest in testing and refuting the testimony of Eppler and Brown in the arson trial as JC Wright would have in the second suit against the insurance carrier, and this testimony from the arson trial would be admissible in the second suit. Under the *narrow* reading, arguably the same result would be proper because JB and JC Wright are in "privity" because they both own the building.

☛ EXAMPLE AND ANALYSIS

After a plane crash, the surviving wife of passenger X sues Airline for wrongful death. The case goes to judgment favoring the Airline, and crucial witness J, whose testimony helped establish that the Airline was not negligent, dies. Now the surviving husband of passenger Y sues the Airline, which offers J's testimony from the first suit.

Reading "predecessor in interest" to mean "privity" means J's testimony must be excluded because the new plaintiff did not succeed to any property interest owned by the prior plaintiff. This reading is probably the right one. Reading the phrase to mean "community of interest," J's testimony could either be (a) admitted because both plaintiffs have the same interest or motivation to prove the negligence of the airline, or (b) excluded because the first plaintiff does not represent the second in any formal or official sense. There is occasional support for this approach, but it is a minority view.

f. Depositions

The civil and criminal rules provide that depositions may be offered at trial if the deponent is unavailable. The former testimony exception applies to depositions too. See FRE 804(b)(1) (mentioning depositions taken in the "current" or a "different" case). In these three places, however, the stated requirements differ slightly, and depositions should be admissible if they satisfy the governing standards in any of these three sources.

☛ EXAMPLE AND ANALYSIS

In a workplace accident suit against an equipment maker, the defense deposes an eyewitness who provides an account suggesting that the accident was caused entirely by plaintiff's misuse of the machine. The eyewitness dies, and the defense offers his deposition at trial.

Under FRCP 32(a)(3), the deposition of a witness may be used at trial "for any purpose" if the witness is dead. Nevertheless plaintiff objects, arguing that he lacked "similar motive" to develop the testimony at the deposition, as required by FRE 804(b)(1), because "depositions are for gathering information, not resolving factual issues or impeaching witnesses." Plaintiff should lose this objection because the deposition satisfies FRCP 32, even if plaintiff's argument about motive were accepted.

g. Preliminary hearing testimony

In criminal cases, preliminary hearings determine whether there is "probable cause" to believe defendant committed an offense. If so, trying him is appropriate; if not, the charges should be dismissed. It is recognized that preliminary hearings function as a discovery device for defendants, who learn much about the prosecutor's witnesses and testimony. If a witness who testifies in a preliminary hearing disappears, or becomes otherwise unavailable at the time of trial, sometimes his testimony from the preliminary hearing is offered at trial, usually by the prosecutor against the defendant (which makes sense because usually only the prosecutor calls witnesses who testify at preliminary hearings, and most of these witnesses testify favorably for the prosecution), but sometimes by the defense (some such witnesses surprise the prosecutor and testify favorably for the defense).

i. Offered against defendants

In practice, courts scrutinize state efforts to use preliminary hearing testimony against defendants at trial, rigorously enforcing the unavailability requirement and sometimes expressing concern on the question whether defendants are actually motivated to test witnesses in this setting on cross. The reason is that defendants expect the witnesses will testify live at trial, and defendants don't want to tip their hand during preliminary hearings. Moreover, the only question at the preliminary hearing is "probable cause," and defendants usually cannot get the case "kicked" at this time. Hence some courts are unwilling to admit such testimony, when offered against defendants, although other courts *do* admit it. *Compare State v. Erickson*, 241 N.W.2d 854 (N.D. 1976) (admitting preliminary hearing testimony against defendant) with *People v. Smith*, 597 P.2d 204 (Colo. 1979) (excluding). While the Supreme Court has upheld the use of preliminary hearing testimony against defendants at trial, when this use was challenged as violating the Confrontation Clause, the Court emphasized that the defendant had *actually* cross-examined the declarant, and of course stressed as well that she was unavailable. See *Ohio v. Roberts*, 448 U.S. 56 (1980) (declining to say that *mere opportunity* to cross-examine would suffice, and stressing that defense engaged in "functional equivalent" of cross-examination).

ii. Against the prosecution

Much the same considerations apply in the unusual case where the *defense* offers preliminary hearing testimony against the prosecution.

While the prosecuting attorney has an interest in developing the testimony of such a witness, still the only question for the hearing is "probable cause," and even a vigorous defense attack is unlikely to be so devastating that the case is dismissed, so the prosecutor does not really have a forceful interest in protecting the witness. See *United States v. Bartelho,* 129 F.3d 663 (1st Cir. 1997) (no error to exclude such testimony, when offered by the defense).

☞ EXAMPLE AND ANALYSIS

In a robbery trial, the state offers testimony given by Sandra in the preliminary hearing. She is the only eyewitness who places defendant Ron at the scene, but has moved to another state to a known address and could not be subpoenaed to attend the trial. Ron was represented in the preliminary hearing, but did not cross-examine Sandra. He objects at trial, claiming (a) the prosecutor must try harder to obtain her live testimony, and (b) the exception does not apply because Ron lacked motive or opportunity to cross-examine before.

Ron should prevail on the first point. The state should take steps to bring Sandra in and offer travel money if necessary. FRE 804(a)(5) requires "reasonable means" beyond subpoena, and Sandra is so important that these steps should be taken. Admittedly the situation in *Barber v. Page,* 390 U.S. 719 (1968) was worse for the defense (no counsel at the preliminary hearing, thus no chance for cross), but *Barber* still means the prosecutor has a constitutional obligation that is not bounded by the subpoena power. In *Ohio v. Roberts,* 448 U.S. 56 (1980), where the defense engaged in the equivalent of cross in the preliminary hearing, the Court still recognized the state's duty to find and produce the witness at trial and only excused the state because she could not be located. But Sandra *can* be located.

On his second claim, Ron will stress that the question in the preliminary hearing was probable cause to think he committed the offense, hence that there was no point in attacking credibility and no incentive to cross-examine. As noted above, jurisdictions split on this point.

---

h. Grand jury testimony

Grand jury testimony does not fit the exception when offered against defendants because the defense cannot cross-examine during (or even attend) grand jury proceedings. But if a grand jury witness testifies at trial, the prosecutor can sometimes use his grand jury testimony as substantive evidence: That testimony may fit FRE 801(d)(1)(A) (sworn inconsistent statement in proceedings under oath; witness can *now* be cross-examined about his statements) or qualify as past recollection recorded under FRE 803(5) (transcript of what the witness said can be admitted if reporter and witness together satisfy requirements of exception).

i.   **Offered against state**

Prosecutors have a good argument that they lack incentive, in the grand jury setting, to cross-examine the witnesses they call. Grand juries serve the same purposes as preliminary hearings—deciding whether there is probable cause to think defendant committed the crime, so he should be tried for it. If there is enough testimony incriminating the defendant, the fact that a witness says exculpatory things won't much matter because the grand jury won't resolve the conflict and should indict. The cases are split: Compare *United States v. DiNapoli*, 8 F.3d 909 (2d Cir. 1993) (indictment had already been obtained when witness testified, so no incentive to cross-examine) with *United States v. Lester*, 749 F.2d 1288 (9th Cir. 1984) (admitting, but court has room for discretion, depending on its appraisal of government's motive and interest in cross-examining).

ii. *Salerno* **case**

In *United States v. Salerno*, 505 U.S. 317 (1992), the Supreme Court ruled against an effort to get grand jury testimony favorable to the defense admitted against the government. The defense argued that because the government refused to immunize the witness (which would have made him available to testify at trial), notions of "adversarial fairness" should block the government from arguing lack of motive to cross-examine during the grand jury proceedings, and that the government should "forfeit" the protection of that requirement. The Court rejected this argument out of hand, and signaled that the requirements of the exception are to be strictly applied even when defendants offer grand jury testimony. (*DiNapoli*, which is cited above, is actually the *Salerno* case on remand.)

3. Dying Declarations

This exception paves the way for statements by a person who knows he is dying and describes the cause or circumstances of his death. At common law, this venerable exception was designed to admit the last words of a victim in the homicide trial of his alleged killer, and usually the exception could be applied only in this setting.

a. Rationale

A moral or religious reluctance to die while speaking a falsehood was thought to provide an assurance of trustworthiness, but in a secular modern age many reject this idea. The unavailability of the speaker provides an element of necessity. Also, it is singularly unattractive to exclude the dying words of a crime victim, and this notion clearly plays a role in the exception.

b. Modern version

Under FRE 804(b)(2), the exception applies in homicide prosecutions and in civil cases as well. Technically, the declarant need not be dead, since other forms of unavailability suffice, and it is at least theoretically possible for one to believe he is dying and to make a statement describing the situation, but yet recover and be unavailable at trial for some entirely different reason.

c. Elements

Apart from unavailability, the two important elements are a settled expectation of imminent death and a statement "concerning the cause or circumstances." See FRE 804(b)(2).

i. Settled expectation

The speaker must believe death is imminent and unavoidable. It is not enough that the declarant knows he has a terminal illness, nor is it enough that he knows he is seriously at risk. It suffices, however, if he thinks death is moments away (as seriously injured victims of crime or accidents may know) or thinks death is certain to come in a few hours or days (as terminally ill patients may know). Proof of this settled expectation may be made by using statements made to the dying person ("you know you can't survive much longer, so tell us now"), by descriptions of his condition (bleeding, labored breath, semi-conscious), or by statements of the declarant himself ("I know I'm dying," or "look after my spouse when I'm gone").

ii. Concerning cause or circumstances

The statement need not describe physical cause of death or injury ("he stabbed me in the chest with a knife"). It suffices that the statement "concern" the cause or circumstances ("Bob snuck up on me from behind, and we were fighting"). Usually these statements identify the assailant in some way.

4. Against–Interest Statements

Until the last quarter of the twentieth century, this exception covered only statements against pecuniary or proprietary interest. Now the Federal Rules and most states recognize a broader exception that also reaches **statements against penal interest**, and most modern cases involve this use of the exception. See FRE 804(b)(3).

a. Rationale

The idea is that one does not usually concede a point that causes one harm or loss unless the point is true. Unavailability of the speaker provides an element of necessity.

b. Admissions doctrine distinguished

The instant exception has an against-interest requirement and an unavailability requirement that the admissions doctrine does not have. Usually the against-interest exception is used for statements by nonparties, but the admissions doctrine reaches only statements by parties (or by their employees, speaking agents, or coconspirators).

c. Requirements

There are two (and sometimes a third): First, the declarant must be unavailable. Second, the statement must be against her interest, and she must *understand* that it is (a subjective standard). Third, for statements against penal interest offered in criminal cases under FRE 803(b)(3), there must be "corroborating circumstances" (a point examined below). Often the unavailability requirement is satisfied (at least with statements against penal interest) when the declarant claims his privilege against self-incrimination, or because he is dead or cannot be found and brought to court. The against-interest element may appear in the facial meaning and presumed understanding: If one says "I killed the President," or "I owe my landlord the rent for April," there is little doubt that what is said can satisfy the against-interest requirement and little doubt that the declarant understands as much. Here the requirement should be considered satisfied unless other facts show the requirement is not met, despite surface appearance.

d. Meaning of against interest

The meaning of the central requirement of the exception is problematic for four main reasons having to do with **context, conflicting interests, collateral points,** and the problem of **facts versus statements** being against interest.

i. Context

Even more than most, the against-interest exception depends on context. Facial meaning is sometimes enough because the fact asserted implicates the speaker in a crime ("I killed the President"). But usually facial meaning does not settle the matter for two reasons. First, a statement may be against interest even though facial meaning does not indicate as much. Suppose the FBI questions the speaker in New Orleans in December about the assassination of the President in Dallas on November 22, and he says, "I was in Dallas from November 18th to the 23rd." In context, the statement could well be against interest even though nothing on its face suggests as much. Second, context may show that *what seems on its face* to be against interest really is not: If this speaker had said "I was involved in a bank robbery in New York on November 22nd," his statement seems on its face to be against interest, but the requirement is not satisfied if he was trying to create an alibi to avoid capital charges for killing the President in Dallas on the same date by confessing to a lesser crime.

ii. Conflicting interests

Unfortunately "interest" is not a unitary concept, and often a person has more than one interest, some of which conflict. When multiple interests appear, the court should compare and weigh them, and admit the statement if it seems to give up more than it gains, if the interest served by the statement is smaller than the interest lost or disserved.

☛ **EXAMPLE AND ANALYSIS**

Depositor claims Bank wrongly paid money from an account on the signature of Depositor's daughter. Bank freezes the account unless Depositor signs a paper saying the payments were proper. She signs and later dies. In surviving husband's suit to recover money paid, Bank offers Depositor's statement.

It should be excluded if Depositor's main interest was to get the balance of the account rather than preserve claims against Bank. Factors that bear on the question are the amount paid versus the remaining balance, the Depositor's need for immediate funds, and the strength or weakness of the claim for wrongful payment. See *Demasi v. Whitney Trust & Sav. Bank*, 176 So. 703 (La. App. 1937) (depositor was uneducated and had already lost a suit against the bank to recover;

she had taken an appeal when she signed the paper; the hope for reversal might suggest that her statement was against interest because it might be offered against her in a second trial, but reversal was not a likely enough prospect to warrant the conclusion that her statement was against interest; the paper she signed did not satisfy the exception).

---

iii. Fact versus statement

Usually "against interest" means **the fact asserted** is against interest, as is true with "I killed the President" because killing the Preisdent is a crime. If the fact asserted is against interest, usually **the statement of the fact is against interest too:** The statement "I killed the President" is against interest because the statement could help convict the speaker of a crime. The exception can be rationalized by against-interest elements in *either the statement or the fact.* Sometimes courts focus mostly on the statement, and sometimes they focus mostly on the facts. Compare *United States v. Barrett,* 539 F.2d 244 (1st Cir. 1976) (admitting statement "Bucky wasn't involved; it was Buzzy" to prove Buzzy committed theft; statement showed speaker had "insider's knowledge" of criminal plot) with *United State v. Goins,* 593 F.2d 88 (8th Cir. 1979) (admitting statement to off-duty policeman friend, even if it did not subject declarant to prosecution in a real or tangible way; people usually admit crimes only to those they trust).

e. **Pecuniary or proprietary interest**

Statements can satisfy the exception by admitting facts that would tend to prove tort liability, conceding misbehavior that might cost the speaker his job or opportunity for advancement, conceding indebtedness or tax obligations, conceding that claims owed by the declarant have been satisfied, or by conceding that another person owns property.

☛ EXAMPLE AND ANALYSIS

A warehouse burns down in an early morning fire apparently caused by a discarded cigarette. The next day Frank, who is employed by the company leasing the warehouse, tells a fire inspector that he and others were on the premises the previous night drinking and smoking. In a civil suit by the building owner against the lessee to recover for loss of the building, plaintiff offers what Frank told the inspector.

Since the statement suggests that Frank might have started the fire, and subjects him to a risk of civil liability and loss of employment, it satisfies the against-interest requirement. See *Gichner v. Antonio Troiano Tile & Marble Co.*, 410 F.2d 238 (D.C. Cir. 1969) (statement is against interest; remanding to determine whether speaker was unavailable).

f. Penal interest

For years the exception did not reach statements against penal interest. Behind this tradition lay fears of "perjured confessions"—false testimony that someone else confessed, or truthful accounts of false confessions by people not worried about being tried themselves. It was feared that guilty defendants would avoid conviction, as prosecutors couldn't show the confessions had not been made or were false (declarant's unavailability compounds the difficulty). But Justice Holmes protested, see *Donnelly v. United States*, 228 U.S. 243 (1913) (no statement is "so much against interest" as a confession of murder), and FRE 804(b)(3) abandoned the common law tradition and extended the exception to declarations against penal interest.

i. Corroboration

Because of the concern about fabricated confessions by third parties who have nothing to lose, Congress added a proviso in FRE 804(b)(3) requiring "corroborating circumstances" when criminal defendants offer against-interest statements by third parties. In 2010, the proviso was amended to require corroboration in criminal cases regardless whether it is the prosecutor who invokes the exception in offering third-party statements implicating the accused or the accused who invokes the exception in offering third-party statements that exonerate the accused. Independent evidence supporting the substance of a third-party confession satisfies this requirement, and courts accept lesser corroboration as well, including factors supporting the veracity or credibility of the declarant.

ii. "Curry favor" statements

When a suspect is arrested, the conversation may turn to cooperation. The suspect incriminates himself while implicating others, believing his best chance is to acknowledge his own guilt so as to show how he can help convict others. Usually courts find such statements to advance the greater interest in leniency while sacrificing a smaller interest in maintaining innocence, and exclude "curry favor" statements. Since such statements are testimonial, they are likely to be excluded in any case under *Crawford*.

iii. **Blame-shifting statements**

When someone says she played a role in a crime in which another played a bigger (more serious or blameworthy) role, the context disclosed by the statement itself suggests that it does more to protect than to harm the declarant. Like curry favor statements, these may advance the greater interest in lenient treatment or excuse while sacrificing the lesser interest in maintaining innocence and therefore are generally found not to be against interest. When such statements are made to law enforcement officers, they are likely to be testimonial, and to be excludable under *Crawford*. When they are made in private settings, they are not testimonial but they may fail the against-interest requirement simply because they do more to excuse or justify behavior than to implicate the speaker in a crime.

iv. **Collateral points**

The whole of this statement could be against interest: "I killed Joe on Saturday June 12th in St. Louis." The specifics referring to date and place are integral parts of admitting to a criminal deed and make the statement more grounded and real. In trying to understand the deed, these specifics help and make the statement more persuasive. Without them, the statement would be against interest to a lesser extent. Suppose the speaker says, "I killed Joe on Saturday June 12th in St. Louis, and Harvey drove up afterwards." The reference to Harvey is not integral to the confession. Absent a showing that Harvey was *also* suspected of killing Joe, *these* specifics are not integral to the substance of the message, and do little or nothing to make the statement more grounded and real. A statement lacking these details would be as much against interest. Such details are sometimes called "collateral." The ACN to FRE 804(b)(1) says the exception applies to "associated statements," but in *Williamson v. United States*, 512 U.S. 594 (1994), the Court held that this provision does not reach "non-self-inculpatory statements" within a "broader narrative that is generally self-inculpatory." The Court concluded that "collateral statements, even ones that are neutral as to interest," do not fit the exception. *Williamson* is authoritative on the meaning of FRE 804(b)(3), but the decision did not rest on the Constitution, so it left states free to apply their own against-interest exception to collateral statements.

v. Postconviction statements

People imprisoned for crimes may have little to fear from (1) describing what they did, (2) confessing other crimes committed before incarceration, (3) describing what they did and exonerating others, or (4) describing what they did and implicating others. Where such statements pose little or no practical risk, they are usually excluded as failing the against-interest requirement.

g. **Statements offered by the accused**

If J confesses to a crime and K is tried for it, J's confession may prove K's innocence. It would if the crime was apparently committed by one person, or the facts suggested by J's confession conflict with the facts shown by the state to prove K's guilt. In the situation described here, third-party confessions are clearly admissible. (In cases governed by FRE 804(b)(3), the corroboration requirement must be met.)

☞ EXAMPLE AND ANALYSIS

In the trial of Alice for trafficking in drugs, the defense offers a statement by Sarah (who is unavailable) to an FBI agent. The agent was investigating *both* Sarah and Alice and suggested in questioning Sarah that there is information indicating that both women are involved in the crime. Sarah told the agent that "the drugs are mine, and Alice has nothing to do with drug selling."

There are two main issues. First, acknowledging guilt to an investigating agent usually suggests an attempt to curry favor, which leads to exclusion. But Sarah did not take this tack, since her statement acknowledges sole responsibility without suggesting that she can help "get" anyone else, so this objection should fail. Second, the part of Sarah's statement exonerating Alice might be excluded as collateral, since that part of the statement does not by itself implicate Sarah. *Williamson* supports this conclusion (holding that the exception reaches only statements that are themselves against interest, and not collateral statements), but there is also room to reach the opposite conclusion. Arguably the second part of Sarah's statement makes the first part *more* against interest by making it clear that Sarah is solely responsible in a situation in which it appears that the FBI Agent thinks both women are involved, so getting Alice off the hook may heighten the suspicion of Sarah and lead investigators and prosecutors to focus on her alone. In this sense Sarah's reference to Alice actually puts Sarah in more trouble, so even that reference is against Sarah's interest. Courts split on this point.

h. Penal interest: Offered against defendants

If L is tried for a crime and M tells a friend about his own role in the crime, facts that M asserts may be relevant evidence in the trial of L. M might say, for instance, "I was the person they said was waiting in front in the truck while the Country Store was being robbed." If there is other proof that L was seen driving off in a truck with M just before the robbery, M's statement helps connect L to the crime scene. The exception reaches statements such as this one, in which the speaker describes his own actions in ways that are useful in convicting others involved in the same offense. But other situations are harder.

i. Penal interest: Defense confrontation rights

In *Crawford,* defendant was tried for an assault allegedly committed because the victim made a pass at defendant's wife. She witnessed the altercation, and made a statement to police afterwards that was understood to mean that the victim may *not* have had a weapon in his hand at the time of the assault, although defendant's statement had indicated that the victim *did* have one. The Supreme Court reversed in a landmark opinion that took a new departure toward confrontation jurisprudence: The Confrontation Clause requires exclusion of "testimonial" statements, and this category includes *at least* statements by eyewitnesses describing crimes to police investigators. *Crawford* indicates that an opportunity to cross-examine the declarant at trial satisfies confrontation concerns, and that a prior opportunity to cross-examine also satisfies those concerns. *Crawford* is described further in Chapter 5.

ii. *Crawford*: Statements to police implicating defendant

Crawford makes clear that statements to police by co-offenders implicating the defendant by name or reference are almost certainly "testimonial." Objections under the Confrontation Clause might still be obviated if the defendant had cross-examined the declarant in proceedings prior to trial (and perhaps merely had an *opportunity* to do so, although this conclusion is less than certain). The against-interest exception is not likely to be available in cases where the declarant is subject to cross-examination at trial because the exception requires unavailability, but conceivably a declarant who claims lack of memory at trial (thus being unavailable under FRE 804(a)) might still be considered sufficiently subject to cross-examination to satisfy the Confrontation Clause, in which case once again there would be a possibility of admitting against-interest statements to police under the exception.

iii. *Crawford*: Statements to friends and acquaintances implicating defendant

Crawford left open the possibility that statements by an alleged co-offender, implicating the defendant by name or reference but made to a friend or acquaintance in a private setting might be admissible. The real question under *Crawford* is whether such a statement can ever be "testimonial," and most decisions answer this question in the negative, but the matter has not yet been definitively resolved.

iv. *Crawford*: Statements that do not implicate the defendant

When a co-offender makes a statement to police investigating a crime that describes *only* his own conduct, it is still "testimonial" under *Crawford*, which means that it is objectionable under the Confrontation Clause, unless the declarant is cross-examinable at trial or was cross-examinable before. Where such a statement is given to friends or acquaintances, it might be admitted, although once again the question would arise whether such a statement is testimonial, and once again the answer is not yet certain, although most decisions say no.

☞ Examples and Analysis

1. In Carl's murder-for-hire trial, arising out of the execution-style killings of Mick and Jim, the prosecutor's theory is that Carl hired Dan to do the killing in revenge after a dispute over territory and money owed in drug transactions. The prosecutor offers Evan's testimony describing a comment by Dan to the effect that "I killed Mick and Jim." Called to testify in Carl's trial, Dan claims his privilege against self-incrimination, and the trial judge upholds the claim. If Carl raises a hearsay objection, can Evan testify to what Dan said because it fits the against-interest exception?

Dan's statement does fit the against-interest exception. It refers only to his own behavior, so it does not appear to be an effort to shift blame to Carl or anyone else. In *Williamson v. United States*, 512 U.S. 594 (1994), the Court commented that a statement like "yes, I killed X" is "likely" admissible under the exception "against accomplices" on trial "under a coconspirator liability theory," and the instant case is very similar to this example. Note that the statement was made in a private setting, so it does not appear that Dan was trying to better his own position by currying favor with police, and note that Dan's claim of the privilege against self-incrimination makes him unavailable as a witness.

It seems probable, although perhaps less than certain, that Dan's statement is *not* "testimonial" under the *Crawford* doctrine, both because it was made in a private setting and because it hardly seems likely that the speaker would have said what he did if he expected his statement to be used during an investigation or prosecution.

2. Again in Carl's murder-for-hire trial, the prosecutor offers Frank's testimony describing another comment by Dan, to the effect that "I got five rocks and a bundle of bucks off of Carl for shooting Mick and Jim." Again Carl raises a hearsay exception, this time arguing that the reference to Carl is "collateral" and "not really self-inculpatory," so it does not fit the against-interest exception as it was construed in the *Williamson* case.

The prosecutor has a good argument that this statement too should be admitted under the against-interest exception. Dan acknowledges a large share of personal guilt in this statement because he refers to his own criminal act ("shooting Mick and Jim") and the reference to Carl increases the degree to which Dan exposes himself to criminal liability because the reference to Carl implicates Dan in a conspiracy and in murder-for-hire (not just murder). *Williamson* acknowledged that the statement "Sam and I went to Joe's house" can fit the exception, so the reference to another person does not prevent use of the exception. Moreover, Dan is not speaking to investigating agents and is clearly not currying favor, as the speaker in *Williamson* was doing, and Dan does not appear to be shifting blame to Carl, because Dan accepts responsibility for actually being the triggerman in the shooting.

On the other hand, there is at least a caveat: Unlike Dan's statement to Evan, Dan's statement to Frank focuses primarily not on what Dan did but on Carl's act in paying Dan. It is arguable, then, that Dan's reference to Carl is "collateral" under *Williamson,* hence lying beyond reach of the exception. It is also at least possible that a court would conclude that Dan's statement to Evan is "testimonial" for purposes of the *Crawford* doctrine because it reports the criminal activity of another. If so, then the Confrontation Clause might require exclusion. Since in this example Dan was speaking to an acquaintance and not to law enforcement officers, however, a court might well conclude that the statement was *not* testimonial.

---

5. Forfeiture Exception

FRE 804(b)(6) paves the way to admit statements by a person who has become unavailable to testify because of wrongdoing committed by the party against whom the statement is offered, where the wrongdoer was "intending" to make the declarant unavailable. In its easiest and perhaps most common application, this exception permits the prosecutor to introduce against a criminal defendant grand jury or preliminary hearing testimony by a prosecution witness who has been murdered by the defendant, or by order of the defendant, where it is clear that the defendant was trying to prevent the speaker from testifying in a similar way at trial. Only a few states have adopted similar provisions (Delaware, Michigan, Ohio, Oregon, Pennsylvania, and Tennessee), but many other states have gone in the same direction by judicial decision, without amending their evidence codes (Arizona, Colorado, Connecticut, District of Columbia, Iowa, Kansas, Minnesota, New Jersey, New Mexico, New York, and Texas).

a. Procedure

Usually the kind of conduct that triggers the exception is itself a crime, and normally the exception is invoked against the defendant in a criminal case. Often the crime that triggers the exception is also the crime for which the accused is now being tried. Nevertheless, it is clear that the question whether defendant committed an act that made the declarant unavailable, and that now justifies admitting the declarant's statement, is decided by *the judge* under FRE 104(a), and not by the jury. It follows that the Rules of Evidence do not themselves apply to this inquiry. It is also clear, despite the fact that the defendant is now on trial for an offense involved in the same act that brings the exception into play, that the preponderance standard applies to the inquiry that the judge conducts, and not the far higher standard required for conviction for the offense ("beyond reasonable doubt").

b. Reach of the Exception: Statements

Clearly the exception paves the way for statements of the most ordinary sort, and it is not limited to statements given in testimony before a grand jury or in a preliminary hearing. Thus the exception applies to statements given directly to police during a criminal investigation, and statements made to friends or to co-offenders in a criminal venture.

c. Reach of the Exception: Intent

As codified in FRE 804(b)(6), the exception applies only if defendant was "intending" to make the declarant unavailable. Originally there was disagreement among state courts on the question whether intent should necessarily be required, and some state rules on forfeiture abandoned the intent requirement. However, in *Giles v. California*, 554 U.S. 353

(2008), the Court held that a defendant's confrontation rights cannot be forfeited unless the defendant had the intent to make the hearsay declarant unavailable as a witness. Therefore, any state forfeiture rules or decisions that purport to eliminate the intent requirement would violate the Sixth Amendment.

d. Reach of the Exception: Conduct

Clearly the exception can pave the way to admit statements where the party against whom they are offered did *far less* than kill the declarant or order his death. Merely frightening the declarant into refusing to testify can be enough. Indeed, one court has held that involvement in a conspiracy, in which one member of the conspiracy kills a witness to keep him from testifying, is itself enough to invoke the exception, provided only that killing the declarant is an event that is "reasonably foreseen as a necessary or natural consequence" of the conspiracy. See *United States v. Cherry*, 217 F.3d 811, 818 (10th Cir. 2000) (noting that under *Pinkerton* doctrine, satisfying this standard is enough to make a conspirator guilty of a murder committed by another member of the venture, and suggesting that it would make no sense to say that one who is guilty of murdering the witness fails to satisfy the forfeiture exception).

☞ EXAMPLE AND ANALYSIS

Tony Emery is charged with killing Christine Elkins, an informant cooperating with the Bureau of Alcohol, Tobacco and Firearms (BATF) in a drug trafficking investigation. During the course of this investigation, Elkins recorded her conversations with Emery. She also talked with BATF Agent Farber, telling him at one point that "Emery spotted some of your guys the other day, and he said he'd kill me if I ever cooperated with you. I told him I didn't know what he was talking about, and I think he believed me, but I'm worried." Two days later Elkins is found dead, and there is substantial evidence that Emery killed her. The prosecutor calls Agent Farber, and offers his testimony describing the statement by Elkins recounting Emery's threats. Emery raises a hearsay objection, and the government invokes the forfeiture exception. Emery argues that the exception applies only in a trial for the very crime to which the declarant was expected to testify, not in a trial for killing the declarant herself. Alternatively, Emery demands that the court hold a preliminary hearing to determine whether the exception applies, and that the court resolve the matter without considering her statement, arguing that "considering the statement in resolving the hearsay issue would be bootstrapping." What result?

Probably Emery should lose. On his first argument, it is true that the exception applies only where the party "intended" to make the witness unavailable, but the language does not say the exception only applies in a trial on the very charges on which the defendant sought to silence the declarant. Emery was apparently trying to prevent Elkins from testifying against him on drug charges, and was presumably not thinking about her availability to testify against him on charges that he murdered her, but that probably does not matter.

Emery will probably come up short on the second argument too. Instead of determining in a pretrial hearing whether Emery killed Elkins for purposes of deciding whether to allow Farber to testify to what she said, the court can probably do what it would do in applying the coconspirator exception. In both situations, an issue on the merits coincides with an issue that determines admissibility: In cases applying the coconspirator exception, the question whether defendant and declarant conspired affects both the exception and guilt or innocence on conspiracy charges. Here the question whether Emery killed Elkins to silence her affects both the forfeiture exception and guilt or innocence on charges of killing a federal witness. In cases applying the coconspirator exception, the statement itself may be considered in deciding whether the predicate facts are proved. Probably the same principle applies here. See *United States v. Emery*, 186 F.3d 921 (8th Cir. 1999) (tracking these facts and finding forfeiture).

E. CATCHALL EXCEPTION

The catchall exception provides flexibility by allowing courts to admit trustworthy hearsay that does not fit any of the categorical exceptions discussed above. The hallmarks of the catchall are trustworthiness and a showing that the hearsay being offered is better than other available proof.

1. Background

The framers of Federal Rules proposed to abandon the system of categorical exceptions in favor of a broad exception for trustworthy hearsay, but professional reaction was negative. The main objections were that the new approach would (1) make life uncertain because lawyers could not know in advance what hearsay would be admitted and what would be excluded, and (2) give judges too much discretionary power. This opposition persuaded the framers to adopt the arrangement we see today: The categorical exceptions dominate, but the catchall is available in exceptional cases. See FRE 807.

2. Requirements

The catchall contains five requirements, including the obligation to give pretrial notice:

a. Trustworthiness

The catchall requires "circumstantial guarantees of trustworthiness" that are "equivalent" to those of the categorical exceptions. Courts look to factors in the categorical exceptions, like spontaneity, careful routine, reliance, and against-interest elements. Courts also appraise the hearsay risks (perception, candor, narration, memory) in the particular setting of the statement being offered. Courts may find hearsay trustworthy if the declarant testifies so his statement can be tested on cross-examination. Finally, courts stress corroborating evidence.

The Supreme Court cast a disapproving eye on the corroboration factor in the setting of hearsay offered against the accused, see *Idaho v. Wright*, 497 U.S. 805 (1990) (corroborative evidence does not count in satisfying the Confrontation Clause), but *Wright* was applying a reliability criterion under the Confrontation Clause, and the Court discarded this approach in *Crawford v. Washington*, 541 U.S. 36 (2004). Hence it seems that there is no bar against considering corroborative evidence in applying the catchall.

b. More probative

Hearsay offered under the catchall must be "more probative" than anything else available. In practice, this requirement may force the proponent to call the declarant if she is available (in preference to offering her statement) and sometimes simply to resort to other kinds of evidence.

c. Material fact

To fit the catchall, hearsay must bear on a "material fact." In practice, this requirement means only that the hearsay must be relevant under FRE 401–402.

d. Interests of justice

Hearsay may be admitted under the catchall only if it serves "the interests of justice." This requirement echoes the content of FRE 102. In practice, courts usually say the interests of justice are served when the hearsay seems reliable, and those interests are not served when the hearsay does not seem reliable.

e. Notice

"Before" the trial or hearing, the proponent must notify adverse parties of the "particulars" of a statement offered under the catchall, including "name and address" of the speaker. This requirement responds to the complaint of practitioners that a broad discretionary exception would make it hard to plan for trial. Despite the wording, courts sometimes admit hearsay without pretrial notice, commenting that adverse parties were aware of what was to be offered (hence already prepared) and sometimes offering a continuance (or noting that none was requested). At least theoretically, the notice requirement forecloses resort to the catchall exceptions for the first time on appeal, either as a way of urging error in a ruling that excluded hearsay or as a way of defending a ruling that admitted hearsay.

3. "Near Miss" Theory

A few decisions hold that hearsay cannot be admitted under a catchall if it *almost* fits a categorical exception, but does not quite fit because of some requirement or limit in the exception.

a. Most courts reject

The "near miss" theory is rejected by most courts that consider it, on the ground that the purpose of the catchalls is to admit reliable hearsay that somehow falls outside one of the categorical exceptions.

b. Blocking use of catchall

Even without the "near miss" theory, resort to the catchall may be improper or unwise because the proffered hearsay fails to satisfy one or another criterion in a categorical exception.

☛ EXAMPLE AND ANALYSIS

In the trial of used car dealers Alf and Bill on charges of conspiracy and related substantive crimes, the government claims they bought and sold stolen cars, committed consumer fraud (turning back odometers), and engaged in money laundering (transfers through foreign banks to disguise funds) and tax evasion. The government offers (1) a report by FBI specialists in banking and currency based on bank records and interviews tracing the movement of money allegedly involved in the transactions, and (2) a report by an insurance adjustment company commissioned by the government to connect cars on the lot with reported thefts across the country. The defense objects that the FBI report cannot be admitted under FRE 803(8) because it fits clause A(iii) (covering "factual findings"), which can only be invoked "against the Government" in a criminal case. The defense objects that the second report cannot be admitted as a business record under FRE 803(6) because it was not "the regular practice" of the adjustment company to prepare such reports and the source of information was outsiders, not "a person with knowledge" in the firm. The defense also claims the second report should be treated as a public record under FRE 803(8)(A)(iii) (government hired the company) and excluded for the same reason as the FBI report. In response, the government invokes the catchall exception for both reports.

The FBI report should be excluded. It is covered by the use restriction in FRE 803(8)(A)(iii) (factual findings can only be admitted "against the Government"), so the government cannot resort to the catchall. The use restrictions in the public records exception embody exclusionary policies, which makes them different from requirements in other exceptions. Those restrictions would be almost meaningless if the proponent could avoid them by invoking the catchall. The report by the insurance adjuster should be excluded too: Either it should be treated as a public record and excluded for the same reason as the FBI report, or it should be treated as a business record and excluded as untrustworthy. Moreover the business records exception requires personal knowledge by a source within the business and routine preparation, which are lacking here. Failing these requirements does not block the proponent from invoking the catchall, but the reports are unreliable for the same reason that keeps them from satisfying the business records exception. To make up for these drawbacks, the government would have to show compensating factors, perhaps that the company has special expertise or an excellent track record. Absent such showing, the report should be excluded.

---

4. Common Use of the Catchall–Child Victim Statements

Among the many cases applying the catchall, the area that stands out as most important is child victim hearsay. Here as elsewhere, the burden is on the proponent to show trustworthiness and there are numerous cases in which child victim statements are excluded, but often the statements are admitted.

a. Favorable factors

Cases admitting child victim statements stress the following factors: spontaneity, age-appropriate language, precocious knowledge, repetition, absence of motive to lie, and (in the common situation in which the child talks to social workers) the training and experience of the interviewer.

b. Unfavorable factors

The presence of motivational factors (like parents splitting up, which brings risks that parents may try to manipulate the child, and that the child might make statements designed to insure that he stays with one parent rather than the other) sometimes points toward exclusion of child victim statements. So do indications of coaching and the use of formal terms not expected in young children.

c. Impact of *Crawford*

In *Crawford,* the Court held that the Confrontation Clause bars the use of "testimonial" hearsay against the accused, and this category is usually viewed as including statements by children describing abuse, when given to police or social service workers. Most modern cases conclude, however, that statements by children to doctors, family members, caretakers or friends are not testimonial. See the discussion of the exception for child victim statements in the next section.

5. Criticism of the Catchall

Modern critics have argued that cases applying the catchall have failed to develop useful standards or coherent doctrine and that courts apply the catchall unevenly. There is no move afoot to repeal this provision, however.

F. NEW HEARSAY; PROTECTED WITNESS TESTIMONY

Beginning in the 1980s, a surge in child abuse prosecutions brought a felt need for new mechanisms to gather and admit statements by victims. Three new provisions are common:

1. Child Victim Statements ("Tender Years" exception)

Special exceptions, now adopted in all states, pave the way for statements describing abuse made by child victims or other children who see the abuse occurring. Typically these provisions include a "trustworthiness" clause and unavailability requirement.

a. Trustworthy

Some experts say children "do not lie" about child abuse, but this view is not generally accepted, and cases applying the exception look to the factors considered in applying the catchall (discussed above).

b. Unavailable

Usually these exceptions require the child to be "psychologically unavailable." One meaning of this term is that she is *completely unable* to testify because of a combination of factors, including tender years, the difficulty of the subject matter, her relationship to the defendant, and the unfamiliar and intimidating nature of the courtroom. Another meaning of the term is that testifying would likely cause severe damage to her psyche.

c. Constitutional constraints

There is a significant constitutional constraint on the use of such exceptions: The decision in *Crawford* means that the prosecutor cannot use them in a criminal case if they are "testimonial," unless the accused has a chance at trial or before trial to cross-examine the child. Hence at the very least, statements given to police investigating crimes after the fact, or to investigators for child or family service agencies, as well a statements given in depositions or in obvious preparation for trial, are often excludable (absent a chance to cross-examine). See *Crawford v. Washington*, 541 U.S. 36 (2004), discussed in Chapter 5.

2. Child Victim Depositions

In criminal cases, depositions are rarely taken. But many states now authorize videotaped depositions of victims in child abuse prosecutions. See also 18 U.S.C. § 3509 (elaborate federal statute providing for deposition testimony by child victims in federal prosecutions). In this less formal setting, the hope is that the factors that disable a child from telling her story can be ameliorated, and her story can be obtained after all.

a. Trial substitute

Unlike typical depositions, in which the deponent is expected to testify at trial, depositions of child abuse victims are taken in the expectation that they will be offered in place of live testimony. Court approval is required, and the matter is raised by pretrial motion.

b. Unavailability

When the motion is made, the court must determine whether the child is "psychologically unavailable" at the time and will continue to be unavailable at time of trial. Usually the issue is resolved by expert testimony or affidavits.

c. Confrontation issues

As with the child victim hearsay exception, here too *Crawford* means that child victim hearsay faces confrontation issues. Again the critical point is that the defense must have a chance to cross-examine, either because the child testifies at trial (but with this particular exception, it is more-or-less expected that the child will *not* testify at trial) or because the defense gets an opportunity during the deposition to cross-examine. The statutes that provide for such depositions ordinarily contemplate that defense counsel will be present (and can cross-examine), but not the defendant himself. Probably these provisions pass constitutional muster, so long as a judge makes a particularized finding that the child would be traumatized by having to face the defendant in person. See *Maryland v. Craig*, 497 U.S. 836 (1990) (noted further immediately below and in Chapter 5).

3. Remote Testimony

Most states have procedures that allow child victims to testify live during trial from a remote setting (typically another room in the courthouse). See also 18 U.S.C. § 3509 (elaborate federal statute providing for remote testimony by child victims in federal prosecutions).

a. Physical arrangements

Usually the lawyers are present in the room with the child, along with parents or a guardian and the court reporter, and the defendant remains in the courtroom. The child's testimony is carried to the courtroom by video monitor, and the defendant is in live voice contact with his lawyer. Sometimes the connection to the courtroom is by one-way video feed, and sometimes courts use a two-way feed in which the child is visible in the courtroom by video monitor and the courtroom scene is visible in the remote setting by video monitor.

b. Unavailability (*Craig* case)

The Court accepted the idea of psychological unavailability in this setting in *Maryland v. Craig*, 497 U.S. 836 (1990). In *Craig*, the Court held that the necessary showing could be made without bringing the child face to face with the defendant in a hearing.

REVIEW QUESTIONS AND ANSWERS

Question: Why do we have exceptions to the rule against hearsay?

Answer: Considerations of trustworthiness and necessity support the existence of most hearsay exceptions. Both these ideas are elastic and mean different things in different settings. Common factors indicating trustworthiness are spontaneity, which reduces the risk of veracity (spontaneous speech is less likely to be calculated to deceive) and organizational routine (diminishing the risk of misperception and narrative misstatement). Necessity too takes different forms: Unavailability of live testimony by the declarant is one indication of necessity and is part of the reason for the exceptions in FRE 804. The fact that the subject of proof is a fleeting event (a violent crime or an accident) produces another kind of necessity.

Question: What's the difference between statements that are "not hearsay" under FRE 801(d) and statements that are nonhearsay because they are offered for nonhearsay uses, like verbal acts (as discussed in Chapter 3)?

Answer: The difference is that the "not hearsay" category defined by FRE 801(d) contains statements that can be used to prove what they assert, but the nonhearsay categories only allow use of statements for some other purpose or purposes. In the former ("not hearsay") category is a prior inconsistent statement, if made under oath in a prior proceeding by a witness who is now testifying and subject to cross-examination about what he said earlier. Under FRE 801(d)(1)(A), such a statement may be used as proof of what it asserts, and also to impeach the witness (since it is inconsistent with what he now says). In the latter category is a statement offered to prove effect on listener or reader, like a sign saying "loose gravel." Such a statement is nonhearsay when it is offered just to prove that motorists were warned to drive more slowly than they might otherwise (and not to prove what they assert, which that there is in fact loose gravel nearby). Another way to make the same point is that the "not hearsay" category in FRE 801 really describes statements that are being used for hearsay purposes and the category itself really creates hearsay exceptions. The nonhearsay category simply falls outside the definition of hearsay because the statements are not being used for hearsay purposes.

Question: What statements fit the "not hearsay" category?

Answer: Basically three different kinds of prior statements by witnesses who are now subject to cross-examination and admissions by a party opponent (of which there are five kinds). The former includes inconsistent statements made under oath in proceedings, certain consistent statements when offered to refute claims of fabrication or improper motive or influence, and statements of identification. The latter includes personal admissions, adoptive admissions, authorized admissions, admissions by servants or agents, and coconspirator statements.

Question: What does fitting an exception mean?

Answer: Only that the hearsay doctrine does not require exclusion. Whether a statement should be admitted depends on whether it is relevant and whether admitting it would violate some other rule. Thus a statement by a defendant that he "robbed the bank" (as charged in the indictment) and "robbed two other banks before that" would fit the admissions doctrine if offered against him in his bank robbery trial. FRE 801 puts admissions in the "not hearsay" category, which is the equivalent of a hearsay exception. Hence the hearsay doctrine does not require exclusion of these statements. The first part of what he said is that he committed the crime. It would likely be admitted, but not if some other principle required exclusion, like the *Miranda* doctrine (which allows the prosecutor to offer statements by arrested persons in answer to police questions *only* if suitable warnings have been given). The second part proves uncharged offenses and might be excluded under FRE 404, which bars proof of other acts if offered for the propensity inference (he did it before, so he probably did it this time). But this part too would likely get in if it fit FRE 404(b) because the other robberies shed light on specific points like intent or modus operandi, or if the defendant had testified on direct that he "never committed any other crime," in which case the second part of his statement would likely be admitted on rebuttal to contradict this overbroad claim.

Question: What is double or multiple hearsay, and how is it handled?

Answer: Double or multiple hearsay refers to layers of hearsay, meaning statements reported in other statements. Assume the purpose is to prove the light was red. If witness Jill testifies "Ken said the light was red," there is one layer of hearsay (Ken's out-of-court statement). If witness Jill testifies, "Ken said that Laura told him the light was red," there are two layers of hearsay (Ken's statement, which asserts that Laura made a statement to *him,* and Laura's statement, which asserts that the light was red). Double or multiple hearsay is admissible only if each layer fits an exception. In a few instances, a single exception actually embraces double or multiple hearsay: The business records exception, for instance, actually embraces multiple or layered hearsay as information is passed along a chain of people and ultimately recorded. When information in the records of one business is taken from a record kept by another business, each record must fit the exception.

Question: Are admissions different from the hearsay exceptions?

Answer: Functionally, the various branches of the admissions doctrine are just like hearsay exceptions and are often called exceptions. Unlike the hearsay exceptions, however, the admissions doctrine is not founded on notions of trustworthiness or even necessity. And unlike the hearsay exceptions, admissions may be used as evidence even if the speaker lacked personal knowledge.

Question: Are admissions subject to constitutional constraints?

Answer: In criminal cases, they are. Two of the most important constraints are the *Miranda* and *Massiah* doctrines. *Miranda* is a Fifth Amendment doctrine (based on the right against self-incrimination) that requires exclusion of admissions made during post-arrest police interrogation unless suitable warnings are given, and *Massiah* is a Sixth Amendment doctrine (based on the right of counsel) that requires exclusion, under certain conditions, of similar statements given after the defendant has a lawyer. (Statements that are blocked by the *Miranda* or *Massiah* doctrines can, however, be used to impeach defendants whose testimony conflicts with those statements, in which case the statements come in not as admissions but as prior inconsistent statements which may be used only to impeach.) Admissions are also subject to the *Bruton* doctrine (resting on the Confrontation Clause of the Sixth Amendment), which requires exclusion, in a trial of two or more defendants, of an admission by one that names and incriminates another.

Question: Are admissions subject to any other restrictions?

Answer: Not many. Personal knowledge is not required; there is no against-interest requirement; even conclusory statements are admissible. Occasional statutes block narrow categories of statements that might otherwise qualify as admissions, and they can be excluded under FRE 403, but the admissions doctrine is a very wide open doctrine.

Question: What are "adoptive" admissions?

Answer: An adoptive admission is a statement by one person that another signs or agrees to, thus making the statement his own. Adoption sometimes happens by silence, and we speak of "tacit" adoption. Here context is important, and the most important factor is the nature of the statement and the setting in which it is made.

Question: What are authorized admissions, and how do they differ from admissions by agents and employees?

Answer: Authorized admissions, which are covered by FRE 801(d)(2)(C), are statements by a person who has been authorized actually to speak for another, offered against the other. Admissions by agents and employees, which are covered by FRE 801(d)(2)(D), are statements by a person employed or retained as an agent by another, on a subject within the scope of the speaker's duties, offered against the other, *regardless* whether the speaker has authority to speak. The former were admissible under common law tradition, and the Rules expanded the admissions doctrine to reach the latter as well. It once was understood that the proponent offering a statement under either of these exceptions had to prove the predicate facts (agency, authority, scope of duties) entirely by independent evidence, but FRE 801(d)(2) was amended in 1997 to permit courts to rely in part on the very statement being offered, although the statement is "not alone sufficient" to prove the predicate facts, so *some* other evidence is still required.

Question: What is the coconspirator exception, and how does it work?

Answer: The coconspirator exception is most useful in conspiracy cases, but it can be invoked even if no conspiracy is charged. The exception requires proof of the predicate facts—that the party against whom the statement is offered (usually the defendant) conspired with the speaker, that the statement furthered the conspiracy, and that it was made during the conspiracy. The exception does not embrace "mere narrative" statements. Under *Bourjaily*, the judge determines the predicate facts, and these must be proved by a preponderance of the evidence, but the statement itself may be considered as partial proof of the predicate facts.

Question: What are the differences between the exceptions for present sense impressions and excited utterances?

Answer: The exception for present sense impressions, which is new with FRE 803(1), requires **contemporaneousness** and the statement must **actu-**

ally describe the act, event, or condition. The exception for excited utterances, which is found in FRE 803(2), requires the speaker to be **excited or startled** as he speaks but the statement may *follow the event* or condition and need only **relate to it** (rather than describe it).

Question: What does the state-of-mind exception cover?

Answer: This exception, which is contained in FRE 803(3), covers statements describing existing physical condition, existing mental state (as an end in itself or as a basis for drawing inferences about future behavior by the speaker), and facts about the speaker's will. The Supreme Court's 1892 opinion in the *Hillmon* case approves use of the exception to prove later conduct by the speaker, but *Hillmon* is problematic because the opinion can be read as approving use of a statement to prove what the speaker and someone else did. This use of the exception involves drawing a backward-looking inference (the speaker must already have met the other person, and the two must have agreed to do something together), and the exception is not supposed to cover statements offered to prove past events. This point is made express in FRE 803(3) (which says the exception cannot be used to prove facts remembered or believed), but modern courts continue to admit at least some statements by crime victims describing plans to meet others (often the defendant) when there is corroborating evidence that the two met.

Question: When a statement is offered to prove something about state of mind, does it fit the exception only if it expressly describes state of mind (as by saying "I am angry" or "I intend to go")?

Answer: Courts disagree about using the exception to prove fact-laden statements, like "My boss told me to go to Chicago," if offered to prove the speaker's state of mind. Some courts say the exception applies only to statements that describe state of mind expressly or by necessary implication ("I intend to go to Chicago" or "I'm going to Chicago"), but not to fact-laden statements. Courts that take this view, however, would likely treat fact-laden statements as nonhearsay "circumstantial evidence of state of mind" and admit them on that theory, or perhaps exclude them if there are other reasons for doing so.

Question: Can statements offered under the exception be used to prove fear, hence supporting inferences about what caused the fear?

Answer: Yes and no. The "yes" part is that statements offered under the exception can prove fear. The "no" part is that the exception cannot be used to prove acts by other people that caused the fear. If a murder victim or an extortion victim makes a fact-laden statement implying fear of the defendant ("X keeps threatening to kill me"), such a statement can properly prove fear but not the conduct to which the statement alludes. In extortion cases, where fear is *an element* of the prosecutor's case, the exception is often used even for fact-laden statements. In murder cases, where fear on the part of the victim is *not* an element of the prosecutor's case, statements by the victim describing fear are usually excluded. Note that fear on the part of the victim is *relevant*, even in a murder case, because it suggests that the defendant made threats or acted in a belligerent or hostile way toward the victim, which would be relevant in showing that when the victim was killed, it was the defendant who killed him. Still, the victim's fear is not something that the prosecutor *must* prove in order to win a murder conviction, and statements by the victim indicating fear of the defendant are usually excluded. (It would be altogether different if the prosecutor could prove that the victim was afraid by showing that he or she *fled* whenever the defendant appeared, because flight is not an assertion—it is not intended to express or communicate an idea—so it is nonhearsay, and flight *can* properly be used to draw inferences about what the defendant might have done to cause the victim to flee.)

Question: Are there any proper uses for statements of fear on the part of the victim in murder cases?

Answer: Yes, if the defendant claims self-defense or claims that the victim committed suicide. In this situation, the defense argument makes the state of mind of the victim more relevant, and if the victim was afraid of the defendant, then the victim is less likely to have attacked the defendant, and arguably suicide is less likely to be the cause of death. In situations such as these, courts are more likely to admit statements by the victim indicating fear of the defendant.

Question: How has the medical statements exception been broadened in recent years?

Answer: In several ways: First, under FRE 803(4) it reaches statements made for purposes of **diagnosis,** which in most cases means statements given to doctors for purposes of preparing them to testify, while the common law version of the exception was limited to statements made for purposes of *treatment*. The theory for this expanded coverage is that doctors rely on statements in making diagnoses, even if they are not treating the person, and those statements are likely to be admitted along with the doctor's opinion, so it is wiser to let the jury use them for any purpose. Second, courts now apply the exception in child abuse prosecutions to admit statements by a child victim describing abuse, and some courts even admit statements identifying the defendant as her abuser. The former is not a particularly surprising use of the exception, but the latter is a considerable expansion, and courts are split on the question whether this expansion is proper.

Question: What are the requirements of the exception?

Answer: The exception reaches statements (1) relating to condition or symptoms, (2) made for purposes of diagnosis or treatment, (3) insofar as pertinent to diagnosis or treatment. While the exception is perhaps most often used for statements by patients to doctors, it is not actually limited to such statements, and it reaches as well statements by parents describing the symptoms of a child, statements by Good Samaritans who bring someone to the hospital, and statements by doctors and hospital or emergency room personnel. The exception does not reach statements attributing fault to other people ("I got run over because he ran the red light").

Question: What can you do with the exception for past recollection recorded?

Answer: You can use it to prove the facts once remembered by a witness who testifies in the case but has forgotten those facts. The exception applies to a written or recorded statement if (1) the witness lacks sufficient memory to testify to the facts, (2) the statement correctly reflects memory that the witness once had, (3) the witness made or adopted the statement himself, and (4) the statement was made while the matter was fresh in the mind of the witness. While the statement may be read to the jury and is admitted into evidence, the usual rule is that it cannot be taken with the jury to its deliberations.

Question: Can the exception apply when two people are involved in preparing the statement?

Answer: Yes it can, in at least two situations. First, the exception reaches statements one person prepares and another adopts. If Andrew writes a statement describing facts known to Brenda, and she signs it with the intent of adopting it as her own, the writing can satisfy the exception. Of course Brenda must testify that she lacks memory of the facts, and the statement must correctly reflect knowledge she once had, and must have been adopted while the memory was fresh in her mind. Second, the exception can reach a jointly produced writing. If Carl sees an event and tells David what he saw, and David writes it down, the writing may satisfy the exception if Carl and David both testify and if between them they satisfy the requirements. Carl must testify that he lacks knowledge but once had it, and that he correctly told David what he knew while the matter was fresh in his mind. David must testify that he correctly recorded what Carl told him, and that he in fact made the writing. Between them, Carl and David have laid the necessary foundation.

Question: What are the foundation requirements for the business records exception?

Answer: There are four requirements. First, there must be a regular business, and the record must be regularly kept. The business may be small or large and need not be a profitmaking operation, but it must be an ongoing enterprise of some kind. And the record cannot be a one-of-a-kind or extraordinary thing, but must be something routinely kept. Second, the record must rest on information acquired from someone with firsthand knowledge. The source need not make the record, however, and it is all right if the information is passed along from person to person acting in routine course of business. The source, however, must be someone within the business, not an outsider. Third, the record must be made contemporaneously with the event. Fourth, a foundation witness familiar with the recordkeeping process must show that these requirements are satisfied. The keeper of the records need not testify, however, and someone having mere "circumstantial knowledge" of the way records are kept may lay the foundation even if he knows nothing specific about the item being offered.

Question: Can business records get in even if they're "self-serving"?

Answer: Yes, but there is a "trustworthiness" factor that allows the adverse party to exclude even business records that satisfy the specific criteria of the exception if they are shown to be untrustworthy (burden being on the objecting party). While many business records may still fit the exception even if they are self-serving in various ways (like statements of account), still records may be excluded as untrustworthy if they are, for instance, prepared in anticipation of litigation.

Question: Is the public records exception different from the business records exception? How?

Answer: Yes, the public records exception is different, although the two exceptions overlap and many public records could satisfy the requirements of the business records exception. Here are the main differences: First, the public records exception does not depend on making a similar foundational showing that the record was prepared in a routine manner or contemporaneously. Second, the public records exception cannot be used freely against criminal defendants, since the result would be a serious infringement of confrontation rights.

Question: What kinds of material does the public records exception reach?

Answer: Three somewhat different kinds of things: First, the exception reaches records that reflect the activities of the office or agency (like disbursing checks or serving papers). Second, it reaches records reflecting matters observed (weather conditions, building code violations). Third, it reaches investigative findings (reports on the nature and spread of diseases).

Question: Are these different categories subject to different limits? What are "use restrictions"?

Answer: There **are** different limits. Investigative findings offered under the exception may rest on hearings or interviews with outsiders to government, but records reflecting agency activities and matters observed require internal sources. And the three categories of the exception, as defined in FRE 803(8), reach different *kinds* of records: A report on the cause and spread of disease based on outside information, for example, can fit the "factual findings" category in clause A(iii) but could not fit clauses A(i) (activities of agency) or A(ii) (matters observed). The use restrictions in clauses A(ii) and A(iii) of FRE 803(8) are mainly designed to protect defense confrontation rights in criminal cases, and they differ from ordinary limits found in hearsay exceptions because they block resort to certain other exceptions, such as the catchall and business records exception. The one in clause A(ii) applies in criminal cases and blocks use of police or law enforcement reports, and the landmark *Oates* case holds that this use restriction applies to public crime laboratories. But courts have approved use against the accused of "routine and nonadversarial" records (like border crossing logs), even when prepared by law enforcement agencies. The one in clause A(iii) blocks the prosecution from offering factual findings in criminal cases. There is no restriction blocking use of such material in civil cases, or blocking defense use of such material in criminal cases.

Question: Can learned treatises now be used as substantive evidence?

Answer: Yes, but only in combination with expert testimony. The common law tradition allowed treatises to be the basis for cross-examining experts, but not to be used to prove what they said. Under FRE 803(18), a treatise may be admitted to prove what it says, under certain conditions: It must be authoritative, and it must be called to the attention of an expert witness or relied on by her in her testimony.

Question: Why do some exceptions require unavailability of the declarant, and what exceptions are they?

Answer: The idea is that some exceptions rest more on necessity than trustworthiness, and unavailability of the declarant's testimony is part of the calculus of necessity. This requirement applies to former testimony, against-interest statements, dying declarations, and statements of family history. The exceptions are codified in FRE 804.

Question: Are there any real issues relating to unavailability?

Answer: Yes, there are some. In the first place, don't forget that unavailability takes many different forms—not just death or being beyond reach of subpoena, but also lack of memory, claim of privilege, and refusal to testify. And while FRE 804(a) defines unavailability in helpful ways, sometimes applying the definition is challenging. Unavailability for lack of memory, for instance, can be troublesome because it is necessary to determine whether the witness/declarant has forgotten the facts or events described in the statement (its "subject matter"), which makes her unavailable. Lack of memory on this point must be distinguished from memory relating to the statement itself, which doesn't count in the calculus. Also, a witness who is beyond reach of process is not unavailable if her deposition was (or could have been) obtained. And in criminal cases with respect to declarants whose statements the prosecutor wants to offer, unavailability has a *constitutional* dimension. Under the *Barber* case, the Confrontation Clause of the Sixth Amendment requires the prosecutor to take reasonable steps to bring a witness to court, like offering transportation and expenses.

Question: What is most important about the former testimony exception?

Answer: First, this exception requires the declarant to be unavailable. Second, the key requirement is that the party *against whom* former testimony is offered must have had *a chance* and *a similar motive* to cross-examine the declarant in the former proceedings. Third, commentators and courts disagree on the question whether the exception should be available for use against a party if *some other party* with similar chance and motive could have cross-examined in the prior proceedings. Under FRE 804(b)(1), the exception can be used against a party who was not a party to the prior proceedings only if a "predecessor in interest" had a chance and motive to cross-examine in the prior proceedings. Fourth, don't forget that the exception covers depositions as well as trial testimony, and that courts often allow use of the exception to admit preliminary hearing testimony too.

Question: What's the use of the dying declaration exception?

Answer: The main value of this exception is that it reaches statements by accident and crime victims who die of their injuries and cannot testify for that reason. To fit the exception, a statement must describe the cause or circumstances of impending death, and the speaker must know he is dying. And in criminal cases the exception is available only if homicide is charged.

Question: What is most important about the against-interest exception?

Answer: The exception has nothing to do with the admissions doctrine, and is usually applied to statements by third persons who are not parties to the suit. The exception can be invoked only if the declarant is unavailable. In recent years, the exception has been extended to reach statements against **penal** interest, making it far more important than it had been when it reached only statements against pecuniary or proprietary interest. Somewhat unexpectedly, this expansion paves the way to prove not only third-party statements confessing criminal involvement and exonerating the accused but also some third-party statements confessing criminal involvement and implicating the accused.

Question: What does "against interest" mean?

Answer: The usual meaning is that the fact asserted in a statement impairs the interest of the speaker in some way. Sometimes facial meaning makes it clear ("I killed the President"). Often, however, you can only know a statement is against interest by looking at broader context, which may show that a facially neutral statement was against interest (such as a statement placing the speaker at a crime) or may show that an apparently against-interest statement really was not against interest (as by confessing to a small crime when the speaker knew he was being investigated for a bigger crime that happened somewhere else at the same time).

Question: Does the whole statement get in, or just the part that is against interest?

Answer: In 1994, the Supreme Court in the *Williamson* case held that the federal version of the exception in FRE 804(b)(3) does not reach "collateral statements." In the statement "I was carrying the drugs, but they belonged to X," arguably the second part of the statement ("but they belonged to X") is collateral and would not fit the exception even if the first part of the statement ("I was carrying the drugs") fits. This is the approach taken by the Court in *Williamson*, but it is hard to be sure that this conclusion is right because the Court there was clearly concerned about the fact that the speaker in that case was talking to federal agents after his arrest. The situation raises the "curry favor" issue (the speaker may have been trying to get lenience by showing he could be helpful) that casts doubt over the whole statement, not just the part that mentions someone else. And arguably the second part of the statement is not just collateral, and is against the interest of the speaker because it implicates him in a conspiracy with X.

Question: Is it *constitutional* to use against-interest statements against the accused?

Answer: Yes and no, but mostly no. In the *Crawford* case, the Supreme Court emphatically disapproved the use against the defendant of an against-interest statement made by the wife of the defendant to investigators after the crime, condemning broadly the use of "testimonial" statements against the accused (at least if the declarant cannot be cross-examined at trial or before). While *Crawford* covers many if not most of the against-interest statements that prosecutors are likely to gather and offer against the accused, *Crawford* probably does not cover against-interest statements made in private settings (declarant speaking to friend or acquaintance outside the setting of police investigation), including statements in which the declarant speaks only of *his own* misconduct (without mentioning the defendant by name or apparent reference).

Question: Is there a corroboration requirement for statements against penal interest?

Answer: In the federal version of the exception in FRE 804(b)(3), "[a] statement tending to expose the declarant to criminal liability and offered in a criminal case is not admissible unless corroborating circumstances clearly indicate the trustworthiness of the statement." Thus, the rule requires corroboration whether the self-inculpatory statement is offered by or against a criminal defendant.

Question: What kinds of statements are against pecuniary or proprietary interest?

Answer: A statement is against pecuniary or proprietary interest if it concedes that someone else owns property, or that the speaker owes a debt to someone, or that money owed by another has already been paid. A statement can also be against pecuniary interest if it states facts indicating that the speaker has committed a tort, or states that he has done something wrong on the job for which he might be fired or penalized.

Question: What is the catchall exception, and how important is it?

Answer: The catchall exists to provide flexibility, in case trustworthy hearsay doesn't fit a categorical exception. In the Rules, the catchall is found in FRE 807, and Congress amended what the drafters had proposed to insure that this exception is used only in exceptional cases. Under the "near miss" theory, the catchall is unavailable for statements that *almost* fit some other exception, but most courts reject this idea because the whole purpose of the catchall is to permit use of reliable statements that don't fit other exceptions.

Question: What are the requirements of the catchall, and how is it used?

Answer: The central requirement is that a statement must have "circumstantial guarantees of trustworthiness" comparable to those found in the categorical exceptions. Factors like spontaneity, careful routine, reliance, and against-interest elements count on this point, and other circumstances count as well (such as testimony by the declarant that is consistent with his statement). A statement offered under the catchall must be "more probative" than other available evidence, must relate to a "material fact," and admitting the statement must serve the interests of justice. The proponent must also give notice before resorting to the catchall. This exception has been used in many different settings, but the most dramatic cases are those that admit grand jury testimony against defendants under the catchall, and statements by child abuse victims. It is by no means the case, however, that all such statements always fit the catchall, and each case must be analyzed on its own facts. Under the Court's decision in *Crawford*, the catchall exception cannot be used to offer "testimonial" hearsay against defendants in criminal cases (unless the declarant testifies and can be cross-examined at trial, or can be cross-examined about the statement in a pretrial proceeding).

Exam Tips

Here are some pointers about issues relating to the hearsay exceptions:

Admissions are statements *by* a party offered *against* him. Admissions need not confess a crime, and need not be against interest, and the term "admission" refers simply to any statement by a party. Remember the five kinds (individual, adoptive, authorized, agent or employee, coconspirator).

Admissions can be excluded for reasons other than hearsay (statement admitting a prior crime may be excluded if the prior crime can't properly be proved).

Admissions by one defendant that name and incriminate another defendant in the same trial may be excludable under the *Bruton doctrine* (based on Confrontation Clause).

Unrestricted exceptions may be invoked regardless whether the declarant testifies and regardless whether she is available as a witness.

When applying the state-of-mind exception, remember especially two things:

The exception cannot be used to prove previous acts, events, or conditions (facts "remembered or believed").

The exception can be used only to prove *present* mental or physical state, not past mental or physical states.

When applying the medical statements exception, remember that the federal version covers statements made for treatment and also statements made for diagnosis even if no treatment is contemplated, and that in child abuse cases courts allow the use of statements describing abuse, and some courts allow the use of statements naming the abuser, although other courts disagree on this point.

When applying the exception for past recollection recorded, remember these points:

The exception is not needed if the attorney succeeds in using a previous statement to refresh the memory of the witness, and she then testifies from present memory.

The exception can reach a statement actually written by one person summing up what a second person said, but both must testify and between them they must satisfy the conditions of the exception.

When applying the business records exception, remember that it covers multiple hearsay within the organization, but only if each person in the chain is acting in course of business and the source has personal knowledge.

When applying the public records exception, remember that it cannot be used to prove police investigative reports in criminal cases, but that certain investigative findings made by government agencies and based on outsider hearsay may be proved in civil cases and against the government in criminal cases.

When applying the exceptions that require the declarant to be unavailable, remember:

Raise and discuss the unavailability point before applying the exception.

There are three important exceptions that require unavailability, including former testimony, dying declarations, and against-interest statements.

Unavailability means not only death and absence from the jurisdiction, but lack of memory about underlying events and claims of privilege that are upheld.

In *criminal cases*, especially where prior testimony is offered against the accused, the unavailability requirement has a constitutional dimension.

In applying the former testimony exception, remember that in the *prior proceedings* the party *against whom* the testimony is now offered must have had a chance and similar motive to cross-examine, and that in *civil cases* applying FRE 804(b)(1) it suffices if a "predecessor in interest" had such motive and opportunity.

In applying the against-interest exception, remember that it reaches statements against *penal* interest (as well as statements against pecuniary interest), and that the exception covers third-party statements that can sometimes be offered by or against criminal defendants, but:

Remember that *Williamson* insists that the exception reaches only statements that are themselves against the interest of the speaker, not associated statements.

Remember too that *Williamson* cites the example "Sam and I went to Joe's house" as a statement that could be against the interest of the speaker, so a reference to another person does not necessarily keep the exception from applying.

Remember too that *Crawford* condemns, under the Confrontation Clause, the use against the accused of the against-interest exception to admit statements to police investigating crimes, and that *Crawford* makes an exception to this blanket rule excluding such statements only if the declarant testifies and can be cross-examined, either at trial or in pretrial proceedings.

In applying the catchall exception, remember the suggestions mentioned above: Normally you should get to these only after discussing categorical exceptions, and not if the professor indicates that you should ignore the catchall. If you do discuss the catchall in connection with a statement offered against a criminal defendant, remember that *Crawford* condemned the use against the defendant of "testimonial" statements (which category includes many statements, like grand jury testimony) that might be offered under the catchall.

CHAPTER 5

Confrontation and Compulsory Process

CHAPTER OVERVIEW

The key points in this chapter are

- The Confrontation Clause of the Sixth Amendment applies in both federal and state courts.

- The Confrontation Clause restricts the admissibility of hearsay against criminal defendants.

- Since the *Crawford* decision in 2004, the central focus of the Confrontation Clause has been "testimonial" hearsay, which means *at least* statements by eyewitnesses describing crimes to police during investigations, as well as actual testimony given in other proceedings, such as depositions, preliminary hearings, plea proceedings, and prior trials.

- Generally "testimonial" hearsay does not include statements made in purely private settings.

- Since the *Davis* decision in 2006, generally statements made for the primary purpose of obtaining emergency assistance are not "testimonial," even if made to police and even if such statements describe apparent criminal acts, and *Davis* was reaffirmed and arguably broadened in the *Bryant* case in 2011.

- Testimonial hearsay is generally inadmissible unless the accused has a chance at trial or before trial (in some earlier proceeding) to cross-examine the declarant.

- Testimonial hearsay in the form of actual testimony given in a prior trial, deposition, or preliminary hearing is probably subject to a constitutional requirement that the declarant be unavailable as a witness to testify at trial.

- All hearsay offered in criminal cases against the accused was once subject to a two-pronged standard that came from the *Roberts* case in 1980. The first prong required that the declarant be unavailable as a witness, but this prong seemed to have only limited application. The second prong required a showing that the hearsay statement was reliable, but this requirement could be satisfied by a showing that the hearsay fits one of the "firmly rooted" exceptions, which included most standard exceptions.

- In the federal system, the *Roberts* standard is a dead letter. Some states, however, continue to implement their own versions of the *Roberts* standard for nontestimonial hearsay, but all states are bound to apply the *Crawford* standard to testimonial hearsay.

- The list of "firmly rooted" exceptions does not include the catchall exception, child victim hearsay exceptions, the against-interest exception (at least for statements against penal interest), nor other new exceptions.

- A criminal defendant may forfeit the right to make a confrontation objection to hearsay by killing the declarant or otherwise making him unavailable.

- The Compulsory Process Clause guarantees criminal defendants the right to subpoena witnesses and present exculpatory evidence.

- The Compulsory Process Clause can override evidence rules that unreasonably restrict a criminal defendants ability to present evidence.

A. THE CONFRONTATION CLAUSE GUARANTEES IMPORTANT RIGHTS TO CRIMINAL DEFENDANTS

1. Text of Clause

The Sixth Amendment of the U.S. Constitution provides, in relevant part, that in criminal cases "the accused shall enjoy the right . . . to be confronted with the witnesses against him." The Supreme Court has repeatedly assumed and sometimes actually held that the term "witness against" includes at least some declarants who make out-of-court statements that are offered against the defendant.

2. Applies to State and Federal Trials

The Supreme Court has held that the Confrontation Clause applies to the states as part of the Fourteenth Amendment Due Process Clause. *Pointer v. Texas*, 380 U.S. 400 (1965).

3. Meaning of Confrontation

a. Right of defendant to be present at trial

It has long been settled that the Confrontation Clause entitles the accused to be present when witnesses testify against him. Normally a defendant cannot be tried in absentia. However, an accused may lose his right to be present at trial by misbehaving in the courtroom. *Illinois v. Allen*, 397 U.S. 337 (1970).

b. Right to have prosecution witnesses present at trial

Confrontation can only occur if the prosecution witnesses are present at trial. In many situations discussed below, the prosecution witnesses must be either produced at trial or shown to be unavailable.

c. Right to have defendant and prosecution witnesses in view of each other

Normally the right to confront means **face to face** confrontation. Thus procedures that block an accused and prosecution witnesses from viewing each other raise constitutional concerns.

i. Screens

In *Coy v. Iowa*, 487 U.S. 1012 (1988), the Supreme Court concluded that using a one-way screen that blocked a teenaged complainant from seeing the defendant while she testified against him in a sexual assault trial (while letting him watch her) violated his confrontation rights.

ii. Closed circuit television

In *Maryland v. Craig*, 497 U.S. 836 (1990), the Court approved use of closed circuit television to present testimony by a young sexual assault victim from a remote location (another room in the courthouse) on the basis of a case-specific finding that testifying in the courtroom itself would harm the health of the child because of the trauma associated with telling the story of a sexual assault. (The defense lawyer could cross-examine in the remote location, and was in electronic or telephone contact with the defendant in the courtroom during the testimony.)

d. Right to cross-examine prosecution witnesses

The most fundamental element of the right to confront witnesses is the right to cross-examine them. Confrontation would be virtually meaningless if it entitled the accused only to watch a prosecution witness give testimony without being able to ask questions of the witness.

i. Refusal to submit to cross-examination

If a witness refuses to submit to cross-examination, his testimony must be stricken.

ii. Denial of earlier statement

The fact that the declarant denies making an earlier out-of-court statement does not mean that cross-examination about it is constitutionally inadequate.

Example. O'Neil and Runnels are tried for kidnapping, robbery, and theft of a Cadillac. According to the police, Runnels made a confession that also implicated O'Neil. Both defendants plead not guilty, go to trial, and both take the witness stand and testify that they borrowed the car from a friend. The prosecutor offers Runnels' out-of-court confession implicating both defendants. Runnels denies making such a confession. O'Neil claims his right to confrontation is violated because he cannot meaningfully cross-examine his codefendant Runnels about a confession that Runnels denies making. (Recall that under the *Bruton* doctrine described in Chapter 4B2, supra, a confession by defendant *A* implicating defendant *B* by name cannot be admitted in the joint trial of *A* and *B*, even with limiting instructions, unless the *B* can cross-examine *A* at trial.) On these facts, the Supreme Court disagreed that the behavior of Runnels frustrated O'Neil's right to cross-examine. The Court concluded that the fact that Runnels denied confessing was more favorable to O'Neil than anything that cross-examination could have produced if Runnels had affirmed the statement as his. *Nelson v. O'Neil*, 402 U.S. 622 (1971).

iii. Loss of memory

Loss of memory by the declarant about the underlying event does not necessarily prevent the declarant from being subject to cross-examination that meets constitutional standards.

☞ EXAMPLE AND ANALYSIS

Owens is charged with a brutal assault on prison guard Foster. At trial, Foster testifies that he cannot remember the assault or who struck him. Invoking FRE 801(d)(1)(C) (covering prior statements of identification by a witness who testifies and is subject to cross "about the statement"), the government offers testimony describing Foster's earlier statement, made in the hospital to a government investigator, identifying Owens as his attacker. Owens objects that admitting this statement would violate his right of confrontation: Foster takes the witness stand and can be questioned, but the defense claims that he is not really subject to cross-examination because he cannot remember the attack itself, although he does remember the statement.

On these facts, the Supreme Court held that admitting Foster's earlier statement was proper. Owens was not denied the right of confrontation because Foster testified, was willing to answer questions to the best of his ability, and was impeached by showing his lack of memory and by suggesting that his earlier statement and recollection may have been implanted by police questioning. *United States v. Owens*, 484 U.S. 554 (1988).

e. Right to impeach prosecution witnesses

If a statute or court ruling unduly interferes with defendant's ability to impeach a prosecution witness, the result may be a denial of defendant's right of confrontation.

☛ **EXAMPLE AND ANALYSIS**

Davis is charged with stealing a safe from a bar. A key witness against him is a teenager named Green, who identifies Davis as the robber and links him to the place where the safe was found. Davis tries to impeach Green by showing that Green was on probation from juvenile court at the time, and would have a motive to cooperate with the prosecutor by concealing his own involvement in the crime charged to Davis and shift blame to someone else. The trial court refuses to allow this impeachment because a state statute makes juvenile records confidential.

Excluding evidence of Green's prior juvenile conviction violates Davis's confrontation rights. In *Davis v. Alaska,* 415 U.S. 308 (1974), the Supreme Court held that the exposure of "witness motivation in testifying" is a proper and important function of "the constitutionally protected right of cross-examination" and that the right of confrontation is "paramount to the State's policy of protecting a juvenile offender." Hence a state cannot "require Davis to bear the full burden of vindicating the State's interest in the secrecy of juvenile records."

B. CONSTITUTIONAL RIGHT TO EXCLUDE "TESTIMONIAL" AND SOME OTHER HEARSAY UNDER THE DOCTRINES OF CRAWFORD AND ROBERTS

1. General Rule

In *Crawford v. Washington,* 541 U.S. 36 (2004), the Supreme Court departed from the approach to confrontation that it had followed for 24 years. It replaced the approach of *Ohio v. Roberts,* 448 U.S. 56 (1980), under which courts required prosecutors to show that a declarant was unavailable before offering her out-of-court statement, and to show that the statement was reliable. Instead, *Crawford* directed courts to determine whether an out-of-court statement is "testimonial" in nature, and to exclude statements that *are* testimonial unless the defendant can cross-examine the declarant at trial or had a previous chance to do so, in some other proceeding.

The Court in *Crawford* offered scathing criticisms of *Roberts,* commenting that *Roberts* departed from "historical principles," that its "malleable standard" was sometimes "too broad" and sometimes "too narrow," and that its "unpardonable vice" was "not its unpredictability, but its demonstrated capacity to admit core testimonial statements that the Confrontation Clause plainly meant to exclude."

2. Defining "Testimonial" for Purposes of the *Crawford* Doctrine

Crawford did not define "testimonial," but did comment that this concept *at the very least* means "*ex parte* testimony at a preliminary hearing" and statements "taken by police officers in the course of interrogations" (using the term "interrogation" in its "colloquial, rather than any technical legal, sense"). In *Crawford* itself, the Court had no doubt that recorded statements given to police by the defendant's wife describing what happened during a fight, which led to charges of assault against both her and her husband, were testimonial in nature.

The Court offered additional descriptions of testimonial statements, without committing itself to any one of them. One description holds that a statement is testimonial if it constitutes "*ex parte* in-court testimony or its functional equivalent," such as "affidavits, custodial examinations, prior testimony that the defendant was unable to cross-examine, or similar pretrial statements that declarants would reasonably expect to be used prosecutorially." In another description, testimonial hearsay includes "extra judicial statements . . . contained in formalized testimonial materials, such as affidavits, depositions, prior testimony, or confessions." Another description holds that statements are testimonial if they are "made under circumstances which would lead an objective witness reasonably to believe that the statement would be available for use at a later trial."

3. The "Emergency" Exception

a. "Emergency" Exception Arrives—The *Davis* Case

Two years after deciding *Crawford*, the Court decided the case of *Davis v. Washington*, 547 U.S. 813 (2006), which held that statements made for purposes of dealing with an ongoing emergency are not testimonial. Obviously *Davis* sharply reduces the reach of the *Crawford* doctrine. To this matter we now turn.

☞ EXAMPLE AND ANALYSIS

Police are dispatched to the home of Hershel and Amy Hammon after Amy placed a 911 call requesting police assistance. In the call, she told the 911 operator that "my husband is hitting me—please send someone quickly," but Hershel yanked the phone away before she could say more. Police arrive shortly thereafter, restrain Hershel, and place him in a separate room while they question Amy. She tells them that Hershel "punched me and shoved me down causing my head to hit the heater." The police arrest Hershel, and he is charged with domestic violence.

At trial, Amy refuses to appear and cannot be located. The prosecutor offers testimony by the police describing her injuries. To prove that Hershel was the assailant, the state also offers (a) Amy's statement to the 911 operator, and (b) her statement to police. Are either or both of these admissible against Hershel?

Answer: Amy's statement to the 911 operator is nontestimonial because it was made for the primary purpose of obtaining police assistance to meet an ongoing emergency. The statement would likely fit the excited utterance exception in FRE 803(2) because it reports a startling or stressful event–the beating that she was experiencing at the hands of her husband. Hence neither the Confrontation Clause nor the hearsay doctrine blocks use of this statement against Hershel Hammon.

Amy's statement to police after they arrive *is* testimonial because there is no longer any ongoing emergency. The primary purpose (perhaps even the sole purpose) of the police questioning was to investigate a possible crime. Hence Amy's statements to them were "testimonial" and must be excluded because she is not subject to cross-examination about them at trial (what would be called *deferred* cross-examination, as is discussed below). Since her statements were not made in court proceedings, such as a preliminary hearing where the defense would have a chance to cross-examine, they were not subject to cross-examination before either (what would be called *prior* cross-examination, as is discussed below). Even if Amy Hammon was still excited at the time she talked in person to the officers, as might well be true because the effect of a beating may produce a kind of excitement or ongoing trauma that makes the excited utterance exception applicable, her statement *still* is not admissible because using it against the accused violates his rights under the Confrontation Clause. See *Davis v. Washington*, 547 U.S. 813 (2006).

b. "Emergency" Exception Evolves—The *Bryant* Case

Five years after *Davis*, the Court revisited the "emergency" exception. In *Michigan v. Bryant*, 131 S.Ct. 1143 (2011), police responding to a reported shooting came upon one Covington in a gas station parking lot at 3:25AM. When asked who had shot him, Covington said "Rick" had done it about 25 minutes earlier (apparently referring to the defendant), that Covington had been talking with Bryant when he was shot "through the back door" of the house. The Court thought the emergency doctrine applied to what Covington told police: Stressing that the situation differed from *Davis* in being nondomestic and involving a gun and an assailant whose location was unknown, the Court clarified *Davis* in three respects. First, the primary purpose standard requires an "objective" assessment that proceeds "by examining the statements and actions of all participants," focusing on "the perspective of the parties" at the time. Second, the Court likened the emergency case to the situation contemplated by the excited utterance exception, where statements are "considered reliable because the declarant, in the excitement, presumably cannot form a falsehood," and it cited "many other exceptions" that are similar, including those for medical statements, business records, and statements against interest. These references suggest the possibility of a broader emergency doctrine than contemplated in the *Davis*. Justice Scalia (author of the opinion in *Davis*) dissented sharply in *Bryant*, both because he thought there was no ongoing emergency and because he thought the hearsay exceptions have nothing to do with the emergency doctrine.

4. Exception to *Crawford*—Testimonial Hearsay by Declarant Subject to Deferred or to Prior Cross–Examination

a. Deferred cross-examination

Crawford stressed that testimonial statements *may be offered* against the accused *after all* if the declarant testifies at trial and can be cross-examined at that time. It is convenient to call cross-examination of this sort "deferred cross-examination" because it comes later, and not when the statement was made. Thus the recorded statement that defendant's wife gave to police in *Crawford* itself could be admitted if she testified at trial and could be cross-examined about those statements. (In fact she did not testify because of the testimonial privilege.)

b. Deferred cross-examination not sufficient under most evidence codes

As a matter of evidence law, the opportunity for delayed cross-examination does not by itself pave the way for out-of-court statements by declarants who testify as witnesses. Most codes treat prior statements by testifying witnesses as inadmissible hearsay, with some exceptions such as the ones contained in FRE 801(d)(1) for prior inconsistent statements given under oath in proceedings, prior consistent statements, and prior statements of identification. See Chapter 3. In this respect, the Confrontation Clause allows more than most evidence codes permit as a matter of hearsay doctrine. But of course *any* out-of-court statement might fit *some* exception, such as the excited utterance exception in FRE 803(2). If so, and if the declarant testifies and is subject to deferred cross-examination, neither the hearsay doctrine nor the Confrontation Clause stands in the way.

c. Prior cross-examination

Crawford also stressed that testimonial statements may be offered against the accused if the declarant was *previously* subject to cross-examination. It is convenient to call cross-examination of this sort "prior cross-examination" because it occurs before trial. Thus testimony given in a preliminary hearing, where the defendant and his lawyer can be present and where the defense may cross-examine witnesses called by the prosecutor, is likely to be admissible. As a matter of hearsay law, if the declarant testifies inconsistently with what he said in the preliminary hearing, FRE 801(d)(1)(A) paves the way to admit his testimony from that hearing, and the Confrontation Clause does not stand in the way, at least if the defense actually cross-examined during the preliminary hearing. If the witness is *unavailable* at trial, his testimony *might* fit the former testimony exception of FRE 804(b)(1), although authorities are split on this point (because neither defendants nor prosecutors have much incentive to cross-examine then, see Chapter 4D2g), and again the Confrontation Clause does not stand in the way, at least if the defense actually cross-examined during the preliminary hearing.

☞ EXAMPLE AND ANALYSIS

Rogers is charged in Ohio state court with possessing stolen credit cards and checks taken from Anita Isaacs, who let him use her apartment. Rogers claims that Anita gave him the cards and checks for his use. At a preliminary hearing, Anita testifies that she did *not* give Rogers permission to use the cards and checks. By the time of trial, Anita has disappeared. The prosecutor offers her preliminary hearing testimony against Rogers, and he is convicted. Before introducing her testimony from the hearing, the prosecutor offers the following evidence to prove that Anita is unavailable to testify at the trial: (1) Anita is no longer living at her apartment; (2) She is not living with her parents (the prosecutor served five subpoenas to the home of her parents but she was not there); (3) Her parents say they have not heard from her since the previous summer; (4) They say she is living or traveling somewhere in California, but neither they nor Anita's brothers know where she is located or how to contact her in an emergency.

The Supreme Court, in the *Roberts* case, found that this proof adequately showed that Anita was unavailable, paving the way to admit her statement. The dissenting justices thought the prosecutor should have done more, including trying to locate a social worker in San Francisco whom Anita's mother spoke with several months earlier and who apparently had contact with Anita. See *Ohio v. Roberts*, 448 U.S. 56 (1980). (Recall that *Crawford* discarded the *Roberts* two-pronged approach to confrontation that required a showing of unavailability and a showing that the proffered statement is reliable, but *Crawford* did not indicate that the *Roberts* approach to defining unavailability was deficient. The *Roberts* holding on this point probably reflects pretty well the approach that courts should take today in deciding whether a witness who previously testified in a preliminary hearing is unavailable. Unavailability appears to be still required, as a constitutional matter, when testimony from a preliminary hearing is offered against the accused.)

5. Other Exceptions to the *Crawford* Scheme

a. Coconspirator Statements

Crawford stated that coconspirator statements are nontestimonial, presumably because conspirators who make such statements do not contemplate their future use in trial or even during a criminal investigation. Such statements fit FRE 801(d)(2)(E) if made "during" and "in furtherance" of a conspiracy, and pretty clearly they have clear sledding under *Crawford*.

b. Dying Declarations

Crawford commented in a footnote that dying declarations represent a "deviation" from a "historical pattern" in which the decided cases, even though they did not rest on the *Crawford* construction of the Confrontation Clause, excluded essentially everything that *Crawford* would exclude. In the footnote, the Court in *Crawford* commented that at least some dying declarations are "clearly testimonial," suggesting that this exception might have to be "accepted on historical" grounds, but that it stands alone. See *Harkins v. State*, 143 P.3d 706 (Nev. 2006) (in murder trial, victim's statement that defendant shot him was dying declaration that can be admitted "as an exception to the Sixth Amendment confrontation right").

c. Business Records

Crawford commented that "business records" are nontestimonial, presumably because the people who make or enter the statements appearing in such records do not contemplate their future use in trial or during a criminal investigation. Such statements are likely to fit FRE 803(6). It is worth noting, however, that some courts resort to the business records exception for police investigative reports that are more at home with the public records exception contained in FRE 803(8), which contains restrictive language blocking use against defendants of such reports. Probably *Crawford* did not mean to endorse this kind of use of the business records exception. The decision in *Melendez–Diaz* in 2009 confirms that forensic lab reports are testimonial (see Chapter 4C7), which strongly suggests that police reports are usually (if not always) testimonial too.

6. Nonhearsay Uses of Out-of-Court Statements Under *Crawford*

a. Confrontation Clause not an obstacle

In a footnote *Crawford* commented that the Confrontation Clause does *not* get in the way of testimonial statements offered "for purposes other than establishing the truth of the matter asserted." The Court cited *Tennessee v. Street*, 471 U.S. 409 (1985), which approved the use against Street of a confession by defendant Peele for the limited purpose of refuting defendant Street's claim that the police had actually read Peele's confession to Street and forced him to sign the same thing.

b. Standard nonhearsay uses

Crawford was not the first case to suggest that nonhearsay uses of out-of-court statements do not offend the Confrontation Clause, but its reiteration of this point is potentially important. The language suggests that the Confrontation Clause is not offended by the use of testimonial statements for any of the standard nonhearsay uses. If so, then prosecutors may offer out-of-court statements when they amount to verbal acts, when they serve to impeach the declarant, or when they are offered to show their effect on the listener.

7. Forfeiture of Right to Exclude Under *Crawford*

Crawford expressly accepted "the rule of forfeiture by wrongdoing," noting that this principle rests on "equitable grounds." Seemingly this statement means that statements that fit FRE 804(b)(6) have clear sledding, although the standard embodied in that provision (forfeiture occurs if the party against whom a statement is offered "wrongfully caused—or acquiesced in wrongfully causing" the unavailability of the declarant, "intending that result") was not vetted or tested in any way in *Crawford*. See *People v. Moreno*, 160 P.3d 242 (Colo. 2007) (discussed in Chapter 4D5, supra).

8. **Nontestimonial Hearsay and the *Roberts* Doctrine**

Prior to *Crawford*, the admissibility of nontestimonial hearsay was governed by *Ohio v. Roberts*, 448 U.S. 56 (1980), which generally required a showing that the hearsay was reliable and the declarant was unavailable to testify. *Crawford* overruled the *Roberts* standard for testimonial hearsay and for a brief period the federal constitutional standard for nontestimonial hearsay remained uncertain. However, in *Davis v. Washington*, 547 U.S. 813 (2006) and *Whorton v. Bockting*, 549 U.S. 406 (2007), the Supreme Court made clear that *Roberts* is overruled in its entirety, even for nontestimonial hearsay. The Court adopted the theory that only declarants who make "testimonial" statements are "witnesses" within the meaning of the Sixth Amendment. Hence nontestimonial hearsay is not governed by the Sixth Amendment, although in extreme cases involving gross unfairness the admission of nontestimonial hearsay against a criminal defendant might violate due process.

9. **Nontestimonial Hearsay Under State Constitutions**

Nontestimonial hearsay may be subject to exclusion, however, under the confrontation clause of state constitutions. A number of states have adopted the *Roberts* two-pronged standard (which used to be the controlling federal standard) as a matter of state constitutional law. Essentially, *Roberts* laid out a two-pronged approach: One prong required hearsay statements offered against the accused to be reliable. The other prong required the prosecutor to demonstrate that the declarant is unavailable to testify.

C. THE *BRUTON* LIMIT

1. **Statements by One Defendant Naming Another Inadmissible**

In its decision in *Bruton v. United States*, 391 U.S. 123 (1968), the Supreme Court decided that a limiting instruction was insufficient to satisfy the rights of the accused under the Confrontation Clause when the prosecutor offers in evidence a statement by a codefendant that incriminates the accused by name. See Chapter 4 Sec. B2a.

2. **Choices for Accommodating *Bruton***

Complying with the *Bruton* restriction means that prosecutors must either forego the use of a statement by one defendant that names and incriminates another or must do one of the following: (A) Try the two defendants separately; (B) empanel two juries, so that the jury that decides the case of the implicated codefendant can be excused when the problematic statement is offered, (C) "redact" the statement by one defendant so that it no longer refers to the other (something that can sometimes be done with written statements, but is much harder to do with oral statements, and sometimes cannot be done at all because redacting can distort meaning too much); (D) use the statement only if the declarant testifies and can be cross-examined by the other defendant (but the prosecutor cannot call a defendant, so this possibility materializes only if the defendant/declarant decides on his own to take the stand).

D. THE RIGHT OF COMPULSORY PROCESS

1. Text of Clause

The Sixth Amendment of the U.S. Constitution provides that in criminal cases the accused "shall enjoy the right . . . to have compulsory process for obtaining witnesses in his favor."

2. Meaning of Compulsory Process

At a basic level, the Compulsory Process Clause guarantees the right of the accused to subpoena defense witnesses and to the assistance of the government in enforcing subpoenas. Under the decided cases, the Clause also entitles defendants in criminal cases to subpoena documents, and to present exculpatory evidence.

3. Overlap with Due Process

In protecting the right to present exculpatory evidence, the Compulsory Process Clause overlaps with the Due Process Clause. The Due Process Clause protects fundamental fairness of trials, and a trial would not conform with due process if a defendant were unreasonably and unfairly denied the opportunity to present exculpatory evidence.

E. A DEFENDANT'S CONSTITUTIONAL RIGHT TO PRESENT EVIDENCE MAY SOMETIMES OVERRIDE EVIDENCE RULES

1. Accomplice Testimony

The Supreme Court has held that preventing accomplices from taking the stand to testify in favor of each other violates the right of compulsory process. In *Washington v. Texas*, 388 U.S. 14 (1967), the Court considered a Texas statute providing that persons charged or convicted as participants in the same crime could not testify for one another (although they could testify as state witnesses against each other). The Court concluded that the statute violated the rights of defendants under the Compulsory Process Clause.

2. Hearsay Rules

Sometimes the constitutional right of a defendant to present evidence overrides the restrictions found in the hearsay law of a state.

☞ EXAMPLES AND ANALYSIS

1. Chambers was charged in Mississippi with murdering a policeman named Sonny Liberty while both were in a hostile crowd. A third person named McDonald gave a sworn written confession to the lawyer for Chambers stating that he killed Liberty, and he made oral confessions to the killing on four other occasions. At trial, Chambers called McDonald to testify and was allowed to read his written confession. But McDonald repudiated his confession, saying on cross by the state that he confessed at the suggestion of another, and in the belief that he would share a sizable tort recovery from the town to be won by Chambers. Invoking both the hearsay doctrine and the state's voucher rule (the party calling the witness may not impeach him), the trial court would not let Chambers question McDonald on his oral confessions or introduce testimony by three witnesses describing them.

    The Supreme Court reversed. It said that testimony about McDonald's confessions was critical, and its exclusion in combination with the refusal to let Chambers cross-examine McDonald denied Chambers a fair trial and violated due process. The Court said that in other situations the exclusion of statements against penal interest might serve a valid state purpose of avoiding untrustworthy testimony. But excluding the other confessions was not justified here because the circumstances provided considerable assurance of their reliability. *Chambers v. Mississippi*, 410 U.S. 284 (1973).

2. Moore and Green were prosecuted separately for raping and murdering Theresa Allen, whom they abducted from the store where she worked and shot two times. Both men were convicted and sentenced to death. During the penalty phase of Green's trial, the court excluded on hearsay grounds testimony by Pasby that Moore said he killed Allen after sending Green on an errand. (The state had argued that the jury could infer that Green had fired one of the shots.)

    Again the Supreme Court reversed because of the exclusion of an exculpatory hearsay confession by another. The Court said the excluded testimony was highly relevant to a critical issue and that there were substantial reasons to think it was reliable. Moore spoke spontaneously to a close friend, there was ample corroborating evidence, the statement was against interest, and there was no reason to think Moore had any ulterior motive. *Green v. Georgia*, 442 U.S. 95 (1979).

3. Other Grounds of Evidentiary Exclusion

A criminal defendant's right to offer exculpatory evidence may also override other evidentiary rules that would otherwise exclude the evidence. For further discussion, see M & K § 4.33 (5th ed. 2012) (discussing constitutional entitlement of the accused, in some cases, to offer evidence of sexual history of the complainant in a sexual assault prosecution despite Rape Shield Statute), § 5.5 (discussing constitutional right to present evidence despite privilege rules that would otherwise exclude such evidence) and § 8.92 (discussing constitutional right to introduce hearsay not fitting exceptions to hearsay rule).

REVIEW QUESTIONS AND ANSWERS

Question: Does the Confrontation Clause affect only the evidence rules pertaining to hearsay?

Answer: No. The Confrontation Clause has an impact on several areas of evidence law, although it only applies in criminal proceedings. It guarantees a criminal defendant the right to be present at trial, and thus comes into play whenever a defendant is excluded from important proceedings or is tried in absentia. It prevents the trial judge from unduly restricting cross-examination or impeachment of prosecution witnesses. In rape trials, the Confrontation Clause may give the defendant the right to bring out evidence pertaining to the complainant's sexual history that would otherwise be excluded by FRE 412 or state Rape Shield laws. The greatest impact of the Confrontation Clause, however, is on hearsay doctrine. Because the term "witnesses against the defendant" has been interpreted to include hearsay declarants, hearsay can be admitted against the defendant only when it satisfies the requirements of the Confrontation Clause.

Question: How does the Confrontation Clause relate to the hearsay doctrine?

Answer: The hearsay doctrine and Confrontation Clause overlap, and both have the effect of restricting the use of hearsay against the accused in a criminal case. But the Confrontation Clause implements a **very different concern** from those underlying the hearsay doctrine. As interpreted in *Crawford*, the Confrontation Clause implements primarily a **procedural concern**: The state may not convict defendants on testimonial statements, such as those given outside of court by eyewitnesses to police investigating crimes, when the defendant has no chance to cross-examine the declarant. In contrast, the hearsay doctrine implements primarily concerns over **reliability and necessity**: Some hearsay is reliable and some is not, and some is more essential and some is less, and the exceptions allow or restrict admissibility accordingly. Moreover, the Confrontation Clause and the hearsay doctrine do not always point to the same conclusion with respect to particular hearsay statements: On the one hand, both would exclude grand jury testimony offered against the accused, for example (it is testimonial under *Crawford,* and generally it does not fit a hearsay exception). On the other hand, statements to police by one defendant incriminating another might qualify as against-interest statements under the hearsay doctrine (making them admissible against both defendants), but such statements would have to be excluded under the Confrontation Clause because they are testimonial.

Question: Can "testimonial" hearsay be offered against criminal defendants?

Answer: In trials in which the declarant does not testify, the answer is, for the most part, no. Testimonial hearsay is inadmissible, if offered against the accused, in cases in which the accused does not have an opportunity to cross-examine (and did not *previously* cross-examine the declarant). In trials in which the declarant does testify, the Confrontation Clause does not block the use of testimonial hearsay for the most part. In this situation, however, it is worth remembering that such hearsay may still be excluded simply because of the hearsay doctrine. (If it does not fit an exception, it is inadmissible as substantive evidence simply because it is *hearsay,* even if the declarant does testify.) It is also worth remembering that the declarant must in fact be cross-examinable, and if he refuses altogether to answer any questions about what he said before, then the opportunity to cross-examine is constitutionally inadequate. (The Supreme Court has given every indication, however, that even a forgetful witness is adequately cross-examinable.) In cases where the declarant *testified before trial* in a preliminary hearing or deposition where the defendant could and did cross-examine on the statements that are later offered at trial, again even this testimonial hearsay is admissible, although this avenue is available to prosecutors only if the witness is unavailable to testify at trial, under a constitutional standard of unavailability (which basically requires the prosecutor to make real efforts to find the witness and bring him to the trial). Finally, bear in mind that out-of-court statements offered for a nonhearsay purpose can also be used against defendants, and that that defendants who kill or threaten witnesses for the purpose of keeping them from testifying may lose the right to exclude what those witnesses have said, in which case objections based on confrontation or hearsay will fail.

Question: What about nontestimonial hearsay?

Answer: For nontestimonial hearsay, such as business records reflecting ordinary transactions (the rental of a car, for example), the Confrontation Clause presents no obstacle. Dying declarations are also admissible, even though these are often testimonial in nature. Co-conspirator statements also count as nontestimonial hearsay that may be used against the accused.

EXAM TIPS

Here are some pointers about constitutional issues of confrontation and compulsory process:

Discuss constitutional issues only if your professor wants you to do so.

The Sixth Amendment applies only in **criminal** cases, and contains critical clauses guaranteeing to the defendant the right to confront witnesses and to have the assistance of compulsory process, and these provisions apply in both state and federal court.

The Confrontation Clause guarantees the right to be present at trial and the right to cross-examine witnesses, which gives rise to the right to limit the use of hearsay against defendants, and to impeach witnesses by asking appropriate questions relating to bias.

For testimonial hearsay, the Confrontation Clause requires exclusion unless the defendant has a chance to cross-examine the declarant, either at trial ("deferred cross-examination") or in proceedings prior to trial ("prior cross-examination").

CHAPTER 6

Character and Habit Evidence

CHAPTER OVERVIEW

The key points in this chapter are

- Character evidence is regulated by rules that say both when evidence of a person's character may be introduced and what form the evidence must take.

- For purposes of evidence law, character means a person's tendency (or "disposition" or "propensity") to engage or not to engage in certain types of behavior. Everyone has multiple traits of character.

- Character evidence generally may not be used to prove conduct reflecting that character on a particular occasion, and this bar against such proof applies across the board in civil cases (with some narrow exceptions made in civil suits arising out of alleged sexual assaults or harassment).

- The bar against proving character in order to show conduct applies in criminal cases too, although important exceptions allow defendants to prove innocence by means of character evidence (and allow prosecutors to rebut), and there are additional exceptions relating to proving behavior by alleged victims of crimes in some cases, as well as exceptions for proving the character of witnesses for truthfulness and an exception for sexual assault cases (where prosecutors can offer character evidence to convict defendants).

- When character evidence is admissible under any of the various exceptions, it generally must take the form of reputation or opinion evidence. Generally specific instances of conduct can only be raised on cross-examination.

- Rape Shield statutes sharply limit proof of the sexual history of rape or sexual assault victims.

- Character evidence is generally admissible when character is an element of a charge, claim, or defense, in which case all three forms of proof are admissible (reputation, opinion, and specific instances).

- Prior crimes, wrongs, or acts are not admissible to prove conduct on a particular occasion.

- Prior crimes, wrongs, or acts are admissible to prove narrower points such as motive, opportunity, intent, preparation, plan, knowledge, identity, or absence of mistake or accident.

- Even when offered on these narrower points, evidence of prior crimes, wrongs, or acts is excluded if it would be unfairly prejudicial to the defendant, or if the jury would be unable to follow a limiting instruction.

- Evidence of the habit of an individual or the routine practice of an organization is generally admissible, and habit is distinguished from character by being more specific, so proof that a person is generally "careful" amounts to character evidence (generally inadmissible), while proof that a person generally drives 75 miles per hour at a particular place on a highway amounts to habit evidence (generally admissible).

A. CHARACTER AND HABIT EVIDENCE GOVERNED BY SPECIFIC RULES

Character and habit evidence present challenging issues of relevancy because the probative value of such evidence must be balanced against significant dangers of unfair prejudice and misleading juries. Admissibility of such evidence is heavily regulated by an intricate and potentially confusing scheme of rules, including FRE 404, 405, 406, 412, 413, 414, and 415. These rules are interrelated but in ways that are not always clear.

B. DEFINITION OF CHARACTER EVIDENCE

"Character" for purposes of evidence law means a person's tendency (disposition or propensity) to engage or not to engage in certain types of behavior, commonly referred to as "traits" of character. Since everyone engages in multiple behaviors, from driving cars to washing dishes to drinking or not drinking such things as coffee and alcohol, everyone has multiple traits of character for purposes of evidence law. A person may have a character for truthfulness or untruthfulness, being peaceable or prone to violence, or qualities of recklessness or carefulness, drunkenness or temperance, or lawfulness or unlawfulness.

C. USES OF CHARACTER EVIDENCE

The key to understanding character evidence is to identify the purpose for which it is being offered. There are three different possible uses for character evidence, and each is subject to different rules of admissibility.

1. Conduct on Specific Occasion

The most common use of character evidence is to prove a person's conduct on a specific occasion (he has a tendency to act in a certain way so he probably acted that way on this occasion). This use of character evidence is known as *circumstantial* or *substantive* use of character evidence. Such use is generally prohibited, subject to important exceptions. The most important of these is the exception allowing the defendant in a criminal case to prove a trait of character that suggests that he did not commit the charged crime. Another important exception lets defendants in criminal cases prove that the alleged victim of the crime was in fact behaving in a criminal manner himself, as happens in assault cases where the defense tries to prove that the alleged victim started the affray by showing that he was generally prone to violence. See FRE 404(a) and the discussion in Section E.

2. Element of Charge, Claim, or Defense

In rare circumstances, a person's character is an element of a criminal charge, a civil claim, or a defense. In such cases, it is sometimes said that the defendant's character is *at issue,* and character evidence is generally admissible. See Section F.

3. To Prove Motive, Intent, or Similar Specific Points

Behavior on specific occasions often reflects traits of character, particularly if the behavior is repeated. For example, a defendant may have been convicted for burglary on three separate occasions. If he is then caught entering someone else's apartment, and he claims that he entered by mistake ("I thought it was a friend's apartment"), his three prior burglaries (as shown by his three convictions) might be proved to show that on this occasion he intended to commit burglary once again, and to rebut his claim of mistake. Evidence of *prior bad acts* to prove intent and similar narrow points is admissible under FRE 404(b), subject to possible exclusion under FRE 403. See Section G.

D. METHODS OF PROVING CHARACTER

There are three traditional methods for proving character: Reputation, opinion, or specific instances of conduct. Which method is allowed depends on the use being made of the evidence—on what it is offered to prove. Permissible methods of proving character are discussed below in conjunction with each permitted use of character evidence.

1. Reputation

A well-accepted method of proving character under both common law and modern codes involves **reputation testimony**, which generally takes the form of accounts offered by a character witness who is familiar with the person's reputation in the community.

a. Relevant community

At one time "community" referred to the geographical area where the person resided. Today most courts allow character witnesses to testify to a person's reputation among colleagues or associates in the workplace, or in a school, church, or other organizational settings. In a cyber age in which relationships sometimes exist largely online or by means of voicemail, email, conference calls, and other "virtual" representations, probably community can include such online centers of activity.

b. Reputation is hearsay

Reputation testimony is hearsay because it is a distillation of the out-of-court statements of community members or associates. An exception to the hearsay rule paves the way for reputation testimony. See FRE 803(21).

2. Opinion

At common law, a character witness could testify *only* to reputation, and could not give an opinion about the person's character. FRE 405(a) discards this limit and also allows **opinion** evidence, provided that the proponent shows that the character witness has an adequate basis in experience to support an opinion. Although this change was controversial, the drafters concluded that reputation testimony is often opinion testimony in disguise. The jury is less likely to be misled when an opinion on a person's character is labeled as such and does not masquerade as reputation.

3. Specific Instances of Conduct

a. Generally not allowed as proof of character

Evidence about **specific instances of behavior** can be a highly revealing indication of the person's character. But for many of the most common uses of character evidence–in criminal cases when the defendant proves his own good character or the prosecutor answers with proof of defendant's bad character under FRE 404(a)(1) and (2)–only reputation or opinion are allowed, and not specific instances of conduct. See FRE 405(a). Evidence of specific instances is excluded because it would consume too much time and divert a trial to side issues (did the person actually do the act to which the character witness would testify?). But sometimes indeed character *can* be proved in order to show conduct, as is true in sexual assault and child abuse prosecutions and civil litigation arising out of such behavior, where the prosecutor (or the claimant in a civil suit) can indeed offer proof of specific instances by the accused (or the defendant in a civil suit). See FRE 412–415.

b. Can be pursued on cross-examination

Even though a character witness generally cannot be asked about specific instances of conduct on direct examination, the cross-examiner can raise such points. See FRE 405(a) (on cross, inquiry is allowed into relevant specific instances of conduct). In a famous decision, the Supreme Court even approved questions asking the character witness whether she had heard about prior *arrests* of the person whose character is being proved (sometimes called the principal or target), although more often the questioner asks about prior acts. See *Michelson v. United States*, 335 U.S. 469 (1948). The acts in question should be at least relevant to the trait of character in question: Thus a character witness who testifies that the principal has a reputation as a peaceful person can be asked whether the principal started a fight on a particular person (which bears on peacefulness), but not whether the principal stole money from his employer (which bears on honesty, but not peacefulness). Seemingly a character witness who testifies simply that the principal is "law abiding" can be asked about any prior criminal conduct, such as violent assault and theft, because any prior crimes bear on the broad "law abiding" character to which the witness has testified.

i.   **Purpose is to test credibility of witness**

The reason to allow the cross-examiner to ask the character witness about specific instances of conduct by the person whose character is being proved (sometimes called the principal or target) is to test the basis for the testimony of the character witness. That is to say, any specific instances of conduct by the principal that come out on cross-examination of the character witness are *not* to be taken as proof of the character of the principal, but rather as some indication of the basis (or lack of basis) for the opinion or reputation being reported. If, for example, a character witness testifies that the defendant has a good reputation for being a peaceable and nonviolent person, then a question asking the character witness whether he "has heard" that the defendant was convicted for violent assault could test the basis of the reputation being reported. If the character witness has not heard of the prior conduct, then perhaps the reputation being reported lacks adequate foundation (how much does the community really know, if the consensus is that the defendant is a peaceful person but nobody ever talks about the assault conviction?). If, on the other hand, the character witness has heard about the prior assault conviction, then perhaps the reputation being reported does reflect relevant information about the defendant, but then one wonders how the reputation could be so good, and the judgment reflected in the good reputation is suspect (how could the community in aggregate think highly of the peaceful disposition of the defendant if he has committed a violent crime?). In this respect, asking questions about prior conduct can make points for the cross-examiner no matter how the witness answers: Either nobody talks about the prior conviction and the reputation reflects *uninformed views* or people do talk about the prior conviction and the reputation reflects *erroneous views*.

ii.   **No extrinsic proof allowed**

Because the proper function of cross-examination about specific instances is only to test the credibility (knowledge and judgment) of the character witness, the questioner is not allowed to prove that the principal actually engaged in the conduct being asked about when the character witness says she has never heard of it (or lacks any knowledge of it, in the case of opinion testimony). Proof that the principal did *not* engage in the conduct being asked about is also normally excluded, unless fundamental fairness mandates another result, in order to correct a groundless insinuation on a critical point.

iii. **Good-faith basis for question**

Before asking about a specific instance of conduct, the cross-examiner must have a demonstrable good-faith basis for believing the conduct actually occurred. A lawyer cannot ask "a groundless question" of the witness, in order "to waft an unwarranted innuendo into the jury box." *Michelson v. United States,* 335 U.S. 469, 481 (1948). A good-faith basis might consist of an official record indicating that the conduct occurred or a statement from a reliable informant with firsthand knowledge. Asking a question without a good-faith basis may constitute grounds for a mistrial as well as professional misconduct by the cross-examiner.

iv. **Exclusion under FRE 403**

The trial court retains discretion to prohibit cross-examination about specific instances of conduct that are insignificant, remote, conjectural, or otherwise unfair.

E. CHARACTER EVIDENCE OFFERED TO PROVE CONDUCT ON SPECIFIC OCCASION IS GENERALLY PROHIBITED

The most fundamental rule is that evidence of a person's character cannot be used to prove conduct in accordance with that character on a specific occasion. The rationale for this rule was set forth by Justice Jackson in the classic case of *Michelson v. United States,* 335 U.S. 469 (1948):

The state may not show defendant's prior trouble with the law, specific criminal acts, or ill name among his neighbors, even though such facts might logically be persuasive that he is by propensity a probable perpetrator of the crime. The inquiry is not rejected because character is irrelevant; on the contrary, it is said to weigh too much with the jury and so overpersuade them as to prejudge one with a bad general record and deny him a fair opportunity to defend against a particular charge. The overriding policy of excluding such evidence, despite its admittedly probative value, is the practical experience that its disallowance tends to prevent confusion of issues, unfair surprise, and undue prejudice.

Example. Sparks is injured in a collision with a truck owned by Gilley Trucking Company. Sparks sues Gilley, alleging that the accident resulted from the negligence of the driver. Gilley asserts that Sparks was guilty of contributory negligence because he was speeding at the time of the accident. To prove that Sparks was speeding, Gilley offers evidence that Sparks was ticketed for speeding on three occasions in the recent past. Even if such tickets are accepted as proof that Sparks was in fact speeding (they are of course hearsay if offered for this purpose, but they may well fit the public records exception in FRE 803(8)), his prior acts of driving faster than the speed limit are not admissible to prove that he was speeding at the time of the accident. Such an inference "is the one specifically prohibited by Rule 404." *Sparks v. Gilley Trucking Co., Inc.*, 992 F.2d 50, 53 (4th Cir. 1993).

1. First Exception: Criminal Defendants

In a criminal trial, FRE 404(a)(1) allows the defendant to offer evidence of a pertinent trait of character to help prove that he did not commit the charged crime. If he does introduce character evidence, the prosecutor may offer character evidence in rebuttal.

a. Exception long recognized

The ACN to FRE 404 describes this exception as "so deeply imbedded in our jurisprudence as to assume almost constitutional proportions and to override doubts of the basic relevancy of the evidence."

b. "Pertinent" trait

The character evidence offered under this Rule must relate to the type of crime charged. An accused may offer evidence of his peaceable disposition when charged with a crime of violence such as assault, or he may offer proof of his honest tendencies when charged with a crime of dishonesty, such as embezzlement. In a trial for assault, however, proof that defendant is "honest" would not be pertinent. Likewise, in a trial for embezzlement, proof that defendant is peaceable would not be pertinent.

c. Form of proof

The character witness, whether called by the defendant or the prosecution, can testify on direct only as to reputation or opinion, and not to specific instances. On cross-examination, however, the character witness can be asked about specific instances of conduct by the person whose character is being proved.

d. When accused attacks victim's character

FRE 404(a)(1) allows the prosecutor to prove the character of the accused in one additional circumstance (in addition to the situation in which the prosecutor offers evidence of the character of the accused in order to rebut his proof of his own good character). The prosecutor may also offer proof going to the character of the accused if he proves the character of the "alleged victim," and in this situation the prosecutor may offer evidence of the defendant's same trait. In a battery trial, for example, if the defendant proves that the alleged victim was an aggressive person (as evidence that he started the affray), then the prosecutor may prove that the *defendant* is an aggressive person (to refute the defense argument, and to prove that in fact the defendant started the affray).

☞ EXAMPLE AND ANALYSIS

Raymond is tried for embezzling from the bank where he worked. He does not deny that funds are missing from accounts under his care, but he denies that he took the money. He calls Reverend Greg Norton, the minister of the church that he has attended for 20 years, as a character witness. Reverend Norton testifies that he has worked closely with Raymond for many years in connection with various church fundraising projects, and that Raymond served as chairman of the Board of Trustees, which manages all the church's financial assets. On the basis of this long acquaintance with Raymond, Reverend Norton gives his opinion that Raymond is "scrupulously honest" and "totally trustworthy in handling other people's money."

This character evidence is offered for the purpose that is generally prohibited by FRE 404—to prove that Raymond has an honest character, hence that he probably acted honestly on the occasion of the charged crime, and therefore that Raymond probably did not embezzle the bank's money. If money is missing from the accounts, there must be some other reason. But such evidence is admissible under FRE 404(a)(1).

2. Second Exception: Crime Victims

In a criminal trial, evidence of a "pertinent trait" of character of an alleged crime victim is admissible in three situations under FRE 404(a)(2): (1) It is admissible when offered by the accused to prove his innocence. (2) It is admissible when offered by the prosecutor to rebut character evidence offered by the accused. (3) It is admissible in a homicide case when the prosecutor offers character evidence pertaining to the peacefulness of the alleged victim to rebut defense evidence that the alleged victim was the first aggressor.

☛ EXAMPLE AND ANALYSIS

During a fight at Humbolt Penitentiary, Quinn is shoved over a railing and falls down three tiers of cell blocks to his death on the concrete floor below. Ramon is charged with his murder. Ramon asserts self-defense and claims that Quinn was coming after him with a steel shank to retaliate for his nonpayment of a gambling debt to a prison gang leader. Ramon says he stepped aside at the last moment and Quinn went flying over the railing. As proof that Quinn was the aggressor, Ramon calls three fellow inmates who testify that Quinn had a reputation in the prison as a "bully" and "hit man" who would attack other prisoners in exchange for drugs or money.

Such evidence relates to a pertinent trait of the victim's character because it suggests that Quinn was the aggressor. If the matter were governed by the general rule stated in FRE 404(a), the evidence would have to be excluded because it is offered to prove that Quinn acted in accordance with his character on the occasion (he was the aggressor). But in fact the evidence is admissible under FRE 404(a)(2). The latter provision also lets the prosecutor call witnesses in rebuttal to give reputation or opinion testimony that Quinn is a peaceable person. In attacking Quinn's character by showing his propensity for violence, Ramon also opened the door to evidence of his own propensity for violence, which the prosecutor could offer under 404(a)(1) to prove that Ramon was the first aggressor.

---

a. **Form of proof**

A character witness, whether called by the defendant or the prosecutor, can testify on direct only about reputation or opinion, not specific instances of conduct. The character witness may, however, be asked about specific instances on cross-examination. In the above example, the character witnesses called by Ramon can give only reputation or opinion testimony about Quinn's character. Such a character witness is not allowed to describe specific instances of Quinn's prior conduct.

b. **Rape Shield statutes**

The general rule that a defendant may prove a pertinent trait of a victim's character has been qualified by "Rape Shield" provisions that are in effect in all states and in the federal system. The federal rape shield statute is FRE 412, and it restricts evidence of a sex crime victim's character that might otherwise be admissible under FRE 404(a)(2). If the latter provision controlled, a defense attorney might offer evidence that an alleged rape victim has a propensity (or trait of character) that would lead her to consent to engage in sexual conduct, which could be offered to prove that she consented on the occasion of the charged crime. But FRE 412 governs in this setting (it was enacted several years after FRE 404). In both civil and criminal proceedings involving alleged sexual misconduct, FRE 412(a) generally bars evidence that the alleged victim "engaged in other sexual behavior" and generally bars proof that the alleged victim has some particular "sexual predisposition." There are four exceptions to this general rule of exclusion.

i. Proving alternative source of semen or injury

One exception to the general rule of exclusion allows the defendant to prove sexual behavior by the alleged victim in order to show that some third person was the **source of the semen, injury, or other physical consequences** of the alleged sexual contact. It would be unfair to allow the prosecutor to offer evidence of semen to prove defendant had intercourse with the alleged victim but not to allow the defendant to prove that the alleged victim recently had intercourse with someone else who could have been the source of the semen.

ii. Prior sexual behavior with accused

A second exception allows evidence of prior instances of sexual behavior by the alleged victim **with the accused** when offered on the issue of consent. In cases of date rape or marital rape in which consent is the only contested issue, the past sexual relationship between the parties may be sufficiently probative to override the general rule of exclusion.

iii. Constitutionally required to be admitted

A third exception allows evidence of prior sexual history or predisposition of the alleged victim when excluding it would violate the **constitutional rights** of the defendant. The scope of this exception is uncertain. Under the Sixth Amendment guarantees of confrontation and compulsory process, defendants sometimes have a constitutional right to introduce exculpatory evidence even when it is inadmissible as a matter of evidence law. For a discussion of circumstances when an accused may be constitutionally entitled to offer evidence of sexual history of an alleged sex crime victim, see M & K § 4.33.

Example. Indicted for kidnapping, rape, and forcible sodomy of Starla Matthews, James Olden claims consent. At trial, Olden seeks to show that Matthews was cohabiting with Bill Russell at the time, and that she had a motive to fabricate the rape charges against Olden to preserve her relationship with Russell. The trial judge excludes this evidence and persists in this ruling even after Matthews testifies that she was living with her mother. This case reached the Supreme Court, which held that refusing to let Olden impeach Matthews by introducing this evidence suggesting that she had a motive to lie deprived the accused of his Sixth Amendment right to confront witnesses against him. *Olden v. Kentucky,* 488 U.S. 227 (1988).

iv. **Civil cases**

A fourth exception applies only in civil cases, and allows proof of the sexual behavior or sexual predisposition of any alleged victim when "its probative value substantially outweighs the danger of harm to any victim and of unfair prejudice to any party" and such evidence is otherwise admissible under the Rules of Evidence. Normally such proof is in the form of specific instances of conduct. The rule specifically prohibits evidence of the alleged victim's reputation unless it has been placed in controversy by her.

v. **Notice of intent to offer**

At least 14 days before trial (unless the court for good cause allows a different time), a party seeking to offer evidence under one of the four exceptions listed in FRE 412(b) must file and serve on all parties a motion specifically describing the evidence and stating the purpose for which it is offered. The party must also notify the alleged victim or, when appropriate, the alleged victim's guardian or representative.

vi. **Hearing** *in camera*

Before admitting evidence under FRE 404(a), the court must conduct a hearing to determine whether the evidence qualifies under one of the exceptions. The victim and parties must be afforded a right to attend and be heard. All papers and records relating to the hearing are required to be sealed and to remain under seal until the court orders otherwise.

3. Third Exception: Witnesses

In both criminal and civil cases, evidence of the character of a witness is admissible to the extent allowed by the rules governing impeachment of witnesses, particularly FRE 607, 608, 609. This exception is necessary to prevent a conflict between FRE 404(a)'s general prohibition against character evidence offered to prove conduct on a particular occasion and the rules governing impeachment, which allow evidence of that a witness is by disposition either truthful or untruthful in order to prove that the witness either is or is not being truthful in testifying.

☛ EXAMPLE AND ANALYSIS

Kelly is charged with filing a false and fraudulent financial statement in order to obtain a loan from a federally insured bank. He testifies in his own defense and denies intentionally misstating any information in the financial statement. On cross, the prosecutor impeaches Kelly by asking him about false statements that he made on his tax returns. (This form of impeachment is allowed by FRE 608(b), discussed in Chapter 10.)

Bringing out false statements on tax returns is part of an effort to show that Kelly is by nature untruthful, hence that his testimony should not be believed (proof of bad character is offered to prove that Kelly is acting in accordance with that untruthful character on the specific occasion of testifying). This mode of impeachment conflicts with the general rule of FRE 404(a) against offering character evidence to prove conduct, but FRE 404(a)(3) creates an exception that paves the way for this attack to go forward.

4. Fourth Exception: Sexual Assault Cases

Three rules (FRE 413–415) significantly expand the permissible use of character evidence in sexual assault and child molestation cases. These rules were enacted by Congress as part of a politically charged crime bill and did not go through the usual rulemaking process. These rules are controversial and were opposed by both the Judicial Conference and the ABA House of Delegates.

Although FRE 413–415 do not refer to FRE 404, they effectively amend it *sub silencio* in allowing the use of character evidence to prove conduct in accordance with such character in sexual assault and child molestation cases.

a. Sexual assault prosecutions

In any criminal case in which defendant is accused of sexual assault, FRE 413 allows evidence that defendant has committed other sexual assaults, and such evidence "may be considered for its bearing on any matter to which it is relevant." Contrary to FRE 404(a), in other words, FRE 413 allows the evidence (prior offenses showing propensity to commit sexual assaults) to prove that defendant committed the assault for which he is prosecuted.

i. **No conviction required**

FRE 413 does not require that the prior offense result in a conviction, or even that it was previously reported or prosecuted.

ii. **Application of FRE 403**

Originally it was unclear whether FRE 403 was available to exclude evidence of prior offenses that would be unfairly prejudicial or misleading to the jury. FRE 413(c) says that the rule "shall not be construed to limit the admission or consideration of evidence under any other rule" but does *not* say that evidence can be excluded under any other rule. But legislative history indicates that FRE 413 is subject to FRE 403, and the courts have so construed FRE 413.

iii. **Notice required**

If the government intends to offer evidence under this rule, the prosecutor is required to disclose the evidence to the defendant (including witness statements and summaries of anticipated testimony) at least 15 days prior to trial unless the court allows a later time for good cause.

iv. **Definition of sexual offense**

FRE 413 includes a wide variety of sexual offenses under both federal and state law, including conspiracy to engage in such sexual offenses. The covered offenses are listed in FRE 413(d).

b. **Child molestation prosecutions**

FRE 414 is virtually identical to FRE 413, except that it applies to prosecutions for child molestation and allows evidence that defendant committed previous molestation offenses (as opposed to sexual offenses, although molestation is often if not always sexual too).

c. **Civil cases involving sexual assault or child molestation**

FRE 415 extends the policy of FRE 413 and FRE 414 into the civil arena. In a civil case in which a claim for damages or other relief is predicated on a party's alleged commission of conduct constituting an offense of sexual assault or child molestation, evidence of that party's commission of another offense of sexual assault or child molestation is admissible. As under FRE 413–414, such evidence "may be considered for its bearing on any matter to which it is relevant."

F. CHARACTER EVIDENCE GENERALLY ADMISSIBLE WHEN CHARACTER IS ELEMENT OF CHARGE, CLAIM, OR DEFENSE

Sometimes character is an element of a charge, claim, or defense. In such cases, which are relatively rare, character evidence is admissible without limitation. FRE 404(a) does not apply because character is being proved for its own sake, not for the "substantive" purpose of supporting an inference that a person behaved in a certain way on a particular occasion.

1. Criminal Cases

Character is rarely an element of a criminal charge or defense. The elements of a crime virtually always relate to the accused's conduct on a particular occasion, not to his general character or propensities.

a. Entrapment defense

The defendant's character may be an element of an entrapment defense, at least in jurisdictions adopting a subjective test of entrapment that focuses on whether the defendant was "predisposed" to commit such a crime rather than an objective standard focusing on the extent of government misconduct. A person's predisposition toward engaging in certain conduct is usually what is meant by character evidence.

b. Habitual offender

Statutes imposing enhanced penalties on persons who are "habitual offenders" present one example in which one might say that character is an element of the charge, but in this setting it seems more accurate to view such statutes as merely requiring proof of a prior conviction, rather than proof of the defendant's character as such.

c. Felon-in-possession

Statutes prohibiting ex-felons from possessing firearms allow proof of the felony convictions as an element of the charge, but again the "character" as such is not really at issue.

2. Civil Cases

There are some important but fairly isolated instances in civil cases where character constitutes an element of a claim or defense. (As in criminal cases, in which conduct on a particular occasion is the central concern, so to in civil cases usually conduct on a particular occasion is the central concern.)

a. Negligent entrustment

Negligent entrustment is a good example of a case in which a person's character is an element of a claim, although it is not the character of the plaintiff or the defendant. In this setting, plaintiff must prove that defendant was negligent in entrusting an instrumentality to a third person, or in hiring or failing to supervise or control a person, and that defendant's negligence consisted in not properly understanding that the person in question was by character or disposition unsuited for the role that the defendant asked him to play. Usually in practice, the claim is that the person entrusted to drive a car or operate some piece of equipment was by disposition careless, or at least not sufficiently careful or mature in his judgment to operate the equipment in question. Hence the character of that third person is an element of the claim that must be proved in order to establish that the defendant was negligent.

b. Defamation

In a defamation case where defendant raises truth as a defense, plaintiff's character is likely to be an element of the defense. Assume, for example that a newspaper publishes a story saying the mayor is corrupt, and that the mayor sues the newspaper for defamation. If the newspaper "stands by the story" and claims that it is true, then the newspaper may prove that in fact the mayor *is* corrupt. That means proving that he is corrupt by disposition or trait character, or that he engages in acts of corruption, to establish the truth of the published story. An important distinction should be noted. Plaintiff's *reputation* is an element in all defamation claims because it is the standard by which damages are measured. But *character* and *reputation* are different. *Character* describes the actual nature or disposition of the person, while *reputation* refers to the community's idea or view of the person. *Character* is an element only when the allegedly defamatory statement impugns plaintiff's character, and defendant asserts truth as a defense in the suit.

c. Wrongful death

In wrongful death cases, the character of the decedent is an element of damages. Thus evidence of the decedent's work habits, criminal record, drunkenness, adultery, gambling, and similar forms of behavior is generally admitted because it bears on such issues as likely future earnings and the degree and nature of the loss suffered by the claimants in the case.

d. Child custody

In child custody disputes, special aspects of the character of the parents or caregivers is almost always in issue. The fitness of each parent or caregiver for good parenting is a central issue, and is viewed as an element of each party's claim, and parental fitness is at least one aspect of character.

3. Form of Proof When Character Is an Element

In cases in which character is an essential element of a charge, claim, or defense, character may be proved not only by reputation and opinion evidence but also by specific instances of that person's conduct. FRE 405(b). In the situations listed above, then, specific instances can be proved. In a negligent entrustment claim, plaintiff can prove prior specific acts of negligence by the person entrusted with the car or other equipment. In a libel suit in which a newspaper stands by its story that the mayor is corrupt (raising truth as a defense), the newspaper can prove specific corrupt acts by the mayor. In a wrongful death case where, for example, a widow sues for the death of her husband, the defendant can prove that the husband had been repeatedly fired from jobs on account of drunkenness or drug abuse. And in a child custody dispute, each parent seeking custody can prove that the other did specific things that bring into question his or her fitness to care for the child.

G. PRIOR ACTS ADMISSIBLE TO PROVE SPECIFIC POINTS

FRE 404(b) restates the principle of FRE 404(a) that evidence of other crimes, wrongs, or acts "is not admissible to prove a person's character in order to show that on a particular occasion the person acted in accordance with the character." But the Rule goes on to say that such evidence is admissible for narrower purposes, such as proving motive, opportunity, intent, preparation, plan, knowledge, identity, or absence of mistake or accident.

1. Listing Not Exclusive

FRE 404(b) lists permissible uses of specific instances of conduct, but the list is exemplary and not exhaustive. Prior crimes, wrongs, or acts are potentially admissible, subject to FRE 403, when offered for any relevant purpose that does not require an inference from character to conduct.

2. Purpose Must Be Specified

The party offering evidence of prior crimes, wrongs, or acts under FRE 404(b) must specify the particular purpose for which it is offered. The proponent should not simply recite the uses listed in the Rule.

3. Listed Purposes

a. Motive

Prior crimes, wrongs, or acts may be used to prove motive. For example, courts admit evidence that defendant has an expensive drug habit to prove motive for a financial crime, such as bank robbery. *United States v. Saniti*, 604 F.2d 603 (9th Cir. 1979). When prior crimes are offered to prove motive, they need not be similar in nature to the charged offense.

b. Opportunity

Prior acts may show that defendant was in the vicinity of the crime when it was committed, or had access to some crucial instrumentality, or had the necessary knowledge, familiarity, or experience to commit the crime. For example, the fact that defendant had escaped from prison could be admitted to establish his presence in the vicinity of a car theft. *United States v. Stover*, 565 F.2d 1010 (8th Cir. 1977).

c. Intent

Prior crimes are sometimes highly probative on the issue of intent, but in this situation generally there must be a close resemblance between the prior crime and the charged crime, or at the very least they must involve the same mental state. In a trial of a prisoner for possessing objects designed or intended for use in escape, proof of defendant's involvement in prior escapes may be admissible to show his intent or state of mind in possessing such objects. See *United States v. Archer*, 843 F.2d 1019 (7th Cir. 1988). Since intent is almost always important in proving guilt of a crime, prosecutors can argue that virtually all previous crimes similar to the charged offense are always relevant, but if this view carried the day, it would sharply undermine the protective policy behind the general bar against proving other acts to show conduct. Hence courts often allow the use of prior crimes to prove intent only if intent is a genuine issue, as in cases where defendant denies intent and vigorously argues the point or offers testimony or evidence that the requisite intent was not there. In a trial for car theft, for example, the claim that defendant only "borrowed the automobile" constitutes a denial of intent that may make it important to show that he committed car theft before. See *United States v. Dudley*, 562 F.2d 965 (5th Cir. 1977) (admitting prior conviction for car theft).

d. Preparation

Sometimes evidence of a prior crime can show preparation for the charged crime. For example, in a trial for attempted bank robbery, proof that on the prior day defendant stole a car to use as the getaway vehicle would be admissible as evidence of preparation.

e. Plan

Prior crimes are often relevant in proving plan. For example, when defendant is charged with conspiracy to import illegal drugs, evidence that he attempted to bribe customs agents and incorporate them into his criminal enterprise would be admissible as evidence of plan.

f. Knowledge

Prior crime evidence is often used to prove knowledge. For example, if defendant is charged with passing counterfeit currency, and he denies knowing it was counterfeit, the fact that he was previously convicted of selling counterfeit currency could be admitted to prove knowledge. *United States v. Beaver*, 524 F.2d 963 (5th Cir. 1975).

g. Identity

Using prior crimes to prove identity overlaps with several other categories. Proof of motive, knowledge, opportunity, intent, plan, and preparation may all tend to identify defendant as the perpetrator of a crime. Usually, however, this category describes cases in which the charged crime was committed by means of a **modus operandi** that is **distinctive and unusual** that also bears **very close resemblance** to some crime that the defendant committed on a prior occasion. In this situation, it is sometimes said that the prior crime and the charged offense are "signature" crimes that were very probably committed by the same person. Hence showing that the defendant committed such a crime before in powerful evidence that he probably committed the charged crime, and the evidence is admitted as proof of identity.

h. Absence of mistake or accident

Proving prior crimes or acts can sometimes rebut a claim that the charged crime was an accident or mistake. In many cases, for example, a defendant charged with unlawfully receiving child pornography claims that he acquired it by mistake, not realizing that he was purchasing images or videos of underage children. To rebut this claim, the government proved that defendant possessed other child pornography. *United States v. Dornhofer*, 859 F.2d 1195 (4th Cir. 1988).

4. Unlisted Purposes

a. Proving context

There are other permissible uses for prior acts that lie beyond those listed in FRE 404(b). Sometimes in the course of proving the charged crime, for example, it is necessary for the prosecutor to prove other crimes to provide background or context that is important to an understanding of the facts surrounding the charged offense. Evidence necessary for a full understanding or to bridge a chronological gap in the government's proof may be admitted under FRE 404(b).

> **Example.** Leichtman is tried for kidnapping. At trial the government offers evidence that the victims were held captive because they had taken delivery from Leichtman and his associates of $1 million of marijuana for which they never paid. Leichtman objects that this evidence improperly alerts the jury to other uncharged crimes, but here such proof is probably necessary. See *United States v. Leichtman*, 742 F.2d 598 (11th Cir. 1984) (approving "marijuana evidence" under FRE 404(b) because it was "necessary to complete the story of the kidnapping" and put the events "in context").

i. Temporal relation not enough

Other crime evidence cannot come in merely because it is temporally related to the charged crime. It must be necessary or helpful to the jury's understanding of the charged crime or to avoid presentation of a time sequence with puzzling gaps in it.

ii. Crimes "inextricably intertwined"

Proof of context must be distinguished from crimes that are "inextricably intertwined." Sometimes several crimes are so interconnected that one cannot be proved without the other. For example, proof that a defendant sold contraband requires proof of possession. Some courts hold that an intertwined crime may be proved without justifying its admission under FRE 404(b) on the theory that the rule restricts only proof of extrinsic or "other" crimes and that intertwined crimes are "intrinsic" to the charged offense. But there is little or no point in exempting this category of proof from FRE 404(b), and the better view is that crimes offered because they are "inextricably intertwined" are still subject to FRE 403.

b. **To rebut insanity defense**

When the accused raises an insanity defense, evidence of prior acts is sometimes admitted on the question whether defendant had cognitive ability or volitional control. For example, prior crimes reveal defendant's mental process and ability to orchestrate a crime. They may also indicate that he appreciated the criminality of his conduct.

c. To rebut entrapment defense

Sometimes courts admit prior crimes evidence to show that defendant was predisposed to committing a certain type of crime, hence was not entrapped by government misconduct (overly aggressive "sting" operations). Some courts admit such evidence of predisposition under FRE 404(b). Others take the view that defendant's character is an element of an entrapment defense. See Section F.

d. To show consciousness of guilt

Sometimes prior acts are used to show defendant's consciousness of guilt. For example, an attempt to escape or to bribe the arresting officer may be introduced to show the defendant's consciousness of guilt.

e. To contradict defendant's testimony

Prior bad act evidence is admissible to contradict an inaccurate statement or misleading suggestion by defendant in his testimony. If, for example, defendant claims that he was never arrested or convicted before, or "never in trouble with the law," or that he never committed a crime before, the prosecutor can rebut such statements by contradicting them in appropriate ways. A claim of never being arrested can lead to counterproof that defendant *was* arrested after all; a claim of never being convicted may lead to proof that defendant *was* convicted; a claim of never being in trouble with the law can lead to proof of prior arrests or convictions; a claim of never having committed a crime can lead to counterproof that defendant was convicted or that he committed prior crimes (which can be proved by eyewitness testimony, often involving testimony by police or law enforcement personnel who describe drug transactions). Such evidence is admissible under the "opening the door" doctrine discussed in Chapter 1, and it is admissible under the theory of impeachment by contradiction discussed in Chapter 10, infra.

5. Degree of Similarity Required

FRE 404(b) does not necessarily require that the prior act be similar to the charged crime. For some uses of prior act evidence, such as showing motive, similarity is not required. For others, such as proving knowledge, similarity may be necessary for the evidence to have probative value. When offered to prove **modus operandi,** the prior act must have *a high degree of distinctive similarity* in order to show that the two crimes bear the "signature" of the accused, so his participation in the first persuasively shows his probable participation in the second.

6. Certainty That Prior Act Was Committed

The proponent of prior act evidence bears the burden of proving that the prior conduct occurred.

a. Forms of proof

The most certain and persuasive way of proving that the prior misconduct occurred is by evidence of a criminal conviction, whether based on a verdict or guilty plea. A conviction is not required, however, and the prior act can be proved by other forms of evidence.

b. Standard of proof

In federal courts, a prior act can be admitted under FRE 404(b) on the basis of proof that is sufficient to support a finding that the defendant committed the prior act. *Huddleston v. United States*, 485 U.S. 681 (1988). Under *Huddleston*, the question whether defendant committed the prior act for the jury to decide under FRE 104(b) as a matter of conditional relevancy, and not a question for the judge to decide under FRE 104(a) as a matter of admissibility. See Chapters 1 and 2. The *Huddleston* approach has been sharply criticized because of the danger of unfair prejudice to a defendant that comes from involving the jury in deciding this point and in allowing the point to be established on the basis of proof satisfying merely the preponderance standard. Some states refuse to follow *Huddleston*, either by requiring that the judge determine whether the defendant committed the prior act or by requiring that the prior act be proved by clear and convincing evidence, or by taking both these steps.

c. Prior acquittals

A prior crime may be proved under FRE 404(b) even if defendant has been charged and acquitted of that crime. See *Dowling v. United States*, 493 U.S. 342 (1990) (such use does not violate Double Jeopardy or Due Process clauses; jury can weigh probative value, and defendant can show fact of acquittal). The acquittal establishes only the presence of reasonable doubt and is not a specific determination that the defendant was not involved in the earlier crime. Under their counterparts to FRE 404(b), however, some states bar proof of crimes of which defendant was acquitted.

7. Exclusion Under FRE 403

Evidence that fits FRE 404(b) is subject to exclusion under FRE 403. The ACN to FRE 404(b) specifically states that a "determination must be made whether the danger of undue prejudice outweighs the probative value of the evidence" under FRE 403. Factors to be considered include:

a. **Whether issue disputed**

Prior crime evidence offered to prove an undisputed issue is less likely to be admitted.

b. **Certainty of proof of prior act**

The more uncertain the proof that the prior act occurred, the less likely it is to be admitted.

c. **Probative force of evidence**

If prior act has only marginal probative force (for example, because of its remoteness in time), it is more likely to be excluded.

d. **Inflammatory or prejudicial effect**

Prior act evidence of an inflammatory nature is more likely to be excluded.

e. **Need for evidence**

If the proponent can establish the point by other evidence (or has already done so), the court is less likely to admit the prior act evidence.

f. **Effectiveness of limiting instruction**

The greater the likelihood of jury confusion between the permissible and impermissible uses of prior act evidence, the stronger the argument for exclusion under FRE 403.

g. **Prolong proceedings**

In undertaking the FRE 403 balancing, courts consider the extent to which other acts evidence will consume time or prolong the proceedings. More trial time is required if the prior acts must be proved by extrinsic evidence. Proof can range from the simple introduction of a prior conviction to eliciting extensive testimony from multiple witnesses.

8. **Notice Required**

In a criminal case, the prosecution must, on request by the defense, provide notice in advance of trial of the general nature of evidence that it intends to offer under FRE 404(b) of other crimes, wrongs, or acts. Such notice may be given during trial if the court excuses pretrial notice for good cause shown.

H. EVIDENCE OF HABIT OR ROUTINE PRACTICE ADMISSIBLE

Under FRE 406, evidence of the habit of a person or the routine practice of an organization is admissible to prove that the conduct of the person or organization on a particular occasion was in conformity with the habit or routine practice. FRE 406 is unusual in stating a principle of admissibility rather than a rule of limitation or exclusion.

1.   Distinction Between Character and Habit Evidence

While evidence of **character** is generally inadmissible to prove conduct under FRE 404, evidence of **habit** is generally admissible for this purpose under FRE 406. The reason for the distinction is that habit describes particular behavior in a specific setting and is by nature at least regular if not invariable. Thus it has greater probative value in proving conduct on a particular occasion than does evidence of general propensities. Also habit evidence is less likely to carry moral overtones or to present serious dangers of unfair prejudice or confusion.

2.   Definition of Habit

Habit is defined by the ACN to FRE 406 as a person's "regular practice of meeting a particular kind of situation with a specific type of conduct" (quoting McCormick). It is hard in practice to distinguish character from habit, but courts generally stress that (a) habit is more specific than character (always signaling a particular turn is habit; driving carefully involves a trait of character), (b) habit involves behavior that is more regular than character (always paying for gas with a credit card is habit; being willing to use credit involves a trait of character), and (c) habit is more automatic or unreflective than character (descending the stairs in two-step rhythmic pairs is habit; generally getting places on time involves a trait of character). These are examples of behaviors that may be considered habits: Carrying the car keys in the left front pants pocket, storing the checkbook in a zipped inner pocket of the purse; always locking the front door before retiring to bed at night. More general behavioral patterns are usually considered to reflect traits of character: Driving carefully, keeping cool in tense situations, being quick to anger; always seeing the humor in unexpected situations; getting quickly upset when plans change are all related to character and would not be considered habits.

Example.   Wanda Lee is the beneficiary on a life insurance policy on her husband Roger. After Roger died and the insurance company refused to pay on the policy, Wanda sues. The insurance company defends on the ground that Roger intentionally made oral misrepresentations about his health and medical history to the medical examiner when he applied for the policy. The company offers the notes taken by the examiner in her interview with Roger. To rebut this evidence, Wanda offers evidence that the "usual practice" of the examiner is not to record answers to health history questions in the same way the applicants "verbally answered them." This evidence is admissible under FRE 406 and may be considered in deciding whether Roger intended to make misrepresentations on his life insurance application. *Lee v. National Life Assurance Co.*, 632 F.2d 524 (5th Cir. 1980).

Example.   Levin is charged with obtaining money through larceny by trick. He asserts an alibi defense, claiming he was home observing the Sabbath. To support this defense, he offers evidence of his alleged "habit" to stay home on the Sabbath. The evidence should be excluded, since such activity is volitional in nature, rather than reflecting unconscious "habits." See *Levin v. United States*, 338 F.2d 265 (D.C. Cir. 1964) (cited in ACN to FRE 406).

3.   Methods of Proving Habit

Habit is usually proved by witnesses describing prior specific instances of conduct. The observations may be "bundled" by a witness who says in substance "he always put his hat on the third peg" and describes a period of observation sufficient to convince the court that the proof shows habit.

a.   Sufficient instances

There must be a large enough sample to establish a pattern of behavior and a sufficient uniformity of response. The court decides under FRE 104(a) whether the witness can describe enough instances to show habit. If not, the testimony may be excluded.

b.   Opinion

Most modern courts also allow habit to be proved by opinion testimony, provided the witness has an adequate basis of personal knowledge. FRE 406 as originally drafted would have specifically allowed opinion evidence to prove habit. This part of the Rule was deleted, but Congress did not disapprove opinion testimony to prove habit.

4.   Common Law Limitations on Habit Evidence

FRE 406 expressly rejects two limitations on habit evidence that were imposed by the common law—one was a requirement that it be corroborated, and the other was that habit was to be proved only if there were no eyewitnesses. These conditions are abolished by FRE 406.

5.   Organizational Routine

Courts are more generous toward proof of organizational routine, perhaps because moral overtones are missing. Examples include warrant service procedures of the Immigration and Naturalization Service, insurance company practices in waiving policy requirements, and mechanics of office mailing mechanisms.

REVIEW QUESTIONS AND ANSWERS

Question: Why is character evidence generally prohibited as a means of proving conduct on a particular occasion?

Answer: There are several reasons. First, character evidence often has relatively low probative value when offered to prove conduct on a particular occasion. The fact that a person has a general tendency to behave in a certain way does not necessarily mean he did so at a particular time. Assume that it can be shown that *A* runs a particular stopsign approximately once a month. This evidence has lower probative value than it might initially seem if *A* drives every day (because the evidence suggests that approximately 29 days out of 30 *A* does *not* run that stopsign). Hence proof that he runs the stopsign once a month has little probative value on the question whether he did so on a particular day. Evidence of *A's* behavior in running the stopsign meets the relevancy standard of FRE 401 because it makes it "more probable" that *A* ran the stop sign on the day in question, but one concern is that such evidence would likely be "overvalued"–given more weight than it deserves. Evidence about a person's character is also thought to be prejudicial because it invites the jury to decide the case on the basis of what kind of person the defendant is, rather than on the basis of what he did or did not do on the occasion in question. A basic tenet of law is that a defendant must be tried for *what he did*, not for *who he is*. Freely admitting evidence of past conduct could deny a party a fair trial despite the justness of his cause and force him not only to answer the specific allegations against him but to defend his entire personal history.

Question: Why are there so many restrictions on the forms of evidence that can be used to prove character and why do they vary so much depending on the use that is being made of character evidence?

Answer: Character evidence presents great dangers of diverting a trial to side issues, prejudicing a party, and invading privacy. Therefore, even when evidence law permits proof of a person's character, courts want the evidence presented in a way that takes the least time and causes the least diversion from central issues. Reputation was the favored method of the common law for proving character because it takes relatively little time to present and focuses directly on the pertinent trait. The Rules expanded the common law to allow proof by opinion testimony. Proving character by specific instances is the least favored form of proof. It is time-consuming and likely to divert the attention of the jury, particularly when parties dispute the question whether the prior acts even occurred and disagree about surrounding circumstances. On cross-examination, however, parties are allowed to ask character witnesses whether they have heard or know about relevant instances of conduct. Simply asking a witness whether he has heard about a particular incident takes little time compared to proving the incident by other witnesses. Permitting such questions on cross is thought to be necessary in order to allow an effective challenge to the reputation or opinion testimony. Special restrictions apply to special cases. For example, in those limited circumstances when sexual history evidence is permitted under FRE 412 or state Rape Shield statutes, it is thought to be less intrusive and prejudicial to prove specific instances rather than adducing reputation or opinion evidence.

Question: While crossing Main Street, Charles is struck by a car driven by Dora. He sues, and she asserts contributory negligence, claiming that Charles was jaywalking. To prove that he was crossing in the marked crosswalk, Charles calls Dan as a witness. If allowed, Dan would testify that he was out of town when the accident occurred, but that he routinely sits on a park bench nearby during noon hour, that he has watched Charles "several times a week for the last few years" crossing the street at noon, and that Charles "always uses the crosswalk." Should Dan's testimony be allowed?

Answer: Yes. This testimony is proof of habit. Using a particular crosswalk satisfies the *specificity* standard; using it on a daily basis satisfies the *regularity* standard; this behavior likely requires little or no reflection, so it is *unreflective* or *semiautomatic*. Dan has seen enough to testify either to specific instances or opinion.

EXAM TIPS

Here are some pointers about issues relating to character and habit evidence:
Character evidence is usually excludable if the purpose is to prove conduct on
a certain occasion, but exceptions permit this use of character evidence. For
example, defendants can prove innocence by means of character evidence,
and in sexual offense cases modern rules make prior acts by the defendant
admissible to prove he committed the charged offense.

Character evidence includes reputation and opinion testimony, as well as prior
specific acts.

Prior specific acts are generally inadmissible, if offered to prove character, but

Usually specific acts may be raised on cross-examination of character
witnesses (to test the knowledge and judgment of the community if
the witness gives reputation evidence, or to test the knowledge and
judgment of the witness himself if he testifies to his opinion of
character).

Often specific acts may be proved in order to show particular points like
intent or knowledge and, if the acts are distinctive and highly similar
to the charged crime, to show modus operandi or identity.

If a party makes a sweeping claim of good character or a clean record, prior
acts may be fair game for cross-examination or extrinsic evidence, to
refute or contradict this claim.

Habit is more specific than character, covering automatic or semiautomatic
behavior in a particular situation, and habit evidence is generally admissible.

Proof that a person always signals a particular turn constitutes habit (both
specific and automatic or semiautomatic).

Proof that a person drives carefully or stays within the speed limit
constitutes character (too general).

Habit may be proved by specific instances, or by opinion testimony.

CHAPTER 7

Relevancy: Specific Applications

CHAPTER OVERVIEW

The key points in this chapter are

- Some principles exclude and limit certain kinds of evidence that might satisfy the basic relevancy standard. There are two reasons:

  - Minimal relevance. Most such evidence is only minimally relevant.

  - Policy. Excluding such evidence implements policies unrelated to truthfinding.

- Subsequent remedial measures. Postaccident precautions, taken to prevent similar accidents, may not be proved to show negligence or culpable conduct, but may be proved to show such points as ownership or control.

  - Broad coverage. The exclusionary principle applies not only to design changes, but to many other measures taken to prevent future accidents, including design and labeling changes.

- Strict liability. Courts split on the question whether this doctrine applies to strict liability claims, in which the main focus is on the fitness of the product rather than conduct by the defendant. Excluding the proof might not achieve anything because product makers must take precautions in light of accidents regardless of evidence doctrine. As amended in 1997, FRE 407 bars such proof in federal courts, but state practice continues to vary.

  - Ownership, impeachment, feasibility. Postaccident measures may be proved to show ownership or control of premises, to impeach witnesses, and to show feasibility (at least if defendant claims otherwise).

- Settlements, negotiations. In civil cases, settlement offers and statements made in negotiations are inadmissible to prove liability, invalidity of a claim, or amount of damages.

  - Form doesn't matter. All statements made in settlement talks are excludable, whether framed conditionally, hypothetically, or as unqualified assertions.

  - Disputed claim. The exclusionary principle applies only to efforts to settle a disputed claim. Demanding payment or filing suit shows a claim exists, and denying liability shows a dispute exists. If one person says another has caused damage and the other agrees to pay, there is not yet a claim or a dispute, and the doctrine does not apply.

  - Exceptions. Despite the exclusionary principle, proof of settlements is sometimes admissible: Nonparty witnesses may be cross-examined on settling with a party if it indicates bias, and proof of settlement, or attempts to settle, may be admissible to refute claims of delay.

- Payment of medical expenses. To encourage responsible and constructive behavior, the payment of medical expenses cannot be proved as a means of showing liability.

- Pleas and plea bargaining. Withdrawn guilty pleas, nolo pleas, and statements by defendants during plea bargaining are generally inadmissible. The most important reason is to encourage the plea bargaining process by making it less risky to defendants.

  - Plea bargaining. Statements by the defendant or his lawyer during plea bargaining are excludable. As formulated in FRE 410, the rule applies to "plea discussions" that involve "an attorney for the prosecuting authority," so statements by defendants to police or other enforcement agents are not covered, except in some unusual cases where such people become involved in the bargaining process.

- Statements sometimes admissible. In rare cases when the defense offers plea bargaining statements by the defendant, the prosecutor may offer others as necessary to provide context. And plea bargaining statements are admissible in the rare case where they form the basis for a prosecution of the defendant for perjury or false statement.

A. INTRODUCTION

This chapter examines a collection of doctrines commonly identified as relevancy rules. They are more specific than the general principles, as codified for the federal system in FRE 401–403, which provide that relevant evidence is admissible unless some particular rule requires exclusion or relevance is outweighed by practical concerns like unfair prejudice (see Chapter 2). The rules examined here exist in part because the categories that they cover are commonplace in trials, and the guidance of specific rules is useful. Another reason for these rules is to implement policies unrelated to the litigation process. The rules examined here do not relate to character, which is governed by elaborate limitations, as codified for the federal system by FRE 404–405 and FRE 413–415 (see Chapter 6).

1. Exclude and Limit

The doctrines examined here exclude or limit the use of evidence. These exclusionary rules apply to proof of postaccident remedial measures, settlement offers, plea bargaining, and liability insurance, although in each case some narrow uses of such proof are permitted.

2. Relevancy Concerns

Each of the exclusionary principles implements a mix of relevancy and policy concerns. Most of the excludable evidence has only minimal relevance. It would likely satisfy the customary standard of relevancy (see FRE 401), but much of it would likely be excluded on an ad hoc basis as confusing or misleading (see FRE 403).

3. Policy

Each exclusionary rule implements a policy unconnected with truthfinding. In one instance, the policy is completely extrinsic to the judicial function:

Proof of postaccident remedial measures is excluded to encourage parties to exercise more care in their behavior outside of court (or avoid discouraging it). In other instances, the policy relates to larger judicial concerns: Proof of settlement offers and plea bargaining is excluded, for instance, to encourage pretrial resolution of civil and criminal matters.

B. SUBSEQUENT REMEDIAL MEASURES (FRE 407)

Postaccident measures, taken to prevent future accidents of the same nature, are excludable when offered to prove what FRE 407 calls "negligence or culpable conduct," or to prove "a defect in a product, a defect in a product's design, or a need for a warning or instruction." The lastquoted phrase was not included in FRE 407 as enacted, but was added by amendment in 1997. But such measures may be shown when the purpose is to prove other points (like ownership or control of the premises), and an important and problematic exception admits such proof when the purpose is to prove feasibility of precautionary measures.

1. Rationale

The exclusionary principle rests on concerns over relevancy and policy. First, subsequent measures do not reliably indicate prior negligence or fault: Even what was reasonably safe before may be made safer by taking further care. Second, parties should be encouraged to make repairs or take other measures to prevent future accidents, and admitting proof that they did so would discourage such measures. Third, regardless whether the policy of encouragement is effective, it seems unfair to penalize responsible behavior by proving it over objection.

2. Application

The exclusionary principle is broad. It covers not only physical changes in the premises or machine involved in an accident, but changes in design, safety modifications (like adding guard rails), labeling changes, new warnings, modifications in instructions, and changes in personnel or procedures.

3. Product Liability Suits

Prior to 1997 courts split on the question whether the principle embodied in FRE 407 should apply in strict liability suits. The 1997 amendment makes it clear that FRE 407 *does* apply in this setting in federal courts. States, however, continue to go their own way, including states that adopted the Federal Rules, since the original version of FRE 407 left room to conclude that the only use covered by the exclusionary principle (proving "negligence or culpable conduct") was not involved in strict liability claims, where the question was fitness for intended use rather than *conduct* by the defendant. See *Ault v. International Harvester Co.*, 528 P.2d 1148 (Cal. 1974) (leading opinion declining to apply statute, on which original FRE 407 was based, to product liability cases). And compare *Forma Scientific, Inc. v. BioSera, Inc.*, 960 P.2d 108 (Colo. 1998) (CRE 407, tracking FRE 407 before the 1997 amendment, does *not* apply in design defect cases) with *Hyjek v. Anthony Industries*, 944 P.2d 1036 (Wash. 1997) (WRE 407, also tracking FRE 407 before the 1997 amendment, *does* apply in strict liability suits).

a. Policy issues

State courts that admit postaccident measures take the view that manufacturers make needed changes without an exclusionary rule, to reduce future claims by stopping accidents and minimize liability for punitive damages for failing to correct known problems. State courts that exclude take the view that the policy of encouraging responsible behavior applies fully in product cases.

b. Terminology issues

As originally enacted, and as found in many state versions, the rule bars proof of subsequent measures to prove "negligence or culpable conduct," but strict liability turns on fitness of the product for intended use rather than defendant's conduct. The legal concept of negligence is not involved in strict liability, and courts disagreed on the question whether making unfit products amounts to "culpable conduct." The 1997 amendment to FRE 407 disposes of such arguments in federal courts, because the amended version clearly does apply to using subsequent measures to prove "a defect in a product, a defect in a product's design, or a need for a warning or instruction."

c. *Erie* problem

Since the main point is to encourage repairs, arguably FRE 407 is "substantive" for *Erie* purposes. Congress can regulate substantive matters of strict liability in products marketed nationwide (and perhaps in others too) under the Commerce Clause, but it is very strange to regulate such matters by means of the Rules of Evidence, and arguably Congress had no intention of doing so when it enacted the Rules in 1975. It is even stranger to regulate such matters by means of the Evidence Rules Advisory Committee, which is comprised of people who are appointed by judges and not elected by the people. Among the federal cases to consider the *Erie* point, most conclude that FRE 407 is procedural for *Erie* purposes, but a few courts thought the matter was substantive prior to the amendment in 1997. Compare *Flaminio v. Honda Motor Co., Ltd.,* 733 F.2d 463 (7th Cir. 1984) (holding that FRE 407, even prior to 1997 amendment, does apply in product liability cases and that the matter is procedural for *Erie* purposes) with *Wheeler v. John Deere Co.,* 862 F.2d 1404 (10th Cir. 1988) (holding that FRE 407, prior to the 1997 amendment, does not apply in this setting, and that the matter is substantive for *Erie* purposes).

4. Exceptions

In cases alleging either negligence or strict liability, the exclusionary principle does not apply to the use of subsequent measures to prove other points, such as ownership or control of the premises. Here are the most important exceptions.

a. Impeachment

Sometimes a defending party offers testimony that the machine or premises in question has a particular safety feature, or that certain procedures are always followed. Proof of postaccident modifications in the machine or premises, or postaccident changes in procedures, is admissible if it tends to refute such testimony, thus impeaching the witness.

b. Feasibility

Sometimes a defending party offers evidence that it would be impossible or impracticable to make a particular change that would prevent similar accidents. Here too, proof of subsequent measures is admissible if it tends to refute the testimony.

c. Fairness issues: The "if controverted" proviso

Care is required in admitting proof of subsequent measures to impeach or prove feasibility. Otherwise claimants might effectively evade the exclusionary principle by (1) tricky cross-examination that forces disclosure of postaccident changes or (2) offering postaccident changes routinely as proof of feasibility. To limit the latter tactic, FRE 407 contains a proviso to the effect that postaccident changes are admissible to prove feasibility only "if controverted."

☛ EXAMPLE AND ANALYSIS

In a suit against the Outrigger Hotel arising out of a fall in the main lobby where two steps lead to a sunken lounge, the manager testifies during the defense case.

On direct, he testifies, "We consider the steps to be safe because potted plants and a handrail alert our guests to the steps and nobody had fallen there before." On cross, the plaintiff asks, "Couldn't you have taken other precautions to alert customers?" The manager replies, "We think the arrangement was perfectly safe, and we don't think other precautions would have made much difference." Plaintiff then proposes to ask, over a defense objection, "Well, didn't you in fact change to carpets of contrasting colors after my client fell?"

The testimony should be disallowed. The direct testimony did not "controvert" any claim that further precautions were feasible because the manager only said the existing arrangement was safe. On cross, the manager did not actually claim that nothing more could be done, although he came very close ("don't think other precautions would make much difference"). Since the testimony sought to be refuted by putting the final question was elicited on cross, any marginal impeaching value of that final question should not count for much. Plaintiff was more intent on avoiding the exclusionary doctrine than making a fair response to the defense case.

C. CIVIL SETTLEMENT OFFERS AND NEGOTIATIONS (FRE 408)

Almost all civil cases settle, and the system would break down if a substantial number of them went to trial. To make settlement possible, all jurisdictions recognize an exclusionary principle that covers settlement agreements and statements made by the parties or their lawyers in the course of trying to reach a settlement. Under FRE 408, such agreements and statements are inadmissible to prove either "liability or the invalidity of the claim or its amount." As amended in 2006, this provision also blocks use of settlement offers or statements made in compromise negotiations to impeach the testimony of a party at trial. Exceptions commonly allow other uses of such proof, however: For example, witnesses who have settled their claims with parties can be impeached by questions inquiring about such matters because they bear on possible bias.

1. Agreements

Ordinarily settlement agreements are performed and result in dismissal of the underlying suit. If a settlement agreement is not performed, and the party entitled to payment sues on the agreement itself, then of course the exclusionary principle does not apply (the settlement agreement is a contract, and the party entitled to performance may sue to recover damages for breach). But if suit is brought on the underlying claim, and if the settlement agreement can no longer be enforced because the obligor breached his duty to pay the agreed sum, then the exclusionary principle normally applies and the agreement itself is excludable.

2. Statements

Since settlement talks may fail to result in agreement, the exclusionary principle can succeed in its purpose only if it applies to statements made during negotiations, including those that come up short.

a. Lawyers and parties

Settlements are usually negotiated by lawyers, whose statements could be used against their clients as authorized admissions under FRE 801(d)(2)(C), so the exclusionary principle applies in this setting. Of course, it applies to statements by parties as well.

b. Form doesn't matter

To avoid making statements that could actually concede anything, lawyers instinctively negotiate by speaking hypothetically ("let's just suppose") or conditionally ("for the sake of settlement, we could say my client was speeding"). Under FRE 408, however, the form of such statements makes no difference. Even unqualified assertions ("my client was speeding") are excludable, so long as the purpose of the parties was to try to settle the case.

3. Disputed Claim

The exclusionary principle comes into play only when there is a claim and a dispute that goes either to validity or amount.

a. Claim

Filing suit means a claim exists, but claims that lead to suit are usually advanced by demands before filing. The exclusionary principle applies at this prior stage, but does not apply merely because someone comments that he should compensate another or receive compensation from another.

b. Dispute

The exclusionary principle does not apply to every statement that follows the events that produce a claim. If a party concedes liability and promises to pay, and also accepts the sum demanded by the other side as correct, then neither the validity nor the amount of the claim is disputed, and the exclusionary principle does not apply.

c. Attempt to settle

Even if a dispute exists, not every statement made by a party constitutes an attempt to settle. If two motorists collide, and one says to the other "What did you do that for, didn't you hear me honk?" and the other replies, "It was all your fault," then neither speaker appears to be trying to reach settlement. The statement "didn't you hear me honk?" appears to be an assertion that the speaker honked his horn, and it could be admitted against him as a statement of a party opponent in the event that the accident led to a suit.

☞ EXAMPLE AND ANALYSIS

After a two-car automobile accident, Driver 1 says, "I'm sorry I damaged your car. You had the light, and I didn't see that it was red for me."

This statement is not excludable as a settlement negotiation because there is no dispute (no claim has been made and there is no disagreement, at least yet, on the validity or amount of any claim that might be made). If Driver 1's statement had come in response to a statement by Driver 2 that "You owe me for the damages to my car," arguably a claim would exist. Still, the statement by Driver 1 would be admissible against him because there is not yet a *dispute* over liability or amount, and indeed Driver 1 appears to be agreeing that he is fully liable.

4. Pre–Existing Materials

The exclusionary principle does not apply to **documents or statements made prior to settlement** negotiations. If lawyers mention or exchange such material during settlement talks, doing so does not bring them within the principle. Congress was concerned enough to add language in FRE 408 stating that the exclusionary principle does not apply to "evidence otherwise discoverable merely because it is presented in the course of compromise negotiations." This addition, however, was unnecessary because the exclusionary principle never did reach such material anyway, and the language of the Rule was not read in that way. The 2006 amendment removed this clause from FRE 408.

5. Third–Party Settlement

In P's suit against D, proof that P settled or negotiated a related dispute with X, or that D settled or negotiated a related dispute with Y, might be relevant on issues relating to liability or damages. The exclusionary principle applies (P can exclude his dealings with X, and D can exclude his dealings with Y) because otherwise the purpose to encourage settlements would be undercut.

6. Criminal Cases

Plea bargaining and plea agreements in criminal cases are subject to a parallel exclusionary principle. See FRE 410.

a. Applicability of FRE 408

Looking only at the *language* in the Rule, one is tempted to conclude that FRE 408 applies only in civil cases—the exclusionary principle blocks use of civil settlements and negotiations to prove "liability for" or "invalidity of" a "claim." There does not appear to be anything that blocks use of statements made in civil settlement negotiations, or of civil settlement agreements themselves, in *criminal* trials. But there is good reason to block the use of civil settlements and negotiations to prove charges in criminal cases: This potential use would discourage civil settlements. Also the provision that *clearly does apply* in criminal cases (FRE 410) does not cover statements by prosecutors (it reaches only statements by defendants), which provides another reason to apply FRE 408 in criminal cases (making what prosecutors say in settling criminal cases excludable after all). In 2006, FRE 408 was amended to make it clear that the Rule applies for the most part in criminal cases too.

b. Extending FRE 408 to criminal cases

The 2006 amendment makes clear that statements made by a party in civil compromise negotiations cannot be used against that party if he becomes a defendant in a later criminal trial, except in cases in which the prior negotiation "related to a claim by a public office or agency in the exercise of its regulatory, investigative, or enforcement authority." Thus a statement made by J, as defendant in a civil case, made in negotiations with a plaintiff seeking to settle the plaintiff's claim for damages resulting from an assault committed by J, cannot be later used against J if he is charged with criminal assault. On the other hand, a statement by K, as defendant in a civil case, made in negotiations with the State Attorney General, in connection with the State's attempt to collect taxes owed by K, can be used against K if he is later charged with a crime in connection with his tax situation.

c. Obstructing investigation

When an act causes damage or loss and also amounts to a crime, private parties may settle civil claims but not necessarily criminal liability.

Suppose L steals M's car and wrecks it, but then enters a settlement agreement in which L agrees to pay the value of the car and M agrees not to sue and "not to testify in any criminal prosecution of defendant for theft of M's car." If L is later charged with theft, the exclusionary principle does not apply, at least if the agreement constitutes obstruction of justice under the applicable law.

7. Exceptions to the Rule

Several exceptions to the exclusionary principle are well established.

a. Proving bias

If a party has settled with a nonparty who testifies as a witness, the point may be explored on cross if it bears on bias. For example, if a defendant in an accident case paid money in settlement of a claim by a passenger who rode in plaintiff's car, this payment might incline the passenger to shade her testimony to favor the defense, and plaintiff may bring out the point on cross.

b. Refuting claim of undue delay

Sometimes failing to negotiate a claim becomes an element in a further claim, as happens if an insurance carrier adds to the liability of its insured by failing to properly investigate a claim, or if delays by the carrier increases its own liability to an injured claimant. When such claims are made, proof of attempts by the carrier to settle is admissible by way of defense.

c. Impeachment

Prior to the 2006 amendment, it was not clear whether the exclusionary principle applies in the situation in which a party who tried to negotiate a settlement later takes the stand as a witness and testifies in a manner that is inconsistent with statements he made during negotiations. The 2006 amendment removed this uncertainty, and it is now clear that FRE 408 does block the use of civil settlement statements to impeach a party by "contradiction" or by arguments that the prior statements are "inconsistent" with his testimony.

☞ EXAMPLE AND ANALYSIS

Edgar gets drunk at a July 4th picnic in a public park in the City of Oakridge. He then lights and plays with fireworks and, as a result of his negligence caused by intoxication, he seriously burns Paul (another person at the picnic) when fireworks explode unexpectedly and a picnic shelter is destroyed in the resultant fire. Paul sues Edgar for personal injuries. Edgar is also charged criminally with reckless endangerment. In the course of compromise negotiations with Paul, Edgar admits that he was intoxicated and that it was he who set off the fireworks that set fire to the shelter. The settlement efforts fail, and both cases go to trial.

1. Paul offers Edgar's statement, made in the failed settlement negotiations involving Paul and Edgar, to prove that Edgar is liable. Edgar objects, and the objection should be sustained. Edgar's statement was made in the course of an attempt to compromise the civil claim, and use of Edgar's statement against him is barred by FRE 408.

2. In the criminal trial of Edgar for reckless endangerment, the prosecutor offers the statement that Edgar made in the civil settlement negotiations as proof of Edgar's guilt of the charged crime. Edgar objects, and the objection should be sustained. FRE 408, as amended in 2006, bars proof of statements made in civil compromise negotiations, when offered against the declarant as a defendant in a criminal trial.

3. Edgar objects, and his objection should be sustained. His statement was made in the course of an attempt to compromise the City's civil claim, and use of the statement is barred by FRE 408.

D. PAYMENT OF MEDICAL EXPENSES

Proof that a party paid the medical expenses of another (or offered or promised to pay them) is inadmissible when offered to show that the party is liable for the injury. The purpose is to encourage this form of responsible and constructive behavior by severing it from liability concerns. Under FRE 409, the principle applies to payment of "similar" expenses, which should cover payment of other expenses related to treatment such as rehabilitation and personal care. The principle does not apply to *statements* made by the party who pays such expenses.

E. PLEAS AND PLEA BARGAINING (FRE 410)

Like civil cases, most criminal cases are resolved without trial. Because the system would be paralyzed if all cases had to be tried, and because most people consider settlements to be good rather than bad things, most courts recognize a strong public policy favoring plea bargaining. To this end, an exclusionary principle covers statements made during plea negotiations and certain pleas as well. See FRE 410.

1. Withdrawn Pleas

When plea bargaining leads to agreement and a plea is entered, it can be withdrawn for good reason with court permission. When a plea is withdrawn under this system and the case goes to trial, the plea and the plea bargain themselves are excludable. The same is true if a plea bargain disposes of some charges but leaves others to be tried. Otherwise the purpose in allowing withdrawal would be undercut. See FRE 410.

2. Nolo Pleas

Pleas of **nolo contendere** ("no contest") may be entered only by court permission. The purpose of such pleas is to allow a person charged with a crime to obviate a criminal trial without admitting to civil liability. To implement this purpose, nolo pleas are excludable from later civil litigation. See FRE 410.

☞ EXAMPLE AND ANALYSIS

Out for a joyride after an evening of drinking, Rhoda drives her car more than 80 mph on a winding suburban street. Ignoring a stopsign, she enters an intersection and broadsides a car driven by Steve and Tara, killing them both. Charged with negligent homicide and driving under the influence, Rhoda obtains court permission to enter a plea of nolo contendere. Based on that plea, she is convicted. In a suit for the wrongful deaths of Steve and Tara, plaintiffs offer Rhoda's nolo contendere plea and conviction.

Both are hearsay, but the plea is an admission by Rhoda that would fit FRE 801(d)(2)(A) (personal) or (C) (authorized). Still, the plea should be excluded under FRE 410(2). The latter provision says nothing about convictions, but the hearsay exception in FRE 803(22) contains a similar restriction (excluding felony conviction that rests "upon a plea of nolo contendere"), and the purpose of a nolo plea would be utterly defeated if it could be offered in the civil suit.

3. Plea Bargaining Statements

Statements made by defendants or their lawyers during plea bargaining are excludable if the process fails to reach agreement and the case goes to trial. In FRE 410(3), the exclusionary principle is narrowly framed: It allows the defendant to exclude statements made during "plea discussions" that involve "an attorney for the prosecuting authority." This principle applies when a defendant and her lawyer talk to prosecutors in private. It also applies when a defendant formally enters her plea in court proceedings, at which time the judge normally asks the defendant to describe her role in the charged offense (in order to insure that the guilty plea has some basis in fact).

a. Statements to police

Statements given by suspects to police are generally not excludable as attempts to engage in plea bargaining. Sometimes such statements are excludable for constitutional reasons under doctrines developed to implement the Fifth and Sixth Amendments, but they do not amount to plea bargaining even if the defendant hopes to attain leniency by cooperating with authorities.

b. Two-tiered standard

Sometimes law enforcement agents get involved in plea bargaining. If statements or actions by such agents make the defendant think that they have authority to conduct plea negotiations, and if that belief is reasonable under the circumstances, then even statements to law enforcement agents should be excluded under FRE 410. Under this two-tiered standard, it is sometimes reasonable to treat such agents as stand-ins or representatives of the prosecutor.

Example. Charged with residential burglary, Mat obtains representation from the Public Defender, who calls the prosecutor and sets up a meeting to discuss possible pleas. At the beginning of the meeting, the prosecutor says, "Best I can do for you is grand larceny with a recommended six-year sentence." During the ensuing discussion, Mat says, "I did enter the house and take the stuff, but Natalie is the one who thought it up and told me the friend who lived there was out of town." His attorney adds, "We know my client had a knife on the fellow in the house, but there was no indication that he intended to use it." Discussions stall, and the parties fail to reach agreement. At trial, Mat can exclude what both he and his lawyer said as plea bargaining statements.

Example. The facts are similar to the prior example. This time the prosecutor says she cannot attend but sends the investigating officers to talk to Mat and his lawyer. They say, "We can't speak for the prosecutor but we'll convey whatever messages you want," and they read Mat his *Miranda* rights. He does not sign a waiver form, but the discussion goes forward. Mat and his lawyer make the same comments as in the prior example. On these facts, applying FRE 410 is hard. Here is the argument for excluding the statements: The defense tried to initiate plea bargaining, and the response by the prosecutor signaled that the agents represented her office. Mat did not sign the waiver, thus indicating his purpose to engage in bargaining. For the prosecutor, one can argue as follows: The agents are not "an attorney for the prosecuting authority." They said they could *not* "speak for the prosecutor" and indicated their investigative intent by providing *Miranda* warnings. *Miranda* rights can be waived even if defendant does not sign the form, and Mat waived them by continuing to talk in this case. FRE 410 doesn't apply.

4. Permissible Uses of Plea Bargaining Statements

The exclusionary principle has a few exceptions. One might expect that there would be an exception for the use of plea bargaining statements to impeach the accused by contradiction: If he said in a plea bargaining statement "I took the gun into the bank" but negotiations later break down and the accused takes the stand and testifies "I did not have a gun in the bank," one might expect that the earlier statement would be admissible to impeach by contradiction. It is clear from the legislative history of FRE 410, however, that Congress intended to block even this use of such statements, and there is no language in the Rule that requires or points toward a different result.

a. Completeness

FRE 410 makes an exception for the rare situation in which the defendant offers his own plea bargaining statement (which might be admissible if it qualified as a prior consistent statement or fit another hearsay exception), in which case the prosecutor can offer a related statement that "ought in fairness" to be considered with what the defendant offers (an application of the "rule of completeness" expressed more generally in FRE 106).

b. Perjury

FRE 410 also allows use of plea bargaining statements by the defendant in trials for **perjury or false statement**. Hence defendants cannot lie with impunity in "guilty plea allocutions" in court (perjury charges remain possible) or in conversations with prosecutors (charges for false statement remain possible).

c. Impeachment

As noted above, no exception authorizes use of plea bargaining statements to impeach, which would include the most obvious possibility of using such statements to contradict the defendant if he testified in a manner that was contrary to some earlier statement made during negotiations. But as is also noted above, legislative history makes it plain that plea bargaining statements are *not* admissible to impeach the defendant if he takes the stand and testifies in a way that is inconsistent with what he said before, and there is no language in the Rule that creates an exception for this use. See M & K § 4.29. In the federal system, however, the Supreme Court held, in a case applying FRE 410, that the accused can *waive* the bar against the impeaching use of plea bargaining statements by signing a plea bargain containing a waiver clause, and this "loophole" has carried the day, as prosecutors routinely demand such waivers as a condition of negotiating and most defendants are willing to sign them. See *United States v. Mezzanatto*, 513 U.S. 196 (1995).

F. PROOF OF LIABILITY INSURANCE (FRE 411)

By longstanding common law tradition, proof of liability insurance cannot be used to show negligence or other wrongful conduct.

1. Rationale

Liability coverage is excluded for two reasons. First, it is irrelevant on issues of carefulness versus negligence (either insurance leads to carelessness because losses are covered or insurance shows foresight, hence careful disposition; both these arguments are foreclosed). Second, proof of liability coverage could easily be misused: The presence of insurance might tempt juries to find liability where none exists or boost recovery unjustifiably, and the absence of coverage might persuade juries to find against liability or reduce recovery unjustifiably.

2. Complements Other Rules

The exclusionary principle complements several other doctrines. One is the **real-party-in-interest principle** in FRCP 17: Despite its name, this principle in common application leads to the result that insurance carriers are hidden from view, as injured parties sue in their own name even when recovery may be channeled to the carrier who already paid the bills, and tortfeasors are sued in person even when a carrier will pay any judgment that is obtained. The other is the **collateral source doctrine**, which often prevents defending parties from proving that claimants have already collected for their injuries.

3. Exceptions

There are several important exceptions to the coverage of the exclusionary principle.

a. Agency, ownership, control

The purchase of liability coverage for a car, machine, or premises obviously indicates that the purchaser has an interest in the thing in question. Proof of coverage is admissible when it tends to show such points.

b. Impeachment

Often insurance investigators or adjusters interview eyewitnesses, and sometimes they prepare statements for eyewitnesses to sign or they make summaries or synopses of such statements. When such investigators or adjusters testify to the substance of eyewitness statements, or when written proof is offered in which investigators or adjusters played a role, their connection with liability carriers may be shown when it bears on the bias in their testimony or the possible accuracy of their written work.

REVIEW QUESTIONS AND ANSWERS

Question: Why do we have rules that exclude specific kinds or categories of proof?

Answer: Partly these rules exist because the problems to which they relate are common, and specific guidance is useful. Also they help implement, in particular settings, the policies set forth in FRE 401–403 (relating to probative worth, prejudice, waste of time, and confusion). Finally, these rules exist in order to implement policies unrelated to litigation, such as encouraging people to take greater care (FRE 407).

Question: What does the subsequent measures rule cover?

Answer: This rule covers all kinds of postaccident measures taken by the person or entity responsible for the place or equipment or process involved in an accident, where the apparent purpose is to improve safety. Thus the rule covers changes in design, safety modifications, labeling changes, new warnings, modifications in instructions, and changes in personnel or procedures.

Question: Does the subsequent measures rule apply in strict liability cases, or only in negligence cases?

Answer: Most courts hold that the rule applies in both contexts. As amended in 1997, the federal rule expressly applies, both in cases involving "negligence" or "culpable conduct" and in cases where the point is to prove product or design "defect" or inadequate warnings. Most courts say the former phrase reaches product liability cases, but some jurisdictions do *not* apply this rule in product liability cases and some states with the Federal Rules did not adopt the 1997 amendment. Partly the disagreement in this area stems from differences in interpretation of the terms "negligence" and "culpable conduct." Partly the disagreement in this area stems from a disagreement over the best policy: Some believe the exclusionary principle plays a useful role in this setting, by encouraging manufacturers to make safer products, and others believe that economic and other pressures force or encourage design changes even without the aid of the exclusionary principle.

Question: Are there important exceptions to the rule against proving subsequent measures?

Answer: Yes. Subsequent measures may be proved for purposes other than showing negligence or culpable conduct, such as demonstrating ownership or control. And in two important and somewhat problematic exceptions to the exclusionary rule, subsequent measures may be proved in order to contradict testimony by a witness, or to demonstrate that improvements or better design or precautions were feasible. But under FRE 407, subsequent measures are admissible for the latter purpose only if feasibility is "controverted."

Question: Why are civil settlement offers and negotiations excludable, and what exactly is excluded?

Answer: The purpose is to encourage litigants to settle instead of try cases. The exclusionary rule covers not only settlement agreements as such, but statements made during settlement negotiations by parties and their lawyers (so it is no longer necessary to couch statements in this setting as "hypothetical" or "conditional" remarks). The exclusionary principle applies not only in civil cases, but in later criminal cases arising out of the same transaction. The exclusionary rule also applies generally to settlement statements made by a party in negotiations that conflict with what that party later says on the witness stand at trial. The earlier statements might impeach his testimony, but those statements are not admissible for this purpose. There is one exception to this principle, and that is an exception that allows the use of settlement statements *made in negotiations with a government agency,* which can be offered *in a later criminal trial* for crimes arising out of the same transaction leading to the civil settlement talks. The rule also applies to statements and agreements between the plaintiff or defendant in a suit and a third party who is not involved in the suit.

Question: When does the rule against proving settlements and negotiations apply?

Answer: The rule comes into play when a claim is made and disputed. That means the rule applies if a suit is filed and contested, but the rule can come into play before suit is filed. If, however, the party against whom a claim is made does not resist or contest the claim at all, the exclusionary rule does not apply. And if the parties simply quarrel with one another in conversations that are not aimed at settlement, the exclusionary rule does not apply. Thus comments made by drivers who speak to one another after an accident may well be admissible in a later lawsuit if the person who makes them seems to be acknowledging responsibility for what happened or if the parties are simply arguing with one another over responsibility.

Question: Are there things that the rule does not cover, that one might easily but mistakenly think are covered?

Answer: There are things like pre-existing documents that are sometimes discussed or exchanged between lawyers during settlement negotiations, and these items are not covered by the rule. The rule covers *statements made* during settlement talks, but not other kinds of already-existing evidence that may get mentioned in such statements or exchanged during the talks. The rule also does not apply to statements or agreements made in an attempt to forestall a criminal prosecution. In addition, there are exceptions to the exclusionary principle, which permit proof of statements or settlement agreements that are relevant (1) to show bias or (2) to refute a claim of unnecessary delay.

Question: What is the rule about payment of medical expenses?

Answer: The rule is that payment of medical expenses on behalf of someone injured in an accident is not admissible to show that the party who makes such payment is responsible for the accident. The purpose is to encourage this form of behavior.

Question: Plea bargains and statements made during bargaining are covered by a principle similar to the one relating to civil settlements, but what about statements by the defendant himself to police or law enforcement officers?

Answer: It's correct that we have a rule in criminal cases that is similar to the civil settlement rule. In the federal system and many states, it is FRE 410 that applies to plea bargaining. This rule clearly covers the bargain and the plea themselves (which are inadmissible if for some reason the agreement is set aside and the defendant goes to trial, or if the agreement covers only some charges, leaving others to be tried). The rule applies when the bargaining process leads to a guilty plea, and it applies when the bargaining process leads to a plea of nolo contendere. It is also true that the exclusionary rule covers statements made during the plea bargaining process, including statements to prosecutors and judges in court, but the rule does *not* normally apply to statements by defendants to police, even if a particular defendant talks in order to improve his chances. In the words of FRE 410, the exclusionary principle applies only to plea discussions involving "an attorney for the prosecuting authority." In unusual cases, however, where a defendant believes he can actually negotiate with police, and where that belief is reasonable under the circumstances, the exclusionary principle may apply.

Question: What about using plea bargaining statements to impeach defendants who testify at trial?

Answer: There is no exception to the rule against using plea bargaining statements that covers impeachment. In the federal system, the legislative history of FRE 410 makes it plain that Congress at least did not apparently intend to allow this use of plea bargaining statements. As a practical matter, however, prosecutors can get around this restriction if they can get defendants to *waive* their right to exclude such statements in the event that the case goes to trial and they testify, and the Supreme Court held in the *Mezzanetto* case that such waivers are enforceable.

Question: Are there other settings in which plea bargaining statements may be used?

Answer: Yes, false statements during plea bargaining may become the basis for a perjury prosecution. And since the exclusionary rule actually bars *prosecutorial* use of plea bargaining statements and not *defense* use of them, there is an exception in FRE 410 that allows prosecutors to offer plea bargaining statements if the defendant offers one of his own statements and a related statement by the defendant is needed in order to provide context.

Question: It seems obvious that proof of insurance should be excluded, since the law normally requires a showing of fault by the insured as the basis for recovery, and having or not having insurance has little or nothing to do with fault, but are there times when insurance is provable, after all?

Answer: It's true that proof of insurance normally is excludable. Arguments that carrying insurance would show either due care (foresight) or negligence (coverage reduces personal cost of careless behavior) are foreclosed. But it's also true that sometimes proof of insurance may be admitted, and there are two important exceptions to the exclusionary principle. First, insurance may be proved in order to show agency, ownership, or control. Second, insurance may be proved when agents or investigators for interested insurance carriers testify in the case, typically describing the substance of eyewitness statements, where affiliation with an insurance company bears on the accuracy of their testimony or written work.

EXAM TIPS

Here are some pointers about issues relating to other specific applications of relevancy rules:

Subsequent remedial measures are excludable if offered to prove negligence or culpable conduct. In federal courts and many states, they are also excludable if offered to prove defect in a design or a product, or inadequate warnings, and this principle is very broad (applying not only to changes in safety equipment, but to measures like firing employees who have caused injuries).

An important exception allows proof of subsequent measures to impeach.

Another important exception allows such proof to prove feasibility, if controverted.

Civil settlement offers and negotiations are excludable if offered to prove liability or the invalidity of a claim, and this rule covers statements made in efforts to settle, *but*

The rule applies only if there is actually a dispute (whether or not a suit has been filed).

The rule covers what is said or done *during negotiations*, not to statements made in other contexts, nor to evidence existing prior to negotiations.

Settlements are sometimes provable when they bear on other points, like the bias of a witness.

Withdrawn pleas and plea bargaining are excludable from criminal cases.

This principle applies to withdrawn guilty pleas and to nolo pleas.

This principle applies to statements made by defendants to prosecuting attorneys, but generally not to statements by defendants to police.

Proof of insurance is generally excludable, when offered to prove negligence or due care, but insurance is sometimes provable to show ownership or control, or to impeach (as happens when statements gathered by insurance adjusters are admitted).

CHAPTER 8

Competency of Witnesses

CHAPTER OVERVIEW

The key points in this chapter are

- There are few incompetent witnesses. The modern approach holds that almost everyone is competent as a witness, although the facts underlying the old common law restrictions may now sometimes be used to impeach if they bear on credibility (as prior convictions sometimes do).

- Courts occasionally take precautions for reasons related to competency. They can, for example, authorize a voir dire examination if serious questions of mental capacity arise, but further measures (like mental examinations) are problematic.

- Drug or alcohol use or addiction can be raised on cross, and testimony can be deferred for witnesses under the influence at trial.

- Posthypnotic testimony is regulated or restricted in many states, but the *Rock* decision by the Supreme Court held that criminal defendants cannot be automatically barred from testifying on account of having undergone hypnosis.

- Children. In most jurisdictions, no legal rule disqualifies children from testifying, no matter what their age. Many states once had statutes that did disqualify some children, but for the most part these have been discarded, at least in the important setting of child abuse prosecutions. If children are too young or immature to testify in court, or if the rigors of court would cause serious trauma, accommodations can be made. Most states authorize remote testimony (televised from elsewhere) or depositions.

- Lawyers and judges. In cases that they try, lawyers would violate ethical rules if they testified on contested points, although there is no evidentiary doctrine that makes lawyers incompetent as witnesses, even in this setting. In cases that they try, judges cannot testify or use their office to gather information about the case outside the courtroom, and in this situation FRE 605 expressly bars judges from testifying in cases in which they preside.

- Dead Man's Statutes. To prevent perjured testimony and to protect estates, these state statutes block some or all testimony by parties who sue estates. These provisions are viewed as substantive and are applied by federal courts in diversity cases.

- Impeachment of verdicts. Juror testimony and affidavits are generally inadmissible when the purpose is to attack or impeach a verdict.

- Policies. The reasons to exclude such evidence are to prevent or reduce jury harassment, to preserve privacy of deliberations, to prevent jury tampering, and to protect and preserve the finality of judgments.

- Broad exclusion. As formulated in FRE 606(b), the exclusionary principle bars testimony or affidavits about "any statement" during deliberations, or "the effect of anything" on mental processes of any jury. This is a very broad principle that covers virtually everything that happens in a jury room during deliberations, but the principle is nevertheless limited (it does not reach some situations) and it admits of several critical exceptions. In the *Tanner* case, the Supreme Court held that this principle applies to the use of alcohol or drugs during trial, and notably this holding means that the principle applies to some things that occur even *before* deliberations begin.

- Limits. The exclusionary principle does not apply generally to predeliberative conduct like lying on voir dire, or to postdeliberative conduct like making a clerical error in filling out the verdict form.

- Exceptions. As formulated in FRE 606(b), the exclusionary principle does not apply to proof of "extraneous prejudicial information" like media reports, or to proof of "outside influence" like threats or bribe offers from parties.

A. INTRODUCTION

Mainly the term "competency" refers to the qualifications needed to enable a person to testify as a witness (traditionally, points like maturity and sanity). The term also refers to a body of principles that disqualify participants in the trial process (judges and jurors) from also testifying as witnesses. Finally, the term refers to a few exclusionary principles that block certain kinds of testimony for extrinsic policy reasons (preventing fraud, preserving verdicts).

1. Witness Qualifications

The old common law approach limited the range of people who could testify, excluding testimony by the very young, the very old, convicted felons, insane persons, and even parties to the suit. All these restrictions have been discarded, and underlying facts that used to constitute the basis for finding witnesses incompetent are now usable, if at all, only insofar as they bear on the credibility of witnesses. In other words, the factors that used to affect competency now affect only credibility. The modern approach is one of universal competency, with a few narrow limitations. See FRE 601 ("every person is competent to be a witness," with few exceptions).

2. Participants

Nothing disqualifies lawyers from testifying, but ethical restrictions block them from testifying on contested points in the cases they try. Judges cannot testify in cases in which they preside, see FRE 605, and jurors may not testify in the cases they try, see FRE 606.

3. Exclusionary Principles

Two bodies of law block certain kinds of testimony for policy reasons. First, so-called "Dead Man's Statutes" block claimants who sue estates from testifying in support of their cases. Second, all states have doctrines, statutes, or rules that block or limit the use of affidavits or testimony by jurors from being used to attack or set aside verdicts, with important exceptions.

B. ORDINARY WITNESSES

The modern approach is to let everyone testify. Under FRE 601, "every person is competent" except as "otherwise provided," and there are no general exceptions. The strong trend over the last century has been to convert the various points thought to affect competency into points that may be raised on cross-examination to attack credibility.

1. Nobody Too Young or Old

In most states, there is no age that is "too young" to testify, but many states once had (and some still have) statutes limiting the use of children as witnesses (described below). In the area of child abuse trials, these restrictions have been abolished everywhere. No age is too old for giving testimony, but ill health or infirmity may make a witness "unavailable" under FRE 804(a), and deposition testimony by such people can then be presented under the former testimony exception, see FRE 804(b)(1). Failing memory, eyesight, or hearing can be raised on cross, or even shown by extrinsic evidence, as matters relating to capacity.

2. Felons

Convicted felons are often disqualified from jury service and from the civil right of voting in elections, but convicted felons are not disqualified from testifying as witnesses. Convictions can be used to impeach, and are treated as matters relating to "character for truth and veracity," subject to elaborate limits and safeguards. See FRE 609.

3. Insane Persons

Persons suffering from mental illness are qualified to testify despite such affliction. Mental problems may be explored on cross-examination–once again as matters that affect credibility, except this time we usually say that such an affliction bears on "capacity" to observe events and to process them mentally in appropriate manners, as well as "capacity" to recount such events in court. Sometimes medical records or psychiatric testimony is admitted.

4. Interest

Parties and their spouses may testify as witnesses. Their interest in the case may be explored on cross-examination, or proved by extrinsic evidence, as matters relating to "bias." Rules of privilege sometimes bar or restrict spousal testimony, but these rules do not cover all spousal testimony and there are many situations in which spouses can in fact testify both for and against one another. See the discussion of privilege rules in Chapter 14.

5. Surviving Restrictions, Precautions

In a few instances, mostly very rare, some restrictions and precautions are still observed.

a. Voir dire; competency examinations

When serious questions are raised about mental capacity (sanity or comprehension), courts can allow the matter to be explored on voir dire, in which both sides can question the witness outside the jury's presence. Courts claim authority to order a psychiatric examination if voir dire suggests a serious problem, but the existence of such authority is doubtful (apart from criminal defendants who raise an insanity defense). A court can certainly exclude testimony by a witness who refuses to undergo such evaluation, but even this measure is problematic because mental incapacity does not disqualify a person from testifying.

b. Drug or alcohol use

If a witness was under the influence of drugs or alcohol at the time of observation, this fact may be raised by way of impeachment. If a witness is under the influence at the time of testifying, the usual solution is to defer his testimony until he has recovered.

c. Hypnosis

If a forgetful witness is hypnotized, serious risks appear: The witness may "confabulate" facts as creative imagination displaces memory and become both more suggestible and more certain of the things he thinks he remembers. For these reasons, some states bar hypnotically refreshed testimony, and others regulate the process. In *Rock v. Arkansas*, 483 U.S. 44 (1987), the Supreme Court held that a state may not impose a per se bar on hypnotically refreshed testimony by a defendant in a murder case.

C. CHILDREN

As noted above, many states once had (and some still have) statutes relating to the competency of children. Typically these statutes disqualified children under a certain age (often seven), provided that children below another age (often twelve) are presumptively incompetent and that children that age or older are presumptively competent. In the area of child abuse, these statutes have been displaced. For an example of an elaborate statutory mechanism to deal with child competency issues (and hearsay problems) in the setting of child abuse prosecutions, see 18 U.S.C. § 3509 (providing that children are "presumed competent," but also providing for competency examinations if "compelling reasons" exist). Apart from these provisions, no rules flatly disqualify children from testifying, no matter what their age, but sensitive and sometimes difficult issues arise with very young witnesses. Mostly these issues are seen in trials for abuse (sexual and otherwise).

1. Depositions, Remote Testimony

For children testifying in abuse cases, most states authorize pretrial depositions or testimony during trial from a remote setting (a room elsewhere in the building where the child can be more comfortable).

2. Unavailable, Incompetent

Typically, depositions and remote testimony are allowed to substitute for live testimony only if the child is psychologically unavailable, which means either that she cannot testify in court (because of shyness, fear, anxiety) or that doing so would cause serious psychological damage (beyond mere fright). See *Maryland v. Craig,* 497 U.S. 836 (1990) (rejecting constitutional challenge to use of remote testimony if child witness would suffer "serious emotional distress" in court). Sometimes the inquiry is framed in terms of "competency," but a finding that she cannot or should not testify in court (she is "incompetent") leads to the use of one of these other mechanisms, and does not result in blocking her testimony.

D. LAWYERS AND JUDGES AS WITNESSES

Like everyone else, judges and lawyers are qualified to testify in court proceedings. Because testifying would conflict with their roles as presiding officer or advocate, however, judges and lawyers usually do not (and often cannot) testify in cases in which they play those roles.

1. Judges

Because testifying and presiding are inconsistent functions, judges cannot testify in the cases where they preside. The rule is slightly broader in that it bars judges from gathering or using information, either personally or by asking court personnel to do so. See FRE 605. But judges can take judicial notice of certain facts (those that are universally known, or verifiable by resort to unimpeachable sources, such as atlases). See FRE 201.

2. Lawyers

No *evidence* rule disqualifies lawyers from testifying, even in the cases they try. Provisions in the Code of Professional Responsibility and Rules of

Professional Conduct, however, state that a lawyer should not accept employment in litigation if he or his firm should be a witness in the case. Other provisions in the Code and Rules state that lawyers trying cases can testify only on "matters of formality" or "uncontested" matters.

E. DEAD MAN'S STATUTES

These provisions, which are in force in most states, block parties who sue the estates of decedents from testifying as witnesses.

1. Purposes

One purpose is to prevent claimants from giving false testimony that the estate cannot rebut because the decedent cannot reply, and the theory is that perjury is a serious possibility here just because the survivor believes he cannot be caught if he lies. Another is to preserve estates for the benefit of heirs (in the days when these statutes were enacted, legislatures had in mind "widows and orphans").

2. Vary in Detail

The statutes differ greatly in detail and breadth, some covering all testimony (others covering only certain kinds), some covering heirs and assignees (others covering only the original claimant).

3. Federal Deference to State Law

Mainly because Dead Man's Statutes are considered substantive in nature, Congress included language in FRE 601 that defers to state competency rules in diversity cases litigated in federal court.

4. Reform

Some states have tried to ameliorate the severe effects of these statutes while still implementing the underlying policies, by passing reform legislation that would allow the survivor to testify while admitting hearsay statements by the decedent that are relevant to the case. The effect of such statutes is to even the playing field to some degree: Surviving claimants are not blocked from testifying (their mouths are not closed) and decedents are "enabled to speak" (their statements before death are admitted).

F. IMPEACHING JURY VERDICTS

The states and the federal system all have rules restricting or blocking use of affidavits or testimony by jurors to "impeach" verdicts.

1. Underlying Concerns

By reducing or eliminating the incentive that would otherwise encourage losing parties to pursue and interview jurors after trial, these doctrines serve four purposes: First, they reduce harassment of jurors. Second, they preserve the privacy of deliberations. Third, they reduce risks of tampering with the process (persuading unhappy jurors, who sympathized with the losing side, into thinking that their own consent to the verdict rested on impermissible considerations, so now they can once again voice their views, which they reluctantly abandoned in order to put an end to deliberations). Fourth, they help preserve the finality of judgments. (Of course judgments, on the day they are rendered, are not quite final anyway, because they can be set aside on post-trial motion or appeal, but they would be far less final if, in addition to all the reasons that can *now* be advanced, on motions and appeals, they could *also* be set aside for juror misconduct as reflected in affidavits.)

2. Variation in Principle

The rule originated in England, where Lord Mansfield derived it from a Latin aphorism that "nobody may allege his own moral turpitude." In America, one popular formulation is the so-called "Iowa rule," which says jurors may not testify on points that "inhere in the verdict" (they may not describe deliberations or reasons for the verdict), but may testify on "independent" or "objective" facts such as contacts with parties and also certain objective facts reflecting misbehavior in reaching a verdict by quotient (adding sums each juror prefers and dividing by the number of jurors) or by chance or lot (drawing straws or flipping coins).

3. Federal Rule

In very broad terms, FRE 606(b) blocks juror testimony or affidavits describing "any matter or statement" during deliberations, "the effect of anything" on the mind of any juror, and "the mental processes" of any juror. These provisions exclude juror testimony or affidavits describing many improprieties, including wrongfully holding it against the accused that he didn't testify, misunderstanding or misapplying instructions, vote trading, reaching agreement simply in order to go home, and speculation on improper matters like the taxability of awards. Despite its similarity to the Iowa rule described above, legislative history makes it plain that FRE 606(b) also blocks juror affidavits or testimony relating to quotient verdicts. The rule contains three exceptions:

a. Extraneous information

Juror testimony and affidavits are admissible to prove "extraneous prejudicial information." Under this exception, jurors may describe, for example, learning the substance of media reports about the trial or the underlying events that are in issue in the trial, or going to the scene of an accident or crime and making their own observations or performing their own investigations.

b. Outside influence

Juror testimony and affidavits are also admissible to prove "outside influence." Under this exception, jurors may describe, for example, threats or bribes transmitted to themselves or their families, and pressures from bailiffs to hurry up and finish deliberating.

c. Error on verdict form

Jury testimony and affidavits are admissible to prove a mistake in entering the verdict onto a verdict form. This exception, which was added by amendment in 2006, is purposefully crafted to be very narrow in scope. It does not pave the way for jurors to testify that they made mistakes in interpreting the evidence or in calculating the amount of damages, but it does allow testimony that jurors entered, for example, $10,000 onto the form when they intended to enter $100,000.

d. Limits of coverage

By its terms, FRE 606(b) covers only the course of deliberations, which suggests that it does not cover *predeliberative* or *postdeliberative* conduct. For this reason, jurors may testify to points that show that one or another juror lied or provided misinformation during voir dire, and jurors may testify that an error was made in transmitting or communicating the intended verdict to the court. Also FRE 606(b) does not block jurors from communicating with judges *during deliberations*, and judges may address problems that arise during deliberations and are reported in this way.

e. The *Tanner* decision

In *Tanner v. United States*, 483 U.S. 107 (1987), the Court held that FRE 606(b) blocks testimony by jurors describing the use of drugs and alcohol during trial. The Court overlooked the fact that this misconduct occurred before deliberations began.

f. Hard cases

In many applications, FRE 606(b) is uncontroversial, but there are at least five settings that pose serious difficulty:

i. Chance or lot

Probably jurors cannot give testimony or affidavits describing verdicts by chance or lot, but this point is not entirely clear, and such misconduct is so serious that there is room to doubt whether proof of this sort could really be excluded.

ii. **Insane juror**

It is uncertain whether juror testimony or affidavits may be admitted to prove that a juror was insane, but the Court in *Tanner* mentioned this situation as especially serious, implying that it could be proved. Occasionally jurors write letters to judges afterwards reporting bizarre reasons or reflecting apparent mental disturbance, but reversals for this reason are rare.

iii. **Prejudice**

Testimony and affidavits indicating racial or gender bias are problematic for purposes of FRE 606(b). Sometimes such bias may be proved by statements or conduct occurring before or after trial, or by proof that a juror lied during voir dire. In such situations, FRE 606(b) does not stand in the way.

iv. **Physical intimidation**

Probably FRE 606(b) bars proof of intimidating behavior by one juror toward another during deliberations. Some have thought FRE 606(b) should be amended to permit proof of violence during deliberations, but this suggestion has not been adopted and the problem does not appear to have arisen very often.

REVIEW QUESTIONS AND ANSWERS

Question: What are competency rules, and what do they do?

Answer: Competency rules limit the persons who are allowed to take the witness stand in trials. Under the common law approach, many people were disqualified from testifying, including people who had been convicted of felonies and the litigants themselves. The modern approach sweeps away most of the old restrictions. Now almost everyone is competent to testify (including people with felony convictions and the litigants). In the modern world, we disqualify only a few categories of people: Judges cannot testify in cases where they preside, nor can sitting jurors. While lawyers are not disqualified from testifying in the cases they try, ethical rules block them from testifying on contested points in this situation. Beyond these restrictions, there are two more restrictions that are commonly considered to be competency rules: Dead Man's Statutes, which exist in many states and block or limit testimony that may be offered against the estates of deceased people, and restrictions against impeaching verdicts by means of testimony or affidavits by jurors.

Question: In a world that no longer disqualifies very many people from testifying, are there any permissible precautions when serious problems appear?

Answer: Yes, when mental capacity seems to be an issue (sanity or comprehension), courts can conduct voir dire examinations, in which the parties question the witness outside the presence of a jury. In extreme cases, courts might ask a witness to undergo a psychiatric examination. Testimony by witnesses under the influence of drugs or alcohol can be deferred until they are no longer under the influence. (Otherwise drug and alcohol use can be explored on cross-examination if it bears on the capacity of the witness at the time of the events.) And hypnotically refreshed testimony is sometimes barred or regulated to guard against risks of confabulation (reciting imagined points as remembered points).

Question: What about children?

Answer: There are statutes in some states that limit testimony by children (often providing that children under seven are incompetent, that children under twelve are presumptively incompetent, and that children twelve or older are presumptively competent). In the important setting of child abuse prosecutions, no American states observe a minimum age for testifying.

Question: Obviously child abuse prosecutions are hard for children and litigants alike. What can be done to obtain testimony by children while protecting the rights of defendants and safeguarding the process?

Answer: Most states authorize pretrial depositions by children in abuse cases, as well as remote testimony (child testifying by videotape from another room). Resort to these measures is allowed only if the child is unavailable. In this setting, the concept of "psychologically unavailable" holds sway: This concept means that the child is so afraid or anxious that she simply cannot testify or would be seriously damaged if forced to do so.

Question: What do Dead Man's Statutes do, and why do we have them?

Answer: These statutes block a claimant who sues the estate of a deceased person from testifying against the estate. The purpose is to block perjury and preserve estates. These statutes vary in detail and coverage, and they are creatures of state law that must be applied in federal court in diversity cases under FRE 601. Some states have adopted a reformist approach that permits claimants to testify in this setting, while trying to even the balance by admitting relevant hearsay statements made by the decedent.

Question: What is the rule on impeaching verdicts, and why do we have it?

Answer: The general principle is that testimony or affidavits by jurors, after returning a verdict, may not be offered in an attempt to set the verdict aside. The reasons are to reduce harassment of jurors, preserve privacy of deliberations, reduce risks of tampering with the process, and protect the finality of verdicts.

Question: What is covered by the principle, and what exceptions are there?

Answer: Coverage and exceptions vary from state to state. FRE 606(b) states the principle and the exceptions in a way that is commonly accepted. It bars testimony or affidavits describing any matter or statement during deliberations, or "the effect of anything" on the mind of any juror or "the mental processes" of any juror. FRE 606(b) recognizes three exceptions to coverage, which provide that testimony or affidavits may show "extraneous prejudicial information" or "outside influence." The first of these exceptions would allow, for instance, juror testimony that media reports relating to contested facts were received by jurors during deliberations. The second would allow, for example, testimony by a juror that he was threatened by one of the parties. Legislative history indicates that the intent of FRE 606(b) is to block testimony or affidavits by jurors indicating that they reached a quotient verdict. The third exception permits proof that the jury made an error in entering a verdict onto the verdict form.

Question: Does the exception cover things that happen before deliberations begin?

Answer: At least in the formulation found in FRE 606(b), the principle applies only to what happens during the course of deliberations. Clearly such predeliberative misconduct as giving false answers on voir dire is not covered, so juror testimony may be admitted on this point. In the *Tanner* case, the Supreme Court held that FRE 606(b) applied to testimony by jurors describing misconduct during trial and prior to deliberations (use of drugs and alcohol), but the Court in *Tanner* did not pay any attention to the fact that it was applying the Rule to pre-deliberative conduct.

Question: Are there some hard cases in which application of the exclusionary doctrine relating to juror affidavits or testimony is open to doubt or dispute?

Answer: Yes, at least four. It is not settled whether the exclusionary principle should block juror testimony or affidavits indicating that (1) a verdict was reached by chance or lot (flipping a coin, drawing straws), (2) a juror was insane or delusional during deliberations, (3) a juror was prejudiced on the basis of race or gender in ways that might have affected deliberations, and (4) a juror engaged in physical intimidation of others during deliberations.

EXAM TIPS

Here are some pointers on issues relating to competency of witnesses:

There are few incompetent witnesses (trend is to allow factors that once affected competency to be used for impeachment instead).

With child victim witnesses, concerns over competency are displaced by concerns over ability to testify in a courtroom setting. For children who can't manage, the usual approach is to offer their depositions or remote testimony. Under *Craig*, the Confrontation Clause allows these expedients only if the child would suffer serious psychological damage if required to testify.

A few competency rules remain important.

Dead Man's Statutes in many states block or limit testimony by a party against a decedent's estate.

Judges cannot testify in the cases where they preside.

Jurors cannot impeach their verdicts, but may testify to certain limited points, which FRE 606(b) defines as "outside influence" and "extraneous prejudicial information" and making a mistake in entering the verdict onto the verdict form.

CHAPTER 9

Direct and Cross–Examination

CHAPTER OVERVIEW

The key points in this chapter are

- Direct examination must normally proceed by nonleading questions. For the most part, leading questions are permitted only on cross-examination.

- In special circumstances, leading is allowed on direct. Thus lawyers are often allowed to lead in covering preliminary matters, such as getting the identity of the witness and placing her at the scene. Leading is also permitted on direct when a witness is hostile, as happens if a witness is aligned with the other side (or is the adverse party herself), and often happens when the witness was simply called by the other side. Even though leading questions bring dangers if used when a witness is forgetful, timid or frightened, leading is generally allowed in such cases because otherwise it is feared that there is no way to get the testimony of the witness at all.

- Lawyers may refresh the recollection of witnesses during or prior to their testimony.

- Writings used to refresh recollection must be produced on request by the adverse party for purposes of aiding in cross-examination.

- Questioning on cross-examination is limited to the scope of the direct examination.

- Leading questions are generally permitted on cross-examination.

- The judge may call and ask questions of witnesses.

- On request, the court must exclude witnesses from the courtroom (subject to certain exceptions), for the purpose of preventing them from hearing testimony by other witnesses. This process is called "sequestering witnesses."

A. ORDER OF EXAMINING WITNESSES

1. Normal Sequence

The normal order of examining witnesses is as follows:

Direct examination by the calling party;

Cross-examination by the adverse party;

Redirect examination by the calling party;

Re-cross by the adverse party;

Further redirect and re-cross as may be necessary.

2. Judge Has Discretion to Alter Order of Proof

Under FRE 611(a), the trial judge is given authority to exercise "reasonable control over the mode and order of interrogating witnesses" in order to make the interrogation "effective for the ascertainment of truth," avoid "undue consumption of time," and protect witnesses from "harassment."

☛ EXAMPLE AND ANALYSIS

Emily files a medical malpractice action against Dr. Corbin for performing surgery on her negligently. She calls Dr. Archer, her current treating physician, as her first witness. Archer describes the later surgery he performed on Emily to remedy complications from the first surgery, but he is not asked his opinion about whether Corbin was negligent in the first surgery. Emily plans to establish negligence through the testimony of Dr. Binder, a famous surgeon whom Emily has retained as an expert. But after the direct and cross-examination of Archer is finished and he has been excused, Emily learns that Binder has had a stroke and will be unable to testify. Emily requests permission to recall Archer and reopen his direct examination so he can now give his opinion that Corbin was negligent.

The court has discretion under FRE 611(a) to allow Emily to do so. Since testimony about Corbin's negligence is essential to Emily's case and she is not responsible for Binder's failure to appear, a court would be very likely to grant her request to admit this evidence outside the normal order.

B. DIRECT EXAMINATION

1. Discretion to Allow Testimony in Narrative Form

The judge has discretion to allow a witness to give testimony in narrative form rather than responding to specific questions. The court is likely to allow narrative testimony only if the witness appears to be able to testify without putting before the jury material that is inadmissible or seriously prejudicial. With narrative testimony, the opposing party can object and move to strike any statement that is inadmissible. Striking testimony after it has been given is not, however, always an adequate remedy. Because narrative testimony is risky, attorneys generally prefer, and courts often require, a question-and-answer approach.

2. Leading Questions Generally Not Allowed on Direct

The most fundamental rule of direct examination is that a party generally cannot ask leading questions of its own witnesses. Direct examination is supposed to be spontaneous (even though the witness has usually been prepared prior to trial). Leading questions undermine the truthseeking process because they enable an attorney to "plant" a selected version of facts in the mind of the witness by artfully phrasing the questions so as to suggest the desired response. Leading questions may evoke false memories or cause a witness to lessen efforts to relate what she actually remembers. Also a witness is likely to have less credibility when she seems merely to "endorse" questions put to her by attorneys rather than presenting her own account.

Example.   Pam sues Reginald for injuries that she sustained after Reginald ran into her in the truck that he was driving. On direct examination, Pam's lawyer asks her: "You were driving well within the speed limit prior to the collision and keeping a careful lookout for other cars, weren't you?" This question is objectionable as leading. It suggests the answer and is essentially testimony in the words of the attorney rather than the witness.

3. Definition of Leading Questions

Leading questions are those that suggest the desired answer. Whether a question is leading depends on many factors other than wording, including the tone of voice of the questioner, the context, and which side is asking the question.

Example.   Dirk is prosecuted for assault and battery of Tom, but claims he never struck a blow. On direct examination of an eyewitness, Dirk's lawyer asks, "Did you see the defendant beat the victim?" Such a question, asked by the defense, would hardly be considered leading. But the same question would likely be considered leading if asked by the prosecutor.

4. Exceptions—Leading Questions Allowed

a. Preliminary matters

Courts may allow leading questions when a lawyer is trying to bring out background information about a witness, such as name, address, place of employment, and similar details. Such information is usually uncontroversial and is intended to introduce the witness to the jury. Courts sometimes allow leading questions on other preliminary matters, such as laying a foundation for an exhibit.

Example.   In her suit against Reginald (above), Pam calls Roland as a witness. He is the deputy sheriff who investigated the accident, but he has trouble remembering the details because the accident happened two years ago. Pam's lawyer lays a foundation to introduce Roland's notes under the hearsay exception for past recollection recorded contained in FRE 803(5). After Roland identifies his notes, Pam's lawyer asks these questions and receives these answers: Q. "I take it these notes were made by you personally?" A. "Yes, sir." Q. "And were they made at or near the time of the accident when the events were fresh in your memory?" A. "They were." Q. "Do they correctly reflect your knowledge at that time?" A. "Yes, sir, they do." Such foundation questions are clearly leading but are routinely allowed.

b.   Adverse party

FRE 611(c) allows an attorney to use leading questions when examining the adverse party. Thus direct examination of an adverse party ordinarily proceeds as though it were cross-examination.

c.   Witness identified with adverse party

Similarly, FRE 611(c) allows leading questions when an attorney examines a witness identified with an adverse party. Examples include an employee of a corporate defendant and the spouse of an individual plaintiff.

d.   Hostile witness

Sometimes a witness proves hostile at trial, even if she is not an adverse party or a person identified with an adverse party. Once a witness is shown to be hostile to the examining lawyer, courts normally allow leading questions on direct examination.

e.   Forgetful witness

Courts may allow leading questions to develop testimony by forgetful witnesses. But courts are usually cautious here, because a forgetful witness may be susceptible to suggestion–to the technique of "planting" testimony through leading questions. Apart from leading questions, an attorney may try to refresh recollection by handing the witness a document that may help restore her memory of the matter. See Section B5.

f.   Timid or frightened witness

Courts usually let lawyers ask leading questions of witnesses who are timid or frightened to the point that they have trouble testifying at all unless gently led to the points that the attorney wants them to address.

g.   Child witness

Courts often give attorneys greater leeway to pose leading questions to young children. Again there is a danger that leading questions may allow the examining attorney to construct the facts in a biased, unfair, or incomplete way.

5.   Refreshing Recollection of Witness

An important technique for dealing with a forgetful witness is to "refresh" her memory by showing her a document or other matter that helps revive her memory. Although the Federal Rules do not require any particular foundation, normally the attorney first shows that the witness does not remember, and then ask her if seeing a particular document would refresh her memory. (Almost always, refreshing memory involves documents that contain information that helps the witness recall something, and typically such documents are ones that the witness herself wrote or prepared or kept, but the process can proceed by showing other objects to the witness, such as an article of clothing or a picture.)

Example.   Plaintiff's attorney is examining the treating physician. Q. "Doctor, on what date did you discharge my client from any further treatment?" A. "I'm sorry, I don't remember the exact date. It was sometime at the end of April, 1996." Q. "Doctor, would it refresh your memory if you reviewed your medical records pertaining to my client?" A. "Certainly." Q. [To court] "May I approach the witness, your honor." A. "You may." Q. "Doctor, would you please review your medical file on the plaintiff which I am now handing to you." [Witness reviews file.] Q. "Thank you, Doctor. Do you now recall the date my client was discharged from any further treatment by you?" A. "Yes, I remember now. It was on April 26." Q. "Thank you, doctor. No further questions."

a. Memory is refreshed

If after reviewing the document the witness is able to testify from **present recollection refreshed,** there is no hearsay problem. The reason is that the lawyer who questions the witness is not introducing a past out-of-court statement. Instead, the lawyer is jogging the memory of the witness, who then testifies from refreshed memory about the acts, events, or conditions in issue. The witness is under oath and her demeanor is on display for the trier of fact to appraise. Hence there is no hearsay problem. It can be hard to determine, however, that the witness really is testifying from current memory, and is not simply testifying to her recollection of what she just read. Sometimes the opposing party asks that the document be removed from the hands of the witness before she proceeds with her testimony, which can at least check some possible abuses.

b. Memory not refreshed

What if the witness's memory is not refreshed and the witness can only answer questions by reading or relying on a statement in the document used to refresh? In this case, there is a hearsay problem. The prior statement is hearsay (whether introduced through the testimony of the witness or as an exhibit). It can only be admitted if it fits an exception to the hearsay rule, and one exception is designed for most such situations. That is the exception for **past recollection recorded** set out in FRE 803(5). This exception reaches certain statements "made or adopted" by a testifying witness and shown to reflect the earlier knowledge of the witness correctly, and usually the foundation for this exception includes a showing that the witness no longer recalls what he wrote down before. See Chapter 4.

c. Impeaching witness with earlier statement

What if, despite being shown the earlier statement, the witness gives contrary testimony? In this case, the earlier statement may be admissible to impeach. Under FRE 607, a party may impeach his own witness, although sometimes this kind of impeachment is considered an abuse of FRE 607 if pursued by the party who called the witness and if it appears that the primary purpose of the calling party is to get the jury to misuse the impeaching evidence as substantive evidence. See the discussion of this point in Chapter 10, Sec. H5, infra. If the prior inconsistent statement was made under oath at a proceeding, it may be admissible under FRE 801(d)(1)(A) not only to impeach but as substantive evidence, in which case concerns over abuse disappear, even if the party offering the statement is the party who called the witness.

C. CROSS–EXAMINATION

1. Cross–Examination as an Entitlement

Cross-examination is a fundamental right. If a witness cannot be cross-examined, his direct testimony may be stricken and sometimes a mistrial is required.

2. Reasons for Requiring Cross–Examination

Wigmore called cross-examination "the greatest engine ever invented for the discovery of truth," 5 Wigmore on Evidence 40571390 (J. Chadbourn rev. 1974). Cross-examination helps check against the four testimonial dangers of misperception, faulty memory, misleading narration, and deception. See Chapter 3. Cross-examination helps guarantee both the reality and the perception of a fair trial and is an important component of due process of law. In criminal cases, the right to cross-examine witnesses is guaranteed by the Confrontation Clause of the Sixth Amendment. See Chapter 5.

3. Cross–Examination Generally Limited to Scope of Direct

a. Majority rule

By far the larger number of states limit cross-examination to the scope of direct. In other words, the cross-examiner is not allowed to explore new issues that were not raised in the direct testimony of the witness. Raising new matter solely for impeachment, however, does not violate the "scope of direct" rule. The majority rule reflects the view that each side should be able to control its order of presentation and make its case without interruption or diversion by the opponent into different issues.

b. Minority rule

Some states (a handful) allow what is known as "wide open" cross-examination. Here the cross-examiner can explore issues beyond the scope of direct. In favor of this approach, it may be argued that the "scope of direct" rule is hard to administer and leads to quibbling. And the "wide open" approach avoids the need to call witnesses back to the stand a second time.

c. Federal rule

FRE 611(b) generally adopts the majority view limiting cross-examination to the scope of direct. But it compromises the matter by authorizing the judge, in the exercise of discretion, to permit inquiry into additional matters. If inquiry into new matter is allowed, the examiner is to proceed "as if on direct," meaning that he is to ask nonleading questions.

d. Scope of cross when witness claims privilege against self-incrimination

When the defendant in a criminal case take the stand, he is subject to cross-examination, but in this setting questioning that goes beyond the scope of the direct threatens to violate the right against compelled self-incrimination protected by the Fifth Amendment. How extensively can he be cross-examined without violating the privilege? Courts generally adopt a waiver rule for Fifth Amendment claims that is similar to the "scope of direct" rule, meaning that the defendant is viewed as waiving his right against self-incrimination as to issues within the scope of his direct testimony, but not his privilege as it applies to new matter that lies beyond the scope of the direct. On the allowable scope of cross-examination of a witness asserting the privilege against self-incrimination, see M & K, § 6.65. See also FRE 104(d) (providing that in "testifying upon a preliminary matter" the accused does not become "subject to cross-examination as to other issues").

4. Leading Questions Generally Allowed

Leading questions are allowed on cross-examination, except in special circumstances. One such circumstance arises when an attorney "cross-examines" her own client after she was called as an adverse witness by the opposing party. In this situation, leading questions would enable an attorney to lead a witness who is already sympathetic to the direction in which the lawyer wants to proceed, and leading questions are undesirable for the same reasons that apply to direct examination in more typical situations.

5. Improper Cross–Examination

Cross-examination cannot be used simply to badger or demean a witness. FRE 611(a) authorizes judges to exercise reasonable control over the questioning process to protect witnesses from "harassment or undue embarrassment." Ethics codes impose similar constraints on attorneys. See ABA Model Code of Professional Responsibility DR 7–106(C)(2) (a lawyer shall not ask "any question that he has no reasonable basis to believe is relevant to the case" or that is "intended to degrade a witness or other person"); ABA Model Rules of Professional Conduct 4.4 (lawyers shall not "use means that have no substantial purpose other than to embarrass, delay or burden a third person").

6. Cross–Examining on Documents Used to Refresh Memory

If the witness uses a writing to refresh memory for purposes of testifying, the cross-examiner can ask to have the writing produced at the hearing.

a. Production mandatory or discretionary

If the witness uses the document to refresh at the hearing, the examiner is *entitled to have it produced*. If the witness used the document or refresh his memory in advance of the hearing, *the trial court has discretion* whether to require production, depending on whether "it is necessary in the interests of justice."

b. Unrelated portions of documents

If it is claimed that the writing contains matters not related to the subject of the testimony, the court may examine the writing *in camera*, excise any unrelated portions, and order delivery of the remainder to the adverse party.

c. Use of documents

Once the documents are produced, the adverse party is entitled "to inspect it, to cross-examine the witness thereon, and to introduce in evidence those portions which relate to the testimony of the witness." FRE 612.

d. Refusal to produce

If a writing used to refresh is not produced or delivered as ordered by the court, the court is authorized to make any order justice requires, including contempt, dismissal, or finding issues against the offender. In criminal cases, FRE 612 limits the remedy to striking the direct testimony or declaring a mistrial if the court determines that the interests of justice so require.

D. REDIRECT EXAMINATION

1. Leading Questions Generally Not Allowed

Redirect is a form of direct examination. A party is posing questions to its own witness. Hence the rules of direct examination apply and leading questions are ordinarily not allowed.

2. Limited to Scope of Cross

Normally the only permitted purpose of redirect is to rebut or otherwise respond to issues raised on cross. If an attorney wishes to go into new issues that were not previously raised, she must ask permission to reopen the direct.

E. FORMAL OBJECTIONS TO QUESTIONS ON DIRECT OR CROSS-EXAMINATION

A party can make "formal" objections to questions asked on direct and cross-examination, in addition to substantive objections such as hearsay, privilege, irrelevancy, and so forth. Formal objections go to the *wording* or *form* of a question. Such objections can usually be overcome by rephrasing the question. The following are some of the most common formal objections:

1. Compound

Sometimes a single question really asks two questions, and any answer could be misleading. For example, "Did you read the instructions and use the drill properly?" An affirmative answer might mean "yes" to both questions or only to one or the other, but the jury has no way to know which.

2. Misleading Witness, Misstating Evidence

If there is evidence that the witness took an hour to drive someplace and that the trip was ten miles, it is misleading to ask "Why did it take you an hour to drive five miles?"

3. Assumes Facts Not in Evidence

It is improper to ask a witness a question that assumes facts not in evidence. For example, the question "Where was X sitting in the car?" is objectionable if there is no evidence that X was even in the car.

4. Uncertain, Ambiguous, and Unintelligible

Sometimes a question is worded in such an incomprehensible way that it is impossible for the witness to give a meaningful answer. Consider this sarcastic gem: "In arranging the lineup, you tried to pick seven men who weighed the same and didn't weigh the same, who looked alike and didn't look alike, didn't you?"

5. Calls for Speculation

It is improper to ask a witness about something she has no way of knowing and about which she can only conjecture. For example, it is normally objectionable to ask a witness "what she would have done" if she knew something that she knows now or what someone else "was thinking when she did that."

6. Asked and Answered

An attorney cannot repeatedly pose the same question to the point of harassment in an attempt to force the desired response. But some pressing is allowed, and the attorney is not required to take the first answer, such as "I don't know." More leeway is usually allowed on cross, and the lawyer can come at the same point from different directions to try to get some sort of answer or to test the credibility of the witness if he continues to be evasive.

7. Argumentative

Questions are objectionable if they do not seek information and seek merely to be rhetorical, sarcastic, or argumentative. For example, the question "How can you seriously expect us to believe what you just said?" is a thinly disguised form of argument.

F. QUESTIONING BY JUDGE

1. Judge May Call Witnesses

Under FRE 614(a), the trial judge can call witnesses on her own or on suggestion by a party. The judge can question such witnesses, and all parties may cross-examine witnesses called by the judge.

2. Judge May Question Witnesses Called by Parties

FRE 614(b) authorizes the trial judge to interrogate witnesses called by a party.

3. Party May Object to Questioning by Judge

FRE 614(c) allows the parties to object to what the judge does (or proposes to do) in calling or questioning witnesses. To avoid prejudice to the parties (or embarrassment to the judge), such objections can be made at the next available opportunity when the jury is not present. Questioning may be improper if it is overly intrusive, deprives attorneys of control over trial, or gives jurors the impression that the judge is biased for or against one side. Questioning by the court is also improper if it reveals knowledge that is not yet in evidence. Such questioning may violate the spirit of FRE 605, which bars judges from testifying in cases in which they preside.

G. EXCLUSION OF WITNESSES

1. Witnesses May Be Excluded

On request by a party, the court must order witnesses excluded so they do not hear testimony by other witnesses. The court may also make such an order on its own motion. See FRE 615. Such orders are often referred to as sequestration orders.

2. Exemptions from Exclusion

a. Parties

Parties are exempt from sequestration orders. It would violate fundamental fairness and probably due process to exclude parties from the trials of their own lawsuits.

b. Representatives of parties

Corporations, governments, and other artificial entities can only be present through representatives. The attorney for such an entity is allowed to designate a representative who is then exempt from sequestration.

c. Other essential persons

Under FRE 615, a witness is also exempt from sequestration if "shown by a party to be essential to the presentation of the party's cause." For example, an expert advising an attorney on how to cross-examine the opposing party's expert would likely fit this exemption.

d. Crime victims

FRE 615 also exempts from sequestration any person "authorized by statute to be present," which in federal courts accommodates victim rights legislation that entitles crime victims to be present in court throughout the proceedings. See 18 U.S.C. §§ 3510 (in noncapital cases, federal court "shall not order any victim of an offense excluded from the trial" because he may make a statement or present information during sentencing; in capital cases federal court "shall not order any victim of an offense excluded from trial" because he is to "testify as to the effect of the offense" during sentencing) and 3771 (crime victims have right "not to be excluded" from court proceeding unless court decides on basis of "clear and convincing evidence" that testimony by the victim would be "materially altered" by hearing other testimony). Many states have similar legislation.

Review Questions and Answers

Question: When are leading questions permitted?

Answer: As a general rule, leading questions are allowed on cross but not on direct examination. But there are exceptions in both situations. On cross, the court may restrict leading questions when the lawyer questions his own client (after the other side called the client as an adverse witness). Similarly, when the court allows a lawyer to cross-examine a witness beyond the scope of direct, leading questions are generally not permitted. On direct examination, leading questions are allowed when necessary to develop testimony, as happens when the witness is timid or forgetful or the lawyer is bringing out preliminary matters. Leading questions are allowed for hostile witnesses, adverse parties, or witnesses identified with adverse parties.

Question: What restrictions govern the process of refreshing the recollection of a witness?

Answer: Very few. The Rules do not require any particular foundation. Ordinarily the attorney brings out through questioning that the witness has some memory loss so the jury understands why it needs to be refreshed. Usually the attorney asks the witness "Would it help refresh your memory to review Document X?" This way the jury hears directly from the witness that Document X would be helpful and understands why the attorney is handing the document to the witness. The primary check against abuse of the process of refreshing recollection is provided by FRE 612, which allows the opponent to see any writing used to refresh, to cross-examine the witness about it, and to introduce relevant portions into evidence. This is thought to be sufficient deterrent against improper "coaching" while witnesses are on the stand.

Question: What are "formal" objections?

Answer: Formal objections are those directed against the form of the question rather than the substance of the testimony being sought. Usually a formal objection can be overcome if the questioner rephrases the question. Examples of formal objections include claims that a question is compound, misleading, ambiguous, argumentative, repetitive, or assumes facts not in evidence.

EXAM TIPS

Here are some tips on issues relating to direct and cross-examination:

Remember that direct examination normally requires nonleading questions, but exceptions allow the lawyer to lead while questioning an adverse party, a witness identified with an adverse party, a hostile witness, and to some extent a forgetful witness (whose memory may be refreshed by questions calling his attention to points he may have forgotten).

Remember that cross-examination is generally limited to the scope of the direct, and generally proceeds by leading questions.

Remember that leading questions are those that suggest the answer sought by the lawyer.

CHAPTER 10

Impeachment and Rehabilitation

Chapter Overview

The key points in this chapter are

- There are five common methods to impeach witnesses–one involves showing bias; another involves showing a defect in sensory or mental capacity; third involves showing bad character for "truth and veracity" (or simply truthfulness); fourth involves questioning or extrinsic evidence of prior inconsistent statements by the witness that conflict with her testimony; fifth involves contradicting the witness by questioning or extrinsic evidence that shows that something she said in her testimony is wrong or mistaken.

- The Federal Rules do not regulate all these methods in any detail, although various Rules do cover some of these impeaching methods in detail, and other provisions address isolated aspects of these methods.

- To impeach by showing bad character for truthfulness of a witness (the "target"), the attacking party may (a) ask about prior specific instances of conduct by the target witness that shows untruthfulness, (b) bring out prior criminal convictions of the target witness, or (c) offer reputation or opinion testimony indicating that the target witness has an untruthful character.

- Parties are entitled to impeach their own witnesses.

- Bias in a witness is always relevant and never collateral.

- When the purpose is to show bad character for truth and veracity under FRE 608(b), the cross-examiner may inquire into prior conduct by the target witness but may not prove such conduct by extrinsic evidence (testimony by other witnesses or documentary evidence).

- An attacking party may impeach the target witness by bringing out his convictions for crimes involving "dishonesty or false statement," and the trial judge lacks discretion to exclude such convictions (FRE 403 is unavailable in this context).

- An attacking party may impeach the target witness by bringing out his convictions for felonies that do not involve "dishonesty or false statement," but in this setting the judge *does* have discretion to exclude (FRE 609 authorizes the trial judge to exclude for unfair prejudice).

- The balancing test in FRE 609 for felony convictions is different for criminal defendants than for other witnesses. In the case of criminal defendants, prior felonies are admissible if probative worth exceeds the risk of unfair prejudice (a "reverse–403 standard" that is weighted slightly in favor of excluding). In the case of other witnesses, prior felonies are admissible unless the risk of unfair prejudice exceeds probative worth (the usual standard contained in FRE 403 that is weighted slightly in favor of admitting).

- A witness impeached by a prior inconsistent statement generally must have an opportunity to deny or explain such statement under FRE 613.

- Evidence offered to contradict a witness generally must also prove some other point that counts in the case.

- A witness may be rehabilitated by evidence of a good character for truthfulness, but only after an impeaching attack that suggests that she has bad character for truth and veracity.

- A witness may be rehabilitated by evidence of a prior consistent statement, but this kind of rehabilitation is not allowed merely because the was impeached by use of a prior inconsistent statement. Instead, this kind of rehabilitation is allowed mainly when an impeaching attack suggests that her testimony reflects recent fabrication or improper motive or influence, which can be suggested by use of prior inconsistent statements or by other forms of impeachment, but not is not suggested in every instance of the use of prior inconsistent statements.

A. IMPEACHMENT: AN OVERVIEW

All witnesses who testify are subject to impeachment. "Impeachment" means asking questions or introducing extrinsic evidence that attacks the credibility of a witness. Some of the most important methods of impeachment, such as bias, are not covered by the Federal Rules, and one method—impeachment by evidence of religious belief—is prohibited by FRE 610. The following is a list of the five most common methods for impeaching a witness, with a cross-reference to the applicable Federal Rule (if any). Each mode of impeachment is discussed in further detail below:

(1) **Bias:** This category includes animus, sympathy, motive, and corruption. No federal rule speaks expressly to this mechanism of impeachment, but there is no doubt that this mechanism is acceptable and it is commonplace in trials and reported opinions.

(2) **Defect in sensory or mental capacity:** No federal rule speaks expressly to this mechanism of impeachment, but again there is no doubt that it is acceptable. It is somewhat less commonly seen in trials and reported opinions.

(3) **Bad character for truth and veracity:** This mechanism of impeachment involves three related techniques. One is asking about prior bad acts indicating dishonesty, which is regulated by FRE 608(b). The second involves asking about prior convictions, which is regulated by FRE 609. The third involves reputation or opinion evidence, which is regulated by FRE 608(a).

(4) **Prior inconsistent statements:** This mechanism of impeachment is partly regulated by FRE 613, and again it is acceptable and commonplace in trials and reported opinions.

(5) **Contradiction:** This mechanism of impeachment is not mentioned in the Rules, but it is once again accepted and commonplace in trials and reported opinions.

B. WHO MAY IMPEACH

Usually a witness is impeached by the adverse party. But under modern codes, a party may impeach its own witnesses. See FRE 607 (providing that credibility "may be attacked by any party, including the party calling the witness").

1. Voucher Rule

At common law, a party could not impeach his own witness. It was said that the calling party "vouches" for the credibility of the witness simply by putting him on the stand and adducing his testimony.

2. Reasons for Abolishing Voucher Rule

The voucher rule was long criticized as unfair and unworkable. Calling a witness is surely a sign that the party thinks she will do more good than harm, but the calling party does not necessarily mean to endorse everything (or even anything) the witness may say. Often the calling party has little or no choice and must call whoever knows the relevant facts, despite concerns that might arise over honesty or accuracy. It is sometimes said that parties "must take witnesses as they find them."

3. Consequences of Abolishing Voucher Rule

Abolishing the voucher rule means that a witness can be impeached on direct as well as on cross-examination, and a party is not "bound" by testimony or other evidence she introduces or sponsors. She remains free to contradict or explain such evidence if it damages her case. All the modes of impeachment available to the adverse party are generally available to the calling party. It is noteworthy, however, that when the calling party impeaches her own witness by means of prior inconsistent statements that are admissible *only* to impeach (they cannot properly be used as substantive evidence), courts sometimes conclude that the right of impeachment is being abused and they block such attempts if the primary purpose of the calling party appears to be encouraging the improper (substantive) use of such statements. See Chapter 10, Sec. H5, infra.

C. BIAS

A witness may be impeached by showing bias for or against a party, which includes animus, sympathy, motive to falsify, corruption, and bribery.

1. No Federal Rule

There is no federal rule governing impeachment by bias. But this mechanism of impeachment continues to be commonplace and fully acceptable. It is recognized as a matter of federal common law that is loosely connected now to the Rules, including especially the relevancy rules (FRE 401–403, which embody the general principle that evidence is admissible only if relevant) and FRE 611 (which says that courts have the power to regulate the examination of witnesses). See *United States v. Abel*, 469 U.S. 45 (1984).

2. Bias Always Relevant

It is commonly said that bias is always relevant, which means at least three things. First, bias is a matter "of consequence in determining the action" under FRE 401, meaning that it is always "relevant." Second, bias may be explored on cross-examination of the witness *and* may also be proved by extrinsic evidence. Third, courts cannot unreasonably limit the attacking party, who must have reasonable latitude on cross-examination to explore bias and must be allowed a reasonable chance to prove bias by extrinsic evidence. Insofar as bias is explored on cross-examination, it is exempt from the usual rule that the cross must stay within the scope of the direct, and of course other forms of impeachment are also exempt. See FRE 611(b) (limiting cross to the "subject matter of the direct" and to "*matters affecting the witness's credibility*").

3. Types of Possible Bias

There are many facts that indicate (or *may* indicate) bias. These include family ties with a party, personal friendship, sexual involvement, membership in clubs or organizations, employment or business or financial relationships, an interest in the outcome of the suit (financial or otherwise), hatred or enmity between witness and a party, fear on the part of the witness for his personal safety or safety of friends or family (relating to the parties or issues in suit), and settlement or attempts to settle a claim between a witness and a party to the suit. Bias is also shown by indications that a party has influenced the witness to testify in a certain way, or by indications that the witness may be subject to criticism or embarrassment for testifying in a certain way, or that the witness has taken or solicited bribes, or made or received threats, or faces a risk of prosecution or engaged in plea bargaining to avoid prosecution.

4. Proving Bias

a. By examination of witness, including questions on direct

Bias is usually brought out on cross, but the calling party may also develop points showing bias on direct (otherwise jurors might think that the calling party was hiding important information). If the witness is impeached by prior statements indicating bias, most courts require that the witness first be asked about them on cross before they can be proved by extrinsic evidence. (This requirement is similar to that imposed by FRE 613 for prior inconsistent statements. See Section H3.) Such a requirement is generally not imposed if the evidence tends to show bias by prior conduct as opposed to prior statements, although some authorities would apply the requirement to both forms of proof.

b. By extrinsic evidence

It is said that bias is never collateral, which means that it can be proved by extrinsic evidence. Examples of extrinsic evidence includes proof that the witness made statements indicating some attitude or connection with the case that supports an inference of bias (at least if he has been asked about them on cross), and proof that the witness was involved in prior or ongoing relationships with one of the parties, or proof of prior specific instances of conduct that point in such directions. Occasional confusion arose from the original language of FRE 608(b), which used to say that specific instances of conduct could not be proved by extrinsic evidence for the purpose of attacking or supporting the witness' *credibility*, but the confusion should have been dispelled by a change in wording adopted in 2003. Now FRE 608(b) states that specific instances of conduct may not be proved by extrinsic evidence for the purpose of attacking or support-ing the witness' *"character for truthfulness."* The new language makes clear what was intended from the beginning–specifically that extrinsic evidence of prior instances of conduct is excluded *only* when it is offered to prove untruthful disposition or character, and *not* when it is offered to impeach in other ways, as by showing bias or lack of capacity or by contradicting the witness. States with their own counterparts of the Rules have not all adopted this change, so the confusion may still appear in state systems.

5. Restricting Proof of Bias

Parties are entitled to reasonable latitude in showing the bias of a witness, whether by cross-examination or extrinsic evidence, and undue restrictions on proving bias may constitute error. In criminal cases, the accused is constitutionally entitled to impeach prosecution witnesses for bias, which means developing the relevant points sufficiently to let the factfinder make an informed evaluation of credibility. See *Alford v. United States*, 282 U.S. 687 (1931). Rulings denying or too narrowly restricting such efforts infringe confrontation and due process rights. *Davis v. Alaska*, 415 U.S. 308 (1974). But the judge has discretion to limit attempts to establish bias in order to prevent harassment of witnesses, confusion of issues, waste of time, and unfair prejudice to parties.

D. DEFECT IN SENSORY OR MENTAL CAPACITY

This method involves showing a defect in sensory or mental capacity if it (a) affected the ability of the witness to observe and understand at the time of the events, or (b) affects her memory and ability to recount the events at trial. Common examples include bad eyesight, poor hearing, or faulty memory. While impaired capacity usually does not make a person incompetent as a witness (see Chapter 8), problems in mental or sensory capacity are relevant in assessing the credibility of the witness and of the testimony that she gives at trial.

1. No Federal Rule

No federal provision addresses this method of impeachment, but there is no doubt that the method remains valid in the federal system and states that have adopted the Rules. If the method were ever challenged as invalid in a state jurisdiction, the court would likely reject the challenge for reasons similar to those cited in *United States v. Abel*, 469 U.S. 45 (1984) (approving impeachment by bias in federal courts even though bias is not mentioned in the Rules; bias is relevant, and the Rules did not end all common law traditions).

2. Forms of Proof; cross-examination and extrinsic evidence; bringing out on direct

The attacking party can inquire on cross-examination about sensory or mental defects, such as limits in visual acuity or mental problems, that affect a witness and bear on his testimony. Sometimes the impeachment is indirect or subtle, as happens when the demeanor of the witness, and difficulty in responding to simple questions, reveal mental incapacity. Sometimes questions about the event at issue expose serious flaws in memory. The attacking party may also call other witnesses to testify to such points, although such proof is less commonly seen. The calling party may also bring out sensory or mental deficiencies on direct: Here the usual purpose is to avoid hiding (or seeming to hide) these matters from the jury, and of course the calling party hopes to show that *despite* any such problems the witness should be believed.

3. Alcohol or Drug Use

Both perception and memory may be affected by the use of drugs and alcohol. Hence the attacking party may go into the matter of intoxication or influence of drugs at the time of the events about which the witness testifies. If he is under the influence of drugs or alcohol at the time of trial (which does happen, but fortunately not often), this matter can be explored as well. But courts generally exclude evidence of drug addiction or alcoholism unless it bears on the ability of the witness to perceive or recall the events at issue.

4. Mental Illness or Disability

a. Impeaching a witness

The attacking party may show by cross-examination or extrinsic evidence that the witness suffers (or once did) from a mental illness that could affect her ability to perceive or recall the events at issue. Evidence of an unrelated mental illness is excluded to protect the personal privacy of the witness. Medical records indicating treatment for a relevant mental problem provide a proper basis for cross-examination, although the records themselves are usually excluded. When the adverse party attacks a witness by questions or extrinsic evidence suggesting mental illness or incapacity, the calling party may offer counterproof in the form of expert testimony that the witness has adequate mental capacity.

b. Court-ordered examinations

Many decisions say courts have inherent authority to order witnesses to undergo mental examinations as a condition of testifying, although courts rarely exercise such authority. See *United States v. Gutman*, 725 F.2d 417, 420 (7th Cir. 1984) (trial judge has power and sometimes duty to hold hearing to determine whether psychiatric examination should be required as condition of allowing witness to testify). The purpose of such court-ordered examinations is to assess mental condition and more specifically capacity to distinguish truth from falsehood. Courts can in effect force parties to undergo examinations by refusing to allow them to testify unless they are examined, or by limiting claims or defenses unless such examinations are performed. But courts lack authority to compel nonparty witnesses to submit to such examinations, and can do no more than to exclude their testimony if they refuse.

E. BAD CHARACTER: PRIOR BAD ACTS

This method of attack involves cross-examination about specific instances of conduct that suggest untruthfulness on the part of the witness, such as lying on employment applications or turning in false reports. Usually described as "impeachment by showing bad acts" or "impeachment by nonconviction misconduct," this method of attack can *only* be mounted on cross. See FRE 608(b) (nonconviction misconduct may be "inquired into on cross-examination" but may not be proved by "extrinsic evidence"). This method is one of three ways of showing what is usually called "bad character for truth and veracity," or simply untruthfulness. The other two ways, taken up separately below, involve the use of convictions or the use of character witnesses who give opinion or reputation testimony to the effect that the target witness is by character or disposition untruthful or untrustworthy.

1. Acts Must Bear on Truthfulness

At common law, some jurisdictions allowed inquiry about past acts bearing on the witness's general morality. FRE 608(b) is much narrower. It limits the inquiry to acts that bear on the truthfulness of the witness, meaning essentially acts that involve falsehood or deception.

a. Examples

Acts that qualify as proper matters to raise on cross-examination of the target witness include use of false identification, making false statements on government forms such as applications or tax returns, making false claims on resumes submitted in support of employment applications, giving false testimony, and making deceptive or fraudulent representations. Acts that do not qualify as proper matters to raise on cross-examination include violent behavior, using or selling drugs, getting into commercial or financial defaults, engaging in prostitution or adultery or other sexual misconduct, and bearing or begetting illegitimate children.

b. Arrests

It is generally improper to ask about being arrested, charged, or indicted because such facts are unreliable proxies for the important point, which is behavior by the witness that bears on truthfulness. Rather than asking "Isn't it true that you were arrested for embezzlement?" the questioner should ask "Isn't it true that you embezzled funds from your employer?"

2. Good Faith Basis

There must be a good faith basis for questions about prior bad acts because a groundless question may "waft an unwarranted innuendo into the jury box." *Michelson v. United States*, 335 U.S. 469, 481 (1948). Forcing a string of denials about past behavior that did not occur may leave a witness effectively impeached. Before allowing the question, the trial judge may require a showing outside the presence of the jury of a good faith basis. Parties may make motions in limine requesting a ruling to prevent (or allow) questioning on particular conduct, but the court may decline to rule on such motions and leave the matter to be resolved if the issue arises at trial.

3. Discretion to Exclude

Trial judges have discretion under FRE 608(b) (and under FRE 403 and 611) to bar questions when probative value is overbalanced by the need to protect parties from undue prejudice, witnesses from harassment and undue embarrassment, juries from being confused and misled, and trials from being unnecessarily prolonged. Thus questions that ask about misconduct involving lies or deception may be barred even though the misconduct tends to indicate untruthfulness. Although FRE 608(b) specifies no time limit on prior bad acts, remoteness in time erodes probative value.

4. No Extrinsic Evidence

Even when a witness denies committing a prior untruthful act, extrinsic evidence of that act is not admissible under FRE 608(b). This limitation is often described by the maxim that the cross-examiner must "take the answer of the witness" when it comes to nonconviction misconduct. It is also sometimes stated as a rule that extrinsic evidence of prior misconduct is deemed "collateral," hence inadmissible.

a. Rationale for limitation

Excluding extrinsic evidence helps keep trials from being sidetracked on peripheral issues. It reduces surprise that might unfairly confront the calling party if he were faced with unexpected proof requiring rebuttal witnesses, as would likely happen if evidence beyond the answer of the witness were allowed. It also limits the risk that the jury might use the evidence for an improper purpose.

b. Need not take first answer

This limitation does not mean the cross-examiner must take the first answer. The very idea of cross-examination implies testing and probing, and the questioner should have a chance to overcome an initial denial. Only after the questioner has been able to press the witness should the lawyer be obliged to take the answer given.

c. Extrinsic evidence admissible under other methods of impeachment

The bar against extrinsic evidence of specific instances of conduct applies only when it is offered to show untruthful disposition. The bar does not apply to extrinsic evidence offered in support of other kinds of impeaching attacks, such as showing bias or sensory or mental defect, or proving prior inconsistent statements, or (sometimes) contradicting the direct testimony of the witness.

F. BAD CHARACTER: PRIOR CRIMINAL CONVICTIONS

This method of attack involves the use of criminal convictions to show that the witness is untruthful. The controversial premise underlying this method of impeachment is that a witness who has been convicted of certain crimes may be dishonest in testifying today (and may disregard the law against committing perjury). Since witnesses are often parties, and since convictions bring explosive risks of unfair prejudice, especially in criminal cases when the defendant is the person testifying and the person on trial, this method of attack is regulated in detail (see FRE 609) and litigated with vigor. This method is also controversial because many convictions have no direct or immediate relationship to veracity.

1. Policy Considerations

There are lots of reasons to limit use of convictions for impeachment. For a nonparty witness, questions about convictions can embarrass or humiliate. For a complaining witness in a criminal case, using prior convictions to impeach may invite the jury to acquit the defendant because "the victim had it coming." For a witness who is a civil litigant, using prior convictions to impeach might cast him in a bad light and lead the jury to become disaffected from his cause. For a witness who is a criminal defendant, using convictions to impeach brings the greatest danger. It may lead the jury to convict on present charges simply because the accused is a bad person (an emotional or angry reaction) or because the jury thinks the prior convictions show criminal propensity, hence guilt of the charged offense (misuse of evidence), and these possibilities track the usual meaning of the term "unfair prejudice" in FRE 403 (the same concept is also embodied in the discretion clause in FRE 609).

2. First Prong: Felony Convictions

Jurisdictions that follow the Federal Rules allow the use of *any* prior felony convictions to impeach, subject to a balancing test and time limitations. See FRE 609(a)(1) (allowing impeachment by convictions punishable by "death or imprisonment for more than one year," which is the usual definition of a felony). It is the *nature and extent of possible punishment* that counts, rather than *punishment actually imposed*, and the nature and extent of possible punishment are set by the law of the jurisdiction where the conviction was obtained.

a. Balancing test for impeaching witnesses other than accused

For witnesses other than the accused, prior felony convictions are admissible to impeach "subject to Rule 403." This lenient standard is cast in favor of *admitting* convictions, since FRE 403 warrants exclusion only if probative value is "substantially outweighed" by the danger of unfair prejudice, confusion of issues, and related concerns.

b. Balancing test for impeaching accused

If the accused is the witness, prior felony convictions are admissible to impeach if the court determines that the probative value of admitting this evidence outweighs its prejudicial effect to the accused. This stricter ("reverse–403") standard is cast in favor of *excluding* convictions, which come in only if probative worth "outweighs" prejudice, in contrast to the more lenient standard that applies for convictions of witnesses other than the accused.

c. Factors to be considered in balancing

i. Nature of prior crime

The more the prior crime reflects adversely on honesty or integrity, the greater its probative worth. Crimes of "dishonesty or false statement" are automatically admissible under FRE 609(a)(2), but some crimes that don't meet this standard nonetheless have probative value on veracity. Such crimes include theft, receiving stolen property, smuggling, or failure to register or report when required. Others are less probative, especially crimes involving violence as the central feature (a category that embraces many sexual assaults). Also low on the scale are drug crimes and crimes against public morality, such as prostitution. Crimes requiring planning or preparation bear more strongly on veracity because planning indicates deliberate violation of standards rather than impulse or anger, and usually it involves some element of deceiving the victim.

ii. Recency or remoteness

FRE 609(b) creates a presumption that a conviction more than ten years old should be excluded, but even the age of a more recent conviction may tip the balance in favor of exclusion. Remoteness as a factor is affected by the presence or absence of more recent convictions. More recent convictions suggest that a defendant has not changed his ways, and strengthen the inference that the witness is willing to violate the law.

iii. Similarity to charged crime

The closer the resemblance between the charged crime and the crime of prior conviction, the greater the potential prejudice to the defendant, and such resemblance weighs heavily in favor of exclusion as unfairly prejudicial.

iv. Extent and nature of record

The probative value of a conviction may be affected by defendant's whole criminal record. All other things being equal, an isolated conviction by one who otherwise leads a "blameless life" carries less probative worth on veracity than a conviction that fits a pattern of criminal behavior.

v. **Importance of defendant's testimony**

For a defendant with a criminal record, the question whether to take the stand is very much affected by the prospect of impeachment by convictions. A judge may decide it is more important for the jury to have the benefit of the defendant's version of the case than to have him remain silent out of fear of impeachment.

vi. **Importance of credibility issues**

In cases in which the trial is a "swearing contest" between the defendant and a prosecution witness (including the complainant), the judge may decide that a wider scope of prior conviction impeachment is justified so the jury can decide who is to be believed.

vii. **Conviction in trial where defendant testified**

Some courts find a conviction after a trial during which the defendant pled not guilty and gave testimony more probative on the issue of veracity than a conviction based on a guilty plea because the former suggests that the defendant gave testimony that the factfinder found to be false.

3. Second Prong: Convictions for Crimes Involving Dishonesty or False Statement

Jurisdictions that follow the Federal Rules allow impeachment by convictions of any crime of dishonesty or false statement. (In 2006, the language in FRE 609(a)(2) was amended, so it no longer covers crimes "involving dishonesty or false statement," and instead it reaches any conviction for a crime if it readily can be determined that establishing the elements of the crime required proof or admission of an act of dishonesty or false statement. We return to the purpose of the amended language below.) The two most important points about these second-prong convictions for crimes of dishonesty or false statement are that (1) the category reaches both felonies and misdemeanors, and (2) convictions within this category are *automatically* admissible, meaning that the trial judge does not have discretion to exclude them. They still may be excluded, however, if they do not satisfy the criteria in FRE 609(b)–(d) (such as being more than 10 years old or being subject to an annulment). If a conviction qualifies under both prongs, as in the case of a perjury conviction, which is *both* a felony *and* a crime of dishonesty or false statement, the fact that it fits the second prong makes it automatically admissible.

a. Crimes included

Legislative history suggests that Congress intended that only a small subset of crimes can fit FRE 609(a)(2), thus becoming automatically admissible. This subset includes convictions for crimes like perjury, false statement, criminal fraud, embezzlement, and false pretense. Courts narrowly construe this provision, in accord with legislative intent, and limit its reach to crimes involving deceit, untruthfulness, or falsification. Forgery and counterfeiting are generally admissible, but courts are divided on the admissibility of convictions for failure to file tax returns.

b. Crimes not included

Crimes that generally do not fit FRE 609(a)(2) include ordinary assault, rape or sexual assault, battery, murder, drunk and disorderly, drug offenses, and prostitution. Because the legislative history focused so strongly on crimes involving false statement or deception of some sort, most courts hold that crimes like burglary, robbery, larceny, and other forms of theft are not automatically admissible under FRE 609(a)(2).

c. Crimes that "involved" dishonesty or false statement: State and pre-amendment practice

Before 2006, FRE 609(a)(2) reached convictions for crimes that "involved" dishonesty or false statement, and many states retain this language. Under this language, the question arose whether a crime that was *committed by means of* dishonesty or false statement fit the second prong. Theft crimes, for instance, might be committed by pocketing merchandise and not paying for it (shoplifting), which arguably involves deception. Or theft might be committed by means of lying: The customer who steals a wrist watch might say to the clerk, "I decided not to get the watch, but I need to pay you for this box of tissues," which is arguably a crime that "involved" false statement. Many courts thought that in such a case a conviction for petty theft fit the second prong. They reached this conclusion even though most courts also thought that *ordinarily* theft does not fit this prong because the *elements of the crime do not require proof* of deception or false statement—just taking something that belongs to another—does not involve either dishonesty or false statement.

d. Crimes in which it can "readily be determined" that the elements "required" proof of dishonesty or false statement

Since 2006, FRE 609(a)(2) has reached convictions for crimes in which it readily can be determined that establishing the elements "required" proof of dishonesty or false statement. Apparently one purpose of the amendment, as stated in the 2006 Advisory Committee Note, was to "limit" convictions that fit the second prong, although the same ACN also says that convictions *may still fit* the second prong regardless "how such crimes are specifically charged." Hence a crime for "making a false claim to a federal agent" fits the second prong even if the charge is obstructing justice, which does not include false statement as a necessary element. Apparently a second purpose, as reflected in the same ACN, was to end detailed inquiries into the proceedings that produced the prior conviction: Thus the proponent should have "ready proof" that the crime required dishonesty or false statement. Recourse to the statute defining the offense is proper, and to the indictment and jury instructions, but perhaps not a more extended examination of the record of proceedings. The meaning of the new language must be developed over time: Apparently theft convictions arising out of shoplifting, as described above, do *not* fit the new language. Certainly theft statutes do not require false statements or dishonesty (if taking is not itself dishonest), and certainly a jury would not be instructed that such a statement is necessary or that they must make a finding of dishonesty. Perhaps, however, a conviction for misdemeanor theft in stealing electricity by tampering with an electric meter would still qualify under the second prong as amended. Again the statute would not require proof of false statement, but the jury would have to find that the defendant rigged the meter (surely a form of deceit or false statement) in order to convict, and arguably this conviction would still fit the second prong, even with the amended language.

4. Meaning of "Conviction"

Normally a conviction for purposes of FRE 609 means a judgment of conviction entered at the end of a criminal trial. But a conviction does not require a contested trial. For purposes of FRE 609, a conviction following a plea of guilty or nolo contendere or an *Alford* plea (where defendant in effect claims to be innocent while consenting to judgment of conviction) is still a conviction. Nor does it matter that conviction leads to a suspended sentence. Both state and federal convictions are admissible under FRE 609 as well as convictions from foreign nations.

5. Ten–Year Limit

FRE 609(b) in effect establishes a presumption that convictions more than ten years old are not admissible to impeach. The beginning point of the ten-year period is the date of the conviction or the release of the witness from confinement for that conviction, whichever is later (and usually release is later). Courts generally count imprisonment for probation or parole violations as part of the confinement period and measure the beginning date from the witness's final release. The end point of the ten-year period is not so clear: It could be the date of the attempted impeachment, the date that the trial began, the date that impeachment occurs, the date that charges were filed, or the date of the charged crime. Choosing the earliest possible end point would maximize the number of convictions that escape the ten-year rule, and choosing the latest would minimize the number of convictions that escape that year rule. Arguably the date when charges are filed is the preferable one (it would create an incentive for prosecutors to bring charges promptly, which is arguably a good thing), and opting instead for the date of impeachment would be undesirable (it would create an incentive for defendants to delay the trial, which is arguably a bad thing). This matter remains unresolved.

a. Exception

The court may admit convictions more than ten years old if it determines, on "specific facts and circumstances," that probative worth outweighs prejudicial effect.

b. Notice requirement

A party wishing to use a conviction more than ten years old must give "advance written notice" sufficient to enable the other side to "contest the use" of such a conviction.

6. Bringing Out Convictions on Direct

Often the calling party brings out the prior convictions of its witness on direct examination to "take the sting out" of anticipated cross-examination. This strategy is perfectly proper (even advisable) because otherwise the calling party could appear (or might be made to appear) to be concealing a criminal past from the jury. Notably, however, a defendant who takes the stand and brings out his own prior convictions on direct waives the right to urge any error on appeal (at least in the federal system), on the theory that he himself caused any mistake. See *Ohler v. United States*, 529 U.S. 753 (2000) (decision applies FRE 609 under Court's supervisory authority; states remain free to take other directions).

7. Extrinsic Evidence of Conviction

Prior convictions are usually proved by asking the witness about them on direct or cross-examination, but extrinsic evidence (like a certified copy of the judgment of conviction) are also admissible.

8. Details About Conviction

Generally the impeaching party may bring out only the date, place and nature of the conviction, and the punishment imposed. Questioning that goes beyond these basic points is usually condemned. Out of respect for the witness, courts usually allow him some opportunity to respond or explain the conviction if he wishes. But if the witness offers an explanation in an effort to exonerate himself, the other side may pursue the matter further in an effort to refute or challenge the explanation.

9. Effect of Pardon, Annulment

A conviction may not be proved under FRE 609 if it has been the subject of a pardon, annulment, or other equivalent procedure based *either* on a finding of innocence, *or a finding of rehabilitation and* the person has not been convicted of a later crime punishable by death or imprisonment in excess of one year.

10. Juvenile Adjudications

Evidence of a juvenile adjudication is generally not admissible to impeach under FRE 609. In a criminal case, the court may admit evidence of a juvenile adjudication to impeach a witness other than the accused if it is one that would be admissible to attack the credibility of an adult, *and admitting the juvenile adjudication is necessary "to fairly determine guilt or innocence."*

11. Pendency of Appeal

A conviction may be introduced under FRE 609 even if it is on appeal. See FRE 609(e). Most convictions are affirmed, so the fact of appeal is viewed as affecting weight rather than admissibility. It is up to the party supporting the witness to bring out that an appeal is pending. If a conviction used for impeachment is ultimately reversed, however, the party hurt by this use of the conviction has an argument for a new trial based on new evidence.

12. Review on Appeal

If a defendant in a criminal case makes and loses a pretrial motion to exclude prior convictions and then declines to take the witness stand, he waives his right to urge that the trial court erred in ruling the convictions admissible, at least in the federal system. See *Luce v. United States*, 469 U.S. 38 (1984) (decision applies FRE 609 under Court's supervisory authority; states remain free to take other directions).

G. BAD CHARACTER: REPUTATION OR OPINION EVIDENCE

This method of attack involves the use of one witness to show that another is untruthful. It is convenient to refer to the former as the "character witness" and the latter as the "principal" or "target" witness. Most jurisdictions permit a character witness to give either "opinion" or "reputation" testimony on the truthfulness of the target witness. See FRE 608(a).

1. Circumstantial Rather Than Direct

This form of impeachment involves circumstantial rather than direct evidence that the principal witness may be lying. In substance, the testimony indicates that the principal witness is by character or disposition untruthful, hence may be lying in his testimony, which is different from testimony that he actually lied. Whether to draw the inference of lying is up to the factfinder. In short, what is being proved is the *character* of the principal witness, which is a circumstantial indicator of possible lying. This use of character evidence requires an exception to the general bar against using character to prove conduct, and the exception is found in FRE 404(a)(3) (allowing proof of character of witnesses in criminal and civil trials).

2. Opinion and Reputation Evidence Both Allowed

Most jurisdictions let character witnesses give either opinion or reputation testimony. See FRE 608(a) (authorizing both opinion and reputation evidence). Thus a character witness may say, "I know [the target witness] and she is not a truthful person, and is prone to lie when it suits her." Alternatively, the character witness may say, "I am acquainted with the reputation of [the target witness] for truth and veracity, and that reputation is very bad." Common law tradition was narrower in allowing only reputation evidence. In a sense, the change from tradition represents nothing new, for it was long suspected that witnesses describing untruthful reputation were really giving disguised opinion testimony. But the change has some real importance because a personal endorsement, particularly if the character witness is engaging and appealing enough to be liked or respected by the jury, is probably more convincing than an endorsement purporting to convey what nameless others think.

3. Foundation for Character Testimony

A character witness called to describe the reputation of the principal witness in the community, or to give her opinion of the principal witness, must have an adequate foundation to testify to such points.

a. Foundation for reputation testimony

For reputation testimony, the character witness must be acquainted with the community where the principal witness spends most of his time–typically where he lives, works, or goes to school. A character witness who testifies about reputation need not actually reside, work, or study in the pertinent community, so long as she is familiar with that community.

b. Foundation for opinion testimony

The foundation requirement for a character witness who is to give her opinion of the principal witness is simply that the former knew the latter for some period of time in some setting–typically personal, business, or professional.

c. Character witness influenced by knowledge of case

If the principal witness is a party to the suit, especially if he is the defendant in a criminal case, impeaching testimony is excluded if it rests on or has been affected by impressions relating to defendant's guilt of the charged offense. See *United States v. Dotson*, 799 F.2d 189 (5th Cir. 1986) (reversible error to admit testimony by four government agents that they would not believe defendant and defense witnesses under oath; agents who know the accused only through criminal investigations did not have adequate basis).

Example. Here is an example illustrating a litany of the kinds of questions that are commonly put to a character witness under FRE 608(a). Q. "Do you know the defendant, Richard Palmer?" A. "Yes, I do." Q. "Please tell the jury how you know him." A. "I am the landlord of the apartment building where he lives." Q. "And how long have you been the landlord?" A. "I've managed the apartment for the last seven years, but Palmer moved in about four years ago. I didn't know him before then." Q. "Have you heard Mr. Palmer discussed by other tenants in the apartment building or by other people in the neighborhood?" A. "Yes, I have." Q. "And have you gotten to know Mr. Palmer personally during the last four years that he has lived there?" A. "Yes, indeed I have." Q. "Are you familiar with his reputation in the neighborhood for truth and veracity?" A. "I am." Q. "What is that reputation?" A. "It is bad." Q. "Do you yourself consider him a truthful person?" A. "I do not." Q. "Would you believe his testimony under oath?" A.

"No, sir, I would not." Q. "Thank you, no further questions." Note that the character witness both testifies to Palmer's reputation and expresses a personal opinion about his truthfulness. Both forms of testimony are proper here because the examiner laid a foundation for both.

4. Cross–Examination of Character Witness

A character witness is, like any other witness, subject to cross-examination and impeachment. Probably the most effective questioning of an adverse character witness aims at testing the knowledge and judgment of the community (in the case of reputation testimony) or her own knowledge or judgment (in the case of opinion testimony).

a. Specific conduct bearing on truthfulness

The character witness who gives reputation or opinion testimony about the untruthful character of the target witness may be cross-examined about specific instances of conduct by the target witness bearing on his truthfulness. In the case of reputation testimony, if the character witness *has not heard* talk in the community about relevant conduct by the target witness (*good* conduct reflecting positively on the latter's veracity), the indicated conclusion is that the community reputation *lacks an adequate basis for the reputation being reported*. And if the character witness *has heard* talk in the community about such relevant conduct, the indicated conclusion is that the community reputation *reflects poor judgment about the veracity of the target witness*. In the case of opinion testimony, if the character witness *does not know* about relevant conduct by the target witness (again presumably *good* conduct), the indicated conclusion is that the character witness *lacks an adequate basis for her opinion*. And if the character witness *does not know* about relevant conduct, the indicated conclusion is that the character witness *has poor judgment about the character of the target witness*. As a moment's reflection reveals, such questions put the cross-examiner in a win-win position: Either a yes or a no answer has impeaching effect. See FRE 608(b)(2) (on cross, character witness may be asked about "specific instances of conduct" by the target witness if probative of "truthfulness or untruthfulness").

b. Goes only to credibility of character witness

The cross-examination described above, in which the party supporting the target witness tries to undercut the negative character witness, does not constitute a proper method of showing that the target witness is truthful. The only legitimate purpose of the cross-examination is to test the character witness. If the latter answers such questions, by saying for example "No, I didn't know the target witness gave a proper accounting of all funds while serving as treasurer of the charity drive," this answer amounts to "extrinsic evidence" of conduct by the target witness. Since truthfulness and untruthfulness may not be shown by extrinsic evidence of conduct, its only legitimate use is to help the jury appraise the testimony of the character witness.

H. PRIOR INCONSISTENT STATEMENTS

A common method of impeachment involves showing that the witness made prior statements inconsistent with her trial testimony. Even though the jury may not know the cause of the inconsistency or which version is true (the prior statement or the trial testimony), the jury can properly infer that a witness who "blows hot and cold" on a point is more likely to be lying or mistaken in either or both statements than one who has not vacillated in this way.

1.   Meaning of "Inconsistent"

Most courts say a prior statement is inconsistent if it differs significantly from the thrust of trial testimony, or if comparing the prior statement with the trial testimony suggests that the witness has changed his view or made a mistake that matters in the case. For example, if an observer ventures an opinion or conclusion on fault or responsibility, such a comment may be admitted as inconsistent if the same person later testifies to facts that seem at odds with his earlier appraisal.

a.   Impeachment by omission

If a prior statement omits a material detail, which under the circumstances would likely have been included if true, the statement is inconsistent with trial testimony that includes this detail.

☛ EXAMPLE AND ANALYSIS

Calvin sees a fatal automobile accident. Immediately afterwards he gives a statement to the investigating police officer that Derrick ran the stopsign at a high rate of speed and plowed into Paul's car, killing him. Paul's estate sues Derrick, and Calvin is called as the principal eyewitness. Calvin testifies to what he saw. Calvin also testifies that when he talked to Derrick immediately after the accident Derrick "reeked of alcohol." On cross, Derrick's lawyer asks, "Did you ever mention anything to the investigating police officer about smelling alcohol on my client?" and Calvin answers "No."

If Calvin omitted such an important detail in his statement to the police immediately after the accident, this fact suggests that what he told the investigating officer is "inconsistent" with his trial testimony including this important detail. This inconsistency tends to impeach his trial testimony and raises the inference that what Calvin said in court about Derrick reeking of alcohol may not be accurate, and may even be a recent fabrication. The factfinder might even take this inconsistency as some indication that Calvin is wrong, and perhaps even lying, in the rest of what he testifies to, including his testimony that Derrick ran the stopsign at a high rate of speed.

b. Lack of memory at trial

If a witness claims lack of memory at trial, most courts view an earlier positive statement about the point to be inconsistent. Some courts find the earlier statement to be inconsistent only if the claim of memory loss at trial appears to be feigned.

☛ EXAMPLE AND ANALYSIS

Del is charged with armed robbery of a liquor store. At trial, Seth, a customer who was in the store at the time of robbery, testifies for the state. The prosecutor asks if Seth can identify the person who robbed the store. Seth testifies that he cannot, that he never got a good look at the robber, and that he has "pretty much forgotten" what happened that night. The prosecutor then calls O'Malley, a police officer, who testifies that on the day after the robbery Seth came to a police lineup and picked out Del as the robber.

This statement identifying Del is generally considered to be inconsistent with trial testimony claiming loss of memory and inability to observe. Therefore it is admissible to impeach. Some courts would insist on a showing that Del is feigning lack of memory. Of course such a showing is hard to accomplish, but in any event the question of lack of memory (and whether it is feigned) is for the trial judge to decide under FRE 104(a). Not all prior inconsistent statements can be used as substantive evidence (as proof of whatever they assert), but this particular one does. The reason is that Del's statement at the police lineup qualifies as a statement of identification under FRE 801(d)(1)(C). Hence it is "not hearsay" and may be considered for its truth, as well as being impeaching evidence. See Chapter 3.

2. Foundation Required

The common law required the attacking party to follow certain niceties in impeaching witnesses by their prior inconsistent statements, but FRE 613(a) significantly relaxes the process.

a. Prior written statements

At common law the rule of *Queen Caroline's Case*, 129 Eng. Rep. 976 (1820) held that the attacking party had to show the witness any prior written statement before cross-examination could proceed. FRE 613(a) provides, however, that the witness need not be given this opportunity before being questioned, but that on request the written statement must be shown to opposing counsel. One reason for this change is that the old rule was seen as a "trap for the unwary," and another is that the old rule was seen as giving the witness too much of an opportunity to prepare for the attack.

b. Prior oral statements

If the prior inconsistent statement was oral, *Queen Caroline's Case* required the lawyer to recite the details to the witness before asking her about it, even providing reminders of surrounding circumstances so the witness would have a chance to call it to mind. FRE 613(a) also abolishes this requirement, although once again on request the other party is entitled to learn of the contents of the statement. Again one reason for this change is that the old rule was seen as a "trap for the unwary," and another is that the old rule was seen as giving the witness too much of an opportunity to prepare for the attack.

3. Opportunity to Explain

A witness who has been impeached by a prior inconsistent statement must have an opportunity to deny or explain it. Under FRE 613(b), extrinsic evidence of a prior inconsistent statement is admissible only if the witness has such an opportunity, although the court may dispense with the requirement if the interests of justice so require. The requirement does not apply to admissions by a party opponent who is present at trial, and therefore always has an opportunity to explain by taking the witness stand.

a. Common law approach

At common law, the attacking party could not prove the prior inconsistent statement by extrinsic evidence unless he had first raised the matter during cross. One reason for this requirement was to save time: Taking extrinsic evidence wastes time if the witness admits on cross that he made the prior statement. Another reason was fairness: The witness under attack should have a chance to deny making the statement or to explain the apparent inconsistency.

b. Federal Rules approach

FRE 613(b) paves the way for extrinsic evidence of a prior inconsistent statement even though the witness was not asked about it on cross. But such proof is admissible only if he gets "an opportunity to explain or deny" the statement and the other side is given a chance "to examine" him on the statement. Thus FRE 613(b) is more flexible than common law practice while recognizing the underlying concerns: The foundation need not be laid first (as once was the case) but extrinsic evidence is admissible only if the witness gets a chance sometime to explain or deny, which means at least that he must be subject to recall when the extrinsic evidence is offered (if he has not already been given a chance to explain or deny).

☞ EXAMPLE AND ANALYSIS

Microcomputer, Inc. sues Macrocomputer, Inc. for unfair competition and violation of fair trade laws. Bunn, an auditor hired by Microcomputer, testifies that annual sales dropped from $10 million a year in 2009 to $2 million a year in 2010 as a result of Macrocomputer's anticompetitive practices. The defense attorney cross-examines Bunn extensively, but does not ask him about prior statements. During its case-in-chief, Macrocomputer calls Reginald, a loan officer in a bank from which Microcomputer sought to borrow money at the end of 2010. Reginald quotes Bunn as telling him that the 2010 drop in Microcomputer's revenue was caused by a "defective computer chip" and "the company has now got the problem remedied."

This statement to Reginald is *extrinsic evidence* of a prior inconsistent statement by Bunn that conflicts with his trial testimony that the drop in revenue was caused by unfair competition from Macrocomputer. This evidence is admissible under FRE 613(b), provided that Bunn has an opportunity at some point in the trial to explain or deny the statement if he wishes to do so.

4. Collateral Matter Limitation

The general rule that a witness cannot be impeached on collateral matters applies to impeachment by prior inconsistent statements. If a prior statement tends neither to undermine an assertion by the witness on some substantive point in the case nor to demonstrate or refute bias, capacity, or truthful disposition on the part of the witness, then the statement relates only to a collateral matter and may be excluded. The collateral matter bar is enforced less rigorously here than for impeachment by prior bad acts (where any extrinsic evidence is deemed "collateral") or impeachment by contradiction, at least when the inconsistency can be brought out on cross-examination without the need for extrinsic proof.

Example. Peter is the first driver to arrive at the scene of an automobile accident. At trial, plaintiff calls Peter to describe what he saw. Peter says he saw the collision while driving to the hardware store. Defendant calls Karen, Peter's next-door neighbor, and offers her testimony that Peter told her he saw the accident while driving to the grocery store. While Peter's earlier statement (about driving to the grocery store) is inconsistent with his testimony (about driving to the hardware store), it relates only to a collateral and insignificant point. Testimony about his earlier statement is likely to be ruled collateral and inadmissible. A court would likely reach the same conclusion if defendant simply asked Peter whether he had said something different to Karen, although the court might permit the question because it takes so little time.

5. Abuse of FRE 607

FRE 607 allows a party to impeach its own witnesses, but this possibility opens up a risk of abuse if a party calls a witness solely for the purpose of impeaching her by parading her prior out-of-court statements before the jury, at least when these prior statements do not fit some exception that would allow their substantive use to prove whatever they assert.

a. Primary purpose test

As a check on this abuse, many courts refuse to allow a party to impeach its own witnesses with prior inconsistent statements if the "primary purpose" is to put otherwise inadmissible statements in front of the jury. Some courts frame the standard slightly differently, asking instead whether the witness was essential or important to the calling party's case (in which case impeaching by prior statements is not an abuse of FRE 607). The danger that courts are seeking to minimize is that the jury may consider the earlier statements for their truth, despite a limiting instruction that they are admitted only for impeachment.

☞ EXAMPLE AND ANALYSIS

Morlang is charged with participating in a scheme to misuse federal funds. The prosecutor seeks to prove that Morlang made a statement to a coconspirator named Wilmoth that "One of us had to take the rap so the other one could stay out and take care of the business." The prosecutor wants to introduce this statement as an admission to prove Morlang's knowledge of and involvement in the conspiracy. Wilmoth initially told prosecutors that Morlang made that statement, but before trial Wilmoth changed his story and denied having had any such conversation with Morlang. The prosecutor calls Wilmoth anyway. True to his latest word, Wilmoth denies having had the conversation with Morlang. To refute the denial, the prosecutor calls Wilmoth's cellmate Crist, who testifies that Wilmoth did, after all, say that Morlang made such a statement. The prosecutor argues that what Wilmoth said to Crist is inconsistent with what Wilmoth says at trial, hence that Crist's testimony is admissible. The defense objects: "Wilmoth's testimony didn't hurt the other side, but just failed to help. It's not fair to let the prosecutor offer Crist's testimony describing Wilmoth's hearsay statement because the jury will take Willmoth's hearsay statement as proof that Morlang did indeed admit involvement, and not just as proof that impeaches Wilmoth. The prosecutor is the one who created the situation in which he needs to use the prior statement, and he shouldn't be allowed to do that." Should this objection be sustained?

Yes, Crist's testimony about Willmoth's prior statement should be excluded. Even though Wilmoth's statement that Morlang admitted his involvement is offered (through Crist's testimony) only to impeach Wilmoth's denial at trial of having talked to Morlang, the prior statement is likely to be taken as actual proof that Morlang *did* admit his involvement. It cannot properly be used for that purpose, because it can only be used to impeach Wilmoth. *United States v. Morlang*, 531 F.2d 183, 189–190 (4th Cir. 1975) (calling party may not impeach its witness by a prior inconsistent statement "as a mere subterfuge to get before the jury evidence not otherwise admissible").

b. Essential witness

The "primary purpose" test has been qualified by some modern dicisions where a party can show that the witness was essential to its case.

☞ EXAMPLE AND ANALYSIS

DeLillo is prosecuted for fraud in a government construction project involving the installation of substandard concrete pipes and hiding the defects. The government first calls Gorman (an accomplice) who testifies that DeLillo told a subordinate to hide the leaks. Next the government calls Monahan and elicits favorable testimony from him corroborating many aspects of the government's case against DeLillo. But when the prosecutor asks Monahan about DeLillo's statement telling a subordinate to hide the leaks (as reported by Gorman), Monahan denies that DeLillo ever said that. To impeach Monahan, the government offers Monahan's prior taped statement saying DeLillo did issue such an order. The defense objects that the government was "just eliciting Monahan's denial as a subterfuge to offer what Monahan said before as proof of what it asserts, which is an abuse of the impeachment process." Should this objection be sustained?

No. The objection should be overruled. The reason is that Monahan was an essential witness for the government, which could properly call him and use the part of his testimony that supported the government's case. The government could then properly bring out the other parts of Monahan's testimony (leaving them out would open the government to a charge of hiding adverse information) and impeach those parts of the testimony that hurt the government's case. See *United States v. DeLillo*, 620 F.2d 939, 946–947 (2d Cir. 1980) (Monahan was not called "as a subterfuge with the primary aim" of putting prior statements in front of the jury; his testimony was "essential in many areas," and government had right to call and question him, and to impeach parts of his testimony that conflicted with other proof).

---

c. Common law approach

To keep parties from parading inadmissible hearsay before juries, the common law had a rule barring a party from impeaching its own witness with her prior inconsistent statement unless the party could show that it was **surprised and damaged** by the testimony. Thus if the calling party knew beforehand that the witness was going to testify inconsistently with an earlier statement, there is no surprise and the calling party could not use the statement. Even if surprise were shown, the calling party could not use a prior statement unless the witness had given damaging testimony, and mere failure to recall did not count as damaging. Some commentators think these restrictions have in effect survived enactment of FRE 607 because of the *Morlang* doctrine, and at least one thinks the restrictions should be formally adopted as part of the rule. See Michael Graham, *Handbook of Federal Evidence* § 607.3 (5th ed. 2001).

6. Impeaching with Plea Bargaining Statements

Statements made in the course of plea discussions with the prosecutor under FRE 410 cannot be used in criminal cases to impeach the defendant's testimony at trial. See discussion in Chapter 7F. But the protection against impeaching use of such statements can be waived. See *United States v. Mezzanatto*, 513 U.S. 196 (1995).

7. Impeaching with Statements Made in Settlement Negotiations

Prior to the 2006 amendment to FRE 408, courts and commentators split on the question whether statements made by a party in the course of civil settlement negotiations could be used to impeach the testimony of that party at trial in the event that settlement talks failed. The 2006 amendment resolved this issue: Statements made by a party in civil settlement negotiations may not be used to impeach that party's testimony at trial, except that *some* such statements *can* be used in a criminal prosecution of the party. The new language provides that statements made in "negotiations related to a claim by a public office in the exercise of its regulatory, investigative, or enforcement authority" *can* be used in a later criminal trial of the party. Thus statements by a defendant in civil settlement negotiations acknowledging fault for an accident cannot be used in a later trial of the suit that led to the negotiations, even if the defendant takes the stand and testifies that he was *not* at fault. Nor can those statements be used in a later criminal trial of the defendant for reckless driving or negligent homicide. On the other hand, a statement by a licensed general contractor, spoken in settlement negotiations relating to the effort of a regulating agency to revoke his contractor's license, could be used in the event that the contractor testifies in a later criminal case in which he has been charged with crimes arising out of the same misconduct, if he testifies inconsistently with what he said during the earlier settlement negotiations with the agency.

8. Impeaching Defendant with *Miranda*–Barred Statements

Statements that are not admissible during the government's case-in-chief because *Miranda* warnings were not given can nonetheless be used to impeach the witness if the witness gives contrary testimony at trial. See *Harris v. New York*, 401 U.S. 222 (1971) (testifying does not include "right to commit perjury," and defendant who takes the stand must speak "truthfully and accurately" and submit to "traditional truth-testing devices," including use of prior statements, even if taken in violation of the *Miranda* rule).

9. Impeaching with Involuntary Statements

If a statement is obtained from a defendant involuntarily, it cannot be used to impeach.

☞ Examples and Analysis

1. James is charged with murder during a late-night fight between two groups of boys. On arrest, James admitted that on the day of the crime his hair was reddish brown, long, and combed straight back. Prior to trial, the defense succeeded in suppressing this statement because it was taken in violation of *Miranda*. At trial, state witnesses say the culprit had reddish shoulder-length hair worn in a slicked-back "butter" style. Henderson (a friend of the defendant) testifies for the defense that she drove James to school that day and that his hair was black. Now the state wants to impeach Henderson's testimony by offering James' admission that his hair was reddish at the time of the crime. Can it do so?

    No. A defense objection based on *Miranda* should be sustained. When the state offers a *Miranda*-barred statement to impeach *the defendant himself*, it tends to impeach because it shows vacillation—a change of position on his part. When such statement is offered to impeach testimony by other witnesses, it has that tendency only if taken as proof of what it asserts. What James said to the arresting officers tends to undermine what Henderson said in his trial testimony only if the jury takes as true the statement by James that his hair was reddish brown, long, and combed straight back on the day of the crime. If that is correct, then Henderson's trial testimony is wrong. If what James said is not correct, then it doesn't impeach Henderson's trial testimony. James' earlier statement would be admissible to impeach his own testimony if *he* had testified that his hair was black the evening of the crime, where the prior statement would tend to impeach *without* taking it as proof of what it asserts (because it shows vacillation). But the statement by James is not admissible to impeach other defense witnesses. See *James v. Illinois*, 493 U.S. 307 (1990).

2. Mincey was hospitalized after being shot in an exchange of gunfire with the arresting officer. While in the emergency room with an intravenous feeding tube, a catheter in his bladder, and tubes in his throat and nose, he was questioned by a police detective. Because he could not speak, he wrote his answers on a piece of paper. The interrogation continued despite his repeated requests for a lawyer. At trial, Mincey's testimony differed from his earlier statements in the emergency room. Should the earlier statements be admissible to impeach, on the theory adopted in the *Harris* case?

    No. *Harris* created an exception to the *Miranda* doctrine, which is designed to force police to give warnings as a way of curbing abuses in the interrogation process. Here Mincey's statements are not merely involuntary in the technical *Miranda* sense, but actually involuntary because of physical and psychological compulsion. Here particularly, concerns arise that the statements may be inaccurate. See *Mincey v. Arizona*, 437 U.S. 385, 398–401 (1978) (excluding "involuntary" statements offered against defendant for impeachment purposes since he was "seriously wounded" at the time, in a "debilitated and helpless condition," and "on the edge of consciousness").

---

10. Impeaching with Statements Obtained Under a Grant of Immunity

Statements obtained from a defendant under a grant of immunity cannot be used to impeach his trial testimony. See *New Jersey v. Portash*, 440 U.S. 450, 459 (1979) (testimony given in response to a grant of immunity is "the essence of coerced testimony," and there is no question of free will, since the witness is told "to talk or face the government's coercive sanctions" in the form of a contempt citation).

11. Impeaching with Silence as Prior Inconsistent "Statement"

Sometimes the earlier silence by a witness can be viewed as an inconsistent "statement," at least under circumstances in which he would reasonably be expected to have related the same facts now disclosed in his testimony at trial.

a.   Pre-arrest, pre-*Miranda* silence

If a crime occurs and the defendant says nothing about it, even though he was involved in it, there is no constitutional impediment to the use at trial of the fact that defendant did not say anything. His silence can be proved at trial, if it is probative, and it can be used to impeach him if he testifies to an exculpatory version of events. See *Jenkins v. Anderson*, 447 U.S. 231 (1980). However, the fact that the accused is silent in this setting can be excluded as a matter of evidence law if silence does not seem probative.

b.   Post-arrest, pre-*Miranda* silence

If defendant is taken into custody and he says nothing and the police ask him no questions, his silence during this time *can* be used as an admission or to impeach his testimony at trial. *Miranda* does not require warnings merely because the accused is arrested. *Miranda* requires warnings when the accused is under arrest *and* is questioned by police. See *Fletcher v. Weir*, 455 U.S. 603 (1982). Again, however, the fact that the accused was silent in this setting can be excluded as a matter of evidence law if silence does not seem probative.

c. Silence after *Miranda* warnings

If a defendant refuses to talk to police during questioning and after receiving *Miranda* warnings, his silence cannot be used against him at trial, either as evidence of guilt or to impeach his testimony at trial. If, on the other hand, the defendant takes the witness stand at trial and testifies that he "told police when they questioned me the very same thing that I'm telling you now," then the prosecutor can offer testimony by the police that he did *not* do so. In other words, post-arrest post-warning silence warnings cannot be proved on the theory that the silence is inconsistent with an exculpatory story given at trial, such silence can be used to contradict positive testimony that the defendant wasn't in fact silent and that he did in fact tell officers the same thing he's saying now. See *Doyle v. Ohio,* 426 U.S. 610 (1976).

☞ EXAMPLE AND ANALYSIS

Weir stabbed Buchanan to death in a parking lot and then left the scene in his truck. Police came to his trailer the next afternoon with an arrest warrant on murder charges. They advised him of the warrant and waited for ten minutes while Weir put on his socks and boots. The arresting officers did not deliver *Miranda* warnings until Weir was placed in the police cruiser. At trial Weir claimed self-defense. He testified that Buchanan attacked him, that he drew a knife from a scabbard at his waist, and that Buchanan "fell on it." He further testified that he put the knife in a toolbox on the back of his truck, but it was never found. On cross, the state proposes to ask Weir why he had not told this story to his friends, why he did not go to the police after the incident, and why he didn't tell the arresting officer where the knife was. The defense objects that these questions violate defendant's *Miranda* rights by asking him about his post-arrest silence. Should the objection be sustained?

No. None of the proposed questions suggests that Weir stood silent *after* receiving *Miranda* warnings. It is true that the last question asks Weir why he was silent after his arrest, but he had not yet received *Miranda* warnings. Those warnings must be given before police question an arrested suspect, but it is *questioning after arrest* that triggers the warning requirement, not arrest by itself. See *Fletcher v. Weir,* 455 U.S. 603 (1982) (questioning about post-arrest silence does not violate Fifth Amendment because *Miranda* warnings had not yet been given).

I. CONTRADICTION

Contradicting a witness is a recognized method of impeachment, even though it is not codified in the Federal Rules. (Remember that impeachment by bias and impeachment by showing lack of sensory capacity are not codified in the Rules either.) Impeaching by contradiction simply means showing that something the witness said is not so. By offering counterproof, the impeaching party may raise doubts in the minds of jurors not only about the specific point contradicted but about the credibility of the witness more generally. Sometimes impeachment by contradiction is accomplished on cross-examination by confronting the witness with facts that rebut what he has said, and he either retreats in uncertainty or confusion or concedes his mistake, or perhaps offers some explanation or even denies that there is any conflict. But dramatic turnarounds are more the stuff of popular fiction than courtroom life. Often impeachment by contradiction proceeds by means of extrinsic evidence, either in the form of testimony by other witnesses or in the form of physical or documentary evidence.

1. Dual Relevancy Requirement

Under the traditional view, evidence to contradict a witness is not admissible if its only relevance is to prove the witness wrong on some specific point in her testimony. Instead, the evidence must have dual relevancy, meaning that it must also be relevant for some *additional* reason, such as proving a point that has substantive significance in the case (going to the merits) or proving one that has some other impeaching significance (such as showing bias or defect in capacity). See 3A Wigmore, *Evidence* §§ 1003–1004 (J. Chadbourn rev. 1970).

2. Collateral Matter Limitation

Courts exclude counterproof that contradicts only on "collateral" points. This limitation is a direct outgrowth of the dual relevancy requirement. Counterproof is collateral if it is relevant in only one way–only in tending to contradict the witness. While such counterproof does (like all counterproof) show that the witness may have lied or erred on some point in his testimony, it has no *other* importance in the case. If, for example, the witness testifies that he was wearing a jacket on the day that he was standing near the scene of an accident, and can be shown that he did not have a jacket and was wearing a sweater instead, the counterproof contradicts his testimony but does not count in any other way (at least in the absence of some special facts that change the picture). The counterproof would normally be excluded as impeachment on a collateral matter. The bar against impeaching on collateral matters prevents a party from contradicting on points that are not independently important in the case–bearing on the merits or on other credibility issues (like bias).

3. Exception to Dual Relevancy Requirement

Occasional modern decisions recognize an exception to the dual relevancy requirement when the counterproof tends to refute a point that the witness simply could not be mistaken about if he is truthful, revealing a "telltale" deception that more broadly undercuts what he said. See M & K § 6.47; McCormick, *Evidence* § 45 (5th ed., J. Strong ed. 1999). In this circumstance, the testimony being attacked is sufficiently important to justify impeachment by contradiction despite the fact that the counterproof serves only to contradict.

☞ EXAMPLE AND ANALYSIS

In the trial of Don for robbing A & J Liquors, Carl testifies for the state that he "saw the defendant running out of A & J at about 1 P.M." and that he was "wearing a ski mask." The prosecutor develops Carl's testimony in three ways. First, the prosecutor asks, "Do you have any prior connection with Alfred and John, who own A & J?" Carl testifies, "No, I don't." Second, the prosecutor asks, "What makes you call it a ski mask?" Carl answers, "It's just like one I had several years ago when I was on Ski Patrol." Third, the prosecutor asks, "Where were you going that day?" Carl replies, "I was on my way to lunch with Jim." The defense counterattacks on all three points. First, on cross it seeks to get Carl to admit he "once loaned money to Alfred and John in connection with an expansion of A & J." Second, on cross it challenges the reference to being "on Ski Patrol," seeking to get Carl to admit that he "actually skied only once many years ago." Third, the defense calls Jim during its case, offering his testimony that he "didn't have a luncheon engagement with Carl" on the week of the robbery and "didn't ever eat lunch with him" during that week. In all three instances, the state objects that the defense is "trying to contradict Carl on collateral points." Should these objections succeed?

On the first point (loaning money to Alfred and John), the objection should be overruled. A prior relationship would indicate possible bias on Carl's part toward the victims, so disproving the claim of "no prior connection" is relevant both in showing that Carl lied or erred and in showing that he may be biased in favor of the victims (dual relevancy). On the second point (whether Carl was on Ski Patrol), the objection should again be overruled. Service on Ski Patrol is not a point on which Carl could be innocently mistaken, at least if the truth is that he has hardly ever skied before, and the point is closely related to a critical matter in his testimony—how he recognized the ski mask. On the third point (lunch with Jim), the objection should be sustained. Luncheon engagements are typically minor matters easily forgotten afterwards. In this case, the point is collateral, and it should certainly not be proved by calling another witness. Proving that Carl was lying or mistaken about where he was going would cast doubt on his testimony on that point (relevant in that one way) but would not affect anything that matters (no substantive issue, no point affecting credibility in any other way).

4. Discretionary Exclusion

Courts also have authority under FRE 403 and 611 to limit or exclude contradictory evidence that is otherwise admissible (because it satisfies the dual relevancy requirement and does not go to collateral points) in order to prevent undue prejudice, confusion, waste of time, or harassment of witnesses.

5. "Setting Up" Impeachment on Cross–Examination

Ordinarily impeachment by contradiction is used to attack a witness's testimony on direct examination. Courts are understandably reluctant to allow lawyers to "set up" a witness by questioning that allows them to "open their own door" to contradictory evidence that would not otherwise be admissible.

☞ EXAMPLE AND ANALYSIS

In a car accident case, plaintiff Paula testifies on direct that she was driving "carefully" at the time. On cross, the defense asks Paula, "Do you consider yourself a good driver?" She answers "yes" (as the defense hoped she would). Now the defense proposes to attack Paula's answer by asking further questions about two accidents in which she was cited for speeding: "Isn't it true that in December of 1995 and again in August of 1996 you were involved in accidents in which you were speeding, according to the investigating officer?" "Objection, Your Honor, they can't ask about prior accidents. They set that up. My client didn't claim on direct that she was a good driver. She just stuck to the facts of this case by saying she was driving carefully at the time. Defendant is just trying to open his own door here." How should the court rule?

The plaintiff's objection should be sustained. In her direct testimony, Paula didn't open herself to contradiction on the general proposition of being a careful driver.

When the defense *broadened the inquiry,* she was put in an impossible position: Either admit that she is not a careful driver or claim to be a careful driver, and of course almost everyone considers herself (or himself) to be in the latter category. Taking the latter course usually leads (as here) to attempts to disprove the broadest aspect of this claim by questions or extrinsic proof of prior careless acts, particularly accidents in which the witness was at fault. Courts are reluctant to reward such manipulation by attacking parties to "set up" the impeachment or "open their own door." Paula's lawyer could have objected to the question as beyond the scope of direct because Paula did not testify to her carefulness generally, but objecting is not a happy solution either, as it would inevitably suggest to the jury the very point that the defendant wants to make, which is that there are other accidents in Paula's past.

---

6. Impeaching with Illegally Seized Evidence

a. Testimony on direct examination

Direct testimony by a witness may be impeached not only with a prior inconsistent statement that was unlawfully obtained, *Harris v. New York,* 401 U.S. 222 (1971), but with physical evidence unlawfully obtained. *Walder v. United States,* 347 U.S. 62 (1954) (defendant made "sweeping claim" on direct that he never possessed or dealt drugs; prosecutor could ask about heroin illegally seized years earlier, to impeach credibility).

b. Testimony on cross-examination

In an early decision, the Supreme Court disapproved the use of illegally seized evidence to impeach a defendant on cross-examination. *Agnello v. United States,* 269 U.S. 20 (1925) (on direct, defendant said he received packages but did not know they were cocaine; prosecutor then asked whether he had "ever seen cocaine," and sought to impeach his denial by proving that cocaine had been seized from him earlier, in an illegal search; here prosecutor "smuggled in" the impeaching opportunity by questions asked on cross, and could not offer the illegally-seized cocaine). But later the Supreme Court approved use of illegally seized evidence to impeach a defendant's answer on cross, where the question was "reasonably suggested" by defendant's direct testimony. *United States v. Havens,* 446 U.S. 620 (1980) (approving use of illegally seized evidence to contradict "false testimony first given on cross-examination" in response to question closely related to defendant's direct testimony).

J. REHABILITATION: AN OVERVIEW

Once a witness is impeached, the calling party may attempt to rehabilitate him. Three general principles govern this process.

1. Rehabilitation Cannot Precede Attack

The first principle is that the calling party cannot repair or rehabilitate a witness until she has been attacked. This principle is usually framed as "the rule against bolstering your own witness." In one of its most important applications, this rule means that the calling party may not offer proof of "good character for truth and veracity" until the other side has attacked the witness in ways that suggest bad character (untruthfulness). See FRE 608(a)(2) (excluding evidence of truthful character until "the character of the witness has been attacked" by opinion or reputation evidence "or otherwise").

2. Can Anticipate Impeachment on Direct

Although bolstering is improper, the calling party may properly anticipate an attack and lay out the impeaching facts during direct examination. This approach is often wise because otherwise it can seem that the calling party is hiding damaging information. Thus the calling party may, on direct, bring out impeaching points, like affinity or rivalry with a party (suggesting bias or favoritism) or prior convictions. Doing so can "take the sting" out of cross-examination on such points, while enabling the calling party both to *seem* and to *be* forthright with the jury ("we're not holding back anything; we want you to know the important facts here"). Sometimes courts and commentators invoke the principle of FRE 607 in this setting (any party may impeach), but the calling party is not so much impeaching the witness as anticipating and disarming an attack by the other side in advance.

3. Rehabilitation Must Respond to Attack

The third general principle of rehabilitation is that the repair must respond to the attack. A witness impeached with evidence of bad eyesight cannot be rehabilitated by evidence of good character for truthfulness. A witness impeached by past criminal convictions cannot be rehabilitated by evidence that he made a prior consistent statement.

K. ALLOWING WITNESS AN OPPORTUNITY TO EXPLAIN

The simplest and least regulated method of rehabilitation is to allow the witness to explain away the impeaching matter, if he can, on redirect examination. If one party asks a witness about nonconviction misconduct, the witness may deny the conduct in question or offer an explanation on redirect examination. Questions about convictions may elicit denials, explanations, or conceivably even proof that there was no conviction. Supporting parties may try to refute or rebut evidence that contradicts the witness and may show that prior inconsistent statements were not made or that they mean something different from what the attacking party suggests.

L. CHARACTER FOR TRUTHFULNESS

Under FRE 608(a), once the character for truthfulness of a witness has been attacked, a supporting character witness may testify in the form of reputation or opinion that the principal witness has a truthful disposition. The character witness can say that the principal witness is truthful—that he is by nature, character or disposition a truthful person—but cannot testify that the testimony that the principal witness gives in the case is itself truthful or correct. Thus FRE 608(a) does *not* pave the way for testimony by a character witness that he has listened to the testimony of the principal witness and that the character witness believes what he said.

1. Attack on Character

This method of rehabilitation can be used only if the character of the witness for truthfulness has been attacked by the opponent. Thus the admissibility of proof of good character for veracity depends on how the witness was impeached.

a. Impeachment with character evidence

Proof of good character for truth and veracity is admissible if the calling party directly assails character, whether by cross-examining the principal witness on prior acts under FRE 608(b) or prior convictions under FRE 609, or by offering negative reputation or opinion testimony under FRE 608(a).

b. Prior inconsistent statements

Impeachment by prior inconsistent statements generally does *not* pave the way for proof of good character for truth and veracity. The reason is that the most obvious explanation for most inconsistencies involves forgetfulness or faults in perception or judgment. In special circumstances, however, inconsistent statements an indeed suggest deliberate falsehood and can thus impugn character. In such cases, rehabilitation by proof of good character is again proper.

c. Bias

Similarly attacks indicating bias do *not* generally imply lack of truthfulness or open the door to proof of the witness's truthful disposition. But attacks that suggest not only a favorable or unfavorable inclination toward one party or another, but determined partisanship that might lead to perjured testimony can impugn character. Again in such cases, rehabilitation by showing good character is proper.

d. Contradiction

Usually impeachment by contradiction does not impugn character. When one witness testifies to one version of the facts and another presents a conflicting version, the conflict in proof does not impugn the character of either witness, and proof of good character is normally excluded.

e. Sharp cross-examination

Usually cross-examination does not impugn character, even if it succeeds in getting the witness to retreat from his direct testimony or to admit to error or uncertainty on important matters. But sharp and suggestive cross-examination sometimes does suggest that the witness is actually lying or purposefully distorting his testimony, which again impugns character. In such cases proof of good character becomes again proper.

2. Foundation for Character Testimony

Before a supporting character witness may attest the good character of the principal witness, the party seeking to rehabilitate must show that the character witness is acquainted with the principal witness (if opinion testimony is to be offered) or knows the prevailing community sentiment about her (if reputation testimony is to be offered).

3. Cross–Examining the Supporting Character Witness

The supporting character witness, who testifies to the good character of the principal witness, may himself be challenged on cross-examination by questions about specific instances of conduct by the principal witness when these bear on her veracity. See FRE 608(b) (on cross, character witness may be asked about specific instances of conduct by the principal witness "in the discretion of the court, if probative of truthfulness or untruthfulness" of the principal witness).

A character witness who has given opinion testimony may be asked whether he "has heard" about particular instances of conduct by the principal witness bearing on his truthfulness (presumably these will be instances of misconduct that suggest untruthfulness). The purpose of such questions is to test the knowledge and judgment of the character witness. If he does not know of the conduct, the indication is that he lacks important information, so his opinion rests on a shaky foundation. If he does know about the conduct, and maintains that the principal witness is truthful anyway, the indication is that his judgment is questionable. Such questions are "win-win" questions for the cross-examiner because *either* a yes or no answer tends to impeach. Of course such questions are proper only if the cross-examiner has a good faith basis for them, and such questions (and the answer given by the character witness) are *not* a proper means to prove character as such—they are proper only as a means of testing the opinion of the character witness.

A character witness who has given reputation testimony may be asked whether he "has heard" about instances of conduct by the principal witness bearing on truthfulness (again these will be instances that suggest untruthfulness). The purpose is to test the knowledge and judgment of the community in which the reputation arose. If the character witness has not heard of the conduct, the indication is that the community simply lacks information about the principal witness that is important, so the favorable reputation doesn't mean much. If the character witness has heard about the conduct, but the reputation of the principal witness is nevertheless good, the indication is that the judgment of the community, as manifested in reputation, is not so good. Again such questions offer the cross-examiner a "win-win" opportunity, because *either* a yes or no answer tends to impeach. Again such questions are proper only if the cross-examiner has a good faith basis for them, and again such questions (and the answer given by the character witness) are *not* a proper means to prove character as such—they are proper only as a means of testing the reputation of the principal witness as it exists in the community.

M. PRIOR CONSISTENT STATEMENTS

Evidence that a witness made prior consistent statements is sometimes admissible to rehabilitate. If his trial testimony is attacked as the product of a poor memory, a prior consistent statement may rehabilitate by showing that his trial testimony is consistent with his memory at an earlier date. If the witness is impeached by a prior inconsistent statement that he denies making, a prior consistent statement may support his denial of making the earlier inconsistent statement. And if the witness is impeached by a prior inconsistent statement and she claims that in fact the prior statement was *not* inconsistent at all, a prior consistent statement may support this claim that the other statement was really consistent with the trial testimony. Finally and most importantly, a prior consistent statement may rehabilitate a witness whose trial testimony has been attacked by an express or implied charge of recent fabrication or improper influence or motive. A consistent statement made prior to time of the alleged motive shows that the trial testimony is not a recent fabrication. The witness said the same thing before that she is saying now. This last use is both the most common one and probably the most important one, and it is the one that is directly addressed by a Federal Rule.

1. Admissible for Truth

FRE 801(d)(1)(B) provides that a statement is "not hearsay" if the declarant testifies at the trial or hearing and is subject to cross examination concerning the statement and the statement is consistent with the declarant's testimony and is offered to rebut an express or implied charge against the declarant of recent fabrication or improper influence or motive. Thus a statement qualifying under this rule may be received not only to rehabilitate but also for the truth of what it asserts. Unlike common law, no limiting instruction is necessary confining the jury's consideration of the statement to rehabilitation.

2. Charge of Recent Fabrication or Improper Motive

FRE 801(d)(1)(B) clearly applies if the impeaching party expressly accuses the witness of making up his testimony, typically on account of some improper motive, such as making a deal with the prosecutor to help convict the defendant in exchange for favorable treatment. The rule also comes into play when the attacks are implied, provided the judge concludes that they indirectly suggest recent fabrication or improper motive.

Example. On cross, the defense lawyer asks the witness "When did you first decide to change your testimony?" This question expressly charges the witness with recent fabrication. Suppose the defense lawyer asks a witness for plaintiff "Did you talk with plaintiff's lawyer about your testimony here today?" Now the question raises an implied charge of improper influence or recent fabrication, or at least it can be construed that way.

3. Consistent Statement Must Be Prior to Motive to Fabricate

The Supreme Court has held that a statement is admissible as substantive evidence (proof of what it asserts) under FRE 801(d)(1)(B) only if offered to disprove a claim of fabrication or motive *and* the statement was made *prior to the time when the alleged motive to fabricate arose*. See *Tome v. United States*, 513 U.S. 150 (1995). The Court acknowledged that "in some cases it may be difficult to ascertain when a particular fabrication, influence or motive arose." But the Court pointed out that "a majority of common law courts were performing this task for well over a century." Moreover, "the thing to be rebutted must be identified, so the date of its origin cannot be that much more difficult to ascertain."

REVIEW QUESTIONS AND ANSWERS

Question: When a party seeks to impeach a witness, can she do so either by asking about the impeaching matter during cross-examination or by offering extrinsic evidence of it?

Answer: It depends on the method of impeachment. Impeachment by prior untruthful acts can proceed only during cross-examination, and extrinsic evidence is prohibited. On the other hand, impeaching a witness by reputation or opinion evidence that he has a bad character for truthfulness by definition requires the use of extrinsic evidence. Impeachment by contradiction often proceeds by means of extrinsic evidence, but sometimes it goes forward during cross-examination when the questioner confronts the witness with facts that refute his testimony. Most other forms of impeachment go forward either during cross or by means of extrinsic evidence. For example, an opposing party can ask during cross-examination about bias, lack of sensory capacity, or prior criminal convictions, but such matters could also be proved by extrinsic evidence. When a witness is impeached with a prior inconsistent statement, the common law required that the witness be asked about it on cross before it could be proved by extrinsic evidence. Under FRE 613(b) a party may introduce extrinsic evidence of the prior inconsistent statement, even when the witness was not asked about it on cross, provided that the witness has a chance later to deny or explain the statement.

Question: What does it mean to say that impeaching evidence is "collateral"?

Answer: The term "collateral" has more than one meaning. Sometimes it is used to express a conclusion that certain evidence is not admissible to impeach. For example, under FRE 608(b) a witness may be asked about prior dishonest acts on cross-examination, but extrinsic evidence of those acts is considered "collateral," meaning inadmissible as a matter of law. Thus the cross-examiner must take the answer of the witness, even if it could be proved false by extrinsic evidence. Other times the term "collateral" is used to explain why impeaching evidence should be excluded or to explain why a question on cross should be disallowed. For example, a party is not allowed to use contradictory evidence or a prior inconsistent statement to impeach a witness on a collateral point (one that has no significance in the case). The reason for the collateral matter bar is to avoid consuming court time with impeaching evidence that has little bearing on a witness's credibility. The collateral matter limitation also applies to cross-examination and prevents the questioner from delving into insignificant points. But courts apply the limitation less strictly to questions asked on cross because they take less time than does the introduction of extrinsic evidence on the same point.

Question: When and how can parties rehabilitate a witness?

Answer: A party can rehabilitate a witness only after the witness was impeached. The method of rehabilitation must be a relevant response to the impeachment. Perhaps the most common method of rehabilitation involves allowing the witness to respond on redirect to any evidence used to attack his credibility. If impeached by evidence of poor eyesight, the witness may explain that she was wearing her eyeglasses at the time. If impeached by evidence of a prior inconsistent statement, she may deny making it or explain that it was inaccurate. No Federal Rule addresses this method of rehabilitation, apart from general principles of relevancy. A second method of rehabilitation is testimony by a character witness that the principal witness has a good reputation for truthfulness or that in the opinion of the character witness the principal witness is truthful. This method of rehabilitation is authorized by FRE 608(a), but is permitted only if the principal witness was impeached by evidence that amounts to an attack on his character. A third method of rehabilitation, which is addressed at least in part by FRE 801(d)(1)(B), involves evidence of a prior consistent statement. Under FRE 801(d)(1)(B), a prior consistent statement can be admitted only to rebut an express or implied charge against the declarant of recent fabrication or improper influence or motive. If admitted under this rule, the prior consistent statement can be used not only to rehabilitate the witness but to prove the truth of what it asserts.

Exam Tips

Here are some tips on issues relating to impeachment of witnesses:

Remember the five impeaching mechanisms. They are showing bias, showing defects in capacity, showing bad character for truthfulness, showing prior inconsistent statements, and contradicting the witness.

Remember that the Voucher Rule is discarded in most jurisdictions, meaning that any party may impeach a witness (including the one who called the witness).

In connection with character for truthfulness, remember there are three ways to raise this attack:

One is questioning on prior acts bearing on veracity, where the attacking party must take the answer of the witness and may not prove the acts by extrinsic evidence.

The second is questioning on prior convictions, which is governed by elaborate restrictions that are mainly designed to protect criminal defendants.

The third involves opinion or reputation testimony.

In connection with prior inconsistent statements, remember that:

Such statements may be used even if they are inadmissible as substantive evidence under the hearsay doctrine.

Such statements may be used even if they are excludable under the *Miranda* doctrine.

The cross-examiner may ask about a statement without first showing it to the witness, but she must have a chance to explain the statement.

When the calling party wants to impeach its own witness in this way, courts sometimes block this strategy as an "abuse" of the process when it seems that the purpose is to get the prior statement before the jury to use as substantive evidence, rather than the testimony of the witness.

In connection with impeachment by contradiction, remember that counterproof contradicting what a witness has said is excludable if it goes to some collateral point that does not bear on the case except for contradicting the witness. Thus evidence offered to contradict a witness must, in addition to contradicting ("you said you were wearing red shoes at the time, but weren't they green"), also tend to prove a point that has some additional impeaching effect ("you said you didn't know the defendant, but in fact the two of you were dating, weren't you") or tend to prove a point that counts substantively in the case ("you said that the light was red, but it was actually green, wasn't it?").

In connection with efforts to rehabilitate a witness, remember that these cannot proceed until the witness has been impeached, and that any attempt to rehabilitate must be responsive to the attack. Hence:

Proof of good character for truth and veracity is admissible only if the other side has impeached in a way that suggests bad character.

The admissibility of prior consistent statements usually turns on whether the witness has been impeached in some way that suggests undue influence or recent fabrication, which is sometimes (but not always) the implication of impeachment by prior inconsistent statements. Remember that prior consistent statements are ordinarily admissible only if made *before* the motive to fabricate arose, or the undue influence was brought to bear. Remember too that sometimes prior consistent statements are also admissible to refute claims of lack of memory, to suggest that a prior inconsistent statement was never made, or to suggest that a prior inconsistent statement was really not inconsistent, after all.

CHAPTER 11

Opinion and Expert Testimony

CHAPTER OVERVIEW

The key points in this chapter are

- FRE 701 adopts a more liberal position toward the admission of lay opinions than the common law.

- Lay opinions are admissible if they are based on personal perception and are helpful to the trier of fact.

- Categorical certainty is not required. A witness may testify to what she "thinks" or "believes," even if she is less than certain, at least if the opinion is rest on personal perception, and is not guesswork or conjecture.

- Expert testimony is admissible when it will assist the trier of fact to understand the evidence or determine a fact in issue.

- Expert testimony may inform the jury of a matter of scientific, technical, or other specialized knowledge.

- Expert testimony may inform the jury of a matter of scientific, technical, or other specialized knowledge.

- A witness may qualify as an expert based on her knowledge, skill, experience, training, or education.

- Determining whether a witness is qualified to testify as an expert is determined by the court. What weight, if any, to give to the testimony is for the jury.

- Under FRE 704(a), an otherwise helpful opinion is not objectionable on the ground that it embraces an ultimate issue to be decided by the trier of fact.

- At common law, an expert's opinion had to be based on facts in evidence.

- Under FRE 703 an expert opinion can be based on facts (1) perceived by the expert, (2) made known to her at trial, or (3) outside knowledge, if it is of a type reasonably relied upon by other experts in the particular field in forming opinions on the subject.

- Under FRE 705, an expert is generally allowed to express an opinion without first testifying to the underlying facts supporting that opinion, although the underlying facts must be disclosed on cross-examination.

- Under FRE 706, the court is allowed to appoint its own expert witnesses.

- In federal courts, the Supreme Court rejected the *Frye* rule for scientific evidence (requiring showing that scientific technique is generally accepted by a consensus of the scientific community) in favor of the *Daubert* rule (requiring showing that technique is reliable).

- In *Kumho Tire*, the Court extended the *Daubert* requirement of reliability to all forms of expert testimony, not just scientific evidence.

- After *Daubert* was decided, FRE 702 was amended to bring its terms more into line with the *Daubert/Kumho* standard by adding the following requirements for expert testimony: "(1) the testimony is based upon sufficient facts or data, (2) the testimony is the product of reliable principles and methods, and (3) the witness has applied the principles and methods reliably to the facts of the case."

A. LAY OPINIONS ADMISSIBLE IF BASED ON PERSONAL PERCEPTION AND HELPFUL TO TRIER OF FACT

1. Common Law Rule

At common law, opinions by lay witnesses (i.e., nonexperts) were generally not allowed. The common law opinion rule developed out of concern that opinion testimony by lay witnesses might mask conjecture and lack of firsthand knowledge. An additional concern was that allowing lay witnesses to express opinions or conclusions would invade the province of the jury. The common law rule often resulted in halting and confused testimony by witnesses confounded by admonitions to "be specific" or "stick to the facts." See *Central R. Co. of New Jersey v. Monahan*, 11 F.2d 212, 214 (2d Cir. 1926) (Hand, J.) (strict enforcement of opinion rule results in "nagging and checking" the witness and the effect is "often to choke him altogether, which is, indeed, usually its purpose").

a. Exceptions to common law rule

The rigid common law rule proved unworkable because much normal discourse includes opinions. Also it is often hard to distinguish facts from opinions because they occupy regions on a continuum, differing only in degree of specificity. Thus most common law courts developed exceptions that permitted at least some lay opinion testimony. For example, witnesses were generally allowed to express opinions about distance, height, identification of a person, intoxication, emotional state of a person, and many other things.

b. Collective facts doctrine

One well-recognized exception to the common law opinion rule was the "collective facts" doctrine, which allowed lay opinion on everyday matters when the witness relies on aggregations of specific details. This exception survived enactment of the Rules and continues to be a feature of the law governing opinion testimony. For example, a witness might describe someone as being or seeming "tired," which might rest on many observable points, such as apparent lack of energy or enthusiasm, drooping posture, lethargic movements, heavy eyelids, circles under the eyes, nodding, yawning, and so forth. Certainly a witness can and should describe the details in addition to the conclusion, which makes her testimony more persuasive than it would be if expressed purely as a conclusion. But courts generally let witnesses who have firsthand knowledge of the specifics distill them into the shorthand conclusion that the person was or seemed "tired."

2. FRE 701 Generally Allows Lay Opinions

FRE 701 modifies the common law approach, departing from the older requirement to give factual testimony and adopting a milder rule of preference for the more specific over the more general. Under FRE 701, lay opinions are generally admissible, unless they are not based on the personal perception of the witness or are not helpful to the trier of fact.

a. Examples of allowable lay opinions

Under FRE 701, lay witnesses may give opinions on a wide range of standard points, even though such opinions sometimes involve characterizing, estimating, or making judgments. FRE 701 incorporates the exceptions recognized at common law and extends them further. Lay witnesses may describe the speed of a car or similar moving object, distances, size, color, shape, texture, resemblance to other objects, quality and apparent source of sound, light, or odor. They may give physical descriptions of a person, whether tall or short, old or young, dark or fair, apparently healthy or sick, strong or weak, tired or alert, and so forth. Lay witnesses may describe the emotional or psychological state of another, testifying that she seemed angry. frightened, upset, or sad. The "collective facts" doctrine described above continues to inform the application of FRE 701.

b. Based on personal perception

FRE 701(a) requires that lay opinions be "rationally based on the witness's perception." The purpose of this requirement is to exclude opinions that are mere speculation or conjecture. This language simply restates the personal knowledge requirement found in FRE 602, and the purpose is to exclude opinions that amount to mere speculation or conjecture.

i.   Categorical certainty not required

The fact that a witness is uncertain, and testifies to what he "thinks" or "believes," does not disqualify her testimony, provided that her testimony rests on firsthand knowledge.

ii. Jury decides personal knowledge

The jury makes the ultimate decision whether the witness perceived the acts, events, or conditions to which her opinion relates. In other words, the jury ultimately decides whether the witness had personal knowledge or not. The judge plays a screening role on this point, excluding opinion testimony where the facts are such that a reasonable jury could not find that the witness had the requisite firsthand knowledge. In other words, the question of personal knowledge is classified as a matter of "conditional relevancy" under FRE 104(b) rather than a matter of "admissibility" under FRE 104(a).

c. Helpful to trier of fact

FRE 701(b) requires that lay opinions be "helpful to a clear understanding of the witness' testimony or to determine a fact in issue." The purpose is to avoid telling the jury something it already knows, which would waste time or be cumulative of other evidence. This restriction also prevents a witness from simply taking sides and telling the jury how to decide the case. The witness normally must give at least a minimal explanation for her view rather than merely stating which party was right or wrong or what conduct was justified or not justified. But if the witness has perceived and related the necessary particulars, she should usually be allowed to add her overall impression. Allowing the witness's ultimate conclusion may help bring the particulars into focus and add dimension, thereby satisfying the "helpfulness" requirement of FRE 702.

☞ EXAMPLE AND ANALYSIS

Abe is working at his sidewalk newsstand in New York City when he hears a loud crash behind him. He turns and sees that a taxicab has crashed into the rear of the car ahead of it, which had stopped for a red light. The driver of the damaged car sues the taxicab company for property damage and calls Abe as a witness. After establishing that Abe was at the scene, the plaintiff's lawyer asks him to describe how fast the taxi was going prior to the collision. Abe responds, "I'm sure that it was speeding."

This opinion is inadmissible. Although normally lay witnesses are allowed to estimate the speed of moving vehicles in miles per hour, here Abe did not see the taxi before the collision. For that reason, his opinion about speed does not rest on personal perception and is not helpful to the trier of fact. On these facts, there is no room for a reasonable jury to conclude that Abe had personal knowledge, which normally is a matter for the jury to decide under FRE 104(b), and the trial judge should exclude Abe's testimony.

B. QUALIFIED EXPERT MAY TESTIFY TO ASSIST TRIER OF FACT

Under FRE 702, when expert testimony will "help the trier of fact to understand the evidence or to determine a fact in issue," a qualified expert "may testify in the form of an opinion or otherwise."

1. Qualified Expert

There is no across-the-board or detailed list of credentials that a witness must have to qualify as an expert. Under FRE 702, one may qualify on the basis of her "knowledge, skill, experience, training, or education."

a. Foundation

Before a witness may testify as an expert, the calling party must lay a foundation showing that she qualifies. Normally this task involves showing academic training, degrees, honors received, length and nature of work experience, areas of specialization, government certifications, organizational memberships, offices held, publications, professional awards, and so forth.

b. Determination for court

Deciding whether a witness is or is not qualified to testify as an expert is a matter for the judge under FRE 104(a) (it affects "admissibility" or "competency"). What weight to give such testimony, if the trial judge decides to allow the witness to testify as an expert, is a matter for the jury.

c. Expertise must relate to matter at issue

It is not enough that the witness qualifies as an expert in a particular field. The expertise must relate to the matter at issue in the case. Thus a urologist, for example, would not qualify as an expert to venture an opinion on the question whether a brain surgeon committed malpractice, no matter how impressive the credentials of the urologist in his area of expertise.

d. Property owners

Property and business owners ordinarily have sufficient knowledge, skill, and experience to testify as experts about the value of their property or business. Thus a homeowner can testify to the approximate value of his house, and the owner of a motel can testify to the approximate value of the motel. See ACN to FRE 702 (rule is "broadly phrased" and includes "not only experts in the strictest sense of the word" but also "skilled" witnesses such as "land-owners testifying to land values").

2. Assist Trier of Fact

Under FRE 702, expert testimony is admissible only if it will "assist the trier of fact to understand the evidence or to determine a fact in issue."

a. Common law rule

The common law took a more restrictive view. The narrowest view was that expert testimony was admissible only when necessary to enable the jury to decide the case. Under a slightly broader view, expert testimony was allowed on matters that were beyond the ken of the jury, meaning matters that the jury could not understand on its own.

b. More liberal federal standard

FRE 702 adopts a more expansive view. It allows expert testimony that helps the trier of fact make a more intelligent and informed decision and excludes testimony that is merely superfluous and a waste of time. Trial courts have broad discretion to determine when expert testimony would assist the trier of fact.

☞ EXAMPLE AND ANALYSIS

Carla suffers serious injuries when the car she was driving is sideswiped by a Tri–Met Bus and run off the road into a telephone pole. Carla sues, claiming that the accident happened when the bus changed lanes without signaling. Tri–Met claims that Carla cut in front of the bus, which was in the lane closest to the curb. Carla calls Browning, a police officer who qualifies as an expert in accident reconstruction in virtue of 25–years experience in investigating accident scenes. He conducted an investigation in this case that included taking measurements and evaluating physical traces at the scene (skidmarks, damage to vehicles, scratches on the road surface, physical debris), and is prepared to testify that the bus had crossed lanes at the time of impact and struck Carla's vehicle.

At common law, such testimony might well have been excluded. Browning's opinion is probably not necessary, and the subject is not beyond the ken of the jury, which can appraise the facts and determine the point of impact. Under FRE 702 and its state counterparts, however, Browning can probably testify. The reason is that testimony from qualified experts on accident reconstruction can be helpful to the trier of fact, and probably would be helpful here. See *Baker v. Elcona Homes Corp.*, 588 F.2d 551 (6th Cir. 1978) (admitting report containing conclusions of state police officer who qualified as expert in accident reconstruction, based on physical measurements taken at the scene, and on "vector analysis" and on eyewitness accounts). Such an opinion must rest on substantial investigative data, such as measurements and appraisals performed by Browning, and probably cannot rest solely on interviews with eyewitnesses, since Browning is an expert in accident analysis, although Browning can probably rely as well on eyewitness accounts. See ACN to FRE 703 (opinion of "accidentologist" as to point of impact inadmissible if based merely on "statements of bystanders").

c. Expert testimony on law

Expert testimony on the controlling law is generally inadmissible. See *Marx & Co., Inc. v. Diners' Club, Inc.*, 550 F.2d 505 (2d Cir. 1977) (error to allow expert to give opinion as to legal obligations of parties under a contract); *Specht v. Jensen*, 853 F.2d 805 (10th Cir. 1988) (error to allow attorney to testify as expert for plaintiff that defendant's action constituted a "search"). Informing the jury of the law is the task of the judge, not witnesses. Also determining the applicable law may require legal interpretation of statutes or case law or other bodies of authority, which is exclusively a judicial function. But courts sometimes allow qualified experts to testify to mixed questions of fact and law, such as whether a condition was "hazardous," when such an opinion has at least some factual content and would assist the trier of fact.

d. Form of testimony

Although the purpose of calling an expert is usually to elicit opinion testimony, FRE 702 applies to expert testimony in other forms. Sometimes an expert provides only factual or conceptual accounts that help the jury appraise the evidence, as happens when a doctor describes a course of treatment or explains the operation of technical equipment. Such testimony too is subject to the helpfulness standard, must be adequately based, and must come from a qualified expert.

e. Degree of certainty required for opinions

When a doctor is asked for her opinion on causation or the permanence of injuries, usually she is first asked if she is able to provide such an opinion "to a reasonable probability" or "reasonable medical certainty." The rule that the expert must have sufficient certainty is derived more from substantive law of torts (or damages) than from FRE 702. If she can say only that it is "possible" that defendant's conduct caused plaintiff's injuries, such an opinion constitutes insufficient evidence to support a jury finding of causation by a preponderance, and this question should be taken from the jury by appropriate motion for partial judgment as a matter of law.

C. ULTIMATE ISSUE RULE REJECTED

At common law, a witness could not testify about an "ultimate issue" in the case because doing so was thought to "invade the province of the jury." FRE 704(a) repudiates this principle, and provides that "an opinion is not objectionable just because it embraces an ultimate issue." Thus FRE 704(a) abandons the older concern that lay factfinders would give up their responsibility to look critically at testimony and take the word of the witness. The modern notion is that juries have authority to reject even decisive and informed testimony and are told as much before retiring to deliberate. But the ACN to FRE 704 states that opinions telling the jury "what result to reach" remain excludable and that the rule does not "lower the bar" to all opinion testimony.

1. Exclusion Under FRE 701 or 702

Even though it is no longer proper to object that an opinion goes to an ultimate issue, hence invades the province of the jury, it is still proper to object to an overbroad opinion that does not assist the jury. FRE 701 supports such an objection against lay opinions, and FRE 702 supports the same objection against expert opinions. For example, an opinion that "The accident was the defendant's fault" offers little or no assistance to a jury that is trying to determine this point. Instead such testimony tells the jury what result to reach, while failing to provide facts or specific insights that could help jurors reach sound conclusions on this matter.

2. Inadequately Explored Legal Criteria

According to the ACN to FRE 704, testimony expressing a conclusion on an ultimate issue is excludable if it is based on inadequately explored legal criteria. The concern is that the witness may base her testimony on a mistaken standard, so a more elaborate statement of criteria is required. Thus a witness may not testify that the decedent "had the capacity to make a will," which does not make clear whether the expert is applying the right standard for testamentary capacity. He may, however, testify that the testator knew "the nature and extent of his property and the natural objects of his bounty," since this testimony is more specific, and speaks to common understandings (the natural objects of one's bounty include spouses and children and other relatives or close friends).

3. Mental Condition Exception

FRE 704(b) was added after John Hinckley was acquitted on grounds of insanity for the attempted assassination of President Reagan. Enacted as part of the Insanity Defense Reform Act of 1984, the new language provides: "No expert witness testifying with respect to the mental state or condition of a defendant in a criminal case may state an opinion or inference as to whether the defendant did or did not have the mental state or condition constituting an element of the crime charged or a defense thereto. Such ultimate issues are matters for the trier of fact alone."

D. PERMISSIBLE BASES FOR EXPERT OPINION TESTIMONY

FRE 703 allows expert opinions to rest on (1) facts or data perceived by the expert, or (2) facts or data made known to him at the trial or hearing, or (3) outside information of the sort that experts in the field would reasonably consider and rely upon. Regardless what the expert relies upon, it must be adequate to support the opinion given. Particularly when the expert relies on knowledge gleaned outside the courtroom, it must encompass data on which other experts in the field would reasonably rely. By way of contrast, the common law tradition generally required that experts rely on personal knowledge or on facts already proved or supported by evidence in the case (the "facts in evidence" rule).

1. Facts Perceived by Expert

Experts may rely on personal knowledge (firsthand observation), which is the standard that FRE 602 sets for lay testimony. A treating or examining doctor has such knowledge, as does a fire marshal who inspects a burned building, or an accident reconstruction expert who examines the accident scene and the wrecked cars.

2. Facts Learned at Trial

An expert opinion may be based on facts or data learned at trial, as by hearing the testimony of other witnesses or listening to a hypothetical question that sums up the relevant facts that are supported by evidence already introduced.

a. Hearing testimony of other witnesses

Often an expert learns the facts that can be the basis for an opinion by watching the proceedings and listening to other witnesses testify. Then the expert is asked a question such as the following: "Doctor, assuming the truth of the earlier testimony that you heard, do you have an opinion as to whether the plaintiff's headaches were caused by the automobile accident?" The jury understands that the opinion is based on the assumption that the facts related by the previous witnesses are accurate. Thus the expert's opinion depends on the persuasive force of earlier testimony, and any weaknesses in that testimony can be explored on cross-examination of the expert.

b. Hypothetical questions

A hypothetical question asks the expert to assume certain facts (each must be supported by evidence already in the case) and provide an opinion based on those facts. Hypothetical questions are proper if the elements of the question are reasonably supported by the evidence, and if the facts suffice to support the opinion that the questioner seeks. Unsupported factual hypotheses must be stricken as an element of the question, and the question itself should be disallowed if its constituent elements taken as a whole are not sufficient to support the opinion sought.

i. Unfairly slanted

A hypothetical question may be disallowed if it unfairly slants the evidence, includes facts not in evidence, omits crucial facts, or is otherwise misleading. Under modern codes, however, hypothetical questions are generally allowed even if they do not exhaustively recite all the evidence previously introduced, provided that they cover the critical elements.

ii. Based on opinions of others

Pre–Rules tradition sometimes disapproved hypothetical questions inviting an expert to base his opinion on the opinion of others, but this tradition does not comport with FRE 703. Now an expert may rely on the opinion of others, so long as the basis is sufficient and reliance is reasonable, meaning that other experts in the field would similarly rely on such opinions.

3. Outside Information

Apart from personal perception and facts learned at trial, FRE 703 allows an expert to base an opinion on outside information obtained from a variety of sources if the information is of a type reasonably relied on by experts in the particular field in forming opinions or inferences upon the subject. The outside information may come from treatises or other authorities, reports by third parties, test results, interviewing bystanders, and independent investigation.

a. Who decides "reasonable reliance"

Courts split on the question whether the expert or the court determines the adequacy of the underlying basis for expert testimony, which in turn raises the question whether the facts underlying the expert's opinion are of a type "reasonably relied upon" by experts in the field. Compare *In re Japanese Elec. Prods. Antitrust Litigation*, 723 F.2d 238, 276–277 (3d Cir. 1983) (reasonable reliance is for expert to decide) with *Soden v. Freightliner Corp.*, 714 F.2d 498, 505 (5th Cir. 1983) (reasonable reliance is for court to decide). The better view, increasingly accepted, is that the court decides this point as a matter of admissibility of evidence under FRE 104(a), and the court need not defer entirely to the expert. Letting the expert determine this matter himself amounts a ceding responsibility for applying FRE 703's reasonable reliance standard to the witness, and courts cannot properly take this course.

b. Evidence can be inadmissible

The information relied upon by the expert need not be already admitted in evidence. More importantly, the outside information need not even be *admissible* in evidence, although that information must satisfy the requirements of FRE 703, which means that it must be sufficient and it must be information of the sort that other experts would rely on. In its most important application, this principle means that an expert may rely on statements made by others outside of court, even if those statements would not fit any exception to the hearsay doctrine and would not be admissible as substantive evidence.

c. Disclosure to jury on direct examination

FRE 703 does *not*, however, authorize experts to act as "mere conduits" for statements made by others out of court. While experts may *rely* on out-of-court statements in forming their opinions, the statements themselves remain hearsay and are not admissible as proof of what they assert unless they fit an exception to the hearsay doctrine. See FRE 703 (providing that facts or data that are otherwise inadmissible "shall not be disclosed to the jury by the proponent" unless the court decides that "probative value in assisting the jury to evaluate the expert's opinion substantially outweighs their prejudicial effect").

d. Right of confrontation

In criminal cases, when an expert bases an important opinion on inadmissible hearsay, the defendant may claim his confrontation rights are violated. Generally such challenges fail, but courts acknowledge the importance of respecting confrontation rights when evidence is offered under FRE 703. Using experts merely as a conduit to report the substance of otherwise inadmissible out-of-court statements by third persons would likely violate defense confrontation rights.

☛ EXAMPLE AND ANALYSIS

After the destruction by fire of the gas station he had owned and tried to sell, Wallace is charged with arson. The state's theory is that he wanted to collect insurance proceeds, but he claims that the fire started accidentally when oily rags ignited after coming in contact with frayed electric wires. The state calls Fire Marshal Harvey Burke, who investigated the blaze. After qualifying as an exert, Burke describes his investigation, which included taking samples of debris and running chemical analysis, tracing the path of the blaze, interviewing eyewitnesses, and examining the wires. The prosecutor then asks: "Based on your investigation, do you have an opinion as to the cause of the fire?" Burke replies, "I do." "And what is that opinion?" "I think the fire was set by some human agency. In other words, it was arson."

Continuing, the prosecutor asks Burke to explain the reasons for his conclusion. "Well," answers Burke, "there was no current in the wires at the time of the blaze, so the wires could not have caused it, and I interviewed two eyewitnesses, one named Gerald Motley and the other named Helen Stoop, and they said. . . ." "Quickly counsel for Wallace rises: Objection, your honor, hearsay. The jury wants to hear what the Marshal thinks, not what someone else said. If the Marshal describes what Motley and Stoop told him, that will violate the hearsay rule and the Confrontation Clause because we can't cross-examine." The prosecutor gets into the act: "Well, your honor, we need to show Marshal Burke didn't just leap to conclusions and has a factual basis for believing arson caused the blaze."

The court excuses the jury, and in aid of his offer of proof the prosecutor develops the following points through Burke: "Motley and Stoop told me they saw a man in back of the station just before the flames erupted. He had a big can and seemed to be pouring some liquid on the woodshed at the rear of the service station. They said he was about 50, balding, just over six feet tall, and heavyset, maybe 200 pounds. He drove away, after the fire started, in an old Toyota pickup." (This description matches Wallace, who owns a Toyota pickup.) Should the testimony be admitted or excluded?

Probably it should be excluded. Even if it is reasonable for arson investigators to rely on eyewitness statements, FRE 703 does not authorize their use as proof of what they assert. If the court concludes that the probative value of the statements in assisting the jury to evaluate the expert's opinion substantially outweighs their prejudicial effect, the court might rule that Burke should be allowed to report that Motley and Stoop said they saw someone pour liquid onto the woodshed. But adding their physical description seems unnecessary in appraising the care Burke brought to his task, and the description brings great risk of prejudice under FRE 403 because the jury might misuse the description by taking it as proof that Wallace was the perpetrator. Wallace also has a good claim that admitting these statements would violate his confrontation rights, particularly if Motley and Stoop never testify and cannot be cross-examined.

E. AN EXPERT GENERALLY MAY GIVE AN OPINION WITHOUT FIRST DISCLOSING UNDERLYING FACTS

Under FRE 705, an expert may give an opinion or inference and give the reasons without first testifying to the underlying facts or data, unless the court requires otherwise. For example, an expert who treated or examined the plaintiff may go right to the point and testify that "In my opinion the plaintiff is not likely to regain use of his legs and will need a wheelchair for the rest of his life."

1. Common Law Comparison

FRE 705 changes common law, which required preliminary disclosure of underlying facts and data before an expert could give an opinion. The most typical method for adducing expert testimony at common law was the hypothetical question.

2. Rationale for FRE 705

The purpose of the change is to discourage the use of hypothetical questions by eliminating the need for them. Hypothetical questions bring major drawbacks: By encouraging lawyers to engage in excessive framing and narrowing of questions, and actually forcing them to do so, they push experts toward partisan positions. They provide an opportunity for lawyers to make speeches in the middle of the case, before the time has come for summation. Worst of all, hypothetical questions are time-consuming and complicated, and they focus attention on the lawyers rather than the expert. See ACN to FRE 705.

3. Court May Order Advance Disclosure

FRE 705 expressly preserves the authority of courts to order advance disclosure of underlying facts by coupling the general elimination of the requirement with the phrase "unless the court requires otherwise." Courts often require advance disclosure when experts are to offer scientific testimony based on complicated theories or processes.

4. Underlying Facts Must Be Disclosed on Cross–Examination

Even though the underlying facts need not be disclosed before the expert gives an opinion on direct examination, FRE 705 provides that the expert may be required to make disclosure on cross-examination. The adversary is entitled to bring out the basis for the expert's opinion so its adequacy can be challenged. In civil cases, the adversary normally has benefited from discovery conducted under FRCP 26(a)(2), which assures that the adversary learns the identity of opposing experts, and obtains a description of their qualifications and publication record, as well as a written report setting forth "all opinions to be expressed" along with the "basis and reasons" and "data or other information" used in forming such opinions. Under FRCP 26(b)(4), a party can even depose the adversary's experts in advance of trial. Not all states have civil discovery procedures as expansive as those in federal court, which may make courts in such states more inclined to require advance disclosure of the underlying data at trial.

F. TRIAL JUDGE MAY APPOINT EXPERT WITNESSES

FRE 706 authorizes the trial judge, acting on her own or on motion by a party, to appoint expert witnesses. The judge may ask the parties to submit nominations and select a person on whom they agree. But the judge is not limited in this way and may appoint an expert of her own selection. An expert cannot be drafted to serve, however, and may be appointed only if he consents.

1. Procedure

An expert appointed under FRE 706 is to advise the parties of his findings, if any. Any party may take the expert's deposition, and any party may call the expert as a witness. The expert is subject to cross-examination by all parties, including the party calling him.

2. Compensation

Experts appointed under FRE 706 are entitled to reasonable compensation, to be determined by the court. In criminal cases and condemnation actions, fees are paid from government funds set aside for that purpose. In other civil cases, the parties pay the compensation in whatever proportion the court determines.

3. Disclosure

Whether the jury should learn that the expert was appointed by the court is a matter for the court to decide in the exercise of sound discretion.

G. SCIENTIFIC EVIDENCE IS ADMISSIBLE WITH PROPER FOUNDATION

There is no rule focused exclusively on the admissibility of scientific evidence. Instead scientific evidence is governed by the rules regulating expert testimony generally.

1. Common Law Rule

In common law tradition, most courts adopted the standard of *Frye v. United States*, 293 F. 1013 (D.C. Cir. 1923), which held that scientific evidence can be admitted only when the scientific principle or technique is generally accepted in the relevant scientific community. The *Frye* test was long criticized as too conservative and too vague. It requires courts to reject techniques that are too new to achieve general acceptance, regardless of reliability. And even though general acceptance does not mean "universal acceptance," the standard is too vague to be applied easily or consistently: One court might cite a few dissenting opinions as proof that a technique is not generally accepted, while another might conclude that general acceptance means that most qualified scientists concur in approving the method or technique, even if some do not.

2. *Daubert* Standard

In *Daubert v. Merrell Dow Pharmaceuticals*, 509 U.S. 579 (1993), the Supreme Court rejected *Frye* for the federal system and adopted a new three-prong approach resting on FRE 702 and 401–403. First, the evidence must present valid science, meaning it must be what the Court called "reliable" (even if not necessarily correct in every instance or application). Second, the science must be pertinent, meaning it must "fit" in the sense of relating directly to the issues and facts so that it can be truly helpful to the trier of fact. Third, the evidence may be excluded under FRE 403 even if it satisfies the first two standards if it seems too likely to confuse or mislead the jury.

a. Preliminary determination by court

The prerequisites of reliability (or scientific validity) and fit are determined by the court before the evidence is admitted, and of course the question whether to exclude under FRE 403 is also for the court to decide. The question of reliability is the most critical question of all, and it is for the court to decide under FRE 104(a) rather than for the jury to decide under FRE 104(b). Thus a trial judge may (and ordinarily should) hold a hearing before trial, and at this time the proponent must demonstrate the reliability (and fit) of the evidence. Since the Rules do not themselves apply in this setting, the hearing can proceed on the basis of affidavits, although it is wise for the parties to call witnesses if the contest is serious or elaborate.

b. Factors for determining reliability

When trial judges perform their "gatekeeping" role of determining the reliability of scientific evidence, the Court in *Daubert* suggested that they consider the following five factors (although none is decisive and the list is not exhaustive).

i. **Testing (or falsifiability)**

One important criterion of scientific evidence is whether the theory or technique in question "can be (and has been) tested." The Court in *Daubert* said that the scientific method rests on "generating" and "testing" hypotheses to "see if they can be falsified," and that this aspect of the scientific method is what distinguishes it from other human undertakings. (Apparently the majority in *Daubert* meant essentially "testable" when it said "falsified," and the dissenters chided the majority for presenting an elaborate description that is likely to confuse trial judges and practicing lawyers.)

ii. **Peer review**

Another factor that counts in the calculus is the presence or absence of peer review and publication. Exposure of this sort gives others in the pertinent field a chance to examine and criticize or endorse the underlying methodology and reasoning, which can enhance or diminish confidence in the proffered evidence.

iii. **Error rate**

In the case of a particular scientific technique, the court ordinarily should consider the known or potential rate of error.

iv. **Operational standards**

Another factor that counts is the presence or absence of standards, whether set by government agencies or private associations, governing the practices or techniques employed to produce the evidence being offered.

v. **General acceptance**

Even though general acceptance in the scientific community is no longer the sine qua non for admissibility, it still can have an important bearing. The Court noted that a scientific technique may be viewed with skepticism if it "has been able to attract only minimal support within the community."

3. States Divided Between *Frye* and *Daubert* Standards

After *Daubert* was decided, some states abandoned *Frye* and adopted the *Daubert* test, but other states stuck with their own versions of the *Frye* standard. As of 2008, approximately 27 generally follow the *Daubert* approach, while approximately 22 states retain state standards that usually rest upon or reformulate the *Frye* approach. Some very large states are in the latter category, including California, New York, and Pennsylvania. A few major states, including Texas and Michigan, have adopted standards that are close to the *Daubert* standard. See generally 5 Mueller & Kirkpatrick, Federal Evidence § 7:10 (3d ed. 2007).

4. *Daubert* Reliability Standard Extended to All Types of Expert Testimony

Originally *Daubert* seemed to apply only to scientific evidence, as the opinion rested heavily on the term "scientific" that appears in FRE 702. A few years after deciding *Daubert*, however, the Supreme Court extended the *Daubert* standard to all expert testimony and stressed that the trial judge has broad discretion in applying *Daubert*. See *Kumho Tire Co., Ltd. v. Carmichael*, 526 U.S. 137 (1999) (all expert testimony must have a reliable basis, including testimony by experts based on experience; the *Daubert* criteria may be helpful in evaluating expert testimony for reliability, but are not exclusive and some are less likely to apply to nonscientific forms of expert testimony; the trial judge has discretion both in applying the *Daubert* criteria and in deciding which of these criteria to apply in any given case). *Kumho Tire* involved testimony by an expert in analyzing tire failure, who had developed a method that employed specific criteria in determining, on the basis of a physical examination of the tire in question, whether the failure was caused by a manufacturing defect or a failure to keep the tire properly inflated. Such testimony was recognizably "technical" in nature (as that term is used in FRE 702) but might not be viewed as "scientific" in nature (because it employed common-sense criteria that did not reflect complex theories or great precision or require extended training in standard scientific disciplines).

5. FRE 702 Amended In Response to *Daubert*

After the decision in *Kumho Tire*, FRE 702 was amended in response to *Daubert*, with the clear purpose of bringing the text of the Rule more closely into alignment with the substance of the approach adopted in *Daubert*, as extended and modified in *Kumho Tire*. Amended FRE 702 states that expert testimony must rest on "sufficient facts or data" and must reflect "reliable principles and methods," and that these principles and methods must be applied "reliably to the facts of the case."

6. Types of Scientific Evidence Commonly Admitted

With a proper foundation, the following types of scientific evidence are commonly admitted: Chemical analysis for alcohol of a person's breath, blood, urine, or saliva; ballistics tests; radar measurements of speed; fingerprint evidence; blood tests to determine paternity; neutron activation analysis; DNA evidence; blood spatter analysis; microscopic hair analysis.

7. More Controversial Forms of Scientific Evidence

The authorities are more divided about the admissibility of the following types of scientific evidence: Voiceprint evidence (spectography); horizontal gaze nystagmus (HGN) tests; psychological syndrome evidence.

REVIEW QUESTIONS AND ANSWERS

Question: On what issues is expert opinion testimony admissible?

Answer: Expert opinion testimony is admissible on a wide range of issues in both criminal and civil cases. Unlike the strict common law rule, which allowed experts to testify only when "necessary" to enable the jury to understand a matter, FRE 702 allows expert opinion whenever it can "assist" the jury to understand other evidence or determine a fact in issue. The expert may testify on matters of "scientific, technical or other specialized knowledge." A witness who lacks specialized knowledge does not qualify as an expert. In contrast to the common law, which prohibited witnesses from testifying about the ultimate issues in the case, FRE 704 allows such testimony and repudiates the objection that opinion testimony invades the province of the jury.

Question: What are the permitted bases for expert opinion testimony?

Answer: Experts can give opinions based on personal knowledge. In contrast to lay witnesses, however, experts do not *have to have* personal knowledge, and can instead rely on opinions or statements by others made outside of court, so long as reliance is reasonable and so long as other experts in the field would rely on such material. The expert can also testify on the basis of facts made known to her at or before the hearing. Sometimes experts are made aware of the relevant facts about which their opinion is sought by sitting in the courtroom and listening to the testimony of other witnesses. Sometimes they are made aware of the relevant facts by being asked a hypothetical question that recites those facts as a prelude to asking the expert for an opinion based on them.

Question: What standards govern the admissibility of scientific evidence?

Answer: In federal courts, the *Daubert* decision controls, which relies on relevancy principles and the rules governing the admissibility of expert testimony to establish standards regulating scientific evidence. Under *Daubert*, the scientific evidence must be shown to be reliable (otherwise it would not really be "scientific knowledge" within the meaning of FRE 702) and must be pertinent to the facts at issue. In deciding whether scientific evidence is reliable, *Daubert* said that trial judges can consider the following factors: whether the theory or technique can be or has been tested; the presence or absence of peer review and publication, error rates, the existence of operational standards governing the technique; and the acceptance of the technique within the scientific community. Some states adopting the Federal Rules have also adopted the *Daubert* standards. Other states continue to follow the old common law standard established in the *Frye* case, which holds that scientific evidence is admissible only when accepted by a consensus of the relevant scientific community.

Question: Do the standards that apply to scientific expertise also apply to other kinds of expertise?

Answer: In federal courts, the *Daubert* decision governs scientific evidence, and *Kumho Tire* both broadened the application of *Daubert* and made it more flexible. Under *Kumho Tire*, the *Daubert* standard applies to all expert testimony, including testimony by an expert in tire failure, but *Kumho Tire* recognized that the *Daubert* criteria would not all apply equally to all expertise, and the Court in *Kumho Tire* stressed that trial judges have discretion both in selecting among the *Daubert* criteria and in deciding whether those criteria are satisfied in any given case.

Exam Tips

Here are some tips on issues relating to opinion and expert testimony:

Under the modern approach, lay opinion testimony is admissible if based on personal perception and helpful to the trier of fact.

Lay opinion is admissible on a variety of standard points, like speed of a car and the demeanor of another person (angry, sad, etc.), and lay opinion can describe points like "fatigue" under the "collective facts" doctrine (allowing a conclusion rather than a catalogue of details).

Expert opinion is admissible on technical subjects, and even familiar subjects, if the expert is qualified by training or experience, if she has an adequate basis for her testimony, and if it will be helpful to the trier of fact.

Expert testimony may rest on facts or data perceived by the expert, made known to her during trial, and on outside information (statements by others, and similar material), so long as the basis is adequate to support the opinion being offered.

Scientific testimony by experts must satisfy a validity standard. Traditionally that standard required general acceptance in the relevant scientific community (the *Frye* standard).

In federal courts and in many states, the traditional *Frye* standard was displaced by the *Daubert* standard, and in federal courts *all expert testimony* must satisfy this standard.

The Supreme Court's new *Daubert* standard has three main parts, including validity (which in turn includes such factors as whether the proof can and has been tested, whether it has been peer-reviewed, and whether it is generally accepted), "fit" with the case (does it bear directly on the issues?), and balancing probative worth against dangers of jury confusion and misuse under FRE 403.

FRE 702 was amended after *Daubert* and *Kumho Tire* to insure that expert testimony rest on sufficient basis, reflect reliable principles and methods, and to insure that the principles and methods are properly applied.

CHAPTER 12

Authentication

Chapter Overview

The key points in this chapter are

- Authenticating a proffered item of evidence means showing that it is what the proponent claims it to be.

- The requirement to authenticate (or "lay the foundation") reflects the view that courts cannot ordinarily "take things at face value," and applies across the board to physical evidence and to everything but live testimony.

- Juries decide authentication issues, and the judge plays only a screening role (requiring the proponent to offer enough evidence to support a finding that an object is what the proponent claims it to be).

- Pretrial procedures solve most authentication issues in civil cases, but most authentication issues in criminal cases must be resolved at trial.

- Appearance, contents, and internal characteristics count and may be considered with other proof in determining authenticity, even though objects are not taken at face value.

- Tangible objects are usually authenticated by (a) testimony by a **witness with knowledge** who relies on **distinctive characteristics** of the object or (b) **chain of custody** evidence.

- Writings are the primary example of objects requiring authentication in which issues of authentication are most often resolved prior to trial. When authentication issues survive in this setting, the most common ways to authenticate a writing are as follows:

  - Lay opinion testimony based on knowledge of handwriting;

  - Expert opinion based on comparison with exemplar;

  - Jury opinion based on comparison with exemplar;

  - Proof of distinctive characteristics, such as internal contents indicating that the writer was making a **reply to an inquiry** that the recipient had earlier directed to the apparent maker of the writing (the "reply letter" doctrine) or the appearance of code words or knowledge that the apparent maker of the writing would have.

- Public records may be authenticated many different ways:

  - By means of certified copy ("self-authentication" of this kind is the most common method);

  - By showing public filing or recording;

  - By testimony from a knowledgeable witness;

  - By other methods generally available for writings, such as lay opinion testimony based on handwriting, which can also be used for public records.

- Ancient documents (20 years or more) are viewed as authentic by virtue of age alone. Age may be shown by testimony or by satisfying these three criteria:

  - The document looks old enough—physical appearance and internal characteristics indicating age (but written or internal dates are not enough);

  - The document was found in appropriate place–finding the document in a place where such a thing would likely be;

- There are no suspicious circumstances—this kind of document would look this way if it were 20 years old or more, and would be found in such a place and would have such contents.

- Audio recordings require caution because they may be edited and altered, and proving part of a conversation raises issues of completeness. Authentication usually involves two steps:

  - Process—the proponent should explain the process, show the people who made the recording were competent, and that there are no material alterations or deletions;

  - Identify the participants—the proponent must show who participated in the conversation and identify the voices;

  - Alternative methods include simply getting a participant or observer to testify that the recording faithfully captures the conversation.

- Photographs may be authenticated by testimony of a knowledgeable witness that photograph accurately depicts the thing or scene (photographer need not testify).

  - Merely illustrative—often photographs are treated as merely illustrating testimony by knowledgeable witnesses, but the trend is to recognize photographs as independently relevant;

  - "Silent witness" doctrine—surveillance photographs taken by automatic cameras are independent evidence and may be authenticated by testimony explaining the process and showing the camera took accurate pictures.

- X-rays and other kinds of medical images are authenticated by proof describing the process and its use in the case (qualifications of operator; nature and acceptability of the machine; procedures followed; when x-ray or image was taken and what it shows).

- Computer output is authenticated by describing the process and showing it reaches an accurate result.

- Phone conversations are authenticated in different ways:

  - Voice recognition—any call can be authenticated by testimony of one participant who knows the voice of the other;

- Incoming calls—these can be authenticated by proof connecting the conversation with events or transactions involving the caller, or an earlier communication with her;

- Outgoing calls—these can be authenticated by proof that the caller dialed the number assigned to a particular individual, or that the caller dialed the number assigned to a business and talked to someone about appropriate business matters.

- Self-authentication means taking things at face value despite the general rule against doing so.

  - Strong but not conclusive—being self-authenticating does not mean authenticity cannot be contested, but the criteria are strong so that satisfying them can lead to a mandatory instruction (but not against criminal defendants).

  - Sealed public documents and certified copies of public documents are self-authenticating. The latter method is most common: A certificate states that the attached copy of a public record is true and correct, and the certificate is signed and sealed by an appropriate public officer.

  - Official publications are self-authenticating, which means the court can rely on a legend, found in the thing itself, stating that it is official.

  - Newspapers and magazines are self-authenticating, which means the trier can rely on appearance alone.

  - Trade inscriptions and labels affixed in course of business are self-authenticating and can be used to show ownership, control, or origin, so product label on a can is competent to prove who made the product.

  - Acknowledged documents (like deeds) and certain commercial paper (like bills of lading) are self-authenticating.

- Demonstrative evidence is best understood to mean evidence that conveys a "firsthand sense impression," which includes both "real" evidence (the things actually involved in the transaction in issue) and "illustrative" evidence (like diagrams illustrating testimony).

- Drawings, charts, diagrams, maps, models—demonstrative evidence of these kinds must be authenticated by testimony or other proof indicating that such items are accurate portrayals.

- Displays involve showing such things as scars or injuries; courts have wide discretion and often permit proof in this form.

- Demonstrations involve parties or witnesses showing how things happened, and sometimes re-enactments out of court that are presented by videotape or film in court, including day-in-the-life films and videotapes showing the effects of injuries; again, courts have wide discretion and often permit such proof.

- Animations involve computer-generated imagery that recreates scenes or events, and may require scientific testimony to lay the necessary foundation; again, courts have wide discretion.

- Experiments may be conducted in court or out, for such purposes as demonstrating scientific principles, or to test or present theories about what happened; again, courts have wide discretion.

- Jury views—these are allowed, in the court's discretion, when a trip to a scene would increase understanding, unless practical considerations indicate otherwise.

A. INTRODUCTION

The requirement to "authenticate" something is often described by the phrase "laying the foundation." Authenticating means showing something is what the offering party (proponent) claims it to be. The requirement reflects an official attitude of agnosticism toward writings and objects, and an insistence on being careful in order to avoid inadvertent mistakes and easy deception: Unless authenticating proof is offered, the thing cannot be admitted, which is to say that it is not "taken at face value."

1. Applies Everywhere

Usually authentication is associated with tangible objects offered as exhibits, but in fact it applies to everything but live testimony: Factfinders may assume, or perhaps "accept the evidence of their senses," that someone who takes the stand and looks like a person *really is* a person (we require identification, a showing of personal knowledge, and, at least for experts, a showing of qualifications), and that testimony that sounds like words *is* words, and so forth. But proof in all other forms must be shown to be what the proponent claims it to be, including documents, phone conversations described in testimony or captured in recordings, photographs, and tangible objects of all kinds.

2. Steps in the Process

Authenticating an object involves (1) marking it for identification, (2) proving that it is what the proponent claims, using testimony of someone with knowledge, (3) offering the exhibit in evidence, (4) letting counsel for the other side examine it, (5) allowing an opportunity for objection, (6) obtaining a ruling if objection is made, and (7) marking the object as an exhibit (meaning that it is now admitted into evidence). The order of these steps sometimes varies, according to local custom.

3. Roles of Judge and Jury

The question of authentication is one of conditional relevancy, which means that the judge plays only a screening role. See FRE 104(b).

a. Jury finally determines

If the proponent offers enough proof to permit a reasonable person to conclude that something is what the proponent claims, the authentication requirement is satisfied and the jury finally determines whether that something is authentic or not. Only at the extremes does the judge control the process.

b. Insufficient

At one extreme, when there is no proof (or not enough) of authenticity, the judge excludes the proffered evidence for failing the requirement.

c. Overwhelming

At the other extreme, when proof of authenticity is overwhelming (or cogent and compelling), the proffered evidence satisfies the requirement and is admitted (assuming no other reason to exclude). The jury may be told (if the proponent asks) to accept the evidence as authentic, although probably such an instruction may not be given against the accused in a criminal case.

4. Burdens

The burden of laying the foundation (authenticating proffered evidence) rests with the proponent.

5. Pretrial Authentication

Particularly in civil cases, discovery and pretrial proceedings often remove all or most authentication issues. In criminal cases, some issues of authenticity are resolved prior to trial by stipulation, but at least some usually remain to be resolved at trial.

6. Liberality of FRE 901(b)(4)

Under this provision, authenticity may be shown by "appearance, contents, substance, internal patterns, or other distinctive characteristics, taken in conjunction with all the circumstances." This provision stops short of abandoning the attitude of agnosticism noted above, but goes far to assure that "face value" at least *counts* in determining authenticity, even if it is not enough by itself to resolve the matter.

B. TANGIBLE OBJECTS

There are many ways to authenticate tangible objects, most depending on some combination of testimony by someone with knowledge and circumstantial evidence.

1. Testimony by Person with Knowledge

In its easiest and most general formulation, authentication requires testimony by someone who has personal knowledge and can identify the object and show how it connects to the matter in suit. See FRE 901(b)(1) (approving testimony by a witness with knowledge that a thing "is what it is claimed to be").

a. Distinctive and well-known objects

An unelaborated statement identifying an object is sufficient if it is distinctive and well known to the witness ("that's my pocket knife"). Here, requiring more would be a waste of time, although cross-examination that exposes a possible lie or mistake would lead the proponent to offer further evidence because the object itself might be excluded if the cross left no room for a reasonable person to find that it was authentic.

b. Other objects

For objects that are less distinctive or less known to the witness, more is usually required. A witness to a bank robbery, for example, could not satisfy the authentication requirement by saying "that's the bag the robber was carrying." More would be required, such as "I remember that the bag he was carrying had that 'Pier 16' label on it, and I remember that it had a tear like that close to the top, so I think that's the bag he was carrying."

c. Marks or tags

Law enforcement officers and other experienced witnesses sometimes mark or tag objects, and a witness who recognizes such a mark or tag can offer the necessary proof even if he is not otherwise certain of the identity of the object. (Typically additional chain-of-custody testimony is also given in such cases, but sometimes a mark or tag by itself is convincing evidence of the identity of an item, as might happen if the item is sealed in a plastic bag with identifying labels backed up by computerized lists or inventories that describe each such item.)

d. Certainty

As is true of witnesses generally, an authenticating witness need not be certain about the relevant points in order to give useful and sufficient evidence. A witness with personal knowledge can identify an object as the one involved in the events in suit even if he is not absolutely sure, and acknowledges some risk of error. See *United States v. Johnson*, 637 F.2d 1224 (9th Cir. 1980) (in trial for assault, victim adequately identified ax as the weapon even though he testified with "some hesitancy" and did not say he could distinguish the ax from others, where he said he was "pretty sure" it was the weapon).

2. Chain of Custody

Authenticating an object by showing chain of custody is useful when the evidence is fungible, or no witness can identify it by personal knowledge of distinctive characteristics, or when great care must be taken because of risks of mistake or deception. Much evidence in criminal cases is authenticated this way, such as drugs seized from the defendant and physical clues found at the scene (the glove in the O.J. Simpson case), and forensic evidence depends on chain of custody (blood spatters, fiber samples).

a. Calling each person

Normally showing chain of custody involves calling each person who handled the object, which convincingly shows the object is the right one and has not been altered or tampered with.

b. Gaps, missing links

Gaps or missing links in the chain may be fatal, but often they are not. With some frequency, it happens that one or more people who handled an item cannot be found to testify. If people who handled the item before and after such a person testify, the missing link may not matter, particularly if other circumstantial clues (like testimony describing or recognizing the object, or tags or labels) provides some assurance that the absent person did not tamper with the object or substitute some other. Unless serious difficulty appears, gaps or missing links affect weight rather than admissibility. See *United States v. Howard–Arias*, 679 F.2d 363 (4th Cir. 1982) (in drug trial, marijuana was shown to have been seized from wreckage of trawler by chain-of-custody evidence, and missing link did not destroy foundation; question is whether testimony was "sufficiently complete" to show that it was "improbable that the original item had been exchanged with another or was otherwise tampered with").

c. Round-the-clock watch

The proponent who depends on chain of custody to authenticate need not keep an object under round-the-clock watch. Storing an object in a sensible location, typically under observation during business hours, locked up when nobody is around, and retrieving it from there are common occurrences that do not undercut the claim of authenticity.

d. Presumption of official care

Public officers (like police and FBI) enjoy what some courts term a presumption of due care in the discharge of their public duties, which helps when there are gaps in the chain of custody.

C. WRITINGS

Written documents are often proved and often critical. Authenticating a writing may involve a witness with personal knowledge, who recognizes the writing itself because of its distinctive characteristics, or who can authenticate the writing by describing how it was kept (as part of business records, for instance) and giving other circumstantial proof. In this setting, however, authenticating often means proving a particular person wrote or signed a document. Here especially, good pretrial procedures can resolve and remove authentication issues in advance. In criminal cases, however, and in civil cases where genuine contests over authenticity sometimes arise, the proponent must be prepared to take trial time to authenticate written evidence.

1. Lay Opinion

On the basis of familiarity with the handwriting of a person, a lay witness can authenticate a document as having been written by the person. See FRE 901(b)(2) (authorizing lay testimony based on familiarity "not acquired for the current litigation").

a. Need not have watched

Such testimony does not require the witness to have been there to watch the preparation or signing of the document.

b. Familiarity

The requisite familiarity may come from watching a person write, or from working with her or carrying on a correspondence with her, or from other forms of acquaintance. Family members, for example, are often in a good position to be familiar with a person's writing.

2. Expert Opinion

Experts can testify that a proffered document was written by some person X by comparing it with a handwriting exemplar known to have come from X. See FRE 901(b)(3) (authorizing comparison by expert witness "with authenticated specimens").

3. Comparison by Trier

On the basis of a handwriting exemplar known to have come from Y, jurors can conduct similar comparisons and can conclude that a proffered document does or does not contain the handwriting of Y. See FRE 901(b)(3) (authorizing comparison by the trier or expert witness "with specimens that have been authenticated").

4. Distinctive Characteristics (and Reply Letter Doctrine)

Often appearance and surrounding circumstances are strong indicators that bear on authenticity. See FRE 901(b)(4) (authentication may be shown by "distinctive characteristics" like appearance, content, substance, and internal patterns, "taken in conjunction with circumstances").

a. Matching knowledge to person

The offering party may show Z wrote a document by showing the author of the document knew things Z knew or used code terms Z used. Where matches are unique to Z (nobody else knew such things or used such codes), the proof is most convincing, but it suffices if relatively few people knew such things and that Z was the most likely among these. See *United States v. Bagaric*, 706 F.2d 42 (2d Cir. 1983) (letter was shown to have been written by B on basis of internal qualities, including references to B's friends, proof that letter came from city where B lived, use of B's nickname at end of letter, and self-descriptions of writer matching facts known about B).

b. Reply doctrine

A letter or other document may be shown to have come from K if it is shown to be an apparent reply to a letter or other inquiry directed to K.

c. Mere name insufficient

The mere fact that a name or signature indicates that a document was authored by L is not enough to authenticate the document as the work of L. Still, a match on this point is a factor that counts, along with others, in authenticating the document.

d. Letterhead

At common law, showing that the printed letterhead on a document matched the letterhead of a particular person or firm was insufficient to show the document originated with that person or firm. Under the more liberal standard of FRE 901(b)(4), such a match certainly counts and may even suffice.

☞ EXAMPLE AND ANALYSIS

J offers a letter that came to him stating "the limit of your coverage for arson is $1 million." The letterhead indicates that the source is "The AllRisk Company," and it bears a signature block stating the name K as the author and a corresponding signature. The proponent offers proof that J wrote a letter to K at The AllRisk Company one week before, asking, "What is the limit of my coverage for arson?"

On these facts, the letter satisfies the authentication requirement. By itself, proof that J wrote the original inquiry to K should suffice, for timing and content suffice to support a finding of authenticity. The letterhead and signature block support the indicated conclusion. The letterhead and signature block might even suffice by themselves. It would certainly be enough, for example, to match the letterhead to AllRisk's standard letterhead and showing that K is an agent of AllRisk having responsibilities in the area covered by the letter, particularly if J were also shown to have an arson policy issued by AllRisk. By itself, however, the signature block and signature would not suffice. (Testimony identifying the signature as K's, coupled with proof that K worked in the appropriate capacity for AllRisk, would also suffice.)

---

5. Public Records and Documents

There are many ways to lay the foundation for proving public records and documents. Some are peculiar to public records, but other mechanisms are more generally available.

a. Certified copy

The most common method of authenticating a public document or record is to offer a certificate of authenticity, and usually what is offered is a machine-made copy of an original. This mechanism is not available for most other documents, and it involves the concept of self-authentication. The subject is discussed further below under that heading.

b. Showing public filing or recording

A document or record may be authenticated by proof that it was recorded or filed as authorized by law in the appropriate public office. Ideally the custodian of records would testify to these points, but it seems that testimony by any knowledgeable person suffices, including one who simply went to the office and obtained the document. See FRE 901(b)(7). This mechanism is not available for other documents.

c. Testimony by knowledgeable witness

A witness familiar with a document or record can testify that it is official and explain whatever may be necessary to know about its preparation. This method of authentication is not limited to public documents and records, but is generally available. See FRE 901(b)(1) (authentication by witness with appropriate knowledge).

d. Other ways

There are other mechanisms generally available for authenticating documents, and these may be used for public records and documents too.

i. Lay testimony on handwriting

If the crucial point is to show authorship (Bertha Smedley is the county coroner), and a letter bearing a signature setting forth that name is offered, lay opinion that the signature is hers suffices. See FRE 901(b)(2).

ii. Expert testimony; comparison

Again if the crucial point is to show authorship, it suffices to present expert testimony based on comparison with an exemplar, or the exemplar may be offered and the jury can decide the point. See FRE 901(b)(3).

iii. Ancient document

The ancient documents rule (discussed below) applies to public records and reports as it applies to all writings.

6. Ancient Documents

The "ancient documents" rule comes from common law tradition, except that the old rule employed a 30–year standard and the modern approach shortens the time to 20 years. Although the "ancient documents" label continues to be used, modern doctrine reaches not only writings but "data compilations" in "any form," which includes computerized material. The requisite age may be shown through testimony by a person with knowledge, who might have seen the preparation or execution of the document or know how long it has been around, and other proof is proper too (like expert testimony). In fact, however, the greatest utility of this doctrine lies in the fact that it allows age to be proved by satisfying three criteria that pose no difficulty in practice: If a document looks old enough, and if it was found in a place that is appropriate of it, and if there are no tellingly suspicious circumstances, it can be taken as what it appears to be (a document that is more than twenty years old).

a. Looks old enough

Physical appearance and internal characteristics (including date) go far toward establishing the requisite age, but a *written or other internal date alone* is not enough.

b. Found in appropriate place

The fact that a writing came from a place where it would likely be found if it were authentic helps establish the requisite age. Thus corporate records should come from the place where such records are kept, and a diary should come from the effects of the person in question.

c. No suspicious circumstances

When these circumstantial indicators are used to prove the requisite age, there must be no suspicious circumstances raising doubts about authenticity.

d. Hearsay issues

With the ancient document rule as with other authentication doctrines, satisfying authentication requirements does not remove hearsay objections. In the case of ancient documents, however, there is a matching or complementary hearsay exception. See FRE 803(16) (exception for statements in a document at least 20 years old the authenticity of which is established).

e. Rationale of rule

While being ancient does not guarantee authenticity (or accuracy), age alone tends to insure that the writing was made before the forces leading to litigation had begun to operate, so one source of error or possible deception is eliminated. Being that old also means that direct proof of authenticity is probably hard to find. If the document is offered as proof of matters asserted in it (under the hearsay exception noted above), it is also probably that live eyewitness testimony will be hard to come by, as witnesses will have forgotten or disappeared.

D. ELECTRONIC RECORDINGS

A recording of a conversation may be authenticated by showing how it was made and identifying the participants. (As with phone calls, authentication does not solve hearsay problems that arise if recorded statements are offered to prove whatever they assert, and applicable exceptions must be invoked.)

1. Caution Required

Since recordings can be altered and manipulated, both by simple techniques of splicing and editing and by highly sophisticated techniques, courts were once very cautious, but contemporary standards are simpler and more flexible.

2. Completeness

Evidence in the form of recorded conversations typically presents problems of completeness under FRE 106, which states that the proponent must offer any other part of a recording that ought in fairness to be considered contemporaneously with the part that the proponent chooses to offer. Sometimes less than all is presented because only part of a conversation is relevant and the recording goes on for a long time, and sometimes the difficulty is that parts of the conversation are not adequately recorded. Usually objections based on incompleteness do not require exclusion of the whole tape.

3. Two–Step Authentication

Usually the required foundation has two major elements:

a. Explaining the process

The first step involves showing what process was followed and why it is reliable. In the common setting of a criminal case, one court put it this way: The government must "go forward with respect to the competency of the operator, the fidelity of the recording equipment, [and] the absence of material deletions, additions, or alterations in the relevant portions." See *United States v. Biggins*, 551 F.2d 64 (5th Cir. 1977) (admitting filtered rerecording despite absence of testimony by trained operator and failure to call person who filtered and rerecorded the original; government showed the rerecording accurately transcribed the original).

b. Identifying the participants

The second step involves showing who participated in the conversation, which can be done by voice identification, testimony by a participant in the conversation, or testimony by people who made the recording if they know who was present and which voice belongs to whom.

4. Alternative Method of Authenticating

Sometimes authenticity is established by getting a participant in the recorded conversation (or an observer) to testify that he listened to the recording and that it fairly, fully, and accurately captures the conversation. Such testimony can obviate the need to explain or validate the process.

5. Transcripts

Often recorded conversations are presented along with transcripts that identify the speakers, and the parties should have an opportunity to compare the transcript and tape prior to trial, so as to be able to object in timely fashion to inaccuracies.

E. PHOTOGRAPHS; X–RAYS AND OTHER MEDICAL IMAGES; COMPUTER OUTPUT

Authentication issues commonly accompany the introduction of proof of this sort.

1. Photographs

Authentication can be accomplished by testimony of a witness with knowledge of the thing or the scene, who states that the photograph accurately depicts the thing or the scene at the relevant time. The photographer can ordinarily testify (if he was personally there operating the camera), but the photographer need not testify.

a. Illustrative versus independent

Because the authenticating witness typically testifies in the manner described above, courts tend to treat photographs as merely "illustrative" evidence, sometimes instructing juries that testimonial accounts control, in case they conflict in any way with photographs. (Similar treatment is sometimes accorded to films and videotapes.) But in some respects photographs are obviously more reliable and complete than testimonial accounts, and the modern trend is to treat photographs (or films or videotapes) as independently relevant and not simply illustrative.

b. "Silent witness" doctrine

In the case of photographs taken by surveillance cameras that take pictures automatically, usually no live witness can describe the scene or attest the accuracy of the picture because no such person was watching. Here photographs are necessarily independent evidence, and the problem of authentication is solved by testimony explaining the process and showing that the camera accurately captures the scene on which it is trained. See FRE 901(b)(9) (authentication may take the form of evidence describing a process or system used to produce a result and showing that the process or system produces an accurate result).

c. Films, videotapes

Modern surveillance cameras sometimes make films or videotaped records of events or scenes. Courts have abandoned their original skepticism toward such proof (as indicated by requirements of elaborate foundation testimony) and now accept it on the basis of testimony describing the process and showing that the camera makes an accurate record. Of course witnesses who have seen with their own eyes the events or scene captured in films or videotape can authenticate such evidence too, just as in the case of photographs.

2. X-rays and Other Medical Images

Since no human eye sees what an x-ray depicts—and many other medical imaging techniques share this same quality, such as ultrasound images—authentication proceeds by testimony describing the process and its use in the case. The foundation witness describes the capability and acceptability of the equipment, qualifications of the operator, procedures followed, development process, when the x-ray or other image was made, and what it shows.

3. Computer Output

Authentication requires a description of the process and a showing that it produces an accurate result, see FRE 901(b)(9). In this setting, the authenticating witness provides evidence that (1) the equipment can perform the functions claimed for it and was in good working order, (2) qualified operators ran the equipment, (3) they followed proper procedures in the input and output phases, (4) the machine used a reliable program that could do what it purports to do, and (5) the operators programmed and operated the computer correctly. (Normally the witness also describes and identifies the output being offered.)

a. Manipulation

When computer output is manipulated for use in court, a more elaborate foundation is necessary, and adverse parties should be given an opportunity prior to trial to examine and raise objections.

b. Hearsay issues

Computer output usually embodies out-of-court statements by human beings, so hearsay issues arise. The business and public records exceptions embrace computerized material, but those exceptions have requirements of their own that the proponent must also satisfy in laying the foundation. See FRE 803(6) (business records) and (8) (public records).

F. TELEPHONE CONVERSATIONS

Telephone conversations raise authentication problems because typically no single witness hears or sees both sides of a conversation. (Remember that statements in phone conversations are hearsay if offered as proof of matters asserted, which is the usual purpose of proving them, and a hearsay exception is necessary. Authenticating a phonecall typically means offering testimony by one party to the conversation and the task is to identify the person talking on the distant end. If the conversation is offered as evidence against that very person, then whatever he said is his admission, and identifying him solves the hearsay problem. In other cases, where the party against whom the conversation is offered is *not* the one on the distant end, the hearsay issue must be solved in some other way.)

1. Incoming Phone Calls

When the witness testifies to something said by another during a call that the witness *received* (an incoming call), usually the witness cannot establish the identity of the calling party merely by testifying that he identified himself as a certain person ("Hello Witness, this is Frank calling"). There are typically two ways to identify the calling party.

a. Voice identification

If the witness knows the person who called her, she may identify that person by testifying that she recognized his voice ("I recognized the person calling me as Frank"). The witness may acquire the requisite personal knowledge either before or after the call, and even casual familiarity suffices as the basis for voice recognition testimony. See FRE 901(b)(5) (witness may identify voice, "whether heard firsthand or through mechanical or electronic transmission or recording," by opinion based on hearing voice "at any time" in circumstances connecting it with the person being identified).

b. Content

Sometimes parties to a phone call discuss an event, transaction, or plan, and other proof connects the person at the distant end to such matters ("the hike mentioned in the meeting of our mountain club begins at 2PM on Saturday"). Or the incoming call indicates that the caller is replying to an earlier query or call from the witness herself ("you asked about meeting for coffee this morning, but I'm tied up"). Such statements by the voice on the distant end of an incoming call are circumstantial of the identity of the caller that can suffice to authenticate the phone call, and self-identification by the caller ("this is Frank") counts in this calculus (even though it is not enough by itself).

2. Outgoing Phone Calls

When the witness is the calling party, the task of identifying the voice at the distant end is made somewhat easier by the fact that the witness may rely at least in part on the number she dialed. If it is programmed into the witness' own telephone, her past experience of reaching the person in question by pressing that button helps prove that *this time* when she pushed that button she reached the same phone (hence the same person). If the witness "looked it up," the very fact that a standard listing stated that a particular number was assigned to a particular person is enough to make the same point. If a court is not convinced by such foundations, there are other common means for supplementing such testimony, and these may make the authenticating proof even more convincing even if more is not, strictly speaking, required. Here are common additional means of authentication phonecalls in this situation.

a. Voice identification

As with incoming calls, the witness may identify the person on the distant end of an outgoing call by voice recognition. See FRE 901(b)(5).

b. Personal calls (number and circumstances)

For calls to a residence, self-authentication and just a few more details about the content of the conversation can be convincing. The witness testifies that she pressed the button programmed to dial Frank's phone, that the answering voice identified itself as Frank ("yes, this is Frank") and that what the answering voice said thereafter was something that fits Frank's situation ("I'm still laid up with that cold I caught last week"). See FRE 901(b)(6) (for outgoing calls to a person, authenticate by showing call was placed to the person's number coupled with "circumstances, including self-identification" indicating that he is the one who answered).

c. Business calls (number and appropriateness)

For calls to a business, dialing the number assigned to the ABC Company and having a conversation on appropriate business matters are strong indications that the call reached the ABC Company and the person who answered was employed there. The authentication requirement is satisfied by testimony showing these points. See FRE 901(b)(6) (for outgoing calls to a business, authenticate by showing call was placed to the number for that business coupled with proof that the conversation "related to business reasonably transacted over the telephone").

G. SELF–AUTHENTICATION

Some written material and some objects *are* taken "at face value" despite the general rule against doing so. See FRE 902 (listing ten categories of self-authenticating evidence). It should be noted here that a self-authenticating item is not necessarily admissible, and that an objection on some other ground may be viable: Newspapers, for example, are self-authenticating, but it does not follow that a story about an automobile accident is admissible to prove that the accident happened in the way described (the newspaper is hearsay if offered to prove such points).

1. Effect of Principle

Being self-authenticating means independent proof is unnecessary to satisfy the authentication requirement.

a. Can still contest

Being self-authenticating does not mean the matter is conclusively settled, and the adverse party may offer counterproof indicating that the matter is not authentic.

b. When no counterproof offered

When the adverse party offers no such counterproof, it is unclear whether a jury should receive a mandatory instruction or remain free to decide against authenticity. An early draft of FRE 902 provided that the self-authentication principle raised a presumption of authenticity, but this language was deleted. Arguably the criteria of the self-authentication principle amount to cogent and compelling proof of authenticity, so material that satisfies the principle can generate a mandatory instruction, at least in civil cases and for items offered by the defense in a criminal case.

2. Sealed Public Documents and Certified Copies

A public document with what appears to be an appropriate seal and signature is self-authenticating. See FRE 902(1). The same is true of a *copy* of a public document to which is attached a certificate of authenticity with what appears to be the appropriate seal and signature, see FRE 902(4). A public document *lacking* such an apparent seal and signature becomes self-authenticating if an appropriate certificate (apparently signed and sealed) is attached. See FRE 902(2) and (4).

a.   The common method

Officials are reluctant to let go of originals, and the certificate procedure is simple and avoids the need for a witness, so the most common method of proof is by certified copy under FRE 902(2) and (4).

b.   Maker and seal

The certificate must be made by the custodian of records or another appropriate person, like a supervisor or superior in the agency or branch, and must be signed and sealed. If the custodian (the one immediately in charge of the record) lacks a seal, a second certificate by someone in the hierarchy who *has* a seal must be attached, and in theory a chain of certificates might be needed.

c.   Substance of certificate

The certificate must say the attached copy is true and correct.

d.   Coverage

Public records covered by this principle include documents recorded or filed in public office (deeds and reports).

e.   Narrower alternative

A narrower provision in the Civil Rules reaches only "official record[s]" and entries (not recorded or filed documents), requires an initial certificate by the "custodian of record" (not some other person), and requires a second certificate attesting that the signer of the first is indeed the custodian. See FRC 44(a).

3.   Foreign Public Documents

The self-authentication principle applies to foreign public documents as well as to copies of such documents, although it differs in this setting on points of detail. See FRE 902(3) and (4).

4.   Official Publications

Federal, state, and local governments publish huge numbers of books, pamphlets, and reports, from instructions on fishing on public lands to reports on the toxicity of products to the Congressional Record. These are self-authenticating on the basis of a mere legend indicating the public source. See FRE 902(5) (books, pamphlets, publications are self-authenticating when "purporting to be issued by public authority").

5. Newspapers and Magazines

Anything that purports to be a newspaper or magazine is self-authenticating, which means that an apparent copy of the *Chicago Tribune* may be offered without proving authenticity. (As noted above, however, the fact that a copy of the *Chicago Tribune* may be taken as authenticate does *not* mean that an article in the paper may be taken as proof of the matters reported in the article: If the newspaper is offered for this purpose, a hearsay exception is necessary.)

6. Trade Inscriptions and Labels

In a notorious case that could be cited as proof of the old adage penned by Dickens in *Oliver Twist* ("If the law supposes that, the law is an ass–an idiot"), a reviewing court held that a can of peas bearing the Green Giant label, which was the basis for a suit by someone who claimed to have ingested a piece of glass while eating the peas, had not been shown to have been made by the defendant because the label was not enough to establish the point. See *Keegan v. Green Giant Co.*, 110 A.2d 599 (Me. 1954). The modern principle is that trade labels and inscriptions apparently affixed in course of business are self-authenticating, which means they can be used to prove ownership, control, or origin. Thus a can of peas that *says* Green Giant on it can be admitted as a can of peas made by that company. See FRE 902(7).

7. Acknowledged Documents

A notarial certificate of acknowledgment makes a document self-authenticating. Deeds and other conveyances are commonly acknowledged as a condition of being recorded, but any document with the appropriate notarial certificate is self-authenticating. See FRE 902(8).

8. Commercial Paper

Under the Uniform Commercial Code, bills of lading are presumptively authentic, and various dates and signatures on negotiable instruments are presumed correct and genuine. Such material also fits the self-authentication principle. See FRE 902(9).

H. SUBSCRIBING WITNESSES

Some documents, most especially wills, require subscribing or attesting witnesses. One purpose is to insure that such documents are executed under appropriate conditions and with due seriousness, and another purpose is to try to insure the availability of authenticating witnesses if the need should arise. States vary on the question whether the proponent of a subscribed document *must* call subscribing witnesses, assuming that they are still alive and can be found. In the federal system, subscribing witnesses must be called only if the law of the state governing the validity of the writing so requires.

I. DEMONSTRATIVE EVIDENCE

This term is sometimes defined as evidence that "appeals to the senses," or more narrowly as evidence that conveys a "firsthand sense impression," or (more narrowly still) as "illustrative evidence." The second definition (proof conveying a "firsthand sense impression") seems most satisfactory because the first describes all proof and the third excludes proof having independent probative force (e.g., bank surveillance photographs).

1. "Real" Versus "Illustrative"

Physical objects actually involved in the events in litigation are known as "real" evidence (a murder weapon in a criminal case, the break pedal that failed in a product liability case). In contrast, physical objects used to illustrate testimony, like a schematic drawing of the floorplan of a room, are called "illustrative" evidence. The term "demonstrative evidence" reaches both these categories, when defined as indicated above to mean proof that provides a firsthand sense impression. Some courts and commentators use "demonstrative" evidence to mean only "illustrative" evidence (and not "real" evidence). It seems more useful to treat both illustrative and real evidence as part of the larger category of demonstrative evidence, and this outline uses the term "demonstrative evidence" in that larger sense.

2. Lodging with Court

To preserve issues on appeal, the party offering demonstrative evidence must take care to insure that it is marked for identification and lodged with the court to become part of the record. If such proof is ultimately *excluded* (ruled inadmissible in evidence), failing to lodge and mark it (the mark serves to connect the evidence with whatever foundational testimony is offered) means the claim of error is lost.

3. To the Jury Room?

Sometimes demonstrative evidence is too large, extensive, or unwieldy to go with the jury to deliberations. Even if it is compact and portable, some courts prefer *not* to allow it to go to the jury room unless it is essentially "substantive" (which usually means "real" evidence). There is some risk that demonstrative evidence taken to the jury room will get undue emphasis, but there is no ironbound rule that demonstrative evidence cannot accompany the jury during deliberations, and in fact it often does.

4. Drawings, Charts, Diagrams, Maps, Models

Such items as these, made specially for use in trial, are common examples of demonstrative evidence. The proponent must simply show, typically by means of testimony by the person who made the item or by testimony of someone familiar with the thing being depicted, that the item is an accurate portrayal.

5. Displays, Demonstrations, Animations

Courts may allow the parties to display or demonstrate events or conditions, and to use films or animations for such purposes. In these areas, the court has wide discretion to control and supervise what occurs.

a. Displays

Parties or witnesses are sometimes allowed to display scars or injuries, or to stand or speak. Such displays may help the jury understand or evaluate testimony and other evidence in the case.

b. Demonstrations

Parties or witnesses are sometimes allowed to show how things happened or might have happened. In the trial of O.J. Simpson on murder charges, for example, Simpson himself put on a glove (part of an attempt by the prosecutor to show it fit, but in the demonstration it appeared too small), and prosecution witnesses demonstrated for the jury how a knife-wielding assailant might have inflicted the fatal wounds on one of the victims.

i. Re-enactments

When events cannot be recreated in court with people and simple props, the parties sometimes do out-of-court re-enactments that are filmed or videotaped. Such recreations of events are often admitted, but courts may and sometimes do insist that adverse parties be notified when material of this sort is prepared, or at least given a chance to see it before it is offered. When the point is to convey the message "this is how it happened," video presentations are quite properly viewed as out-of-court statements: Those who prepare them, and of course the claimant himself or herself often participates and may largely inform and direct such efforts, are purposefully communicating the idea that "this is the way it actually happened," and video presentations are hearsay. If the claimant takes the witness stand and provides a running account or at least testifies in court after the video is show that it accurately shows what happened, hearsay concerns are to some extent satisfied by the fact that the other side can question the witness and cross-examine her about the substance of the video presentation. Cautionary instructions can help too: The court can tell the jury that the video presentation is not itself evidence, but can be considered insofar as it illustrates or helps understand courtroom testimony and other evidence in the case.

ii.   Day-in-the-life films

This method of showing the effects of serious injuries has become popular and is routinely used. When offered by a claimant to show the difficulties he experiences, hearsay issues and risks of unfairness in the presentation become matters of paramount concern, and once again advance notice to adverse parties seems crucial.

c.   Animations

Computer-generated imagery can recreate scenes with special vividness and can be structured and edited to make whatever point the proponent wants to emphasize. Such proof may require a special foundation: If the imagery relies on scientific principles, scientific testimony may be needed, along with more usual proof relating to the facts, the techniques used to recreate these facts or embody the available information in visible images, and the reliability or accuracy of the final result.

6.   Experiments

Experiments may be conducted in court or out, in order to demonstrate scientific principles, to test or present theories about what happened, to measure the capabilities of humans, animals, or products, or to recreate events. The proponent of such proof must show that the experiment was conducted under circumstances substantially similar to the event, and the court has discretion to allow or exclude such proof depending on probative worth and risks of confusion, prejudice, or waste of time.

7.   Jury Views

Taking the jury to an important scene (like the place of the murder or accident) is one way to provide what amounts to demonstrative evidence. In deciding whether to allow a jury view, courts have broad discretion, and they consider such factors as the importance of the matter to be viewed, the extent to which a view would increase understanding, the time, distance, and expense involved, whether conditions have changed, and what risks the journey would entail. Risks include exposure to outside influences, too much unsupervised mingling with lawyers or others, and similar things.

REVIEW QUESTIONS AND ANSWERS

Question: What does authentication mean, and why do we have such a requirement, and where does it apply?

Answer: Authenticating means proving that something is what the offering party claims it to be. We have the requirement in order to insist on taking care with proof, to avoid inadvertent mistakes and easy deception. The requirement applies across the board to everything but live testimony, where we do have an analogous requirement (identifying the witness, showing personal knowledge, and so forth).

Question: What does authenticating an object entail?

Answer: The steps vary among jurisdictions, but most would require the proponent to do the following: First, mark the exhibit for identification; second, prove that it is what the proponent claims (usually by live testimony); third, offer the exhibit in evidence; fourth, let opposing counsel examine the exhibit; fifth, allow opportunity for objection; sixth, obtain a ruling if objection is made; seventh, mark the item as an exhibit.

Question: Who determines authenticity, judge or jury, and which party bears what burden?

Answer: Questions of authenticity are for the jury to determine under FRE 104(b), which means that the court admits an item requiring authentication if there is sufficient evidence of authenticity to enable a reasonable jury to decide the item is authentic. If insufficient proof of authenticity is offered, the item must be excluded. If overwhelming proof of authenticity is introduced, the court might instruct the jury to treat the item as authentic (but such an instruction probably cannot be given against a criminal defendant). The burden is on the proponent to establish authenticity.

Question: How do you authenticate tangible objects?

Answer: There are many ways, but the most common and direct way is to offer testimony by a person with knowledge that the object is what the proponent says it is. The witness may give such testimony on the basis of direct and specific knowledge if the object is sufficiently distinctive ("that's my pocket knife"), or may give more general testimony that connects the object in question to prior experience (the bag carried by the robber "had that 'Pier 16' label" and had "a tear like that close to the top," so "I think that's the bag he was carrying"). Experienced witnesses, like law enforcement officers, may give the appropriate testimony by referring to marks or tags placed on objects.

Question: What does "chain of custody" entail?

Answer: In criminal cases particularly, this method of authentication is common because the prosecuting authority is expected to take great care and often no witness is available to give specific authenticating proof relying on distinctive features. In this setting, authentication by "chain of custody" involves calling all the people who handled an object from the time it was retrieved to the time it was offered. If someone who handled an object is missing, her absence may not be fatal, at least if circumstances support reasonable inferences that the object was not changed or tampered with. Even in criminal cases with respect to objects offered by the prosecutor, it is not critical that they be kept under round-the-clock watch, so long as they are kept in a reasonably secure area. A presumption of due care on the part of police officers sometimes helps overcome minor gaps in proof.

Question: How do you authenticate writings?

Answer: Again there are many ways. (Parenthetically it should be noted, in civil cases especially, that pretrial procedures typically resolve authentication issues that relate to writings that are of central importance in the case, and often resolve authentication issues for all writings.) Lay witnesses can testify on the basis of personal knowledge, either because they recognize the document itself or know enough about surrounding circumstances to show its authenticity. When the important point is to identify a signature or handwriting in the body of a document, a lay witness familiar with the writing of a particular person may say whether the signature or writing came from that person. Experts too can testify to the authenticity of handwriting or signatures, on the basis of a handwriting exemplar. Jurors also can determine authenticity by comparing a writing with an exemplar of known origin.

Question: Can writings be authenticated circumstantially? What about the "reply" doctrine?

Answer: Yes, writings can be authenticated by circumstantial evidence, and the reply doctrine is a common form of circumstantial proof. If a witness testifies that she wrote a letter to K, and that after a suitable interval she received what appears to be a reply to what she wrote (because the reply indicates that it came from K and it alludes to material in the initial letter), this fact is sufficient evidence to authenticate the reply. Circumstantial proof of authenticity also includes internal references in a writing that in some way matches the person in question, particularly if the writing reflects knowledge that only that person would have, or that few others would have. The mere fact that a name appears in the signature line is not enough by itself to prove that a particular person by that name signed the document, but additional indicators (like letterhead) and other circumstances may suffice.

Question: What about public records?

Answer: The most common way of authenticating public records is to offer a certified copy, which usually means a machine-made copy to which the custodian of the record has attached a notarized certificate of authenticity. Short of such proof, the proponent can authenticate a public record by showing that it was recorded or filed as authorized by law in the appropriate office, or by testimony from a witness who has firsthand knowledge that the object is a public record as claimed by the proponent. Other mechanisms to prove the authenticity of public records include lay and expert opinion on handwriting or signatures, and proof that the object satisfies the "ancient documents" rule (taken up below).

Question: What is the "ancient documents" rule, and why do we have it?

Answer: The "ancient documents" rule allows a writing to be authenticated by proving that it has been in existence for 20 years or more (the common law requirement was 30 years). Practically speaking, the proponent usually satisfies this rule by showing that the document *looks old enough,* and was *found in an appropriate place,* which justifies treating the document as authentic unless *suspicious circumstances* appear. A related hearsay exception allows use of ancient documents to prove matters asserted in them. While age alone does not guarantee either authenticity or accuracy, being more than 20 years old helps assure that the document was created before the forces resulting in litigation had gathered, and the ancient documents doctrines (both the authentication rule and the hearsay exception) help accommodate the absence of witnesses with good memory extending back that far.

Question: What problems come with authenticating recordings?

Answer: A recording of a conversation is commonly authenticated by testimony describing the way the recording was made (the process) and identifying the participants. Recordings are problematic because they can be altered and manipulated, they may not capture all of a relevant conversation, and the proponent might not offer the whole conversation. (The rule of completeness applies, which requires the proponent to prove everything that ought in fairness to be considered. See FRE 106.) In proving the process, usually the proponent offers proof of the qualifications of the person operating the recording equipment and shows that no alterations were made in the recording itself. Identifying the participants involves proving who participated, whether by voice identification, by testimony of participants, or by testimony from those who made the recording describing the situation.

Question: How does one authenticate photographs, videotapes, and films?

Answer: One way to do it is by means of testimony by a witness who saw whatever a photograph depicts, who states that the depiction is accurate. The photographer can testify on such points, but he need not be called if another witness can do so. Videotapes and films can be authenticated in similar ways. Sometimes courts treat such proof as merely "illustrative" of live testimony and tell jurors to rely on testimonial accounts if photographs (or films or videotapes) conflict with that testimony. Under the "silent witness" doctrine, photographs (or films or videotapes) are treated as independent evidence if the process of preparation is adequately described, and this approach is often taken in the case of surveillance cameras that operate automatically.

Question: How does one authenticate phone conversations?

Answer: For *incoming* calls described by a witness who received the call, authentication can rest on voice identification (witness knows voice of caller) or on internal content (if the subject of the call is some event or transaction in which the witness engaged with the apparent caller). In this setting, self-identification by the calling person is part of the authenticating proof, but is not enough by itself. For *outgoing* calls, the witness can once again identify the person on the distant end by voice recognition, which suffices to authenticate a call. But it also suffices if the caller can testify that he called the number belonging to a particular person X, coupled with self-identification by that person. In the case of outgoing calls to a business, proof of the number called, coupled with proof that the conversation related to business appropriately conducted by phone from that business, suffices to authenticate the call.

Question: What does "self-authentication" mean?

Answer: Self-authentication refers to a collection of rules that dispense with independent proof of authenticity. If something is self-authenticating, its authenticity may still be contested by the other side. If no proof is offered contesting authenticity of a self-authenticating object, it is not clear whether the jury is given any instruction or remains free to disregard it.

Question: When are public records self-authenticating?

Answer: When such a record (more often a copy of such a record) is offered with a signed and sealed certificate attesting authenticity, the record (or copy) is self-authenticating. The certificate must be made by the custodian who keeps the record, or by some appropriate person in the office or agency (such as a supervisor or superior of the custodian who actually keeps the record), and must be both signed and sealed. (If the person in charge lacks a seal, a second certificate is needed, with a seal, attesting the authority of the person who signs the first certificate, and conceivably a whole chain of certificates might be needed.)

Question: What other things are self-authenticating?

Answer: Official publications are self-authenticating on the basis of a legend indicating a public source. Materials purporting to be newspapers and magazines are self-authenticating. Trade inscriptions (like the label on a can of Green Giant peas) are self-authenticating if they are apparently affixed in the course of business. Acknowledged documents are self-authenticating (deeds). And various forms of commercial paper are self-authenticating under the commercial code (including signatures on negotiable instruments).

Question: What is "demonstrative evidence," and when is it admissible?

Answer: Demonstrative evidence is proof that conveys a "firsthand sense impression," such as a photograph. The concept of demonstrative evidence includes proof that is sometimes called "real" evidence (the murder weapon in a homicide prosecution) and "illustrative" evidence (the floorplan of a room, drawn in court or prepared in advance for purpose of helping to "flesh out" a testimonial account describing the layout and contents of the room). In the former case, the proponent must offer authenticating proof of the sort described throughout this chapter. In the latter case, the proponent must show, in ways appropriate to the specific evidence being offered, that it accurately depicts what it is supposed to depict. Demonstrative evidence includes items specially made for use at trial, like drawings (or a floorplan of a room), charts, and models. It also includes displays (plaintiff shows his wounded hand), demonstrations (murder suspect dons glove), and re-enactments performed out of court and captured on film or videotape, a category that includes day-in-the-life films. In today's world, animations are becoming more commonplace ("here's how the robber held the gun").

Question: What about experiments and jury views?

Answer: An experiment performed outside the courtroom may be proved in court if the proponent satisfies the court that the experiment was conducted under circumstances substantially similar to the event in question, subject to the discretionary power of the court to exclude proof because it would take more time than it is worth or might confuse or mislead. Jury views involve taking the jury to a place that is significant in the case (the crime scene), and courts have discretion, which they exercise by considering the time, distance, and expense involved, whether conditions have changed, and what risks the trip would entail.

Exam Tips

Here are some tips on issues relating to authentication:

Remember that authenticating an object means proving it is what the proponent claims, and that the question whether something is authentic is for the jury to resolve, not the judge, so the requirement is satisfied if enough evidence of authenticity is offered to support a finding in favor of the proponent.

Remember that authenticating physical objects and traces (such as guns and blood drops), especially in criminal cases, usually involves "chain of custody" testimony in which every person who handled the object or trace testifies.

Remember that some things are "self-authenticating," especially objects that carry trade labels (like a can of peas), acknowledged documents (like deeds), and copies of public records that are accompanied by signed and sealed certificates indicating genuineness.

CHAPTER 13

Best Evidence Doctrine

CHAPTER OVERVIEW

The key points in this chapter are

- Content of writings is the main concern of the Best Evidence Doctrine, which requires content to be proved by the writing itself, unless it is unavailable through no fault of the party seeking to prove content.

- The rationale for the doctrine is that writings are of central importance in law, other evidence is inferior, and producing the writing helps insure completeness and prevent forgery or fraud.

- The traditional formulation covered only writings, and required production of originals rather than copies, but modern formulation extends the doctrine to **recordings** and **photographs** and allows proof by means of **duplicates.**

- The term "writing" is broadly defined for purposes of the Best Evidence Doctrine to reach anything that contains or memorializes numbers, letters, or words, including computer output, but courts sometimes exempt "inscribed chattels" (like roadsigns and product labels) from the doctrine even though these fit the modern definition of writings.

- Recordings are within the doctrine in Rules jurisdictions whenever they memorialize letters, words, or numbers.

- Photographs are within the doctrine in Rules jurisdictions, and this concept includes x-rays.

- Originals of writings, recordings, or photographs are the counterparts that have the most relevance in light of the claim or defense being made, the circumstances, party intent, and the substantive law.

  - The original of a letter is the counterpart delivered to the recipient if the purpose is to show what the recipient got.

  - The original of a letter is the counterpart retained by the sender if the purpose is to prove what the sender actually dispatched (mailed) to the recipient.

  - The original of a business record may be any record that fits the business records exception, including a record made after some other record in which the later record incorporates data drawn from the earlier record.

  - Multiple originals exist when the parties intend each to have equal dignity (contracts executed in multiple counterparts; sales slips given to buyer and kept by seller).

- Duplicates, meaning primarily machine-made copies, have special status under the Federal Rules, and are almost as admissible as originals.

- The doctrine applies in two common situations:

  - Substantive law forces a party to prove content of original (as suits on written contracts where Parol Evidence Rule has this effect, barring testimony or other evidence outside the written document if offered to "alter" or "vary" the contract).

  - Party strategy may require proof of content, as in cases in which someone relies on a business record under FRE 803(6) to prove the truth of statements found therein.

- The doctrine does not apply in the following situations:

  - Matters incidentally recorded may be proved in other ways, meaning that the mere existence of a writing does not require its use to prove what it says, so (for example) a party may prove payment by testifying that he paid even if he has a receipt that could be used to prove the point (an admission by the other side or a business record).

  - Absence of content may be proved without the document (one could testify that an item was not on a list without producing the list itself).

  - Matters other than content may be proved without the document, such as preparation or execution of a document.

- Recordings are rarely required (even when the doctrine reaches them) because usually the purpose is to prove what was said, not the content of the recording itself, so recordings usually fit the category of matters incidentally recorded.

- Photographs too are rarely required (even when the doctrine reaches them) because usually the point is to prove the appearance of the thing or person depicted, and not the content of the photograph itself, but x-rays must sometimes be produced because nobody saw what an x-ray depicts (although experts can sometimes testify on the basis of x-rays without producing them) and surveillance photographs must be produced if there is no eyewitness.

- Duplicates are almost as admissible as originals in Rules jurisdictions under FRE 1003, except that duplicates are excluded when:

  - Genuine question is raised as to the authenticity of original, although this outcome is often anomalous and duplicates should be admitted when they shed light on authenticity of originals and when originals are unavailable.

  - Unfairness would result from admitting a proffered duplicate that omits parts of the original needed for cross-examination, or has significant gaps or omissions, or if the proponent has lost or destroyed the original in bad faith, or actually has and could offer the original.

- Production is excused in these situations:

  - The original was lost or destroyed, except when proponent was acting in bad faith;

  - The original was not obtainable by court process, but when a copy can be produced (as by deposition), the copy should be offered;

  - The original is in the possession of opponent who knew its contents would likely be proved; or

  - The writing relates to a collateral matter, rather than a central issue, particularly if production would be hard and content is simple.

- No degrees of secondary evidence are recognized in modern formulations of the doctrine, meaning that when production is excused the doctrine does not prefer one form of proof over another (testimony may be used even if a compared copy is available).

- Public records may be proved by certified copy, and originals are not required.

- Summaries of voluminous writings may be offered, provided that the writings are made available to the other side, they would be admissible, and the summaries are shown to be accurate.

- Judges decide most questions on application of the doctrine, but juries decide questions relating to the existence and authenticity of writings and whether other evidence correctly reflects content.

A. INTRODUCTION

The Best Evidence Doctrine forces the proponent seeking to prove the content of a writing to produce the writing itself. The root idea is that the writing itself is more reliable than testimony describing what it contains. The doctrine does not apply across the board. For instance, a party wishing to prove what kind of gun was used in a crime may offer testimonial accounts, even if the gun itself is available and can easily be produced. The doctrine also admits of exceptions: Most importantly, it does not require the proponent to produce a writing that is unavailable through no fault of the proponent herself.

1. Rationale

The main reasons for the Best Evidence Doctrine are three in number. First, writings occupy a central position in the law, which justifies more stringent proof requirements. Second, other evidence is distinctly inferior when the content of a writing is what counts Third, producing the writing itself helps insure completeness and provides some assurance against forgery or fraud.

2. Traditional Versus Modern Formulation

Traditionally the doctrine reached only writings, and traditionally it required production of the **original** when the purpose was to prove content. In its modern formulation, the Federal Rules change the doctrine in two important ways.

a. Expanded reach (recordings and photographs)

Traditionally the doctrine did not reach recordings of conversations or statements, or photographs. But recordings share with writings the quality of being permanent and accurate memorials of words (writings preserve written words; recordings preserve spoken words), and the Federal Rules extend the Best Evidence Doctrine to recordings. In many respects, photographs too are permanent and accurate memorials, not usually of words but of people, places, and things. In another departure from tradition, the Federal Rules extend the Best Evidence Doctrine to photographs and videos. See FRE 1001 and 1002.

b. Reduced bite (copies admissible)

Traditionally, producing a writing meant producing the original of a writing. But the Federal Rules make **"duplicates"** (virtually any machine-made copy) almost as good as the original. See FRE 1003.

3. Proving Content

The key concept is that the Best Evidence Doctrine applies when the purpose is to prove the **content of a writing** (or, under the Rules, a recording or photograph), but the doctrine does not apply when the purpose is to prove some act, event, or condition outside the writing, even if the writing *could be used* to prove the act, event, or condition. This point is covered in more depth under the heading "Matters Incidentally Recorded" below.

☞ EXAMPLE AND ANALYSIS

Suppose Peter sues Donna on a promissory note. Donna claims that she paid off the note. She is prepared to testify that she personally handed over to Peter the cash that was necessary to pay off the note, and she has a receipt for the cash signed by Peter. Must she offer the receipt, or can she testify to the fact of payment?

The answer is that she does not need to offer the receipt and can testify that she paid off the note to Peter. When she testifies to her action in handing Peter the cash, she is not proving the content of a writing. Instead she is proving payment, and for this reason the Best Evidence Doctrine does not require her to offer the receipt. Of course she *can* offer it: Any hearsay objection would be overcome because the receipt is Peter's *admission* that he was paid. And if Donna chose to prove payment by using the receipt, then the Best Evidence Doctrine would require her to offer the receipt itself. If she tried to testify, "Peter gave me a receipt indicating payment in full," a Best Evidence objection would be sustained (unless the receipt were unavailable through no fault of her own). See *Timmons v. Royal Globe Ins. Co.*, 653 P.2d 907 (Okla. 1982) (admitting testimony to show payment; receipt not required).

---

4. Excused Nonproduction

The Best Evidence Doctrine is flexible in operation and does not require production when production is impossible. When writings (or recordings or photographs in jurisdictions where the doctrine applies to them) have been lost or destroyed without fault by the proponent, and in some other situations of unavailability, other proof is admissible after all, including testimony describing content.

5. Collateral

Sometimes writings are only marginally relevant in cases, and for one reason or another they are hard to produce. Particularly when these conditions are met *and* the writing is relatively simple in nature, courts often excuse nonproduction of the original and accept other proof of content, and often they label such writings as "collateral" to the case.

B. DEFINITIONS (SCOPE AND COVERAGE)

As noted above, traditionally the doctrine applies only to writings, but the Federal Rules extend coverage to recordings and photographs as well.

1. Writings

The doctrine reaches writings of all sorts. Thus it applies to "legally operative" documents like contracts and "formally kept" material like business records, and it *also* applies to essentially *all* written material. Thus the doctrine applies to personal letters, memoranda, or notes, and to books and articles. In other words, the concept of "writings" is broadly interpreted.

Technically, it reaches anything that contains or memorializes numbers, letters, or words. See FRE 1001(a) (writing means "letters, words, or numbers, or their equivalent, set down in any form").

a. Computer output

In its modern form, the Best Evidence Doctrine reaches computer output, meaning hardcopy printouts and the content of disks. See FRE 101(b)(6) ("a reference to any kind of written material . . . includes electronically stored information").

b. Inscribed chattels

The root concept of "writing" reaches what is traditionally described as inscribed chattels, such as road signs ("No Right Turn") and labels ("Green Giant Peas"), and FRE 1001(a) clearly embraces such material. But courts often decline to require production of such items, describing them as "inscribed chattels" rather than "writings." Alternatively, courts treat such inscriptions as "collateral" rather than central, or decline to require production because the object cannot be had. See generally *United States v. Duffy*, 454 F.2d 809 (5th Cir. 1972) (government need not produce shirt found in trunk of car bearing laundry mark with initials D–U–F because court had discretion with inscribed chattels, the writing involved here was simple, and its terms "were by no means central" in the case). See also FRE 1004(2) (other evidence admissible if original unavailable) and (4) (other evidence admissible if writing "is not closely related to a controlling issue").

2. Recordings

As noted above, traditionally the doctrine did not reach recordings of conversations or statements, but the Federal Rules extend the doctrine to recordings. See FRE 1001(b) (recordings include "letters, words, or numbers, or their equivalent" captured by mechanical or electronic recording); FRE 1002 (doctrine applies to proving content of "recording").

3. Photographs

As also noted above, traditionally the doctrine did not reach photographs either, but the Federal Rules extend the doctrine to photographs. See FRE 1001(c) (defining photographs); FRE 1002 (doctrine applies to proving content of "photograph").

4. Definition of "Original"

Since production of a writing meant production of the original at common law, it was important to know the difference between originals and copies.

Under the Rules, the distinction is less important because machine-made copies are commonplace, and such "duplicates" are almost as admissible as originals under FRE 1003. Even under the Rules, however, it is sometimes important to distinguish originals from duplicates.

a. Greatest relevance

What constitutes an "original" depends on the nature of the claim or defense, surrounding circumstances, party intention, and substantive legal principles. See FRE 1001(d) (original is "the writing or recording itself" and any counterpart "intended to have the same effect").

☞ EXAMPLE AND ANALYSIS

Dora is a government employee who is prosecuted for submitting false expense claims in the form of credit card slips that actually reflect vacation expenditures. Commonly, credit card transactions generate either two or three slips: The top slip is printed by machine or by hand (the customer physically signs this slip, and the seller keeps it); next is a yellow "carbonless copy" given to the customer; there may be a third "bottom copy" that the seller retains.

If Dora submitted her yellow copy in claiming reimbursement, *that* is the original in her criminal trial. The reason is that this copy was the one actually used in the transaction, and it is what Dora invited the government to rely on.

b. Letters and telegrams

If the purpose is to prove the message delivered at the distant end, the letter or telegram *delivered to the recipient* is the original. If the purpose is to prove what the sender meant to say or what the sender thought, the original of a telegram is the version given to the telegraph company. See *Hall v. Pierce*, 307 P.2d 292 (Or. 1957) (for this purpose, original of letter is copy retained by sender).

c. Photographs

Any print from the original negative is an original photograph under FRE 1001(d). A print made from a print is a duplicate under FRE 1001(e).

d. Computer output

Any output from a computer that is readable by sight and shown to be accurate is an original. See FRE 1001(d).

e. Business records

When a business record is offered for its truth, the hearsay exception may apply even if the record incorporates data from other records maintained within the business, and indeed the exception may apply to a whole chain of entries. See FRE 803(6). Here application of the Best Evidence Doctrine depends on which record or entry is to be proved. Occasionally, however, the doctrine is interpreted to require the proponent to offer the entry that has the more complete information, in preference to a more abbreviated summary.

f. Multiple originals

Often documents are executed in multiples to provide records to everyone involved in the transaction. Thus written contracts are often executed in multiple counterparts (with appropriate language in the agreement itself stipulating that it is being "executed in four counterparts"), and credit card transactions generate two or three slips at the point of purchase. In this situation, each counterpart can constitute an original if the parties so intend. See FRE 1001(d) (original includes "any counterpart intended to have the same effect").

5. Definition of "Duplicate"

The Federal Rules, which make "duplicates" almost as admissible as originals, defines "duplicate" broadly to reach any machine-made copy. That means essentially any copy that does not require human faculties to comprehend the original and recreate it. The definition reaches the common product of all modern office copiers, as well as old-style carbon copies. See FRE 1001(e) (defining duplicate).

a. Authentication (laying the foundation)

In offering a duplicate, the proponent must show not only that the item is a machine-made copy, but that it is a copy that was made from an original that is itself authentic. The judge decides the first point (whether the item is a machine-made copy) and ordinarily the jury decides the second (whether it was made from an authentic original), since authentication issues are generally for juries to decide under FRE 901.

b. Rerecordings

A rerecording, meaning essentially a recording made from another recording (whether the original is a tape or disk, to refer to older technology, or takes the form of electronic memory typically captured on a "memory stick" or "flash drive" to refer to more current technology) qualifies as a duplicate. Since the rerecording process can be used to edit, enhance, or otherwise alter the original, ordinarily testimony by the preparer is necessary in order to establish that the rerecording accurately captures the substance of the original. A rerecording can qualify as a duplicate even if it is enhanced to modified by use of technology that eliminates background noise or augments parts of the sound spectrum to increase audibility. A transcript of a recording is not a duplicate, however, if it is prepared by a human being who listens to the recording and transcribes it into writing.

c. Photographs

Prints made from an original negative are themselves originals, but enlargements or miniatures, or prints made from prints, are duplicates. See FRE 1001(4).

C. THE BEST EVIDENCE DOCTRINE IN OPERATION

The Best Evidence Doctrine applies in two common situations, but does not apply in several others in which one could easily (but mistakenly) think it does.

1. Substantive Law Requires Proof of Content

Sometimes substantive principles require a party who relies on a particular claim or defense to prove the content of a writing, or the content of a recording or photograph. In a libel case, for example, the proponent must prove the content of the defamatory writing, and in a suit on an integrated written agreement the Parol Evidence Rule requires the claimant to prove the content of the writing. In a suit alleging copyright infringement based on unauthorized use or distribution of a photograph, substantive law requires the claimant to prove the content of the photograph in question.

☞ EXAMPLES AND ANALYSIS

1. Fred and Gordon enter into a written sales agreement, in which Fred is to sell his old Harley–Davidson motorcycle to Gordon for $8000. The applicable Statute of Frauds states that a sales contract for a price exceeding $1000 must be in writing. Gordon gets the motorcycle, but later Fred brings suit, claiming that Gordon paid only half the price at the time of delivery and still owes $4000. Fred proposes to testify to the substance of their agreement, but Gordon raises a Best Evidence objection.

   Fred should be required to produce the writing (or a satisfactory excuse for nonproduction). The Statute of Frauds requires a writing in this situation, so the content of any such writing is in issue in this case. The Best Evidence Doctrine requires the party who would prove this content to produce the writing itself (or a satisfactory excuse for nonproduction).

2. Lamar is tried for giving perjured testimony to a Committee of the United States Senate. To prove the substance of his testimony, the government calls Rogers as a witness. Rogers was chief counsel to the Committee, and he heard Lamar testify. Lamar objects, "the government must offer the transcript, since it is the Best Evidence of what Lamar said and the substantive law requires the government to prove what he said."

The objection should be overruled. There is no doubt that a verbatim transcript is more reliable as proof of what Lamar said than the memory of a witness who heard him, but that is not the test. The crime of perjury involves "giving false statements under oath," not "making a transcript that contains falsehoods," so the substantive law does not force the government to prove the transcript. Rogers can testify. See *Meyers v. United States,* 171 F.2d 800 (D.C. Cir. 1948) (testimony may be used; transcript not required; dissent argues that government should be forced to offer transcript because it is more reliable proof).

2. Party Strategy Requires Proof of Content

Sometimes content must be proved because a litigant simply chooses to rely on the content of a writing (or, in a Rules jurisdiction, a recording or photograph) to prove some point in the case. If, for example, a party chooses to prove a medical diagnosis by relying on records prepared by a physician, which may fit the business records exception in FRE 803(6) (reaching records reflecting "diagnoses"), the records themselves must be offered. In most imaginable settings, no substantive rule of law would require a party to prove a diagnosis in this way, and expert testimony is the usual method of proof. But if a party chose to prove the diagnosis by means of the record, the Best Evidence Doctrine applies and the record must be produced.

☞ EXAMPLE AND ANALYSIS

Suppose Rogers (from the prior example) did not hear Lamar testify, and instead familiarized himself with what Lamar had said by reading the transcript of proceedings. The government calls Rogers to testify against Lamar, who again argues that "under the Best Evidence Doctrine the government must offer the transcript."

This time the objection should be sustained. This time the government *is* trying to prove the content of the transcript since it is the only basis for the testimony by Rogers. While substantive law does not require proof of the transcript, the government has chosen to rely on the transcript as the basis of its proof (rather than calling some member of the Committee who listened to Lamar). The Best Evidence Doctrine requires production of the transcript (or an excuse for nonproduction).

It is worth remembering that a transcript of testimony, if prepared in the usual way by a reporter who was present and listened to the proceedings (or recorded them and later prepared the transcript from the recording), is itself *hearsay* if offered to prove what was said at the proceedings. The reason is that the transcript is the reporter's written out-of-court statement that in effect asserts that Lamar actually spoke all the words attributed to him at the time. But any hearsay objection would likely be overcome by resort to the public records exception contained in FRE 803(8), or by resort to various statutes, which typically provide that transcripts may be used to prove the content of judicial (and often legislative) proceedings.

---

3. Matters Incidentally Recorded

The mere fact that a writing exists (or, in a Rules jurisdiction, a recording or photograph) and could be used to prove the point in question does not mean that it must be used for this purpose. The common way of making this point is to say that the Best Evidence Doctrine does not require use of a writing to prove "matters incidentally recorded." Suppose, for example, that under-cover officers listen to and record a conversation among drug dealers. Even in a Rules jurisdiction where the doctrine includes "recordings," the officers may testify to the substance of that conversation, and they may do so even though they also have a recording of the conversation. And consider the situation in which Rogers (in the first version of the example involving Lamar's testimony before the Senate Committee) actually heard Lamar's testimony and then testified to what Lamar said. It would be correct to say that the transcript of the Committee proceedings setting forth Lamar's testimony represents another example of "matters incidentally recorded." That is so even though the transcript is a better and more convincing record of what Lamar said than any human recollection could provide, including the testimony given by Rogers.

4. Other Situations in Which Doctrine Does Not Apply

There are several other situations in which the Best Evidence Doctrine does not apply, even though on first glance one might think it does.

a. Proving absence of content

When the point is to show that a certain entry or certain words do **not** appear in a writing, the proponent may offer testimony without producing the writing. See *United States v. Madera*, 574 F.2d 1320 (5th Cir. 1978) (admitting testimony that a particular auto body shop was not listed in a phone directory). To the extent that absence of an entry might be taken as a statement that something didn't happen or didn't exist, several hearsay exceptions pave the way for such proof. See FRE 803(7) (absence of business entry); FRE 803(10) (absence of public entry). It is also plausible to argue that failure to mention something isn't hearsay at all because not saying something is inaction that lacks any assertive purpose. See Chapter 3, Sec. D5, supra. It may still be plausible to argue that silence or the absence of mention means something. For example, the fact that an auto body shop was not listed in a phone directory is some indication that there is no such auto body shop, even though the compilers of the directory had no purpose in suggesting as much. (The reason is that any such shop would likely see to it that its name is listed in the phone directory, and if the name does not appear, that is some indication that there is no such shop.)

b. Proving matters other than content

Offering documents (or photographs or recordings) typically requires foundation testimony that alludes to content. Often such testimony shows that a particular person prepared or signed or delivered the document in question, or verifies the existence of the document in some way. Such testimony, offered to prove such points, is not considered proof of content and does not itself offend the Best Evidence Doctrine.

D. RECORDINGS, PHOTOGRAPHS, X–RAYS

The foregoing points apply to recordings and photographs (including x-rays and other kinds of medical images) in Rules jurisdictions where the Best Evidence Doctrine covers such material. But recordings and photographs bring a few special problems and some surprises, and application of the doctrine is worth a further look in these settings.

1. Recordings

Only rarely does the Best Evidence Doctrine require production of recordings. The substantive law might force a party to introduce a recording, but only in an unusual case like a claim of copyright infringement involving recorded material. Party strategy would require use of a recording only if a party *chose* to prove a statement or conversation by means of a recording, or by testimony from someone who had listened to a recording but not to the conversation itself.

a. Incidentally recorded

The mere fact that a recording exists, even if it is the most reliable proof of a statement or conversation, does not mean a party must offer the recording. Instead, the party may offer testimony by someone who heard the statement or conversation, and the situation is subject to the rule on matters "incidentally recorded."

b. Transcripts

When recordings are offered, problems in audibility often lead to the use of transcripts to help the trier understand the recording. The proponent must show that the transcript is accurate, and disagreements may lead the parties to offer competing transcripts of important segments. Transcripts are *not* the Best Evidence, and usually courts admit them with instructions that the recording itself controls in case of any discrepancy, collecting them before deliberations begin.

2. Photographs

The Best Evidence Doctrine seldom requires production of photographs. Only rarely does substantive law force a party to prove a photograph (one example is an infringement suit involving photographs). Party strategy would require production of a photograph, but only if a party *chose* to prove a point by this means, as might happen if a prosecutor used surveillance pictures to show that defendant committed a robbery or other crime, rather than relying on eyewitness accounts. Still the mere fact that photographs exist does not require a party to rely on them. In accident litigation, for example, one may prove the appearance of the scene or wreckage by offering testimonial accounts rather than photographs, even if the latter would be in some senses more informative or reliable.

3. X-rays

Since x-rays capture images that no human eye can see, and the same is true of many other kinds of medical imaging techniques, faithful application of the Best Evidence Doctrine would require production of x-rays and other medical images whenever a radiologist or other expert uses them as a basis for testimony. But the ACN to FRE 1002 observes that an expert may "give an opinion based on matters not in evidence" under FRE 703, and concludes that FRE 1002 is accordingly "limited" in its application. It seems, then, that it is proper to offer expert testimony describing and interpreting x-rays and other medical images, and at least arguably a party can offer expert testimony based on x-rays or other medical imaging techniques without producing the x-rays or images themselves. It seems, however, that one who offers testimony that actually describes or evokes x-rays or other medical images as part of the expert's presentation should be required to produce them produce them as the Best Evidence of their actual content.

E. ADMISSIBILITY OF DUPLICATES

In Rules jurisdictions, FRE 1003 significantly modifies common law tradition. This provision opens the door by providing that a duplicate is admissible "to the same extent as an original" unless "a genuine question is raised" as to the authenticity of the original or it would be "unfair" under the circumstances to admit the duplicate.

1. Duplicates

FRE 1003 makes machine-made copies *almost* as acceptable as originals, and thus shifts away from requiring originals toward requiring originals or duplicates. Don't forget, however, that the party who offers a writing (or in Rules jurisdictions a writing, recording, or photograph) must *authenticate* what is offered, and this point holds true whether the party is offering what he says is the original or what he says is a duplicate. In other words, the offering party must show that what he is placing in evidence is really what he claims that it is, whether original or duplicate. See FRE 901.

2. The Genuine Question Proviso

Under FRE 1003, a duplicate is excludable if a "genuine question" is raised as to the authenticity of the original. The purpose is to require production of the supposed original so the trier of fact may examine the actual document. Applying this exception may lead to anomalous results.

a. Authenticity of original contested

If a writing is offered as a duplicate and the other side offers evidence that the source of the copy is not the original, a genuine question on authenticity of the original has been raised. Excluding the proffered duplicate would deprive the fact-finder of evidence (the claimed duplicate itself) bearing on this very question. If two differing documents are available and both are offered, one as the original and the other as a duplicate, both should be admitted on suitable foundation. The aim of the Best Evidence Doctrine, which is to exclude secondary evidence in preference for writings themselves, is not violated if both forms of proof are offered.

b. Contest over existence of original

If a writing is offered as a duplicate and the opponent offers evidence that there never was an original, again it seems that a genuine question on the authenticity of the source of the copy has been raised. Here production of the original may be required, but if it is unavailable through no fault of the party offering the duplicate, then the duplicate may be admitted as other evidence of content under FRE 1004.

3. Unfair

A duplicate may be excluded on grounds of fairness under FRE 1003 in several situations. The ACN suggests that this clause requires exclusion if only part of the original is reproduced in the duplicate and the remainder is needed for cross-examination. Also, it seems that a duplicate may be excluded if it has gaps or omissions, or if the party offering the duplicate has lost or destroyed the original in bad faith, or actually has and can offer the original.

F. PRODUCTION OF ORIGINAL EXCUSED

When the original writing (or, in Rules jurisdictions, the recording or photograph) cannot be had, production is excused and other evidence of content may be offered. See FRE 1004.

1. Originals Lost or Destroyed

Loss or destruction of originals paves the way for other evidence, unless the proponent "lost or destroyed them in bad faith." See FRE 1004(a).

2. Original Not Obtainable

If originals cannot be obtained by judicial process, other evidence is admissible. See FRE 1004(b). When originals are in the possession of nonparties, ordinarily judicial process leads to a deposition, with copies (rather than originals) attached to the transcripts as exhibits. While a wooden reading of the Rule might suggest that **any** other evidence is admissible (because the "original" cannot be produced), the preferable and apparently intended result is to require proof by means of the copies produced in this manner. Such copies, if made by ordinary office machines, will also qualify as "duplicates" for purposes of the Best Evidence Doctrine.

3. Original in Possession of Opponent

When the original is in the possession of a party who knew the contents would likely be proved, the other side may offer other evidence of content. See FRE 1004(c) (if one side is "on notice" that contents would be "a subject of proof," other evidence admissible).

4. Collateral Matters

If the content of a document is not closely related to critical issues in the case, other evidence may be offered, particularly if production would be difficult and the writing is simple in nature. See FRE 1004(d) (other evidence admissible if writing, recording, or photograph "is not closely related to a controlling issue"). See ACN to FRE 1004(d) (citing examples of newspaper in a suit for the price of publishing an ad, and streetcar transfer where plaintiff claims status as passenger).

5. Judge Decides

The court (not the jury) decides whether production of originals is excused, and the issue is one of the admissibility of evidence. See FRE 104(a) (questions of admissibility are for judge) and 1008 (when admissibility of other evidence of content depends on "fulfillment of a condition of fact," the judge decides).

6. Degrees of Secondary Evidence

When production is excused, common law tradition recognized a preferred hierarchy of proof, called "degrees" of secondary evidence. For example, typically the proponent had to offer a copy that had been compared with the original in preference to a testimonial account of the original, and there were other degrees and preferences. The modern approach does not recognize "degrees" of secondary evidence. If the writing, recording, or photograph need not be produced, the proponent may choose the method of proof. See ACN to FRE 1004 (stating that Rule recognizes no degrees of secondary evidence).

G. OTHER EXEMPTIONS

Through special adjustments, the Best Evidence Doctrine accommodates proof of public records and summaries and allows proponents who would prove content to take advantage of concessions made by adverse parties.

1. Public Records

The easiest means of proving public records is to offer certified copies, partly because it is often hard to get originals and insisting on them would work a hardship on public officials, and partly because certified copies are "self-authenticating," which means they need no foundation witnesses. See FRE 902, as discussed in Chapter 12.

a. Copies acceptable

Answering the special needs in this area (and complementing the self-authentication doctrine for public records) is a feature of the Best

Evidence Doctrine that says copies of public records are as acceptable as originals. See FRE 1005 (inviting proof by "copy, certified as correct in accordance with rule 902").

b.   Reach of doctrine

This special accommodation applies to all public records (state, federal, and local), and also to filed and recorded documents (deeds and mortgages, land sale contracts, and similar things).

c.   Compared copies

Proof by certified copy almost always means offering what amounts to a machine-made duplicate. But FRE 1005 is actually broader than FRE 1003 (which makes duplicates *almost* as admissible as originals), because FRE 1005 allows proof of public records by means of a compared copy—one that is verified as "correct" by someone who has "compared it with the original"—which would *not* qualify as a "duplicate" under FRE 1003. FRE 1005 would also pave the way to admit a handmade copy of a public record, which also would not qualify as a "duplicate" under FRE 1003.

d.   Effects of FRE 1005

In Rules jurisdictions, one effect of FRE 1005 is to encourage proof by certified copy or compared copy. Such proof may be offered without accounting for the original. And such proof is not subject to the sorts of objection that FRE 1003 allows for other "duplicates" (exclusion where "genuine question" is raised about authenticity of original, or for reasons of fairness). Another effect of FRE 1005 is to *prefer* proof by certified copy or compared copy. The final sentence of that provision states that *if* such a copy cannot be obtained, *then* other proof may be used.

2.   Summaries

When writings are too voluminous to be conveniently examined in court, the proponent may use written or testimonial summaries instead, subject to certain restrictions. See FRE 1006 (voluminous writings may be presented by means of "chart, summary, or calculation," provided that originals or duplicates are made available "for examination or copying"). While FRE 1006 reaches recordings and photographs too, and contemplates charts and calculations as well as summaries, almost always these issues are associated with writings and with summaries offered in their stead.

a.   Requirements for summaries

Because of concerns relating to accuracy and distortion (essentially hearsay issues), and because of the general policy of the Best Evidence

Doctrine to insist that content be proved by use of the written documents themselves, summaries are admissible as substitutes for the documents only on three conditions.

i. Originals made available

Summaries are admissible only if the originals have been first made available for inspection and copying. This precaution helps assure that opposing parties have an adequate opportunity to refute, impeach, or otherwise attack summaries as inaccurate or distorted.

ii. Writings admissible

Summaries are admissible only if, and to the same extent as, the writings themselves are admissible. Hence the proponent of a summary must show the writings in question are admissible. Typically writings are offered as proof of what they assert, so they are admissible only if they fit exceptions to the hearsay rule, the two most common being the exceptions for business records and public records. See FRE 803(6) and (8).

iii. Authenticating summaries

The proponent who offers a summary must show not only that the summary fairly and accurately captures the original writings, but that the original writings themselves are what the proponent claims.

b. Summaries as evidence

When summaries are offered *in lieu of* the documents themselves under FRE 1006, the summaries are in fact evidence. Even when the original documents are offered, it still may be wise to admit summaries as evidence under FRE 1006 because necessarily the documents are so voluminous that they cannot be conveniently examined or analyzed in the courtroom setting. But sometimes summaries, charts, or other illustrative material are offered purely for pedagogical purposes, as illustrative or demonstrative material that offers shortcuts to understanding the original writings, in which case FRE 1006 is not involved. In this setting, summaries or charts are not evidence, and the jury may be instructed that in case of any discrepancy the originals should control.

c. Written or testimonial admission

The content of writings may be established by using the written or testimonial admission of adverse parties. See FRE 1007. Oral out-of-court admissions, which generally fit the hearsay exception in FRE 801(d)(2)(A) just as much as written admissions do, are nevertheless not accepted as a substitute for the document itself in proving its content. The reason is that the same complexities that lead to preferring the document itself also suggest that oral admissions are not reliable as proof of content.

H. JUDGE AND JURY

Not surprisingly, many issues affecting the application of the Best Evidence Doctrine are for the judge to decide, since the doctrine largely regulates "admissibility" of evidence. See FRE 104(a) (admissibility questions are for judge to decide). Some issues in applying the Best Evidence Doctrine, however, overlap with or constitute authentication issues, which are viewed as matters of "conditional relevancy," and here the judge plays only a screening role and juries make the actual decision. See FRE 104(b) (juries determine issues of conditional relevancy).

1. Judge–Determined Issues

Judges decide most questions relating to application of the doctrine, including the questions whether an item constitutes a writing (or, in Rules jurisdictions, a recording or photograph), whether it is an original, and whether production of a writing (or recording or photograph) is excused because it is lost or destroyed, beyond reach of process, or relates to a collateral matter. In Rules jurisdictions, the judge decides under FRE 1003 whether a "genuine question" has been raised on the authenticity of the original, and whether admitting a duplicate would be unfair. See FRE 1008.

2. Jury–Determined Issues

Juries decide three major questions relating to Best Evidence issues that are in the nature of issues of authenticity. One is the question whether a writing, the content of which a party seeks to prove, ever existed at all. Another is the question whether some other writing is the original. The third is whether other evidence of contents (such as a duplicate) correctly reflects the original. See FRE 1008.

REVIEW QUESTIONS AND ANSWERS

Question: Why do we have a Best Evidence Doctrine, and what does it cover?

Answer: The Best Evidence Doctrine serves three overlapping purposes. First, it protects the centrality of writings in legal transactions, by imposing stricter proof requirements for written materials. Second, the Best

Evidence Doctrine implements the view that alternative forms of proof, such as testimony by someone who has seen a writing, are distinctly inferior and less reliable when it comes to proving the content of writings. Third, the Best Evidence Doctrine implements the view that completeness and physical appearance are important in proving written material, and requiring production of the writing itself helps insure completeness and provides at least some physical information that may help deter forgery or fraud. In its modern formulation, the Best Evidence Doctrine covers not only writings, but photographs (including films, videotapes, x-rays and other medical images) and recordings.

Question: When does the Best Evidence Doctrine apply?

Answer: The doctrine applies whenever the purpose is to prove content. Sometimes substantive legal doctrine requires the parties to prove content, as is true in libel suits and in contract suits where the Parol Evidence Rule applies. Sometimes party strategy requires proof of content, as is true where someone decides to prove that a patient received some particular medical treatment by resorting to medical records kept by a doctor or a hospital.

Question: What are the main situations where the Best Evidence Doctrine might seem to apply, when actually it does not apply?

Answer: The main situation where the doctrine does not apply is that of "matters incidentally recorded." This phrase describes the situation in which a writing depicts the point or embodies the statement to be proved, but the proponent chooses to offer evidence that does not depend on the writing because the witness has independent knowledge of the point or statement. Thus, an undercover agent who hears a conversation may testify to its substance even though a recording exists, and a doctor may describe the treatment he gave even though he has written records that describe the treatment. Other situations where the doctrine does not apply include proving the absence of content or the absence of a writing, and proving other facts about a writing, such as that the writing was delivered or was executed on a certain date.

Question: What is the status of duplicates under the Best Evidence Doctrine, and how do you tell the difference between duplicates and originals?

Answer: Under the Best Evidence Doctrine in its modern form, duplicates are almost as freely admissible as originals. Essentially a duplicate is a machine-made copy (any copy produced by modern office duplicators), and duplicates are as admissible as originals under FRE 1003 unless a "genuine question" is raised as to the authenticity of the original or it would be "unfair" to use the duplicate. The best way to distinguish between originals and duplicates is to consider the purposes of the proof and the circumstances in which the writings were produced: The original is the writing that is most relevant in light of these considerations. Thus if the point is to prove that someone submitted a false claim, the original is the writing actually submitted to make good on the claim, and if the point is to prove what message was actually given to someone by a written document, the original is the writing that was delivered to that person.

Question: What about photographs and recordings?

Answer: In its modern formulation, the Best Evidence Doctrine applies to photographs and recordings too. But in fact the doctrine seldom requires parties to produce photographs or recordings. The reason is that such materials are rarely made important by substantive principles. One rare instance is the copyright infringement suit, where substantive law might force a party to prove the content of a recording or a photograph if it were the object that was allegedly infringed. Somewhat more often, party strategy makes recordings or photographs important: Someone who wants to prove the content of a conversation, for example, could not introduce testimony by a witness who heard only a recording of the conversation, but would have to produce the recording itself. But when a party has a percipient witness, who heard a conversation or saw the place of an accident, proof by means of testimony is proper even if a recording or photograph exists.

Question: Are there times when production of a writing, recording, or photograph is excused even though the doctrine applies?

Answer: Yes. If a writing, recording, or photograph has been lost or destroyed (through no fault of the party wishing to prove what it contains), then testimonial proof may be offered. The same is true if the writing, recording, or photograph cannot be obtained by judicial process, or if the original is in the hands of the adverse party (who knew its content was to be proved), and if the point to be proved is "collateral" (not central) to the suit.

Exam Tips

Here are some tips on issues relating to best evidence:

Remember that under FRE 1001 the Best Evidence Doctrine applies to writings, recordings, and photographs, and not just to writings (as was true at common law), but that the doctrine does not apply to other things (like guns and parts of automobiles, which may be described without being produced).

The Best Evidence Doctrine applies only when "content" is to be proved, which is true when *substantive law* requires proof of content (as in contract cases, where the Parol Evidence Rule may require proof of a writing) and when *party strategy* makes content important (as in cases where a party relies on a written statement to prove the truth of the matter asserted).

The doctrine does not apply to matters that just happen to be recorded if a witness who saw those matters can testify and describe them.

Under FRE 1003, a duplicate (machine-made copy) is almost as admissible as an original except where a genuine issue is raised as to the authenticity of the original or use of the duplicate would be unfair.

CHAPTER 14

Privileges

CHAPTER OVERVIEW

The key points in this chapter are

- Privileges differ from other evidence rules because they implement extrinsic policies, usually protecting important relationships outside of court.

- Privileges have both *statutory* and *common law* sources.

- Privileges are *substantive* for *Erie* purposes, and federal courts apply state privileges in diversity cases, a point recognized and reinforced in FRE 501.

- Privileges serve both instrumental and privacy interests, encouraging certain conduct and protecting privacy simply because privacy is important in itself.

- The attorney-client privilege protects **confidential communications** between client and lawyer providing **legal services**, and exists to encourage candor by the client so the lawyer can provide good representation.

- The **client is the holder.** A client can be an individual or entity (corporation, partnership, government agency). The privilege applies not only to conversations between a lawyer and her client, but also to conversations between a lawyer and **representatives of her client** (agents of a corporation, accountants retained by the client to help deal with the lawyer, and similar people).

- A lawyer is someone authorized to practice law in any jurisdiction, or someone reasonably believed by the client to be a lawyer.

- The privilege also covers **communications among lawyers** if the client has more than one, and communications with **representatives of the lawyer,** including law office functionaries and outside experts retained to help the lawyer.

- Legal services include but are not limited to litigating lawsuits, but do not include such things as business or investment advice.

- Communication includes oral and written statements, but not matters observed by the lawyer that are not communicative (like the appearance of the client).

- **Confidential** means the communication is kept from outsiders, who are not agents or representatives of the client or lawyer helping in providing legal representation, and the privilege does not apply if the communication is disclosed or intended for disclosure.

- **Joint clients** are covered by the privilege, as happens when two or more people consult a lawyer on a matter of common interest, where the privilege applies against outsiders but not between the clients.

- **Pooled information** is covered by the privilege, if two or more clients, each represented by lawyers, consult on matters of common interest or strategy, and here the privilege applies against outsiders and among the clients as well, so each can block the other from using statements spoken in the course of such cooperative efforts.

- **Corporate clients** are covered by the privilege, and there are different views of the breadth of the privilege here. Under the *Upjohn* standard, which prevails in federal court, the key element is that the agent of the corporation communicated with a lawyer on a point within the subject matter of the agent's duties in the corporation.

- Client identity, which is ordinarily *not* privileged, but may be privileged after all under the *Baird* doctrine if disclosing identity would reveal the substance of communications covered by the privilege (the "confidential communication" version of the client identity exception; there are other versions of this exception, but this is the soundest and prevailing version). Identity is often protected when a client retains a lawyer to make restitution, or report misconduct, or when an outsider seeks the identity of a client to whom specific advice was given. Identity is typically *not* protected when one hires a lawyer to represent another (paying fees does not make one a client) or make a cash payment (although *Baird* itself involved the use of a lawyer to make a cash payment of past-due taxes).

- Lawyer observations relating to the client's mental qualities may be privileged to the extent necessary to protect client confidences.

- Under the prevailing view, **physical evidence** that the client delivers to the lawyer must be turned over to the prosecutor, although the lawyer should not disclose that he received the item in question from the client (the act of turning over the evidence to the client is treated as a communication that is within the privilege).

- Under an exception for **ongoing crimes or frauds**, the privilege does not apply to statements made by the client in furtherance of such undertakings. The party seeking or offering the information must show that the exception applies, and the judge may make an *in camera* inspection when the party seeking disclosure makes an appropriate showing that the exception applies.

- Under the **breach-of-duty** exception, the privilege does not apply when the lawyer sues the client for breach of duty (usually nonpayment of fees) or the client sues the lawyer for breach of duty (usually legal malpractice), and the privilege gives way to the extent necessary to litigate such disputes.

- Under the exception for **claimants through same deceased client**, the privilege does not apply in will contests and other suits to determine who inherits property from a deceased client.

- Under the exception for **lawyer as attesting witness**, the privilege does not apply when a lawyer serves as an attesting witness for her client.

- The privilege **must be claimed** or it is lost, and the lawyer is obliged to claim the privilege on the client's behalf.

- Ordinarily a ruling on a privilege claim **cannot be immediately appealed.** Where a privilege claim is *denied* and the claimant then disobeys an order to disclose and is held in *criminal* contempt, an appeal may be taken, although it is not clear whether a disobedient privilege claimant can obtain review of the *merits* of the privilege decision in this manner if the claimant is a party to the suit in which the privilege claim was made. If the claimant is not a party in that suit, the merits of the privilege claim can be reviewed (because the privilege claimant has no other options for obtaining review). If a disobedient privilege claimant is held in *civil* contempt and is a party in the action in which the claim of privilege was made, ordinarily an appeal from the judgment of civil contempt is not allowed. If a disobedient privilege claimant is *not* a party to the suit, then an appeal from the judgment of civil contempt is allowed, and the merits of the privilege claim can be reached (once again because there is no other option for obtaining review).

- Under the *Perlman* doctrine, the client is sometimes allowed to intervene and appeal from a contempt citation if his lawyer holds the information and refuses to disclose. A ruling *upholding* a privilege claim is ordinarily not appealable.

- The privilege is *waived* by voluntary disclosure or failure to claim when privileged information is sought. Disclosure to outsiders also waives the privilege, but private agreements during discovery may preserve the privilege in cases of inadvertent disclosure, at least as between the parties, and protective orders entered by a court during discovery may also preserve privilege claims in cases of inadvertent disclosure.

- When a client asserts a claim or defense based on privileged communications, many courts treat this tactic as waiving the privilege to the extent necessary to respond to the claim or defense. Such waiver occurs when the client claims that an attorney committed malpractice with respect to certain advice, which waives the privilege to the extent necessary to test this point. Courts split on the question how to handle an insanity defense when the accused has communicated with a psychotherapist hired by the lawyer, but most courts find that waiver occurs to the extent necessary to test the psychotherapist if she testifies.

- The **spousal testimonial privilege** is recognized in criminal cases in about 30 states. In some states, this privilege means that a witness-spouse may refuse to testify against her spouse. In others, this privilege means a party may block his spouse from testifying. In some states, the privilege belongs both to the witness spouse and the party spouse, and either can invoke the privilege (the testimony is allowed only if neither invokes it). In the federal system under the *Trammel* doctrine, the privilege belongs only to the witness spouse.

  - The privilege covers all **testimony**, but it does not block proof of out-of-court statements by one spouse (which may be offered against the other if they fit a hearsay exception and there is an outside witness–someone who is not the other spouse–who can testify to them).

  - The privilege applies only if the witness spouse and the party spouse are *married at the time the testimony is sought,* and common law marriage counts if recognized by the state where the two reside, but not "sham" marriages entered into for fraudulent purposes.

  - Under well-recognized exceptions, the privilege does not apply (a) when one spouse is charged with a crime or tort against the other, the minor child of either, or the property of the other, or (b) the spouses are joint participants in a crime.

- The **marital confidences privilege** is recognized almost everywhere in both civil and criminal cases, and it covers confidential communications between husband and wife during marriage.

  - Under a traditional broad view, both spouses hold the privilege for all confidential communications, and can thus refuse to disclose and prevent the other from disclosing what either said. Under a narrower view, each spouse holds the privilege only for what he or she said.

  - When one discloses without the consent of the other, the latter may still assert the privilege in legal proceedings.

  - This privilege covers, for all time, **communications uttered in confidence** during marriage, but not **noncommunicative** conduct.

- The parties must be married at the time of the communication, and common law marriage counts if recognized in the state of residence. Some states also extend the privilege to same sex couples in civil unions or domestic partnerships.

- There are exceptions for suits involving familial or spousal crimes or torts, and for statements relating to ongoing or future crimes in which both spouses are participating.

- The **physician-patient privilege** rests on statutes that exist in most states. Coverage varies, but the privilege always applies to confidential statements by patient to doctor for purposes of treatment, and sometimes also to information gleaned by the doctor from examining the patient.

  - Statements made in the presence of family members who speak for or assist the patient are privileged, but statements intended for disclosure to outsiders are not.

  - Exceptions severely limit the utility of the privilege. The important ones include a **patient-litigant exception** that applies when the patient puts his physical condition in issue as part of a claim or defense, and when the patient undergoes a court-ordered physical examination.

- The **psychotherapist-patient privilege** grew out of the physician-patient privilege, but is now better accepted, especially after being recognized in the Supreme Court's 1996 decision in *Jaffee v. Redmond* (where the court applied it to a clinical social worker). This privilege too is statutory. The privilege covers statements uttered in confidence to a psychotherapist in the course of treatment, whether in an individual or group setting.

  - The privilege applies to conversations with psychiatrists and psychologists, and under the lead of *Jaffee* the privilege may be expanded to cover others who render psychotherapeutic services.

  - In what amounts to offshoots or extensions of this privilege, some states recognize a rape counselor privilege as well.

  - Exceptions mean that the basic psychotherapist-patient privilege does not apply where the patient (or someone acting for the patient) relies on her mental or emotional condition as an element in a claim or defense (as in criminal cases where the accused claims insanity or another mental status as a defense), and the exception gives way in the case of court-ordered examinations, at least to the extent necessary to serve the underlying purpose of ordering the exam in the first place.

- The **clergy-penitent privilege** covers confidential communications by a person seeking spiritual counseling from a member of the clergy of any organized religion (but not "mail-order" or "self-proclaimed" ministers).

- A **social worker privilege** exists by statute in many states, covering confidential communications with social workers.

- The **journalist-source privilege** provides qualified protection for the identity of confidential sources, and sometimes sweeps more broadly to protect the work product of the journalist.

  - The privilege is subject to a balancing standard that weighs litigation need against the policy of encouraging a free press.

- The privilege often gives way in criminal cases when the journalist has information needed by the defense, and in defamation cases where the information is directly relevant in the case.

  - An **accountant-client privilege** is part of the law in a few states, but not a feature of federal law. The privilege covers confidential communications.

  - A **researcher/academic privilege** is occasionally recognized, but in the *University of Pennsylvania* case the Supreme Court refused to recognize a privilege covering peer review materials relevant to a tenure decision.

  - A qualified **trade secrets privilege** protects trade secrets during litigation, and ordinarily results in protective orders that limit access or use of commercial information (including customer lists, design and manufacturing specifications).

  - A **political vote privilege** entitles a person not to disclose the tenor of his ballot in a political election, but not when the vote was cast illegally.

  - **Required report privileges**, covering materials that citizens and businesses are required to file, are sometimes created by reporting statutes.

  - Governmental privileges cover many different areas:

- A **state secrets** privilege covers military and diplomatic secrets.

- An **official information** privilege covers both deliberative materials used in official decision making and investigative materials used in law enforcement investigations.

    - A qualified **informer's identity** privilege covers the identity of persons who cooperate with law enforcement agents.

    - A **presidential** privilege provides qualified protection for confidential presidential communications.

- The **privilege against self-incrimination** is the only one recognized expressly in the Constitution, and it applies to the state courts as well as a matter of due process under the *Malloy* decision.

    - The privilege protects **persons** and not entities such as corporations, but a corporate custodian of records has no privilege to refuse to produce corporate records even if they incriminate him.

    - The privilege means that a **criminal defendant** cannot be forced to testify, and cannot even be called as a witness by the prosecutor. If he chooses to testify, he must submit to cross-examination related to the direct, but the privilege blocks the prosecutor from going into unrelated matters.

    - The privilege covers **mere witnesses** who are not being prosecuted, but they must take the stand and claim the privilege where the answer to questions would tend to incriminate them.

    - The privilege covers **testimonial proof** (meaning words and communicative acts), but not physical evidence like bodily fluids.

    - The privilege covers **compelled statements** that might tend to incriminate the privilege claimant. It does not apply to statements that are humiliating or embarrassing, or might lead to civil liability. The court determines whether the risk of incrimination is sufficient to support a claim of privilege, and the privilege applies only if there is an actual risk of prosecution.

    - A grant of **use immunity,** under which prosecution is possible but statements compelled from the witness will not be used against him at trial or during investigation, removes the risk of incrimination and the witness must answer. When a statement could incriminate the claimant under both state and federal law, immunity is adequate only if it protects him from prosecution by both sovereigns, and it seems that immunity granted by either must be honored by the other.

- Under the *Griffin* doctrine, no adverse comment or argument can be made about the failure of the defendant in a criminal case to testify, or his claim of the privilege, and the accused is entitled to an instruction directing the jury to draw no inference.

- Under the *Doyle* doctrine, post-arrest, post-warning silence may not be used to impeach the defendant if he testifies in court, but pre-arrest silence and post-arrest, pre-warning silence may be used in this way.

- Argument and inference from a claim of the privilege are permissible in civil cases.

- The privilege does not apply to pre-existing documents. Under the *Doe* doctrine, however, the privilege does prevent the government from asking the accused to produce documents that might incriminate him because the act of production would prove the authenticity of the documents, but production is required if the government can authenticate the documents independently.

- Under the *Grosso* doctrine, the privilege does not block the use against the accused of records he is required by law to keep, provided that there is a valid regulatory purpose, the records are of a kind that the regulated party normally keeps, and the records themselves have acquired "public aspects."

A. INTRODUCTION

In general, privileges differ from other principles of evidence law because their purpose is to implement extrinsic policies, not to regulate the fact-finding process or improve its reliability. Mostly those underlying policies involve protecting important relationships, like those of attorney and client, physician and patient, and spouses. Privileges operate by enabling their holders to block others from proving privileged matters (usually communications), and privileges apply during discovery phases of litigation as well as trial, and thus enable their holders to block attempts to acquire certain kinds of evidence.

1. Statutory Sources

In many states, important privileges (like attorney-client, marital, and psychotherapist-patient) are codified. Where they exist, such statutes control. Sometimes they are detailed, and they vary considerably.

2. Common Law Sources

Under FRE 501, and counterparts adopted in many states, privileges are creatures of common law, at least in the absence of statutes governing the subject. Often the source of important privileges (like attorney-client and marital) is common law tradition.

3. Substantive for *Erie* Purposes

Under FRE 501, federal courts apply state privilege law in connection with substantive issues that are governed by state law (mostly diversity cases), but otherwise apply federal privilege law. In the federal system, the main privileges (attorney-client, marital, and psychotherapist-patient) are the product of uncodified common law tradition.

4. Instrumental and Privacy Rationales

Privilege law serves both instrumental (or utilitarian) interests and privacy interests. The attorney-client privilege, for example, rests on the view that clients will only convey the important facts to their lawyers if confidentiality is respected, and that without such candor the quality of legal representation would suffer (an instrumental or utilitarian interest), and the privilege also rests on the view that what lawyers and clients say to one another in the course of their professional relationship ought not to become a public matter (a privacy interest). The marital confidences privilege reflects the view that privacy in this intimate personal setting is important in fostering a good relationship between spouses, and the view that privacy in this setting deserves protection in its own right. As is true in these examples, both the instrumental and privacy rationales apply to most privileges, including attorney-client and marital. Some courts and theorists emphasize a purely instrumental approach, but others stress privacy concerns.

B. ATTORNEY–CLIENT PRIVILEGE

Every American jurisdiction recognizes an attorney-client privilege covering confidential communications by the client to the lawyer.

1. Purposes

The purpose of the privilege that is most often mentioned is to encourage candor by the client so the lawyer can provide quality legal representation.

Without a privilege, lawyers would feel obliged to warn clients that what they say could be discovered and used by adverse parties, which would discourage candor and diminish the quality of legal services. The privilege also protects privacy as a value in itself, and in criminal cases it has constitutional underpinnings because the Sixth Amendment right of counsel requires at least some protection of confidences.

2. Elements of Privilege

a. Client

The holder of the privilege is the client, who may be a person, organization, or entity (including corporations, unincorporated associations, and governmental units).

i. Becoming a client

One becomes a client by consulting a lawyer for purposes of securing professional legal services, and the privilege applies to preliminary discussions before the lawyer is formally retained or fees are paid. These preliminaries are covered even if the lawyer ultimately declines to go forward by providing legal services.

ii. Representative of client

Corporations and other entities can communicate with a lawyer only through representatives. Also individual clients may *choose* to communicate with lawyers through intermediaries, sometimes because the subject matter benefits from expertise in some form (like accounting). In these situations, the privilege covers communications by such representatives and intermediaries.

b. Lawyer

For purposes of the privilege, a lawyer is a person **authorized to practice law** in some jurisdiction (even if not in the place where the client seeks legal services). Also for purposes of the privilege, a lawyer is any person whom the client *reasonably believes* to be authorized to practice law, including (for example) a law student working in a law office after her second year of law school.

i. Multiple lawyers

If a client consults more than one lawyer, the privilege applies to the client's communications with each, and applies as well to communications among the lawyers while they are rendering legal services.

ii. Representative of lawyer

The privilege covers not only communications with a lawyer, but also communications with representatives of a lawyer, including law office functionaries (people employed to help provide legal services, such as secretaries, clerks, paralegals, and office staff).

iii. Outside experts

The privilege reaches outside experts employed to help the lawyer provide legal services, including accountants, doctors, appraisers, and similar experts. (The privilege does not apply when the client retains such experts on his own.)

c. **Legal services**

The privilege applies when the lawyer provides **legal services**, regardless whether they involve litigation. But the privilege does *not* apply if the attorney acts in another capacity, such as business partner or advisor, investment counselor, accountant, or claims adjuster.

d. **Communication**

The privilege applies to "communications" between client and lawyer, whether written or oral, and to nonverbal conduct that is communicative in nature.

i. Observations

The privilege does not apply to matters observed by the lawyer that are not communicative in nature. Thus lawyers can testify to the appearance or demeanor of a client (whether drunk or injured, for instance), and to the apparent sanity of the client, at least so long as the lawyer does not reveal the substance of communications from the client.

ii. Facts not covered

The privilege applies to communications, not to the facts embodied in communications. Suppose the client is asked in a deposition whether the traffic light was green for him: If he knows, he must answer, and the privilege does not cover his knowledge about the traffic light even if he told his lawyer in confidence what color the light was. On the other hand, if the lawyer is asked what the client said about the light, the privilege applies because in substance the lawyer is being asked what his client told him, and the lawyer should claim the privilege on his client's behalf (assuming that the other requirements of the privilege are satisfied). (The client too could claim the privilege if the questioner asked "what did you tell your lawyer about the color of the traffic light?")

iii. Pre-existing writings

The privilege does not cover pre-existing documents, such as letters from the client to her spouse, merely because she turns them over to her lawyer. On the other hand, the privilege does cover documents that the client *prepares as communications* to the lawyer, such as a letter explaining the facts as the client understands them (assuming once again that the other requirements of the privilege are satisfied).

iv. Lawyer's statements

Although the purpose is to protect what the client says, and not what the lawyer says in response, most courts hold that the privilege applies as well to statements by the lawyer. For the most part, these are likely to be relevant only insofar as they reflect what the client has said, so it would undermine the purpose of the privilege to exclude the lawyer's statements from coverage.

e. Confidentiality

The privilege applies only to communications that are intended to be confidential. The necessary intent may be inferred from the circumstances (such as a private conversation in the lawyer's office). The presence of outsiders who are representatives of the lawyer or client, or communicative intermediaries of the client, or experts hired to help the lawyer provide legal services, does not destroy the requisite confidentiality.

i. Other outsiders

The presence of other outsiders, who are not representatives of client or lawyer or communicative intermediaries or experts hired to help the lawyer, indicates that confidentiality was not intended. Thus a conversation between client, lawyer, and casual friends in a public setting is not within the privilege.

ii. Disclosure intended

If a client intends that her communication with her lawyer be made public, confidentiality is missing and the privilege does not apply, even if disclosure is not made. Thus information given to the attorney for use in tax returns, applications, or reports is generally not privileged.

iii. Voluntary disclosure

If a communication is voluntarily disclosed, and the disclosure is not itself privileged, then disclosure waives the privilege. Thus a wife who consults a lawyer and describes to a friend the statements she made to her lawyer waives the privilege. (Merely talking about the underlying facts of the case, however, does not waive the privilege: If the client tells her lawyer "the traffic light was green" and later talks to her friend about the color of the traffic light, the privilege still applies to what the client told her lawyer. If she tells her friend "I told my lawyer that the light was green," then she has waived the privilege: It is disclosure of the statements made to the lawyer, not disclosure of the facts communicated in such statements, that waives the privilege.) If the wife describes to her husband in confidence the statements she made to the lawyer, however, she does *not* waive her privilege because her statement to her husband is itself privileged (it fits the spousal confidences privilege).

iv. Eavesdroppers

Modern cases have abandoned the older strict view that protection is lost if the communication is overheard by eavesdroppers, in favor of the view that the privilege remains intact if the client took reasonable precautions to maintain confidentiality.

3. Joint Clients

If two or more clients consult one lawyer on a matter of common interest, communications between clients and lawyer are privileged as against outsiders. That means each may assert the privilege with respect to outsiders, but each may also waive the privilege with respect to his own statement, so long as disclosure of that statement does not also disclose the substance of a statement by the other client.

a. Exception for suits by one client against another

Such communications are not privileged if the clients become adversaries in litigation. In this situation, each may offer whatever the other said to the lawyer, even in confidence.

b. Reason for exception

The reason for not applying the privilege in suits between clients is that neither intended to keep the other in the dark (the requisite confidentiality is missing) and there is no basis for deciding which position to honor in case one client wants to invoke the privilege and the other does not.

4. Pooled Defense; Allied Lawyers

When two or more clients are not jointly represented (typically because each has her own lawyer), ordinarily communications shared among the clients and lawyers are not privileged because nobody intends to maintain secrecy (or confidentiality) as against the others. But even separately represented clients often find it in their mutual interest to enter into conversations involving both clients and lawyers for purposes of mapping out cooperative strategies, and this process involves communicating and sharing information with lawyers for other clients. To encourage these collaborative efforts, which may reduce time and expense to the system as well as the clients, courts usually apply the privilege. Usually the situation is described in terms of "pooled defense" (the clients being criminal defendants), but cooperative efforts among separately represented clients occur in other settings, and the term "allied lawyers" describes more broadly what is going on in such cases.

a. Privilege against outsiders

When separately represented clients consult on matters of mutual interest, the privilege applies *as against outsiders.* Thus two defendants and their lawyers may meet and discuss the case, and what they say in confidence in meetings involving all of them, for purposes of mapping out common strategies, is privileged and need not be disclosed to the prosecutor.

b. Privilege among clients

There is little authority on the question whether the privilege applies *as against the other clients* in this setting. The policy of applying the privilege in the situation of pooled defense (or allied lawyers) supports its application here, where one client offers the statement of another against him. Note that in the setting of joint clients (two clients seeing the same lawyer), we *don't* let one invoke the privilege for his own statement when the other wants to use it. But the assumption there is that the clients have unified interests (that's why they have a single lawyer). In the setting of allied lawyers, however, refusing to apply the privilege *among the clients* and insisting that it *only* applies when outsiders seek to offer statements would make it pretty risky for separately represented clients to consult or cooperate. They are already likely to know that they have separate and possibly divergent interests (that's one reason why they have separate lawyers), and getting together to plan joint strategies would be a very dangerous thing if each had to bear the risk that another client would use whatever might be said in such meetings.

c. Common interest

The privilege only applies to conversations among separately represented clients who have some common ground or interest, and agree expressly or by implication to cooperate. It does not apply where separately represented clients and their lawyers engage in adversarial or arm's-length discussions.

5. Corporate Client

The privilege applies to corporate clients, but the extent of application is problematic. With large corporations, there is a fear that extending the privilege to communications by any agent who talks to a lawyer would cast too large a cloak of secrecy around corporate communications that are relevant and otherwise discoverable. The Advisory Committee that drafted the Rules considered this matter "too hot to handle," leaving it to caselaw development, and various standards emerged over time.

a. Control group

The most restrictive standard confines the privilege to communications by people in the corporate managerial hierarchy who have authority to act on any advice given. This group includes officers and directors, and presumably people of lesser rank when they have authority to act on the advice given. See *Philadelphia v. Westinghouse Electric Corp.*, 210 F.Supp. 483, 485 (E.D. Pa. 1962). Some states follow this standard, but the Supreme Court criticized and rejected this standard as too narrow in *Upjohn Co. v. United States*, 449 U.S. 383 (1981), which is the leading modern decision, and the trend is in the direction charted by *Upjohn*. In that decision, the Court said the control group standard was (a) inconsistent with the realities of the modern corporation where middle management may be best situated to talk to lawyers, (b) inadequate in failing to protect information that attorneys need in order to give sound legal advice, and (3) unpredictable in application.

b. Subject matter

Under what came to be known as the "subject matter standard," the privilege for corporate clients applies to communications by any employee relating to subject matter that is within the scope of his job or responsibilities to the corporation. See *Harper & Row Publishers, Inc. v. Decker*, 423 F.2d 487, 491–492 (7th Cir. 1970), *aff'd by equally divided court*, 400 U.S. 348 (1971).

c. *Upjohn* approach

In its 1981 decision in *Upjohn*, supra, the Supreme Court endorsed something very close to the "subject matter" standard. *Upjohn* stressed four factors in defining the scope of the privilege, but the opinion is unusually modest in tone, and it disclaimed any intent to settle the matter comprehensively. *Upjohn* involved an attempt by the government to obtain, by means of subpoena issued in a tax investigation, the responses that employees had given to an internal questionnaire in which upper management, on advice of the corporation's lawyer, sought information on under-the-counter payoffs made to government officials in foreign countries, as well as notes and memoranda relating to those responses. The Supreme Court in *Upjohn* concluded that the privilege applied to this material. Here are the points stressed by the Court:

i.   Obtain legal advice

   Corporate employees made the communications in talks with corporate counsel for the purpose of obtaining legal advice for the corporation, and the employees shared in this purpose. (The privilege *never* applies when people consult lawyers for other purposes, so this element seems essential but is not peculiar to corporate clients, and would apply regardless whether the corporate attorney-client privilege was framed broadly or narrowly.)

ii. Request by superiors

   The employees made the communications at the direction of their superiors in the organization. (Such a request helps show that the purpose really was to secure legal advice, but this element does not seem essential.)

iii. Scope of duties, or subject matter

   The communications related to subject matter within the scope of the duties of the employees. This element is the absolutely critical one, and it is *central* to the *Upjohn* approach. It is similar if not identical to the "subject matter" standard described above.

iv. Treated as confidential

   The corporation (people within the corporation) treated the communications as confidential from beginning to end: They were gathered in private interviews, memorialized in notes and memoranda that were not shown to outsiders and were not circulated broadly in the company to people not connected with the issues at hand. (Of course confidentiality is always a necessary element of privileged communications, but the matter takes on a special dimension in the setting of the corporate client because it is not *just* a matter of keeping the communication confidential as against *outsiders*, and is also a matter of limiting access to the communication *within the corporation itself.*)

d. Mere eyewitnesses excluded

For courts that do *not* take the control group approach, the scope-of-duties or subject matter standard serves the important function of insuring that communications by corporate employees who are "mere eyewitnesses" to events are not covered by the privilege. In a case better known as a landmark in the law of work product, the Court pointedly said that statements to corporate counsel by seamen on a tugboat who had actually seen the events that led to the sinking of the boat were not within the attorney-client privilege, see *Hickman v. Taylor*, 329 U.S. 495 (1947). Excluding communications by mere observers who happen to be company employees seems important as a way of limiting the reach of the privilege.

e. Corporation as holder

The privilege belongs to the corporation, which means that corporate management ultimately decides whether to claim or waive it, and *current* management makes the decision. See *Commodity Futures Trading Comm'n v. Weintraub*, 471 U.S. 343 (1985). Hence former managers, who made statements during their employment that would be covered by the privilege, cannot prevent waiver, and of course lower-echelon employees cannot prevent waiver of the corporate privilege (although former employees and lower-echelon employees may have their own privilege if a lawyer represents both them and the corporation).

f. Mixed reaction

Defenders argue that *Upjohn* provides an important incentive for corporate management to conduct internal investigations for the purpose of complying with legal standards. Critics argue that a privilege broader than that allowed by the control group standard is unnecessary. Agents and employees can be required to give information to counsel as part of their job, and the corporation rather than individuals owns the privilege and can waive it anyway. But an answer to this objection is that corporations often make common cause with agents and employees, so the privilege encourages corporations to ask them to cooperate. Also, it is often the case that the interests of the corporation and its agents mesh, so corporate counsel represents both the entity and the people, which often means that both hold the privilege and each may claim its protection.

g. Shareholder litigation

When shareholders bring derivative or other suits alleging corporate mismanagement, the privilege must be qualified because managers have a conflict of interest and they might shield their own misconduct rather than represent the best interests of the corporation. A landmark decision holds that shareholders can overcome a claim of the privilege by making a showing of good cause. See *Garner v. Wolfinbarger*, 430 F.2d 1093, 1103–1104 (5th Cir. 1970) (court should consider number of shareholders bringing suit and percentage of stock they hold, their bona fides, nature and strength of claims, need for the information, possible criminality of alleged misconduct, whether communication relates to past or future acts, whether it concerns the suit itself, extent to which those seeking information are "blindly fishing" and risks to corporation if trade secrets or other confidential information is disclosed), *cert. denied*, 401 U.S. 974 (1971).

6. Hard Cases

In a number of situations, the privilege gives way to other considerations that have greater importance.

a. Client identity

Ordinarily the identity of the client is not covered by the privilege because it is not a confidential matter and opposing litigants are entitled to know who they are up against. But in exceptional situations the identity of the client is privileged after all: In the landmark case of *Baird v. Koerner*, 279 F.2d 623 (9th Cir. 1960), a client had hired a lawyer to make an anonymous payment of back taxes, in an attempt to minimize potential penalties that might be assessed later. The government sought from the lawyer the identity of his client, but the court concluded that under these circumstances the identity of the client was privileged. There are several versions of the exception crafted in *Baird*, but the prevailing and soundest version holds that identity is protected if disclosure would reveal confidential communications between client and lawyer (the **confidential communications** version). Other versions hold that identity is protected if disclosure would implicate the client in the matter for which he consulted the lawyer (the **legal advice** version), or would be a link that could complete the chain of testimony needed to convict (the **last link** version). This exception holding identity to be privileged is invoked, with varying outcomes, in five recurring situations.

i. Restitution

When retained for purposes of making some form of anonymous payment or restitution, the lawyer seemingly acts merely as messenger or transmitting agent, which does not constitute rendering legal services. Arguably the privilege should not apply, but *Baird* was such a case and the court there held that the privilege did apply.

ii. Reporting illegal conduct

In cases where the lawyer is hired to report misconduct by an undisclosed client or others, courts often find that the lawyer has rendered legal services and apply the privilege (protecting nondisclosure of the client's identity).

iii. Hiring lawyer to represent another

When one person hires a lawyer to represent another (as may happen in drug cases in which lower-echelon participants are arrested, and "drug kingpins," who are involved with these underlings, provide lawyers so underlings do not turn against them), application of the privilege turns on whether the fee payer is a client. Merely paying a fee does not bring the privilege into play, nor is identity protected if payment of the fee is itself part of an ongoing conspiracy, but the privilege does apply if the lawyer acts on related matters for a client who also asks the lawyer to help by representing another, where disclosure of the identity of the fee payer would reveal his confidential communications.

iv. Cash payments

When clients make cash payments exceeding $10,000 for legal services, federal reporting requirements apply, and these overcome claims of privilege on the identity of the client.

v. Clients getting certain advice

When a lawyer is asked to identify a client to whom he gave certain legal advice, giving the name would clearly uncover a confidence under *Baird*, and often the privilege applies.

b. **Other basic facts**

Apart from identity, most other basic facts about the attorney-client relationship are unprivileged, including the following:

i. Fee arrangements

The nature and status of fee arrangements. Courts order disclosure of the fee agreement, identity of the payer, amounts billed, moneys received, and dates and duration of consultation.

ii. Fact of consultation

The fact of consulting a lawyer, and the identity of the lawyer. Here too, courts order disclosure.

iii. Client's whereabouts

Location of the client. Except where the lawyer's knowledge of the client's whereabouts is linked closely to the purpose of consultation, the lawyer's knowledge on this point may be discovered and is not within the privilege.

c. Lawyer's observations of client

Demeanor or mental qualities or characteristics of the client. The privilege applies to **communications** between client and lawyer, and not to observations that a lawyer make about the demeanor (complexion, dress, even sobriety) or mental qualities or characteristics of her client. It is sometimes said that such observations could be made by anybody who saw the client, so the requisite confidentiality is lacking and the privilege does not apply. Lawyers are not often called to testify to such points, but sometimes they are.

i. Physical appearance

Physical appearance of the client. If a lawyer is asked to describe the physical appearance of his client (height, weight, hair color, dress), the privilege does not apply because these matters are not communications (usually they are not confidential either).

ii. Mental or psychological qualities

Mental or psychological qualities. If a lawyer is asked to describe mental or psychological qualities of his client, sorting out privilege issues is difficult because any such assessment is likely to rest at least partly on confidential communications from the client. While the lawyer might testify in purely conclusory terms, adequate testing of his opinion is likely to involve cross-questions on what the client said that forms the basis of the opinion. Some courts try to allow the former while limiting the latter, and others simply exclude such testimony.

d. Evidence delivered to lawyer

Ethical rules bar attorneys from receiving physical evidence from a client or third person for the purpose of concealing or destroying it, and from counseling a client to destroy or conceal evidence. At least in criminal cases, hard problems arise when physical evidence is delivered to a lawyer.

i.   Turn over

The prevailing view is that a lawyer must turn over to the prosecutor any physical evidence received from a client or third party that is either an instrumentality or a fruit of the crime. Some courts require the lawyer to turn over other physical evidence, but usually not documents that are incriminating (like financial records). If the lawyer does not turn over such material voluntarily, the prosecutor may compel production.

ii.   Disclosing source

If a lawyer receives physical evidence from someone other than a client, the lawyer must disclose the source if asked. But if a lawyer obtains physical evidence from her client, usually courts say the source is protected by the privilege, which means that a prosecutor can use that physical evidence only if he can lay the necessary foundation without calling the lawyer or offering proof that the lawyer turned it over. In effect, this approach lets the accused sever his connection to the evidence, but at least it achieves some accommodation of the need to maintain confidentiality and the need for evidence.

iii.   Removing, concealing, altering evidence

If a lawyer removes evidence after being guided to it by her client, not only must the lawyer turn it over to the prosecutor, but a leading decision holds that the attorney may be compelled to disclose the location from which she took it, on the theory that otherwise the attorney's conduct might impede law enforcement efforts by preventing discovery that could otherwise have gone forward. See *People v. Meredith*, 631 P.2d 46, 54 (Cal. 1981) (investigator for lawyer removed remains of murder victim's wallet from burn barrel at defendant's residence, after defendant told lawyer about wallet; investigator was required to disclose where it was found).

iv.   Mere observation

When a lawyer merely sees damaging evidence, this fact does not trigger any disclosure obligation.

7.   Exceptions to Coverage

In the following cases, the attorney-client privilege does not apply.

a. Future crime or fraud

The privilege shields statements relating to past misconduct, but not ongoing or future crimes or frauds. The idea is to help clients obtain legal representation, not to create a mechanism that enables them to continue to behave wrongfully.

i. Two-part test

The party seeking disclosure must make a prima facie showing that (1) the client was engaging in criminal or fraudulent conduct and (2) the attorney's assistance was obtained in furtherance of such activity.

ii. Client knowledge

This exception applies only if the client knew or should have known that the conduct was criminal or fraudulent, and the exception does not apply if the client innocently inquires about the legality or advisability of a possible future course of action.

iii. Past versus ongoing

The line between past and ongoing misconduct may be hard to draw: If a client engages in drug running, copyright violations, or racketeering, for example, and is sued or prosecuted in connection with such activities, advice from a lawyer may relate both to the ongoing activities and to the suit or prosecution. For consultations relating to ongoing criminal activities, the privilege does not apply, but it does apply to consultations about the suit or prosecution. Here courts must balance the conflicting policies as best they can, and no clear answer seems possible.

iv. Applying the crime-fraud exception

The information seeker bears the burden of proving that the crime-fraud exception applies. In *United States v. Zolin*, 491 U.S. 554 (1989), the Supreme Court held that the judge may conduct an *in camera* inspection of the material on which the opposing party claims a privilege, in order to rule on the privilege claim itself, but first the information seeker must adduce facts that support a good-faith belief that the exception applies. This showing may be made ex parte, and the court has discretion whether to undertake the *in camera* examination. This mechanism holds out the prospect of intruding less into privileged material than would occur if the crime-fraud exception actually applies, and prior to full disclosure the privilege claimant is given a chance to be heard. *Zolin* does not answer the question what quantum of evidence is necessary in order to establish that the exception applies, but the traditional rule is that the information seeker must make only a **prima facie showing** (offering evidence sufficient to show the exception applies). When the court undertakes an *in camera* inspection, it seems that the information seeker must show by a preponderance of the evidence that the exception applies.

b. Breach of duty by lawyer or client

In suits by a lawyer against her client (typically to collect fees) and suits by a client against his lawyer (typically for malpractice), the privilege gives way to the extent that communications are relevant to the claims and defenses being raised.

i. Formal charges unnecessary

The exception applies where the client publishes allegations damaging to the attorney, even if no formal charges or proceedings are brought.

ii. Third-party charges

Even though charges brought against the lawyer by a third party cannot be viewed as a waiver of protection by the client, here too lawyers can disclose privileged communications to the extent necessary to defend the charges.

iii. Loss limited by need

In these situations, the privilege gives way only to the extent it covers communications that are relevant in the situation.

c. Claimants through same deceased client

The privilege survives the death of the client, but there is an exception for communications by a deceased client that are relevant in suits between parties claiming through that client. The idea is that in will contests and similar disputes among those claiming to inherit from the client, the court cannot know which of two competing claimants stands in the shoes of the decedent, and his communications may be important in resolving the competing claims. But the privilege continues to apply against "outsiders" who bring claims against the estate, as happens when creditors and tort claimants sue the estate.

d. Lawyer as attesting witness

When the lawyer acts as attesting witness, the privilege does not apply because this role does not involve legal services, and what the lawyer sees is not confidential because it is understood that attesting witnesses testify to the relevant facts (courts sometimes say the situation is covered by an exception to the privilege).

8. Duration of Privilege

The privilege continues to protect confidential communications after the death of a client who is a person, but it is unclear whether the privilege survives the dissolution of a corporate client.

a. Client's death

After the client's death, the attorney (or the personal representative if there is one) may claim or waive the privilege. See *Swidler & Berlin v. United States*, 524 U.S. 399 (1998) (in connection with investigation by independent counsel on question whether various people made false statements or obstructed justice during investigation of White House Travel Office, refusing to recognize exception to attorney-client privilege for communications by client now deceased).

b. Corporate dissolution

While provisions in the proposed Federal Rules would have continued the privilege of a corporate client after dissolution, to be asserted by the successor, trustee, or similar representative, earlier codifications (the original Uniform Rules and the Model Code) provided that the privilege terminated on dissolution.

c. Confession by deceased client

When a deceased client has confessed to a serious criminal act, and another is later charged with having committed the act, arguably the privilege should give way. While the privacy interest of the client extends to the protection of his heirs and successors from difficulties and embarrassment that might come with disclosure, arguably these are at least sometimes less important than the interest of the third person in obtaining evidence that may protect him from an unjust conviction. But see *Swidler & Berlin v. United States*, 524 U.S. 399 (1998) (refusing to recognize exception where statements by deceased client might incriminate others).

9. Claiming the Privilege

The privilege is not self-enforcing, and the privilege holder must claim the privilege when asked to disclose matters covered by the privilege, and failing to claim the privilege on such occasions means that the privilege is lost. When the privilege is claimed, the court (and not a jury) resolves the matter under FRE 104(a) (court determines, among other things, issues of privilege).

a. Lawyer's obligation

While the client holds the privilege, the lawyer has an ethical duty to advise the client of the privilege and to claim it on the client's behalf whenever necessary, and the lawyer's authority to claim the privilege is presumed in the absence of evidence to the contrary.

b. Corporate clients

Corporate management has the duty to assert the privilege on behalf of a corporate client (and here too the lawyer may act on behalf of management).

c. Burdens of persuasion

The burden of claiming the privilege, and of showing that the privilege applies, rests on the person or entity claiming the privilege. If, in the face of a proper claim of privilege, the proponent or information seeker claims an exception applies, it is the proponent or information seeker who bears the burden of showing that the exception applies.

d. Specificity requirement

Blanket claims of privilege do not fare well, and courts usually require the claim to be made "document by document."

e. No privilege from being called

The attorney has no privilege against being called, and may (if called) have to take the stand and claim the privilege. Some courts require a preliminary showing that the information sought from a lawyer is relevant, nonprivileged, and unavailable by other means before allowing a lawyer to be deposed.

f. *In camera* inspection

To determine whether a privilege applies, the court may require production of the material in question for *in camera* inspection, and the task may be delegated to a special master if the quantity is large. Often such inspection and delegation involves ex parte proceedings from which the party seeking disclosure is excluded.

g. Appellate review

If the privilege claim is *sustained*, ordinarily the information seeker or proponent has no immediate appeal, but must await the final judgment and raise the issue then. If a privilege claim by a party to the suit is *denied*, usually the same result obtains, and the privilege claimant must await the final judgment and raise the issue then.

h. Refusal to disclose

If a privilege claim is rejected and the privilege claimant refuses to disclose, the court may hold him in contempt. The usual rule is that a privilege claimant may obtain immediate review of a **criminal contempt citation**, but it is not entirely clear that he may test the ruling on the privilege issue in this manner if the client is a party to the suit (the reason being that the privilege claimant can test the ruling by appealing an adverse judgment at the end of the suit). If he is **not** a party, the merits of the privilege claim can be reviewed on this appeal from the judgment of contempt(the reason being that a nonparty privilege claimant has no other mechanism to obtain review). If a disobedient privilege claimant is held in **civil contempt** and is a party in the action, ordinarily an appeal from the judgment of civil contempt is not allowed (one reason is that normally the privilege claimant can "holds the key" to the cell because he can gain release by complying with the request to produce, in the case of civil contempt citations; another reason being once again that the privilege claimant can test the ruling by appealing an adverse judgment at the end of the suit). If a disobedient privilege claimant is not a party to the suit, then an appeal from the judgment of civil contempt is allowed, and the merits of the privilege claim can be reviewed (even though the nonparty ordinarily "holds the key" to the cell and can gain release by complying with the request to produce, we feel uncomfortable with this degree of coercion on nonparties; another reason being once again that a nonparty has no other mechanism to obtain review).

    i.   Rationale

These rules restricting interlocutory appeal minimize disruption and delay of ongoing proceedings in which privilege claims are made. Preventing a party to a suit from appealing from civil contempt orders can be justified, as noted above, on the basis that the party "holds the key" to his own discharge. In any case parties to a suit may appeal an adverse judgment eventually and obtain review of privilege rulings at that time.

    ii.   *Perlman* doctrine

Attorneys are often the source from whom privileged matter is sought, and they may be unwilling as a practical matter to go to jail to vindicate a client's privilege claim. Hence courts following the doctrine of *Perlman v. United States*, 247 U.S. 7 (1918) may allow the client to intervene if the court orders the attorney to disclose privileged material, and seek interlocutory review. Courts may require a showing that the person with the information will disclose rather than risk contempt.

iii. **Other forms of review**

Sometimes privilege rulings may be tested by interlocutory writ of mandamus, but this mechanism is entirely discretionary, and reviewing courts usually refuse to intervene in this way, even when asked.

10. Waiver by Voluntary Disclosure or Failure to Claim

Voluntary disclosure of any significant part of privileged matter waives the privilege, and so does failure to claim the privilege when disclosure is sought. Such waiver may occur during discovery or outside the litigation context.

a. Facts versus communication

Discussing or disclosing the facts expressed in a privileged communication does not waive the privilege, which covers the communication with lawyers, and not the facts themselves or the client's knowledge of the facts. Thus a client who tells her lawyer in confidence "I did not go near the bank on Tuesday" does *not* waive a claim of privilege for that statement if she tells a friend "I did not go near the bank on Tuesday." (She *would* waive the privilege, however, if she told the friend "I told my lawyer that I did not go near the bank on Tuesday.")

b. Fraud, deception, theft

Disclosure is viewed as involuntary (no waiver) if the communication gets out by means of fraud, deception, or theft.

c. Court order

Disclosure pursuant to court order is not a waiver, and if the order is reversed the privilege may be reclaimed. In other words, if a client turns over a letter that she wrote to her attorney after claiming a privilege with respect to the letter that the court rejects, the client may still appeal from the adverse ruling on the privilege claim (the appeal may have to be delayed until the court enters a final judgment on the underlying claims), and the fact that she has in the meantime disclosed the letter after being ordered by the court to do so does not cause loss of the claim that the letter is, after all, privileged.

d. Privileged disclosure

When disclosure of confidences is itself privileged, no waiver occurs. Privileged disclosures might occur if a client tells his spouse about the statements he made to his attorney or if a client or attorney discloses the substance of such statements to another client or attorney in a situation where the attorney-client privilege itself applies, as in the case of joint clients or pooled information (discussed above).

e. Selective disclosure

Generally speaking, selective disclosure is not allowed. Thus clients waive or lose the privilege by disclosing to adverse parties or auditors, and most courts say that the privilege is lost by disclosing to government agencies in connection with ongoing investigations.

f. Pretrial agreements, orders

By private agreement, parties may share confidences while preventing broader disclosure, but such agreements probably do not bind third persons. Court-approved protective orders, which may permit disclosure during discovery in complex cases in order to expedite the process while preserving privilege claims intact, have greater force.

g. Writings used to refresh memory

If a witness uses privileged communications to refresh her memory before testifying, waiver issues arise. If she is outside the charmed circle covered by the privilege, granting her use of the material is already a disclosure that waives the privilege for the client. If the witness *is* the client, the question arises whether her use of privileged material in this way also waives the privilege. Under FRE 612, the court has discretion to require the proponent of testimony to turn over to the adverse party material used to refresh recollection before giving testimony, and it is possible to read this provision to mean that this use does waive the privilege. Among courts addressing the question, most conclude that courts may order disclosure of privileged material under FRE 612, but significant authority attempts to preserve the privilege by permitting disclosure only if shown to be necessary or if the writing did in fact refresh memory, and some courts undertake *in camera* review to determine whether there is any discrepancy between the testimony and documents used to refresh.

h. Scope of waiver

Traditionally disclosure of any significant part of a communication waived the privilege not only for what was disclosed but for other related material, on the theory that the client should not be able to make selective use of privileged material. However, FRE 502 now provides that disclosure is limited to the material disclosed unless the court finds that other related communications "ought in fairness be considered together" with the material already disclosed.

11. Waiver: Inadvertent Disclosure

Under FRE 502, an inadvertent disclosure in a federal or state proceeding does not operate as a waiver if the holder took reasonable steps to prevent disclosure (i.e., was not negligent) and also took reasonable steps to rectify the error, such as by asserting the privilege and attempting in a timely manner to reclaim the privileged material.

12. Waiver by Asserting Claims or Defenses

When a client asserts a claim or defense based on communications within the privilege, this tactic often amounts to waiver. If, for instance, the client claims that an attorney committed malpractice by giving or failing to give advice, the privilege is lost with respect to whatever was said by the attorney and the client relating to this point.

a. Insanity defense

Courts are divided on the question whether claiming an insanity defense waives the attorney-client privilege with respect to communications to a psychotherapist retained by the defense. When the psychotherapist testifies, almost all courts find the privilege waived for communications necessary for a fair evaluation of the testimony. Some courts do not allow a psychotherapist retained by the defense to be called by the state. Others permit the prosecutor to call the psychotherapist, but limit her testimony to opinions relating to sanity and to nonincriminating statements made by the defendant that bear on this point.

b. Utility versus fairness

In the concept of waiver by claim assertion, the key is not that the adverse party would find that the privileged statements are useful, which is always true when privileged statements are sought. Rather, the key is that the privilege claimant should play fair: If he relies on privileged statements, they should be disclosed. From this perspective, it is the actual use of privileged material, and not merely the assertion of a claim, that is the key.

C. MARITAL PRIVILEGE: SPOUSAL TESTIMONY

The federal system and about 30 states recognize a spousal testimony privilege. In most jurisdictions, this privilege applies only in criminal cases. Depending on how it is constructed (see discussion of "holder" below), the privilege either permits a witness who is married to the accused to refuse to testify for the prosecution, or permits the accused to block his spouse from testifying for the prosecution, or it operates in both these ways.

1. Rationale

The reason for the privilege is to preserve and protect the marital relationship. Testifying against a spouse in a criminal case would likely amount to an "unforgivable act" that would destroy a marriage. See *Hawkins v. United States*, 358 U.S. 74, 78–79 (1958). Moreover, forcing one spouse to testify against another in this setting, over the objection of one or both, would offend basic societal values.

2. Holder

There are three possible approaches, and each has some following. One possibility is to vest the privilege both in the party spouse and the witness spouse. Another is to vest the privilege only in the witness spouse. The third possibility is to vest the privilege only in the party spouse.

a. Both hold privilege (some states)

Giving the privilege to both spouses means the witness spouse can refuse to testify, and the party spouse can block the witness from testifying. Before adopting a narrower view (below), the Supreme Court had taken this approach in the federal system as a matter of federal common law, see *Hawkins* case, supra, and some states continue to follow this approach.

b. Witness only (federal rule)

Giving the privilege only to the witness spouse means that she may refuse to testify, but that the accused cannot block her from testifying if she is willing to do so. In 1980 the Supreme Court decided, as a matter of federal law under FRE 501, that only the witness spouse holds the privilege, see *Trammel v. United States*, 445 U.S. 40, 53 (1980), and some states take this approach too. The main consequence of following the *Trammel* doctrine is that prosecutors who have evidence that both spouses are involved in a crime may bring or threaten to bring charges against one and use the leverage thus gained to force the other to agree to testify.

c. Party only (some states)

Giving the privilege only to the party spouse means that the accused may block his spouse from testifying, but that she may not refuse to testify if he does not raise the objection. About a dozen states follow this approach.

Example. Roger and Nancy Miller are arrested for smuggling drugs as they get off a commercial airliner in Miami. They are married to each other. A search discloses that Nancy is carrying drugs on her person, and that Roger is carrying a large sum of cash and ledgers that appear to describe drug transactions. Prosecutors believe Roger is the source of the funds used to purchase drugs abroad, and that he has been involved in other smuggling operations using other people as "mules" or carriers. Federal charges are brought against Roger, and prosecutors agree to drop charges against Nancy in exchange for her testimony. At trial, Roger invokes the spousal testimony privilege to prevent Nancy from testifying. Roger's claim of privilege fails because in the federal system only the witness spouse (Nancy) holds the privilege. If she is willing to testify, Roger cannot prevent her from doing so.

3. Scope

When it applies, the privilege covers all testimony and is not limited to testimony describing marital confidences. The privilege does not apply to proof of out-of-court statements that a party has made. Ordinarily such statements are hearsay, if offered to prove the truth of the matter asserted, but if a hearsay objection is overcome and the statement is offered, the spousal testimony privilege does not stand in the way.

4. Marital Relationship

The privilege requires that the witness and the party be married at the time the testimony is sought. Some states also recognize the privilege for civil unions or domestic partnerships.

a. Marriage after events in issue

It does not matter that the parties were not married at the time of the events that the testimony would describe, so a marriage that begins after those events *does* support a privilege claim (provided that it is ongoing at the time of trial).

b. "Sham" marriage

If the parties do not intend to remain married and are using their marital status for a fraudulent purpose (like violating immigration laws), such a marriage does not count for purposes of the privilege.

c. Moribund marriage

Some courts hold that the privilege does not apply if the marriage is "moribund," but most courts are reluctant to get into the question whether the marriage is healthy or not. All agree that divorce ends the privilege.

d. Common law marriage

A common law marriage, if recognized in the jurisdiction where the couple resides, does give rise to the privilege.

5. Exceptions

The spousal testimony privilege is subject to well-recognized exceptions.

a. Familial or spousal crimes or torts

The privilege does not apply when one spouse is charged with a crime or tort against the other, or against the minor child of either, or against the property of the other.

b. Joint participants

Most courts recognize an exception to the privilege when the spouses are joint participants in the charged crime, but a few conclude that the privilege should apply even in this setting. (Even if the privilege is not applied, the witness spouse may claim her privilege against self-incrimination.)

D. MARITAL PRIVILEGE: MARITAL CONFIDENCES

In the federal system and almost all states, courts recognize a privilege for marital confidences that covers private communications between spouses during marriage. This privilege, which applies in civil and criminal cases alike, enables each spouse to refuse to testify to the substance of such communications and to block the other spouse from doing so.

1. Rationale

Like the spousal testimony privilege, the marital confidences privilege is designed to preserve and protect the marital relationship.

2. Holders

Under the traditional broad view, both spouses hold the privilege for statements made by either, so each can (a) refuse to disclose and (b) prevent the other spouse from disclosing any confidential communications between them.

a. Narrower view

Some authorities say each spouse holds the privilege only with respect to his or her own statements, see URE 504, but this somewhat artificial distinction invites attempts to prove circumstantially the statements of one spouse by proof of what the other said.

b. Unconsented disclosure

If one spouse discloses a confidential marital communication without the consent of the other spouse, the latter may still assert the privilege to block the use of this communication in legal proceedings.

3. Scope

The privilege covers for all time all communications uttered in confidence during a marriage, and it does not cover noncommunicative conduct.

a. For all time

For communications uttered in confidence during marriage, the privilege applies, and it does not matter if the marriage has ended at the time the communications are sought or offered. The privilege even survives the death of a spouse and may be asserted by the personal representative of the spouse.

b. In confidence

The privilege does not apply to statements made in the presence of outsiders persons, or to statements that are intended to be disclosed. The requisite confidence may exist even if spouses talk to one another in the presence of children of tender years, but there is no confidence (hence no privilege claim) when spouses talk in the presence of older children, friends, relatives, or anyone else.

c. During marriage

The privilege applies only to statements uttered during the course of a marital relationship, not to statements uttered before or after marriage. If a man and woman are married from 2004 through 2008, what they said to each other in confidence in 2003 is not privileged, but what they said to each other in confidence from 2004 through 2008 is privileged forever.

d. Communications

Assertive or expressive conduct that is designed to carry a message or meaning is a communication. It makes no difference whether the communication is oral or written (or even recorded). In *United States v. Montgomery*, 384 F.3d 1050 (9th Cir. 2004), for example, the court found that a note written by a wife and left for her husband on the kitchen counter was within the privilege. Even *conduct* that is communicative can be within the privilege. Thus in *United States v. Estes*, 793 F.2d 465, 467 (2d Cir. 1986), for example, the court found that the act of a husband in dumping onto the marital bed cash stolen from a robbery was privileged because it was part of his account of committing the robbery. The privilege does not apply, however, to ordinary noncommunicative acts. Thus the court said in *Estes* that the privilege does not reach testimony describing the behavior of a husband leaving the house by car and driving in a certain direction and returning at a certain time, nor would it apply if the wife had actually see the husband committing the crime. (In such situations, the spousal testimony privilege might apply, but if the two have been divorced the latter privilege would not apply, and the spouse could describe this behavior because the marital confidences privilege does not apply to noncommunicative conduct.)

4. Marital Relationship

The privilege applies only to parties who are legally married. A few states also recognize the privilege for civil unions or domestic partnerships. It applies to common law marriages if such are recognized in the state where the parties reside. Some courts refuse to apply the privilege when the spouses are separated or the marriage is moribund, but other courts apply the privilege without inquiring into such matters.

5. Exceptions

There are two important exceptions to the privilege.

a. Familial or spousal crimes or torts

As is true of the spousal testimony privilege, the marital confidences privilege does not apply where one spouse is charged with a crime or tort against the other, or against the minor child of either, or against the property of the other.

b. Ongoing crimes

Again as is true of the spousal testimony privilege, the marital confidences privilege may not apply to statements relating to ongoing or future crimes in which both spouses are participants.

E. PHYSICIAN–PATIENT PRIVILEGE

Most states have a statutory physician-patient privilege, which was not part of common law tradition. Coverage varies substantially and the terms of the statutes control many of the issues that arise in applying the privilege, which covers mainly confidential statements made by a patient to a doctor during the course of treatment.

1. Rationale
The purpose of the privilege is to promote full disclosure between patient and doctor, and to protect the privacy of the patient.

2. Holder
The patient (not the doctor) holds the privilege.

3. Scope
Wherever the privilege is recognized, it covers confidential communications to a doctor for purposes of treatment.

a. Confidentiality
Statements by the patient are privileged only if made in confidence, but the presence of family members or others who are assisting or communicating for the patient does not destroy the privilege. Nor does the presence of nurses, medical assistants, or others who help the doctor. Statements intended for disclosure to a third person (such as an employer or insurance carrier) are not privileged.

b. Information
Some states recognize a broader privilege covering information that a doctor acquires by examining or testing the patient, at least to the extent that such information would not be generally observable by others.

c. Testimony and records
The privilege generally applies not only to testimony by the doctor, but also to medical and hospital records that would reveal matters covered by the privilege.

d. Fee arrangements, etc.
Such matters as fee arrangements, time and date of visits, or consultation are not within the privilege.

e. Identity
Patient identity is covered to the extent disclosure would reveal the substance of a privileged communication or matter.

4. Exceptions

Many exceptions severely limit the scope of the privilege, so much so that the framers of the Federal Rules believed there was "little if any basis" for the privilege.

a. Patient-litigant

Most statutes provide that a patient who puts his physical condition in issue as an element of a claim or defense waives the privilege, although merely denying a claim of physical disability made by another does not have the effect of waiver.

b. Reporting statutes

When statutes require doctors to report certain types of illnesses or injuries, such as gunshot or stab wounds, venereal disease or AIDS or other ailments, or child abuse, the privilege gives way to the extent required for the underlying purpose, although the degree to which protection is thus reduced depends entirely on the statute.

c. Criminal cases and related matters

Statutes often make the privilege inapplicable in criminal cases, will contests, commitment proceedings, malpractice suits, and disciplinary proceedings.

d. Court-ordered exams; contemplated disclosure

Commonly the privilege does not apply to court-ordered examinations or to examinations taken for the benefit of others like insurance carriers, employers, or opposing litigants.

F. PSYCHOTHERAPIST–PATIENT PRIVILEGE

This privilege grew out of the physician-patient privilege, but it has taken on a life of its own and now enjoys more acceptance than the other privilege. The Supreme Court's 1996 decision in *Jaffee v. Redmond*, 518 U.S. 1 (1996), recognizing the privilege in the federal system under FRE 501, gives it strong modern support. Virtually all states provide for such a privilege by rule or statute. Essentially this privilege covers statements made in confidence to a psychotherapist for purposes of treatment.

1. Rationale

The reason for the privilege is to encourage disclosure to a psychotherapist, which is necessary for effective treatment, and to protect privacy.

2. Holder

The holder of the privilege is the patient (not the psychotherapist).

3. Scope

The privilege applies to confidential communications by a patient to a psychiatrist or psychologist made in the course of obtaining therapy individually or in a group setting.

a. Confidential communications

The privilege covers only communications, but the concept is often construed broadly to include conclusions derived from observation of the patient or from what he says.

b. Psychiatrist, psychologist

Normally the privilege applies to communications with psychiatrists (who are medical doctors) and licensed psychologists or other psychotherapists (who ordinarily are not medical doctors), and in *Jaffee* the Supreme Court pointedly applied the privilege to a clinical social worker (noting that "the poor and those of modest means" may not be able to afford to see a psychiatrist or psychologist).

c. Individual, group

While the privilege covers only confidential communications, courts recognize the privilege when others are present to further the interests of the patient in obtaining treatment, including family members and others participating in group therapy.

4. Exceptions

Critical exceptions limit the reach of the privilege.

a. Court-ordered examinations

There is a generally recognized exception for court-ordered examinations, although the judge has discretion to limit the degree of disclosure so as to protect privacy where possible.

b. Claim or defense

The privilege does not apply when the patient, or someone acting on her behalf, relies on her mental or emotional condition as an element of a claim or defense.

i. Child custody proceedings

Courts disagree on the question whether a party (typically the mother or father) puts her mental condition in issue in child custody proceedings, with some courts finding the privilege to be waived and others finding that it applies.

ii. Insanity defense

When the accused claims insanity or asserts another mental status defense, many courts hold the privilege is waived and apply the waiver to other psychotherapists consulted on the condition.

c. **Endangerment**

Following the lead of the landmark California decision in *Tarasoff v. Regents of University of California*, 551 P.2d 334 (Cal. 1976), many jurisdictions recognize a kind of "exception" to the privilege under which the psychotherapist is obligated to warn law enforcement authorities or potential victims of threats uttered by the patient to kill or harm another person. *Tarasoff* did not actually create an exception in this situation, but rather built on an express exception to the statutory version of the privilege, imposing on the psychotherapist a duty to warn that would give rise to a cause of action in the event that the required warning was not given and the patient then acted on his threat: In this situation, the victim or his estate could hold the psychotherapist liable in damages. In the federal system, some authority construes this duty to warn as a reporting requirement and *not* as an exception, which presumably means that threatening utterances continue to be covered by the privilege but that the warning must still be delivered and that law enforcement authorities may act on the warnings.

d. **Reporting requirements**

Many states have statutes requiring psychotherapists and others to report child abuse. As in the case of the doctor-patient privilege, the psychotherapist-patient privilege gives way to the extent required for the underlying purpose, but again the degree to which protection is thus reduced depends on the statute.

G. OTHER PRIVILEGES

In addition to the five often-invoked privileges discussed above (attorney-client, spousal testimony, marital confidences, physician-patient, psychotherapist-patient), courts often recognize a host of other privileges that are somewhat less often seen. Some depend on statutes, but others are part of common law tradition.

1. Clergy–Penitent

This privilege reflects governmental deference to the Catholic sacrament of confession, but has been expanded to embrace less formal counseling undertaken by members of the clergy in other religious traditions, whether such counseling is termed "confession" or something else. The privilege, which is recognized almost everywhere, belongs to the penitent (and sometimes to the clergymember as well) and covers confidential communications between a lay person and a clergymember for the purpose of spiritual counseling.

a. Clergy

The privilege covers counseling with clergymembers of any organized religion, but not to holders of religious titles conferred by mail order or by people who simply call themselves ministers.

b. Marriage counseling

The privilege does not cover marriage counseling as such, but couples who engage in counseling sessions with members of the clergy usually seek spiritual advice, which justifies applying the privilege.

2. Social Workers

At common law, there was no privilege for confidential conversations with social workers, but many states have adopted statutes creating a privilege in this setting. Movement in this direction received support from the decision in *Jaffee*, which applied the psychotherapist-patient privilege to counseling with a clinical social worker.

3. Journalists

This privilege did not exist at common law, but a qualified journalist privilege has been widely adopted by statute in the states, and sometimes by judicial decisions, including many federal decisions recognizing such a privilege as a matter of common law. The instrumental purpose is to encourage the gathering and reporting of news by enabling journalists to interview sources with an assurance of confidentiality.

a. Coverage

The privilege covers identity of sources, and occasional modern decisions extend the privilege to cover essentially the work product of journalists, such as notes and memoranda, photographs, and tapes. Such an extension supports the enterprise of news reporting by providing some assurance that the efforts of the reporter are in effect his or her property and cannot be freely used by others.

b. Holder

The holder of the privilege is the journalist, who may disclose or not regardless of the preferences of people acting as sources.

c. Balancing

The privilege is qualified, meaning that it gives way in the face of compelling need. Courts have not settled on a formula, but try to balance what amounts to constitutional concerns of encouraging a free press against the relevance and salience of the information being sought.

d. Defamation suits

In defamation suits, the privilege commonly yields when the existence, identity, and reliability of the source is directly relevant in the case.

e. Criminal cases

When journalists hold information obtained in confidence that is relevant to the defense of criminal charges, constitutional concerns rooted in the Compulsory Process and Confrontation Clauses may require the privilege to give way. See *In re Farber*, 394 A.2d 330 (N.J. 1978) (requiring investigative reporter to disclose notes of his investigation of unsolved hospital deaths, where this information was central to the defense of a doctor charged with murder), *cert. denied*, 439 U.S. 997 (1978).

4. Accountants

A few states recognize a privilege covering confidential communications with accountants. The federal courts do not recognize this privilege, but confidential communications with accountants retained by lawyers to aid in providing legal representation may be covered by the attorney-client privilege.

5. Researchers and Academics

Some decisions recognize a privilege for researchers and academics that protects confidential research conducted for purposes of serious scholarly inquiry, but others reject claims of such a privilege. Statutes sometimes require confidentiality in connection with the identity of human subjects and other research records. In 1990, the Supreme Court refused to recognize a privilege for academic peer review materials, where these related to claims of discrimination in a tenure decision. See *University of Pennsylvania v. EEOC*, 493 U.S. 182 (1990).

6. Trade Secrets

Courts have long recognized what amounts to a qualified privilege that protects trade secrets during litigation. This privilege covers valuable commercial information (from customer lists to pricing policy to design and manufacturing specifications). Usually such information must be disclosed during discovery when it is relevant in suits involving the privilege claimant, but protective orders limit access and bar publication or distribution of such information.

7. Political Vote

Under a common law "political vote" privilege that is sometimes thought to be rooted in statutory "ballot" requirements and constitutional considerations, a person may refuse to disclose the tenor of his or her vote in a political election. An exception is recognized where the vote was cast illegally.

8. Required Reports

A great many state and federal statutes require citizens and businesses to file periodic reports on certain subjects, and commonly these statutes provide that such reports cannot be used in evidence. Sometimes these provisions are viewed as establishing a privilege, either absolute or qualified.

9. Governmental Privileges

Courts have long recognized certain governmental privileges, which are viewed as essential to the conduct of official business, and sometimes as important to national security.

a. State secrets (military and diplomatic)

There is a privilege that covers information about intelligence activities, and the information generated by such activities, as well as information about weapons systems, military operations, arms sales, and diplomatic contacts and negotiations.

i. Procedure

Under the leading case of *United States v. Reynolds,* 345 U.S. 1 (1953), the government invokes this privilege by showing that disclosure will "expose military matters" that should not be divulged "in the interests of national security." The required showing is to be made by testimony or written statement, and on government request the showing may be made ex parte and *in camera.*

ii. Government litigation

If the government is a party to a suit in which the privilege is claimed, and sustaining the privilege deprives the other side of information important to a claim or defense, the court may adopt appropriate remedies such as striking testimony or finding against the government on the issue to which the privilege pertains, or dismissing the action.

b. Official information

There is a privilege covering information collected by government agencies for use in policy deliberations or during investigations.

i. Deliberative materials

This part of the privilege is designed to encourage the free flow of ideas and uninhibited exchange of views among decision makers. The privilege covers recommendations, proposals, and opinions expressed or advanced prior to final decision, but it does not cover purely factual materials, and it does not shield final agency actions that amount to law or have the effect of law.

ii. Investigative materials

This part of the privilege is designed to avoid compromising the identity of confidential sources, alerting targets of investigation, unfairly stigmatizing people who have not been charged with crimes or wrongdoing, and shielding from public view the techniques of law enforcement agencies.

iii. Agency head claims privilege

Most courts require the head of the agency having the information to claim the privilege rather than the attorney representing the state or government in the case.

iv. Qualified protection

The official information privilege is qualified under a standard in which the need for accurate fact-finding in litigation is weighed against the public interest in governmental functioning. To make the necessary decision, courts sometimes order disclosure of the underlying material for *in camera* inspection. Disclosure is often ordered in connection with investigations of misconduct by public officials.

v. Freedom of Information Act (FOIA)

While this statute entitles citizens to obtain vast amounts of official information, the FOIA also contains major exemptions which largely match the official information privilege, thus leaving room for it to operate (because the exemptions in the FOIA mean that disclosure will not be ordered for most information that would be covered by the official information privilege described here).

c. Informer's identity

The government holds a qualified privilege to refuse to disclose the identity of an informer who provides information assisting law enforcement. The privilege normally covers only the identity of sources, but it covers information provided by such sources to the extent necessary to protect identity itself. The purpose of the privilege is to aid in effective law enforcement by making it possible for law enforcement agents to promise confidentiality to people who cooperate.

i. Trials

In the leading case of *Roviaro v. United States*, 353 U.S. 53 (1957), the Court held that the privilege is qualified and requires balancing "the public interest in protecting the flow of information against the individual's right to prepare his defense," taking into account the crime charged, possible defenses, and possible significance of the informer's testimony. Courts are more likely to order disclosure when the informer played a significant role in the crime, and less likely to order disclosure if the informer was a mere observer (or "tipster") or if the court determines that he would give only testimony tending to incriminate the defendant. To obtain disclosure, the defendant must make a showing that the informer may be able to give relevant testimony, which may be done by means of affidavits. The court may conduct an ex parte hearing (excluding the defense) to determine this matter.

ii. Probable cause hearings

Sometimes defendants seek disclosure of an informer's identity in proceedings testing probable cause (suppression motions under the Fourth or Fifth Amendment, or motions to dismiss an indictment). In *McCray v. Illinois*, 386 U.S. 300 (1967), the Court held that the defense is not constitutionally entitled to disclosure of an informer's identity in this setting if the government produces independent evidence that the informer is reliable. But if the court "doubts the credibility of the affiant" who attests the reliability of the informer, the court may order that the informer be produced or identified.

d. Presidential

In *United States v. Nixon*, 418 U.S. 683 (1974), the Court recognized an executive privilege that protects confidential presidential communications. The Court found that the privilege was necessary to the operation of government and rooted in the separation of powers doctrine.

i. **Qualified protection**

At least for ordinary conversations involving the President and others, the privilege is qualified, and the Court held in the *Nixon* case that the privilege may give way to a "demonstrated, specific need" for the information.

ii. **Absolute protection**

For communications involving state or military secrets, the decision in *Nixon* suggests that the privilege is absolute.

iii. **President must claim**

The privilege can be invoked only by the President, not by his aides (of course a lawyer representing the President may claim the privilege on the President's behalf).

H. PRIVILEGE AGAINST SELF–INCRIMINATION

This privilege is the only privilege expressly recognized by the Constitution, which states in the Fifth Amendment that "No person shall be . . . compelled in any criminal case to be a witness against himself." In *Malloy v. Hogan*, 378 U.S. 1 (1964), the Supreme Court held that this privilege applies against the states as well, as an element of due process under the Fourteenth Amendment.

1. Rationale

The Supreme Court has commented that the privilege reflects "fundamental values" and "noble aspirations," and explained the underlying idea by saying that the privilege expresses our unwillingness as a society to subject those accused of crime to what it called "the cruel trilemma of self-accusation, perjury or contempt." Hence the privilege implements our "preference for an accusatorial rather than an inquisitorial system of justice," and expresses our fear that without the privilege people accused of crime would be subjected to "inhumane treatment." See *Murphy v. Waterfront Commission*, 378 U.S. 52, 55 (1964).

2. Persons Protected

The privilege applies only to individuals and cannot be asserted by entities such as corporations, labor unions, or partnerships.

a. Cannot claim for another

Because the privilege is personal, one defendant in a criminal case cannot raise the Fifth Amendment privilege of another.

b. Corporate agent

Since a corporation has no Fifth Amendment privilege, and since the custodian of corporate records is a corporate agent when acting in that capacity, such an agent may not refuse to turn over records even if they might incriminate him personally.

3. Scope of Privilege

The privilege applies to criminal defendants and to witnesses who have not been charged with crimes (although in slightly different ways), but it applies only to proof that is testimonial or communicative in nature.

a. Criminal defendants

In a criminal case, the defendant has not only the right not to testify against himself but the right not even to be called to the witness stand by the prosecution.

i. Cross-examining the defendant

If a defendant in a criminal case does take the stand, however, he is subject to cross-examination on every matter to which he testified on direct.

ii. Not broader cross

Trial judges have discretion to permit cross-examination beyond the scope of direct, see FRE 611(b) (providing that in this situation the examination proceeds "as if on direct," meaning for the most part by nonleading questions). The accused, however, may object to questioning that goes beyond the scope of "relevant cross-examination" by invoking the privilege, which means that the Fifth Amendment comes close to *requiring*, in the situation of cross-examination of the accused by the prosecutor, something that is pretty close to the scope-of-direct rule that FRE 611(b) adopts as the usual or normal rule across the board. In the situation of cross-examining the accused, then, the court probably lacks the discretion it would otherwise have to permit broader cross-examination. See *Brown v. United States*, 356 U.S. 148, 154–155 (1958).

b. Witnesses

A person who is not the defendant in a criminal case has no privilege not to be called as a witness, but does have a Fifth Amendment privilege not to give answers that would incriminate himself.

c. Nontestimonial proof

The privilege applies to testimonial proof (essentially words and communicative acts), but not to physical evidence, including bodily fluids.

Thus even a person accused of a crime may be forced to give a blood or hair sample, fingerprint, handwriting exemplar, and even to utter words to aid in identification.

d. Written statements

Not surprisingly, the privilege applies to forced written statements as well as oral utterances, although pre-existing writings are another matter (see below).

e. Compulsion and immunity

The privilege applies to "compelled" self-incrimination, not to statements made voluntarily to police or others. Statements given by arrested suspects in response to police questioning may be excludable under the *Miranda* doctrine, which is a particular application of this privilege, if arresting officers fail to provide the required warnings or fail to honor defendant's request for a lawyer or his stated wish not to answer questions. See *Miranda v. Arizona*, 384 U.S. 436 (1966).

4. Incrimination; Procedural Issues

The Fifth Amendment covers compelled statements that might subject the speaker to a risk of incrimination, not statements that might be damaging in other ways. When the privilege is claimed during judicial proceedings, the court (not the witness) decides whether an answer would incriminate the witness under the Fifth Amendment.

a. Humiliation, embarrassment, civil liability

The privilege does not apply to statements or answers that might subject the speaker to humiliation or embarrassment, or to civil liability.

b. Tendency to incriminate

The court determines whether a claim of the privilege should be sustained, considering the implications of the question in the setting in which it was asked and deciding whether an answer might tend to incriminate the witness. A statement is incriminating if it would tend to prove the maker of the statement guilty of a crime and would be relevant evidence against him in a criminal trial. There must be an actual danger of prosecution, not a mere fanciful danger, and a privilege claim should be denied if the claimant cannot be prosecuted because the statute of limitations has run or because he has already been tried for the offense (or related offenses) in situations where the Double Jeopardy Clause would bar a second prosecution.

c. Immunity

The Supreme Court has held that a person may be forced to make self-incriminating statements if he is given so-called "use immunity" (statements cannot be used against him, either at trial or during ensuing investigation), although broader "transactional immunity" (blocking all prosecution) is not required. See *Kastigar v. United States*, 406 U.S. 441 (1972). When the requisite immunity is granted, the person may no longer claim the privilege and must answer questions even if those answers tend to incriminate him.

d. State and federal criminal liability

A person may claim the Fifth Amendment even where the risk of incrimination involves another sovereign. Thus a witness testifying in federal court may claim the privilege on the basis that his answer might be used against him in a state prosecution, and a witness testifying in state court may claim the privilege on the basis that his answer might be used against him in federal court. See *Murphy v. Waterfront Commission*, 378 U.S. 52 (1964) (one who was compelled to testify in state court has privilege to block use of this testimony against him in federal court). Often the state or the federal government grants use immunity to obtain testimony in a situation in which the answers incriminate the witness under the law of the other sovereign, and here it seems that state courts must honor a federal grant of immunity and federal courts must honor a state grant of immunity.

5. Adverse Inferences and Argument

In a variety of situations the question has arisen whether a claim of privilege or failure to speak or testify can support adverse inferences and be the subject of argument that the defendant must have done something wrong because otherwise he would testify or protest his innocence.

a. Same proceeding (inference and argument barred)

It may be humanly impossible to prevent jurors from drawing adverse inferences when the accused expressly invokes the Fifth Amendment, or does so implicitly by declining to take the witness stand, but the Supreme Court has held that the Fifth Amendment includes a right on the part of the defendant in a criminal proceeding not to have his failure to testify or his claim of the privilege held against him.

i. No comment or argument

One practical meaning of the "no adverse inference" rule is that the judge may not comment adversely on the failure of the accused to testify, or on his claim of the privilege, and the prosecutor may not urge the jury to draw an adverse inference. See *Griffin v. California*, 380 U.S. 609 (1965).

ii. Instruction

Another practical meaning of this rule is that the accused is entitled, on request, to an instruction advising the jury that it should not consider the fact that the defendant did not testify or that he claimed the privilege. See *Carter v. Kentucky*, 450 U.S. 288 (1981).

b. Pretrial investigation (the *Doyle* doctrine)

In cases where the accused testifies at trial and says things that he did not say to police during the investigative phase, the question whether prior silence may be used to impeach is affected by the *Miranda* doctrine (requiring warnings before police question arrested suspects). See *Doyle v. Ohio*, 426 U.S. 610 (1976) (use of post-warning, post-arrest silence to impeach testimony by the accused at trial violates *Miranda* doctrine).

i. Pre-arrest silence

Asking the defendant, on cross-examination at trial, about his failure to offer explanation *prior to arrest* does not violate *Miranda*. The reason is that *Miranda* warnings have not been given at this point, and it is the use of post-*warning* silence, not the use of silence itself, that violates the Fifth Amendment. See *Jenkins v. Anderson*, 447 U.S. 231 (1980) (approving use of pre-arrest silence to impeach).

ii. Post-arrest, pre-warning silence

Asking the defendant, on cross-examination at trial, about his failure to offer explanation *after arrest but before receiving Miranda warnings* also does not violate *Miranda*. Again the reason is that *Miranda* warnings have not been given, and in fact there is no need to give them at the moment of arrest because it is the combined fact of *custody and questioning by police* that triggers the obligation to give *Miranda* warnings. See *Fletcher v. Weir*, 455 U.S. 603 (1982) (absent *Miranda* warnings, state may cross-examine about post-arrest pre-warning silence, in order to impeach).

c. Contradicting a positive claim

In *Doyle*, the Supreme Court carefully noted, in a considered dictum going beyond the holding of the case, that if the accused had said in his testimony that he told police at the time of his arrest the same story that he was telling at trial, then it would be proper to show that he had not done so. Thus, in a case in which the defendant is tried for selling marijuana, if he testifies "I wasn't selling marijuana, but was trying to buy it," the prosecutor *cannot* properly ask why defendant "didn't tell arresting officers that story when he was arrested and questioned after receiving *Miranda* warnings." If, on the other hand, defendant testifies "I wasn't selling marijuana, but was trying to buy it, and when the police arrested me and gave me the *Miranda* warnings I told them exactly what was going on," then the prosecutor can seek to establish by cross-examination that defendant did *not* say that at the time. In other words, *Miranda* shields defendant from questions about post-arrest post-warning silence, but does not shield him if he claims that in fact he was not silent at all, and that he told officers the same thing that he says in court.

d. Civil cases

In civil litigation, there is no constitutional rule against comment and argument based on a claim by a party of the privilege. See *Baxter v. Palmigiano,* 425 U.S. 308 (1976) (in prison disciplinary hearing, civil in nature, permissible to draw adverse inferences against inmate who declines to testify on Fifth Amendment grounds).

6. Writings

The Fifth Amendment privilege certainly does apply to a written confession that law enforcement officers force a defendant to execute or sign, and it certainly does not apply to documents that a person prepares on his own, free of any government pressure or requirement, since such material is not "compelled."

a. Pre-existing documents

Pre-existing documents, like business and financial records made voluntarily before any charges are brought, are not within the privilege. See *Fisher v. United States,* 425 U.S. 391 (1976) (privilege does not apply to tax records as such).

b. Production and authentication

A prosecutor who wants to obtain documentary evidence ordinarily serves the person in possession with a subpoena duces tecum, which has the effect of requiring the person to produce what is sought. The records themselves may not be privileged (made voluntarily and independent of the proceedings), and yet those records may strongly tend to incriminate the person in possession, and could easily be admissible against him under the hearsay doctrine if they are his own records (they would be admissions or fit the business records exception). In this situation, merely producing the records has an incriminating effect, since the act of production is also a concession that the records are what the government has described, which often means conceding that the taxpayer himself (or his agent) made them. For this reason, the Supreme Court has held that forcing the person to produce the records by subpoena *presumptively* violates his privilege against self-incrimination, unless the government rebuts this presumption by showing that it can establish the authenticity of the desired materials independent of the act of production. See *United States v. Doe*, 465 U.S. 605 (1984).

7. Required Reports

Required **production** of an incriminating document may violate the privilege against self-incrimination under *Doe* (unless the government shows it can authenticate the documents independently), but the use of required records against the accused passes muster if there is an adequate regulatory purpose.

a. *Grosso* standard

In its decision in the *Grosso* case, the Supreme Court held that the government may both require records to be kept and use those records to prove criminal acts on three conditions: First, the purpose of the requirement to keep records must be "essentially regulatory." Second, the records that the government requires must be the kind that the party in question would regularly or customarily keep. Third, the records themselves must have taken on "public aspects" that make them similar to public documents. See *Grosso v. United States*, 390 U.S. 62 (1968).

Example. The Emergency Price Control Act requires businesses to keep records reflecting prices and sales. In a trial for violating the Act, the government offers those records against the defendant. This use of such records does not violate the Fifth Amendment because the purpose of the statute is regulatory, the records in question are the sort that are customarily kept, and the records themselves have public aspects in light of the regulating scheme. See *Shapiro v. United States*, 335 U.S. 1 (1948).

b. Penal statutes

In a number of cases, where the purpose of the statute was more punishment than regulation, using required reports against the defendant was found to violate the Fifth Amendment. See *Albertson v. Subversive Activities Control Board*, 382 U.S. 70 (1965) (requiring officers of Communist Party to file registration statement violates Fifth Amendment); *Marchetti v. United States*, 390 U.S. 39 (1968) (requiring wagering registration statement violates Fifth Amendment); *Haynes v. United States*, 390 U.S. 85 (1968) (requiring registration of regulated firearm violates Fifth Amendment).

REVIEW QUESTIONS AND ANSWERS

Question: What are privileges, and what are the sources of privilege law?

Answer: Privileges protect important relationships, like that between a lawyer and her client, and they enable their holder to block others from proving privileged matters. Since privileges apply outside the trial setting as well, they can also be invoked to block certain attempts at discovery. Many important privileges are codified in the various states, but in the absence of statute many privileges are recognized as a matter of common law tradition. Under FRE 501, privileges are viewed as substantive, which means that in diversity cases state privilege law applies, but otherwise federal courts apply federal privilege law. In the federal system, most privileges are rooted in common law tradition rather than statutes.

Question: What is the rationale of privileges?

Answer: There are actually two rationales. One is instrumental: Privileges exist to insure certain results (like proper legal representation). The second rationale stresses the importance of privacy in certain relationships (like the relationship between spouses), treating privacy as an important social good in itself.

Question: What are the elements in the attorney-client privilege?

Answer: First, there must be a client. The client may be a person or entity, and the privilege attaches when a person or entity seeks legal advice and thus covers preliminary conversations even if the lawyer does not go forward. Corporations and other entities can only act through human agents, so in this setting the privilege covers communications by these human agents to the lawyer. Second, there must be a lawyer. For purposes of the privilege, a lawyer is a person authorized to practice law *somewhere,* even if not in the place where the client seeks legal services. The privilege also applies to communications with someone that the client reasonably believes to be a lawyer. The privilege extends to law office functionaries (staff, paralegals) who assist the lawyer in his work, and to people whom the lawyer retains for this purpose (experts). Third, the privilege applies when the lawyer provides legal services, but not when the lawyer performs in other capacities (like business advisor). Fourth, the privilege applies to **communications** between the client and the lawyer. The privilege does not extend to **observations** by the lawyer relating to such matters as the physical appearance of the client, and it does not cover **facts** as such (a client cannot refuse to describe an accident merely because he has already described it to his lawyer, although he need not disclose the statement that he made to his lawyer), and the privilege does not apply to pre-existing documents that the client might turn over to the lawyer (even though the privilege *does* apply to letters by the client to the lawyer that seek legal advice or help provide information about the case). Fifth, the privilege requires that communications be kept confidential. If the client speaks to the lawyer with the intent of disclosing what he says, the privilege does not apply. And if the client speaks to the lawyer in the presence of outsiders (apart from law office functionaries and others retained to help provide legal services), the privilege does not apply.

Question: Can the privilege apply if two clients consult the same lawyer at the same time?

Answer: Yes, two or more people may become **joint clients,** in which case what they say to the lawyer is privileged as against outsiders. But what each client says to the lawyer in this situation is not privileged as between the clients. If the clients later become adversaries in litigation, neither can block the other from inquiring into (and using) what the other has said to the lawyer.

Question: What if several clients have different lawyers, but all confer together on matters of mutual interest?

Answer: There is a **"pooled defense"** or **"allied lawyers"** privilege that arises in this setting. As in the case of joint clients, what gets said by the clients is privileged as against outsiders. Unlike the joint client situation, however, the various clients in the pooled defense setting also have a privilege that applies among themselves. If one client were to try to prove what another said to one of the lawyers in this setting, the latter could probably invoke the privilege and block the proof (the point is not entirely clear in the cases, but this is the better conclusion, and it is the clear implication of most descriptions of the privilege in this situation).

Question: With corporate clients, how far does the privilege extend?

Answer: The prevailing view is that the privilege does not apply to literally every communication by any corporate agent to counsel for the corporation because such a broad approach would cast too large a cloak of secrecy around internal communications. Some states follow the "control group" approach, under which the privilege applies to communications by persons in the corporation who have the authority to act on whatever advice a lawyer might give. In the federal system, where FRE 501 leaves the matter for common law development, the Supreme Court in *Upjohn* adopted a version of the "subject matter" standard under which the privilege applies to communications to those who talk to the corporation's lawyer on matters within the scope of their duties. The opinion in *Upjohn* disclaims any intent to resolve these issues across the board, and the opinion stresses three other factors: One is that the purpose of speaking to the lawyer was to obtain legal advice (and of course this element is always essential, regardless whether the client is a corporation or a person). Another is that the people who spoke to the lawyer in *Upjohn* did so at the request of their superiors (a point that helps show that the purpose was to secure legal advice). Finally, the court in *Upjohn* stressed that the communications were treated as confidential from beginning to end (the element of confidentiality is necessary for the privilege in all settings).

Question: How does the corporate attorney-client privilege apply in shareholder litigation?

Answer: In derivative suits, where shareholders typically sue corporate management for the corporation (meaning any recovery goes to the entity, not the shareholders personally), the people with power to claim the privilege are often the same people who have allegedly mismanaged the entity. In this setting, the directors have a conflict of interest (protecting themselves as opposed to helping the company), and the prevailing view, which was developed in the *Garner* case, is that the shareholders can overcome a claim of the corporate attorney-client privilege by making a showing of good cause.

Question: When, if ever, is the identity of the client protected by the privilege?

Answer: Under the landmark Ninth Circuit opinion in *Baird*, the identity of the client is privileged if, under the circumstances, disclosure of identity would reveal the nature of confidential communications between the client and the lawyer. In *Baird* itself, a taxpayer hired a lawyer to make an anonymous payment of taxes, and the IRS sought to learn the identity of the client, but disclosing identity would also disclose the substance of the communication (which is that the taxpayer asked the lawyer to make the payment). Under the *Baird* rationale, courts have held the identity of the taxpayer to be privileged when the client hires a lawyer for the purpose of making an anonymous payment or restitution or reporting misconduct by the client or others. Results are mixed when a client hires a lawyer to represent another (merely paying fees does not make someone a client, and identity can be protected in this setting only if the person paying the fees also gets legal representation by the lawyer on some related matter). And identity is protected if the lawyer is simply asked to name the client to whom the lawyer gave certain specific advice.

Question: Can lawyers be asked to testify about the appearance or mental or psychological qualities of their clients?

Answer: Yes, since the privilege applies to **communications,** not matters observed about the client that others could observe too. With respect to mental or psychological qualities, conclusory accounts would not necessarily disclose confidential communications, but testing the lawyer's opinion would likely involve questions that get into communications from the client (where the privilege applies), and some courts either exclude the testimony or try to limit the disclosure of confidences.

Question: Does the attorney-client privilege apply to physical evidence delivered by the client to the lawyer?

Answer: No, certainly not in full force: The prevailing view is that the lawyer must turn over to the prosecutor physical evidence delivered by the client that is either an instrumentality or a fruit of the crime. But usually courts also say that **the source of such evidence** need not be disclosed, which has the effect of applying the privilege in a very limited sense. The result is to enable the client to sever his connection to evidence by delivering it to his lawyer. In the slightly different case when the client tells the lawyer where physical evidence may be found and the lawyer retrieves it, the leading decision in *Meredith* holds that the lawyer must turn it over *and* can be forced to disclose the place where he got the item. It is a different matter altogether if the client simply tells the lawyer where critical evidence is located: Such statements are privileged, assuming that the client is seeking legal advice and that no exception to the privilege applies (like the one for consultation in furtherance of ongoing crimes).

Question: What happens to communications between client and lawyer that are part of a future or an ongoing crime or fraud?

Answer: These are not privileged, under what amounts to an exception to the coverage of the privilege. To invoke this exception, the party seeking to overcome a claim of privilege must show that the client was engaging in criminal or fraudulent conduct and that the attorney's assistance was obtained in furtherance of this activity. The client must know (or must reasonably be expected to know) that the conduct is criminal or fraudulent, and the exception does not apply if the client simply inquires into the legality or advisability of a course of action. In determining whether the exception applies, the judge may undertake an ex parte *in camera* inspection of the material in question. The Supreme Court approved this procedure in the *Zolin* case, but did not address the standard of proof. Traditionally it is said that the information seeker need make only a **prima facie showing** that the client is engaging in ongoing fraudulent or criminal acts.

Question: What happens to the privilege if the client and lawyer get into a dispute over fees or the adequacy of legal representation?

Answer: Here the privilege gives way, at least to the extent necessary to enable each side to support the claims or defenses being advanced.

Question: How does the privilege apply when the lawyer has represented a deceased person (and now represents the estate)?

Answer: The privilege survives the death of the client, as the Supreme Court recognized in the *Swidler & Berlin* case, but an exception to coverage exists with respect to statements by a decedent that are relevant in suits between persons claiming to inherit from the decedent. Here it is usually said that it cannot be known which of two competing claimants stands in the shoes of the decedent. The privilege does apply, however, with respect to claims against the estate by outsiders (creditors of the decedent). It often happens that the lawyer who represented the decedent witnessed the signing of the will, and it is usually said that the lawyer can testify on the point of due execution because the privilege was not intended to apply to what the lawyer saw.

Question: What happens to the privilege if a corporate client dissolves?

Answer: Under the modern approach, successors to the corporation (a trustee or similar representative) can claim the privilege, but earlier codifications indicated that dissolution of the corporation terminated the privilege.

Question: What about confessions of criminal acts made to lawyers by clients who have died? If another person is prosecuted for the same crime, can he or she obtain the confession?

Answer: Arguably the privilege should give way in this setting because the interests of the person charged with the crime outweigh the privacy concerns of the family of the deceased person. In the *Swidler & Berlin* case, however, the Supreme Court refused to recognize an exception where statements by a deceased client might help the prosecutor prove that some other person had committed criminal acts.

Question: Who claims or asserts the privilege?

Answer: While the privilege belongs to the client (not the lawyer), the lawyer has an ethical duty to claim it and may do so on the client's behalf. Corporate management (or the lawyer acting on behalf of the corporation) claims the privilege for corporate clients.

Question: How are privilege claims decided? Who bears what burden? And how can a party dissatisfied with a trial court ruling on a privilege issue obtain review?

Answer: The court determines privilege claims (these issues are not for juries), and the privilege claimant has the burden of persuasion. Where it is claimed that an exception applies, the party seeking information or offering the proof bears the burden of persuasion on issues relating to the exception. The privilege must be claimed for specific answers or documents and cannot be asserted as a blanket claim by general subject matter. The court may resolve issues that arise by *in camera* review of documents, or by assigning the matter to a special master. Such *in camera* review often goes forward ex parte, meaning that the information seeker is excluded. Rulings on privilege claims are typically viewed as interlocutory, and orders that either require or deny disclosure are usually not appealable. The dissatisfied party must usually await final judgment in the suit before raising the issue on appeal. Refusing to produce when disclosure is ordered can result in a civil contempt citation, and usually parties to a suit are not allowed to contest the propriety of a privilege ruling by appealing from the citation. (A nonparty may appeal if he is held in civil contempt, and anyone who is held in criminal contempt may appeal, whether or not she is a party in the underlying suit, although it is not so clear that anyone *apart from* a nonparty to the suit may obtain a review of the privilege ruling in this way.) Under the *Perlman* doctrine, a party to a suit is allowed to intervene and take an appeal from an order to disclose that is directed to an attorney who holds privileged material, on the theory that the attorney may not be willing to risk a contempt citation (leading to incarceration or a fine) to protect a right that belongs to her client, obtaining a review of the privilege ruling in this manner.

Question: Does disclosure always result in loss of privilege protection?

Answer: Generally speaking, intentional disclosure results in loss of protection (waiver of the privilege) for the material disclosed. The privilege holder must claim or assert the privilege when disclosure is sought. Disclosing **facts** relating to the case (light was red at the time of the accident) does *not* waive the privilege, however, because the privilege covers **communications** (I told my lawyer the light was red), not facts. And disclosure pursuant to court order is not a waiver because eventually an appeal may be taken, and the privilege may be reclaimed if the disclosure order is found to be error. A disclosure that is itself privileged does not waive the attorney-client privilege. Nor does a disclosure to another in a situation covered by the joint clients or pooled information situation waive the privilege.

In two other situations, the question whether disclosure waives the privilege is complicated by other facts. One is the situation in which a pretrial protective order or a stipulation between the parties provides that inadvertent production of privileged material during discovery does not waive the privilege. Such court orders are authorized by FRE 502 and protect against waiver. The other situation is the one in which writings are used to prepare or refresh memories of witnesses. Disclosure to a nonparty for such purposes is already a waiver of the privilege, but use by clients is not a waiver. Under FRE 612, however, a court may order disclosure of material used prior to trial to prepare witnesses, and most courts construe this provision to mean that disclosure of privileged material may be ordered in this setting, although significant authority indicates that care should be taken to preserve the privilege as much as possible through *in camera* inspection and other precautions.

Question: Does even inadvertent disclosure waive the privilege?

Answer: FRE 502 states that inadvertent disclosure does not waive the privilege provided the holder of the privilege took reasonable steps to prevent disclosure and also took reasonable steps to rectify the error, such as asserting the privilege and attempting in a timely manner to reclaim the privileged material.

Question: Can the privilege be lost merely because a client brings a claim or raises a defense?

Answer: Substantial authority holds that bringing some claims does waive the privilege. Bringing a malpractice suit against a lawyer can be seen as waiving the client's privilege insofar as what the client said to the lawyer is relevant to the claim. Courts split on the question whether raising an insanity defense in a criminal case waives the attorney-client privilege with respect to communications by the client to a psychotherapist retained by the defense. When the psychotherapist testifies, most courts find the privilege waived with respect to communications that must be examined in order to appraise the testimony being given. Some courts do not let the prosecutor call a psychotherapist retained by the defense, and others let the prosecutor call the expert but limit the testimony to nonincriminating statements made by the defendant. A better way to view this area is in terms of fairness.

Question: What does the spousal testimony privilege cover?

Answer: This privilege covers **all testimony** against the accused in a criminal case by the spouse of the accused. There is a wide variation among jurisdictions on the question who holds the privilege. In some states, the privilege belongs to both, so in a trial of the wife for a crime the husband can refuse to testify against her, and she may prevent him from doing so even if he is willing. In the federal system and some states, the privilege belongs only to the witness spouse (in her trial, he may refuse to testify but she cannot stop him). In other states, the privilege belongs only to the defendant (so she may stop him from testifying, but he cannot refuse if she does not object).

Question: When must the spouses be married?

Answer: At the time the testimony is sought. That means the privilege applies if the trial is on Wednesday and the spouses got married on Tuesday, even if the events in issue occurred on Monday. That means as well that the privilege does not apply if the trial is on Wednesday and the spouses got divorced on Tuesday and the events in issue took place on Monday, even though the spouses were still married on Monday. Courts refuse to allow the privilege, however, if the marriage is a "sham" (which is perhaps most likely if the spouses married hastily just before trial). And courts sometimes refuse to allow the privilege if the marriage is "moribund" even if a divorce has not yet been obtained.

Question: What exceptions are there to the spousal testimony privilege?

Answer: There are two common situations. First, the privilege does not apply when one spouse is charged with a tort or crime against the other (including a property offense) or the minor child of either. Second, most jurisdictions say the privilege does not apply when the spouses are joint participants in the charged crime. And remember that the privilege does not apply in civil cases at all.

Question: What is the marital confidences privilege, and what does it cover?

Answer: This privilege, which applies in civil and criminal cases alike, covers communications made in confidence between spouses. By the better view, both parties hold the privilege, meaning both the person who speaks and the person who listens, and each may refuse to testify and may block the other from testifying to what was said. The privilege covers only **communications,** not testimony describing behavior, and it covers only communications uttered **during the marriage** and **in confidence.** The privilege applies to marital confidences, uttered during the marriage, even if the spouses are not married at the time of trial, and the privilege does not cover confidences uttered before the spouses marry or after they divorce.

The latter requirement means that communications in the presence of children of tender years can be privileged, but that the presence of older children prevents the privilege from applying.

Question: What are the exceptions to coverage?

Answer: The exceptions are similar to those that apply to the testimonial privilege, which is to say that the marital confidences privilege does not apply in prosecutions of one spouse for a tort or crime against the other (including property offenses), nor in cases where the two spouses are charged with being joint participants in a criminal venture.

Question: What is the physician-patient privilege, and how important is it?

Answer: This privilege, which is statutory in nature, covers confidential communications by a patient to his doctor for purposes of obtaining medical treatment. An exception exists for required reports by physicians, to the extent necessary to the underlying purpose (such as investigating crimes or tracking venereal diseases), and many statutes provide that where a patient puts physical condition in issue as an element of a claim or defense, the privilege does not apply. Further statutory exceptions often make the privilege inapplicable in criminal cases and inapplicable in the case of court-ordered examinations. The privilege has limited significance in litigation because of these important exceptions.

Question: What are the essentials of the psychotherapist-patient privilege?

Answer: This privilege, which covers statements made in confidence to a psychotherapist for purpose of treatment, got a boost in the Supreme Court's 1996 decision in *Jaffee*, which recognized the privilege as a matter of federal common law in federal courts. In most formulations, the privilege applies in the setting of group counseling, but does not apply to court-ordered examinations (where the judge has discretion to limit the degree of subsequent disclosure to protect privacy concerns), and it does not apply where the patient (or someone acting on her behalf) puts mental condition in issue. In child custody proceedings, some courts find that the contesting adults have put their mental condition in issue, and some disagree on this point. Many courts hold that the privilege is waived when the accused pleads insanity. Exceptions in state statutes on the subject provide that the privilege gives way to the extent necessary to enable the psychotherapist to report suspected child abuse to authorities.

Question: What other privileges are there?

Answer: Among the more common are the clergy-penitent privilege (covering conversations with a member of the clergy by a believer seeking spiritual counseling), a privilege covering clinical social workers (in their counseling functions), and a qualified journalist-source privilege (entitling journalists sometimes to refuse to disclose the name of sources and to withhold their notes). A few jurisdictions recognize a privilege for accountants, and some jurisdictions recognize a privilege covering researchers and academics engaged in research. A qualified privilege for trade secrets has long been recognized, but this privilege operates to limit the degree of disclosure and the use to which disclosed material can be put, rather than blocking disclosure altogether. A narrow privilege exists covering political votes. Numerous specific statutory privileges cover reports that citizens must file with government agencies.

Question: What are the important governmental privileges?

Answer: There are four major governmental privileges. One covers state secrets, both military and diplomatic. Another covers official information, including deliberative materials and investigative materials. The third privilege covers confidential informers and applies both to informers who give information used to obtain warrants and make arrests and to informers who give information relevant to guilt. The fourth privilege covers confidential presidential communications.

Question: Who is covered by the Fifth Amendment privilege against self-incrimination, and when does the privilege apply?

Answer: The privilege against self-incrimination applies to persons, but not to corporations or other entities. Hence a corporate agent, when asked to produce corporate records, must do so even if those records tend to incriminate the agent (although good authority indicates that fact of production cannot be used against the agent). The privilege applies to **testimonial** material (essentially words, whether written or oral, and communicative acts), but not to physical evidence such as bodily fluids, fingerprints, and handwriting exemplars. The privilege applies to defendants in criminal cases, and to people who have not been charged with crimes. Under the Fifth Amendment, a person who is a defendant in a criminal case is entitled not to take the witness stand and not to be called as a witness. If a defendant testifies, he must submit to cross-examination, but the Fifth Amendment limits the prosecutor to "relevant cross-examination." Persons who are not defendants in criminal cases have no privilege against being called, but they do have a privilege not to give answers that would be self-incriminating.

Question: Why are statements made to police officers admissible against criminal defendants?

Answer: Of course some statements by defendants to police officers are excludable, such as those given after arrest in response to police questioning if *Miranda* warnings have not been given. But the Fifth Amendment creates a right against compelled self-incrimination, not against voluntary statements.

Question: What does incrimination mean?

Answer: For purposes of the Fifth Amendment, a statement is incriminating if it would be relevant in a criminal trial against the maker of the statement, and the question whether a statement is incriminating is resolved by reference to the implications of the question in the setting in which it is asked. There must be some actual danger of prosecution, not a mere fanciful danger, and the privilege does not apply if the claimant cannot be prosecuted because the statute of limitations has run or because he has already been tried for the offense and could not be tried again under the Double Jeopardy Clause. If a person has been given use immunity under the *Kastigar* case, meaning that the government has agreed not to use his statement against him, there is no longer a privilege to refuse to give answers. Broader "transactional immunity" blocking prosecution for the underlying criminal acts is not necessary. But a person may claim the privilege if he may be prosecuted by any sovereign, so immunity is effective as the basis to compel testimony only if it is effective against use of the testimony by any sovereign. In the United States, testimony given under a grant of federal immunity may not be used in state court, and vice versa.

Question: When, if ever, can triers of fact draw inferences from a claim of the Fifth Amendment privilege?

Answer: In civil cases, there appears to be no constitutional bar to comment and inference based on a party's claim of the privilege, under the *Palmigiano* case. In the narrow circumstance in which an accused defendant in a criminal case testifies positively that he told police the same story he repeats at trial, the prosecutor can rebut by showing that on the prior occasion the accused said nothing, even though saying nothing could be viewed as an exercise of rights under the Fifth Amendment. Under the *Jenkins* case, the prosecutor can show that the accused did not come forward and report the crime to police (which is occasionally probative, but not always), and under the *Weir* case the prosecutor can report that after arrest (but before police questioning, or the warnings that must be given before custodial interrogation proceeds) the defendant did not speak. But in most other settings, comment and argument on claims of the privilege (or exercises of the right not to speak or testify) are impermissible. Under *Griffin,* the prosecutor cannot comment or argue that failing to take the stand indicates guilt, and indeed the defense is entitled to an instruction directing juries not to consider this point. Under the *Doyle* doctrine, the prosecutor cannot show that the accused declined to talk after receiving *Miranda* warnings.

Question: Does the Fifth Amendment privilege apply to writings?

Answer: Mostly not, although the privilege certainly does apply to any written confession that the accused signs or executes under duress by law enforcement officers. Pre-existing documents, made voluntarily and without any government pressure or official requirement, however, are not covered because there is no coercion. But the self-incrimination privilege does play a role, even with respect to pre-existing documents: In its 1984 decision in the *Doe* case, the Supreme Court recognized that merely producing records in response to a subpoena duces tecum has the effect of acknowledging that what is produced is what the government sought in the first place, and this effect amounts to self-incrimination. Hence the Court held obtaining records this way *presumptively* violates the privilege against self-incrimination held by the person in question, and the government may not do so unless it can establish the authenticity of the materials in question without relying on the fact of production.

And the Court has recognized that when the government requires a person to keep records, offering such records against the person can violate her privilege against self-incrimination. Under the decisions in *Grosso* and *Albertson* and others, required records may be used against the person who keeps them only if the purpose of requiring records was "regulatory," the records are of the sort that the person customarily keeps, and the records themselves have "public aspects" that make them at least "analogous" to public documents.

EXAM TIPS

Here are some tips on issues relating to privileges:

Remember that privileges are generally lost if not claimed when privileged matter is sought.

In connection with the attorney-client privilege, remember that the privilege belongs to the client (not the lawyer), and it covers **communications** and not the underlying facts, which the client must still disclose if asked. Remember too that there are important exceptions, including:

The crime/fraud exception, under which the privilege does not apply to communications in furtherance of **future or ongoing** crimes or frauds.

The exception for **identity of the client**, under which the privilege does not cover name, address, and fee arrangements of the client, except that the privilege applies after all to such material under the *Baird* doctrine if disclosure would reveal the legal advice given by the lawyer.

In connection with the spousal privileges, remember that there are two of them, including:

The spousal testimony privilege, which applies to testimony by one spouse against another in *criminal* trials. Some states say *both* the party and the witness hold the privilege (testimony is allowed only if neither claims it). Others say only the *party* holds the privilege (witness cannot refuse if defendant doesn't claim privilege). In federal courts (and some states have followed), the *Trammel* doctrine states the privilege belongs only to the witness (defendant cannot block testimony that the witness is willing to give). The spouses must be married at the time of trial.

The marital confidences privilege, which applies in both civil and criminal cases and covers confidential statements *during marriage*. The spouses need not be married at the time of trial.

There are professional privileges covering communications to doctors, psycho-therapists, members of the clergy, social workers, and journalists.

There are governmental privileges that cover state secrets, certain official information (deliberative and investigative materials), informers' identity, and presidential communications.

The privilege against self-incrimination is the only privilege created by the Constitution, and it applies only to persons, not entities. Under this privilege:

A defendant need not testify, and his silence at trial cannot be made the subject of comment or argument.

Post-arrest post-*Miranda*-warning silence in the face of police questioning may not be used against the defendant.

A grant of **use immunity** can remove the privilege claim, which means the defendant would have to testify even if he can still be prosecuted for the underlying offense on the basis of other evidence (in other words, **transactional immunity** is not required).

CHAPTER 15

Burdens and Presumptions

CHAPTER OVERVIEW

The key points in this chapter are

- The term burden of proof can refer either to the burden of production or to the burden of persuasion.

- There are three standards of proof, or persuasion: Preponderance of the evidence, clear and convincing evidence, and proof beyond reasonable doubt.

- The term burden of production refers to the burden of producing **sufficient evidence** to enable a reasonable factfinder (the jury in a jury-tried case) to find all the elements in a a charge, claim or defense.

- The term burden of persuasion refers to the burden of **actually persuading** the factfinder (the jury in a jury-tried case) on all the elements in a charge, claim or defense.

- In a criminal case, the prosecutor has the burden of persuasion on all elements of the charge beyond a reasonable doubt.

- In most cases the party having the burden of production also has the burden of persuasion.

- Generally the term presumption describes a mandatory conclusion, and the term inference describes a permitted conclusion (one that the factfinder can reach, but need not), but in criminal cases the term presumption is often understood to mean inference (a permitted conclusion) because the jury in a criminal case **cannot be instructed** that it must find any fact against the accused.

- In civil cases, a presumption usually arises on proof of certain basic facts, and the presumption means that *if* the basic facts are established, *then* the presumed fact must be found unless there is other proof indicating that the presumed fact is not so.

- In civil cases, a presumption **shifts the burden of production** and, if the presumed fact is not contested, requires a finding of the presumed fact. If the presumed fact is contested, there are differing views on the effect of the presumption.

- In civil cases, FRE 301 provides that presumptions **do not shift the burden of persuasion**, and many states also follow this Rule, but some states adhere to the view that civil presumptions do shift the burden of persuasion.

- Presumptions, in the sense described above for civil cases, generally cannot operate against defendants in criminal cases. Although courts speak of presumptions in this setting, for the most part they are simply using that term to describe a **permissive inference.**

- In criminal cases the proper way of communicating to juries the role of a presumption (more precisely, a permissive inference) requires the court to stress the overall evidentiary context and the requirement that the prosecutor prove every element of the offense beyond reasonable doubt. If a court gives such a **contextual instruction,** then the relationship between the facts giving rise to the presumption and the presumed fact need only satisfy the preponderance standard (the former must make the latter "more likely than not").

A. BURDEN OF PROOF DEFINED

The term "burden of proof" has two very different meanings. It can refer to either the burden of production or the burden of persuasion.

1. Burden of Production

This term describes the requirement imposed on each party to produce **sufficient evidence** to support a jury finding in its favor on the elements of its charge, claim, or defense. Carrying the burden of production means producing sufficient evidence on every element. Failing to carry this burden means that the other side should prevail on a motion to dismiss or on a motion for a directed verdict or judgment as a matter of law.

a. Shifting burden of production

If a party succeeds spectacularly well in carrying its burden of production by offering evidence of such great persuasive force (what might be called "cogent and compelling") that a reasonable jury would have to find in its favor on all the elements in its case, *then the burden of production shifts* to the other side. Unless the other side then carries its burden by offering sufficient counterproof to enable a jury to find in its favor, the original party may prevail on a motion to dismiss, or for a directed verdict or for judgment as a matter of law.

b. Prosecutor cannot win such motions

In criminal cases, the special consideration given to defendants on the basis of the Constitution means that prosecutors cannot win motions for judgment as a matter of law. The only exception to this rule is that prosecutors can win motions to dismiss affirmative defenses, like insanity and self-defense, if the defendant fails to carry its burden of production on such defenses.

2. Burden of Persuasion

This term describes the requirement of persuading the factfinder (the jury if there is one, or the court in a bench trial) on every element of its charge, claim, or defense.

a. Standard of proof

The burden of persuasion is usually described in terms of a standard of proof (in most civil cases, it is the preponderance standard; in all criminal cases it is the standard of proof beyond a reasonable doubt), and this subject is taken up below. If the factfinder considers the evidence evenly balanced, the party bearing the burden of persuasion loses (plaintiff in a civil case, prosecutor in a criminal case), and the prosecutor also loses in a criminal case if the factfinder believes the elements in its case probably exist, but is not convinced beyond a reasonable doubt.

b. Burdens coincide

At the beginning of trial, normally the party who bears the burden of persuasion also bears the burden of production. In a sense, the larger burden (persuasion) embraces the smaller (production), and it is necessary to carry the latter if one is to succeed in the former.

c. Burden of persuasion never shifts

As noted above, the burden of production sometimes shifts from one side to the other, as happens if a party offers cogent and compelling evidence that a reasonable jury would be required to accept. It is usually said, however, that the burden of persuasion never shifts. Normally the burden of persuasion is set at the beginning of the case, and it only operates when the case goes to the jury or is submitted to the judge for decision. Under one approach to presumptions, however, the burden of persuasion *can* shift (a point explored below).

B. STANDARDS OF PROOF

1. Three Common Standards

There are three common standards of proof by which the factfinder must be persuaded in order for a litigant to satisfy its burden of persuasion.

a. Preponderance of the evidence

The preponderance standard requires convincing the jury that the existence of a particular fact is more probable than its nonexistence. Most civil claims and defenses require proof by only a preponderance of the evidence. Similarly the preponderance standard applies to most (but not all) affirmative defenses in criminal cases.

b. Clear and convincing

In connection with some claims and defenses, a standard that is more stringent than the preponderance standard applies. In civil cases based on claims of fraud, for example, the plaintiff is often required to satisfy the clear and convincing evidence standard. Likewise in federal criminal cases, the defense of insanity must be proven by clear and convincing evidence. See 18 U.S.C. § 17(b). Similarly, before a person may be civilly committed, the state must demonstrate by clear and convincing evidence that he is mentally ill and dangerous. See *Addington v. Texas*, 441 U.S. 418 (1979).

c. Beyond reasonable doubt

In criminal cases, the prosecution must prove all elements of the charged offense beyond a reasonable doubt. This requirement comes not only from the common law, but is now a constitutional requirement, and this constitutional requirement applies in both state and federal courts. See *In re Winship*, 397 U.S. 358 (1970) (Due Process Clause of 14th Amendment requires states to observe this standard).

C. ASSIGNMENT OF BURDENS IN CIVIL CASES

1. Burden of Pleading

As a general rule, a party making a claim or asserting a defense must plead the elements of that claim or defense. However, common law tradition or local practice may control the matter of details in pleadings. For example, in a contract action normally a plaintiff need allege only agreement, consideration, performance, breach, and resultant damages and not additional points that bear on the right to recover, such as capacity to contract.

2. Burden of Production

As a general rule, a party has the burden of producing evidence whenever a finding against the party on a point would be required in absence of further evidence. Normally a party is assigned the burden of production with respect to the allegations it has made in its pleadings. There are certain exceptions. For example, plaintiff in an action to collect money on a promissory note is required to allege nonpayment, but the defendant has the burden of producing evidence of payment (and also the burden of persuasion on this point) if she claims that payment was made.

3. Burden of Persuasion

As a general matter, a party has the burden of persuasion on each fact, the existence or nonexistence of which is essential to his claim or defense. The essential elements of a claim or defense are determined by the substantive law, not the law of evidence. The burden of persuasion usually follows the burden of production as well as the burden of pleading. Thus a litigant is normally required to persuade the factfinder (as well as produce evidence) on each claim or defense it has asserted. As noted above, defendant in a suit on a promissory note bears the burden of persuasion on the question of payment if she raises in her answer the affirmative defense of payment.

D. ASSIGNMENT OF BURDENS IN CRIMINAL CASES

1. Burden of Production

a. Prosecution burdens

The prosecution is required to carry the burden of production with respect to each element of the charge. If it fails to produce evidence sufficient to support a jury finding beyond a reasonable doubt with respect to *all* elements, a motion for directed verdict of acquittal must be granted.

b. Defense burdens

i. **"Defenses" that only negate an element of the charge**
Sometimes lawyers speak of "defenses" that are not true affirmative defenses because they merely negate an element of the prosecution's case. For example, the "defense" of consent in a rape case merely rebuts the allegation of nonconsent, which is an element that the prosecution is required to prove. Defendants do not have to carry a burden of production on these types of "defenses"—at least they do not have to carry such a burden in the sense of that they would lose on the issue if they failed to produce evidence. Even though they produce no evidence whatsoever, they do not *necessarily* or *automatically* lose on such a point, although it is probably true in most cases that their risk of losing is greater if the do not offer any evidence in their favor.

ii. **Affirmative defenses**
A true affirmative defense is one that goes beyond negating an element of the charge and alleges new matter that mitigates or eliminates criminal liability. The defendant can be required to carry the burden of production with respect to affirmative defenses. For example, if the defendant fails to produce any evidence of duress, the court will not submit a duress defense to the jury.

2. Burden of Persuasion

a. Prosecution burdens
The prosecution carries the burden of persuading the jury beyond a reasonable doubt on all elements of the charge. See *In re Winship*, 397 U.S. 358 (1970).

b. Defense burdens

i. **"Defenses" that only negate an element of the charge**
The defendant has no burden of persuasion with respect to "defenses" that merely negate an element of the charge. If the prosecution fails to carry its burden of persuasion beyond a reasonable doubt, the defendant should be acquitted even if he produces no evidence in his favor.

ii. Affirmative defenses

Whether the defendant is required to carry the burden of persuasion on an affirmative defense depends on local law and which defense is being asserted. Sometimes the prosecution is required to disprove an affirmative defense once it has been raised by the defendant. More commonly, the defendant is required to carry both the burden of production and the burden of persuasion with respect to affirmative defenses. Usually the defendant is required to establish the affirmative defense by only a preponderance of the evidence. But under federal law, a defendant must prove the insanity defense by clear and convincing evidence.

E. PRESUMPTIONS AND RELATED CONCEPTS DEFINED

1. Presumption

In civil cases, a presumption is a rule of law that *if* a certain basic fact or facts are established, *then* the presumed fact *must* be found *in absence of evidence rebutting that presumed fact* (sometimes called "counterproof"). The same term appears in criminal cases, but presumptions cannot operate against criminal defendants in the same way that they operate in civil cases because a verdict cannot be directed against the defendant in a criminal case, in whole or in part. In both civil and criminal cases, the term "presumption" is sometimes modified by terms like "mandatory" or "rebuttable." These adjectives are accurate enough, at least in civil cases, but they are also unnecessary because the term "presumption" standing already carries the meaning of a device that requires a finding of the presumed facts once the basic facts are shown, unless the other side offers proof in rebuttal.

2. Inference

An inference is a rule of law that *if* a particular basic fact is established, *then* another inferred fact *may* be found. An inference is sometimes confusingly and improperly referred to as a permissive presumption. When a civil presumption is met with counterproof, sometimes an inference is left (the conclusion *can* still be drawn but the factfinder is not *required* to draw it). In criminal cases, with respect to presumptions operating against the defendant, a presumption generally operates as an inference from the very beginning, even though the term presumption is still used.

3. Conclusive or Irrebuttable Presumption

An irrebuttable presumption is a rule of law that if a particular basic fact is established a certain presumed fact must be found. The finding is mandatory even if evidence rebutting the presumed fact is offered, thereby distinguishing this concept from a true presumption. An irrebuttable presumption is simply a rule of substantive law that does not belong in an evidence code. Some states, for example, observe an irrebuttable presumption that a child born of a woman and man who are married to each other is the child of both, absent proof that the man is impotent or proof of nonaccess. In effect, this rule is substantive rather than evidentiary in nature.

4. Prima Facie Case

The term prima facie case has two meanings. Sometimes it is used to indicate that a party has carried its burden of production (the party "has made out a prima facie case") and is therefore entitled to submit its case to the jury. Other times the term is used to mean that the party has carried its burden of production so successfully that the burden of production has shifted to the opponent. If the opponent fails to produce counterproof, then a finding in accordance with the prima facie case is required as a matter of law. Under this latter interpretation, prima facie case has essentially the same meaning and operative effect as a presumption.

F. SOURCES AND EXAMPLES OF PRESUMPTIONS

1. Sources

a. Evidence codes

Many state evidence codes contain a nonexclusive list of the presumptions that are part of the law in that state, but the Federal Rules do not contain a list of presumptions recognized in federal courts.

b. Statutes

Many federal and state statutes set forth presumptions applicable to certain types of lawsuits. For example, the Uniform Commercial Code contains several presumptions applicable in commercial litigation, and federal legislation creates presumptions relating to employment discrimination claims.

c. Caselaw

In many jurisdictions, there are important presumptions that have not been codified but that can be found in appellate caselaw.

2. Examples

The following are examples of commonly recognized presumptions.

a. Absent seven years

A person not heard from in seven years is presumed to be dead.

b. Receipt from proper mailing

A letter properly mailed is presumed to have been delivered to the recipient in due course (usually three days).

c. Continuing status or condition

A status or condition once shown to exist is presumed to continue to exist.

d. Sudden, violent death is accidental

A death that occurs suddenly and violently is presumed to be accidental (rather than suicide or the result of crime).

e. Negligence by bailee

If goods are entrusted to a bailee in good condition and returned in damaged condition, it is presumed that the bailee was negligent and that this negligence caused the damage.

f. Causation of disease

If it is shown that someone suffering from black lung disease worked at least ten years in a coal mine, it is presumed that the disease came from mining. See 30 U.S.C. § 921.

g. Official duty performed

Official duty has been regularly performed.

h. Intent of actor

A person intends the ordinary consequences of voluntary acts.

i. Suppressed evidence

Evidence willfully suppressed would be adverse to the party suppressing it.

j. Date on writing

A writing has been truly dated.

k. Marriage

There are several presumptions relating to marriage. One important presumption arises on proof that a man and woman have gone through a ceremonial marriage, and the presumed fact is that the marriage is valid. Another presumption is that a marriage continues in effect unless shown to have been ended. And it is sometimes presumed that a man and woman who believe themselves to be married and who act as though they are married are in fact lawfully married.

l. Legitimacy of child

A child born in lawful wedlock is presumed legitimate.

m. Capacity to contract

A person is presumed to have capacity to contract.

n. Scope of employment

A person shown to be an employee is presumed to have been within the scope of his employment.

o. Permission of owner

A person driving a loaned car is presumed to have had the owner's permission, and is sometimes presumed to have been driving within the scope of that permission.

G. REASONS FOR CREATING PRESUMPTIONS

1. Probability

One common reason for creating a presumption is to resolve a point that is hard to prove by resorting to probability instead of requiring actual proof. Receipt of a letter is often difficult for the sender to prove, but despite occasional lapses by the Postal Service, the overwhelming majority of properly posted letters are properly delivered to the intended recipient. Therefore a presumption to this effect, shifting the burden of production to the party contending that the letter was not received, makes perfect sense as a matter of probability.

2. Access to Evidence

Sometimes evidence relating to a disputed issue is more readily accessible to one party than the other. For example, it is hard for a bailor to know whether bailed goods were damaged by the negligence of the bailee or by act of God. A presumption of negligence by the bailee shifts to the party in custody of the goods the burden to produce evidence on this point. Since the bailee is also the party who is more likely to know and have ready access to prove relating to the cause of the damage, this presumption makes sense from the perspective of putting the burden on the party who is more likely to be able to carry it.

3. Social Policy

Many presumptions rest on social policy. A good example is the presumption described above, to the effect that a child of a woman who is married to a man is the child of both of them (absent proof of nonaccess or impotence), which serves the important social policy of keeping families in tact and assuring that children have parental figures in their life, and it achieves the desirable result that fewer children can be labeled "illegitimate."

H. CONFLICTING PRESUMPTIONS

Sometimes two presumptions conflict. If, for example, a man marries first one woman and then another, it is presumed that the first marriage is valid and ongoing, and it is also presumed that the second marriage is valid and ongoing. But they cannot both be valid and ongoing, and sometimes the conflict is resolved by presuming that the later of the two marriages is valid, hence that the first marriage lawfully ended before the second began.

1. General Rule

When presumptions conflict, the general rule is that the presumption applies that is founded on weightier considerations of policy and logic.

2. Equally Strong Presumptions

If the considerations of policy and logic underlying each presumption are of equal weight, neither presumption applies.

I. RELATIONSHIP BETWEEN PRESUMPTIONS AND BURDENS

In civil cases, presumptions affect both the burden of production and the burden of persuasion, but the nature of this effect turns in part on the approach taken to presumptions.

1. Presumption Both Satisfies and Shifts Burden of Production

When the basic facts are established and the presumption comes into play, it satisfies the burden of production for the party for whom the presumption operates, and it also shifts the burden of production to the other side.

☛ **EXAMPLE AND ANALYSIS**

Paul is the beneficiary on his sister Karen's life insurance policy, and he sues the insurance carrier to collect. Paul cannot directly prove that Karen has died, but he offers cogent and compelling evidence (proof any reasonable juror would accept) that she disappeared more than seven years ago, and nobody has heard from her. The insurance carrier offers no proof to the contrary.

Paul can take advantage of a presumption that "a person not heard from in seven years is dead." He has satisfied his *burden of production* on the issue of her death, and the presumption means that the burden of production shifted to the carrier. In failing to present proof that Karen was still alive, the carrier failed to rebut the presumption, and the factfinder must find that Karen is dead. The jury can be so instructed.

---

2. **Presumption Can Satisfy Burden of Persuasion**

In the example just considered, the presumption of death shifts the burden of production to the insurance carrier, and it also satisfies Paul's burden of persuasion if the carrier fails to present proof that Karen is still alive.

3. **In Some Jurisdictions Presumptions Can Shift Burden of Persuasion**

Under what is commonly called the Morgan view of presumptions, which is followed in a substantial minority of states, presumptions actually shift the burden of persuasion. This point is examined further below. In the example just considered, this view would mean that the insurance carrier now bears the burden of persuasion on the question whether Karen is still alive. If it offers testimony that one of her friends thinks that he saw Karen recently, that might suffice to enable a jury to find that Karen was still alive. But the jury would be instructed that the carrier bears the burden of persuasion on this point and that the jury should find in favor of the insurance company only if it believes by a preponderance of the evidence that Karen is still alive.

J. EFFECT OF PRESUMPTION WHEN COUNTERPROOF CONTESTS THE BASIC FACT

If the opponent introduces counterproof contesting the basic fact only, then the presumption applies only if the jury finds the basic fact to be established.

☛ EXAMPLE AND ANALYSIS

In the problem above, assume that at trial the insurance company calls Helen, a cousin of Paul's, who testifies that she remembers receiving a Christmas card from Karen three years ago. On cross-examination, Paul challenges Helen's memory and raises significant doubts about her credibility.

The insurance company has produced counterproof contesting the basic fact ("not heard from in seven years"). Before the jury can rely on the presumption to find the presumed fact (Karen is dead), it must first resolve the dispute over the basic fact (whether Karen has been heard from during the last seven years). Thus, the presumption must be presented to the jury conditionally. The jury will be instructed that the presumption of death applies only if the jury finds that Karen has not been heard from for seven years.

K. EFFECT OF PRESUMPTION WHEN COUNTERPROOF CONTESTS THE PRESUMED FACT

There are differing views on the question what should be done if the party opposing the presumption offers evidence challenging the existence of the presumed fact.

1. Thayer View

The common law follows the view of Professor Thayer, set forth in writings in the early part of the twentieth century, that a presumption shifts only the burden of production. Under this approach, the presumption disappears from the case in the face of sufficient counterproof challenging the presumed fact. Thus it is sometimes referred to as the "bursting bubble" view.

2. Morgan View

The position long advocated by Professor Morgan in the middle of the twentieth century is that a presumption shifts the burden of persuasion to the opponent to disprove the existence of the presumed fact. This view was adopted by the drafters of the Federal Rules but rejected by Congress. But URE II adopts the Morgan view, and a significant number of states also take this approach. See URE 301 (a presumption "imposes upon the party against whom it is directed the burden of proving that the nonexistence of the presumed fact is more probable than its existence").

3. Intermediate Views

Between Thayer and Morgan, there are at least three intermediate views under which presumptions do not automatically disappear when counterproof is offered that is sufficient to support a finding of the nonexistence of the presumed fact. First is the view that presumptions play a role until "substantial and uncontradicted" evidence is offered against the presumed fact. Second is the view that presumptions play a role until the adverse party offers counterproof that the jury believes. Third is the "equipoise" view, which holds that presumptions play a role until the factfinders believe the nonexistence of the presumed fact is as likely as its existence. These intermediate views give presumptions more effect than the Thayer view, but less than the Morgan view. The bottom line is that these intermediate views allow presumptions to take the case to the jury, even when there is counterproof against the presumed fact.

4. Presumption as "Evidence" View

Another approach is known as the presumption as "evidence" view. Congress considered this approach as an alternative to what is now FRE 301. The House of Representatives adopted it in the following form (although it was ultimately rejected by the Senate): "[A] presumption imposes on the party against whom it is directed the burden of going forward with the evidence, and, even though met with contradicting evidence, a presumption is sufficient evidence of the fact presumed, to be considered by the trier of facts." This approach has now been abandoned by almost all jurisdictions.

5. California Combined Approach

California and several other states follow the common law view (presumption shifts only burden of production) for presumptions based on probability and logical inference. It follows the Uniform Rules view (presumption shifts burden of persuasion) for presumptions based on public policy. See Cal. Ev. Code §§ 630–660.

L. EFFECT OF PRESUMPTIONS UNDER FRE 301

Under FRE 301, a presumption shifts only the burden of production but not the burden of persuasion ("the risk of nonpersuasion").

1. Extent of Counterproof Required

By shifting the burden of production, FRE 301 requires the opponent to produce counterproof in order to prevent a finding of the presumed fact as a matter of law. While the opponent need not disprove the presumed fact by a preponderance of evidence, the opponent must introduce *sufficient evidence* to support a jury finding that the presumed fact is not so.

2. Federal Statutory Presumptions

When a presumption is created by federal statute, FRE 301 does not necessarily control its effect because the Rule applies only where "not otherwise provided." Often courts conclude that statutory presumptions, including presumptions that simply implement specific statutory schemes, do not behave in the manner prescribed by FRE 301.

M. RECOGNITION OF STATE PRESUMPTIONS IN FEDERAL CIVIL CASES

1. Presumptions Are Substantive

FRE 302 adopts the view that presumptions are matters of substance rather than procedure. See *Erie R.R. Co. v. Tompkins,* 304 U.S. 64 (1938). In other words, federal courts apply state presumptions, and give them the effect called for by state law, when such presumptions bear on elements of claims or defenses governed by state law.

2. Tactical Presumptions

State law controls only presumptions bearing on elements of claims or defenses. It does not apply to presumptions having a lesser effect, which are referred to by the ACN to FRE 302 as "tactical" presumptions.

N. PRESUMPTIONS IN CRIMINAL CASES

In criminal cases, presumptions cannot operate as they do in civil cases because courts cannot direct a verdict in whole or in part against the accused. In a drug case, there might be a presumption, arising from proof that drugs were found in the defendant's bedroom (in a space that he controlled), that the defendant possessed those drugs. Even if the basic fact is established, and indeed even if the defendant *concedes* that the drugs were found in his bedroom, and even if he *offers no counterproof* indicating that the drugs belonged to someone else (or at least not to him), *nevertheless* a court cannot direct a jury that it must find that the defendant possessed the drugs. At most, a court could instruct a jury that it might be infer, if it chooses, on the basis of the presence of the drugs in the defendant's bedroom and all the other evidence in the case, that the defendant possessed the drugs, if the jury believes that fact to be proved beyond reasonable doubt. In effect, the presumption in a criminal case operates in the manner of a permissive inference. Still courts speak of presumptions in criminal cases, and it is important to recognize that they mean something very different from what they mean when they use the same term in civil cases.

1. Irrebuttable Presumptions

Irrebuttable presumptions are not allowed because they would relieve the prosecution of its proof burdens and violate the due process rights of a defendant to challenge the prosecution's case. See *Sandstrom v. Montana,* 442 U.S. 510 (1979).

2. Presumptions That Shift Burden of Persuasion

Presumptions that shift the burden of persuasion to the defendant are not permitted in criminal cases. They would violate the rule that the prosecution is required to prove each element of the charge beyond a reasonable doubt. See *In re Winship*, 397 U.S. 358 (1970).

3. Presumptions That Shift Burden of Production

In its leading decision in *Sandstrom*, the Supreme Court did not say whether a presumption operating against the accused could constitutionally shift to the defense the burden of production. It is, however, highly doubtful that such a presumption could be constitutional because, once again, the prosecution could not get an instruction requiring the jury to find an element of the charge against the accused if he failed to produce evidence tending to show the nonexistence of the presumed fact. See *Sandstrom v. Montana*, 442 U.S. 510 (1979).

4. Presumptions on Matters Other Than Guilt

It is constitutional to recognize presumptions that operate against defendants in criminal cases on matters not directly related to the issue of guilt. For example, the Court once approved a presumption that "a defendant is presumed competent to stand trial unless it is proved by a preponderance of the evidence that the defendant is mentally incompetent." This presumption addresses only competency to stand trial, and does not relate to elements of the charge, so the Court decided that *Winship* and *Sandstrom* were not controlling. See *Medina v. California*, 505 U.S. 437 (1992). But see *Cooper v. Oklahoma*, 517 U.S. 348 (1996) (cannot make criminal defendant prove incompetence by clear and convincing evidence).

O. INFERENCES IN CRIMINAL CASES

1. Generally Permitted

Inference instructions, unlike instructions telling the jury to find in accordance with a presumption, are permitted in criminal cases if they satisfy constitutional standards. In some states inference instructions are not allowed on the ground that they violate state policy against judges commenting on the evidence.

2. Constitutional Limitation

In a pathbreaking decision in the *Allen* case, the Supreme Court held as a matter of due process that a presumption can operate against the accused in the manner of a permissive inference, but only if the relationship between the basic fact and the presumed (or inferred) fact satisfies a "rational basis" standard. The Court did not elaborate what it meant by "rational basis," but pretty clearly this standard is best captured in the phrase "more likely than not" or "preponderance." In other words, *Allen* requires that the basic fact support an inference of the presumed (or inferred) fact because the former makes the latter likely true than not. See *County Court of Ulster County v. Allen,* 442 U.S. 140 (1979).

Allen stressed that in conveying the sense of such a presumption to the jury, it is to be judged by this rather lenient "rational basis" (or "more likely than not") standard *only if* the judge gives what amounts to contextual instructions stressing that (a) the question whether the presumed (or inferred) fact exists is to be decided on the basis of all the evidence, including the basic fact, and (b) every element in the case must be proved beyond reasonable doubt. If an instruction does not describe the presumption (or inference) in context, and instead *isolates* the presumption (or inference), inviting the jury to infer the truth of the presumed (or inferred) fact by looking only to the basic fact, then the presumption must pass a much higher constitutional standard, under which it can be said that the basic fact proves the presumed (or inferred) fact beyond a reasonable doubt. As a practical matter, almost no imaginable presumption can satisfy this high standard.

☞ EXAMPLE AND ANALYSIS

Dr. Timothy Leary, a professor at Harvard University, is stopped by customs inspectors in Laredo, Texas, as he returns from Mexico. Marijuana seeds and a silver snuffbox filled with marijuana and three partially smoked marijuana cigarettes are discovered in his car. Leary is charged with transporting marijuana while knowing that it had been illegally imported into the country. At trial, Leary admits possessing the marijuana but denies it was illegally imported from a foreign country. He claims he carried it from New York to Mexico and then back. Under a federal statute, the judge tells the jury that it can infer, from the fact that Leary possessed the marijuana, that he knew it had been illegally imported.

This inference is irrational and unconstitutional because much marijuana is grown domestically rather than imported. Therefore, the inferred fact (importation) does not follow more likely than not from the basic fact (possession). See *Leary v. United States,* 395 U.S. 6 (1969) (reversing conviction).

REVIEW QUESTIONS AND ANSWERS

Question: What is the relationship between burdens and presumptions in civil cases?

Answer: In civil cases, presumptions help litigants satisfy their burdens of production and persuasion, and in fact presumptions shift the burden of production to the other side. If the proponent establishes the basic fact by cogent and compelling evidence and there is no counterproof contesting either the basic fact or the presumed fact, the presumption satisfies the burden of production, shifts that burden to the other side, and satisfies the burden of persuasion on the presumed fact. In this setting, the jury must find the presumed fact. If the opponent produces counterproof contesting only the basic fact (but not such strong counterproof that it requires rejecting the basic fact as a matter of law), then the presumption can still operate if the jury finds that the basic fact is established. If so, once again the presumption satisfies the burden of production, shifts it to the other side, and satisfies the burden of persuasion on the presumed fact. If the opponent produces counterproof indicating that the presumed fact is not so, then the effect of the presumption depends on whether the jurisdiction adopts the Thayer or Morgan view. Under the Thayer view, the presumption disappears in the face of evidence sufficient to support a finding of the nonexistence of the presumed fact. Thus the presumption drops from the case and no longer helps the party for whom it operated. Under the Morgan view, the presumption has a much stronger effect. It still satisfies the burden of production (although the counterproof has satisfied the opponent's burden of production), and it shifts the burden of persuasion to the opponent to prove the nonexistence of the presumed fact.

Question: Why do we have presumptions?

Answer: Presumptions serve several useful purposes. They sometimes help litigants establish facts that are likely to exist but may be hard to prove (a properly posted letter reached the person to whom it was addressed in due course). Sometimes they allocate the burden of producing evidence to the party having best access to such evidence (the bailee must come up with proof relating to its own due care and the cause of damage to goods). Sometimes presumptions favor or disfavor certain results for reasons of social policy (the presumption that sudden violent death was accidental favors recovery for surviving family members suing insurance companies and reduces occasions when survivors must face not only loss from death but the sadness of knowing that death was self-inflicted).

Question: What burdens can criminal defendants be required to carry?

Answer: Since the prosecution must prove every element of a charge beyond reasonable doubt, defendant cannot be required to shoulder any burdens on such elements. If the defendant asserts a defense that does no more than negate an element of the charge (consent in a rape case), then the defense is simply a way of contesting the element of nonconsent, which the prosecutor must prove beyond reasonable doubt. Hence defendant has no burden with respect to this element. For true affirmative defenses (those raising new matter going beyond elements of the charge), both the burden of production and the burden of persuasion can be allocated to the defendant. For virtually all affirmative defenses, the defendant must produce evidence or the defense is not submitted to the jury in instructions. Once the defendant satisfies the burden of production and raises the defense, it is a matter of legislative choice whether to allocate the burden of persuasion to the defendant or to the government. Some jurisdictions allocate to the defendant the burden of persuasion on almost all affirmative defenses (the preponderance standard applies here). Other jurisdictions place on the prosecutor the burden of disproving most affirmative defenses, once they have been raised.

EXAM TIPS

Here are some tips on issues relating to burdens and presumptions:

Burden of proof means *either* burden of production *or* burden of persuasion.

Having the burden of production on a point means being required to produce enough evidence to support a jury finding on the point. The burden of production can shift as the trial unfolds, but carrying the burden of production does not shift it to the other side, except that in civil cases carrying the burden of production by "cogent and compelling" evidence can have this effect. Failing to carry this burden can result in judgment as a matter of law in a civil case, or dismissal in a criminal case (where the defense, but not the prosecutor, can win on motion if the other side fails to carry this burden).

Having the burden of persuasion on a point means being required to persuade the factfinder on this point, and this burden does not shift.

In civil cases, a **presumption** is a rule of law that if a basic fact is shown, then the presumed fact must be found, absent rebutting evidence. In contrast,

An **inference** is a conclusion that a jury may (but need not) draw on the basis of a particular fact.

A **conclusive** or **irrebuttable** presumption is a legal rule that if a certain fact is found, another must be found, no matter what.

Prima facie case describes the situation of a party who has carried his burden of production (hence is entitled to get her case to the jury for decision) or the situation of a party who has carried his burden of production so well it now shifts to his opponent.

In civil cases, presumptions shift the burden of production, and in some jurisdictions they shift the burden of persuasion as well.

If the basic facts are established (letter properly posted), the presumed fact must be found absent counterproof. Thus the burden of production has shifted.

If counterproof is offered in a jurisdiction where the presumption shifts only the burden of production (FRE 301), there are differing views of what happens. By one view, the presumption vanishes ("bursting bubble"). There are other views, under which the presumption protects an inference from extinction.

If counterproof is offered in a jurisdiction where the presumption affects the burden of persuasion, the presumption does not disappear. The case goes to the jury with instructions that the party against whom it operates bears the burden of showing the presumed fact is not so.

In civil cases, presumptions are substantive law, so federal courts in diversity cases apply state presumption law under FRE 302.

In criminal cases, presumptions of the sort described above cannot be used against the accused if they bear on elements of a crime. The reason is that the accused cannot be required to bear the burden of persuasion on such elements, and the burden of production probably cannot be shifted to the accused because an instruction requiring the jury to find the element if the accused does not carry that burden would be unconstitutional. Under the *Allen* case, however, *presumptions can operate as inferences* if they are rationally based, and if they are conveyed to the jury by instructions that stress context rather than inviting an inference from the basic fact alone, and if the instruction emphasizes the beyond reasonable doubt standard for all essential findings.

CHAPTER 16

Judicial Notice

CHAPTER OVERVIEW

The key points in this chapter are

- Judicial notice puts facts into lawsuits without requiring formal proof.

    - **Adjudicative facts,** such as who did what and when, are the ones on which trials focus and are the most important facts in deciding cases. These can be judicially noticed only if **indisputable,** which means:

    - **Generally known** to informed people, or to informed people in the jurisdiction, or

    - **Verifiable** by resort to unimpeachable sources.

- Judicial notice came from common law tradition, in which judicially noticed facts were binding and the process was not subject to any formal rules.

- FRE 201 governs judicial notice of adjudicative facts, and

    - Allows judicial notice to be taken at any stage of proceedings;

- Requires notification to parties and an opportunity to be heard on the propriety of taking judicial notice;

- Makes noticed facts binding in civil cases; and

- Makes noticed facts nonbinding in criminal cases.

- In criminal cases, some special concerns arise.

  - Post-trial notice of facts that help the prosecution and hurt the defendant is improper because the defense has no chance to offer counterproof against the noticed fact.

  - Facts relating to jurisdiction or venue are subject to this bar, but some courts allow post-trial judicial notice of such facts, on the theory that they relate only to jurisdiction and not to culpability, and that the right to offer counterproof against noticeable facts applies only to facts relating to culpability.

- **Basic facts** of two kinds are also sometimes introduced into cases through judicial notice, although FRE 201 does not apply to such facts.

  - **Communicative** facts relate to the meaning of words and language and have to do with the ways that the factfinder interprets testimony and other evidence in verbal form (such as documents). The fact that the term "car" can mean an automobile that runs on gasoline (or sometimes electricity or natural gas) and transports people from place to place on roadways is an example of a "communicative" fact that factfinders "know" and bring to bear in deciding cases.

  - **Evaluative** facts relate to ordinary human experience, and serve to assist the factfinder in understanding testimony. The fact that cars are driven on the righthand side of streets and highways in this country is an evaluative fact that factfinders

- **Legislative facts** are what courts consider in construing and applying laws, and in deciding whether laws are reasonable or rational. The fact that working long hours is deleterious to health is a legislative fact that would help a court determine the reasonableness of a law that limited to eight the number of hours that employers could expect employees to work.

- Notice of these facts is unregulated.

- Such facts need not be indisputable.

- Judicial notice of law is regulated by rules of procedure, not evidence law, and courts (rather than juries) determine what the law is.

A. INTRODUCTION

Judicial notice is the process by which courts introduce into the litigation, or take as settled, certain facts or factual propositions without formal proof. The idea is to save time and, at least in civil cases, to implement some controls and limits on what juries can do.

1. Adjudicative Facts

For any adjudicative fact, such as who did what and when, judicial notice is only proper if the fact is indisputable and either generally known (Boston is northeast of New York City) or readily ascertainable (September 22, 2007 was a Saturday).

2. Procedural Issues

Judicial notice may be taken at any stage of the proceedings. The process of taking judicial notice derives from common law tradition, where it went forward informally without notification to the parties, and in this process judicially noticed facts were usually considered binding. Under FRE 201, which covers only adjudicative facts, notification to the parties and an opportunity for input is required, and noticed facts are **binding in civil cases** but **nonbinding in criminal cases**.

3. Other Facts (Basic and Legislative)

Basic facts relate to verbal communication ("dog" means a four-legged mammal, usually smaller than grown humans) and ordinary experience (dogs are often pets and they bark and sometimes bite). Legislative facts relate to the meaning of laws (a statute barring "motorized vehicles" in the park includes motorcycles but not motorized wheelchairs). Such facts are sometimes judicially noticed, but the process is not regulated by FRE 201.

4. Judicial Notice of Law

The content of domestic law is made known to courts through a form of judicial notice, but the process is governed by provisions in the Federal Rules of Civil Procedure and the Federal Rules of Criminal Procedure.

B. ADJUDICATIVE FACTS

The "who, what, where, when, and how" of lawsuits are adjudicative facts. These are the facts to which the law is applied and the ones juries are asked to determine. See ACN to FRE 201 (quoting Davis). Formal proof is required for almost every adjudicative fact—testimonial or written evidence—but not when truth is apparent and a fact is indisputable for all practical purposes. See FRE 201 (providing for judicial notice of indisputable adjudicative facts).

1. Generally Known

Facts generally known, or generally known by informed people in the jurisdiction, may be judicially noticed. A judge in San Francisco, for example, could take judicial notice that there is regular passenger ferry service between there and Sausalito. See FRE 201(b)(1) (generally known within the jurisdiction of the trial court).

a. Not personal

The standard refers to what informed people in the area know. That a judge personally knows something is not enough if the point is not generally known. Thus a judge who has done business at First Western Bank and knows that Jordan Alford has been the branch manager for the last ten years cannot properly take judicial notice of this fact because it would not be generally known.

b. Not universal

The fact that some people in the jurisdiction might not know the fact does not matter. Doubtless some people in San Francisco do not know there is passenger ferry service between there and Sausalito, but that would not make judicial notice improper.

c. Examples

Geographical facts of a general nature and their obvious human implications readily qualify. Thus a Colorado judge may take judicial notice that traveling Interstate 70 between Denver and Vail takes motorists through the Eisenhower Tunnel, and that the drive takes more than an hour. Also qualifying are current events, language and word usage, history and politics, and economic conditions.

2. Verifiable

Facts readily verifiable by unimpeachable sources may be noticed, like the exact time of sunrise on a particular date. See FRE 201(b)(2) ("capable of accurate and ready determination" by resorting to sources that "cannot reasonably be questioned").

a. Scientific facts

Firmly established and generally accepted scientific principles, methods, or techniques may be noticed, sometimes with reference to standard treatises, expert testimony, or appellate decisions. Here taking notice can pave the way to admit expert testimony, shortening substantially the foundation that would otherwise be required. When courts in Rules jurisdictions take this kind of notice for this purpose, FRE 201 does not apply because such facts are in the nature of legislative or evaluative facts (see further discussion below) rather than adjudicative facts.

b. Geography

Courts may take judicial notice of a specific geographical fact that is not generally known, typically on the basis of referring to a map or atlas. Thus a judge in New York could take judicial notice that the distance between New York City and Albany is 325 miles, a point that she might not know but could readily ascertain.

c. History and politics

Courts may take judicial notice of historical and political facts. A judge in Illinois could take judicial notice of the date when the current governor took office, for example, and could take judicial notice that the state joined the Union in 1818.

d. Court records

Courts can take judicial notice of the content of court records, including indictments, transcripts, judgments, and appellate rulings. Such notice can establish the judicial acts and events that the record reflects, but not points that testimony or documents in such records might tend to prove. If the purpose is to prove such points, the records are hearsay, which raises the separate question of whether some exception would allow this use.

☞ EXAMPLE AND ANALYSIS

Matt is charged with armed robbery of Vista Liquors and murder of the clerk. The evidence shows that Matt and Nick acted together, with Matt firing the shot that killed the clerk. Nick pled guilty to charges and made a sworn statement in his plea proceedings. There he said the clerk made a sudden movement before being shot.

The judge has not yet decided whether to accept the plea and pass sentence on Nick in accord with the understanding reached with the prosecutor. In Matt's case, Nick testifies for the state. On cross he denies playing any role and denies "being under pressure to say what the prosecutor wants." Matt asks the judge to take judicial notice that Nick has been charged but not sentenced, and that the clerk made a sudden movement.

The judge should take judicial notice on the first point but not the second. The court record satisfies the indisputability standard in showing that charges are pending and that Nick pled guilty but has not been sentenced. The record does not satisfy the standard when offered to prove the clerk made a sudden movement, and the record is hearsay if offered to prove this point. No obvious exception is available.

C. PROCEDURAL ISSUES

Before the Federal Rules were adopted, the procedural aspects of judicial notice were largely unregulated. Various provisions in FRE 201 address procedural issues, mostly in flexible terms, and the main innovation is a provision that insures an opportunity for party input.

1. Initiating Notice

Courts may take judicial notice on their own ("sua sponte") or on request by a party. See FRE 201(c) and (d), which provide that if the criteria for taking notice are satisfied because an adjudicative fact that counts in the case is indisputably true, the court "may" take judicial notice on its own and "must" take notice on request, if supplied with relevant information such as an almanac if the fact is one that can be learned by resort to indisputable sources.

2. Party Input

Common law tradition did not include providing the parties an opportunity to be heard. But in Rules jurisdictions, FRE 201(e) states that the parties are entitled, on timely request, to an opportunity to be heard on the propriety of taking judicial notice, and that this request may be made after notice was taken if there was no prior notification.

a. Notice taken on request

When one party asks the court to take judicial notice, the request itself serves as notification to the other side, which should (if it wants a hearing) make timely request for a hearing.

b. Notice sua sponte

If the court takes judicial notice on its own, a party who might want to contest the propriety of taking this step might not have prior notification, and a request to be heard may be timely even if made after the fact.

3. Time for Taking Judicial Notice

Courts often take judicial notice during trial, but they may actually notice adjudicative facts at any stage of the proceedings, from pretrial through the appeal process. In criminal trials, however, the jury cannot be told it must find a fact adverse to the defendant, and post-trial notice would have the effect of taking away from the defendant the possibility that the jury might reject the noticed fact. See *United States v. Jones*, 580 F.2d 219 (6th Cir. 1978) (refusing to take post-trial notice that Southern Bell was a common carrier, which was essential to federal jurisdiction on charges of unlawful interception of phone messages; doing so would prevent jury from considering the issue). Even in civil cases, reliance issues may surface if a party forgoes the opportunity to offer proof in the belief that a certain fact is not in the case, and this point alone may make it improper to take judicial notice after trial.

4. Effect of Notice: Civil Cases

Here judicial notice establishes a fact conclusively, and the jury is instructed accordingly. See FRE 201(f) (jury instructed "to accept as conclusive" any noticed fact). The party adversely affected by the fact cannot offer counterproof to refute it. In a hearing on the propriety of taking judicial notice, however, such a party may attempt to show that the indisputability standard is not met by offering counterproof that the fact in question is not true. In other words, one way of showing that a fact is *not* indisputable is to dispute it in a reasonable fashion.

5. Effect of Notice: Criminal Cases

In a criminal case, judicial notice cannot conclusively establish a point, and the point to be noticed is conveyed to the jury as a permissive inference (one that the jury may draw or not as it chooses). Here arguably the party adversely affected by the point may offer counterproof. FRE 201(f), however, is silent on this particular point, and it may not be entirely free of doubt. Certainly it is preferable for such proof to be offered in the first instance in a hearing on the propriety of taking notice.

D. SPECIAL PROBLEMS IN CRIMINAL CASES

Taking judicial notice of an adjudicative fact against the accused would raise constitutional concerns because criminal defendants are entitled to have juries decide essentially every factual issue. In the analogous setting of presumptions, which sometimes operate against criminal defendants, it is settled that mandatory instructions cannot be given. See Chapter 15. A similar principle should apply in the setting of judicial notice. See *State v. Lawrence*, 234 P.2d 600 (Utah 1951) (landmark case reversing larceny conviction where trial court took judicial notice that value of stolen car exceeded $50; this procedure violated state constitution, and reviewing court asks "where would the process stop" if such notice can be taken?).

1. FRE 201(f) Is Overbroad

The special concerns that apply to criminal defendants do not seem applicable to the prosecution. Hence FRE 201(f) appears overbroad in requiring that *all* noticed facts in criminal cases be communicated to juries by permissive instructions.

2. Post–Trial Notice

As suggested above, taking post-trial judicial notice against criminal defendants is improper. Doing so would deprive the defendant of an opportunity for the jury to reject the fact. This opportunity may be constitutionally required and is required under FRE 201(f) as well.

3. Facts Relating to Jurisdiction and Venue

Sometimes reviewing courts refuse even to take post-trial notice of facts that relate only to jurisdiction or venue. See *United States v. Jones*, 580 F.2d 219 (6th Cir. 1978) (refusing to take judicial notice that Southern Bell is a common carrier). Some courts, however, allow judicial notice of facts relating to federal jurisdiction and venue in criminal cases, even where the effect of taking judicial notice is to prevent a jury from rejecting the necessary point. Arguably facts of this sort are not "adjudicative" under FRE 201, and arguably there is no entitlement to a jury trial on such points (see the discussion below). See *State v. Detrich*, 873 P.2d 1302, 1306 (Ariz. 1994) (taking judicial notice that crime, shown to have been committed in Tucson, was committed in Pima County, so venue was proper).

E. OTHER KINDS OF FACTS

Adjudicative facts (the who, what, where, when, and how) are not the only sort of facts that count in deciding cases. In Rules jurisdictions where FRE 201 governs judicial notice of adjudicative facts but not other kinds, it is sometimes important to distinguish such facts from other kinds.

1. Basic Facts

In order to avoid beginning on the most basic level, trials must go forward on the assumption that jurors have an ordinary understanding of the world. They must know, for example, that the term "car," when used in a description of a trip across town, means a self-propelled vehicle that can carry passengers and ordinary cargo like bags of groceries. And they must know, for example, that cars drive on the righthand side of the street and are required to stop when a traffic light is red.

a. Communicative facts

These are involved in the ordinary meaning of language and words. That the term "car," when used in an account of driving from home to work means a self-propelled four-wheel vehicle capable of carrying passengers, is a "communicative fact," and such knowledge is essential in *understanding testimony* in trials.

b. Evaluative facts

Knowing that cars are driven on the righthand side of the street and that motorists are required to stop at a red traffic light involves an ordinary knowledge of "evaluative facts" that are essential in *evaluating or appraising* testimony presented at trial.

c. Juries and judges

Both juries and judges "notice" these basic communicative and evaluative facts in the sense of already being aware of them and bringing them to bear in listening to and appraising the evidence presented in trials.

d. Unregulated, invisible, unconscious

Notice of these basic facts is largely unregulated and indeed largely invisible and even unconscious. FRE 201 does not apply, which means not that notice cannot be taken but that the various safeguards and limits of that provision simply do not apply in this setting.

e. Limited

The background facts that we expect juries to know are of limited scope. While jurors are expected to know, for instance, what a car is and what a red light means, they are not expected to know that the particular car involved in a suit (or cars of that kind) is powerful or sluggish, or that a particular intersection has a long or a short red light. In other words, we expect jurors to know basic facts of a general nature drawn from a lifetime of experiences, but we do not expect (and we take pains to avoid) jurors having specific factual knowledge that relates directly to the case.

☛ EXAMPLE AND ANALYSIS

In a Rules jurisdiction, the state charges Doris with criminal negligence in the death of a child in the street near a school in a snowstorm. She was driving 35 mph, according to police radar (posted speed was 25) and she braked when the child appeared in front of her but was unable to stop or even slow down in time. Afraid that the jury might acquit because the standard ("gross and willful negligence") is much higher than civil negligence, the prosecutor asks the court to take judicial notice and instruct the jury that "cars slide easily in icy conditions, and exceeding the speed limit by as little as ten miles per hour puts cars and pedestrians at risk of collision leading to damage, injury and even death." The defense objects that "the jury doesn't need such an instruction, and it is not authorized by FRE 201." Should the instruction be given?

No. The defense is right that FRE 201 does not authorize this instruction because it communicates an evaluative fact and the Rule applies only to adjudicative facts. It is also true, however, that FRE 201 does not *bar* such an instruction for the same reason: The Rule applies to adjudicative facts and leaves the matter of evaluative facts unregulated. In fact, evaluative facts sometimes find direct expression in opinions, sometimes buttressed by references to sources. Still, they are not usually communicated to juries by instruction, and part of the reason is that such an instruction would appear to be a heavy-handed judicial comment on the evidence, which courts generally avoid doing. Particularly in criminal cases where evaluative facts are likely to count against defendants, such instructions are problematic. Even in common law jurisdictions, courts would not likely give such an instruction.

2. Legislative Facts

These are the facts which courts consider in construing and applying laws, and sometimes in deciding whether they satisfy some higher standard (like constitutional standards or standards of reasonableness or rationality). Among the most famous examples are the psychological studies on effects of racially separate primary education, to which the Supreme Court adverted in construing the Equal Protection Clause in *Brown v. Board of Education*, 347 U.S. 483 (1954).

a. Invisible

Legislative facts sometimes become the subject of proof at trials, but often they are simply known to judges or introduced into the case by briefs or consultation with outside sources, and in this sense they are developed off the record. Appellate court opinions, especially Supreme Court decisions construing constitutional standards, often make express reference to historical, cultural, social, and scientific facts and may cite authorities supporting their observations. But these may be simply assumed or alluded to, and in the work of trial court judges such facts are usually invisible to outside observers.

b. Unregulated

Notice of legislative facts is unregulated, both as a matter of common law tradition and in Rules jurisdictions. As is true with basic facts, FRE 201 simply does not apply. That does not mean notice cannot be taken. Instead, it means the safeguards and limits of FRE 201 do not apply.

c. Necessary latitude

The strongest arguments for exempting legislative facts from procedural constraints stress that the law (at least judge-made law) would stop growing if judges could not take into account the facts they believe, as opposed to those that satisfy the "indisputability" criterion of judicial notice. Some have argued, however, that the parties to lawsuits should play a role in the process by which such facts are introduced into decisions, and that courts should provide notice of their intent to consider such matters so party input can be provided.

☞ EXAMPLE AND ANALYSIS

In a federal trial for illegally importing a "derivative of coca leaves," the evidence shows that defendant Ezra imported cocaine hydrochloride. Over defense objection, the trial judge instructs the jury that "cocaine hydrochloride is a derivative of coca leaves." Ezra is convicted, and he argues on appeal that the judge violated FRE 201(f) by conveying the substance of judicial notice by a mandatory instruction.

This claim should probably be rejected. Whether or not cocaine hydrochloride is a derivative of coca leaves is a matter of legislative fact to which FRE 201 does not apply. See *United States v. Gould*, 536 F.2d 216 (8th Cir. 1976) (legislative fact; instruction proper). But this matter presents some difficulty. In an analogous setting in which the question is whether a particular implement is a deadly weapon, courts tend to give mandatory instructions for guns but permit the jury to decide whether such things as bottles can be deadly weapons. See generally M & K § 2.3.

F. JUDICIAL NOTICE OF LAW

Courts take judicial notice of federal and state law, including constitutional provisions, statutes, caselaw, and administrative regulations. Foreign law is proved by way of any "relevant material or source," and a party who relies on elements of foreign law is to give notice (through pleadings or otherwise). See FRCP 44.1 and FRCrimP 26.1. Ascertaining the content of law is itself a matter of law rather than fact, and juries as such play no role.

1. Common Law Tradition

In common law tradition, the content of foreign law was considered a matter of fact to be proved at trial, but courts took judicial notice of domestic law, and thus relieved the parties of the burden of offering formal proof.

2. Rules of Evidence Inapplicable

Under the modern approach, evidence law as such has nothing to say on these subjects. See ACN to FRE 201 (commenting that the manner by which law enters the judicial process is "never a proper concern of the rules of evidence" and is a subject for rules of procedure).

REVIEW QUESTIONS AND ANSWERS

Question: What is judicial notice? Why do we have it, and what kinds of things can be noticed?

Answer: Judicial notice is the process by which courts inform themselves of commonplace facts that bear on the case, but without formal proof. One reason for taking judicial notice is to save time. In civil cases, another reason is to put some constraints on what a jury might otherwise do. Judicial notice is appropriate for certain scientific facts (water freezes at 32 degrees Fahrenheit), geographical facts (New York City is east of Chicago), history and politics (in the presidential election of 2004, Bush defeated Kerry), and court records (in a prior action, the same plaintiff sued the same defendant for injuries arising out of the same accident).

Question: What are adjudicative facts, and how do we know whether they may be properly noticed?

Answer: Adjudicative facts are the "who, what, where, when, and how" of law-suits—the kinds of facts that trials spend the most time on. Under the modern formulation of the judicial notice doctrine in FRE 201, adjudicative facts may be introduced into the case by judicial notice if they satisfy one of two standards. First are facts generally known by informed people in the jurisdiction. Thus a judge in

Denver could take judicial notice that the road through Rocky Mountain National Park is closed in the winter because of snow in the high country. Second are facts that are verifiable by resort to sources like almanacs that cannot reasonably be questioned. Thus a judge could consult an almanac or yearly calendar to determine that January 17, 1994 fell on a Friday.

Question: What is the effect of taking judicial notice? Is it the same in criminal and civil cases? Are there any safeguards against mistakes in taking notice?

Answer: In civil cases, judicial notice is binding on the trier of fact, which means that evidence may not be admitted to contradict the point that has been judicially noticed. It is different in criminal cases, where juries cannot be directed to find any fact against the accused. In this setting, FRE 201(f) says that trial judges are to instruct juries that they may (but need not) find the fact suggested by judicial notice. To prevent mistakes, and to provide for procedural fairness, FRE 201 provides that parties have a right to be heard on the propriety of taking judicial notice.

Question: For purposes of the judicial notice doctrine, are there other kinds of facts than adjudicative facts? Does judicial notice apply to the content of the laws that are applied in a case?

Answer: There are, in addition to adjudicative facts, basic facts and legislative facts. Basic facts are the ones that everyone carries around in his mind as a matter of common experience and communicative skill: The term "automobile" refers to a self-propelled vehicle that carries people (a basic fact that is often called a "communicative" fact), and automobiles travel on the righthand side of streets and highways (a basic fact that is often called an "evaluative" fact). Legislative facts are the ones that bear on the meaning and construction of laws, as exemplified by the psychological studies noticed in *Brown* relating to the effects of segregation in public education. Judicial notice of basic and legislative facts proceeds in courtrooms every day, and the process is not covered or regulated by FRE 201. Finally, courts also take judicial notice of law, but the process once again is not regulated by FRE 201. In this area, courts make the necessary determinations alone because questions relating to the content of applicable law are themselves questions of law in which juries play no role.

EXAM TIPS

Here are some tips on issues relating to judicial notice:

Judicial notice means introducing facts into a suit without formal proof.

Judicial notice of an **adjudicative fact** (who did what and when) is proper only if the fact is indisputable and either generally known (Boston is north of New York) or readily ascertainable (September 22, 1992 was a Tuesday).

Judicial notice of **adjudicative facts** is regulated by FRE 201, which provides for party input on the propriety of taking notice, makes the noticed fact binding on juries in civil cases, and requires a permissive instruction in criminal cases.

Judicial notice of **basic facts,** which include communicative facts ("car" means automobile) and evaluative facts (cars are driven on the right side of the street), as well as judicial notice of **legislative facts** (racially separate primary education is injurious) and **law** are unregulated.

APPENDIX A

Sample Exam Questions

FACT SITUATION: ANN'S ACCIDENT

While crossing a street in a residential area, Ann is struck by a car driven by Brett, who is employed as a driver for Davis Foods. Ann sues Davis Foods for injuries she sustained in the accident. In support of her claim that Brett was speeding, Ann calls Cliff as a witness. Cliff used to work with Brett at Davis Foods, but has changed jobs. After showing that Cliff had often driven on company business with Brett and was acquainted with Brett's "driving habits," Ann's lawyer asks Cliff, "Would you say Brett was a careful driver, or did he often drive too fast on residential streets?" Rising to her feet, the lawyer for defendant Davis Foods says "Objection, your honor, she can't ask questions like that."

Question 1: Is the objection by Davis Foods adequate to preserve a claim of error in case the trial court lets Cliff testify?

Answer: The objection is inadequate because it fails to state a ground. Stating the ground helps inform the court of the problem and the applicable legal rule, alerts the proponent to the problem in her proof (so she can correct it or take other steps to prove the point), and helps insure that the objecting party has reasonable but not endless opportunities to achieve a fair trial.

Question 2: What more particular point or points might Davis Foods reasonably raise in an objection?

Answer: The lawyer for Davis Foods had three good grounds on which to object. One is that the question was leading. On direct examination of its own witness, Ann should ask nonleading questions, and this question is leading because it suggests the desired answer (Brett often drove too fast on residential streets). The reason to discourage leading questions on direct is that they may plant false memories in the mind of the witness or discourage him from searching his memory and being accurate in his response.

A second good ground for objection is that the question is compound. If Cliff answered by saying either "yes" or "no" (the question invites a yes-or-no answer), the answer might relate to the first clause in the question (Brett was or was not a careful driver), or the second (he did or did not drive too fast on residential streets)? Hence the answer apparently invited by the question would be uncertain in meaning, which is why such questions are improper.

A third good ground for objection is that the question asks Cliff to give "character evidence" suggesting general carefulness in driving. Under FRE 404, character may not be used to prove conduct in a civil case (and is only sometimes admissible in criminal cases). Ann's lawyer might argue that Cliff's answer would prove the "habit" of Brett or "routine practice" by Davis Foods, which is allowable under FRE 406. But this argument should fail because driving too fast on residential streets is not sufficiently specific or focused to count as habit evidence. Habit is considered more relevant than character (it has greater tendency to prove conduct on a particular occasion), but it must be specific and must refer to things that one does automatically or semi-automatically. Speeding in a particular block or stretch of road would count as habit, but not speeding in residential areas.

Question 3: If the judge sustains the objection and Ann loses and appeals, would any inadequacy in the objection matter if the reviewing court thought the testimony was properly excluded?

Answer: No, an objection that states no ground would be treated like one that states a wrong ground. If the trial judge acted correctly for reasons that nobody thought of at the time, the ruling does not count as error on appeal from the judgment. Ann cannot get the judgment reversed merely because Davis Foods did not state the ground for its objection.

FACT SITUATION: TERMINATION OF EMPLOYMENT

Ellen sues Garfield Industries for alleged wrongful termination of employment, arguing that she was fired in violation of Garfield's contractual commitment to utilize her talents on its sales force for not less than three years. She seeks damages and reinstatement. Garfield resists, invoking a clause in the "letter of understanding" that says termination before three years is allowed if Ellen "fails to achieve a sales volume of $200,000 per month" in each of three successive quarters. Frank, as Garfield's General Manager for marketing, prepared a summary of sales generated by Ellen over the three quarters preceding her termination. Hal, as lawyer for Garfield, had asked the company president to "have your General Manager prepare a summary of Ellen's sales during the relevant period," and Frank prepared and sent this summary to Hal. In getting ready for trial, Hal asked Frank to review this summary, which Frank did.

At trial, Frank testified that Ellen "didn't meet her sales quota for three quarters, which is why we let her go." On cross conducted by Ellen's counsel, Frank admits that "I reviewed a memorandum I prepared for Hal, using it to refresh my memory, before testifying today." Ellen's counsel demands to see the memorandum, but Garfield's lawyer claims the memo is "covered by the attorney-client privilege," explaining to the judge how it was prepared.

Question 4: Putting aside any question of waiving the privilege, does the memorandum fit the attorney-client privilege?

Answer: Yes, Frank's memorandum was privileged, at least if the waiver question is ignored. Under the *Upjohn* approach, the crucial point is not whether Frank was a member of the control group in Garfield, but whether Frank was speaking of matters within the scope of his duties for the company. That is certainly true here. *Upjohn* also stressed that the purpose must be to obtain legal advice (which is true here), and indicated that it helps establish the privilege claim if the spokesperson communicated with the lawyer at the request of his superior (which happened in this case). Finally, *Upjohn* stressed that the communication must be treated as confidential, and not circulated generally. Apparently that is true here, since Frank sent the memorandum to Hal, but the defense must establish this point.

Question 5: Does Ellen's lawyer have a reasonable argument that the memorandum must be produced? Can she overcome a claim of privilege by arguing that Frank's use of the memorandum to prepare for trial waived the privilege?

Answer: Ellen's lawyer can argue that use of the memorandum to prepare Frank as a witness means the memorandum should be produced, so Frank's credibility as a witness may be explored. If Frank's testimony differs from the memorandum, the latter would be an inconsistent statement, hence an indication that Frank changed his story and perhaps should not be believed. If Frank does not actually remember Ellen's sales figures, and has just memorized what the memorandum said, his testimony is technically improper because it is just indirect hearsay. Then the memorandum itself would have to qualify under a hearsay exception, such as the one for past recollection recorded in FRE 803(5).

Under FRE 612, the calling party is *required* to disclose to the other side writings to refresh memory of the witness "while testifying." For writings used "before testifying," however, disclosure is discretionary and should be ordered only if "necessary in the interests of justice." The arguments sketched above might persuade the judge to order disclosure, but are not so powerful that the judge would *have* to order disclosure (there would probably be no abuse of discretion if the judge did not order disclosure). Since the memorandum was privileged when written, Ellen's lawyer must argue that its use in trial preparation waives the privilege. Most courts that have considered this question have concluded that the privilege claim gives way, but numerous decisions take the view that the policies of the privilege should be honored as much as possible, and that disclosure should be required only if necessary or the facts show that the witness really did depend on the writing to refresh memory. The privilege issue makes it harder to obtain disclosure here, but not necessarily impossible.

Question 6: Suppose the court orders the memorandum turned over to the plaintiff. If Ellen's lawyer thinks the sales volume reflected in the memorandum actually helps Ellen, can Ellen's lawyer introduce the memorandum as proof that Ellen achieved that volume?

Answer: Almost certainly Ellen can offer the memorandum against Garfield. If the writing is produced in response to the request by Ellen because it is important in probing the testimony given by Frank, then Ellen can introduce the writing insofar as it may bear on the accuracy of what Frank says. See FRE 612 (adverse party may introduce into evidence "those portions" of the writing that relate to the testimony of the witness).

The memorandum probably does not fit the **business records** exception because (1) it was prepared in preparation for litigation rather than as a matter of routine business practice, (2) it was not prepared contemporaneously with events, and (3) it would likely fail the trustworthiness standard because it was prepared in a litigation setting. But Ellen need not rely on that exception, and can offer the memorandum as an **admission** by the company. Frank was authorized to speak on this subject, so the memorandum fits FRE 801(d)(2)(C). Also he was speaking on matters within the scope of his employment, so the memorandum also fits FRE 801(d)(1)(D). It does not matter that the memorandum was intended to stay "in-house," since internal statements count as admissions.

FACT SITUATION: BAD BRAKES

On November 14th, while driving his expensive panel truck (used in his carpet cleaning business to get to his various jobsites), Jim is broadsided by a pickup truck driven by Kyle and owned by Laura. The panel truck is totaled, and the cleaning equipment is damaged beyond repair. Jim sues Kyle, whose insurance policy covers this accident if Kyle was negligent. Kyle claims he wasn't negligent and that the brakes on the pickup were bad, so he couldn't stop. (Laura is not named as a party defendant because she is uninsured, has little money, and has left the jurisdiction with the truck.) Assume that the applicable substantive rule is that Kyle is not liable to Jim if he couldn't stop because the brakes on Laura's pickup were in disrepair.

Kyle offers testimony by Marsha about some conversations and events that happened on November 12th. If allowed, Marsha would testify that Laura told her, while the two were having a soda in Laura's kitchen, "the brakes on my truck aren't holding, so I need to get new pads at least, and maybe new disk rotors as well."

Kyle also offers testimony by Nick Nelson (owner of Nelson's Repair) and a page from the appointment log kept regularly by Nick at his place of business. If allowed, Nick would testify that "Laura, whom I've known for years, came in that day and made an appointment. I wrote it down right then in my daily appointment log, just the way I always do, and as it says here the date was November 12th and she wanted us to fix her brakes, including new pads and rotors." Jim raises hearsay objections to both these proofs.

Question 7: In aid of his offer of Marsha's testimony, Kyle invokes the exceptions for present sense impressions in FRE 803(1) and state-of-mind statements in FRE 803(3). Kyle argues, "Laura was saying her brakes were bad at that very time," and anyway her statement "shows what she knew, so we can use the state-of-mind exception too." What result on these proffers, and why?

Answer: Neither exception applies, so Kyle should lose and Marsha's testimony should be excluded. The exception for present sense impressions only reaches statements describing an event or condition "while" the declarant perceives it or "immediately thereafter." Hence Laura could not have been perceiving what she described as she spoke or immediately before that. The state-of-mind exception does not apply either. What Laura knew about the condition of her brakes might bear on a negligence claim brought against her (and her statement could be offered against her as her admission in that setting), but it does not bear on a negligence claim against Kyle. What Laura knew or thought is some evidence of the underlying facts (if she knew or thought her brakes were bad, that is some evidence that they were), but the state-of-mind exception does not allow use of statements to prove facts remembered or believed. See FRE 803(3).

Question 8: Kyle invokes the business records exception to get the log admitted. He also argues that Nelson can testify, and the log itself can prove, that Laura went to the shop and set up an appointment to fix her brakes: "That isn't even hearsay, it's conduct, your honor." Should these arguments prevail? (Don't worry about Best Evidence issues arising out of Nelson's description of what the log says, since Kyle didn't argue that point.)

Answer: The business records exception should work here, at least to prove Laura came in and what she wanted done. Whether that can prove the brakes were bad is harder, but the best answer is yes.

The log fits the business record exception if Nelson testifies that he runs a regular business and kept the log as a matter of regular practice. What he actually said is a good indicator that he keeps a regular log as well. Hence the regular business and regular record requirement is satisfied. Nelson has personal knowledge that Laura came: He knows her and heard her say what she wants, so the second requirement (personal knowledge on the part of the source of the entry) is satisfied. Nelson wrote it down right away, so the third requirement (entry made close in time to the event recorded) is satisfied. (The event is Laura's visit and her verbal behavior setting up an appointment.) Apparently Nelson himself keeps the log, and as the proprietor he certainly knows how it is kept, so he is an appropriate foundation witness, satisfying the fourth requirement of the business records exception. See FRE 803(6).

But can the Nelson testimony and the log prove the most important point—that Laura's brakes were bad? This question is harder.

The better answer is yes, this proof can properly show that Laura's brakes were bad. Laura's behavior is a mix of nonassertive conduct, performative speech, and assertion. She came to Nelson's to set up an appointment, which is nonassertive conduct indicating that she thought something was wrong with her truck, which is nonhearsay evidence that there *was* something wrong with her truck. She set up an appointment to fix her brakes, which is speech with a significant performative aspect: She set events in motion (Nelson's would be ready to take her pickup on the appointed occasion); she didn't just talk about an appointment, but actually made one. While her words assert that the brakes were bad, they also act upon that belief, which provides a good argument for treating what she said as nonhearsay.

Some courts might not accept this analysis. Seeing that Laura's words assert that her brakes are bad, a court might say, "There's no hearsay exception for what Laura said; her action in going to the shop can't by itself show her brakes were bad; only what she said shows that, and it's hearsay." This analysis ignores the performative aspect of Laura's words, and arguably extends the reach of the hearsay doctrine too far.

It is important to note that the business records exception by itself can't prove Laura's brakes were bad because Nelson didn't examine the truck and the business records exception does not reach statements by an outsider as proof of what they assert. But the business records exception can be used to prove what Laura did and said since Nelson did see and hear (and record) these points in his records.

FACT SITUATION: HOUSE BURGLARS

Oliver and Paula are jointly tried for house burglary. In its case against Paula, the state depends partly on eyewitness testimony placing her at the scene in a car, partly on proof that her fingerprints were found on the front door, and partly on forensic evidence that someone "jimmied the lock." In its case against Oliver, the state depends on proof that his fingerprints were found in the house, and the state's theory is that they were in on the robbery together.

As proof against both Oliver and Paula, the state also offers testimony by Rick describing himself as a "fence" and stating that Oliver and Paula fenced items stolen from the house during the burglary. The prosecutor also offers testimony by Paula's friend Quinn that that Paula "told me she picked the lock and that she and Oliver broke into the house and later fenced the stuff with Rick."

Oliver claims Paula did it alone, and that his prints were in the house because he had visited the people who lived there some weeks earlier (the people were friends of both Oliver and Paula).

Prior to trial, Oliver and Paula hired separate lawyers. The two clients and the two lawyers met to discuss strategy. Tempers flared at one point, and Oliver yelled at Paula, "You know I didn't do anything, how come you don't just come clean?" Paula replied, "I broke in myself, all right, but it was your dumb idea." At trial, Oliver proposes to testify to what Paula said during their meeting, and to testify that in fact Paula really did do it by herself without any help from him.

Question 9: Oliver objects to Quinn's testimony describing Paula's statement is "inadmissible hearsay." In response, the prosecutor argues that Paula's statement fits the against-interest exception, and that Paula is "unavailable as a witness" because the prosecutor cannot call her to testify.

Answer: What Paula told Quinn is hearsay if offered to prove any or all of the facts that she described. Of course Paula herself cannot object to the use of the statement against her because it is her admission, but the question is whether *Oliver* can object. Oliver may not care much whether Paula's statement is taken as proof of what *Paula* did, but Oliver certainly cares about use of the statement to prove what *Oliver* did, and Paula's statement does say that Oliver entered the house with her.

The prosecutor should prevail on the point that Paula is unavailable as a witness. Ordinarily the proponent is expected actually to put a witness on the stand and force the witness to invoke a privilege or refuse to testify, but the prosecutor cannot properly call Paula to the stand and force her to invoke her privilege against self-incrimination because that privilege entitles Paula not even to be called.

Oliver has a pretty strong argument that Paula's statement does not fit the against-interest exception insofar as it describes what Oliver did because that is "collateral" under the *Williamson* case. Oliver can forcibly argue that Paula's description of her own conduct (picking the lock and later fencing the stuff) is against Paula's interest, but that the reference to Oliver is not against Paula's interest and is just "collateral" under *Williamson*, just as the statement by Harris offered in *Williamson* was viewed as collateral insofar as it described the actions of Williamson and claimed that Williamson owned the contraband that Harris was carrying in his trunk. Many post-*Williamson* cases conclude that such statements are indeed excludable as collateral.

But Oliver's argument is not watertight. *Williamson* involved statements by Harris that attributed most of the blame to Williamson, but in this case Paula shoulders most of the blame herself, scarcely mentioning Oliver. Moreover, *Williamson* involved statements to police officers who were arresting the declarant, and he had an obvious motive to "curry favor" with authorities, which introduces a strong reason to mistrust the statement and to conclude that it is not against interest after all because the declarant is trying to make a deal by attributing major criminality to the other person. Paula is not talking to police, and she is not shifting blame to Oliver, and she seems to be taking the lion's share of responsibility herself.

Williamson left room for a conclusion that a statement naming another, as Paula names Oliver here, might fit the against-interest exception. *Williamson* said that the statement "Sam and I went to Joe's house" might be against interest if a reasonable person would know that linking herself to Sam and Joe might implicate her in a conspiracy. On the facts given here, Paula might reasonably know that linking herself to Oliver and Rick would flesh out her role in a burglary, creating a fuller picture of the crime, and that linking herself to Oliver and Rick might even help build a conspiracy case against her (even though she is not charged here with conspiracy).

In cases like this, probably modern decisions would exclude Paula's statement mentioning Oliver as collateral. But courts are actually split on such questions. At least some would conclude that phrases mentioning others have sufficient tendency to implicate the speaker to satisfy the exception, and some would admit such statements.

Question 10: Oliver also objects to Quinn's testimony describing Paula's as violating Oliver's "confrontation rights under the *Crawford* case, which holds that 'testimonial' hearsay cannot be offered against he accused." In response, the prosecutor argues that Paula's statement is not testimonial under *Crawford* because it was not made to a police officer investigating the crime, but was made instead to a friend in a purely private setting.

Answer: Probably the statement is not "testimonial" under *Crawford* because Paula was talking to her friend Quinn and would not anticipate that her statement would become part of an investigation or prosecution of a crime. Still, these conclusions are less than certain because some formulations of the idea of "testimonial" statements in *Crawford* might conceivably reach Paula's statement.

Question 11: Oliver objects to Quinn's testimony, arguing thus: "It can't come in because it's just Paula's admission and the *Bruton* doctrine means you can't admit it when we're being tried together because the part about fencing stuff implicates me." How should the court rule on this objection, and why?

Answer: Oliver's *Bruton* objection will likely fail if the court concludes that Paula's statement fits the against-interest exception, although the objection would succeed if the court concludes that Paula's statement does not fit that exception.

Like the *Crawford* objection, this *Bruton* objection rests on the Confrontation Clause of the Sixth Amendment, and it applies to statements by one defendant that refer to another by name or obvious reference. Paula did mention Oliver by name, indicating that he was in the house with her. Of course Paula's statement is her admission and can come in *against her* under FRE 801(d)(2)(A), but the latter provision does not make her statement admissible *against Oliver.* In this setting, the *Bruton* doctrine indicates that admitting the statement against Paula with an instruction not to consider the statement against Oliver will not work. While the Rules of Evidence may permit such an approach, the Confrontation Clause does not. Unless Paula takes the stand and testifies (so that Oliver can cross-examine her), or the statement is "redacted" to delete reference to Oliver, or the trial is severed so that Paula is tried alone, or two juries are empaneled (so that the one trying Oliver does not hear about Paula's statement), Oliver should prevail on the *Bruton* objection in the event that the only basis for admitting Paula's statement is that it fits FRE 801(d)(2)(A).

The *Bruton* objection will likely fail, however, if the court concludes that Paula's statement fits the against-interest exception. If it does, then the we have an exception that makes Paula's statement admissible *against Oliver.* A footnote in the *Bruton* opinion carefully notes that the Court had before it "no recognized exception" to the hearsay rule that would make the statement admissible against the party raising objection. The Court went on to comment that its holding does not reach that situation, and the Court cited the coconspirator exception. On the facts of the case at hand, the against-interest exception could serve the same purpose. If Paula's statement fits that exception, Oliver's *Bruton* objection would fail.

Question 12:   The state raises a hearsay objection to Oliver's testimony about what Paula said during the meeting. Oliver counters that Paula's statement constitutes a declaration against interest, so it is admissible. Who should prevail on this argument, and why?

Answer: The testimony describing Paula's statement is offered to exonerate Oliver from responsibility for the charged crime. Thus the testimony is offered *against* the state even though it might increase the likelihood that Paula will be convicted (something the state wants). Hence the state should be able to raise any proper objection. That objection should fail, subject to some uncertainty over the corroboration requirement.

First, Paula satisfies the unavailability requirement under FRE 804(a)(1). She is present, but she is unavailable because she has a Fifth Amendment privilege not to take the witness stand. (In the typical case, that privilege blocks the state from calling the defendant, but it also blocks one defendant from calling another as a witness.)

Second, at least the first part of what Paula said ("I did it all right") is against interest because it implicates her in the charged crime. Paula may never have thought her statement would be offered because it was privileged or she thought they were speaking off the record (she didn't think the statement was against her interest), but the exception applies when the fact asserted is against interest, which it is here. (Courts often refuse to apply the exception to post-trial statements, where the declarant cannot be prosecuted again and her statements cannot be used against her, but this limit on the exception would not apply here.)

Third, the corroboration requirement is satisfied. There is eyewitness testimony placing Paula at the crime scene. Oliver too is prepared to testify that Paula did commit the crime by herself, although this testimony (since it comes from the same witness who would testify to her statement) might not satisfy the corroboration requirement, even though it appears that he would testify to two points (her statement and whatever he knows about what she did).

Finally, if the first part of Paula's statement is admitted, the state (and Paula too) might insist that the rest be admitted as well ("it was your dumb idea"), to avoid distorting the meaning of the first part. See FRE 106 (rule of completeness for written statements).

Question 13:   Assume that the state's objection does not carry the day. Paula also objects to Oliver's testimony about what she said, invoking the attorney-client privilege. Who should prevail on this argument, and why?

Answer: Paula should prevail on the privilege claim. She and Oliver fit the "pooled defense" or "allied lawyers" doctrine because each of the two clients has a lawyer, and the clients and lawyers met to plan matters of strategy in an area of common interest. In this setting, the rule is that each client has a privilege against outsiders (so both Oliver and Paula can block attempts by the state to obtain or offer statements made during the meeting) and each has a privilege against the other client (so Paula can block Oliver from testifying to what Paula said during the meeting).

FACT SITUATION: DISAPPEARED EIGHT YEARS AGO

In her suit against Toledo Life Insurance Company to recover on a policy insuring the life of her husband Saul, Rene invokes the presumption of death after seven years. That presumption arises when it is shown that a person has disappeared without tidings for seven years or more. Toledo has denied Rene's claim that Saul is dead. At trial, Rene testifies that Saul was 40 when he left for work at an accounting firm in Wichita more than eight years previously, and that she has never heard from him since. She offers testimony by five friends of Saul's, by his parents and only sibling (a sister), and by Saul's former boss and colleagues at work, all indicating that they have not seen or heard from him since that time.

Toledo calls Vickie as a witness. She testifies that she is an accountant, that she met Saul about ten years ago at a professional meeting in Wichita, and that she has seen him "several times since then" in Chicago during national conventions for accountants specializing in "payroll and benefit tracking," including "one occasion two years ago," adding that "each time I saw him he was with the same woman." Toledo's theory is that Saul deserted Rene for another woman and left town, but that Saul is still alive. On cross, Vickie concedes that "I might be mistaken about the person I saw those times in Chicago," that "a few times I said 'Hi Saul' to him but he only smiled back and we didn't get into any conversations." She admits as well, "I didn't know Saul really well here in Wichita." In this suit, Rene bears the burden of proving that Saul is dead. Assume that the jurisdiction follows the common law relating to civil presumptions, but that the judge might be influenced by FRE 301 as an authoritative statement of what the law should be.

Question 14: At the close of the case, Toledo moves for judgment as a matter of law, arguing that Rene failed to make out a prima facie case that Saul is dead and that "there can be no presumption of death" because Vickie's testimony either "keeps the presumption from arising" or "rebuts the presumption." How should the court rule, and why?

Answer: Toledo's motion should be overruled.

Toledo's first claim is mistaken, at least in the terms in which it was cast. It is true that the presumption only arises on proof that the person in question is missing without tidings, so evidence that he was seen alive in the last seven years could be viewed as proof that refutes one of the basic facts that must be shown to bring the presumption into play. But when there is a conflict in proof on the basic facts, and enough evidence to support a jury finding on those facts either way, the right approach is to give a conditional instruction telling the jury it must decide whether the basic facts are established, and that if so the presumption applies. Rene's witnesses provide powerful proof that Saul has not been heard from, and Vickie's testimony is uncertain and might be rejected as wrong. Hence the jury could find Saul has not been heard from, and it would be appropriate to give a conditional instruction telling the jury to decide this point, and to find that Saul is dead if it concludes that he has not been heard from in the last seven years.

Toledo's second objection is problematic. Arguably Vickie's testimony also goes to the presumed fact (Saul is still alive), and does therefore tend to rebut the presumption even if it applies in the case. If the court were applying FRE 301, the presumption would affect the burden of production, but not the burden of persuasion. Vickie's testimony does satisfy Toledo's burden of production (it constitutes sufficient evidence to support a reasonable jury finding that Saul is alive). Under the "bursting bubble" theory that courts often say FRE 301 embodies, the presumption disappears in this circumstance, and the case is decided as if there were no presumption at all.

Under other views, the presumption does not disappear, but still suffices to take the case to the jury. The Morgan view would say the presumption affects the burden of persuasion, and the case would go to the jury with instructions to find that Saul is dead unless the jury is persuaded by Toledo's proof that Saul still lives. Under three other views, presumptions do not shift the burden of persuasion but have more effect than the bursting bubble view would permit. A court might conclude that the presumption continues in the case, which means that the jury must find that Saul is dead, unless (1) the counterproof is "substantial and uncontradicted" (which is not true of Vickie's testimony here, in light of the strength of Rene's proof), or (2) the jury believes the counterproof (it stays unless the jury believes Vickie really did see Saul), or that (3) the jury decides Saul is just as likely to be alive as to be dead ("equipoise" view).

Even if the presumption disappeared, Toledo's motion should be denied. Deciding the case without the presumption, the jury could still conclude, on the basis of all the testimony offered by Rene, that Saul died. The natural probative force of that circumstantial evidence, even without aid of a presumption, suffices to take Rene's case to the jury.

FACT SITUATION: MURDER IN CHARLESTON

In the trial of Will for the murder of Xavier in Charleston on August 14th, the state offers in evidence a handgun. Yuri was the first police officer on the scene, and he ultimately arrested Xavier on August 20th, giving him *Miranda* warnings before asking him questions about the murder. Yuri testifies that he found the gun beside Xavier's body and turned it over to his colleague Zora. She testifies that she bagged and labeled the gun and gave it to Abe. Over Will's objection, the state offers a labeled plastic bag containing a gun. On the label are signatures reflecting the names "Zora," "Abe," and "Bob" (who is described on the label as being the "Police Department Property Clerk"). Zora identifies her own signature and testifies that she obtained the gun from Bob in the property room before trial. She also testifies that guns found at crime scenes are routinely handled in this way, with each person who handles the weapon adding his name to the label. She testifies that Bob is the Property Clerk, and she recognizes his signature on the label.

The prosecutor also calls Bob, the Property Clerk, who identifies the bag. He testifies that his signature is on the label and states that "Abe brought the bag to me, with Zora's signature on it, which I recognize from having worked with her, and Abe's own signature on it, which I recognized for the same reason." Clark, a police ballistics expert, testifies that he got the gun from Bob and tested it in the laboratory, and determined that it fired the fatal bullet recovered from the body of Xavier. Clark also testifies that he tested the gun for fingerprints, but that no recoverable prints were found.

The prosecutor also calls witnesses who testify that Will had a grudge against Xavier, that Will had a gun similar to the one offered in evidence, and that Will had bragged about "having gotten even" with Xavier after Xavier's body was found.

During the defense case-in-chief, Will takes the stand. He testifies that he "never had or handled or used a gun before," and was "visiting my uncle Dan in Knoxville on August 14th." On cross, the prosecutor asks Will, "isn't it a fact that you pled guilty to and were convicted for the crime of embezzlement three years ago, and that you were convicted for unlawful possession of a firearm twelve years ago?" The prosecutor also asks Will, "Why didn't you tell Yuri, the officer who arrested you, that you were out of town on the day of the crime?"

Question 15: Will objects to the introduction of the gun, arguing that "the prosecutor hasn't laid the right foundation, since Abe didn't testify." Continuing, Will argues that "Abe represents a serious gap in the chain of custody." Finally, "the prosecutor never showed that Will ever touched the gun." What result on these objections, and why?

Answer: Will's chain-of-custody objection fails for many reasons. First, a missing link in a chain of custody does not require exclusion unless a serious problem appears. The absence from trial of one of the three persons who retrieved the evidence from the crime scene and got it stored in the police property room is not itself enough to require exclusion. A presumption of due care by police is sometimes invoked to overcome such objections. Second, Yuri testified that he found the gun by the body and gave it to Zora, and she testified that she bagged it and signed the label, recognizes her signature, and retrieved it from Bob. Zora's testimony bridges the gap between discovery and trial, and offers some proof that the gun being offered is really the one found at the scene. Third, Zora testifies that Bob is the Property Clerk and recognizes his signature on the bag, which is some evidence that the gun (which Zora testifies that she bagged) arrived intact at the right place. Hence the absence of Abe seems minor. Fourth, the ballistics testimony also tends to confirm that the gun got to the right place, since Clark says he got the gun from Bob and determined that it fired the shot that killed Xavier. Clark thus gives evidence that the gun delivered to Bob was the gun that killed Xavier.

Lack of physical evidence connecting Will to the gun doesn't matter. There is enough proof that the gun offered in evidence is the murder weapon, which suffices to make it relevant in the case as proof that Xavier was murdered. It would certainly help the state's case if the prosecutor had fingerprint evidence connecting Will to the weapon, and the state would lose on a motion to dismiss if there were *no* proof that Will fired the fatal shot. But there is other evidence, including testimony showing that Will had motive and means, and that he made incriminating statements later. And of course it helps that the prosecutor showed that Will owned a gun that might be the gun found at the scene (he owns a gun of that kind).

Question 16: Will objects to the questions on his convictions for embezzlement three years earlier, and unlawful possession of a firearm twelve years ago. He argues that both are "prejudicial and irrelevant" and that the latter is "barred by the ten-year rule." (Assume FRE 609 has been adopted by the jurisdiction.)

Answer: The question about the embezzlement conviction is proper as a means of showing that Will is by character or disposition untruthful. To begin with, embezzlement is a crime "involving dishonesty or false statement" that fits FRE 609(a)(2). An element in this crime is that the defendant took something entrusted to him, so by definition the crime involves dishonesty. It usually involves false statement as well, because embezzlers usually make false entries to disguise the theft. Convictions that fit FRE 609(a)(2) are *automatically* admissible, and there is no discretion to block the questioning. Express language in FRE 609(a)(1) authorizes the court to exclude *felony* convictions for unfair prejudice, and embezzlement is a felony. But there is no similar language in FRE 609(a)(2) covering convictions for crimes involving dishonesty or false statement, and it is settled that there is no discretion to exclude either. A crime that fits *both* provisions is automatically admissible because it fits the no-discretion prong. Finally, a conviction based on a plea qualifies just as much as a conviction after trial on a plea of innocence.

Will's objection to the twelve-year-old unlawful possession conviction might succeed if the prosecutor argued only that the purpose is to show untruthful disposition. FRE 609(b) says convictions more than ten years old are not admissible "unless" the court determines that probative worth outweighs prejudicial effect, which in effect creates a presumption against admitting stale convictions. Also notice is required, and there's no indication that notice was given here.

But Will's objection would likely fail if the prosecutor argued that the purpose of proving the twelve-year-old conviction was to contradict the testimony by Will indicating that he had never handled a gun before. FRE 609 limits questions about convictions when the purpose is to show a disposition toward untruthfulness (bad character for "truth and veracity"), but does not limit the use of prior convictions for other impeaching purposes. Here the prior conviction contradicts Will's direct testimony by showing that he has had or handled a firearm before. (Of course the conviction is hearsay when offered to prove that he had or handled a gun on that occasion, even though the purpose is to impeach Will's testimony. The reason is that the unlawful possession conviction only shows that he had or handled a gun if taken as proof that he actually did have or handle a gun. But prior felony convictions of the defendant fit a hearsay exception found in FRE 803(22) when offered to prove any fact essential to the judgment in the prior case.)

Question 17: Will also objects to the question asking why he hadn't told Yuri about being out of town on the day of the crime, arguing that the question "violates the Supreme Court's decisions in the *Miranda* and *Doyle* cases." What result, and why?

Answer: Will should win this objection. Under the decision in *Doyle*, the prosecutor may not impeach testimony by a defendant who testifies to an alibi or excuse by proving that (or asking whether) defendant failed to provide a similar explanation while in custody after receiving *Miranda* warnings. The decision in *Jenkins* holds that it is permissible to ask a defendant why he didn't come forward *before* his arrest and explain the incriminating circumstances (as he is now doing), and the decision in *Weir* holds that the defendant may be asked why he did not offer a similar explanation *after* arrest but *prior* to receiving *Miranda* warnings. In this case, however, the situation falls squarely within the prohibition of *Doyle* itself. The rationale of *Doyle* is that the warnings assure the defendant that what he says may be used against him, which makes the exercise of his right to silence ambiguous (he might be silent simply to avoid creating trouble, rather than because he has no defense that he can make). *Doyle* also rests on the view that it is unfair to use silence against a defendant who is in custody after receiving *Miranda* warnings if we can also use what he says: Combining these possibilities would mean that a defendant in this situation cannot avoid making evidence against himself, since both what he says and what he does not say can be used against him at trial. The notion is that it is simply unfair—in effect a "double bind"—to put defendant in such a position.

FACT SITUATION: GOINGS–ON AT THE ALPINE HOTEL

In a sexual assault trial, the complaining witness Cora testifies that she had gone to bed in her own room at the Alpine Hotel after attending a party there that involved groups of college students. She states that it was the second of two nights at the hotel, and that the defendant Arlin entered her room and raped her. She testifies that she and the others (including Arlin) drank a considerable amount before she left, that Arlin had climbed into her bed and "made penetration" when she awakened, that she said, "Let me alone, I'm already asleep and don't want to do that," but that he continued.

Arlin testifies that Cora "said something about being asleep" but that thereafter she "responded in a positive way" and "did not resist in any way, so she clearly consented to what happened." During its case-in-chief, the state offers evidence that Arlin had committed a sexual assault three years earlier against

Brenda during a date: If allowed, Brenda would testify that after seeing a movie they returned to Arlin's room in a fraternity house near campus, that they "made out" for awhile, and that eventually he unbuttoned and tried to pull down her pants and panties, but that she repeatedly told him "stop doing that," and he used physical force in trying to remove her clothing while she resisted, ran out of the room, and went home.

Prior to trial, Arlin made a motion seeking permission to introduce testimony by Drew that there was a party on the first night at the Alpine Hotel too, that much drinking and carousing happened then too, and that as things were winding down Drew and Cora went to his room and had sex. Arlin also sought permission to cross-examine Cora on this subject.

> **Question 18:**   In the pretrial motion, Arlin argues that the activities of Cora and Drew the night before the alleged crime show that she was "in a partying mood" and "interested in having sex," which supports his claim that she consented. Assume that the jurisdiction has adopted FRE 412. How should the court rule, and why?
>
> **Answer:**   The court should rule against Arlin. The proffered testimony and proposed cross-examination are improper under FRE 412.

The general rule is that criminal defendants may prove pertinent traits of the alleged victim that tend to show how she behaved at the time of the offense, but the Rape Shield Rule carves out an exception that applies in this case. That Rule makes the proposed testimony and cross-examination improper.

It is not entirely clear that Arlin could offer testimony relating to a specific instance anyway, since proof of traits of the alleged victim is usually limited to testimony describing reputation or opinion. FRE 404(a)(1) makes it clear that the defendant may prove a pertinent trait of the victim, but FRE 405(a) ordinarily limits proof of character to opinion or reputation testimony. It is true that proof of specific instances may be introduced under FRE 405(b) where character is "an essential element" of a charge or defense, but an inclination to engage in sex on the part of Cora is not an essential element in a charge of rape or a defense of consent: Arlin may be guilty of rape regardless whether Cora is a person who is inclined to engage in sex, and Arlin's claim of consent does not depend upon (and is not established by) proof that Cora is a person who is inclined to engage in sex. In order to be entitled to show that Cora engaged in sex the prior evening with Drew, Arlin would have to show that her doing so was proof of intent or plan, thus fitting FRE 404(b), but this argument would probably fail.

In any event, the more important point is that FRE 412 excludes opinion or reputation testimony on the disposition of the complaining witness toward engaging in sexual acts *even if* such proof were otherwise admissible under the rules governing character evidence. FRE 412 does allow proof of acts, but only in situations other than the one described here. Such proof can get in if it involves acts with the defendant (here the proof involves Cora and Drew, not Carla and Arlin), or tends to prove the source of semen or injury (but there is no indication of issues relating to semen or injury here). A third exception to FRE 412 reaches the situation in which the accused is constitutionally entitled to offer proof that would otherwise be barred by the Rule. But proof that Cora had sex with Drew would be viewed as irrelevant on the question whether she consented to have sex the next night with Arlin, or at best as marginally relevant, so exclusion for reasons of protecting privacy and encouraging the investigation and prosecution of rape cases would be viewed as justified. In cases like *Olden,* where the Supreme Court held that blocking defense cross-examination of the complainant in an effort to show she brought rape charges to protect an ongoing relationship with another man, the reasons to allow the questioning were more powerful than they are here.

Question 19:   Arlin objects to Brenda's testimony, claiming it is "irrelevant and prejudicial" on the question of consent in the present case. Assume the jurisdiction has adopted FRE 413. The prosecutor argues that Brenda's testimony "fits this provision and is admissible." How should the court rule, and why?

Answer: Arlin will likely lose the relevancy argument, but the prejudice argument presents a closer question and he might prevail there. Probably Brenda's testimony is admissible under FRE 413. That provision states that proof of prior sexual assaults "is admissible" and "may be considered . . . on any matter to which it is relevant." The apparent purpose is to permit use of sexual assaults to show that the defendant is by character or disposition inclined to commit such assaults, which makes it more likely that he would assault Cora on the occasion in question. This "general propensity" argument is normally forbidden, and a party who offers prior acts must make a more particular argument under FRE 404(b) that the acts show something other than general propensity. If FRE 404(b) set the standard, Arlin could argue with some force that Brenda's testimony is irrelevant: What Arlin did in trying to remove Brenda's clothing has no direct bearing on the question whether he would force himself physically on a woman who says no. While the "character" inference is plausible (Arlin's the kind of person who assaults women sexually, so it is more likely that he assaulted Cora), a more specific inference (he tried to take off Brenda's clothes without her consent, so it is more likely that he wouldn't respect a verbal refusal to have intercourse) is not plausible.

On the prejudice point, one difficulty comes from the strong verb in FRE 413, which says proof of prior assaults "is admissible." That verb might mean "automatically admissible," hence that FRE 403 cannot be invoked to exclude evidence where probative value is substantially outweighed by prejudicial effect. Under the "plain meaning" approach taken in many Supreme Court cases construing the Rules, perhaps that strong verb will be interpreted in this way. But legislative history indicates that FRE 403 *does* apply in this setting, and that seems the better answer.

Assuming FRE 403 applies, Arlin would argue that evidence of the incident with Brenda should be excluded because it is unfairly prejudicial and has little probative value. At most, Arlin would argue, what he did with Brenda was to initiate sexual contact during the course of "making out," which she rebuffed. He did not seek to overcome her resistance by pursuing her when she left, but accepted her refusal to go further toward intimacy. Hence the evidence does not show a propensity on the part of Arlin to force himself on women without their consent. While the standard in FRE 403 is cast in favor of admitting evidence (exclusion is warranted only when relevance is "substantially outweighed" by unfair prejudice), Arlin would assert that relevance is low and potential for prejudice is high. This is at least a plausible argument, and Arlin might well prevail on this point, but obviously the court has considerable room to exercise discretion.

FACT SITUATION: THE HOMESITE SCHEME

Ed Erston is charged with criminal fraud in selling land as homesites, allegedly by means of letters bearing Erston's signature misrepresenting the physical situation and availability of water needed for residential use, by brochures repeating the same misrepresentations, and in oral conversations with prospective buyers. The prosecutor shows that multiple copies of the letters and brochures in question were found on the business premises operated by Ed Erston, and shows that an identical letter and brochure were received by numerous victims, including Frank. The prosecutor also calls Frank, who testifies over defense objection that "that letter and brochure said the water table was only 20 feet down, within easy reach of standard well-drilling equipment," and that "a fella who said he was Ed Erston called me up a couple of days after I got the letter and brochure in the mail, and asked me about them, and he said the same thing about water being readily available."

During the defense case, Ed Erston takes the stand. Erston testifies that "I was raised by first-generation Americans who came over from Ireland during hard times with hardly any money, and my father always told me that a man's word is his bond. So I didn't lie to Frank about water on that land, but I might have been mistaken. Anyway, I tried to set people straight on the subject when I talked to them personally." Over defense objection, the prosecutor asks Erston on cross "whether you falsely claimed, when you applied for a sales job with 21st Century Realty last year, that you had obtained a real estate license?"

During its case in rebuttal, the prosecutor calls George as a witness, develops his testimony that he has lived for 20 years in the same town with Erston and knows him personally and by reputation. Then over defense objection, the prosecutor asks George to "give us your opinion on whether Erston is a law-abiding citizen, and tell us about his reputation on that score." If allowed, George would testify that he believes that Erston "is not a law-abiding citizen" and that "he is reputed in the community to be the sort of realtor who would misrepresent the facts to potential buyers."

Question 20: Erston's first objection is that "the state can't use Frank to describe what's in any letters or brochures because the Best Evidence Doctrine requires the state to introduce the letters and brochures themselves." Erston also raises a second objection: "Frank can't testify to some conversation with an unknown caller. Just because a fellow who says his name is Erston calls someone–that isn't reason enough to assume that my client had anything to do with the call. Anyway, the Best Evidence Doctrine requires the prosecutor to prove fraud in the letters and brochures, not in any phone conversations, which are irrelevant in this case." How should the court rule on these objections, and why?

Answer: The first objection based on the Best Evidence Doctrine should be sustained. Frank's testimony describes the content of the letters and brochures, and the Best Evidence Doctrine states that when the purpose is to prove "content," the documents themselves are the Best Evidence of content and must be produced unless there is some excuse for not doing so. See FRE 1002. Not only has the prosecutor chosen to try to prove the content of written materials (which is enough by itself to bring the Best Evidence Doctrine into play), but the prosecutor *is required* to prove the content of this material since the charged fraud specifically alleges false statements in the letters and brochures. Absent some justification for nonproduction of the letters and brochures (like all having been destroyed through no fault of the state), the prosecutor must produce the letters and brochures themselves.

The second objection raises issues of authentication ("Frank can't testify to some conversation with an unknown caller"), Best Evidence and relevancy (prosecutor must prove "fraud in the letters and brochures, not in any phone conversations," which are "irrelevant in this case"). The authentication objection should fail. The reason is that the prosecutor has shown enough about the circumstances to support an inference that the call came from Erston. The prosecutor showed that Erston had multiple copies of letters bearing his signature, plus accompanying brochures, and that one such letter and brochure were sent to Frank. In this setting, proof that a call was placed to Frank, in which a person using the name Erston initiated a conversation on the same subject as the letters and brochures, is enough to justify an inference that Erston made the call. The defense is right that self-identification by itself isn't enough, but in this case there is additional proof identifying Erston as the caller.

The Best Evidence objection to testimony describing the call from Erston is partly correct. The state *does* have to prove the content of the letters and brochure because those are the main instruments of the alleged fraud. Whatever Erston told Frank is not relevant if the question is what the letters and brochure said. If that were the only reason to prove what Erston said, Frank's testimony should be excluded. On the other hand, the state has also charged Erston with orally misrepresenting the facts relating to availability of water, and Erston's statements on the phone on this subject directly support the charge of oral misrepresentation. Moreover, Erston has said in his own defense that he "tried to set people straight" when he talked to them. To the extent that this may suggest that he clarified any ambiguities in the written materials, the actual statements Erston made on the phone become relevant in dealing with this defense. For these reasons, Frank would be allowed to testify to his conversations with Erston.

Question 21: When the prosecutor asks Erston about the job application with 21st Century Realty, counsel for Erston asks to approach the bench, and says to the court, "He can't ask that question because Erston was never charged with anything in connection with any real estate license, and anyway the prosecutor is just fishing and has no reason to think Erston ever lied about having a real estate license." The prosecutor replies, "I can ask about dishonest acts on cross." Does it matter whether Erston was convicted of anything? Does it matter whether the prosecutor has reliable information about the application, or is the question proper anyway because it goes to veracity?

Answer: In common law tradition, questions on acts bearing on moral character were proper as a way to suggest untruthful disposition, and convictions were not required. In Rules jurisdictions too, convictions are not required, so it doesn't matter that Erston was never charged or convicted of anything. FRE 608(b) narrows the range of permissible inquiry to acts bearing on veracity, but false statements on employment applications fit the bill. The judge, however, has discretion to allow or disallow such questions.

The other objection has some merit (the prosecutor is "just fishing and has no reason to think Erston ever lied about having a real estate license"), since questions on nonconviction misconduct are proper only if the questioner has a good-faith basis. At the very least, the prosecutor must have reliable information that Erston made a false statement in that setting.

Question 22: To George's testimony, counsel for Erston objects "they can't prove anything about my client's character because we didn't offer any character evidence." The prosecutor replies, "Goes to veracity, your honor." Who should prevail here, and why?

Answer: The objection raises a difficult issue, but the prosecutor's response is wholly inadequate. The defense should prevail, although a proper response by the prosecutor might lead to a different result.

The objection rests on the principle that the state cannot prove guilt by evidence that the defendant is a person of bad character who is *for that reason* likely to have committed the charged offense, unless the defense first seeks to prove innocence by proof that the defendant is a person of good character who is for that reason unlikely to have committed the charged offense. The defense says, "We didn't offer any character evidence," and it is true that the defense did not call any character witness. But Ed Erston took the stand and came very close to offering proof that he is a person of good character: He described his background ("I was raised by first-generation Americans") and recites his own father's advice ("a man's word is his bond") and *implies* that he (Ed Erston) took that advice to heart ("So I didn't lie to Frank"). That's pretty close to a claim that he didn't commit fraud because he is by character an honest man. On such facts, the trial judge has room to exercise discretion. It could decide that the defense had offered proof of Erston's good character, which would justify admitting the testimony by George in evidence, or that Erston's testimony stops short of making a defense based on character and exclude the testimony by George.

The prosecutor's response is misguided and unhelpful ("Goes to veracity"). It is true enough that a character witness could give reputation testimony that Erston "has a bad reputation for truth and veracity," and in a Rules jurisdiction a character witness could give his opinion that Erston is an untruthful person. See FRE 608. But George's testimony does not fit this description. George would address the question whether Erston is a law-abiding citizen, which is another thing altogether. Merely taking the witness stand and claiming innocence does not make an issue out of the defendant's character as a law-abiding or lawless citizen. What the prosecutor should have said, in reply to Erston's objection, is that Erston "claimed he was an honest man who would not commit fraud of the sort alleged here, so Erston opened the door on the matter of character evidence, and we can prove that he is not what he claims to be." This argument has some force, and might prevail if it were made.

APPENDIX B

Glossary

A

Admissions* Statements by a party offered against the party. Important concept in applying hearsay doctrine since admissions are treated as hearsay exceptions or nonhearsay. Hence they are not excludable on a hearsay objection. There are five commonly recognized varieties of admissions, including (1) individual admissions (statement by X admitted against X), (2) adoptive admissions (statement by X admitted against Y where Y has adopted the statement as her own), (3) authorized admissions (statement by X offered against Y where Y authorized X to speak), (4) admissions by employees and agents (statement by X offered against Y, where X was an agent or employee of Y and the statement related to matters within the scope of the agency or employment and was made during the period of agency or employment), (5) coconspirator statements (statement by X offered against Y where the two were coconspirators, the statement furthered the conspiracy, and was made during the course thereof).

Against-interest statement A statement that was against the pecuniary, proprietary, or penal interest of the declarant, meaning that it might subject her to civil or criminal liability, or cause her to lose a claim or defense or to lose money or property. Common hearsay exception, recognized in FRE 804(b)(3), which can be invoked if the declarant is unavailable as a witness.

Ancient documents Category that includes, in its modern formulation, writings and recordings that are 20 years old or older. In the authentication doc-

---

* The restyled Federal Rules of Evidence that became effective December 1, 2011 eliminated the term "admission" from FRE 801(d)(2) and replaced it with the term "opposing party's statement." This change was intended to emphasize that an opposing party's statement is admissible even if it is not against the interest of the party making it.

trine, a writing or recording that appears to be that old may be treated as authentic without further proof of authenticity if its appearance raises no suspicion and it was found in a place where it would naturally be. See FRE 901(b)(8). In the hearsay doctrine, there is an exception for documents that are that old. See FRE 803(16).

Assertion Conduct or words by which the actor or declarant intentionally communicates or expresses some point. Crucial concept in applying the hearsay doctrine, which reaches only assertions, as opposed to nonassertive conduct. Thus a statement that "it is raining" constitutes an assertion because it intentionally expresses or communicates the point that it is raining, which means that this statement (this assertion) is hearsay if offered to prove that it is raining. In ordinary situations, putting up an umbrella is not an assertion, so proving that someone put up an umbrella is not hearsay if offered to prove that it is raining. But if U tells O, "watch me, and I'll find out whether it is raining or not, and I'll put up my umbrella if it is raining," then proof that U put up his umbrella would be an assertion by conduct (in effect a coded signal), and it too would be hearsay if offered to prove that it was raining.

Assertive conduct Human behavior that is intended to assert (express or communicate) some point. The concept is important in applying the hearsay doctrine since conduct intended as an assertion is hearsay if offered to prove the matter asserted. Nodding the head "yes" is assertive conduct. And the example immediately above, an agreed-upon signal ("I'll put up my umbrella if it is raining") is another example of assertive conduct.

Attorney-client privilege Doctrine allowing clients to exclude evidence of their confidential statements to lawyers providing legal representation. This doctrine is among the most important privileges. It covers **communications** but not facts as such, so a client who tells his lawyer that "the light was red" has a privilege to block discovery or introduction of that statement into evidence, but does not have a privilege to refuse to testify about the color of the light. There are important exceptions, including the situation where the client sues the lawyer or vice versa, and where the communication furthers a crime or fraud.

Authentication Proving that an item of evidence is what the proponent claims it to be. Unless covered by pretrial stipulation (common in civil cases and occasionally seen in criminal cases), ordinarily such proof is necessary for physical evidence of all kinds (including writings, recordings, and photographs), and for such matters as phone conversations. See FRE 901.

B

Best Evidence Doctrine Set of rules that, in common law tradition, requires a party who wishes to prove the content of a writing to offer the writing itself for this purpose. In its modern formulation, the doctrine (1) has been broadened to reach recordings and photographs as well as writings (FRE 1002), and (2) permits the use of duplicates (machine-made copies) in lieu of originals, with some limitations (FRE 1003). Both traditionally and under the Rules, the doctrine applies only where substantive law or party strategy makes content important and does not require production of writings (or recordings or photographs) merely because they exist and would be reliable proof. There are important exceptions allowing other forms of proof if the writing (or recording or photograph) cannot be obtained, and for other reasons.

Bias Animus, sympathy, or motive on the part of a witness that might affect her testimony at trial. Bias may be shown by way of impeachment, either on cross-examination or by extrinsic evidence (testimony by another witness). Bias is one of five recognized means of impeachment (the others are showing bad character for truth and veracity, showing lack of capacity, contradiction, and showing prior inconsistent statements).

***Bruton* doctrine** Constitutional rule based on Confrontation Clause, under which a statement by defendant A naming and incriminating codefendant B cannot be introduced *as the admission of A* in the joint trial of A and B. The reason is that the admissions doctrine authorizes the use of A's statement only against A, and B is not adequately protected by a mere limiting instruction directing the jury to consider A's statement only against A. *Bruton* can be accommodated by (a) doing without A's admission, (b) severing the trials of A and B, so that in A's trial A's statement can be admitted without doing any damage to B, (c) empanelling multiple juries, so that only A's jury hears A's statement, (d) A's taking the stand

so that B can cross-examine, or (e) redacting A's statement so that it no longer mentions B. All these "solutions" to the *Bruton* problem are problematic in various ways.

Burden of persuasion Term describing the burden a party must carry to prevail in a case. Usually the burden is described in terms of a standard of proof: In civil cases, usually the party bearing this burden must persuade the fact-finder by a preponderance of the evidence. In criminal cases, the prosecution must persuade the fact-finder beyond reasonable doubt.

Burden of production Term describing the requirement imposed on a party to produce sufficient evidence to support a finding in its favor. In a jury-tried case, success in carrying this burden ordinarily means the party gets its case to the jury for decision. In extraordinary cases, where a party succeeds in carrying this burden in a spectacular way by introducing cogent and compelling evidence in its favor, then the burden of production shifts to the other party. Failing to carry this burden means losing automatically, on appropriate motion for judgment as a matter of law or acquittal, except that criminal defendants cannot lose automatically in this way.

Burden of proof Ambiguous term that is sometimes used to mean the burden of production and sometimes used to mean the burden of persuasion (see above).

Business records exception Hearsay exception covering records of a regularly conducted business activity, made at or near the time of the events or acts recorded, on the basis of personal knowledge on the part of the source of the information, where each person involved in making the record acts in regular course of the business and the record is regularly kept. See FRE 803(6). Business records may be excluded if shown to be untrustworthy.

C

Capacity Term referring to mental or sensory capabilities of a witness, such as short-sightedness. Usually defects are viewed as factors that affect credibility of a witness. Such defects may be shown, in an impeaching effort, either on cross-examination or by extrinsic evidence (testimony by another witness). There are four other methods of impeachment (showing bias, showing bad character for truth and veracity, contradiction, and showing prior inconsistent statements).

Catchall exception Hearsay exception having broad and general criteria emphasizing trustworthiness, as contrasted with exceptions having specific criteria, which are known as "categorical" exceptions. The catchall is found in FRE 807. The catchall is also known as the "residual exception." Usually courts say that the catchall exception may be invoked only in rare or special circumstances.

Categorical exceptions Hearsay exceptions having specific criteria, such as the excited utterance exception codified in FRE 803(2) (declarant must be under the stress of excitement; statement must

relate to the exciting event or condition). Contrasted with "catchall" exception having broad and general criteria emphasizing trustworthiness.

Chain of custody Important aspect of authentication, which refers to the series of people who possess an object between the time of the events in litigation and the time of trial. For items that are fungible, and whenever there is no witness who knows that what is offered at court is the same object that the witness saw at the important time, proving chain of custody may be crucial.

Character evidence Proof relating to the general propensities of a person, such as being peaceful or truthful (or their opposites). Character evidence includes opinion and reputation testimony, and proof of specific instances of conduct (which is generally admissible only if character itself is an element of a charge, claim, or defense). In certain situations, important rules allow the "substantive use" of character evidence to prove conduct on a particular occasion, and in other situations the rules limit or block this use of character evidence. See FRE 404, 405. Other rules allow the use of some forms of character evidence to impeach or repair credibility in certain situations, and limit or block other forms or character evidence and impose other restrictions. See FRE 608 and 609. Yet other rules govern additional aspects of character evidence in sexual assault cases, see FRE 412 (Rape Shield provision) and 413 (special provision relating to prior offenses by defendants). And see FRE 414–415 (applying to child abuse prosecutions and to civil cases involving sexual assaults or child abuse).

Character for truth and veracity The propensity of a witness with respect to being truthful or untruthful. Bad character for truth and veracity may be shown by way of impeachment, and is one of five recognized methods. Typically bad character may be shown in three ways: One is by cross-examination on acts of misconduct indicating a propensity to be untruthful (false statements on an employment application). See FRE 608(b). Another is by opinion or reputation testimony relating to character. See FRE 608(a). A third way is by proof that the witness was convicted of a serious offense (a felony such as murder) or **any** offense involving dishonesty or false statement (such as fraud), subject to certain limits designed mainly to protect defendants in criminal cases who testify on their own behalf. See FRE 609. The other four methods of impeachment include showing bias, lack of capacity, contradiction, and showing prior inconsistent statements.

Circumstantial evidence Proof that does not directly suggest a fact, but provides a basis on which a fact-finder may draw an inference that the fact is more likely true than it was without the circumstantial evidence. Fingerprints at the crime scene are often circumstantial evidence tending to place the defendant there, from which the fact-finder may draw the inference that he was there, or that it is more likely that he was there than it was without proof of the fingerprints. Often distinguished from direct evidence, such as eyewit-ness testimony that defendant committed the crime.

Circumstantial evidence of knowledge, memory, or belief Somewhat risky theory supporting rare use of out-of-court statements to prove knowledge, memory, or belief, from which the trier of fact may infer that the point known, remembered, or believed is true. If, for example, the question is whether J had ever been in M's house, the prosecutor might offer evidence that J and M never met, that J had no occasion to be in M's house, that J said, "M keeps his first edition of *The Grapes of Wrath* hidden behind the frying pans in the second cupboard to the left of the stove," and that in fact M does keep that book in that place. Arguably what J said is nonhearsay circumstantial evidence of his knowledge or memory of M's house, hence proof that J has been in M's house. Key elements in this argument are that J's statement expresses knowledge, shown independently to be correct, about points that he would not likely know if he had not had the experience his statement suggests. If this argument were accepted in this situation, it would overcome objections based on the hearsay doctrine.

Circumstantial evidence of state of mind Common but problematic theory under which an out-of-court statement is considered nonhearsay when offered to prove state of mind. Sometimes courts apply this analysis to statements asserting facts ("it's raining outside") when offered to prove what the declarant thinks (he thinks it is raining outside). Realistically, such statements *do assert that the declarant thinks the fact that he* *asserts*, and the statement may be admitted to prove state of mind by using the state-of-mind exception (FRE 803(3)): Every time we say "it's raining outside," we are also saying "I think (or believe or know or suspect) it's raining outside," so such descriptors of state of mind are always implicit in factual statements. Some other statements, like "I am Louis XIV," are more realistically viewed as circumstantial evidence of state of mind when offered to prove that someone is not in his right mind because they amount to behavior that tends to prove this point, and here the theory of circumstantial evidence of state of mind makes good sense.

Collateral matters In connection with impeachment by contradiction, there is a bar against impeaching on collateral matters. This bar means that an attacking party is not allowed to show that the witness was wrong on a point that does not count in some way in the case, by shedding light on the merits or tending to impeach in some additional way beyond contradicting what the witness has said (as by indicating bias that the witness has denied). The collateral matters concept also applies in connection with the Best Evidence Doctrine, which includes an exception that allows proof of content of writings (or recordings or photographs) on points that are far removed from the center of the controversy (hence collateral).

Collective facts Phrase describing aggregations of details which lay witnesses may present in general terms if they relate to everyday matters, despite the preference for specific factual testimony. Under the collective facts doctrine, a lay witness who has observed another at a party would likely be allowed to testify that the other appeared "intoxicated" or "sober" since the details that underlie these conclusions are understood by most people as everyday matters.

Competency Qualifications that a person must have in order to testify as a witness. For lay witnesses, there are few restrictions, although experts must qualify by special training or experience. Most historical limits on the competency of lay witnesses (such as having a felony conviction) have been changed to points that may be raised in attacks on credibility. Special provisions relate to child witnesses in abuse cases. Other special rules bar judges from being witnesses in cases where they preside, and bar testimony by jurors that "impeach" their verdicts. See FRE 606. Many states also have "Dead Man's Statutes" that bar certain testimony by people who sue decedent's estates.

Conclusive (or irrebuttable) presumption Rule of law that holds that if one fact is established (the "basic fact"), another fact (the "presumed fact") must be found *even if* other evidence tends to refute the latter, and *even if* such other evidence would be viewed as conclusive on the point. In effect, a conclusive or irrebuttable presumption is a rule of substantive law. This concept is to be contrasted with "presumption" or "mandatory" presumption (below). If it were, for example, conclusively presumed that a small child is competent to testify about abuse inflicted upon himself or herself, then proving that a particular child has no concept of truth and no way to distinguish reality from fantasy would make no difference in deciding whether the child can testify.

Confrontation Right guaranteed to defendants in criminal trials by the Sixth Amendment's Confrontation Clause, the most important element of which is the right to cross-examine witnesses against the defendant. The right of confrontation also limits the use of hearsay against criminal defendants. The right of confrontation also requires witnesses who testify against criminal defendants to be present in court, although some special exceptions exist, especially in abuse prosecutions where children sometimes testify by videotaped deposition or from remote settings.

Constitutional error Admitting or excluding evidence in violation of a constitutional provision. Generally such a violation requires reversal in a criminal case unless the error was harmless beyond a reasonable doubt, and in a few instances such error requires automatic reversal.

Contradiction Method of impeachment that involves showing that something to which a witness has testified is not so. Contradiction may be pursued on cross-examination or by extrinsic evidence (typically testimony by another witness). Under certain circumstances, evidence that is otherwise excludable under other rules may be introduced to contradict testimony by a witness. Some rules that may give way in this setting include those relating to character evidence (FRE 404–405) and constitutional exclusionary doctrines (Fourth, Fifth, or Sixth Amendments). Contradiction is one of five recognized means of impeachment (the others are showing bias, showing lack of capacity, showing bad character for truth and veracity, and showing prior inconsistent statements).

Control group Description of people who control the actions of a corporate or other business entity, including directors and officers, and other managers. In connection with the attorney-client privilege, where the client is a corporation or other business entity, some states follow a doctrine that limits application of the attorney-client privilege to statements made by members of the control group to the lawyer. In the federal system, the Supreme Court rejected this approach in the *Upjohn* case in 1981, preferring the "scope of duties" or "subject matter" approach (see below, under "*Upjohn* standard").

***Crawford* doctrine** Authoritative modern approach to the meaning of the Confrontation Clause when it comes to hearsay offered against defendants in criminal cases. Under this doctrine, the Confrontation Clause applies to statements that are "testimonial" in nature, meaning *at least* statements describing criminal acts given to police investigators, and perhaps to other statements describing such acts in other settings, at least where the speaker understands that what he says is likely to be used in the investigation or prosecution of crimes. *Crawford* indicates that the Confrontation Clause is satisfied, even as to "testimonial" statements, if the speaker is subject to cross-examination prior to trial about such statements, or is subject to cross-examination *at trial* about such statements. *Crawford* also indicates that some forms of hearsay are admissible against the accused, citing hearsay that fits the business records exception and hearsay that fits the coconspirator exception. *Crawford* also indicates that objections to testimonial hearsay under the Confrontation Clause can be forfeited if the defendant engages in wrongdoing that prevents the declarant from testifying. *Crawford* also says that nonhearsay uses of out-of-court statements do not violate the Confrontation Clause.

Cross-examination Questioning of a witness conducted by parties who are adverse to the party who called the witness. Ordinarily conducted by leading questions.

Curative instruction Directive instructing jury to disregard certain evidence or testimony, ordinarily given in appropriate cases only on request by a party.

D

Davis "emergency" doctrine Important modification of the *Crawford* doctrine as the modern expression of the meaning of the Confrontation Clause with respect to hearsay offered against the accused. See **Crawford doctrine,** above. Under the *Davis* "emergency" doctrine (which is sometimes descried as an "exception" to the *Crawford* doctrine), statements to police or to agents of law enforcement (including 911 operators) are not excludable as "testimonial" statements if the primary purpose of the speaker is to obtain help during an ongoing emergency. *Davis* makes it implicitly clear that the "emergency" concept means an ongoing emergency in which life or wellbeing are in danger,

and that when the emergency passes and police shift from trying to protect the speaker to investigating a crime, then the emergency doctrine no longer applies and statements to police in this setting are "testimonial" for purposes of *Crawford* and are generally excludable unless the declarant testifies and can be cross-examined.

***Daubert* standard** Modern standard for scientific evidence, based on a 1993 Supreme Court case, which requires such evidence to be reliable and to fit the facts and issues of the case, although evidence that satisfies these criteria may still be executed under FRE 403 for reasons such as unfair prejudice, confusion of issues, or because it would be misleading. Under the Court's 1998 decision in *Kumho Tire,* the *Daubert* standard applies to all expert testimony, not just scientific evidence. *Daubert* factors bearing on reliability include (1) testability, (2) peer review, (3) error rate, (4) operational standards, and (5) general acceptance. The *Daubert* standard is contrasted with the common law *Frye* standard, which stresses only general acceptance in the pertinent disciplines (which *Daubert* includes as one of many factors). Many states follow *Daubert* and *Kumho Tire,* but many other states have retained their own standards, and do not follow the lead of the Supreme Court in this area.

Demonstration Term referring to the use of parties or witnesses, and sometimes by lawyers using physical props or electronic visual aids, to show by physical behavior or graphic depiction how events may or may not have happened.

Demonstrative evidence Evidence that conveys a firsthand sense impression, like photographs, drawings, charts, maps, models, and computer simulations. Demonstrative evidence is said to be "real" when it is an object actually involved in the events in litigation, and "illustrative" if it was created later to aid at trial.

Direct evidence Evidence that asserts a fact or embodies or represents the fact, such as testimony by an eyewitness that defendant shot the victim. Often distinguished from circumstantial evidence, such as proof that defendant's fingerprints were found at the crime scene.

Direct examination Questioning of a witness conducted by the party who called the witness. Ordinarily direct examination proceeds by nonleading questions.

Double or multiple hearsay Situation in which one statement incorporates another. Important in applying the hearsay doctrine because one out-of-court statement that incorporates another is admissible to prove what the two statements assert only if both fit a hearsay exception. Suppose these facts: C hears B say that "A told me the truck ran a red light." Suppose C is called to testify to what B told him that A said, and that the purpose is to prove the truck ran a red light. There is double hearsay: B's statement is hearsay because it is taken as proof that A made a statement. A's statement is hearsay because it says what happened and the purpose is to prove this point. If both B's statement and A's statement fit hearsay excep-

tions, then a hearsay objection would not prevent C from testifying. If either of the two statements does not fit an exception, then a hearsay objection would block C's testimony. See FRE 805.

Duplicate In connection with the Best Evidence Doctrine as formulated in the Federal Rules, a duplicate is a machine-made copy that is almost as admissible as the original. See FRE 1003 (allowing use of duplicates unless "genuine question" is raised as to authenticity of original or it would be "unfair" to admit the duplicate in lieu of an original).

Dying declarations Statement made by a person in the belief that death is imminent, concerning the cause or circumstances. Hearsay exception, recognized in FRE 804(b)(2), which may be invoked in homicide or civil cases if the declarant is unavailable at the time of trial (usually as a practical matter, the declarant has died).

E

Effect on listener or reader Well-recognized nonhearsay use of an out-of-court statement, in which the purpose is to show what someone had been told or warned about. If the purpose is to show plaintiff knew he should not take certain pills if he were going to drive, proving a label on the pills that says "can cause drowsiness" involves this nonhearsay use.

Excited utterance Statement made under the stress of an exciting event and relating to the event. Common hearsay exception, recognized in FRE 803(2).

F

"Fighting fire with fire" Phrase used to describe the reason to admit counterproof that would normally be excludable, but should come in because it tends to contradict testimony or other proof in the case. Often it is said that the original proof "opened the door" to the counterproof, and admitting the counterproof amounts to "fighting fire with fire." Often the original proof could itself have been excluded on appropriate objection, and admitting the counterproof is a way of curing an error or mistake.

Forfeiture exception Relatively new hearsay exception paving the way to use, against a party who engages or acquiesces in wrongdoing that is intended to and does make a witness unavailable to testify, any statement made by that witness. See FRE 804(b)(6). The exception is mainly designed to prevent criminal defendants from avoiding conviction by killing or frightening the witnesses on whom the prosecution depends.

Former testimony exception An exception to the hearsay doctrine that can be invoked if the declarant is unavailable as a witness. In its modern formulation in FRE 804(b)(1), the exception reaches testimony given in a prior proceeding, if the party against whom this testimony is offered had an opportunity and motive to develop the testimony that is similar to the motive the party now has. In civil cases, FRE 804(b)(1) authorizes use of prior testimony if either the party against whom it is offered or a predecessor in interest of the party had motive and opportunity to cross-examine in the prior proceeding.

Frye **standard** The prevailing common law standard for scientific evidence, based on a 1923 federal case, which requires that such evidence be "generally accepted" in the pertinent scientific field or fields. As contrasted with the *Daubert* standard (above), resting on a 1993 Supreme Court case by that name, which substitutes a new standard incorporating multiple criteria.

G

Governmental privileges A series of privileges that protect the conduct of public business. These include privileges covering state secrets, official information (deliberative and investigative material), informer's identity, and confidential presidential communications.

H

Harmless error Error that did not affect a substantial right of a party. Ordinarily a judgment is not reversed if errors committed during trial are found to be harmless on appeal. See FRE 103(a).

Hearsay Out-of-court statement offered to prove the truth of the matter asserted. If a declarant says outside of court, "the light was red for the truck," and somebody testifies to this statement for purposes of proving the light was red for the truck, then the statement is being offered to prove the truth of the matter asserted, and it is hearsay. Generally out-of-court statements are not excluded as hearsay if they are offered for some nonhearsay use (see below). If an out-of-court statement is offered to prove the truth of the matter asserted, it is excludable unless it fits an exception to the hearsay doctrine, in which case the fact that it is hearsay does not require exclusion, although it might be excluded for other reasons.

Hearsay dangers or risks Umbrella term describing the risks associated with accepting statements as proof of what they assert, which are problems relating to (1) perception, (2) memory, (3) narration or ambiguity, and (4) veracity. All statements bring such risks, but the trial safeguards help cope with these risks in the case of courtroom testimony. In other words, statements that are made in courtroom testimony are subject to cross-examination, and the witness is under oath, and the demeanor of the witness may be observed by the trier of fact, which means that the risks of relying upon the say-so of a human being are at least reduced and more readily assessed.

Hearsay exceptions Series of doctrines, based largely on elements of necessity and trustworthiness, that exempt certain kinds of statements from exclusion as hearsay. Some exceptions may be invoked regardless whether the person who made the statement ("declarant") is available or not, and some exceptions may be invoked only if the declarant is unavailable as a witness. Most of the exceptions are "categorical," which means they have specific criteria governing their application. The "catchall" exception turns on general criteria of reliability and necessity.

Illustrative evidence Proof made after the events involved in litigation, to help understand other proof. Examples include drawings, charts, and models. Illustrative evidence comprises part of the larger category of "demonstrative" evidence, which also includes "real" evidence comprised of objects actually involved in the events in litigation.

Impeachment Attacking the credibility of a witness. There are five recognized methods of impeachment, including attacks showing (1) bias, (2) defects in sensory or mental capacity, (3) bad character for truth and veracity, (4) prior inconsistent statements, or (5) contradiction of something to which the witness has testified. The third method (bad character for truth and veracity) may normally be proved by cross-examination on prior acts, by opinion or reputation evidence on veracity, and by proof of prior convictions. See FRE 608 and 609.

Implied assertion Description of statement that implies something beyond its literal meaning, which is important in applying the hearsay doctrine. Sometimes "implied assertion" describes a meaning that the declarant intended to convey: If, for example, one of two arrested defendants said to the other "it would be better for us to take the blame than Kay, because he couldn't stand it," the statement seems intentionally to express the point that Kay is involved in the crime. This implied assertion makes the statement hearsay if offered to prove Kay's involvement. Sometimes "implied assertion" describes a meaning that the declarant did not intend to convey, in which case the statement is not hearsay if offered to prove this point, but it is often very difficult to determine whether the speaker meant to convey the point in question or not. In the famous nineteenth-century decision in *Wright*, for example, letters written to a testator seemed to assume that the testator was competent, although the letters did not expressly say so or indicate any intention on the part of the writers of the letters to express or communicate this point. One might still describe the letters as "implied" assertions that the testator was competent, but "imply" would **not** then refer to something that the writers of the letters were trying to express.

Inference Rule of law stating that if a certain fact is established, another fact may be found.

Interlocutory appeal Review of court ruling prior to final judgment in a case. Usually rulings on evidence issues are not subject to review on interlocutory appeal, and review must await the outcome of trial.

Invited error Error caused by the conduct of the party who now complains of the error, which normally means that the complaining party cannot obtain a reversal, since the error is viewed as being the fault of this party.

Irrebuttable presumption Same as conclusive presumption (see above).

J

Joint clients Situation in which two or more clients consult a single lawyer on a matter of joint interest, as happens in the formation of business partnerships. In the setting of the attorney-client privilege, the usual rule is that each joint client can prevent disclosure or use of confidential statements if an outsider seeks them or offers them in evidence, but in litigation pitting one client against the other there is no privilege. To be contrasted with the "pooled defense" situation (below), where the privilege applies against outsiders and also among the clients.

Judicial notice Process by which courts find facts without formal proof. Under FRE 201, courts may take judicial notice of adjudicative facts (who did what and when) that are generally known (New York is east of Chicago) or verifiable by resort to unimpeachable sources (the moon was full on April 10th). In this setting, FRE 201 includes procedural safeguards, providing an opportunity for the parties to be heard on the propriety of notice. Courts may also take judicial notice of legislative facts (those that bear on the meaning of laws, such as that segregation in education is injurious to excluded groups), basic facts (the word "car" ordinarily means automobile; icy roads are slippery), and the content of law (such as that contracts for the sale of goods exceeding a certain value must be in writing), and in these settings the process is unregulated.

L

Leading question A question to a witness that is framed in a manner that suggests the response sought by the questioner. Normally leading questions are allowed on cross-examination but not direct examination.

Limiting instruction A charge by the judge directing the jury to consider evidence only for specified purposes, or not for other specified purposes, or only for or against certain parties. Ordinarily such a charge is given only if requested by one of the parties. See FRE 105.

M

Mandatory presumption Same as presumption (see below).

Marital confidences privilege Doctrine that allows a married person to block introduction of evidence that reveals confidential statements by the privilege claimant or the spouse of the claimant to each other. The spouses must be married at the time the statements are made, but need not be married at the time the proof is offered. There are some exceptions to coverage.

Medical statements exception Hearsay exception authorizing use of certain out-of-court statements to physicians to prove the nature and history of pain or physical condition, including cause. In its modern formulation in FRE 803(4), the exception reaches statements given for "diagnosis" as well as "treatment," although the common law predecessor reached only statements made for the latter purpose. The exception reaches statements by people other than the patient (Good Samaritans, parents), but does not reach statements offered to prove "fault" for whatever happened to the speaker.

Motion in limine A motion "at the threshold," which means prior to trial, seeking a ruling to admit or exclude evidence.

Motion to strike Delayed objection, raised after testimony has been given, claiming that it should be excluded by means of a motion to disregard or a new trial. A motion to strike satisfies the requirement to object if the witness jumps the gun or the answer simply comes too quickly to be anticipated, or if the ground to exclude only became apparent later. Like an objection, a motion to strike should include the grounds for excluding the proof.

N

Nonassertive conduct Conduct in which the actor does not intend to assert something. Putting up an umbrella is normally nonassertive conduct. This concept is important in applying the hearsay doctrine, which in its modern formulation in FRE 801 does not reach nonassertive conduct. When offered in support of the two-step inference (act suggests belief; belief suggests some act, event, or condition in the world), nonassertive conduct raises the hearsay risks of perception, memory, and ambiguity. Still, nonassertive conduct is not hearsay under FRE 801. Thus, putting up an umbrella is ordinarily nonhearsay evidence of rain. This proof depends on the two-step inference: The first inference is that putting up the umbrella suggests the person believes it is raining. The second inference is that this belief suggests that it is raining in fact. The qualifier "ordinarily" is necessary because *sometimes* conduct that *appears* nonassertive is assertive after all, as would be true if the person who put up the umbrella had agreed in advance that he would put up the umbrella in view of another to tell the latter that it was raining.

Nonhearsay uses Series of purposes for which out-of-court statements are offered that does not involve taking them as proof of the matter asserted. The most common categories of nonhearsay use are impeachment, verbal acts (or parts of acts), proving effect on listener or reader, verbal object, circumstantial evidence of state of mind, and circumstantial evidence of memory, knowledge, or belief.

O

Objection An objection is a claim, advanced by a party at the time that testimony or other evidence is offered, that it should not be admitted. Ordinarily an objection or motion to strike (see above) is required in order to preserve the claim that a ruling admitting evidence amounts to error. It must be timely made, must state the ground for exclusion, and must refer to the evidence to be excluded. See FRE 103(a)(1).

Offer of proof An offer of proof is (1) a statement by a lawyer describing evidence that he or she wants admitted, or (2) the evidence itself, typically in the form of answers by a witness to questions put by the lawyer, where the jury has been excused so that the evidence in question may be made known to the court without being disclosed to the jury. Ordinarily an offer must be made after an objection is sustained, in order to preserve the claim by the offering party that a ruling excluding the evi-

dence amounts to error. See FRE 103(a)(2).

"Open door" doctrine Set of principles under which courts admit counterproof that would normally be excluded simply because it tends to refute proof that the other side has offered. Often the original proof could have been excluded as well, and admitting the counterproof is a way of curing the error or mistake. Often it is said that the original proof "opened the door" to the counterproof. It is also said that admitting the counterproof amounts to "fighting fire with fire."

Opinion testimony Term describing testimony that is general rather than specific. Opinion testimony is often contrasted with factual testimony, but no bright line separates what is specific from what is general or fact from opinion. Most courts would say testimony that "the light was red" is specific and factual, and testimony that "he wasn't being careful" is general and amounts to an opinion. Under the modern approach, a lay witness is normally expected to be as specific and factual as possible, but is allowed to give opinion testimony if it is adequately based on knowledge and helpful to the trier of fact. See FRE 701. An expert witness is allowed to give opinion testimony on technical or scientific matters if he is qualified as an expert, if such testimony would be helpful to the trier of fact, and if such testimony rests on information that similar experts would reasonably rely upon. See FRE 702–703.

P

Past recollection recorded Hearsay exception for written or recorded statements by a witness who lacks present memory, if made when he had knowledge, if and when the matter was fresh in memory, and if the writing or recording reflects that memory correctly. See FRE 803(5). This exception differs from the process of refreshing recollection, where the examining lawyer calls the attention of the witness to statements or other matters and the witness says he now remembers what he had forgotten before. See "recollection refreshed," below.

Performativity Description of one aspect of a statement, which counts in deciding whether the proposed use of that statement should be viewed as hearsay or as nonhearsay. Most statements have both "assertive" aspects and "performative" aspects, and the more prominent the performative aspect in light of the point to be proved, the more plausible it is to treat the statement as nonhearsay. Recall the example given in Chapter 3, where a party guest named Carl tells Derrick, "Please wait. I've got a cab coming for you in just three minutes." Under the circumstances, this statement *asserts* that Carl called a cab, and seems to *imply* (in the strong sense of intentionally suggesting) that Carl thinks Derrick is drunk and shouldn't drive home. The statement is also *conduct* that seeks to prevent Derrick from driving home by providing an alternative. This performative aspect of the statement makes it very similar to the act of calling a cab and putting Derrick in the cab, and constitutes a solid basis for treating the statement as nonhearsay, when offered to prove that Derrick was not fit to drive home.

Personal knowledge Basis in personal experience (typically firsthand visual observation) required of every lay (as opposed to expert) witness. See FRE 602.

Physician-patient privilege Doctrine covering confidential statements by patients to treating physicians, but many important exceptions exist (including an exception in cases where the patient puts physical condition in issue).

Plain error Error that requires reversal even though no objection was made. Usually plain error describes mistakes that are both serious (having major effect on outcome) and obvious (the law clearly requires the court to do otherwise).

Pooled defense (or allied lawyer) Description of the situation in which two or more clients, each having separate lawyers, consult or discuss matters of mutual interest. In the setting of the attorney-client privilege, the rule in this situation is that each client has a privilege to block disclosure of what she has said, and this privilege applies when outsiders offer or seek disclosure of such statements and when another client in the group offers such statements. To be contrasted with the "joint clients" situation (above), where the privilege applies against outsiders but not between the clients.

Preliminary question This term describes (1) an issue of fact or law that must be resolved to determine whether evidence is admissible, in which case the judge makes the decision under FRE 104(a), or (2) an issue of "conditional relevancy" that a jury resolves under FRE 104(b).

Present sense impression Statement describing an act, event, or condition, made while the act or event is occurring or while the speaker observes the condition. Hearsay exception, recognized in FRE 803(1).

Presumption Rule of law holding that in *civil* cases if a particular fact is established (commonly called the "basic fact"), another fact *must* be found (commonly called the "presumed fact") in the absence of evidence that the latter fact is not so. In *criminal* cases, with respect to presumptions that operate against the accused, the rule *permits* the factfinder to infer that the presumed fact is so, but does not require such a finding.

Prima facie case Term indicating either (1) that a party has carried its burden of production, so its case may go to a jury to be decided either way, or (2) that a party has carried its burden of production so spectacularly that the burden of production has shifted to the adverse party.

Prior consistent statement A statement by somebody who is now testifying that is consistent with his testimony. When offered to repair an attack on credibility, such a statement may be admissible, under certain conditions, as nonhearsay evidence because it shows consistency of position. Under FRE 801(d)(1)(B), such a statement is defined as "not hearsay," and may be admitted under certain conditions both to repair an attack on credibility and to prove what it asserts. Often courts allow prior consistent statements to be used in these ways only if the declarant (who is also testifying as a witness) was impeached in a manner that suggests that his testimony amounts to recent fabrication or is the product of undue influence, and most courts require in such cases that the prior consistent statement be made after the motive to fabricate or the undue influence came into play.

Prior inconsistent statement A statement by somebody who is now testifying that is inconsistent with his testimony. When offered to impeach, such a statement is viewed as nonhearsay because it is offered to show change of position. When offered to prove what it asserts, such a statement is hearsay. Under FRE 801(d)(1)(A), *some* prior inconsistent statements are defined as nonhearsay, which means they can be used both to impeach and to prove what they assert. The prior inconsistent statements defined in this way are those given in proceedings under oath subject to the penalty of perjury, when the declarant now testifies and is subject to cross-examination concerning what he said before.

Privilege A rule, of which there are many, that allows a person to refuse to testify or to refuse to disclose certain matters. Examples include the attorney-client privilege, the spousal testimony privilege, and the marital confidences privilege. Most privilege rules exist to protect relationships out of court, and to protect important areas of privacy. Most privileges are created by common law development, see FRE 501, but statutes in many states create and define some privileges.

Psychotherapist-patient privilege Doctrine covering confidential statements to a psychotherapist in course of treatment, with important exceptions (including one covering the case in which the patient relies on mental condition as an element of a claim or defense), and subject usually to an important requirement that the therapist report, to law enforcement officers or targeted victims, credible threats that the patient makes toward such victims.

Public records exception Hearsay exception covering records of a public office or agency. In its modern formulation in FRE 803(8), the exception reaches records describing the activities of the office or agency, records reflecting matters observed under legal duty (but not police reports offered in criminal cases), and records reflecting factual findings made on the basis of investigation (but not against criminal defendants). Records in the latter category may rest on statements by outsiders to government. Important modern cases hold that police and investigative records that are excluded by restrictions in the exception cannot be offered under other exceptions, but arguably they may be admitted if they qualify as past recollection recorded or fit certain narrow exceptions such as the one for records of vital statistics. Public records may be excluded if shown to be untrustworthy.

R

Rape shield statute Rule or statute blocking or limiting use of evidence of the character of the complaining wit-

ness in sexual assault cases, typically blocking proof in the form of reputation or opinion evidence relating to sexual propensities, as well as proof of specific instances of sexual conduct, but with exceptions allowing proof of specific instances of sexual conduct with the defendant and specific instances that might account for injury or semen. See FRE 412.

Real evidence Physical objects actually involved in the events in litigation. Real evidence comprises part of the larger category of "demonstrative" evidence, which also includes "illustrative" evidence made after the events in litigation to help at trial.

Recollection refreshed End product of a process in which examining lawyer calls the attention of the witness to statements or other proof on some point which the witness says he has forgotten, but now says he remembers. This process differs in important ways from the hearsay exception for past recollection recorded (above): With recollection refreshed, the material used to refresh memory is not itself the evidence (rather, the testimony is the evidence), and the material need not be something the witness has written himself. Procedural safeguards allow the adverse party to inspect any writing shown to the witness to refresh memory, and to examine or offer relevant portions. See FRE 612. With past recollection recorded, the prior statement is evidence, and it must have been made or adopted by the witness.

Redaction Editing a statement to remove words that are not admissible. Usually redaction is done with writings and less often with oral statements. Redaction is one means to accommodate an objection based on the *Bruton* doctrine (above), but redaction must be done carefully, and the decision in *Gray* held that redacting a statement to read "me, blank, and blank beat the victim" does not adequately protect codefendants against the risk that the confession will be taken as evidence against them.

Re-enactment Filmed or videotaped recreations of events using parties or actors to show the way things happened.

Refreshing recollection See "recollection refreshed" (above).

Rehabilitation or repair Process by which a party may seek to restore the credibility of a witness after it has been attacked. The most common methods of rehabilitation or repair are (1) proving good character for truth and veracity, which may be done if an attack has been made against truth and veracity, and (2) proving prior consistent statements by the witness, which may typically be done, subject to certain limitations, if an attack has been made that suggests that the testimony of the witness is a recent fabrication or is the product of improper influence or motivation.

Relevant Required by FRE 401–402 for all evidence, relevance describes the tendency of proof to make more probable or less probable a point that matters in the case. Evidence may be relevant but insufficient, meaning it has some tendency to prove a point that matters, but does not suffice by itself to prove the point. Thus relevance differs from sufficiency in that evidence may tend to prove a point that matters (so it is relevant) without being strong enough to prove the point by itself (so it is insufficient). In modern terminology, the concept of relevance means both that the proof tends to prove a point (in the words of FRE 401, it has a "tendency to make the existence of a fact . . . more or less probable") and that the point matters (in the words of FRE 401, it is a fact "of consequence to the determination of the action"). In older tradition, these ideas were split: The first was called "relevance," the second "materiality." Now "relevant" means proof that has both these qualities.

Reply doctrine Technique for authenticating a letter or other item (such as a phone call) by showing that it apparently replies to an earlier communication. See FRE 901(b)(4) (allowing authenticity to be shown by reference to content and circumstances).

***Roberts* doctrine** From 1980 to 2004, prevailing theory on the meaning of the Confrontation Clause when it comes to the use against criminal defendants of out-of-court statements. In 2004, the Court discarded *Roberts* in the *Crawford* decision (see **"*Crawford* doctrine"** above). Because *Crawford* only applies to "testimonial" statements, it seemed at first that *Roberts* might continue to apply to other "nontestimonial" statements offered against the defendant, which could include "private party" hearsay such as conversations among friends. In its decisions in *Davis* and *Bockting,* however, the Court made it clear that *Roberts* no longer applies at all, and that federal confrontation rights relating to hearsay are stated exclusively in the *Crawford* doctrine. *Roberts* may continue to find some application in state courts, however, as states across the country sometimes adopted the *Roberts* standard in applying their own state confrontation clauses. Basically *Roberts* mandated a two-pronged approach: First, the statement had to be reliable, which means satisfying a "firmly rooted" hearsay exception or a "particularized showing" of reliability if the statement does not satisfy such an exception. Second, the declarant had to be unavailable, although this requirement was largely abandoned, and seemed only to apply to "former testimony" offered under FRE 804(b)(1). (Former testimony is now subject to the *Crawford* doctrine because "former testimony" is clearly "testimonial," but *Crawford* seems to continue the *Roberts* notion that former testimony may be offered only if the declarant is unavailable, and both *Roberts* and *Crawford* also seem to require that there was an opportunity for the defense to cross-examine when the former testimony was given.) Importantly, when a statement was offered under some hearsay exception that was not "firmly rooted" (like the catchall exception or the exceptions for child victim hearsay), the constitutional reliability standard had to be satisfied under the *Roberts* regime *without* looking at "corroborative evidence."

Rule of completeness Rule stating that if one part of a written or recorded statement is admitted, other parts should also be admitted if necessary for proper understanding of the first part. As framed in FRE 106, the rule requires the propo-nent of the first part to offer the additional parts (when the point is raised by the adverse party), and it also authorizes the adverse party to offer the additional parts.

S

Self-authentication Doctrine allowing certain kinds of evidence, such as newspapers and products commercially marked with trade labels, to be admitted without proof of authenticity on the basis of surface appearance. See FRE 902(6) and (7). Copies of public records are self-authenticating when accompanied by appropriate signed and sealed certificates of authenticity. See FRE 902(1), (2), and (4).

Self-incrimination, privilege against This privilege is part of the Fifth Amendment, and it entitles a defendant in a criminal case not to testify nor to be called as a witness by the prosecutor. It also entitles witnesses not to give self-incriminating testimony, whether they are criminal defendants or not. The privilege also applies where the government requires production of incriminating documents, but not to documents that the government requires a person to keep for a valid regulatory purpose.

Sidebar A conference among lawyers and judge at the bench, outside the hearing of the jury.

Spousal testimonial privilege Doctrine that allows one spouse to refuse to testify against another in a criminal case, or allows one spouse to block the other from testifying in this setting, or does both these things. In federal courts under the Supreme Court's decision in *Trammel*, the witness spouse holds the privilege and can refuse to testify, but the party spouse cannot prevent the witness spouse from testifying. The witness and party must be married when the privilege is invoked, and there are some exceptions to coverage.

State-of-mind exception Crucial exception to the hearsay doctrine for statements that describe either (1) existing physical condition, (2) existing mental state, or (3) certain facts relating to wills. In its most common application, the exception reaches statements describing the intent of the speaker ("I intend to go to Chicago"). A statement describing intent may also be used to prove that the speaker thereafter acted in accord with her intent. Thus, the statement "I intend to go to Chicago" may be used to prove not only that the speaker intended to go to Chicago, but that she did go. The major challenge in applying the exception is that it does not allow use of a statement to prove some previous fact: In the words of FRE 803(3), the exception does not authorize use of a statement to prove "a fact remembered or believed." Thus, the statement "I have to go to Chicago tomorrow because my father had an accident and is hospitalized" might fit the exception if offered to prove that the speaker intended to go to Chicago, and that she did go to Chicago, but it may not be used to prove that her father had an accident or was hospitalized.

Subsequent remedial measures Term referring to changes that affect the likelihood of accident or injury, typically changes in design, labels, instructions, employment, or procedures. Generally proof of such changes, if taken after an accident that is the subject of suit, is inadmissible, with certain exceptions. See FRE 407.

U

Unavailability as a witness A concept that is important in applying the hearsay doctrine, since some exceptions (notably former testimony, against-interest statements, and dying declarations) can be invoked only if the declarant is unavailable as a witness. In its modern formulation in FRE 804(a), unavailability as a witness includes not only death and absence from the jurisdiction, but also lack of memory, refusal to testify, and a claim of privilege that is upheld.

***Upjohn* standard** An approach to the attorney-client privilege where a corporation or other business entity is the client, in which the privilege applies to statements by a corporate employee or agent who speaks to the lawyer about matters within the scope of the speaker's duties, or on a subject matter that is within the speaker's duties. In the federal system, the Supreme Court adopted this approach in the *Upjohn* case in 1981, rejecting the "control group" standard.

V

Verbal act (or part of act) Term describing nonhearsay use of out-of-court statement, in which the important point is that the statement was made rather than that the statement is true. In civil cases, examples include words constituting libel or slander and words constituting contracts (or offers and acceptance). In criminal cases, examples include words of extortion ("pay me or I'll expose you") or theft ("give me your money or I'll shoot"). Verbal parts of acts are also nonhearsay, as in the case of someone who gives a gift by handing the object to the recipient and saying at the same time, "Here, this is yours now," where the words give character and meaning to the act.

Verbal marker Nonhearsay use of words to identify something, where the words have this effect without relying on what they assert. If, for example, a defendant is prosecuted for robbery, and the prosecutor offers (a) eyewitness testimony that the perpetrator was wearing a shirt that said "Kansas City Chiefs" on it, and (b) testimonial or other proof that defendant owned a shirt with such a legend on it, this use of those words would not be subject to objection under the hearsay doctrine. The words are verbal markers that help identify the shirt as possibly belonging to the defendant, hence increasing the likelihood that he was the thief.

Voucher rule A principle that blocked the calling party from attacking the credibility of her own witness. This rule has been abolished in most jurisdictions. See FRE 607.

APPENDIX C

Table of Cases

APPENDIX D

Index

†